VOICES

UPPER INTERMEDIATE

CLAIRE HART WITH MIKE SAYER

NATIONAL GEOGRAPHIC LEARNING

Australia • Brazil • Canada • Mexico • Singapore • United Kingdom • United States

National Geographic Learning,
a Cengage Company

Voices Upper Intermediate Teacher's Book,
1st Edition
Claire Hart with Mike Sayer

Publisher: Rachael Gibbon
Commissioning Editor: Kayleigh Buller
Development Editor: Laura Brant
Director of Global Marketing: Ian Martin
Product Marketing Manager: Caitlin Thomas
Heads of Regional Marketing:
Charlotte Ellis (Europe, Middle East and Africa)
Irina Pereyra (Latin America)
Justin Kaley (Asia)
Joy MacFarland (US and Canada)
Production Manager: Daisy Sosa
Media Researcher: Leila Hishmeh
Art Director: Brenda Carmichael
Operations Support: Hayley Chwazik-Gee
Manufacturing Manager: Eyvett Davis
Composition: Composure
Audio Producer: James Richardson
Advisors: A. Pilar Calatayud Díez, Bárbara Cuesta Bellido and Nieves Gómez Belda

Teacher's Book:
ISBN: 978-0-357-44339-2

National Geographic Learning
Cheriton House, North Way,
Andover, Hampshire, SP10 5BE
United Kingdom

Locate your local office at **international.cengage.com/region**

Visit National Geographic Learning online at **ELTNGL.com**
Visit our corporate website at **www.cengage.com**

Printed in the United Kingdom by Ashford Colour Press
Print Number: 01 Print Year: 2021

MIX
Paper from responsible sources
FSC® C011748

Contents

Scope and Sequence

READING	LISTENING	WRITING	COMMUNICATION SKILL	CRITICAL THINKING	USEFUL LANGUAGE
an article about how sound affects us; identifying reasons	explorers talk about a memorable experience; inferring emotions	an informal email giving news; writing informal emails and messages	considering other people's emotions	evaluating evidence	expressing emotions; empathizing
an article about communication in the natural world; scanning and skimming	a podcast about English as a global language; identifying discourse markers	a formal email enquiry; organizing formal emails	building relationships using your first language identity	identifying the main message	talking about your first language identity; formal emails
a blog post about exploring your own city; active reading by annotating	an audiobook extract about Polynesian voyages; using visual information to help you listen	a blog post about travel; engaging the reader	fixing misunderstandings	ranking information	telling personal stories; fixing misunderstandings; making recommendations
an article about reconnecting with nature; summarizing	an interview about keeping in touch with friends and family; understanding accents	a story; making a story entertaining	adapting your turn-taking style	synthesizing information	taking turns
three success stories of projects tackling loneliness; identifying and understanding cause and effect	explorers talk about keeping mentally and physically fit; listening for keywords to understand the general meaning	a for and against essay; using discourse markers	adapting your English to be understood	distinguishing cause from correlation	essay introductions

Scope and Sequence

Welcome to VOICES

As educators, we want students to transfer what they learn in the classroom into meaningful interactions in the real world. *Voices* focuses on building language skills, and also the intercultural and interpersonal skills students need for communicative success.

Each lesson of *Voices* features real world content that students can relate to, while carefully sequenced tasks develop students' reading, listening, writing and speaking skills and offer a progressive level of challenge designed to motivate and build confidence.

STUDENT'S BOOK

In the *Voices* Upper Intermediate Student's Book, teachers and students are presented with twelve topic-related units. Each unit has the same structure and clear signposting throughout (see '**Student's Book unit walkthrough**' for a detailed overview) so that teachers and students know what to expect in every unit.

- At the beginning of each unit and lesson, teachers and students are presented with a **set of goals** so that learning is focused and purposeful.
- **National Geographic explorers** feature throughout the Student's Book, sharing everyday stories that students can relate to and modelling language for students to use as a springboard to develop their own voices.
- Reading lessons introduce **real world topics through a variety of text types** whilst also developing students' reading sub-skills and critical thinking.
- Each *Voices* unit has a main **grammar focus** contextualized within a reading or listening text. Activities move from controlled practice to freer, more personalized tasks. The 'Focus on' section looks at a **second grammar point or lexical focus**.
- Each unit has a **clear topic-related vocabulary** set which students can put into practice through activities and personalized speaking tasks.
- Listening lessons expose students to a wide variety of **authentic accents and listening text types**.
- Writing lessons follow a **process writing** approach, providing a model and **scaffolded steps** to enable students to produce a wide variety of text types independently.
- Communication skills give students the opportunity to learn **strategies to become confident and successful communicators**. These lessons engage students with a range of hypothetical situations, and get them to analyse and reflect on the way that they communicate inside, and outside, of the classroom.

- Students are encouraged to communicate in every lesson of *Voices* – we don't believe in a silent classroom! *Voices* provides **opportunities to communicate** in a wide variety of formats, including pair and group activities, classroom discussions, roleplays and debates.
- **Two 'Clear Voice' pronunciation sections** in every unit focus on intelligibility and developing students' ability to express themselves clearly and confidently.
- A **rich reference section** at the back of each Student's Book provides students with structured language support. It includes a **vocabulary reference** complete with wordlists and activities, a **grammar reference** with detailed explanations and extra activities and the **Student's Book audio script**.
- At the end of each unit, students are invited to **'reflect and review'** what they have learned so far – using the learning goals at the beginning of each unit as a guide. The **'Explore More!'** feature, which can be found throughout each unit, suggests ways in which the teacher and student might want to learn more about the topic featured in each lesson.

WORKBOOK

The *Voices* Workbook provides extended practice of the skills and language students have already encountered in the Student's Book.

In addition, the Workbook provides students with opportunities to take ownership of their learning through an integrated *learn to learn* development programme. These features provide learner guidance on methods of improving language learning and study skills outside the classroom to equip students to become lifelong learners.

Each Workbook unit has been separated into sections rather than lessons so that teachers can take a flexible approach to assigning homework, depending on how much of the lesson or unit is covered in the lesson. There are suggestions for how to assign these sections in the teacher's notes.

The *Voices* Workbook includes:

- Topic-related reading and listening texts with related activities.
- Further practice of all the grammar and vocabulary covered in the Student's Book, plus more pronunciation activities and audio.
- Optional 'Learning to learn' activities.
- Review sections for each unit, including exam tasks, enabling students to check their progress.
- Audio available on the student and teacher companion sites.

The Workbook is available with or without answer key.

TEACHER'S BOOK

The *Voices* Teacher's Book provides a comprehensive set of resources to help you effectively plan and teach your lessons. It includes:

- An overview of the goals of each lesson, and a list of related photocopiable and Workbook resources.
- Extra activities to suggest ways to further exploit, or build on, the Student's Book activities.
- Language notes that provide guidance on explaining the main grammar, vocabulary and pronunciation points of the lesson.
- Extra photocopiable grammar, vocabulary and pronunciation worksheets to consolidate learning, which can be used in-class, or assigned as out-of-class additional language practice.
- Two communication worksheets per unit, which can be used to provide extra speaking opportunities.
- A mediation worksheet for each unit to practise various mediation techniques, as well as clear notes, answer keys and a CEFR-mapped mediation chart to help identify what the mediation task is practising.
- A bank of practical teaching tips for managing classroom interaction, conducting language practice activities and providing feedback and correction.

Voices Digital Resources for . . .

PREPARATION

- The **Virtual *Voices* ToolKit** is a set of video-based professional development resources developed by the *Voices* author team and designed to help as you prepare to deliver engaging courses using *Voices* in all classrooms.
- Instructor resources available on the companion site at **ELTNGL.com/ voicesresources** support lesson-planning through downloadable materials like Teacher's Books, video, audio, answer keys, assessment materials, worksheets and more.

LIVE LESSONS

- The ***Voices* Classroom Presentation Tool** includes the complete Student's Book, Workbook, and corresponding video, audio and answer keys, as well as fun language games for use in class. The CPT is an effective classroom management tool for in person and online learning.
- Available through the Online Practice in the Learning Management System, interactive **Student's eBooks** provide a print alternative and include everything that a student needs to be an active participant in any classroom.

SELF-STUDY

- ***Voices* Online Practice** enables students to practise and consolidate learning on the go or catch up with missed lessons. It is mobile compatible, with an inbuilt Gradebook to assign work, automatically mark activities and provide teachers with individual and whole class reports. The Online Practice includes: full skills coverage, progress checks with remediation function and voice recognition abilities.

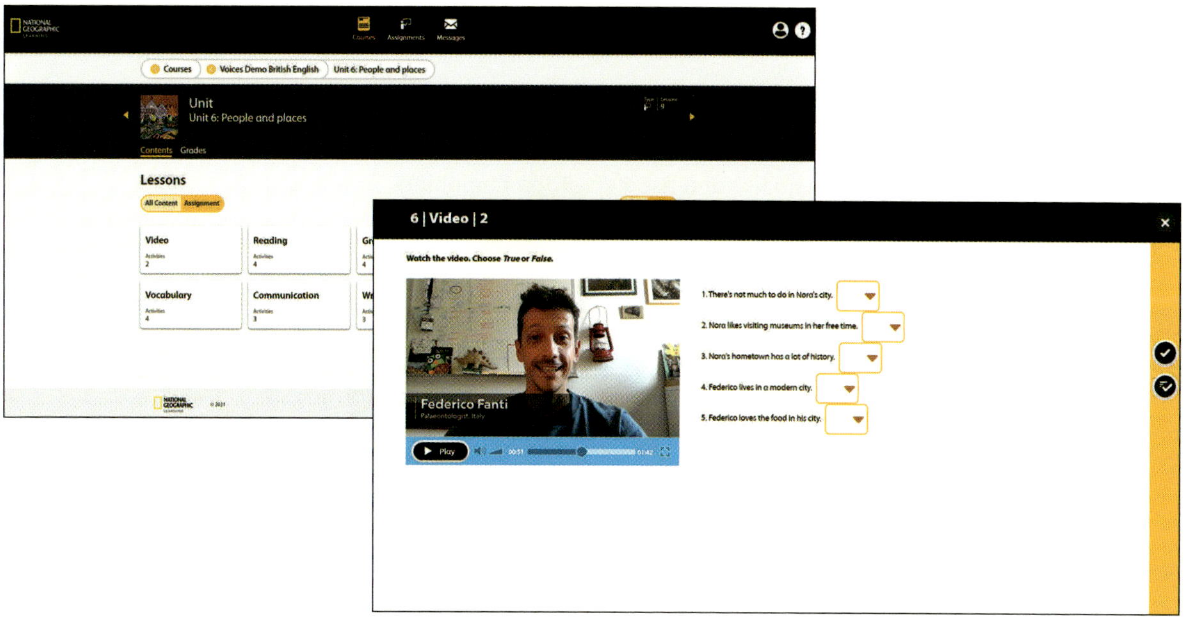

ASSESSMENT

Voices supports teachers and learners throughout their English learning journey to achieve real-world success. Its approach to assessment centres on supplying students with the strategies and opportunities for reflection they need to become self-directed learners, and providing teachers with a toolkit to place learners, to monitor progress and to evaluate learning.

For students:

- The clearly articulated goals in the Student's Book at the start of each unit and lesson help students set clear learning objectives.
- 'Reflect and Review' sections in the Student's Book and 'Learning to learn' strategies in the Workbook encourage students to reflect on their own progress towards meeting their goals.
- Progress checks in the Online Practice provide students with adaptive remediation tutorials and activities that reinforce the lessons in the Student's Books.

For teachers:

- For simple and reliable placement, the **National Geographic Learning Online Placement Test** is a mobile-friendly solution that provides student alignment to the CEFR, recommends placement within the *Voices* programme and delivers a skill-specific report for each test-taker.
- The integrated Gradebook in *Voices* Online Practice generates reports on student and class performance, functioning as a formative assessment resource and a teacher time-saving tool.
- The ***Voices* Cognero® Assessment Suite** offers pre-made and customizable tests and quizzes for monitoring and evaluating student progress, providing both formative and summative assessment.

Teach with confidence through a consistent lesson sequence.

The **Unit Opener** spread introduces students to the topic and sets their expectations for the unit through vibrant photography, real and relatable National Geographic Explorer videos and clear learner goals.

Learner goals are presented at the beginning of each unit so that students know exactly what to expect.

Students are introduced to National Geographic Explorers through bite-sized personal videos. They share snapshots from their everyday experiences that students can easily relate to and use as a model for interaction. Guided speaking activities encourage them to make connections with their own lives.

Lesson A provides students with a rich, topical input as a springboard for reading and critical skills development, as well as opportunities for peer interaction.

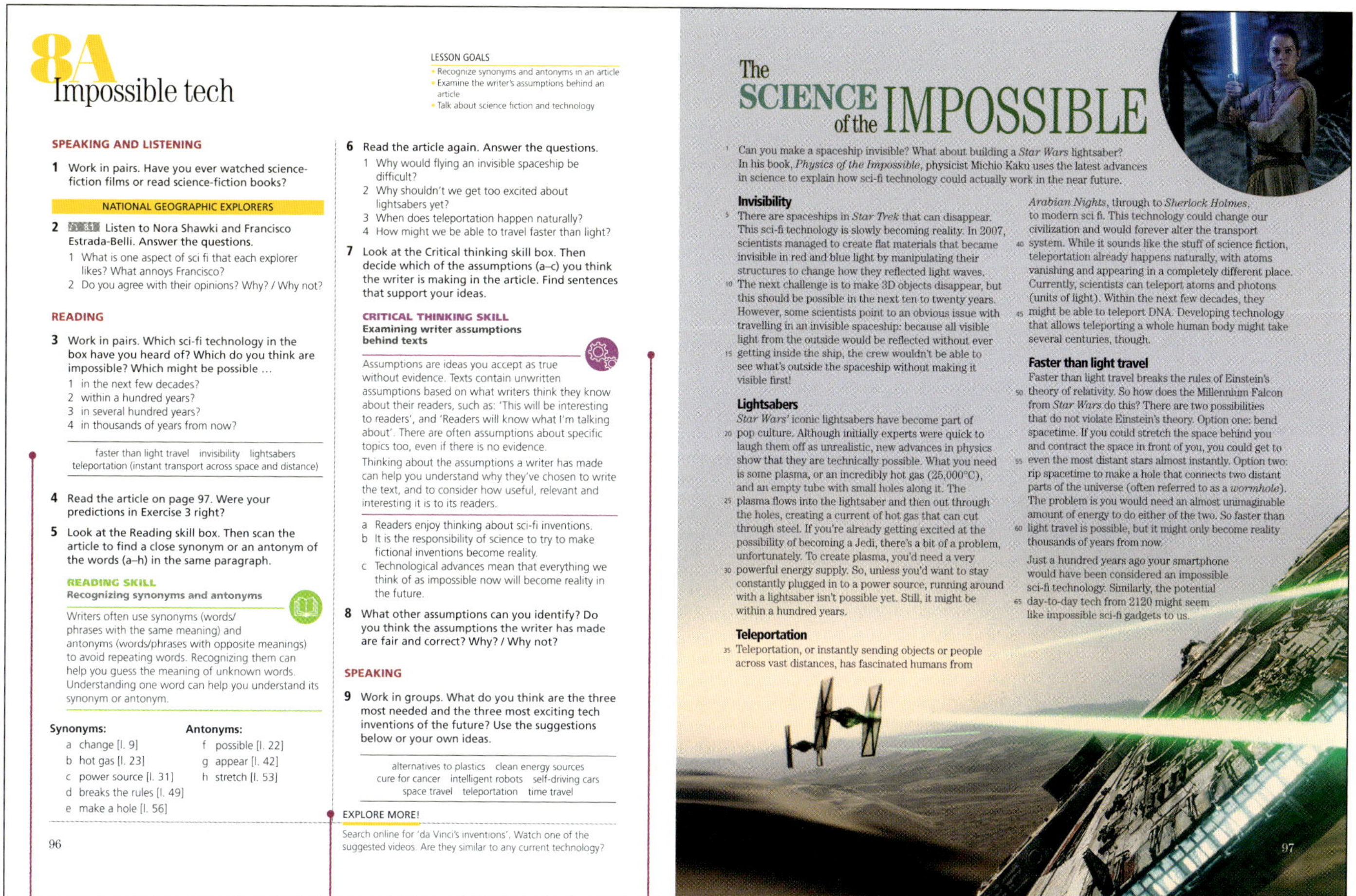

8A Impossible tech

LESSON GOALS
- Recognize synonyms and antonyms in an article
- Examine the writer's assumptions behind an article
- Talk about science fiction and technology

SPEAKING AND LISTENING

1 Work in pairs. Have you ever watched science-fiction films or read science-fiction books?

NATIONAL GEOGRAPHIC EXPLORERS

2 8.1 Listen to Nora Shawki and Francisco Estrada-Belli. Answer the questions.
1 What is one aspect of sci fi that each explorer likes? What annoys Francisco?
2 Do you agree with their opinions? Why? / Why not?

READING

3 Work in pairs. Which sci-fi technology in the box have you heard of? Which do you think are impossible? Which might be possible …
1 in the next few decades?
2 within a hundred years?
3 in several hundred years?
4 in thousands of years from now?

faster than light travel invisibility lightsabers teleportation (instant transport across space and distance)

4 Read the article on page 97. Were your predictions in Exercise 3 right?

5 Look at the Reading skill box. Then scan the article to find a close synonym or an antonym of the words (a–h) in the same paragraph.

READING SKILL
Recognizing synonyms and antonyms

Writers often use synonyms (words/phrases with the same meaning) and antonyms (words/phrases with opposite meanings) to avoid repeating words. Recognizing them can help you guess the meaning of unknown words. Understanding one word can help you understand its synonym or antonym.

Synonyms:
a change [l. 9]
b hot gas [l. 23]
c power source [l. 31]
d breaks the rules [l. 49]
e make a hole [l. 56]

Antonyms:
f possible [l. 22]
g appear [l. 42]
h stretch [l. 53]

96

6 Read the article again. Answer the questions.
1 Why would flying an invisible spaceship be difficult?
2 Why shouldn't we get too excited about lightsabers yet?
3 When does teleportation happen naturally?
4 How might we be able to travel faster than light?

7 Look at the Critical thinking skill box. Then decide which of the assumptions (a–c) you think the writer is making in the article. Find sentences that support your ideas.

CRITICAL THINKING SKILL
Examining writer assumptions behind texts

Assumptions are ideas you accept as true without evidence. Texts contain unwritten assumptions based on what writers think they know about their readers, such as: 'This will be interesting to readers', and 'Readers will know what I'm talking about'. There are often assumptions about specific topics too, even if there is no evidence.

Thinking about the assumptions a writer has made can help you understand why they've chosen to write the text, and to consider how useful, relevant and interesting it is to its readers.

a Readers enjoy thinking about sci-fi inventions.
b It is the responsibility of science to try to make fictional inventions become reality.
c Technological advances mean that everything we think of as impossible now will become reality in the future.

8 What other assumptions can you identify? Do you think the assumptions the writer has made are fair and correct? Why? / Why not?

SPEAKING

9 Work in groups. What do you think are the three most needed and the three most exciting tech inventions of the future? Use the suggestions below or your own ideas.

alternatives to plastics clean energy sources cure for cancer intelligent robots self-driving cars space travel teleportation time travel

EXPLORE MORE!
Search online for 'da Vinci's inventions'. Watch one of the suggested videos. Are they similar to any current technology?

The SCIENCE of the IMPOSSIBLE

Can you make a spaceship invisible? What about building a *Star Wars* lightsaber? In his book, *Physics of the Impossible*, physicist Michio Kaku uses the latest advances in science to explain how sci-fi technology could actually work in the near future.

Invisibility
There are spaceships in *Star Trek* that can disappear. This sci-fi technology is slowly becoming reality. In 2007, scientists managed to create flat materials that became invisible in red and blue light by manipulating their structures to change how they reflected light waves. The next challenge is to make 3D objects disappear, but this should be possible in the next ten to twenty years. However, some scientists point to an obvious issue with travelling in an invisible spaceship: because all visible light from the outside would be reflected without ever getting inside the ship, the crew wouldn't be able to see what's outside the spaceship without making it visible first!

Lightsabers
Star Wars' iconic lightsabers have become part of pop culture. Although initially experts were quick to laugh them off as unrealistic, new advances in physics show that they are technically possible. What you need is some plasma, or an incredibly hot gas (25,000°C), and an empty tube with small holes along it. The plasma flows into the lightsaber and then out through the holes, creating a current of hot gas that can cut through steel. If you're already getting excited at the possibility of becoming a Jedi, there's a bit of a problem, unfortunately. To create plasma, you'd need a very powerful energy supply. So, unless you'd want to stay constantly plugged in to a power source, running around with a lightsaber isn't possible yet. Still, it might be within a hundred years.

Teleportation
Teleportation, or instantly sending objects or people across vast distances, has fascinated humans from *Arabian Nights*, through to *Sherlock Holmes*, to modern sci fi. This technology could change our civilization and would forever alter the transport system. While it sounds like the stuff of science fiction, teleportation already happens naturally, with atoms vanishing and appearing in a completely different place. Currently, scientists can teleport atoms and photons (units of light). Within the next few decades, they might be able to teleport DNA. Developing technology that allows teleporting a whole human body might take several centuries, though.

Faster than light travel
Faster than light travel breaks the rules of Einstein's theory of relativity. So how does the Millennium Falcon from *Star Wars* do this? There are two possibilities that do not violate Einstein's theory. Option one: bend spacetime. If you could stretch the space behind you and contract the space in front of you, you could get to even the most distant stars almost instantly. Option two: rip spacetime to make a hole that connects two distant parts of the universe (often referred to as a *wormhole*). The problem is you would need an almost unimaginable amount of energy to do either of the two. So faster than light travel is possible, but it might only become reality thousands of years from now.

Just a hundred years ago your smartphone would have been considered an impossible sci-fi technology. Similarly, the potential day-to-day tech from 2120 might seem like impossible sci-fi gadgets to us.

97

Carefully sequenced activities give students practice at applying strategies to help them become more confident readers inside, and outside, of the classroom.

'Explore More' activities propose a variety of optional ways teachers and students can engage with the unit topic and develop learner autonomy. Further guidance on how to exploit this is in the Teacher's Book notes.

Explicit Critical Thinking instruction guides students to critically evaluate the reading text and to reflect on their own thought processes, encouraging them to think more analytically.

STUDENT'S BOOK UNIT WALKTHROUGH

Lesson B introduces the main grammar focus of the unit. The grammar is introduced in context through a short text, an infographic, or a listening that often features the National Geographic Explorers of the unit. Students progress through a series of controlled activities that build to more personalized communicative tasks. Extended explanations and additional practice are provided in the grammar reference section at the back of the book.

A guided discovery approach makes grammar memorable: students first see the language in context, then see the form explicitly presented, and are encouraged to notice its features. Practice activities progress from controlled exercises to more open-ended tasks that require students to use the language independently.

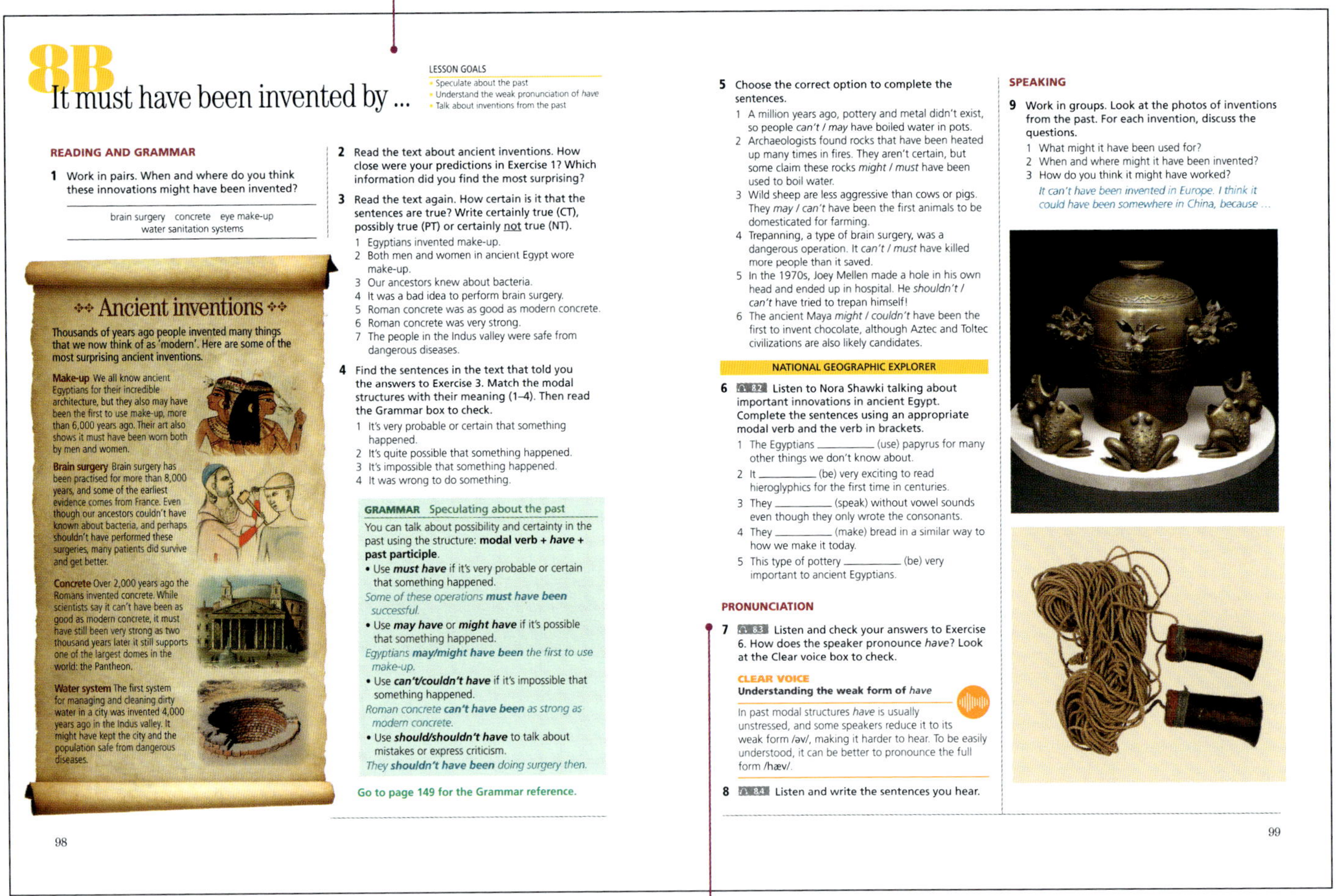

8B It must have been invented by ...

LESSON GOALS
- Speculate about the past
- Understand the weak pronunciation of *have*
- Talk about inventions from the past

READING AND GRAMMAR

1 Work in pairs. When and where do you think these innovations might have been invented?

brain surgery concrete eye make-up water sanitation systems

Ancient inventions

Thousands of years ago people invented many things that we now think of as 'modern'. Here are some of the most surprising ancient inventions.

Make-up We all know ancient Egyptians for their incredible architecture, but they also may have been the first to use make-up, more than 6,000 years ago. Their art also shows it must have been worn both by men and women.

Brain surgery Brain surgery has been practised for more than 8,000 years, and some of the earliest evidence comes from France. Even though our ancestors couldn't have known about bacteria, and perhaps shouldn't have performed these surgeries, many patients did survive and get better.

Concrete Over 2,000 years ago the Romans invented concrete. While scientists say it can't have been as good as modern concrete, it must have still been very strong as two thousand years later it still supports one of the largest domes in the world: the Pantheon.

Water system The first system for managing and cleaning dirty water in a city was invented 4,000 years ago in the Indus valley. It might have kept the city and the population safe from dangerous diseases.

2 Read the text about ancient inventions. How close were your predictions in Exercise 1? Which information did you find the most surprising?

3 Read the text again. How certain is it that the sentences are true? Write certainly true (CT), possibly true (PT) or certainly not true (NT).
1 Egyptians invented make-up.
2 Both men and women in ancient Egypt wore make-up.
3 Our ancestors knew about bacteria.
4 It was a bad idea to perform brain surgery.
5 Roman concrete was as good as modern concrete.
6 Roman concrete was very strong.
7 The people in the Indus valley were safe from dangerous diseases.

4 Find the sentences in the text that told you the answers to Exercise 3. Match the modal structures with their meaning (1–4). Then read the Grammar box to check.
1 It's very probable or certain that something happened.
2 It's quite possible that something happened.
3 It's impossible that something happened.
4 It was wrong to do something.

GRAMMAR Speculating about the past

You can talk about possibility and certainty in the past using the structure: **modal verb + *have* + past participle**.
- Use ***must have*** if it's very probable or certain that something happened.
*Some of these operations **must have been** successful.*
- Use ***may have*** or ***might have*** if it's possible that something happened.
*Egyptians **may/might have been** the first to use make-up.*
- Use ***can't/couldn't have*** if it's impossible that something happened.
*Roman concrete **can't have been** as strong as modern concrete.*
- Use ***should/shouldn't have*** to talk about mistakes or express criticism.
*They **shouldn't have been** doing surgery then.*

Go to page 149 for the Grammar reference.

98

5 Choose the correct option to complete the sentences.
1 A million years ago, pottery and metal didn't exist, so people *can't / may* have boiled water in pots.
2 Archaeologists found rocks that have been heated up many times in fires. They aren't certain, but some claim these rocks *might / must* have been used to boil water.
3 Wild sheep are less aggressive than cows or pigs. They *may / can't* have been the first animals to be domesticated for farming.
4 Trepanning, a type of brain surgery, was a dangerous operation. It *can't / must* have killed more people than it saved.
5 In the 1970s, Joey Mellen made a hole in his own head and ended up in hospital. He *shouldn't / can't* have tried to trepan himself!
6 The ancient Maya *might / couldn't* have been the first to invent chocolate, although Aztec and Toltec civilizations are also likely candidates.

NATIONAL GEOGRAPHIC EXPLORER

6 8.2 Listen to Nora Shawki talking about important innovations in ancient Egypt. Complete the sentences using an appropriate modal verb and the verb in brackets.
1 The Egyptians ______ (use) papyrus for many other things we don't know about.
2 It ______ (be) very exciting to read hieroglyphics for the first time in centuries.
3 They ______ (speak) without vowel sounds even though they only wrote the consonants.
4 They ______ (make) bread in a similar way to how we make it today.
5 This type of pottery ______ (be) very important to ancient Egyptians.

PRONUNCIATION

7 8.3 Listen and check your answers to Exercise 6. How does the speaker pronounce *have*? Look at the Clear voice box to check.

CLEAR VOICE
Understanding the weak form of *have*
In past modal structures *have* is usually unstressed, and some speakers reduce it to its weak form /əv/, making it harder to hear. To be easily understood, it can be better to pronounce the full form /hæv/.

8 8.4 Listen and write the sentences you hear.

SPEAKING

9 Work in groups. Look at the photos of inventions from the past. For each invention, discuss the questions.
1 What might it have been used for?
2 When and where might it have been invented?
3 How do you think it might have worked?
It can't have been invented in Europe. I think it could have been somewhere in China, because ...

99

With mutual comprehension as a goal, pronunciation points are integrated into the lesson sequence. As well as presenting students with productive points, giving them the opportunity to practise what they hear, students also explore receptive points, taking the time to notice and understand without being encouraged to produce them.

Lesson C develops transferable listening skills, presents topic-related vocabulary and introduces the 'Focus on' point which has a grammatical or lexical focus. There is a strong focus on language needed for everyday communication.

Listening activities simulate real-world situations and often feature National Geographic explorers.

8C Two sides to tech

LESSON GOALS

- Talk about gadgets and technology
- Form nouns, verbs and adjectives in word families
- Understand prepositions in connected speech
- Pronounce long and short 'o' sounds clearly

Francisco Estrada-Belli and his team use technology called LIDAR to find Maya ruins in the Guatemalan jungle.

VOCABULARY AND LISTENING

1 **Work in pairs. Look at the technology in the box and discuss the questions.**

driverless vehicles   electric scooters   self-service checkouts   sharing apps (e.g. Uber, Airbnb)   video conferencing

1 What are the advantages of each technology: to the company? to workers? to customers?
2 What disadvantages can you think of?
3 Which technology have you used or experienced yourself? Why did you use it?

NATIONAL GEOGRAPHIC EXPLORER

2 8.5 **Listen to Francisco Estrada-Belli talk about technology in his work. What advantages and disadvantages does he mention about ...**

1 LIDAR?
2 his smartphone?

3 8.5 **Listen again. Complete each sentence with one word.**

1 Remote sensing uses a number of ________ to find ancient remains.
2 LIDAR is really ________ but it's not very ________. You need a lot of training because it's so ________.
3 Francisco couldn't work without his smartphone because it is so ________. It's a ________ collection of ________: G.P.S., compass, flashlight, camera and notepad.
4 But on the flip side, it's not ________, so it might get wet and damaged.

4 **Match the words (1–10) with the definitions (a–j).**

1 gadget
2 handy
3 innovative
4 outdated
5 perform
6 pocket-sized
7 recharge
8 sophisticated
9 user-friendly
10 waterproof

a a small machine with a particular purpose
b advanced in design so it can do complex things
c small enough to carry in your pocket
d fill something with electricity so it keeps working
e complete an action or job, especially a difficult one
f using new and different ideas and methods
g not allowing water to enter it
h old and no longer as good as more modern things
i useful
j simple for people to use

100

5 **Write sentences using the words from Exercise 4 to describe ...**

1 the technology you often use.
2 the technology in Exercise 1.

Go to page 138 for the Vocabulary reference.

6 **Which words from Exercise 4 (1–10) are in the same word families as the bold words (a–c)? Are they nouns, verbs or adjectives? Read the Focus on box to check.**

a a computer with high **performance**
b the latest **innovations**
c **rechargeable** batteries

FOCUS ON Forming nouns, verbs and adjectives

You can expand your vocabulary by exploring the word families of words you are learning.
Notice some common suffixes that are typically added to words to create different parts of speech.
Nouns: -ion, -ment, -ity, -e/ance, -ness
complicated → complication, achieve → achievement, complex – complexity, silent → silence, happy → happiness
Adjectives: -al, -ical, -able, -ous, -ive
universe → universal, technology → technological, afford → affordable, danger → dangerous, act → active
Verbs: -ate, -ize, -ify, -en
active → activate, memory → memorize, simple → simplify, strength → strengthen

Go to page 149 for the Focus on reference.

7 **Complete the sentences, using suffixes to change the words in the box to the correct part of speech. Then use a dictionary to check.**

invent   memory   sense

1 The Chinese are typically credited with the ________ of paper.
2 This app saves you from having to ________ all your passwords.
3 The alarm is ________ to movement and beeps as soon as someone enters the room.

LISTENING

8 8.6 **You are going to listen to a radio phone-in about a new sharing app. First, look at the Listening skill box. Then listen to three extracts and complete the sentences (1–3).**

LISTENING SKILL
Understanding prepositions in connected speech

In connected speech, prepositions might not be heard clearly. They will often be connected to the words next to them, so *for example* might sound like /frəˈzɑːmpl/. Note that speaking like this might make you *less* easy to understand.

1 We've had them ________.
2 MyCarYourCar is revolutionizing ________.
3 That way they share the cost ________.

9 8.7 **Listen to the phone-in. Match the statements (1–5) with the person who said them: the host, Marsha, Yuki or Jens.**

1 One benefit of carpooling is the interesting conversations you can have.
2 Carpooling is cheaper than the alternatives.
3 Carpooling isn't the most environmentally-friendly way of travelling.
4 Personal safety is an issue when carpooling.
5 There is an important difference between carpooling and hitchhiking.

PRONUNCIATION

10 8.8 **Look at the Clear voice box and listen to the words (1–6). Do they have a short or long 'o' sound? Practise saying the words.**

CLEAR VOICE
Pronouncing long and short 'o'

In English there are two different 'o' sounds: a short one /ɒ/ (usually spelled 'o') and a long one /ɔː/. (often spelled as 'au' or 'or').

1 automatic
2 complex
3 laptop
4 performance
5 pocket-sized
6 waterproof

SPEAKING

11 **Work in groups of three. Read the statement and discuss whether you agree or not, and why.**

The internet has damaged our personal and professional lives more than it has helped them.

101

Every pronunciation point is accompanied by an audio track. In many of the productive pronunciation points, students will hear two models – a speaker of British English first, followed by another global English speaker.

STUDENT'S BOOK UNIT WALKTHROUGH

Lesson D equips students with the language and communicative strategies to navigate a wide range of interpersonal and intercultural situations. Guidance is provided through videos and carefully staged tasks to enable students to formulate their own response to hypothetical situations in the safe environment of the classroom.

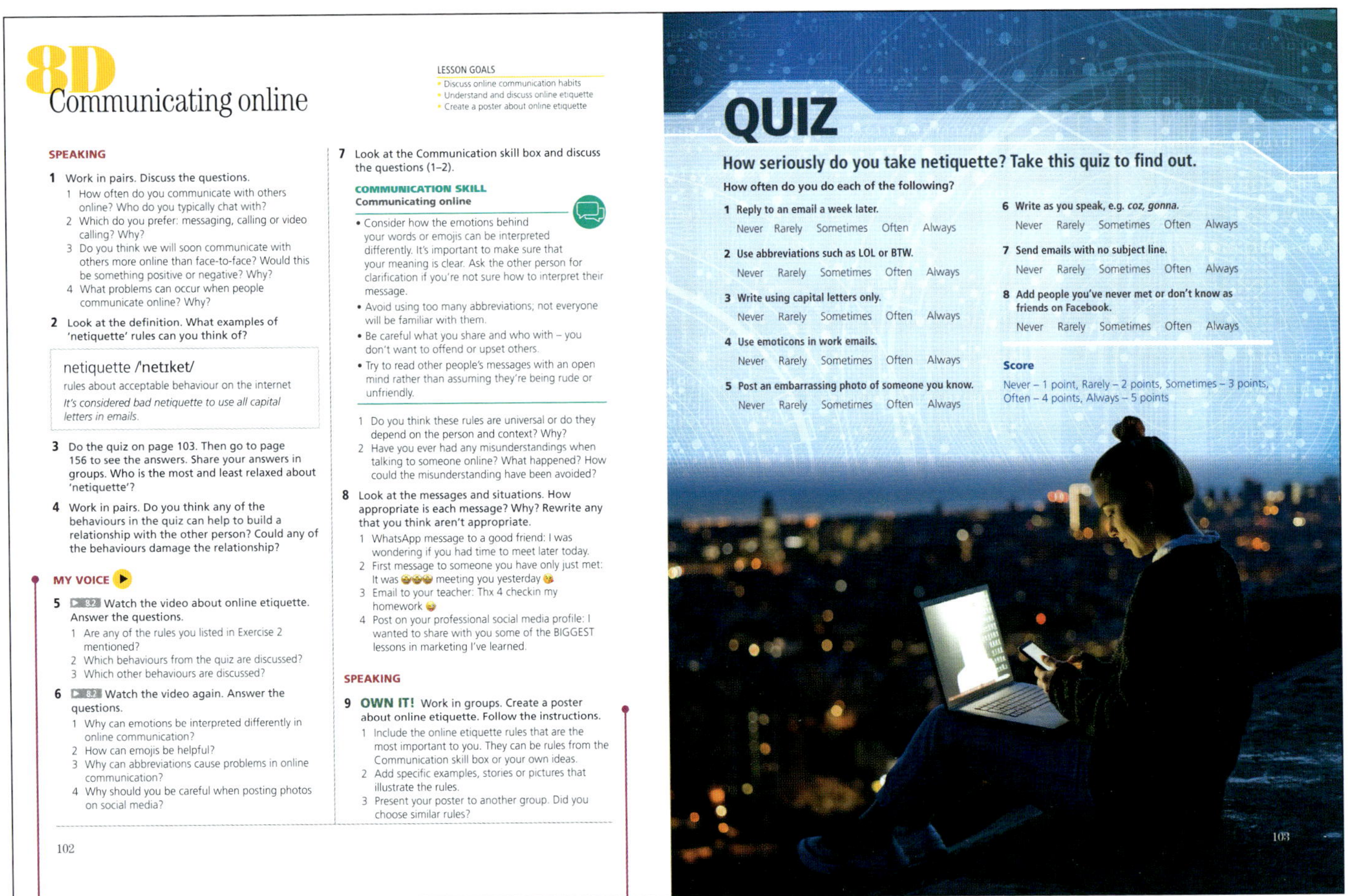

8D Communicating online

LESSON GOALS
- Discuss online communication habits
- Understand and discuss online etiquette
- Create a poster about online etiquette

SPEAKING

1 Work in pairs. Discuss the questions.
1. How often do you communicate with others online? Who do you typically chat with?
2. Which do you prefer: messaging, calling or video calling? Why?
3. Do you think we will soon communicate with others more online than face-to-face? Would this be something positive or negative? Why?
4. What problems can occur when people communicate online? Why?

2 Look at the definition. What examples of 'netiquette' rules can you think of?

netiquette /ˈnetɪket/
rules about acceptable behaviour on the internet
It's considered bad netiquette to use all capital letters in emails.

3 Do the quiz on page 103. Then go to page 156 to see the answers. Share your answers in groups. Who is the most and least relaxed about 'netiquette'?

4 Work in pairs. Do you think any of the behaviours in the quiz can help to build a relationship with the other person? Could any of the behaviours damage the relationship?

MY VOICE

5 8.2 Watch the video about online etiquette. Answer the questions.
1. Are any of the rules you listed in Exercise 2 mentioned?
2. Which behaviours from the quiz are discussed?
3. Which other behaviours are discussed?

6 8.2 Watch the video again. Answer the questions.
1. Why can emotions be interpreted differently in online communication?
2. How can emojis be helpful?
3. Why can abbreviations cause problems in online communication?
4. Why should you be careful when posting photos on social media?

7 Look at the Communication skill box and discuss the questions (1–2).

COMMUNICATION SKILL
Communicating online
- Consider how the emotions behind your words or emojis can be interpreted differently. It's important to make sure that your meaning is clear. Ask the other person for clarification if you're not sure how to interpret their message.
- Avoid using too many abbreviations; not everyone will be familiar with them.
- Be careful what you share and who with – you don't want to offend or upset others.
- Try to read other people's messages with an open mind rather than assuming they're being rude or unfriendly.

1. Do you think these rules are universal or do they depend on the person and context? Why?
2. Have you ever had any misunderstandings when talking to someone online? What happened? How could the misunderstanding have been avoided?

8 Look at the messages and situations. How appropriate is each message? Why? Rewrite any that you think aren't appropriate.
1. WhatsApp message to a good friend: I was wondering if you had time to meet later today.
2. First message to someone you have only just met: It was 🤩🤩🤩 meeting you yesterday 😘
3. Email to your teacher: Thx 4 checkin my homework 😜
4. Post on your professional social media profile: I wanted to share with you some of the BIGGEST lessons in marketing I've learned.

SPEAKING

9 **OWN IT!** Work in groups. Create a poster about online etiquette. Follow the instructions.
1. Include the online etiquette rules that are the most important to you. They can be rules from the Communication skill box or your own ideas.
2. Add specific examples, stories or pictures that illustrate the rules.
3. Present your poster to another group. Did you choose similar rules?

102

QUIZ

How seriously do you take netiquette? Take this quiz to find out.

How often do you do each of the following?

1 Reply to an email a week later.
Never Rarely Sometimes Often Always

2 Use abbreviations such as LOL or BTW.
Never Rarely Sometimes Often Always

3 Write using capital letters only.
Never Rarely Sometimes Often Always

4 Use emoticons in work emails.
Never Rarely Sometimes Often Always

5 Post an embarrassing photo of someone you know.
Never Rarely Sometimes Often Always

6 Write as you speak, e.g. *coz, gonna.*
Never Rarely Sometimes Often Always

7 Send emails with no subject line.
Never Rarely Sometimes Often Always

8 Add people you've never met or don't know as friends on Facebook.
Never Rarely Sometimes Often Always

Score
Never – 1 point, Rarely – 2 points, Sometimes – 3 points, Often – 4 points, Always – 5 points

103

Lively lesson videos illustrate communicative scenarios and provide insight into different communication styles. Students are encouraged to reflect on their own interactions and are provided with ready-to-use tips to promote effective communication.

The 'Own it' task at the end of each lesson encourages learner collaboration as students apply the language and communication skills to real-world scenarios.

Lesson E develops transferable writing skills through a clear, step-by-step approach that guides learners to put the grammar and vocabulary from the unit to use in their own writing.

As well as topic-related vocabulary sets, students are presented with everyday useful language chunks throughout the unit ready to pick up and use in spoken and written interaction inside and outside the classroom.

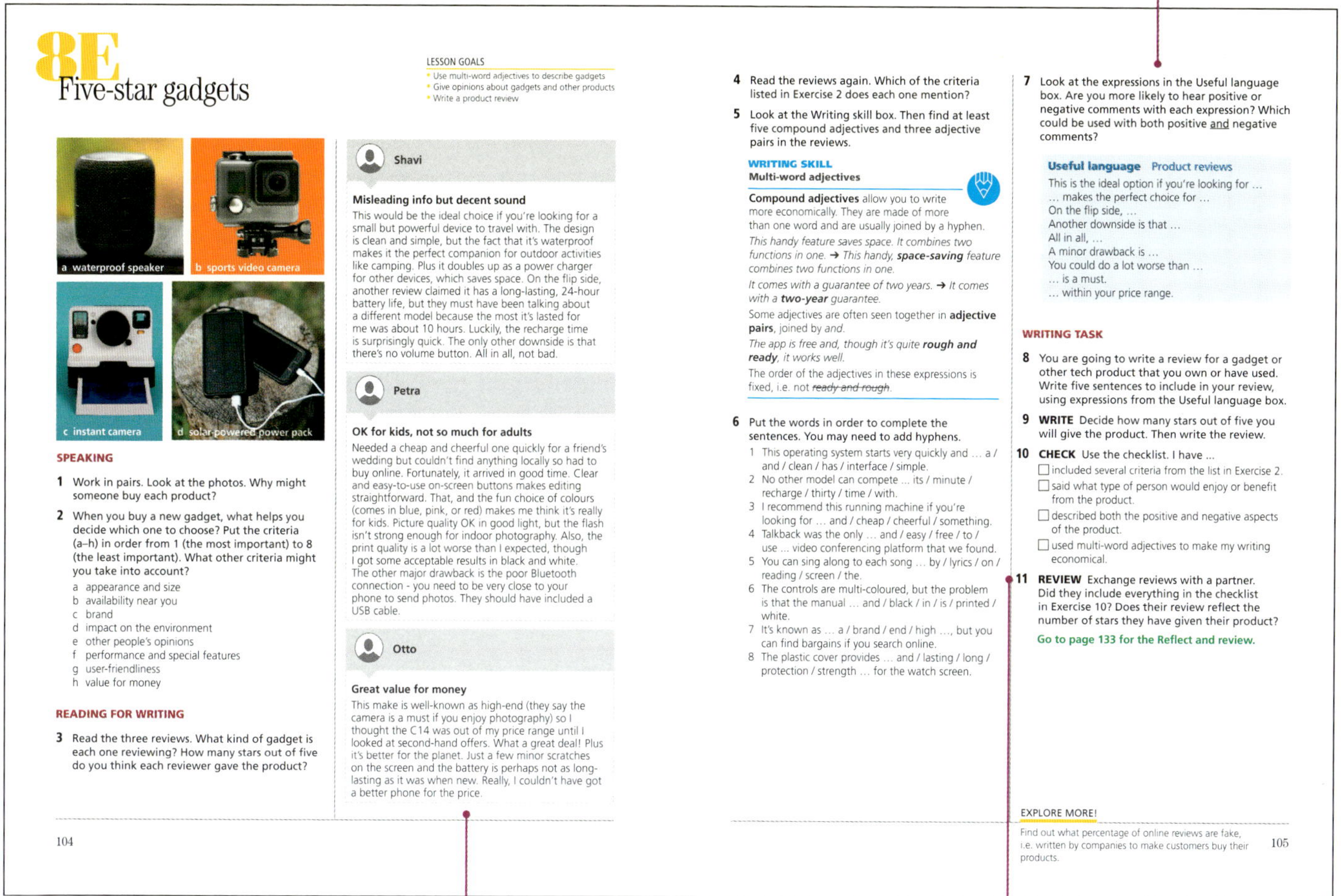

8E Five-star gadgets

LESSON GOALS

- Use multi-word adjectives to describe gadgets
- Give opinions about gadgets and other products
- Write a product review

a waterproof speaker

b sports video camera

c instant camera

d solar-powered power pack

SPEAKING

1 Work in pairs. Look at the photos. Why might someone buy each product?

2 When you buy a new gadget, what helps you decide which one to choose? Put the criteria (a–h) in order from 1 (the most important) to 8 (the least important). What other criteria might you take into account?

a appearance and size
b availability near you
c brand
d impact on the environment
e other people's opinions
f performance and special features
g user-friendliness
h value for money

READING FOR WRITING

3 Read the three reviews. What kind of gadget is each one reviewing? How many stars out of five do you think each reviewer gave the product?

Shavi

Misleading info but decent sound

This would be the ideal choice if you're looking for a small but powerful device to travel with. The design is clean and simple, but the fact that it's waterproof makes it the perfect companion for outdoor activities like camping. Plus it doubles up as a power charger for other devices, which saves space. On the flip side, another review claimed it has a long-lasting, 24-hour battery life, but they must have been talking about a different model because the most it's lasted for me was about 10 hours. Luckily, the recharge time is surprisingly quick. The only other downside is that there's no volume button. All in all, not bad.

Petra

OK for kids, not so much for adults

Needed a cheap and cheerful one quickly for a friend's wedding but couldn't find anything locally so had to buy online. Fortunately, it arrived in good time. Clear and easy-to-use on-screen buttons makes editing straightforward. That, and the fun choice of colours (comes in blue, pink, or red) makes me think it's really for kids. Picture quality OK in good light, but the flash isn't strong enough for indoor photography. Also, the print quality is a lot worse than I expected, though I got some acceptable results in black and white. The other major drawback is the poor Bluetooth connection - you need to be very close to your phone to send photos. They should have included a USB cable.

Otto

Great value for money

This make is well-known as high-end (they say the camera is a must if you enjoy photography) so I thought the C14 was out of my price range until I looked at second-hand offers. What a great deal! Plus it's better for the planet. Just a few minor scratches on the screen and the battery is perhaps not as long-lasting as it was when new. Really, I couldn't have got a better phone for the price.

104

4 Read the reviews again. Which of the criteria listed in Exercise 2 does each one mention?

5 Look at the Writing skill box. Then find at least five compound adjectives and three adjective pairs in the reviews.

WRITING SKILL
Multi-word adjectives

Compound adjectives allow you to write more economically. They are made of more than one word and are usually joined by a hyphen.

This handy feature saves space. It combines two functions in one. → *This handy,* ***space-saving*** *feature combines two functions in one.*

It comes with a guarantee of two years. → *It comes with a* ***two-year*** *guarantee.*

Some adjectives are often seen together in **adjective pairs**, joined by *and*.

The app is free and, though it's quite ***rough and ready****, it works well.*

The order of the adjectives in these expressions is fixed, i.e. not ~~ready and rough~~.

6 Put the words in order to complete the sentences. You may need to add hyphens.

1 This operating system starts very quickly and … a / and / clean / has / interface / simple.
2 No other model can compete ... its / minute / recharge / thirty / time / with.
3 I recommend this running machine if you're looking for … and / cheap / cheerful / something.
4 Talkback was the only … and / easy / free / to / use ... video conferencing platform that we found.
5 You can sing along to each song … by / lyrics / on / reading / screen / the.
6 The controls are multi-coloured, but the problem is that the manual … and / black / in / is / printed / white.
7 It's known as … a / brand / end / high …, but you can find bargains if you search online.
8 The plastic cover provides … and / lasting / long / protection / strength … for the watch screen.

7 Look at the expressions in the Useful language box. Are you more likely to hear positive or negative comments with each expression? Which could be used with both positive and negative comments?

Useful language Product reviews

This is the ideal option if you're looking for …
… makes the perfect choice for …
On the flip side, …
Another downside is that …
All in all, …
A minor drawback is …
You could do a lot worse than …
… is a must.
… within your price range.

WRITING TASK

8 You are going to write a review for a gadget or other tech product that you own or have used. Write five sentences to include in your review, using expressions from the Useful language box.

9 **WRITE** Decide how many stars out of five you will give the product. Then write the review.

10 **CHECK** Use the checklist. I have ...

- ☐ included several criteria from the list in Exercise 2.
- ☐ said what type of person would enjoy or benefit from the product.
- ☐ described both the positive and negative aspects of the product.
- ☐ used multi-word adjectives to make my writing economical.

11 **REVIEW** Exchange reviews with a partner. Did they include everything in the checklist in Exercise 10? Does their review reflect the number of stars they have given their product?

Go to page 133 for the Reflect and review.

EXPLORE MORE!

Find out what percentage of online reviews are fake, i.e. written by companies to make customers buy their products.

105

A practical writing model acts as a point of reference and an aspirational goal for students as they are supported to produce a personalized text of the same genre.

The 'Check' and 'Review' sections at the end of the lesson get students into the habit of reviewing their own work and that of their peers to identify ways to improve it through subsequent edits.

Learn More About *Voices* . . .

We asked the *Voices* author team some questions to understand the thinking behind the series and what makes *Voices* unique . . .

Q: How do the National Geographic Explorers in *Voices* help make the course more relatable for students?

DANIEL BARBER

A: Learners need the chance to use English to talk about their own experience. When they meet the National Geographic Explorers, they are getting to know interesting people who lead exciting lives, but who are also like them in many ways. They do talk about their jobs, but they also talk about their private lives, funny accidents, travel routines, future desires and worst fears. Importantly, many of them are language learners themselves, using English to express themselves and succeed internationally. They're ideal role models and great examples to emulate!

Q: *Voices* represents the real world through its range of Englishes. Why is that important?

LEWIS LANFORD

A: Every day, people from all over the world communicate with one another in English. Colleagues from Germany, Argentina and Japan working together in Saudi Arabia will use English even when no one in the group has it as a first language. Hotel staff in Beijing will speak English with guests from Thailand or Bahrain because it's a global lingua franca. English is also a major medium for the exchange of information and ideas online. To prepare for real-world communication, learners need to be exposed to a wide variety of international English input. That's why *Voices* includes listening and video material featuring a broad range of both first- and second-language English users, and explores accents and pronunciation features that learners will encounter in real life. Not only does this help learners become better communicators, it also demonstrates that English is their own language – and their passport to the wider world.

Q: Can you tell us more about how *Voices* develops communication skills?

CHIA SUAN CHONG

A: As our learners use English, they're going to need skills and strategies to build trust, manage impressions, deal with conflict, and mediate in a space where people from different cultural backgrounds are coming together to convey their messages and develop relationships. The communication skills in *Voices* allow the learner to dive into different areas of interpersonal communication, offering teachers and students useful tips, strategies and useful language which they can then practise using in a variety of realistic scenarios. These relatable scenarios allow us to push the learner to develop an awareness of the issues and their own reactions to them. In my experience, they are also a great way of motivating students to engage in extended speaking practice. After all, the best speaking activities are those where learners can't wait to share their thoughts and opinions about the topic!

Q: What is special about the pronunciation strand in *Voices*?

MAREK KICZKOWIAK

A: There are a few things that make it unique. First, it is based on research. In other words, in developing it, we used research findings to identify which pronunciation features are most likely to lead to misunderstandings in international contexts. Second, it recognizes the beautiful diversity of English, and is the first to use 'second language speakers of English' as models of pronunciation. Third, students are given clear instructions drawing their attention to how a specific sound is produced. Finally, our pronunciation strands emphasizes clear pronunciation, rather than proximity with an idealized standard 'first language speaker of English' model, helping students take ownership of the language and promoting inclusivity.

Q: How does *Voices* support the evolving needs of learners?

EMILY BRYSON

A: Every learner is different, and as such, every learner has different needs. What's so great about *Voices* is that it is a comprehensive course which equips all learners with a multitude of life skills for today's world. The digital components of the course support learners to develop their online learning and self-skills while the Explore More! features encourage learners to enhance their research skills. Each unit provides tips on reading, listening, writing and critical thinking skills to enhance their language as well as their work and study skills. The world is getting smaller, and students on this course will gain international communication skills and knowledge of authentic topics to succeed in an ever-evolving global environment.

Q: Reflecting on your experiences as a teacher, what do you think your three favourite things would be about *Voices*?

CHRISTIEN LEE

A: For me, the focus on real people, including the National Geographic Explorers, is really interesting. I feel that getting glimpses into the lives of real people from all over the world increases the intrinsic interest of the material, and provides a context that makes the grammar, vocabulary, and other content natural and relatable. I also like how the units strike a good balance between being new and familiar. There are some units that focus on topics not commonly seen in ELT materials, which is nice. But even those topics that seem familiar at first glance are typically approached from an unusual angle, which adds both interest and excitement. Above all, though, I like the overall quality of the material. I was impressed with the tremendous passion, extensive knowledge and deep commitment of all of the other authors, and when I see the material they produced, the top-to-bottom quality shines through.

Q: How does *Voices* prepare students for assessment?

GARY PATHARE

A: To prepare for important English exams like IELTS, FCE and TOEFL, teachers need a course that not only systematically builds the real-world skills and language required, but also keeps learners interested and motivated. *Voices* has a rigorous, structured approach based on the international framework of skills and language for each level, but at the same time it engages learners in content-rich lessons with authentic tasks featuring real people from around the world. The unique communication skills and comprehensible pronunciation focus will help *Voices* learners perform confidently in speaking tests, and the contemporary photos and infographics are designed both to stimulate students to develop their productive skills and to input interesting ideas to talk and write about. As all skills are clearly signposted and explained, teachers can easily target specific exam techniques and strategies for them, and there is plenty of extra grammar and vocabulary practice to help learners secure the language they need.

UNIT 1

Reactions

People queue to participate in 'Inside Out: The People's Art Project' by artist JR in Paris, France.

UNIT GOALS

1A Reading, speaking

- read an article to identify reasons and use critical thinking skills to evaluate the reliability of evidence; discuss the most appropriate background noises for different places and activities

1B Listening and grammar, pronunciation, speaking

- review and practise asking questions; practise using word stress on different words to change the meaning of a sentence; design and carry out a questionnaire, then report interesting findings to the class

1C Vocabulary, pronunciation, listening, speaking

- learn and practise using adverbs of degree to describe emotions; practise inferring the speakers' emotions when listening; practise short and long vowel sounds

1D Speaking

- discuss how you would deal with a difficult situation; practise demonstrating empathy in a conversation; help other people see a situation from another perspective

1E Writing

- use informal language to sound friendly in an email; write an informal email giving news; write an email reply to respond to someone else's news

Photocopiable resources

Communication activities: pp. 212–213
Vocabulary activity: p. 233
Grammar activity: p. 245
Focus on … activity: p. 246
Pronunciation activity: p. 268
Mediation activity: p. 283

Workbook

Unit 1 pp. 4–11

ABOUT THE PHOTO

The photo shows an installation that is part of 'Inside Out: The People's Art Project'. The project began in Paris, France, but people from all over the world have participated in it. The project's aim is to increase the representation of 'ordinary people' from diverse backgrounds who may be overlooked by mainstream art. The project was initiated by Paris-born photographer and street artist JR, who is known for posting large black and white photographs on walls in public places.

1

- **Optional step** Provide a model by choosing a person in the photo and describing him/her to the class.
- Students take turns describing the people in the photo. Their partners should guess who is being described.
- Students answer the other questions.

1 Reactions

GOALS

- Identify reasons in an article
- Review and practise asking questions
- Talk about strong emotions
- Infer emotions when listening
- Demonstrate empathy in a conversation
- Write an informal email giving news

1 Work in pairs. Look at the photo and complete the tasks.

1 Take turns to describe people in the photo. Can you guess who your partner is describing?
2 What do you think the artist is trying to show through the portraits?
3 Would you like to participate in a project like this?

WATCH ▶

2 ▶ 1.1 Watch the video. Which person, Francisco (F) or Tsiory (T), talks about feeling ...

a annoyed? T
b excited? T
c happy? F
d impatient? F

NATIONAL GEOGRAPHIC EXPLORERS

FRANCISCO ESTRADA-BELLI
TSIORY ANDRIANAVALONA

3 ▶ 1.1 Watch the video again. Make notes about the reasons for Francisco and Tsiory's feelings.

4 Make connections. When do you feel the emotions that Francisco and Tsiory mention?

Unlike Francisco, I don't mind waiting in traffic. But I get impatient when ...

Sample answer

The artist could be trying to show how interesting 'ordinary' people are; that art is all about the experience of being a human; the public will be more interested in art if they are involved in creating it.

Extra activity

Ask students to write four interview questions to ask someone who took part in the Inside Out project – for example, why they took part or why they chose their pose. In pairs, students take turns to ask and answer their questions. The student being interviewed can answer as themselves or as one of the people in the photo.

WATCH ▶

2 ▶ 1.1

- **Optional step** Elicit the difference in meaning between *excited* and *happy* and between *annoyed* and *impatient*.
- Play the video and encourage students to listen for synonyms for the adjectives.
- Students compare answers in pairs before checking as a class.

Extra activity

Ask students to recall phrases they heard in the video that told them what feelings the explorers were describing: excited – *what excites me*; happy – *the thing that makes me happiest*; annoyed – *frustrating, pointless*; impatient – *I'm stuck for an hour in traffic, get angry at myself*.

3 ▶ 1.1

- Play the video again. Students make notes on the reasons for Francisco and Tsiory's feelings.

Answers

Francisco: happy – goes camping with his kids; impatient – when he's stuck in traffic, or when he has to wait for equipment at work
Tsiory: excited – a project she is running about science education with young people; annoyed – people talking with no purpose, or talking about people

4

- Direct students to the example sentences. Elicit that students can use *unlike* + [name] to say that they have different emotions to Francisco or Tsiory. Elicit other words or expressions to express contrast or say you have something in common, for example: *In contrast to* [name], *I'm (a lot) like* [name] *because ...*
- Students take turns to explain when they feel the four emotions from Exercise 2.

ABOUT THE EXPLORERS

FRANCISCO ESTRADA-BELLI is an Italian-born archaeologist, based in the US. His research focuses on Maya civilizations in Guatemala. He is the co-founder of the Maya Archaeology Initiative which supports heritage conservation in Guatemala's Maya Biosphere Reserve. Francisco searches for ancient Maya cities using aerial laser mapping. This requires special digital technologies such as LiDAR (light detection and ranging).

TSIORY ANDRIANAVALONA is a palaeontologist and a National Geographic Explorer from Madagascar. Her research focuses on Madagascar's fossil sharks. She is the leader of ExplorerHome which aims to infuse curiosity and love for science among young people in Madagascar and have a positive impact on her country.

LESSON GOALS

- **READING** The main aim is for students to learn how to recognize different structures used to give reasons in a discursive text and then use their critical thinking skills to practise evaluating scientific evidence in a text.
- **SPEAKING** The speaking aim is for students to discuss which sounds they find annoying and which sounds would be appropriate for different places and activities.

SPEAKING

1 1.1

- **Optional step** Direct students to the lesson title. Ask, *In what situation might someone say*, 'I can't stand that noise!'? Elicit noises that students find irritating.
- Students read through the list of sounds. If they aren't familiar with any of the words in the list, encourage them to deduce their meaning from the words they collocate with.
- Play the audio. Students match the sounds with the descriptions.

2

- Students order the sounds from Exercise 1 by numbering them.

3

- Students share their rankings and take turns to give reasons why they find some sounds particularly annoying or particularly pleasant. Encourage them to talk about their experiences of situations in which they have heard these sounds, where appropriate.
- **Optional step** You could extend this task by asking students to share their single most annoying and favourite sounds and their reasons why. Students must reach a group consensus together. Encourage students to compare and contrast their feelings about sounds with other group members' feelings, e.g. *Unlike* [name] *I find that sound quite pleasant because …* or *I agree with* [name] *that that's the most annoying sound.*

Sample answers
pleasant sounds include natural sounds, gentle sounds that make us feel relaxed; annoying sounds include sounds with

1A I can't stand that noise!

LESSON GOALS
- Identify reasons in an article
- Evaluate evidence in an article
- Talk about pleasing and annoying noises

SPEAKING

1 1.1 Listen to ten sounds. Match the sounds with the descriptions (a-j).

a a dentist's drill 10
b a fire crackling 2
c someone eating with their mouth open 3
d a workmate humming 6
e a baby crying 8
f bicycle brakes squealing 4
g birds singing 1
h rain on a tent 5
i thunder 9
j water flowing in a stream 7

2 Which of the sounds are the most and least annoying? Order them from 1 to 10 (10 = the most annoying).

3 Work in groups. Discuss the questions.

1 Which sounds in Exercise 1 are the most and least popular among the group?
2 Can you think of reasons why some sounds are pleasant and some are annoying?

READING

4 Read the article on page 13 quickly. Work in pairs and discuss the questions.

1 Which sounds from Exercise 1 are mentioned?
2 Which fact did you find the most interesting?

5 Read the article again. Choose from the sentences (1–5) the one that best fits each space in the text (a–e).

1 Because long-term stress can lead to illness, noise pollution is a real danger to your health. d
2 Next, high-pitched tools such as drills were extremely unpopular, perhaps because they remind people of visits to the dentist. c
3 That's why unpleasant noises can cause strong emotional reactions. a
4 One theory is that birds may be anxious due to an inability to listen out for danger. e
5 A simpler explanation is that these sounds can be physically painful at close range. b

6 Look at the Reading skill box. Then underline words in Exercise 5 that signal reasons.

READING SKILL
Identifying reasons

Identifying reasons helps you better understand the connection between ideas. Look for words and phrases such as *because (of)*, *since*, and *due to* to help you identify reasons. They may appear before or after the action or effect.

7 Write why the three types of sound in the final paragraph of the article might be pleasant.

8 Read the sentences from the article (a–d). Discuss which give strong evidence and which weaker evidence. Then look at the Critical thinking skill box to check.

a According to a survey of two thousand people, bird calls came in as the fifth most popular sound.
b One theory suggests that alarm calls our ancestors might have heard were made at these frequencies.
c Noise pollution … is likely to cause serious health issues too.
d And there is a great deal of scientific research to show that noise causes stress.

CRITICAL THINKING SKILL
Evaluating evidence

Articles might refer to scientific studies, but it's important to recognize how strong the evidence is. Verbs such as *may*, *might*, *suggest* and *seem to* or adverbs such as *likely* and *probably* tell you that scientists are not 100% certain. While phrases such as *a great deal of scientific research* tell you the evidence is based on research, you should always check the original sources and be suspicious if no sources are provided.

SPEAKING

9 Work in groups. What types of background noises or music would you choose for these places and activities? Why?

1 grammar study
2 getting to sleep
3 driving long distances
4 going for a run

I'd choose the sound of rain for grammar study. It's really relaxing and might help me concentrate.

12

negative associations, sounds that accompany bad habits, alarming sounds and other loud noises

READING

ABOUT THE TEXT

The text type is a magazine article. It presents the results of several scientific studies whose aim was to find out which sounds people find the most annoying or the most pleasing. It also explores the physical and mental health issues linked to long exposure to noise pollution, as well as looking at evidence showing the negative effect that noises from human activity can have on wildlife.

Sound is measured in decibels. Sounds that reach 85 decibels or higher can damage a person's hearing. Sound sources that exceed this limit include power lawn mowers (90 decibels), subway trains (90 to 115 decibels) and loud music concerts (110 to 120 decibels).

4

- Students scan the article to find the sounds from Exercise 1.
- Ask students to read the article again. In pairs, they find the sounds and discuss which facts they find the most interesting and why.

The world's MOST (and least) annoying sounds

When people are asked what annoys them, it isn't surprising that many of the most irritating things have noises associated with them: people slapping their lips while eating, humming or tapping their fingers. Scientists have used MRI technology to see what happens in the brain when we hear noises like these. They played people different sounds and studied the brain's activity. They found that the most annoying sounds affected the part of the brain that deals with emotions – the amygdala. **a** 3

More interesting perhaps, is that most of the 'worst' sounds were within a specific frequency range, from 2,000 to 5,000 Hertz. Why might we be more sensitive to these high-pitched noises? One theory suggests that alarm calls our ancestors might have heard were made at these frequencies. They would have needed to jump into action after hearing the squeal of a monkey, for example, as it was likely to warn about danger close by. **b** 5

So what are the most annoying sounds? Well, according to the research, scraping sounds like nails on a blackboard or metal on glass were 'highly unpleasant'. **c** 2. Also in the top ten were two sounds that indicate pain and suffering of other people: a female scream and a baby crying.

But some sounds aren't just unpleasant. Noise pollution, being exposed to loud sounds for long periods of time, is likely to cause serious health issues too. We often think of noise pollution as a problem of big cities. Increasingly, however, it can also be found in suburban neighbourhoods, in the form of low-flying aircraft, barking dogs or garden machines, and within homes and workplaces – even your fridge makes a low hum. And there is a great deal of scientific research to show that noise causes stress. **d** 1. It has been linked to heart disease, high blood pressure and poorer sleep quality.

Some people are more sensitive to noise than others. People with autism sometimes find even normal noises unbearable and everyday sounds at home and in the street can cause pain and even panic. And it's not just humans that suffer. Birds living in areas with high levels of noise have been shown to have increased levels of the stress hormone, corticosterone, resulting in smaller babies. **e** 4. Just the sound of human voices has been shown to result in greater stress levels of wild animals.

In contrast, one of the most pleasing noises to the human ear is bird song. According to a survey of two thousand people, bird calls came in as the fifth most popular sound. The sounds of nature dominate the top fifty, especially water sounds, such as rain or waves crashing on rocks, and other weather sounds, such as thunder. Also popular was food – the crunch of an apple, or popcorn popping, for example – and sounds like laughter and screams of delight on a roller coaster. The conclusion? If you're feeling stressed, the best place to be is the countryside … or a theme park!

A low-flying plane over houses near Heathrow Airport, UK.

13

- **Optional step** Encourage students to help each other to clarify the meaning of any words, phrases or structures in the article they don't fully understand.

Answers

sounds mentioned in the article: someone eating with their mouth open (slapping their lips while eating) (line 3); someone humming (line 4); a baby crying (line 30); birds singing (line 55); rain (line 58), thunder (line 60).

VOCABULARY NOTES

associate /ə'səʊsi,eɪt/ = to connect something with something else in your mind

frequency /'friːkwənsi/ = in the context of sound: the rate per second of a vibration in a material

scraping /'skreɪpɪŋ/ = the sound or action of dragging or rubbing a hard or sharp object over a surface

suburban /sə'bɜːb(ə)n/ = describing something in or typical of a suburb, an area on the edge of a town or city where people live

autism /'ɔːtɪz(ə)m/ = a condition related to brain development that affects how a person makes sense of the world and interacts with other people

hormone /'hɔːməʊn/ = a chemical substance made in the body that controls what cells and organs do

5

- Students read the article again. They then read the sentences and think about which part of the article they could be used in, based on what they can remember from their first reading of the article.
- Tell students to look carefully at the last sentence before each gap in the text and the word or phrase at the start of the sentences (1–5) to help them match the sentences with the gaps.
- Students choose the correct sentence to fill each gap.
- **Optional step** Students explain to their partner how they identified which gap each sentence should go in.

6

- Tell students to read the Reading skill box and notice the words that signal reasons.
- **Optional step** Ask, *Which other words or expressions for signalling reasons do you know?*
- Students read the five sentences in Exercise 5 again and identify the words which signal reasons.
- **Optional step** Ask students whether any of these words that signal reasons are new to them and which words they already know.

7

- Students read the final paragraph of the article again and identify the three types of sounds mentioned (nature sounds, food sounds and sounds of happiness).
- Students write a sentence for each of the three types of sounds, explaining why it might be pleasant. Tell them to use a different expression for giving reasons in each of their sentences.
- Students compare their sentences in pairs and give each other feedback on whether they have correctly used words for giving reasons.

Sample answers

Nature sounds: 'Humans need water. That's why natural water sounds like rain may be pleasant to us.'
Food sounds: 'It's easy to understand why people like food sounds because most people love eating!'
Sounds of happiness: 'We love hearing others feeling happy because it gives us similar feelings.'

Extra activity

Ask students to choose four or five of the sounds from Exercise 1 or their own ideas. Encourage them to choose a mixture of sounds they find pleasant and annoying. Tell students to think about why they find each sound either pleasant or annoying. Then ask them to use the expressions for identifying reasons in the Reading skill box to write a sentence that explains their feelings about each sound, for example: *I find the sound of a fire crackling pleasant because it reminds me of enjoyable camping trips from my childhood.*

8

- Elicit the meaning of 'evaluate evidence' from a stronger student in class. Ensure that students don't read the Critical thinking skill box until they have completed the task.
- Work through the first sentence with students. Tell them to consider which words indicate that it is giving either strong or weak evidence. They can compare their ideas in pairs, then read the Critical thinking skill box and use it to check their answers.

Sample answers

strongest to weakest evidence: d ('a great deal of scientific evidence to show' – the evidence is based on plenty of scientific research); a ('According to a survey' - the fact that the survey had 2,000 respondents is an indication that the information is quite reliable); c ('is likely to' – suggests that scientists aren't 100% sure); b ('theory suggests … might have' – vague language, suggests no real evidence)

Extra activity

Ask students to search for an online article in English that reports the findings of scientific research, a survey or another kind of study. They could find this kind of text in an online newspaper or magazine or in the news section of a university website. Alternatively, find an article yourself to share with the class. Ask students to read the article and apply the strategies from the Critical thinking skill box to evaluate how strong the evidence presented is. Students can then discuss and compare their ideas in pairs or small groups.

SPEAKING

9

- Put students into groups to think of suitable background noises or music for each activity. Mix students before the Speaking task so they can share ideas with different people.
- Encourage students to think about how people need to or want to feel in each of the situations given and then what background noises or music can help them to have those feelings.
- Remind students that there are no right or wrong answers and to respect other students' opinions even if they differ from their own.
- Ask individuals to tell the class what choices they made and give reasons for them.

Extra activity

Extend Exercise 9 by asking students to think of background noises or music for these additional activities: speaking activities in class, doing chores at home, having dinner with friends. Students present their ideas to the other groups in the class. Encourage them to give reasons for their decisions using words and phrases from the Reading skill box and the article. If the class can agree about the best type of background noise or music for different parts of a lesson, you could discuss whether to incorporate this into future lessons.

See **Workbook** pages 4–5 for extra practice.

LESSON GOALS

- **GRAMMAR** The main aim is for students to review and practise asking questions. Students use short questions, subject questions, indirect questions and question tags to ask for information, ask for confirmation and show surprise.
- **PRONUNCIATION** A sub-aim is for students to practise using word stress to change the meaning of a question.
- **SPEAKING** The speaking aim is to get students to design a questionnaire, ask the questions in it and report their findings to the class.

LISTENING AND GRAMMAR

1

- Students look at the infographic and discuss the questions in pairs. Tell students to give reasons for their answers and give examples of emoticons or emojis they have seen or used themselves.

Answers

1 :-D happy :O shock, surprise))))) very happy
>:(angry D: unhappy
(-_-) stressed (T_T) crying, sadness (^^) or ^^ happy
(눈_눈) dissatisfied, unhappy

2 Sample answers: Normally not the nose (which is why noses are optional in emoticons). In Asia more importance is placed on the eyes, whilst in Europe it is more on the mouth.

Extra activity

Students discuss the following questions in groups. If permitted, they can look at messages on their phones to help them.

- Which emoticons and emojis do you think are used most frequently?
- Which do you use most frequently? What do you think this says about your personality?
- Do you ever need an emoji which doesn't exist? What is it and what emotion would it convey?
- Do you think the use of emoticons and emojis has had more of a positive or negative effect on communication? Why?

2 1.2

- Explain that students are going to listen to a conversation about the infographic that they have just looked at.
- Ask students to read the sentences before they listen.
- Play the audio. Students choose T (true) or F (false).
- Students compare answers in pairs before checking as a class.

3 1.2

- Students choose the correct options in the questions based on their existing knowledge and what they can remember from listening the first time.
- Play the audio again so students can check their answers.
- **Optional step** Either say questions 1 and 3 with the correct intonation or ask a confident student to do so. Elicit or explain that fall-rise intonation is used in each question, which means that the voice goes down in tone with the first word and then up on the second word. Ask students to practise saying these two questions to themselves to practise using the correct intonation.

4

- **Optional step** Tell students to read the questions from Exercise 3 out loud as this should help them make the function of each one clearer.
- Students match the questions in Exercise 3 with their functions, then read the Grammar box and check their answers.

For further information and practice, see **Grammar reference Unit 1B** on page 140 of the Student's Book.

GRAMMAR NOTES

Check understanding of the terms 'auxiliary verb' and 'main verb'. Ask *In the question* 'What do you think?' *which verb is the auxiliary verb?* (do) *Which verb is the main verb?* (think). Draw students' attention to the change in word order in indirect questions. No auxiliary verb is used and after the introductory phrase, such as 'Do you think ... ?' the rest of the question retains the same word order it would have in a statement.
Remind students that question tags that follow positive statements contain negative verb forms (e.g. *don't, doesn't, haven't, didn't*). Question tags that follow negative statements contain affirmative verb forms (e.g. *do, does, have, did*).

5 1.3

- Tell students they are going to read and listen to a conversation that includes the types of questions they read about in the Grammar box.
- Students read and complete the conversation.
- Play the audio and ask students to listen and check their answers.
- **Optional step** Pause after each of the questions that students completed if necessary, to check answers.

For additional practice, refer to the **Grammar activity** on page 245 of the Teacher's Book.

PRONUNCIATION

6 1.4

- Elicit or explain that when we stress a word, we say it noticeably more loudly or strongly than the other words in the sentence.
- Play the audio so students can listen and underline the correct word.

PRONUNCIATION NOTES

Sentence stress is the pattern of stressed and unstressed words in a sentence or question. Stress is typically placed on key content words in order to make it clear that these words communicate the most important information in a sentence or question. However, the speaker may stress other words in order to convey a specific meaning or point of view. Students need to learn how to interpret different sentence stress patterns so they can accurately and fully understand a speaker's message.

7 1.5

- Students read the Clear voice box. Check understanding of prepositions (*after, before, under, inside*, etc.), determiners (articles, numbers, possessive adjectives (*my, his, their*, etc.) and demonstratives (*this, that, these, those*).
- **Optional step** Ask, *Is the information in the Clear voice box also true for your first language(s)? Can you think of a short sentence or question in your first language where you could change the stress to emphasize a particular meaning?*
- Ask students to read the three possible meanings before they listen, then play the audio.
- Students match the questions with the meanings and compare answers in pairs.

8

- Students practise emphasizing different words in the question. Tell them to really stress the word they have chosen each time. Their partner guesses the meaning they want to communicate.
- Students give their partner feedback on whether they have emphasized their chosen word clearly enough.
- Monitor the activity. If necessary, model the word students want to stress.

1B Universal emotions?

LESSON GOALS
- Review and practise asking questions
- Use word stress to change the meaning of a sentence
- Design a questionnaire and report findings to the class

LISTENING AND GRAMMAR

1 Work in pairs. Discuss the questions.

1 Look at the infographic. What emotions do you think the different emoticons express?
2 Which parts of the face do you think express emotion most strongly: the eyes, nose or mouth?
3 Do you use emoticons and emojis? When? Which ones?

2 1.2 Listen to a conversation between two friends. Are the sentences true (T) or false (F)?

1 Fatima doesn't think a smile has the same meaning for everyone on the planet. F
2 Tomoya was surprised about how emoticons look in Europe. T
3 People in different countries don't smile for different reasons. F
4 Fatima sometimes smiles at strangers to be polite. T

3 1.2 Choose the correct option to complete the questions from the conversation. Then listen again to check.

1 Tomoya, you studied psychology, *did* / **didn't** you?
2 I'd like to know whether a smile *does mean* / **means** the same thing all over the world.
3 You've noticed, *you have* / **haven't you**?
4 **Don't** / *Do* you do it in the same way in Japan?
5 *At who do you smile* / **Who do you smile at**?

4 Look at the questions in Exercise 3 again and answer the questions (1–4). Then read the Grammar box on page 15 to check.

1 Which question is used to check the listener agrees? 3
2 Which question asks for confirmation of something the speaker already believes? 1
3 Which question shows surprise about some new information? 4
4 Which question asks for the information in an indirect way? 2

EMOTICONS AROUND THE WORLD

Emojis are here to stay 😀👋, but good old emoticons still have their place in emails and texts. Do different styles of emoticons around the world tell us anything about the culture they come from? ¯_(ツ)_/¯

European style

eyes to the left, mouth to the right	nose optional	symbol repeated for emphasis (Russians often don't include eyes)	other variations
:-D	:O	)))))	>:(D:

Asian style

upright, brackets show face outline	emotion expressed through the eyes	mouth sometimes left off and brackets are also optional	use of extended characters e.g. Korean *jamo*
(-_-)	(T_T)	(^^) ^^	(눈_눈)

DID YOU KNOW?

The first use of an emoticon? A poet called Robert Herrick used a smiley emoticon :) in a 1648 poem. That's more than three hundred years before the first computer! :-0

14

Extra activity

Write the indirect question example from the Grammar box on the board: *I'd like to know whether a smile means the same thing all over the world.* Put students into pairs and ask them to choose three or more different words in the sentence which you could stress in order to change its meaning. They should decide what meaning that stress would emphasize, for example:

- stressing *I'd* indicates that it is something you are personally interested in as opposed to other things other people may have expressed a preference to find out about.
- stressing *(a) smile* suggests that you want to focus specifically on the meaning of a smile, as opposed to other expressions.
- stressing *all (over)* suggests you want to focus on whether a smile means the same thing everywhere, not just in certain countries or cultures.

SPEAKING

9

- Go through the instructions in class and check students understand the task. Tell students to go through each of the steps in order.

GRAMMAR Forming questions

You can form questions with **question word** + **auxiliary verb** + **subject** + **main verb**.
What do you think?

Negative questions often express surprise or annoyance.
Don't you do it in the same way in Japan?

There are several other types of questions that you form differently.
Short questions: do not have the main verb and you often use them to express surprise or interest
Wasn't it? Did you?

Subject questions: do not use an auxiliary verb
*Who **makes** you laugh?*

Indirect questions: use them to be more polite or less direct; they follow **subject** + **verb** word order
*I'd like to know whether **a smile means** the same thing all over the world.*

Question tags: use them to confirm what you are saying or check that the listener agrees
*Tomoya, you studied psychology, **didn't you**?*

Go to page 140 for the Grammar reference.

5 1.3 **Complete the conversation with one word in each space. Then listen to check.**

A: Do you know what the difference [1] ___is___ between emoticons and emojis?

B: Yes, emoticons are symbols used to represent faces and emojis are actual pictures.

A: Oh, OK!

B: You know you have to be careful with emojis, [2] ___don't___ you? What you see when you send it isn't necessarily what the other person sees.

A: [3] ___Isn't___ it?!

B: No! A friend of mine texted his wife 'Do you know how beautiful you [4] ___are___?' and sent the Spanish dancer emoji. Except the emoji on her phone was a fat yellow dancing blob!

A: Oh no! Who [5] ___designs___ these emojis – the phone companies? By the way, why [6] ___did___ you send me a surprised face when I told you I got the tickets for the match yesterday?

B: What? [7] ___Didn't___ I send you a smiley?

PRONUNCIATION

6 1.4 **Listen to the question. Underline the stressed word.**

Were you surprised?

7 1.5 **Look at the Clear voice box. Then listen to the question from Exercise 6 said three times, with different sentence stress. Match the questions (1–3) with the meanings (a–c).**

CLEAR VOICE
Using stress for emphasis (1)

In English, content words (nouns, verbs, adjectives, adverbs) are normally stressed. Grammar words like prepositions, determiners and auxiliary words are not stressed. However, this can change if the speaker wants to emphasize a particular meaning.

Question 1 c
Question 2 b
Question 3 a

a I wasn't surprised, but I'm curious to know if you were.
b I want to know how you felt.
c You said you were surprised, but I'm not sure I believe you.

8 **Work in pairs. Take turns to say the question from Exercise 6, putting the stress on one of the three words. Your partner should choose which meaning from Exercise 7 (a, b or c) you were thinking of.**

SPEAKING

9 **Work in pairs. Design a questionnaire to ask your classmates about emotions, emojis and emoticons. Follow the instructions.**

1 Write at least six questions. Use the Grammar box to help you.
What's your favourite emoticon or emoji? Why? Have you ever cried when watching a film?
2 Individually, interview your classmates and write down their answers. Ask follow-up questions.
3 Share the answers with your partner. Which answers were the most interesting? Report these to the class.

EXPLORE MORE!

Search online for the 'app that knows how you feel from the look on your face'. How does it work?

15

- Students should write questions about emotions and the use of emoticons and emojis. Encourage them to strike a balance between the two topics.
- Monitor students while they are writing their questions, offering feedback and support where necessary.
- If possible, tell students to interview at least six other people and remind them to ask follow-up questions, e.g. *When do you usually use this emoticon?*
- Remind students to make notes on any examples of interesting information they hear from their interviewees so they can report these to the class afterwards.
- **Optional step** When students are reporting what they found out, tell them to paraphrase what their interviewees said or summarize it in their own words.
- Ask students to share their answers in pairs and then discuss and decide on the most interesting findings. Invite pairs to share their most interesting findings with the class.

Extra activity

Students write a report on their findings, using proportions or percentages.

EXPLORE MORE!

The aim of the Explore more! sections is to encourage students to do more research into the topic of the lesson. Adapt the task depending on the interest and situation of your students. How you exploit Explore more! will depend on the internet access in your class.
Students do an online search using the search term given in the Student's Book. They should find several articles on the app, as well as a TED Talk called *This app knows how you feel – from the look on your face*, given by computer scientist Rana el Kaliouby in May 2015.
The app she describes has the ability to read people's facial expressions and match them with the corresponding emotions. el Kaliouby has suggested that this has the power to change how we interact with both machines and with each other.
After students have read about the app, or watched the TED Talk, they could write an explanation or prepare a verbal presentation of how the app works to give in the next or a future lesson. Students could also discuss the possible impact that this technology could have on our lives and whether they think this would be a positive, negative or neutral impact.

For additional practice, refer to the **Communication activity** on page 212 of the Teacher's Book.

See **Workbook** pages 6–7 for extra practice.

LESSON GOALS

- **VOCABULARY** A main aim is for students to learn and practise using adjectives to describe emotions and to practise using adverbs of degree to change the strength of an emotion.
- **PRONUNCIATION** A sub-aim is for students to practise short and long vowel sounds.
- **LISTENING** A further main aim is for students to practise inferring emotions when listening.
- **SPEAKING** The speaking aim is for students to tell a story about a time they experienced a strong emotion.

VOCABULARY

1

- **Optional step** Direct students to the title and elicit the emotion someone would be feeling if they said this (surprise).
- Students look at the photo, then ask and answer the questions. Elicit adjectives for the feelings of the people in the photo and write these on the board so students can refer back to them later.

ABOUT THE PHOTO

The photo is of Washington Capitals ice hockey fans during Game 5 of the Stanley Cup Final against the Vegas Golden Knights, Washington, DC.

Sample answers

1 the people are at a match; a player might be about to take a penalty shot
2 excited, nervous, scared

2

- **Optional step** Read the first sentence aloud as an example. Elicit that the sentence contains two adjectives (*massive* and *petrified*) but only *petrified* describes emotions.
- Students check their answers in pairs and then check answers as a class. Model and drill the pronunciation of any adjectives students struggle with.

3

- Students match the adjectives to the definitions. If they are unsure about the meaning of any adjectives, encourage them to use the sentence contexts in Exercise 2 to help them.
- Students compare answers in pairs.

For further information and practice, see **Vocabulary reference Unit 1** on page 135 of the Student's Book.

Extra activity

Ask students to think of more adjectives for emotions, then write an example sentence for each adjective that describes how they have felt at specific points in their lives or when certain things happened to them.

4

- **Optional step** Quickly check students understand the difference between an adjective and an adverb. Ask, *Which type of word would you use to describe a noun? Which type of word would you use to describe a verb?* Elicit or explain that adverbs usually end with *-ly*.
- Students circle the adverbs first and then check answers in pairs. They then discuss and decide whether each adverb makes the emotion stronger or weaker.

1C I couldn't believe my eyes!

LESSON GOALS
- Talk about strong emotions using adverbs of degree
- Infer emotions when listening
- Practise short and long vowel sounds

VOCABULARY

1 Work in pairs. Look at the photo and discuss the questions.
1 Where are the people in the photo? What do you think might be happening?
2 How do you think the people might be feeling? Why?
3 Have you ever been in a similar situation? When?

2 Read the sentences. Underline the adjectives that describe emotions.
1 I saw a massive spider the other day. I was completely petrified!
2 I'm a bit concerned I might not pass the exam. Some of the questions were tricky.
3 The queue wasn't moving and I started to feel slightly impatient.
4 I'd been waiting for the book for months, so I was really thrilled when it finally came out.
5 I was tremendously relieved nobody noticed my mistake. I thought my boss would be angry.
6 I'm feeling relatively optimistic now that I know I will get to keep my job.
7 I was totally astonished when Germany beat Brazil 7-1. I really didn't see it coming!
8 I feel more motivated doing practical class projects than listening to a lecture.
9 The boss was absolutely furious with her. She'd missed the deadline again.

3 Match the adjectives from Exercise 2 (1–9) with their definition (a–i).
a very happy and excited 4
b no longer feeling worried 5
c positive 6
d very angry 9
e very scared 1
f very surprised 7
g wanting something to happen 3
h wanting to do the work 8
i worried 2

Go to page 135 for the Vocabulary reference.

4 Circle any adverbs used with the adjectives in Exercise 2. Which are used to make the emotion stronger? Which are used to make it weaker?

5 Read the Focus on box to check your answers to Exercise 4.

FOCUS ON Adverbs of degree

Many adverbs affect the strength of the word they modify, e.g. ***very*** *happy,* ***a little*** *annoyed.*

Adverbs that make the word stronger
absolutely, completely, really, totally, tremendously

Adverbs that make the word weaker
a bit, relatively, slightly

Go to page 141 for the Focus on reference.

6 Write three sentences about yourself using adjectives from Exercise 2. Use adverbs to make the emotion stronger or weaker.

16

PRONUNCIATION

7 Look at the adjectives, paying attention to the sound of the letters in red. Then complete the table.

astonished delighted impatient optimistic pleased relieved thrilled

/ɪ/	/iː/	/eɪ/	/aɪ/
exhausted	weak	afraid	excited
astonished	pleased	impatient	delighted
optimistic	relieved		
thrilled			

8 1.6 Listen and check your answers to Exercise 7. Then practise saying the adjectives. Use the Clear voice box to help you.

CLEAR VOICE
Pronouncing short and long vowels

In English there is a difference between long and short vowel sounds that is important for clear pronunciation. The sounds /eɪ/, /aɪ/ and /iː/ are always long while /ɪ/ is always short.

LISTENING

NATIONAL GEOGRAPHIC EXPLORERS

9 1.7 Look at the Listening skill box. Then listen to Francisco Estrada-Belli and Tsiory Andrianavalona. Try to infer which emotions they felt in each situation.

LISTENING SKILL
Inferring emotions

Sometimes people might not state how they feel directly and you will need to infer it from the description of the situation. For example, if your friend says 'I passed my driving test yesterday!', you can infer that they are probably feeling happy. To infer emotions, listen to the tone of voice, the type of situation described and for words or expressions that give you a clue.

10 1.7 Listen again. Who, Francisco (F), Tsiory (T) or both explorers (B) ...

1 couldn't see anyone else? T
2 found it difficult to speak? F
3 got help from other people? F
4 is better prepared if the experience happens again? T
5 was prepared for the experience? T
6 was indoors when it happened? B

SPEAKING

11 Look at the Useful language box. Then match the phrases in bold with the emotions (1–5).

Useful language Expressing emotions

I **can't stand** waiting in queues.
It really **gets on my nerves** when people are late to meetings.
My dad really **lost his temper** when he found out I'd been skipping classes again.
I couldn't believe my eyes when I saw the exam results. I got 100%!
I never thought that my best friend could **let me down** so much.

1 annoyed gets on my nerves
2 astonished I couldn't believe my eyes
3 disappointed let me down
4 angry lost his temper
5 impatient can't stand

12 Work in pairs. Help each other memorize the expressions in the Useful language box. Take turns to read out a part of each expression. The other person must complete the expression without looking at their book.

A: I can't stand ...
B: ... waiting in queues!
A: Yes!

13 You are going to tell a story about a time when you experienced a strong emotion. Make notes to prepare. Use expressions from the Useful language box to help you.

14 Work in groups. Take turns to share your story. Don't say what emotions you felt. Can the rest of the group infer the emotions you felt?

17

5

- Students read the Focus on box and check their answers to Exercise 4.
- **Optional step** Ask students to explain, if possible, how they knew whether an adverb made the emotion stronger or weaker. Clarify that while *a bit* and *slightly* are used to mean 'a small amount', *relatively* is used to compare the qualities of the thing or person being described with other things or people of the same type. As a result, *relatively* normally makes the adjective it describes weaker.

Answers
Adverbs that make emotions stronger:
1 completely 4 really 5 tremendously
7 totally 8 more 9 absolutely
Adverbs that make emotions weaker:
2 a bit 3 slightly 6 relatively

For further information and practice, see **Focus on reference Unit 1C** on page 141 of the Student's Book.

6

- Model the activity for students using an adjective from Exercise 2 and an adverb from the Focus on box.
- Students write sentences about themselves.
- **Optional step** Students exchange their sentences in pairs or small groups and give each other feedback on their use of adjectives and adverbs.

Sample answer
I was really concerned when my aunt had to go to hospital last week, but she's fine now.

For additional practice, refer to the **Vocabulary activity** on page 233 and the **Focus on activity** on page 246 of the Teacher's Book.

PRONUNCIATION

7

- Students read the adjectives. Explain that the phonemic symbols at the top of each column represent the sounds of the vowel sound in red.
- Ask students to read the adjectives in the table out loud so they can hear the differences between the four different vowel sounds. They then read the adjectives above the table out loud and match them to the sound.

PRONUNCIATION NOTES

If a word only contains one vowel and that vowel is in the middle of the word, it is usually pronounced as a short vowel. For example: *bed*, *sad*. Long vowel sounds are often created when two vowels appear in the same syllable but the second vowel is silent, e.g. *weak* (*a* = silent), *afraid* (*i* = silent).

8 1.6

- Play the audio so students can check their answers to Exercise 7 and make corrections if necessary.
- Ask students to read the Clear voice box and then practise saying the adjectives from Exercise 7 again.

For additional practice, refer to the **Pronunciation activity** on page 268 of the Teacher's Book.

Extra activity

Students add more adjectives, or other words, to the table in Exercise 7 under each vowel sound header.

LISTENING

9 1.7

- Elicit that Francisco and Tsiory are the two explorers that students watched at the start of the unit.
- Direct students to the Listening skill box and check their understanding of 'infer' (to guess that something is true or form an opinion about something based on the information available).
- Ask students to listen to the explorers and make notes on the emotions they think they felt. Remind them that they will have to infer how the explorers felt from their descriptions of each situation. Play the audio.
- **Optional step** Students compare their notes in pairs and check if they agree with each other's inferences. They can use their partner's notes to add to or modify their ideas.

Sample answers

Francisco - confused ('It took me a few seconds to realize what had happened to me'), shocked ('I still could not believe my bad luck'), terrified ('I tried to breathe and I couldn't'), frustrated ('I tried to say a few words to let them know I was actually not dead'), desperate ('we had to drive around the village looking for help, a doctor, someone'), happy/joy (stated), relief ('I was not paralyzed!' and stated)
Tsiory - nervous ('I wrote my speech … 50 times and repeated it in front of the mirror'), frightened ('cold stream running down my back'), surprised ('When the light turned to red, my mouth opened and words came out!'), confident (stated), proud ('I had overcome one of my biggest fears')

VOCABULARY NOTES

(be) paralyzed /(biː) ˈpær(ə)laɪzd/ = to not be able to move a part or parts of your body

tingle /ˈtɪŋg(ə)l/ = to feel as if sharp points are being put into your body quickly and lightly

backstage /ˌbækˈsteɪdʒ/ = the area behind the stage in a theatre or auditorium

cross your mind /krɒs jɔː maɪnd/ = when something enters your thoughts for a short amount of time

mumble /ˈmʌmb(ə)l/ = to say something quietly and unclearly so that it is difficult to understand

overcome /ˌəʊvəˈkʌm/ = to succeed in controlling or dealing with a problem or feeling

rollercoaster of emotions /ˈrəʊləˌkəʊstə(r) ɒv ɪˈməʊʃ(ə)nz/ = a situation or experience that makes you feel a wide range of different emotions

10 1.7

- **Optional step** Ask students to read the questions first and try to guess the answers based on what they can remember.
- Play the audio again so students can answer the questions.
- Students check their answers in pairs. Play the audio again so students can check their answers if necessary.

SPEAKING

11

- Read through the Useful language box with the class. Tell students that these phrases are all colloquial phrases for describing emotions.
- Students try to guess the meaning of the expressions in bold from the context of each sentence.
- Students match the phrases with the emotions, then check their answers in pairs.

12

- Set a two-minute time limit for students to complete the expressions. Once they've done this, change pairs so students have a new partner to practise with.
- **Optional step** In feedback, ask students what they did or thought about to help them remember the expressions.

13

- Students think of a time when they felt a strong emotion and brainstorm details about what happened, e.g. what caused it, what the consequences were, where and when it happened, etc.
- Students prepare their stories in note form. Remind them not to write out the story in full sentences. Also remind them not to explicitly state what emotions they were feeling.
- Tell students that they are going to share their stories, so they should only write about situations they feel comfortable telling other students about. If not, they can invent a situation to tell a story about.

14

- Students take turns to tell their stories in groups. The students in the group listen and try to infer which emotion the storyteller was feeling.
- In feedback, ask students what they heard in other students' stories that helped them infer the emotion they were feeling.

Extra activity

Students use their phones to make an audio or video recording of themselves telling the story. They then listen to or watch it and consider how they can improve their clarity of communication, accuracy and use of vocabulary and useful expressions for talking about emotions.

For additional practice, refer to the **Communication activity** on page 213 of the Teacher's Book.

See **Workbook** pages 8–10 for extra practice.

LESSON GOALS

- **SPEAKING** This lesson integrates speaking, reading and listening. Its main aim is to raise students' awareness of the importance of demonstrating empathy in communication and to provide opportunities for students to practise this. Students learn phrases to show empathy and encourage others to see a situation from another perspective. The lesson ends with a roleplay task in which students put the tips and language they have used into practice.

SPEAKING

1

- Students read the situation and options and then discuss what they would do, why they would do it and what the possible implications of this choice could be.

MY VOICE ▶

COMMUNICATION SKILL NOTES

Empathy is the capacity to understand or feel what another person is experiencing by placing oneself in another's position and imagining what it's like to be them. Demonstrating empathy can help us resolve differences of opinion, develop relationships and collaborate effectively with others. Good empathy skills can also help us mediate between two parties where there is a conflict of opinion or misunderstanding. Students will already be aware of what empathy is but may be less confident about demonstrating it in English. This lesson gives students practical tips on how they can improve their empathy skills as well as the language they need to help them demonstrate this in conversation.

ABOUT THE SPEAKER

CHIA SUAN CHONG, one of the authors of *Voices*, is a communications skills trainer, writer and teacher trainer. She has delivered many interactive workshops on intercultural communication and collaboration and is the author of *Successful International Communication*.

2 ▶ 1.2

- Tell students that their aim while watching the video the first time is to come up with their own definitions for empathy. Students watch the video.
- Students compare ideas in groups.

Sample answers

Empathy is trying to understand people by experiencing what they are experiencing. / Empathy is feeling other people's emotions. / Empathy is really listening to people. / Empathy is not the same as sympathizing. / Empathy is seeing a situation from another person's point of view. / Empathy takes imagination. / Empathy can be difficult / uncomfortable.

3

- Tell students they are now going to apply what they learned from the video to talk about how to manage situations like the one in Exercise 1.
- Give students one or two minutes to read the questions and make notes on their ideas and then discuss them together.

Sample answers

By empathizing with Andrea, you can see the situation from her perspective rather than reacting immediately in a negative way. She may be feeling under pressure in her new role and may feel more valued if she is listened to. It will help build a good working relationship between you, Andrea and the rest of the team. If you don't show empathy, this could damage your relationship and prevent you from resolving the issue/working together effectively.

4 ▶ 1.2

- Ask students to think about possible reasons why empathy is important and ways of empathizing.
- **Optional step** Tell students that they could make notes in a list or draw a mind map.
- Play the video again and ask students to note down key phrases relating to the two points.

Sample answers

Why empathy is important: By really listening to each other in a team, you show that other people's opinions are important. If you don't fully understand their point of view, it may be harder to look for a solution to problems. In negotiations and other situations when people might feel they are on opposite sides, everyone can feel they got what they wanted if they have been listened to.
Ways of empathizing effectively: It's easier to listen if you don't speak. Focus on what the person is saying rather than planning your response. One way to show that you are listening and to check you understand is to summarize what they have said and repeat it back to them. Remember to consider someone's point of view, even if you disagree with it.

Extra activity

Put students into pairs or small groups. Ask students to each think of a situation where they used empathy to deal with what was happening (e.g. you realize that a member of your project group is contributing nothing or very little to the project work, or you want to complain about the quality of the food you have been given in a restaurant). Students take turns to describe the situation and explain how empathy helped them deal with it.

5

- Students read the four situations individually and think about ways of empathizing that could have a positive impact in each case.
- Students discuss their ideas and try to reach a consensus on the best way to deal with each situation.

Sample answers

1 You are probably feeling quite angry that someone has stolen your seat. Is it possible that they didn't see you? Or perhaps they were being rude but have had a very bad day. You might be able to politely explain that you were going to sit there but there's a good chance that the woman isn't in the mood to listen, and you can probably sit somewhere else. If you are able to, though, you could ask her if she is OK.

2 Do you show your support for your classmate in the middle of the lesson, by speaking against the bully? That may seem like the right thing to do, but he may not feel comfortable being the centre of attention. Instead, you could talk to him after the lesson and check he's OK.

3 It's possible that the neighbour didn't hear about the party. It may also be possible to enjoy the party but a bit more quietly. The first thing to do would be to find out why this neighbour in particular is upset.

4 Your flatmate is understandably upset, and telling her how much cleaner the city will be now probably won't help. But it might help if you can say how sorry you are that this has happened to her. By listening you may discover other information that helps you suggest some practical solutions.

6

- In pairs, students read the advice in the Communication skill box and check their ideas from Exercise 5 against the advice.
- Students think of at least one more piece of advice to add to the list.
- Elicit the additional advice each pair thought of in class.

Sample answers

- Do not assume that other people will have the same reactions and feelings as you in a certain situation.
- Remember that aspects of a person's personality might make them more sensitive to certain things or situations than you may be.
- Try not to make negative judgements about people based on their actions or how they express themselves.

1D Empathizing with others

LESSON GOALS
- Discuss how to deal with difficult situations
- Demonstrate empathy in a conversation
- Consider other people's emotions and help others see the other side

SPEAKING

1 Read the situation. What would you do? Why? Discuss with a partner.

Andrea is the new leader of a team working on a project. In a meeting, she is angry with you and tells you off in front of the rest of the team for not completing your work. You have explained that you needed more information to complete the job. You remember times in the past, before Andrea was leader, when she didn't finish her work on time. Do you …

a think about why Andrea may be angry and talk to her about it after the meeting?
b remind Andrea of the times in the past when she didn't finish her work?
c decide that Andrea is a bad leader and complain about her to other team members?

MY VOICE

2 1.2 Watch the video. Complete the sentence in at least two ways. Then compare your sentences with your classmates.

Empathy is ____________.

3 Work in pairs. How do you think empathy can help you manage situations like the one in Exercise 1? What might happen if you don't show empathy?

4 1.2 Watch the video again. Make notes on …

1 why empathy is important.
2 ways of empathizing effectively.

5 Work in pairs. Read the four situations on page 19. Decide on the best way of dealing with each situation.

6 Look at the Communication skill box. Do the courses of action that you decided on in Exercise 5 follow its advice? What other advice could you add to the box?

COMMUNICATION SKILL
Considering other people's emotions

- Before reacting to a situation, consider how the other person might be feeling. Use this to decide on the most appropriate way to respond.
- Focus on similarities you share rather than differences. If you have trouble connecting with someone, try to think of three things you and the other person have in common.
- When talking to another person, try to listen more than you speak. Check you've understood by summarizing their point of view. This will also show them that you're listening.
- Try not to judge the other person. It's possible to disagree and still understand why the other person feels differently about a certain matter.

7 1.8

- Students listen to the audio and identify the things the speakers do that show that they are not (or not fully) considering the other person's emotions. They should also think of what the speakers could have done to deal with the situation better. Students can use the advice from the Communication skill box to help them.
- Students discuss their ideas in pairs.

Sample answers

Laurent could have apologized immediately and not shown surprise that Gurpreet has been waiting; they could have discussed the problem more constructively and talked about how to improve the situation for next time; Gurpreet could have shown understanding about the fact that Laurent is very busy at work.

8

- Students match the phrases in the Useful language box with the categories.

Exercise your empathy!

Consider the role of empathy in these four situations. In each, ask yourself: What might the other person be thinking and feeling? How would you feel?

1 You are just about to sit down on a crowded bus when another passenger pushes in front of you and sits down herself. It is very clear that you were going to sit down. Even so, she doesn't say anything or look at you.

What do you do?

2 You are a student in class. Your friend makes an unkind comment about a classmate. Other people laugh. This classmate doesn't have any friends in the class and he sometimes disturbs the lesson, which you find annoying. He doesn't look unhappy, but this is probably because he is used to comments like this – it's not the first time.

What do you do?

3 You have just finished your exams and are celebrating at home. Quite early in the evening, your next-door neighbour complains about the noise and says he can't sleep. You and your friends have been looking forward to this party for a long time. You had warned the neighbours a few days before, but this neighbour is talking about calling the police if you don't stop the party immediately.

What do you do?

4 You cycle to work and find it difficult because the traffic is noisy and dirty. Your flatmate recently bought a car so that she could drive to work. However, the council has now banned cars from the city centre, which means her journey will now take an extra hour each day and cost her more money. She is annoyed and upset.

What do you do?

7 1.8 Listen to a conversation between two friends. How could each person deal with the situation better? Discuss with a partner, using the advice from Exercise 6.

8 Look at the Useful language box. Match the phrases in the box with the categories (1–4).

Useful language Empathizing

I'm sorry to hear that. It must be hard for you.
I can see how that would be difficult.
I'm glad you told me. Let me know if I can help.
I want to make sure I understand. Are you saying that …?
It sounds like you're feeling … Is that right?
Have you thought about how they might feel?
I imagine they're feeling quite …

1 Acknowledging difficulties
2 Helping others see the other side
3 Being there for others
4 Checking you've understood

SPEAKING

9 OWN IT! Work in pairs. Follow the instructions.

Student A: Choose to be either Gurpreet or Laurent from Exercise 7. You've just got back from the restaurant and you're angry/upset.

Student B: You are Student A's flatmate. Try to get your friend to calm down and help them see the situation from the other person's point of view.

Use the tips from the Communication skill box and the Useful language to help you.

B: Are you OK? You seem a bit down.
A: Yeah, well, I met up with Gurpreet / Laurent …

10 Work with another pair. Take turns to act out your conversations from Exercise 9. Did both pairs demonstrate empathy?

19

Answers

1 I'm sorry to hear that. It must be hard for you. / I can see how that would be difficult.
2 Have you thought about how they might feel? / I imagine they're feeling quite …
3 I'm glad you told me. Let me know if I can help.
4 I want to make sure I understand. Are you saying that … ? / It sounds like you're feeling … Is that right?

Extra activity

Tell students that their tone of voice and the word stress they use for the sentences in the Useful language box will determine whether or not someone perceives them as being empathetic. Give students an example by saying: *I'm sorry to hear that. It must be hard for you.* in a monotone way with stress on the word *must* so that the sentence sounds slightly patronizing. Then say the same sentence with more vocal variety and as if you care about the person you are talking to by stressing the words *sorry*, *hear* and *hard*. Ask students if they can notice the difference. Then put students into pairs and ask them to practise using tone and word stress to show empathy as they say the sentences in the Useful language box.

SPEAKING

9 OWN IT!

- Give pairs five minutes to prepare for the roleplay. Ask them to begin by assigning roles (A or B) with Student A taking the role of Gurpreet or Laurent and Student B playing the flatmate of the person their partner chose.
- Tell students to think about how they can use the phrases in the Useful language box and the advice in the Communication skill box in the roleplay.
- Pairs roleplay the conversation.
- **Optional step** If time allows, students change roles and roleplay the conversation again.

Sample answers
(If Student A is Gurpreet)
B: Are you OK? You seem a bit down.
A: Yeah, well, I met up with Laurent. I'm really fed up because he's always late when we arrange to go out together.
B: I can see how that might be frustrating, but have you thought about how Laurent might be feeling? He's probably worrying that he's lost a good friend. Maybe it isn't his fault he's always late.
A: Yes, you could be right there.

10

- Organize the class into groups of two pairs to perform their conversations.
- **Optional step** Ask students to make notes on how effectively the other pair demonstrated empathy during their conversation and then use these to give the other pair feedback.

Extra activity

Students choose one of the scenarios from page 19 and roleplay a conversation about it in pairs. Student A is the person who has a problem and Student B is going to empathize with him/her. If time allows, they could choose another scenario and change roles so that both students have had a chance to practise empathizing.

LESSON GOALS

- **WRITING** The aim of the lesson is to guide students to produce an informal email giving news and an informal email that responds to someone else's news. The reading text provides a model. Students practise the skill of sounding friendly by writing in an informal style.

SPEAKING

1

- Students look at the photos and decide which type of news (good or bad) each person has just received.

Answers

The man has just received good news. The woman has just received bad news.

2

- Students think about their own experiences and tell their partner an anecdote.

READING FOR WRITING

3

- Students read the email and answer the questions.
- **Optional step** Tell students to think of explanations for their answers to questions 1 and 3.
- Students compare their answers in pairs.

Answers

1 They are old university friends.
2 He's got a new job, one he's wanted for a long time.
3 Ioana's email will probably include; congratulations on the new job; one or two questions about the job; information about the reunion party; update about Aida's health; a promise to arrange to get together.

4

- Students read the email again and answer the questions. They then read the Writing skill box to check if their answers are correct.

Answers

1 greeting and introductory phrase; questions about the other person's current situation and their recent activities; details of the good news; enquiry about a friend; invitation to meet.

2 *Hi!, been in touch, drop you a line, been up to, chatted, couldn't make it, what's the latest?, Guess what?, couldn't believe my ears*, etc.

Extra activity

Ask students to re-read the email in Exercise 3 and find examples of the following features of an email giving news: greeting and introduction; details of the news; questions about the other person's current situation; invitation to meet/speak.

5

- Students read the email again and identify informal phrases with the same meaning as the formal phrases.
- Students compare their answers in pairs and then check answers as a class.

Answers

1 been in touch; 2 drop you a line; 3 up to; 4 the latest; 5 went for; 6 getting wind of; 7 keep you posted; 8 had no idea; 9 catch up; 10 ages

6

- Students read the response and answer the questions, referring back to their answers from Exercise 3.

1E Great news!

LESSON GOALS
- Use informal language to sound friendly
- Write an email giving news
- Respond to someone else's news

SPEAKING

1 Look at the photos. What news do you think each person has just received?

2 Work in pairs. Tell each other about a time you wrote to someone with good or bad news, or received news. How did it make you feel?

READING FOR WRITING

3 Read the email. Answer the questions.

1 What's the relationship between Erik and Ioana?
2 What's Erik's good news?
3 What do you think Ioana's response will say?

New Message

Hi Ioana!

How are things? Sorry I haven't been in touch for a while, but I've been really busy at work. Thought I'd drop you a line while I have a few minutes.

What have you been up to since we last chatted? Did you go to that university reunion party last week? I got the invitation, but I couldn't make it because I had to go to a family event. But I really wanted to see the old crowd and find out what everyone's up to these days. Who did you see? What's the latest? I'd love to know!

Do you remember that design job I told you about? Guess what? I went for it and I got it! 😉 I'm so thrilled. It's the perfect company for me. To be honest, I didn't think the interview had gone too well, so I couldn't believe my ears when I got the call today. It'll mean getting up early and commuting into town, but I'm sure I'll get used to it. By the way, don't mention it to anyone yet, will you? I don't want my boss getting wind of it just yet! I'll keep you posted.

I hear Aida's been in hospital. I had no idea she was ill. I hope she's better soon. Let's catch up properly soon. It's been ages. Just give me a ring when you're free and we can arrange to meet up.

Take care,

Erik

20

4 Read the email again and answer the questions. Then look at the Writing skill box to check.

1 How is the email organized?
2 What informal language can you find?

WRITING SKILL
Informal emails and messages

If emails and messages in informal contexts (e.g. to people you know personally) are too formal, they can sound unfriendly.

- Informal messages with good or bad news typically contain these elements: greeting and introductory phrase; details of the news; questions about the other person's current situation; invitation to meet/speak.
- Ask about the other person in the first paragraph – you don't have to say why you're writing straight away.
- Talk about the next time you might talk or see each other in the final paragraph.
- Use informal expressions for beginning and ending emails (*How're things?; Take care!*) and in the body of the email (*What have you been up to?; I'll keep you posted.*).

5 Find informal words and phrases in Erik's email that have the same meaning as these more formal phrases (1–10). They are in the same order as they appear in the email.

1 contacted you	6 finding out about
2 write to you	7 inform you
3 doing	8 didn't know
4 recent news	9 exchange news
5 applied for	10 a long time

6 Read Ioana's response to Erik. Answer the questions.

1 Does it include the points you predicted in Exercise 3?
2 Is the email organized into paragraphs appropriately? Yes, it is.
3 Is the language suitably informal? No, the language is very formal.
4 How would you feel if you were Erik and you received this from your friend? Why?
Sample answer: Erik may not be happy to receive this email because the style is too formal, suggesting that they don't know each other very well, or even that Ioana is unsympathetic.

Dear Erik,

Thank you for your email yesterday. It was very good to hear from you.

I would like to offer my congratulations on your new position. I am extremely pleased for you. Please inform me about it once you have started work. I would be interested to learn all your news.

You enquired about the reunion party. I talked with Jenny for a long time. It was good to hear her news. She said she would like to exchange news with you as well, so I will inform you of our arrangements.

Thank you for your concern about Aida. She has fully recovered now and returned to college.

I look forward to seeing you in the near future.

Yours, with best regards,

Ioana

7 Rewrite Ioana's email so that it sounds less formal.

WRITING TASK

8 **WRITE** Write an informal email to a classmate giving your own good or bad news. Use one of these ideas or your own idea.

an exam you failed/passed a job you got
something got stolen/broken
your team won/lost an important game

9 **CHECK** Use the checklist. I have …
☐ included all the typical elements for this type of email (greetings, details of the news, etc.).
☐ organized the information appropriately.
☐ used informal language to sound friendly.

10 **REVIEW** Exchange emails with your partner. Did their email include everything from the checklist in Exercise 9? Take turns to give feedback.

11 Write a response to your partner's email. Remember to sound empathetic. Use the Useful language on page 19 to help you.

Go to page 130 for the Reflect and review.

EXPLORE MORE!

Write an email to someone you haven't spoken to for a while. Share your news and ask about theirs.

- Check answers as a class, focusing on eliciting the feelings that Erik would have on reading Ioana's response.

7

- Tell students to read the email again and identify the examples of formal language.
- Students rewrite the email, replacing the examples of formal language with informal language.

Sample answer

Hi Erik!
Great to hear from you!
That's brilliant news about the new job! Do you have any idea where you'll be working yet? Please keep me posted once you start work. I'd love to hear how it goes.
You wanted to know how the party was. I chatted with Jenny for ages and it was good to catch up. She also has a new job, which she's happy about. We are planning to meet up soon. She said she'd love to catch up with you too, so I'll let you know our plans. I'll give you a ring next week.
Thanks for asking about Aida. She is better now and went back to college last week.
Looking forward to seeing you very soon!
Ioana

Extra activity

Ask students to review the changes they made to the email in Exercise 7. Tell them to find a few pairs of phrases in the original email and their revised version that show the difference between more and less formal language, e.g. *I look forward to seeing you in the near future* and *Looking forward to seeing you very soon*. The aim is for students to notice the differences between the language used in the two different email styles.

WRITING TASK

8 WRITE

- Students choose an idea and write the first draft of their email.
- Refer students back to the Writing skill box for a reminder of how to organize an informal email. Remind them to use the informal language they have learned in this lesson in their email.

9 CHECK

- Ask students to use the checklist and then make changes to their emails if necessary.

10 REVIEW

- Students read their partner's email.
- Students take turns to give feedback to their partner on what they have done well in their email as well as things to improve, using the checklist in Exercise 9 to help them.

11

- Students plan and write a response to their partner's email.
- Remind students to demonstrate empathy when responding to good or bad news in their emails.
- Tell students to use the checklist from Exercise 9 to check their email when they have finished writing.

EXPLORE MORE!

Encourage students to write and send an email in English to someone they know outside of the class. If possible, this could be the start of frequent correspondence so that students can get additional practice with writing emails.

For **Unit 1 Reflect and review**, see Student's Book page 130.

For additional practice, refer to the **Mediation activity** on page 283 of the Teacher's Book.

See **Workbook** page 11 for extra practice.

VIDEO 1.1

Francisco: *I have two kids, they're eleven and nine, and I think the thing that makes me happiest is when we go on holiday together. We like to go camping. We go to the western United States where there are canyons and mountains, or we go to the beach somewhere.*

Tsiory: *I am a scientist, but I also work on science education. My husband and I co-founded a non-profit organization that works to promote science and scientific thinking in Madagascar. We are planning to develop programmes for younger audiences – school groups, for example. To make this dream a reality is what excites me most right now.*

Francisco: *In my line of work there are constant delays. Everything is delayed – you might be waiting for new equipment to be delivered for a long time, for example, so the work isn't really moving along. Everything is always delayed. I get frustrated! The other thing I hate is traffic. I hate traffic. I will always choose to go a longer way around traffic. That's the way I am. If I take the wrong turn, I get angry at myself for taking the wrong turn and I'm stuck for an hour in traffic, when I could have avoided it. So yeah, I'd say I am an impatient person!*

Tsiory: *In my work, I am used to being honest and straight talking. I am not very talkative, but I mean every word I say. So I find people who talk with no purpose very frustrating. They have a habit of talking about other people and I think it is pointless and can even hold people back. So yes, chitchatting for me is annoying. It is better to talk about ideas and work.*

AUDIO 1.1

1 [Sound of birds singing]; 2 [Sound of a fire crackling]; 3 [Sound of someone eating with their mouth open]; 4 [Sound of bicycle brakes squealing]; 5 [Sound of rain on a tent]; 6 [Sound of a workmate humming]; 7 [Sound of water flowing in a stream]; 8 [Sound of baby crying]; 9 [Sound of thunder]; 10 [Sound of a dentist's drill]

AUDIO 1.2

Fatima: *Tomoya, you studied psychology, didn't you?*

Tomoya: *Yes. Why?*

Fatima: *Well, do you think people's feelings are expressed in the same way by everyone?*

Tomoya: *What do you mean?*

Fatima: *Erm, I guess I'd like to know whether a smile means the same thing all over the world.*

Tomoya: *That's a great question! What do you think, Fatima?*

Fatima: *Yes, I guess. I mean, I think whoever I met, even if we were from opposite sides of the world and spoke different languages, one thing we'd understand about each other would be our smiles.*

Tomoya: *You're right, but that wasn't what many people thought before.*

Fatima: *Wasn't it?*

Tomoya: *No. The general idea many years ago was that showing emotions was learned behaviour, so you might learn one facial expression for an emotion in one society but another one in another society.*

Fatima: *Huh! That reminds me of the differences in how emoticons look in different cultures. You've noticed, haven't you?*

Tomoya: *You're right! It's always surprised me that in Europe the emoticons are from left to right: first eyes, then sometimes nose and then the mouth.*

Fatima: *Really? Don't you do it in the same way in Japan?*

Tomoya: *No! Ours are upright, just like your face is.*

Fatima: *Do you think it means that how we express emotions is different from culture to culture?*

Tomoya: *Kind of. For example, you might find that people smile less in some places, or smile for different social reasons. Some cultures smile in embarrassing situations, or just to be friendly and polite to strangers.*

Fatima: *I do that!*

Tomoya: *Who do you smile at?*

Fatima: *Sometimes I smile at people I pass on the street, even if I don't know them.*

Tomoya: *OK, well in some countries they might think that's strange!*

Fatima: *Haha! Thanks a lot!*

AUDIO 1.3

A: *Do you know what the difference is between emoticons and emojis?*

B: *Yes, emoticons are symbols used to represent faces and emojis are actual pictures.*

A: *Oh, OK!*

B: *You know you have to be careful with emojis, don't you? What you see when you send it isn't necessarily what the other person sees.*

A: *Isn't it?!*

B: *No! A friend of mine texted his wife 'Do you know how beautiful you are?' and sent the Spanish dancer emoji. Except the emoji on her phone was a fat yellow dancing blob!*

A: *Oh no! Who designs these emojis – the phone companies? By the way, why did you send me a surprised face when I told you I got the tickets for the match yesterday?*

B: *What? Didn't I send you a smiley? Oops!*

AUDIO 1.4

Were you ***surprised****?*

AUDIO 1.5

1 ***Were*** *you surprised?; 2 Were you* ***surprised****?; 3 Were* ***you*** *surprised?*

AUDIO 1.6

/ɪ/ … /ɪ/: exhausted, thrilled, optimistic, astonished

/iː/ … /iː/: weak, relieved, pleased

/eɪ/ … /eɪ/: afraid, impatient

/aɪ/ … /aɪ/: excited, delighted

AUDIO 1.7

Francisco: *When I got struck by lightning several years ago, I went through a real rollercoaster of emotions. It took me a few seconds to realize what had happened to me. As I lay on the ground, not being able to hear anything after the explosion, I saw all the woodchips falling like snow on me, from all the beams in the roof above me that had been split in half. That's when I realized I had been hit by lightning, but I still could not believe my bad luck. Then, I tried to breathe and I couldn't. I had to hit my chest a few times before I could take a breath. It was an* emotional few seconds. Then I realized that, except for my right arm, I could not move or even feel the rest of my body. Was I paralyzed? As people around me began screaming, I tried to say a few words to let them know I was actually not dead. The next few hours were also very extreme. We were in a remote area and we had to drive around the village looking for help, a doctor, someone. It took four hours for us to connect with an actual ambulance that had to come from a nearby town. Just before the ambulance arrived I started feeling tingling in my legs, and shortly after I began being able to move them. I felt enormous joy at that point. I was not paralyzed! After a brief visit, the doctor told me I was going to be fine! I still wasn't so sure that was true, but I was relieved and happy I could walk again anyway.

Tsiory: *In 2017, I was invited to give a talk on the stage of the National Geographic Grosvenor Auditorium in Washington, DC. It was my first time there. It's always hard to give a speech in English, as I always feel my English is bad. I wrote my speech no less than 50 times and repeated it in front of the mirror. Backstage, millions of questions crossed my mind. What if I mumble in front of the audience? What if no words came out of my mouth? And even stupid questions like: what if I miss the steps and I fall in front of all those people?*

My turn arrives to be on stage. The stage was bright but the audience was in the dark which made me feel more comfortable. I felt a cold stream running down my back. When the light turned to red, my mouth opened and words came out! I had repeated those words a hundred times and I was holding my notes, so I thought 'Everything is going to be alright'. When the clock said three seconds left, I was very confident. I realized that something had changed in me. I had overcome one of my biggest fears: talking to an audience and what an audience! I will have to do more speeches like this, but I just have to remember that I did it once and I can do it again.

VIDEO 1.2

Before we look at how empathy can help in communication, we need to define what 'empathy' is. A good way to explain it is through the saying: 'Never judge another person until you have walked a mile in their shoes'. I think what this means is that we cannot fully understand someone else's actions or emotions unless we try to find out what they are experiencing.

Related to empathy is sympathy, but these aren't the same things. Imagine you see someone crying in the street, for example. You can feel sympathy for them – you can be worried or sad, without knowing anything about them. But empathy can only happen once you've listened to their story.

So empathy involves listening first. When we try to empathize with someone, we try to see a situation from their point of view, to 'walk in their shoes', in order to understand what they are feeling. It can take a lot of imagination to empathize. It's easier to empathize with a friend than a stranger. And it's easier to empathize with someone whose views you share than someone you disagree with.

So why work on our empathy skills? Because it can help us to be more understanding, sort out differences of opinion and in the long term, help to develop positive relationships. It's essential when collaborating in teams for everyone to know they are being listened to and that their opinions are important to the rest of the group. And when there are problems or arguments, it helps to recognize each member's point of view; to try and find a solution that everyone is happy with.

But also, when two sides are looking to get the best from a situation, such as in negotiations or disputes, everyone is more likely to come out of the discussion happy if they feel they have been listened to.

Many of us admit that we aren't always empathetic, but there are ways to improve this skill. First, try to listen more than you speak. Instead of planning your response while the other person is talking, give yourself time to listen and reflect. Think about what they are saying, and why they might be saying it.

Another way to show you are listening is to acknowledge what the other person is saying and even to summarize the point that they're making. You can also use this to check that you've understood them correctly. Remember that empathizing is not about agreeing or disagreeing with someone. You can consider someone's point of view, even if it's different from your own.

So, in your next conversations with friends, and strangers, try exercising your empathy skills by following these techniques.

AUDIO 1.8

Waiter: *Would you like to order anything yet?*

Gurpreet: *Sorry, I'm still waiting for my friend. He shouldn't be much longer.*

Waiter: *That's no problem. I'll pop back when they get here.*

Gurpreet: *Come on. Why is it always me waiting?*

Laurent: *Hi there! Sorry I'm a bit late. The metro.*

Gurpreet: *A bit? I've been waiting for 30 minutes!*

Laurent: *Have you? I'm really sorry. I got stuck at work and the metro was really slow.*

Gurpreet: *The metro is always slow at this time. I came on the metro as well, you know.*

Laurent: *Listen, it's only a few minutes. It won't happen again. Come on, let's order.*

Gurpreet: *Look, this isn't the first time, is it? You're always doing this to me!*

Laurent: *And I've told you before, it isn't always easy to get out of work on time – things come up at the last minute.*

Gurpreet: *Hmm. I'm really annoyed right now.*

Laurent: *What can I say? I'm doing my best here. Come on. Let's order.*

Gurpreet: *I'm not sure I'm hungry right now.*

Waiter: *Erm, do you need a couple more minutes?*

Gurpreet: *I'm so fed up! This happens every time we meet for dinner, or whatever. He's always late, and I always feel so stupid – I hate sitting on my own in the restaurant. I don't understand why, if you're meant to meet someone at seven o'clock and it takes twenty minutes to get there, why you don't leave at twenty to seven! It's so rude!*

Laurent: *He takes it so badly. I mean, I was really surprised at how angry he got. I was only a few minutes late. Plus, when you arrange seven o'clock for something, who actually gets there at seven? If this isn't the first time, maybe he could arrive late too, if he expects me to be late anyway. I'm really busy at work at the moment, so I was actually working until seven tonight.*

UNIT 2

Language and communication

UNIT GOALS

2A Reading, speaking and writing

- read an article to practise skimming and scanning; use critical thinking skills to identify the main message in a text; write a social media post that summarizes an article

2B Listening and grammar, pronunciation, speaking and listening

- review and practise present tenses; notice the difference in pronunciation between auxiliary verbs with full and weak forms and practise saying auxiliary verbs clearly; talk about language learning experiences and give tips for language learning

2C Listening, vocabulary and pronunciation

- use discourse markers to understand a podcast; practise producing the /r/ sound clearly; learn how to use separable and inseparable phrasal verbs; use phrasal verbs in a discussion

2D Speaking, listening

- understand the role of first language identity in relationship building; talk about the similarities and differences between languages and cultures; talk about aspects of one's first language identity

2E Writing

- practise organizing formal emails in an appropriate way; practise using formal language and polite requests; write a formal email to ask for information about a course

Two women from Nigeria braid a customer's hair at their salon in Como, Italy.

Photocopiable resources

Communication activities: pp. 214–215
Vocabulary activity: p. 234
Grammar activity: p. 247
Focus on … activity: p. 248
Pronunciation activity: p. 269
Mediation activity: p. 284

Workbook

Unit 2 pp. 12–19

ABOUT THE PHOTO

The topic of this unit is language and communication. The photo shows two Nigerian women talking to a customer at a hairdressing salon in Como, Italy, where they work. There has been a significant Nigerian community in Italy since the 1980s. The Nigerian women are likely to be using either Italian, a second language for them, or a shared second language such as English, to communicate with their customer.

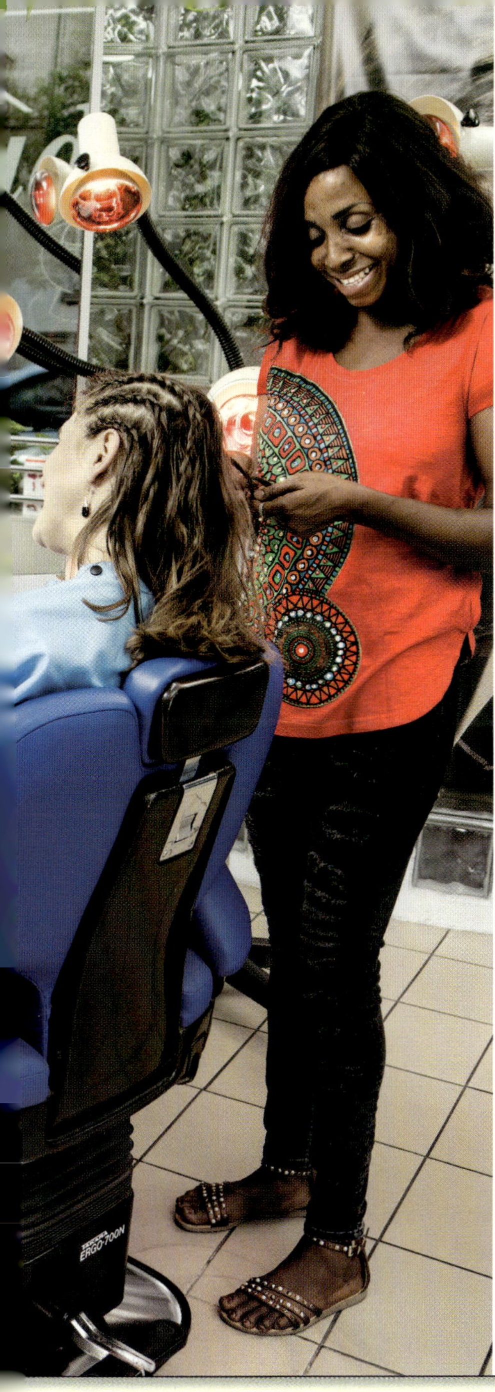

2

Language and communication

GOALS

- Skim and scan an article to identify the main ideas
- Discuss language learning experience and tips
- Talk about communication using phrasal verbs
- Use discourse markers to understand a podcast
- Understand how first language identity can be used in building relationships
- Write a formal email asking for information

1 Work in pairs. Look at the photo. How might knowing another language have helped the women?

WATCH ▶

2 ▶ 2.1 Watch the video. Match the sentences with the explorer, Maria (M) or Arianna (A).

NATIONAL GEOGRAPHIC EXPLORERS

MARIA FADIMAN ARIANNA SOLDATI

1 Learning French helped me professionally. A
2 I always try to learn a few words of the language of the local people I'm working with. M
3 I have worked as a Spanish to English translator for naturalist guides in Costa Rica. M
4 I am currently learning German. A

3 Make connections. How are Maria and Arianna's experiences similar to your own?

23

1

- Tell students to look carefully at the main photo and read the caption.
- **Optional step** Ask, *Do you think the Nigerian women are speaking to the other woman in Italian? Or do you think the three women are talking to each other in a common language that isn't their first language, such as English?*
- Students discuss the question. If they struggle to come up with ideas, suggest they think about topics such as friendship, business, integration and understanding other cultures.

Sample answers

Knowing another language might have helped the women to integrate, to make friends, find work/set up a business, communicate with customers/people from other countries who work in shops, hair salons, etc.

Extra activity

Ask students to think of a time when having some knowledge of another language has helped them. Tell students to work in pairs and tell their partner about the situation, where they were, who they were talking to and why, and how having knowledge of the other language helped them.

WATCH ▶

2 ▶ 2.1

- Ask students to read the sentences. Check students' understanding of *translator* (someone who can change texts from one language into another language).
- Play the video and encourage students to listen for the words in the sentences, or their synonyms, to help them match the explorers with the sentences.

Extra activity

In pairs, ask students to verbally summarize what the explorers said and make notes on the key points from their summaries. They can then use these key points to help them compare their experiences with the explorers' experiences in Exercise 3.

3

- Students talk about similarities between themselves and the explorers in pairs. If students are unsure about possible similarities, you could ask if English was also the first foreign language they learned or talk about your own experiences of learning languages to give them some ideas.

ABOUT THE EXPLORERS

MARIA FADIMAN is a conservationist and professor in the department of geosciences at Florida Atlantic University. She is American and lives in the US. She studies ethnobotany, which examines the relationship between people and plants. For more than 25 years, she has been working in the rainforests of Ecuador as well as in other countries such as Tanzania and Zimbabwe.

ARIANNA SOLDATI is an assistant professor in volcanology. Originally from Italy, she relocated to Germany for work. She has always been fascinated by volcanoes, especially the interaction between the physical properties of lava. Arianna combines observations in the field with laboratory work in order to better understand volcanoes and protect the 500 million people living in the shadow of active volcanoes worldwide.

LESSON GOALS

- **READING** The main aim is for students to practise skimming and scanning an article to identify the main ideas. A sub-aim is for students to practise identifying the main message in an article.
- **WRITING** A further sub-aim is for students to summarize an article in a social media post.
- **SPEAKING** The speaking aim is for students to practise discussing the content of social media posts they write.

ABOUT THE TEXT

The article mentions the following animals, insects and plants that students may not be familiar with:

- The **mockingbird** is a small, grey bird found in North and South America. It is known for mimicking the songs of other birds and the sounds of insects and amphibians.
- The **fork-tailed drongo** is a medium-sized dark brown bird found in Sub-Saharan Africa which is named for its fork-shaped tail. It is known for its *strink strink* call and for stealing food from other birds and animals.
- The **humpback whale** is one of the larger species of whales found in seas and oceans around the world. It is known for breaching, a kind of surfacing behaviour that involves throwing about two-thirds of its body out of the water and then splashing back down into the ocean.
- The **chameleon** is a type of lizard that comes in a range of colours. Many species have the ability to change colour to match their surroundings so they can camouflage themselves.
- The **treehopper** is a type of insect found all over the world. It is recognizable by its vertical face and enlarged thorax (middle section of the body). It lives and feeds on plants.
- The **firefly** is an insect in the beetle family known for its ability to glow. It uses chemicals to produce light from its lower abdomen that may be yellow, green, or pale red in colour.
- **'Corn root'** refers to the root of a corn plant that produces sweetcorn.

2A Talking nature

LESSON GOALS
- Skim and scan an article to identify the main ideas
- Identify the main message in an article
- Summarize an article in a social media post

READING

1 Work in pairs. How do you think the animals and plants in the photos on page 25 communicate with each other? Match the photos (A–E) with the forms of communication (1–5).

1 sound C
2 light E
3 vibrations (small movements) B
4 facial expression D
5 colour A

2 Look at the first part of the Reading skill box (Scanning). Then scan the article on page 25 to find which paragraph gives most of the answers to Exercise 1. Were your predictions correct?

READING SKILL
Scanning and skimming

Scanning: To find specific information quickly, look around the text to find relevant words and expressions.

Skimming: Skim to get the main idea of a text. Run your eyes quickly over the text, focusing only on the main content words: nouns, adjectives and verbs.

3 Look at the second part of the Reading skill box (Skimming). Then match the subheadings (a–g) with the paragraphs (1–7) in the article. Use these tips to help you:
- Scan the paragraphs for key words that match words and ideas in the headings.
- Skim the paragraphs to check your choice of heading was correct.

a Creating songs and music
b Achoo!
c The corn has ears
d Not just humans
e Many means of communication
f Tricks and lies
g Where's that accent from?

4 Find a word or phrase in the article for each definition.

1 ways of sharing information (l. 5) means of communication
2 parts of a subject (l. 7) aspects
3 is different from each other (l. 16) varies
4 change to suit different situations (l. 19) adapt
5 the form of a language spoken in an area (l. 19) dialect
6 copies the way someone or something moves or speaks (l. 22) mimics
7 an action that communicates a message (l. 38) signal
8 loudly blow air out of your nose and mouth in an uncontrolled way (l. 55) sneeze

5 Work in pairs. Look at the Critical thinking skill box. Then choose the main message (a–c) of the article. Where does the writer support the message?

CRITICAL THINKING SKILL
Identifying the main message

A text usually has one main message, or argument, that the writer wants to persuade the reader is true. Look for the same point being repeated in different ways throughout to identify the main argument. It may be mentioned near the beginning and end.

a Means of communication in the natural world are more complicated than human ones.
(b) We need to question the idea that human communication is special and unique.
c We know very little about how animals communicate and need to learn more.

SPEAKING AND WRITING

6 Imagine you want to post a link to the article on social media. Write a short summary to include with your post. Think about how you could persuade people to read the article (e.g. an image or surprising facts from the article).
I've just read an amazing article about animal communication. Did you know that … ?

7 Compare posts with your classmates. Which posts are the most persuasive?

EXPLORE MORE!
Search online for 'amazing animal communication' to find another strange means of communication in the natural world.

24

- The **African wild dog**, also called the painted dog or Cape hunting dog, is found in Sub-Saharan Africa. It is a highly sociable animal that lives in packs.

1

- **Optional step** With books closed, write 'Talking nature' on the board and elicit ideas about what it could refer to. Ask, *How do plants and animals communicate with each other?*
- Students may be surprised by the possibility of plants being able to communicate with each other. If so, tell them to use a wider definition of 'communicate' (to give a signal or move in a certain way), and to be open to the possibility of plants communicating with each other.
- Students look at the photos and decide how they think each animal or plant communicates with each other. They then match the animals and plants with the ways of communicating.
- **Optional step** Ask, *Which communication methods did you already know about? Which communication method surprised you the most?*

A chameleon
B treehopper
C corn
D horse

1 d ______________

It's often thought that only humans have the ability to use language. But animals do talk, of course, just not very often in words we'd understand. It turns out that, throughout the natural world, there are means of communication that are just as innovative as any technology we can invent. Even more surprisingly, aspects of communication that we thought were limited to humans, such as accents, culture and lying, are known to feature in the daily chitchat of many species.

2 g ______________

Take birdsong, for example. Did you know that many birds' calls change depending on where the bird comes from? A mockingbird from Kansas, US pronounces his chirps differently from another mockingbird in Virginia, US. And birds aren't the only group in which accent varies from place to place; sperm whales recognize where strangers are from by their voice and monkeys have been shown to adapt to new places by learning the local dialect.

3 f ______________

Some birds can even use the language of other birds to deceive them. The fork-tailed drongo mimics the alarm calls of more than thirty species. It does so when it sees a bird with food in its mouth. The idea is that the other bird drops the food on hearing the call, which is when the drongo steps in to collect the food. A human equivalent would be to shout 'Fire!' in a restaurant and then eat everyone's meals after they run out of the building.

4 a ______________

If you thought that humans are the only species to use language creatively, think again. The humpback whale in the South Pacific invents new songs every year or two. Other groups living far away hear these songs and learn them if they like them. You might hear a song that started off the Australian coast near the island of Tahiti, six thousand miles away!

5 e ______________

Many animals use sounds, but there are other strategies for getting your message across. The skin colour of chameleons constantly changes as a signal of their emotions and intentions. Treehoppers, tiny insects, shake their bodies to send vibrations through plants to other treehoppers. Fireflies use light and can send signals between thousands of individuals. Remarkably, horses make facial expressions to show emotions.

6 c ______________

What about plants? We've known that they produce chemicals to warn other plants of dangers, such as insects, but recent research shows that some plants even use sound. Corn roots, for example, make regular clicking noises that its neighbours respond to. And scientists have shown that when a plant 'hears' a neighbour is growing next to it, it responds by growing faster.

7 b ______________

Finally, no article about communication in the animal kingdom would be complete without mentioning African wild dogs. These sociable creatures make decisions by sneezing! Yes, according to scientists, they get together in groups and sneeze to decide whether to go on a hunt or not. If more than half sneezes, it's a yes. So it turns out even democracy wasn't invented by us!

E fireflies

25

2

- Ask students to read the information about scanning in the Reading skill box.
- Tell students they are now going to practise scanning by identifying the correct paragraph of the text.
- Students compare their answers for both Exercises 1 and 2 in pairs, then check answers as a class.

Answers

Paragraph 5 contains 4 out of 5 answers

3

- Students read the information about skimming in the Reading skill box.
- Students skim each paragraph to identify its main message and then match the paragraphs with the subheadings.
- Students compare their answers in pairs, then check answers as a class.
- **Optional step** Check students' understanding of how to skim and scan effectively. In pairs or small groups, ask students to brainstorm situations where they need to read texts quickly to identify the main ideas or message (e.g. reading social media posts or news articles with a lot of content that has to be prioritised). Then ask them to discuss what helps them to do this effectively, for example looking at the headline and sub-headline(s) in a news article.

Extra activity

Focus students' attention on the subheadings and elicit the type of language used in each them, for example a) a noun phrase that starts with a verb in the gerund form; b) a one-word exclamation; c) d) e) f) noun phrases, including a use of alliteration in e) ('many means') and two nouns separated by 'and' in f); g) a question. In pairs or small groups, students write alternative subheadings for some or all of the paragraphs in this article using these techniques or other creative alternatives.

VOCABULARY NOTES

turn out /tɜːn aʊt/ = to prove to be true

innovative /ɪnəvətɪv/ = describing something that has new or original features or is technologically advanced

species /ˈspiːʃiːz/ = a group of living organisms that are similar and able to reproduce with each other

chirp (n) /ʧɜːp/ = a high-pitched sound made by a bird

fork-tailed /fɔːk-teɪld/ = describing a tail that is split into two, pointed parts, so it looks like a letter 'y'

remarkably /rɪˈmɑːkəbli/ = describing an action that is surprising and worthy of attention

4

- Tell students to use the line numbers in the text while doing the activity and remind them that they may be looking for either a single word or a multi-word phrase.
- Students find the relevant lines in the text and identify the correct words or phrases.
- **Optional step** Invite different students to say the words or phrases out loud. Check that their pronunciation is correct. Model and drill any words that students struggle to pronounce correctly.

Extra activity

Ask students to choose a few other words or phrases in the text and think of a definition for each one. In pairs, students then tell each other their definitions (with or without the line number) and guess the word or phrase for each one.

5

- **Optional step** Elicit reasons why it is useful to identify a writer's main message, for example: it is easier to remember the main message of an article than specific details; it can help you understand the writer's opinion or argument, which you can then compare with other writers' opinions or arguments, etc.
- Tell students to read the Critical thinking skill box and use the information in it to identify the main message in the article.
- Students look for and make notes on the things the writer describes or explains in the article to support his/her main message then compare their notes in pairs.

Answer

b. The writer supports this message in: Paragraph 1 - sentences 1 and 2 (Paragraph 1 introduces the point explicitly); Paragraphs 2, 3 and 4 describe how accent, deception and creativity are not unique to humans; Paragraph 5 emphasizes the variety of animals' means of communication; Paragraph 6 explains that even plants communicate using sound; Paragraph 7 describes extraordinary findings that wild dogs make democratic decisions.

SPEAKING AND WRITING

6

- Ask students to read the instructions and the sample sentences for the task. Tell them to keep in mind that the aim of their social media post is to persuade people to read the article.
- **Optional step** Brainstorm (as a class, or in groups or pairs) techniques that students could use to persuade the reader of their post to read the article, for example: rhetorical questions, (e.g. *Did you know ... ?*), repeating or emphasizing key points and using adjectives that emphasize how interesting or positive something is, e.g. fascinating, amazing, etc.
- Students write their social media posts.

Sample answer

I've just read an interesting article about animal communication. It talks about all the amazing means of communication that animals (and plants) use and the clever things that they can do with language. It suggests that perhaps human communication is not unique. Did you know that plants listen to other plants, for example, or that some animals have different accents?

7

- When students are reading and preparing feedback on other students' posts, remind them to focus primarily on how persuasive the posts are.
- Students exchange texts in groups and then give verbal feedback to each other directly.
- **Optional step** Stick or pin students' anonymous social media posts to the walls of the classroom or place them on desks. Ask students to walk around and choose one post to give feedback on. Check that all students get feedback on their work by either assigning each student another student's post to read before they begin, or monitoring students as they walk around and read the posts to check that every post is being read, for example by prompting students who haven't yet chosen a post to choose one that nobody else has chosen. Students read their assigned or chosen post carefully and prepare feedback on it, that they could then share in class after indicating which post on the wall they are talking about.

See **Workbook** pages 12–13 for extra practice.

LESSON GOALS

- **LISTENING AND GRAMMAR** The main aim is for students to review and practise using present tenses to talk about language learning.
- **PRONUNCIATION** A sub-aim is for students to practise saying auxiliary verbs clearly in order to be understood.
- **SPEAKING AND LISTENING** The speaking and listening aim is to get students to listen to and discuss examples of language learning experience and tips.

LISTENING AND GRAMMAR

1

- Give students about a minute to read the questions and think about their answers. In pairs, students discuss the questions.
- Ask students to give reasons and examples or even tell short anecdotes to expand on their answers to the questions.

2 2.1

- **Optional step** Ask students to tell a partner what they can remember about Arianna's language learning experiences from the video they have already watched.
- Students read the questions. Check understanding of 'struggle' (to find it difficult to do something).
- Play the audio and ask students to write key words for each question.

Answers

1 English, French, Spanish and German
2 Since she was eleven
3 No
4 German

3 2.2

- Students read the sentences and identify the tenses needed to fill the gaps. This should be a revision exercise for students but remind them to look for key words in the sentences that indicate the tense needed, for example *often* (present simple).
- Students complete the sentences, then listen to the audio to check their answers.

4 2.2

- **Optional step** Draw students' attention to key words in the questions that will help them to identify the correct verb form for each one: 1) regularly; 2) past, present, future; 3) in progress; 4) entire life.
- Students complete the sentences, then listen to the audio again to check their answers.

Extra activity

Use the example sentences in the Grammar box to create prompts, for example: *I often ... with ...; I'm ... at the moment; Unfortunately, I've never had the chance to ...; I've been ... since I was ...* Students use these prompts to write personalized sentences about their own lives. They could focus specifically on their language-learning experiences or write about other life experiences of their choice.

GRAMMAR NOTES

Present simple
Remind students that the present simple is used to say that you do an activity regularly or to say how often you do something. It is irrelevant whether the activity is happening now or not.
Present continuous
Remind students that the present continuous is used more frequently for activities happening around now than for activities happening right now. When we say 'around now', we mean the activity started before now and will continue in the future.
Present perfect simple
The present perfect simple can be used for both past actions and actions that are not yet finished. This may be difficult for students to understand if they don't have a tense in their first language that can be used in these ways.
The form *have* + past participle may be used to form a past tense in students' first language. If that is the case, check they are aware that in English the present perfect simple can only be used for past actions if these have an impact on the present.
Present perfect continuous
Students need to differentiate between the present perfect continuous and simple tenses and this is especially important if one or both of these tenses do not exist in their first language. Tell students that the present perfect simple focuses on the effects of an action or activity in the present, and the present perfect continuous focuses on a process or an activity that is still happening or only finished a short time ago.

For further information and practice, see **Grammar reference Unit 2B** on page 141 of the Student's Book.

5

- Tell students that the incorrect tense is used in each sentence.
- If students are unsure what the correct tense should be, tell them to re-read the Grammar box and look for key words in the sentences, such as *since*, to help them.

Answers

1 She's been studying languages since 2015.
2 I've watched this film several times already.
3 Technology is currently changing how people study languages.
4 She's been reading this book all day without stopping – it must be really fascinating.
5 I can't talk right now because I'm still writing the report.
6 My parents have never learned a foreign language.
7 I call my parents every Saturday.

Extra activity

In pairs, students write four sentences, each of which uses a different tense from the Grammar box. These sentences could be about language learning or about anything students are interested in. Students then re-write their sentences on another piece of paper so that each one has a mistake in the grammar used in it (e.g. *we has* instead of *we have*). Students exchange and correct each other's sentences.

For additional practice, refer to the **Grammar activity** on page 247 of the Teacher's Book.

PRONUNCIATION

6 2.3

- Tell students to read the sentences and identify the auxiliary verb in each one.
- Tell students they will hear each of the sentences twice. They will then identify the version of the sentence (A or B) in which the auxiliary verb was easier to understand.
- Play the audio so students can listen and write their answers.

PRONUNCIATION NOTES

Auxiliary verbs are usually pronounced as weak forms because they are not the key content words in a sentence. Students should be able to understand and produce both the strong and weak forms of auxiliary verbs, and be able to adapt this feature of their pronunciation according to their listener.

First language users will usually use weak forms. In official speaking exams, such as the Cambridge exams and IELTS, examiners will often listen out for weak forms as examples of 'natural pronunciation'. In contrast, it can be better to use strong forms in international contexts, when speaking to listeners for whom English is a second or other language. Strong forms make the auxiliary verbs easier to hear and can help to ensure that the listener understands which tense is being used.

2B I'm taking classes at the moment

LESSON GOALS
- Review present tenses
- Say auxiliary verbs clearly
- Discuss language learning experience and tips

LISTENING AND GRAMMAR

1 Work in pairs. Discuss the questions.
1. How many languages do you speak? How have you learned them?
2. Are there any other languages that you would like to learn?
3. Do you know anyone who speaks a lot of languages? How do they manage to learn so many?
4. What do you think is more important when learning a language: talent or hard work? Why?

NATIONAL GEOGRAPHIC EXPLORER

Arianna (centre right) with her German-speaking and French-speaking friends.

2 2.1 Listen to Arianna Soldati talk about her language learning experiences. Answer the questions.
1. Which foreign languages does Arianna speak?
2. How long has she been using French?
3. Has she ever lived in a Spanish-speaking country?
4. Which language is she currently struggling with?

3 2.2 Complete the sentences with the correct form of the verbs in brackets. Then listen to check.
1. I've ___studied___ (study) English for a long time.
2. I also speak French and I've been ___using___ (use) it since I was 11.
3. I often ___speak___ (speak) it with some French-speaking friends.
4. Our language has always ___been___ (be) French, so we speak in French.
5. Unfortunately, I've never ___had___ (have) the chance to live in a Spanish-speaking country.
6. It has ___not (n't) been___ (not/be) that difficult to learn.
7. The last language I've been ___trying___ (try) to pick up is German.
8. I'm ___taking___ (take) classes at the moment, so hopefully I will improve soon.

4 Look at the sentences in Exercise 3 again. Answer the questions. Then read the Grammar box to check.
1. Which sentence refers to something that happens regularly? 3
2. Which sentences refer to an action that started in the past, continues into the present and is likely to continue in the future? 1, 2, 7
3. Which sentence describes an action in progress at the current moment? 8
4. Which sentence refers to Arianna's entire life? 5

GRAMMAR Present tenses

Present simple
Use to refer to present habits, actions that happen regularly and facts.
*I often **speak** it with some French-speaking friends.*

Present continuous
Use to refer to things happening at this moment or around the present moment (but not exactly right now).
*I'**m taking** classes at the moment.*

Present perfect simple
Use to describe present results of past actions when the time is not specified.
*Unfortunately, I'**ve never had** the chance to live in a Spanish-speaking country.*
Use to describe the results of actions that began in the past and continued into the present.
*I'**ve studied** English for a long time.*

Present perfect continuous
Use to refer to actions that began in the past, are still in progress and are likely to continue in the future.
*I'**ve been using** it since I was 11.*

Go to page 141 for the Grammar reference.

26

- Direct students to the Clear voice box and ask them to read it. Note that the main aim of this section is to develop students' receptive skills. The subsequent activities focus on listening rather than on producing this pronunciation feature themselves.
- **Optional step** Encourage students to reflect on whether the contents of the Clear voice box would also apply to their first language. Ask *Are auxiliary verbs typically reduced to weak forms in your first language(s)?*
- Students practise saying the sentences with both strong and weak auxiliary verbs.

For additional practice, refer to the **Pronunciation activity** on page 269 of the Teacher's Book.

SPEAKING AND LISTENING

7

- **Optional step** Refer students to the Grammar reference section on page 140 to review how to form questions.
- Students complete the questions and write two of their own. Refer students to the Grammar box if they are unsure about which tense to use.
- Students ask and answer the questions in pairs.

5 Find and correct the mistakes in the sentences.
1 She's studying languages since 2015.
2 I've been watching this film several times already.
3 Technology currently changes how people study languages.
4 She's read this book all day without stopping – it must be really fascinating.
5 I can't talk right now because I still write the report.
6 My parents have never been learning a foreign language.
7 I'm calling my parents every Saturday.

PRONUNCIATION

6 2.3 Listen to two sentences said in two ways. In which version is the auxiliary verb easier to hear? Then look at the Clear voice box to learn more.
1 I am taking classes at the moment. A
2 I have been using it since I was 11. A

CLEAR VOICE
Understanding weak forms of auxiliary verbs

In fast speech, auxiliary verbs (e.g. *am, have been*) are typically reduced to weak forms (i.e. *'m* /əm/, *'ve* /əv/, *been* /bɪn/) and are unstressed. This can make them more difficult to hear. To be easy to understand, especially in international contexts, it can be better to pronounce the full forms of auxiliary verbs (/æm/, /hæv/, /biːn/).

SPEAKING AND LISTENING

7 Use the words to form questions. Then write two of your own questions about language learning. Ask and answer the questions with a partner.
1 English / you / how long / learn
2 study / another / language / you / currently / foreign
3 language / speak / ever / you / meet / someone / lots of
4 what / difficult / language / you / most / learn
5 study / most / you / what / enjoy / about / a foreign language
6 ______
7 ______

8 2.4 Listen and write down the language learning tips Arianna gives. Which tip do you think is the best? Why?

9 Work in groups. Discuss the questions. Then decide on the three best tips for learning languages.
1 What do you find difficult when you are studying a language? What do you find easy?
2 What are you currently struggling with? Why?
3 How have you practised your English outside the class since this course started?
4 Which language learning tips have worked best for you?

EXPLORE MORE!
Search online for 'language learning tips'. Choose one tip and apply it to your language learning.

27

8 2.4

- Play the audio. Tell students to identify and write key words or phrases that Arianna uses and then use their notes to summarize each tip.
- Ask students to tell their partner which tip they think is the best and why.

Answers
Speaking to people.
Watching things in their original language.
Cutting out all the other languages you speak.
Changing the language on your laptop and phone.

9

- Put students into groups of three or four for the discussion. Remind them that the aim of their discussion is to decide on the three best tips for learning English.
- Students ask and answer the questions in their groups.
- **Optional step** Open up a class discussion and invite different students to share their tips. Compile a list of students' tips on the board.

EXPLORE MORE!
Tell students that they will get thousands, if not millions, of search results for 'language learning tips', so they will need to be selective about which websites they look at and use tips from. Encourage them to evaluate the credibility and reliability of their search results, for example by looking at websites from institutions such as The British Council, rather than blogs produced by private individuals or companies. Once students have found suitable sources, they will need to skim through the contents of the webpage to find out the main message for each of the tips given.

For additional practice, refer to the **Communication activity** on page 214 of the Teacher's Book.

See **Workbook** pages 14–15 for extra practice.

Answers
1 How long have you been learning English?
2 Are you currently studying another foreign language?
3 Have you ever met someone who speaks lots of languages?
4 What is the most difficult language you have learned?
5 What do you enjoy most about studying a foreign language?
6 and 7 Students' own answers

Extra activity
Ask students to use their seven questions from Exercise 7 to do a class survey on other students' language learning experiences. Give students ten to fifteen minutes to move around the room and talk to as many students as possible. For homework, students write a summary of what they found out from the other students they talked to.

2C The rise of English

LESSON GOALS
- Use discourse markers to understand a podcast
- Produce the /r/ sound clearly
- Talk about communication using phrasal verbs
- Use separable and inseparable phrasal verbs correctly

LISTENING

1 Work in pairs. Discuss the questions.
1. If you could study English anywhere in the world, where would it be? Why?
2. Are there a lot of English users where you're from? Do you think this number is growing?
3. Do you currently use your English more with people from English-speaking countries or people for whom English is a second language?

2 Look at the sentences from a podcast. Underline the words or phrases that introduce ideas.
1. Basically, whether you're from Ho Chi Minh City, New York, Warsaw, São Paolo or Nairobi doesn't matter.
2. On the other hand, when speaking Chinese, Spanish or Arabic, you're most likely to do it with first language users.
3. Interestingly, more than eighty per cent of them do not speak it as their mother tongue.
4. According to many experts, a foreign accent isn't usually a problem.
5. This brings me to my next point.

3 Match the words you underlined in Exercise 2 with the type of information that comes after them (a–e). Then look at the Listening skill box to check.

a contrast 2
b different subject 5
c explanation 1
d reference to sources 4
e surprising information 3

LISTENING SKILL
Identifying discourse markers

Listen out for the discourse markers a speaker uses. They will help you predict what type of information will come next.

New, surprising or interesting fact: *surprisingly, interestingly, funnily enough*
Contrast: *however, while, on the other hand*
Referring to sources: *according to*
Moving to a different subject: *this brings me to, moving on to*
Explaining: *basically*

4 2.5 Listen to the podcast. Write down three things the speaker says that you either agree with or disagree with. Then discuss in pairs.

5 2.5 Listen to the podcast again. Answer the questions.
1. How do English and languages such as Chinese or Arabic differ, according to the speaker?
2. What were the two things that the speaker believed about English?
3. How did travelling and working change her perspective?
4. What did she learn from research about communicating in English?
5. How did the speaker's identity as an English user evolve?

28

LESSON GOALS

- **LISTENING** A main aim is for students to use discourse markers to understand a podcast.
- **VOCABULARY** A further main aim is to review and practise using phrasal verbs to talk about communication, and how to use separable and inseparable phrasal verbs correctly.
- **PRONUNCIATION** A sub-aim is to practise producing the /r/ sound clearly.
- **SPEAKING** The speaking aim is to talk about communication.

LISTENING

1
- **Optional step** Direct students to the lesson title and elicit what it could refer to. Ask *In what ways has the English language 'risen' over recent decades? What have been the effects of this rise on you personally and on the world in general?*
- Put students into pairs for the discussion.
- Draw students' attention to the verb forms in each question (1 second conditional; 2 present simple, present continuous; 3 present simple). Remind them to use the appropriate tenses during their discussion.
- Students ask and answer the questions.

2
- **Optional step** Ask students how often they listen to podcasts and what types of podcasts they like, for example: comedy, crime, news, science, etc.
- Elicit the meaning of 'introduce an idea' from a stronger student. (e.g. to say/write something to indicate you are going to present an idea).

3
- Check students' understanding of 'reference to sources' (to say where the information you are going to give comes from, e.g. experts, a specific person, a specific book, etc.).
- Students identify the function of the words and phrases that introduce ideas in the sentences from Exercise 2 by looking at the whole sentence. Tell them not to look at the Listening skill box at this stage.
- Students check their answers by reading the information in the Listening skill box. Elicit or explain that a 'discourse marker' is a word or phrase that shows what you are going to say/write next.
- **Optional step** Ask students to decide whether the discourse markers in the Listening skill box would be more commonly used in writing or in speaking. (Speaking: *funnily enough*, *this brings me to*, *moving on to*, *basically*; Writing: *surprisingly*, *interestingly*, *however*, *while*, *on the other hand*, *according to*)

Extra activity

Ask students to choose a discourse marker from each category that wasn't used in Exercise 2 (they can re-use 'according to' and 'basically') and use them to write a paragraph about their experience of learning English or how people learn English in their country. This will consolidate their understanding of how to use these discourse markers in context.

VOCABULARY AND PRONUNCIATION

NATIONAL GEOGRAPHIC EXPLORER

6 Read Maria Fadiman's reaction to the podcast. Then discuss the questions (1–3) in pairs.

> One thing that came up in the podcast and surprised me was how many people speak English as second language users. It made me feel lucky that I get to speak English as my first language and that I can easily get my message across to so many people! But I also felt guilty that I get to do that so easily, simply because of where I was born.
>
> In terms of culture, it might be fun to read up on, but I wouldn't say there is a culture of English-speaking people, anyway. And I'm not sure this would help you use English better.
>
> It's worth pointing out there is no real American accent. When I lived in the South, I started to pick up a southern accent (of which there are many variations). In New York, as a child, I tried to pick up the accent there and my mum told me that my grandfather, originally from New York, had tried to *lose* his New York accent. It's similar in Spanish. I've kind of made up my own personal Spanish accent.

1 Were you surprised by how many people speak English as second language users?
2 Do you like to read up on the culture of a country when learning a new language? Why? / Why not?
3 Have you ever picked up a different accent?

7 Match the phrasal verbs (1–8) with the correct definition (a–h).

1 bring up d	a think of an idea
2 come up f	b draw someone's attention to
3 come up with a	c learn more by reading
4 get across e	d mention a topic
5 make up h	e explain (ideas)
6 pick up g	f be mentioned (topic)
7 point out b	g learn to do without much effort
8 read up on c	h invent

Go to page 135 for the Vocabulary reference.

8 2.6 Look at the Clear voice box. Then listen and practise saying the words and phrases (1–4).

CLEAR VOICE
Saying the /r/ sound

Pronunciation of the /r/ sound can vary a lot among users of English. Be careful not to pronounce it as an /h/ or /l/. However, don't worry if your /r/ sounds different to how a first language user might pronounce it.

1 bring up
2 in contrast
3 surprisingly
4 read up on

9 Read the Focus on box. Then correct the mistakes in the sentences (1–3).

FOCUS ON Separable and inseparable phrasal verbs

Most phrasal verbs can be separated, e.g. ***pick up** an accent* and ***pick** an accent **up***. You must always put the pronoun before the preposition (~~*pick up it*~~ → *pick it up*).

Phrasal verbs followed by an adverb and a preposition or two prepositions (e.g. *come up with*) can't be separated.

There are a few phrasal verbs which must always be separated, e.g. ***get** my ideas **across***.

Go to page 142 for the Focus on reference.

1 At first I believed her, but then it turned out she'd made up it.
2 When I'm nervous, I find it difficult to get across my meaning.
3 She's incredibly creative and comes up new ideas with all the time.

10 Work in pairs. Complete the questions with phrasal verbs from this lesson. Then choose three of the questions to discuss.

1 Have you ever been in a situation when you brought up an embarrassing conversation topic by mistake?
2 Do you know a person who is good at making up stories?
3 Can you think of a time when you couldn't get your message across?
4 Have you ever had to point out a mistake to someone?
5 What's something you've picked up quite easily?

EXPLORE MORE!
Search online for 'a short history of the English language' to learn more about how English became the global language of communication.

29

4 2.5

- Play the audio so students can identify and take notes on the points the speaker makes.
- Students tell each other which points they agreed and disagreed with. Ask them to explain their opinions, giving reasons, examples or other evidence to support them.

VOCABULARY NOTES

spread (n) /spred/ = the expansion or distribution of something over a larger area or amongst a larger group of people

mother tongue /ˈmʌðə tʌŋ/ = the first language that someone learned to speak

first language user /fɜːst ˈlæŋgwɪʤ ˈjuːzə/ = a person who speaks a language as their first language, i.e. it is the first language that the person learned to speak

idiom /ˈɪdɪəm/ a phrase that has a different meaning to the meaning of its individual words

imitate /ˈɪmɪteɪt/ = to copy what someone or something else says or does

5 2.5

- Ask students to read the questions.
- Check students' understanding of *perspective* (point of view, how someone sees something) and *evolve* (to gradually change or develop over time).
- Tell students that they will hear the answers in the same order as the questions. Ask students to listen for the key content words in the questions (e.g. 'Chinese' and 'Arabic' in question 1) and use these to find the answers.
- Play the audio so students can write the answers.

Answers

1 Eighty per cent of people who speak Arabic and Chinese are first language users, but eighty per cent of those who speak English are not first language users.
2 She used to believe English was only spoken in the UK, the US and Australia. She also thought it was important to speak like first language users.
3 She realized that most people who use English aren't first language users and that using British or American idioms does not always help her communicate.
4 A foreign accent isn't usually a problem. First language users might often be the most difficult to understand in international contexts.
5 She now feels much more comfortable about her accent. She doesn't try to imitate others' pronunciation but tries to be herself.

Extra activity

Put students into pairs or small groups to discuss the following questions:

1 What were some things you believed about English before or when you started learning it?
2 Do you still believe those things to be true?
3 If your perspective has changed, say what has changed and explain why.

VOCABULARY AND PRONUNICATION

6

- **Optional step** Elicit what students remember about Maria Fadiman's experiences of learning languages from the video they watched at the start of this unit. Students then work in pairs and briefly tell their partner what they think her response to the podcast might be.
- Students read Maria's response and use it as a guide for their responses to the questions. Tell students they do not have to agree with Maria's arguments.

Extra activity

Ask students to read the text again and identify useful phrases they could use when giving their answers to the questions. Alternatively, you could write the phrases on the board: *One thing that came up ... It made me feel ... In terms of ..., I would/wouldn't say ..., It's worth pointing out ...* Clarify the meaning of phrases if necessary. Ask students to choose two or three of these phrases to use when they are discussing the questions or in their next discussion on another topic.

7

- Ask students to read the list of phrasal verbs and match them with the correct meanings. Remind students that they have either heard these phrasal verbs in the podcast or read them in Maria's response to it.
- Several of the phrasal verbs have similar meanings, for example the active *to mention a topic* and the passive *be mentioned (topic)*. Students need to ensure they choose the exact meaning for each phrasal verb.
- Students compare answers in pairs and then check answers as a class.

For further information and practice, see **Vocabulary reference Unit 2** on page 135 of the Student's Book.

For additional practice, refer to the **Vocabulary activity** on page 234 of the Teacher's Book.

8 2.6

- Students read the Clear voice box. A key point here is that students don't need to replicate the pronunciation of the /r/ sound exactly as a first language user would to be understood in an international communication context.
- Play the audio so students can listen and practise saying the four words with /r/ sounds.
- **Optional step** One of the speakers in the audio is a first language user and the other is someone for whom English is a second or other language. Ask students if they noticed a difference in the two speakers' pronunciation and which one they found easier/more difficult to understand and why.

PRONUNCIATION NOTES

Note that several Asian languages, including Japanese and Korean, do not distinguish between the /r/ and the /l/ sound, as the English language does. Speakers of these languages may, therefore, pronounce an /r/ sound as an /l/ sound or vice versa.

If necessary, give your students extra practice to say and identify the /r/ and /l/ sounds. You could do this through games or tongue twisters, e.g, *Lara looked left and right and ran across the road; Red lorries and yellow lorries rarely race on Friday; Rory lit the fire and the roaring lion ran away.*

9

- Ask students to read the Focus on box.
- Ask students to read and correct the mistake in each sentence.
- Students compare their answers in pairs and then check answers as a class.

Answers

1 At first I believed her, but then it turned out she'd made it up.
2 When I'm nervous, I find it difficult to get my meaning across.
3 She's incredibly creative and comes up with new ideas all the time.

LANGUAGE NOTES

Phrasal verbs are verbs that are made up of two or three words. They are frequently used in more informal spoken English and using them in this context can help students sound more natural.
Draw students' attention to the fact that in some cases, putting the pronoun in the wrong position will mean that you communicate a different meaning than you intended to. For example: *pick up* + pronoun (physically move into the air) has a different meaning to *pick* + pronoun + *up* (collect).

For further information and practice, see **Focus on reference Unit 2C** on page 142 of the Student's Book.

10

- Students read and complete the questions with the correct form of a phrasal verb from Exercise 7.
- Remind them that they will also need to put the phrasal verb into the correct tense for the question.
- Students check their answers in pairs, then choose three of the questions and take turns to ask and answer them.

For additional practice, refer to the **Focus on activity** on page 248 and the **Mediation activity** on page 284 of the Teacher's Book.

EXPLORE MORE!

Once students have gone online and found out information about the history of the English language, you could ask them to use the information to prepare a presentation or report about how English became the global language of communication.

See **Workbook** pages 15–17 for extra practice.

LESSON GOALS

- **SPEAKING** This lesson integrates speaking and listening. Its main aim is to raise students' awareness of how they can use their first language identity as a tool to build relationships. Students practise explaining aspects of their first language identity and showing interest in other people's backgrounds. The lesson ends with a group discussion where students share aspects of their culture and first language that they would like others to know about.

LISTENING

1

- Encourage students to use any personal experience they have of talking to people from different countries who they do not know very well to order the topics.
- Ask students to share their lists with a partner and give reasons for their choices. Then ask them to add a few more topics to their lists and put them in order.
- **Optional step** Elicit feedback from the class on the topics that students are most likely to talk about. Then create a class ranking for the topics on the board.

Answers

Suggested additional topics: weather, your age, TV shows, things you know about the other person's country such as politics, celebrities, beautiful places, etc.

2 2.7

- Tell students they are going to listen to two conversations between people from different countries using English to communicate with each other.
- Give students time to read the task.
- Play the audio and ask students to make notes on their answers to the questions.

Answers

1 Similarities: share their love of capoeira, the reason they are together. The male speaker is interested in capoeira in Sibel's home country. They share their tiredness and hunger. Both languages have an idiom for hungry. Differences: hunger is expressed differently in each language (but they share an interest in these differences).

2 Similarities: Both enjoy football and play with friends; José Luis is interested in football in Hassan's country. Differences: Spanish has a specific word for a good goal that doesn't exist in Hassan's first language.

3 2.7

- Ask students to read the questions and try to remember any answers from the first time they listened.
- Play the audio again and ask students to listen for the information they need to identify.
- Students compare answers in pairs. Check answers in class.

Answers

1 I'm as hungry as a wolf / I could eat my arm / Students' own answers.

2 What its football scene is like.

Extra activity

Students write a comprehension question for each conversation. Their questions could either be about an aspect of a topic the speakers talk about, a story they tell or an expression they use. Students can refer to the audioscript to help them prepare their questions. They then take turns to ask and answer their questions in pairs, referencing the audioscript to give the correct answers where necessary.

4

- Check students' understanding of 'switch between languages' (to speak in one language and then change to speaking in another language) and 'first language identity' (the communication style, accent and culture shared by speakers of your first language).
- Give students ten to fifteen minutes to discuss the questions in pairs. Encourage them to go into as much depth as they can, for example by giving specific examples or telling relevant anecdotes.

Answers

1 a) conversation 2 ('golazo'); b) conversation 2 (football); c) conversations 1 and 2

2 Sample answers: if the word is clear in context because it is so expressive (e.g. 'golazo', Wow!); if it refers to something unique to the first language culture (e.g. karaoke, paella); if you don't know the word in the language you are speaking; if you prefer the word in the other language; if you are having fun and playing with languages; if you want to avoid stopping the flow of conversation.

3 Students' own answers. Sample answers: people's sense of national pride; the national personality; sense of humour.

MY VOICE

COMMUNICATION SKILL NOTES

Building rapport when you meet someone for the first time is an important part of forming relationships. A student's first language identity, including their cultural background and the language itself, is a great tool that students can use in international situations to build relationships. It is something that students should be encouraged to share and be proud of, both in and outside of the classroom. The lesson encourages students to find things in common with other people and to celebrate and take interest in differences between themselves and others. They are provided with language to help them ask about aspects of someone else's culture and language and to explain aspects of their own culture and language.

5 ▶ 2.2

- Give students time to read the information they need to watch for and think about possible ways in which their first language identity could help people to build relationships.
- Play the video so students can make notes.

Sample answers

Reasons: people are often interested in other cultures, and your identity is a source of information; by sharing aspects of your cultural identity, you can find things you have in common with another person; by showing curiosity about differences, you make someone feel valued.

Advice: ask lots of questions; look for things in common, and don't be afraid to ask about differences; be proud of your accent and your first language, and don't be afraid to use it sometimes.

6

- Give students a few minutes to discuss and make a list of the relationships they have built or may build in the future with people who have a different first language identity from them.
- **Optional step** Students choose at least one time when this happened to them in the past and one time when it might happen in the future and either tell a partner about what happened/will happen or write sentences describing the experience. Remind students to use the correct present, past or future tense to do this.
- Students discuss which pieces of advice from the Communication skill box are or will be most useful for them. Tell students to give reasons or justifications for their choices.

7 2.8

- Give students time to read the extracts and guess the missing words.
- Play the audio so students can complete the extracts.
- Students compare answers in pairs and then check answers as a class.

8

- Students read the Useful language box and rewrite the sentences from Exercise 7.
- Students compare their answers in pairs and then check answers as a class.

2D Building relationships

LESSON GOALS
- Understand how first language identity can be used in building relationships
- Talk about similarities and differences between languages and cultures
- Practise sharing aspects of your first language identity

LISTENING

1 Imagine you are talking to someone from a different country who you don't know very well. Put the topics in order from the one you would most likely talk about to the least likely. Then compare with a partner. What other topics could you add to the list?

- your families
- food customs in your countries
- living and working conditions in your countries
- language similarities and differences
- current news stories from your countries
- the reason you are together that day
- sport teams and recent matches
- tourist attractions in each other's countries

2 2.7 Listen to two conversations. What things in common do the speakers use to build their relationships? What differences do they use for the same reason?

3 2.7 Listen again and answer the questions.

1 In the first conversation, what two ways of saying 'very hungry' are used? What do you say in your language?
2 In the second conversation, what does José Luis want to know about the UAE?

4 Work in pairs. Discuss the questions.

1 In which conversation …
  a was a speaker's first language used?
  b did the speakers find similar interests?
  c did the speakers compare their first languages?
2 Do you sometimes switch between languages? When and why?
3 What aspects of people's first language identity do you find interesting?

MY VOICE ▶

5 ▶ 2.2 Watch the video. Write down …

1 at least one way your first language identity can help build relationships.
2 two pieces of advice that are given.

A group of friends talk in a coffee shop in Germany.

30

Sample answers

1 Is capoeira popular in Turkey?; 2 We have a similar expression in my language that translates as 'I'm as hungry as a wolf'; 3 It sounds a bit like a phrase that goes 'I could eat my arm'; 4 How do you say that in Arabic?; 5 It's on the tip of my tongue!

SPEAKING

9 OWN IT!

- Give students a few minutes to think of three words, phrases or cultural concepts from their first language and prepare explanations for them.
- If students find it difficult to think of appropriate things to explain, suggest they choose something that people from another culture might not be familiar with an idea, an idiom, an attitude or a specific way of doing something, for example.
- Students take turns to explain the three things they have chosen.

6 Work in pairs. Make a list of times when you have built a relationship with someone with a different first language identity to you, or when you may do so in the future. What advice in the Communication skill box do you think is the most useful to you? Why?

I'd like to work in a large international company, where I imagine I will work with people from different countries. It will be important for me not to feel embarrassed about my accent.

COMMUNICATION SKILL
Building relationships using your first language identity

Your language and cultural background are a great tool to help you build relationships with people from other countries.

- Be open about who you are and where you come from. Be proud of your culture, your first language and your accent!
- Ask open questions to find out about the other person's background.
- Look for things in common. Key moments in establishing friendships happen when you share similar experiences or realize that you aren't so different from one another.
- Celebrate the differences between you and show interest in understanding them.

7 2.8 Listen to extracts from the conversations in Exercise 2. Complete the extracts with one word in each space.

1 Is capoeira _practised_ _much_ in Turkey?
2 In my language, we _would_ _say_: 'I'm as hungry as a wolf'.
3 The _equivalent_ for us is: 'I could eat my arm'.
4 Do you have a word _for_ _that_ in Arabic?
5 I can't _quite_ _get_ it!

8 Rewrite the sentences in Exercise 7 in a different way, using the expressions in the Useful language box.

Useful language Talking about your first language identity

Showing interest in others
How popular is [hip hop] where you live?
How does that compare with [the way you normally do that in your family]?
How do you say that in [Russian]?

Explaining your first language identity
I'd say we [give tips] in a slightly different way to how people do it here.
It sounds a bit like [a children's game in Kenya we call 'Escape the lions'].
We have a similar expression that translates as ['It's raining seas!']
I'm sure we have a phrase in [Urdu]. It's on the tip of my tongue!

SPEAKING

9 **OWN IT!** Think of three words, phrases or cultural concepts from your first language or another language. Explain them to a partner, using the Useful language.

My city is famous for this idea called cachondeo. *When we say someone has* cachondeo, *it means they're always joking and having fun.*

10 Work in groups. For each category, think of aspects of your culture and first language that you would like people from other countries to know. Make a list. What other categories can you think of?

- a word or expression that you think is special
- a festival, dance or celebration unique to your culture
- a type of humour that you would miss if you were away
- an important place that isn't well known abroad
- a grammatical structure that is different from other languages you know
- a well-loved TV show, film, song or book that represents your culture
- a dish that reflects the best food from home
- an aspect of the national character that you want people from other countries to know about

11 Share your ideas from Exercise 10 in new groups. Explain any cultural aspects that other members of the group do not know about.

EXPLORE MORE!

Listen to how you and the people around you talk about your language and culture. How often do you talk about different cultural concepts?

31

- **Optional step** If students all have the same first language identity, tell them to imagine that their partner is giving them new and interesting information, for example by asking follow-up questions. If there is a range of first language identities in the class, pair students with different identities.

10

- Put students into groups of four or five.
- **Optional step** In multilingual classes, group students according to their nationality and/or first language identity. If students don't share the same first language identity with any other students, they can make their own lists to explain to other students.
- Students brainstorm ideas for each category and then think of a few more different categories.

Extra activity 1

Students choose to either prepare a one- to two-minute explanation of one of the aspects of culture they discussed in groups, or provide a two- to three-minute overview of all of the aspects of culture they talked about.

Extra activity 2

If students come from different countries, ask them to think of and share something interesting that they have learned about someone else's culture or language – either during this lesson or at another time – with the class. They could compare their chosen cultural aspect with something similar in their own first language culture to help them do this.

11

- Organize students into new groups. Students share their ideas from Exercise 10.
- Remind students to use language from the Useful language box to present their explanations.
- Encourage students to show interest in what other group members say.

For additional practice, refer to the **Communication activity** on page 215 of the Teacher's Book.

EXPLORE MORE!

The aim of this activity is to encourage students to learn more about themselves, their language and their culture by observing the people around them. Suggest that students pay attention to what people around them have to say about their own language and culture, for example what they say about people from their country or culture, any insights they offer about their country or culture, or the stories they tell about it.

LESSON GOALS

- **WRITING** The aim of the lesson is to guide students to produce a formal email asking for information about a course. The reading text provides a model. Students practise the skill of using formal language and making polite requests by writing a formal email.

SPEAKING

Extra activity

Before students look at the infographic in Exercise 1, ask them to guess the world languages with the highest number of first language speakers. Alternatively, you could write the languages from the infographic on the board and ask students to guess the order.

1

- Students discuss the questions in pairs.
- **Optional step** Elicit feedback on the courses that students would like to take and create an ordered list of the most popular courses in the class.

2

- Students read the advert and think of three questions about it.
- Tell students any questions they have about the advert's contents, e.g. What is in an 'intensive course'? should be included in their list of three questions.

READING FOR WRITING

3

- Students read the email and identify the questions that the writer asks.
- Students compare Son's questions with their own questions from Exercise 2.

Answers

Son asks about course start date, number of hours per week and the course duration; certificate; course fee and how to pay; accommodation; necessary language level

4

- Students read the list of elements. Check understanding of the word 'enquiry' (a formal request for information in an email, in a letter or on the telephone).
- Tell students to look for language with the functions on the list, e.g. a phrase that is used to give a reason for writing (c), or synonyms for the words in the elements, for example: 'necessary language level' (e).
- Students match the elements with the sections of the email, then read the Writing skill box to see a summary of the organization of a formal email.
- Check answers as a class.

5

- Students re-read the email to find the formal equivalents of the informal words and phrases.

Answers

2 advertisement; 3 enquire; 4 (course) fees; 5 currently; 6 accommodation; 7 regarding, concerning; 8 whether; 9 I look forward to hearing from you in the near future; 10 Yours faithfully

2E I am writing to enquire

LESSON GOALS

- Organize a formal email appropriately
- Use formal language and polite requests
- Write to ask for information about a course

SPEAKING

1 Work in pairs. Discuss the questions.

1 Do you speak any of the languages in the infographic? Which would it be useful to learn, e.g. for business, tourism, job opportunities? Why?
2 Why are you taking this English course? Is it for any of the reasons you mentioned for Question 1?
3 Which other types of courses (e.g. yoga, website design, creative writing) have you done, or would you like to do?

Languages with the highest number of first language speakers

Chinese – 1.3 billion
Spanish – 460 million
English – 379 million
Hindi – 342 million
Arabic – 315 million
Bengali – 228 million

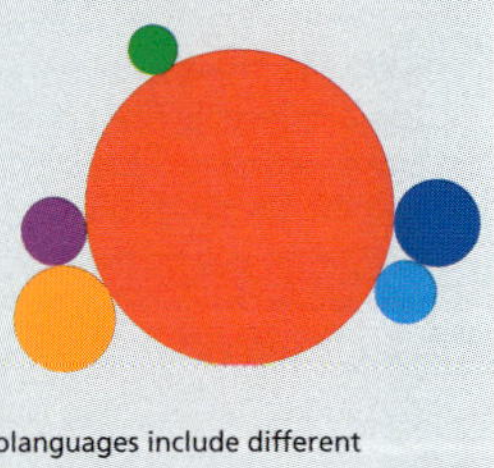

*figures are approximate
Chinese and Hindi as macrolanguages include different languages and dialects

2 Read the advert. Imagine you are thinking of applying for the course. In pairs, think of three questions that you would want to ask about it.

Learn Arabic in Marrakesh!
Come and learn Arabic with us in the heart of this ancient city

- Intensive courses
- Four-week courses throughout the year
- Small groups
- Accommodation available close to the school and city centre

For more information, email
admisssions@olivebranch.mr

READING FOR WRITING

3 Read the email. Does Son ask the same questions that you thought of in Exercise 2?

New Message

Subject: Enquiry about Arabic course

Dear Sir or Madam,

[1] I saw your advertisement for Arabic courses in Marrakesh and I am interested in enrolling. I am writing to enquire about the next course.

[2] I do have a few questions. Firstly, please could you confirm the start date of the next course? The advertisement says the course is 'intensive', but I would be interested to know how many hours per week this is and what the course duration is. I would also like to know whether I will receive a formal certificate at the end of the course as I would like to use it in my application for jobs in my country. Would the certificate be recognized abroad?

[3] I would also be grateful for more information concerning course fees and accommodation. First, I am not entirely sure how I would need to pay and whether I would need to do this in advance. Second, since I am from Vietnam and currently live there, I was glad to see you offer accommodation. Could you give me some idea of the price? Finally, please also let me know whether a host family or hotel would be preferable for someone who is very keen to improve their Arabic quickly and whether you can arrange the accommodation for me.

[4] Regarding the level of the course, I was wondering whether you have courses for complete beginners. In addition, I would like to know whether you would recommend I study first to become slightly more proficient in Arabic before I sign up for your course.

[5] I look forward to hearing from you in the near future.

[6] Yours faithfully,

Son Ngo

4 Put the elements (a–e) in the order they appear in Son's email. Then look at the Writing skill box to learn more about the structure of formal emails.

a enquiry about course fees and accommodation 3
b enquiry about the course itself 2
c reason for writing 1
d asking for a reply 5
e question about the necessary language level 4

WRITING SKILL
Organizing formal emails

Formal emails are much more structured than informal ones. They typically begin with the reason for writing (*I am writing to enquire about …*). Then each paragraph focuses on one clear topic that is stated in the first sentence (*Regarding the course itself …*). Each paragraph is clearly structured (*First/Second/In addition*).
The email finishes with a polite request for a reply (*I look forward to hearing from you./I would appreciate a reply at your earliest convenience.*)

5 Find formal words and expressions in Son's email that have the same meaning as these more informal words and phrases (1–10).

1 Hi *Dear*
2 ad
3 ask about
4 price
5 at the moment
6 a place to stay
7 about (para 3 and 4)
8 if (para 2 and 4)
9 hoping to hear from you soon
10 Bye for now!

6 Read Son's email again and underline any examples of indirect questions or polite requests.

7 Rewrite Eugenio's email to make it more formal. Use the information in the Writing skill box and the Useful language to help you. Then compare with a partner.

~~Hi there!~~ *Dear Sir or Madam*,

A friend told me your driving school is really good, so just wanna ask how much it costs to do a driving course with you. No info about it on your site. Never driven before, so a total beginner. Also, when can we start?

Write back asap.

Bye for now,
Eugenio

Useful language Formal emails

Formal forms of address
Dear Mr/Ms [last name] / Dear Sir or Madam

Reason for writing
I am writing with regard to/to enquire about …

Polite requests
Could you tell me …
I was wondering if you could …
I would appreciate a reply at your earliest convenience.
I look forward to hearing back from you.

Formal endings
Kind regards / Yours sincerely / Yours faithfully

WRITING TASK

8 Imagine you are interested in doing a course. You are going to write an email to make enquiries about it. Follow the instructions.

1 Work in pairs. Discuss what courses you are interested in (e.g. driving, dancing, art).
2 Individually, decide which questions you need to ask (e.g. course fees, start and end date).
3 Plan your email by deciding how many paragraphs you need and what to include in them.

9 **WRITE** Write your email. Use formal language and organize your email appropriately.

10 **CHECK** Use the checklist. I have …

☐ written a formal beginning and ending to the email.
☐ included a clear reason for writing.
☐ written well-organized paragraphs.
☐ used indirect questions.
☐ used suitable formal words and expressions.

11 **REVIEW** Exchange emails with a partner. Write down two things that you think they did better than you and one thing that they could improve. Share your feedback with each other.

Go to page 130 for the Reflect and review.

6

- **Optional step** Refer students back to the Grammar box in Unit 1 Lesson 1B and the corresponding Grammar reference on page 140 for a reminder of how indirect questions are formed.
- Ask students to read Son's email again and underline the indirect questions and polite requests.

7

- Tell students to read Eugenio's email and identify the examples of informal language, e.g. 'Hi there!'.
- Students replace the examples of informal language with examples of formal language.
- Direct students to the Useful language box for examples of formal language.

Sample answer
Dear Sir or Madam,
I am writing to enquire about the driving courses you run. A friend has highly recommended your driving school.
First, I would like to ask about the course fee. I could not find any information about it on your website.
I was also wondering whether you accept complete beginners. I have never driven before nor attempted to learn.
Finally, could you also please let me know about the course start dates?
I look forward to hearing back from you.
Yours faithfully,
Eugenio

Extra activity

For an extra challenge, students could also write an informal email thanking the friend for recommending the driving school.

WRITING TASK

8

- Students work in pairs to think of an idea for a course they can enquire about.
- Students work individually to choose questions and plan their email.

9 WRITE

- Refer students back to the Writing skill box for useful language for formal emails and to Son's email for a guide to an appropriate structure for their emails.
- Students write the first draft of their email.

10 CHECK

- Ask students to use the checklist and then make changes to their emails if necessary.

11 REVIEW

- Students exchange emails with their partner. A sub-aim of this exercise is for students to develop the ability to concede that other students' work can be better than their own in some respects and that they can, therefore, learn from other students.
- Tell students to use the points from the checklist from Exercise 10 to help them assess which aspects of their partner's email are better than theirs or need improvement.

For **Unit 2 Reflect and review**, see Student's Book page 130.

See **Workbook** pages 18–19 for extra practice.

See **Workbook** pages 20–21 for Units 1 and 2 Review.

VIDEO 2.1

Maria: *Language for me is huge. I've been learning Spanish since 1987. I grew up in California where lots of people speak Spanish. I'd never learned another language until high school and they said 'what do you want to learn?' and I said 'Spanish'. I knew exactly what I wanted because I wanted to be able to communicate with the people who lived where I lived.*

Soon, I could walk out of the classroom and I could talk to people that I couldn't talk to before. I thought 'oh my gosh, this is real!' So Spanish has been a real bridge to the people around me in California.

And then in college I took Spanish and I went out to volunteer as a translator for the naturalist guides in the Costa Rican rainforest. In this moment, the language opened the door for me for what I do with my whole life.

When I've worked in other places, I've always tried to learn as much as I can of the local language. Even if I only pick up a few basic words. This helps to really create relationships with the local people. It also shows those people I respect their culture. I respect their way of speaking. It just really touches other people, and me.

Arianna: *The first foreign language I know is English. I've been studying it since I was a child. I'm really grateful I learned it because of all the opportunities it's opened up – in education and now for work. It means that I can go basically wherever I want.*

French has also been incredibly useful for work. At one point I went to the French island of Réunion as a National Geographic Explorer. I don't think I would have got my funding if I didn't speak French.

I've also managed to pick up Spanish. And it's helped me a lot too in my career, especially when I was on a field trip in Guatemala. It was a real bridge to the local community. I managed to get a lot of useful details from them about the volcano's activity, which, for example, my supervisor had not been able to get because he only speaks English.

I've also been learning German lately. I'm living in Germany now, so it's important for me personally to learn it, but it's been really tough. Perhaps the reason is that it is very different from the other languages I speak. So for example, when I don't know the right word in Spanish, I can just make it up, because it's probably something similar in either French or Italian. And usually people understand me. But with German, it's not like that.

AUDIO 2.1

Arianna: *I've studied English for a long time. I started in primary school and have been using it ever since. It's been immensely helpful for me in terms of the opportunities that it has opened up. And right now, it's really the main language that I use in my life. More so than Italian, my first language. To the point that when I think to myself, I do it in English. I dream in English!*

I also speak French and I've been using it since I was eleven. I often speak it with some French-speaking friends I met when I was an Erasmus student in Paris. Their native language is actually German, and because I'm currently trying to learn German, I should probably be practising it with them. But our language has always been French, so we speak in French. Right?

I've also been studying Spanish for several years, starting in high school. Mainly afternoon and evening classes. Unfortunately, I've never had the chance to live in a Spanish-speaking country. However, Spanish is the closest to my mother tongue, so it hasn't been that difficult to learn.

The last language I've been trying to pick up is German. And it's because my job is in Germany. But I have to admit that I'm struggling with that. Like really, really bad. I'm taking classes at the moment, so hopefully I will improve soon.

AUDIO 2.2

1 I've studied English for a long time.

2 I also speak French and I've been using it since I was eleven.

3 I often speak it with some French-speaking friends.

4 Our language has always been French, so we speak in French.

5 Unfortunately, I've never had the chance to live in a Spanish-speaking country.

6 So it hasn't been that difficult to learn.

7 The last language I've been trying to pick up is German.

8 I'm taking classes at the moment, so hopefully I will improve soon.

AUDIO 2.3

1 ***A*** *I am taking classes at the moment.*

B *I'm taking classes at the moment.*

2 ***A*** *I have been using it since I was eleven.*

B *I've been using it since I was eleven.*

AUDIO 2.4

Arianna: *I think speaking to people is the best, but I also find it the most stressful. I also watch shows regularly. I can't say this has helped me very much in English because, you know, at the time when I was learning, that wasn't a thing. There was no Netflix, right? But for French, watching shows has definitely helped. And now, more and more, I'm trying to watch things in their original language.*

One thing I found that helps me the most is not so much as to speak the new language as much as possible, but to cut out the other languages I know. If you still have the option to speak your own language or another one that you know better, I feel like that's too much of an easy fallback. For example, the first thing I do when I move to a different place is change the language on my laptop and on my phone.

AUDIO 2.5

Today, we are going to chat about the global spread of English. It's a topic that has been brought up a few times recently in your comments on social media.

As some of you may know, there are nearly two billion people that speak English. Interestingly, more than eighty per cent of them do not speak it as their mother tongue. In contrast, a similar number of people also speak Chinese, but more than eighty per cent of them speak it as their first language.

Clearly, this means that when you're using English, you're four times as likely to be speaking with people for whom English is a second or third language, rather than someone who speaks it as their first language. Even in places like New York or London, you are very likely to speak English with people for whom it is a second, third or fourth language. On the other hand, when speaking Chinese, Spanish or Arabic, you're most likely to do it with first language users.

This brings me to my next point. I don't know about you, but it's certainly not how I used to think about English when I was learning it. For instance, I believed that English was only spoken in the UK, North America and Australia. We learned a lot about British and American culture. But interestingly, English is an official language in over sixty countries, including India, Kenya, Barbados and Kiribati. I also thought it was really important to speak like 'native speakers'.

It was only when I started travelling and working that I realized that, actually, most people I interact with don't speak English as their first language. And in fact, some of those difficult British or American idioms I was proud I'd learned weren't helping me get my message across. I started to be fascinated by what it actually takes to become a successful communicator in the global English-speaking community.

When I read up a bit more on it, I found out that, funnily enough, according to many experts, a foreign accent isn't usually a problem. And I used to worry about it so much. Surprisingly, researchers point out that first language users might often be the most difficult to understand in international contexts.

Obviously, this had a huge impact on my identity as an English user. While in the past I very much worried about picking up the 'wrong' accent, I now feel much more comfortable just speaking like I do, rather than trying to imitate someone else.

So, I personally feel that English belongs to all of us who use it. Basically, whether we're from Ho Chi Minh City, New York, Warsaw, São Paolo or Nairobi doesn't matter. What do you think?

AUDIO 2.6

1 bring up; 2 in contrast; 3 surprisingly; 4 read up on

AUDIO 2.7

One

The speakers are attending capoeira classes. Capoeira is a martial art from Brazil, a combination of fighting and dance.

A: *… So, Sibel, I can tell you are enjoying the course. You are so good already!*

B: *Thank you. Yes, I'm learning so much. Aren't you?*

A: *Absolutely! Andreza is a very good teacher. Is capoeira practised much in Turkey?*

B: *I've never seen it, but it's probably around in the big cities. It is loads of fun!*

A: *Yes, but I am exhausted though!*

B: *So am I! It's been a very long morning. I'm looking forward to sitting down for lunch.*

A: *I don't know about you, but I am starving!*

B: *Ha ha! In my language, we would say: 'I'm as hungry as a wolf'.*

A: *'Hungry as a wolf'! Wolf is the wild dog?*

B: *Yes. Don't you say 'hungry like a wolf'?*

A: *No, but I know what you mean. The equivalent for us is 'I could eat my arm'!*

B: *'I could eat my arm'?! Ha ha! I love it! Well, I could definitely eat my arm right now …*

A: *Ha ha!*

Two

Hassan and José Luis are colleagues who work in an office in Buenos Aires in Argentina. Hassan, from the UAE, has recently arrived in Argentina.

C: *… But there must be things you miss about your country?*

D: *Sure, but it's more people that I miss than places or food or whatever. I miss my friends of course. I miss a game of football in the park in the evening with them.*

C: *I didn't know you played football in the UAE!*

D: *Yeah! It's really big!*

C: *What's your national team like? I've never heard about them.*

D: *Ha! We're not very good, but we're getting better.*

C: *Hey! You should come with me next Friday. My friends and I play at the sports centre.*

D: *I'd love that. Thanks! Hey! Did you see the match last night?*

C: *Yes! Wasn't it amazing? 4–2 in the end, but I really thought Boca were going to win.*

D: *I know. The last ten minutes were so exciting.*

C: *Yeah, and that* golazo *from Vila, I mean, it was exceptional!*

D: *In Spanish you say* golazo *for a beautiful goal?*

C: *Yeah, exactly. Do you have a word for that in Arabic?*

D: *Erm, that's so annoying! I think there is, but I can't quite get it! In Arabic or in English. Golazo. I'm going to use it. What a golazo by Vila!*

AUDIO 2.8

1 Is capoeira practised much in Turkey?

2 In my language, we would say: 'I'm as hungry as a wolf.'

3 The equivalent for us is: 'I could eat my arm.'

4 Do you have a word for that in Arabic?

5 I can't quite get it!

VIDEO 2.2

If you're like me, you love meeting and talking with people. We all come to conversations with interesting things to say – things about ourselves that reflect who we are. Good communicators are also curious to know about the other person.

It is through being interested in, and learning about, people that we build relationships with them. And in international situations, people are potentially even more interesting because you get the chance to find out about a whole new culture and language as well as a person.

And it works the other way round; you are interesting to other people. Your cultural identity is a strength in building relationships; a tool you can use.

By sharing things about your background and identity you can find things in common. These things emphasize the fact that we are similar, that we can understand each other and that we can get on well. Discovering something surprising you have in common can be a 'wow' moment that starts a friendship.

… And when we discover interesting differences between cultures, our interest in them can make them feel valued and special. If people see that you want to understand the differences between you, they will appreciate the effort you are making to build the relationship. Remember, it's important to go into any conversation with the right attitude. Ask questions to show your curiosity and interest in new things.

Remember, the way you speak is an important part of who you are, so don't worry if your accent makes it clear to everyone where you come from. Be proud of it!

There's no problem, either, in sometimes using words in your own language. Again, the words and expressions you use express aspects of your identity which people will be interested to learn more about.

UNIT 3

Unfamiliar places

UNIT GOALS

3A Reading, speaking

- use annotations as an active reading technique; use critical thinking skills to rank ideas according to their usefulness; plan a trip in your own town/region during a group discussion

3B Listening and grammar, pronunciation, speaking

- listen to someone talking about a memorable travel experience; practise using narrative tenses to tell a story; pronounce groups of consonants accurately

3C Speaking, listening, vocabulary

- use visual information as an aid for listening comprehension; use travel collocations to talk about interesting or unusual journeys; learn and practise using travel collocations with *go on*; plan a very long journey

3D Speaking, listening

- listen to conversations and identify the misunderstandings that occur; learn and practise using three ways of repairing misunderstandings; explain a situation where a misunderstanding occurred and how the problem could have been fixed

3E Writing

- practise using descriptive language to engage the reader of a blog post; make recommendations and give advice about a place; write a blog post about a trip or a place

Campervan in Sequoia National Park, US.

34

Photocopiable resources

Communication activities: pp. 216–217
Vocabulary activity: p. 235
Grammar activity: p. 249
Focus on … activity: p. 250
Pronunciation activity: p. 270
Mediation activity: p. 285

Workbook

Unit 3 pp. 22–29

ABOUT THE PHOTO

The photo shows the Sequoia National Park which is located in California's southern Sierra Nevada mountains. The park is well-known for its huge sequoia trees. The most well-known tree in the park is called General Sherman. This tree is 84 metres high and, in terms of volume, it is the largest known living single-stem tree on Earth. The American national parks are popular holiday spots for both American and international tourists who enjoy exploring their beautiful landscapes.

3

Unfamiliar places

GOALS

- Practise active reading by annotating
- Use narrative tenses to tell personal travel stories
- Talk about journeys
- Use visual information to help you listen
- Repair misunderstandings and confirm understanding
- Write a blog post

1 Work in pairs. Discuss the questions.

1 Look at the photo. What message(s) about travel does it send? Why?
   a An unfamiliar place is anywhere that gets you away from your normal life.
   b Everybody should travel – it broadens the mind.
   c The best thing about travel is coming home at the end.
2 Do you agree with the ideas (a–c) about travel? Why? / Why not?

WATCH

2 ▶ 3.1 Watch the video. Write the name of each place that Andrej and Ellie mention and the reason(s) they like it.

NATIONAL GEOGRAPHIC EXPLORERS

ANDREJ GAJIĆ

ELLIE DE CASTRO

3 Make connections. Discuss the questions.

1 Which of the places that Andrej and Ellie mention would you like to visit? Why?
2 What are your three favourite places? Why?

35

1

- Tell students to look carefully at the unit title, the main photo and the caption.
- Check students' understanding of 'broadens the mind' (increases the range of your knowledge or experience, e.g. by travelling).
- In pairs, students discuss the questions. Encourage students to use their own travel experiences or other ideas to justify their opinions.

Extra activity

If students are allowed phones in class, ask them to find a personal photo that shows an example of one of the messages from Exercise 1 (a–c). Ask students to show their photo to a partner and either explain why or how it illustrates the message, or ask their partner to guess which message it illustrates.

WATCH

2 ▶ 3.1

- Tell students that two explorers are going to take turns to talk about a place.
- Play the video and tell students to write down the names of the places they hear and key words that the explorers use to say why they like each one.

Answers

Andrej: Istanbul (Eminönü) – see the real Turkey there; Egypt – diving (Red Sea), pyramids (Giza) and Egyptian Museum (Cairo); New York – positive energy, landmarks, food

Ellie: Ulaanbaatar, Mongolia – different environment; Dewil Valley – National Geographic project, fun with friends; University of Philippines Diliman campus – fond memories

3

- In pairs, students discuss which of the places mentioned by the explorers they would like to visit.
- When they are talking about their three favourite places, tell students that they can also choose places they haven't visited.

Extra activity

Ask students to prepare a brief presentation about one of the favourite places they chose in Exercise 3 that includes: location, what you can see and do, anything special or different about it, and what the student likes about it and why. Students could give their presentations in pairs or groups.

ABOUT THE EXPLORERS

ANDREJ GAJIĆ is Bosnian. He juggles many different roles – research scientist, author, underwater photographer and ROV (remote operated vehicle) pilot. Andrej has dedicated his career to understanding the effect of pollution on sharks, skates and rays, and improving conservation efforts in the Mediterranean and other marine environments. He is head of National Geographic's Shark Tales team, whose research is focused on the effects of habitat loss and pollution on sharks.

LLENEL (ELLIE) DE CASTRO is an archaeologist based in the Philippines. She is interested in finding ways to encourage young people to engage with their heritage. Ellie created the Dewil Valley Community Museum in the north of the Philippines as her National Geographic Young Explorer project. This museum is located directly next to the archaeological site from which its artefacts came and is designed to bring archaeology closer to the local community.

LESSON GOALS

- **READING** The main aim is for students to read a blog post and practise annotating a text in order to focus on important information so they can remember it later. They then use their critical thinking skills to practise ranking ideas in order of usefulness as a means of organizing ideas effectively before giving an opinion or drawing a conclusion.
- **SPEAKING** The speaking aim is for students to collaborate in groups to design a two-day holiday in their town or region.

READING

ABOUT THE TEXT

Note that students will need to annotate the blog post during this lesson, so if you don't want them to write in their books, make photocopies of the text before the lesson and then distribute them to students.

The text type is a blog post about how to enjoy time in your hometown rather than travelling a long way away for a holiday. The writer describes their personal experience of exploring their hometown of Toronto, Canada after previously always travelling out of the city for a holiday. The writer then gives five tips to help people make the most out of a holiday at home, which is also known as having a 'staycation'.

Toronto is the most populous city in Canada (with almost three million inhabitants). It is the capital city of the province of Ontario and is located on the north-western shore of Lake Ontario in the south-east of the country. The city is known for its skyline that consists of many skyscrapers and the CN Tower.

Staying at home on holiday, or staying in your home region or country, has become increasingly popular in recent years. The reasons for this seem to be an increased awareness of the damage that flying can do to the environment through the release of carbon emissions, coupled with a greater appreciation of local life (e.g. eating locally produced food, supporting local businesses).

3A No place like home

LESSON GOALS
- Practise active reading by annotating
- Rank ideas in order of usefulness
- Plan a trip in your own town/region

READING

1 Work in pairs. Discuss the questions.
1 How well would you say you know your own town, region and country? Why?
2 In Polish, there is an expression: *You praise the foreign, but don't know the local.* What do you think it means?

2 Read the title of the blog post on page 37. What do you think it will be about?

3 Read the blog post quickly to check whether your idea about the topic was correct. Does the writer persuade you to do more sightseeing in your town? Why? / Why not?

4 Read the blog post again. Are the sentences true (T) or false (F), according to the text?
1 The post is about something the writer has been doing for a while. F
2 She's not happy about her normal travel habits. T
3 Taking a tourist bus can teach you about a place's past. T
4 Being a tourist is a lonely activity. F
5 You can decide to be a tourist for the day that same morning. F
6 It's easy to make small changes to your lifestyle to become a tourist in your own town. T

5 Look at the Reading skill box and the example annotations in the blog post. Then annotate the rest of the blog post to prepare to give your opinion about it.

READING SKILL
Active reading by annotating

As you read a text, it can be useful to mark or annotate it. This helps you focus on important information to remember later. Ask questions about ideas and language in the text and notice new vocabulary.
- Use colours to highlight the main ideas.
- Add your own comments and reactions.
- Circle important information.
- Use symbols (e.g. ?, !, ★) next to things you don't understand, surprising information, etc.

6 Work in pairs. Use your annotations from Exercise 5 to discuss the questions.
1 Do you agree with the main idea of the blog post?
2 What information was the most interesting or surprising to you? Why?
3 Were there any words or expressions you didn't understand? Can you explain them to each other?
4 What words or expressions in the post would you like to learn?

7 Work in pairs. Look at the Critical thinking skill box. Then rank the five tips in the blog post from the most to the least useful. Give reasons for your choices.

CRITICAL THINKING SKILL
Ranking information

Ranking ideas from the most to the least useful can help you to organize your thoughts before you give your opinion. To do this effectively, …
- analyse the quality of each idea. What are the problems in doing it? (e.g. Is it expensive? Time-consuming?) What are the benefits of doing it?
- decide how relevant the ideas are to the specific situation e.g. Is it possible for everyone to do?

I think tip number 1 is the least useful. Bus tours are only available in big cities in certain countries. Lots of people, like me, don't have this option.

SPEAKING

8 Work in groups. Design a two-day holiday for yourselves in your town or region. Follow the instructions.
1 Find out what everyone in the group likes doing. Decide what places and activities in your area would appeal to everyone in the group.
2 Plan your two-day trip. Decide …
- what you will do in the morning, afternoon and evening of each day.
- where you will stay overnight.
- where you will eat.

36

1
- **Optional step** Direct students to the lesson title and elicit that this expression is typically used to say that home is the best place you can be. Ask, *Is there an expression in your first language that expresses the same idea?*
- Students tell each other how well they know their town, region and country and then discuss what they think the Polish expression means.
- Elicit feedback on the meaning of the Polish expression in class.
- **Optional step** Ask students if an expression with a similar meaning exists in their language and, if so, what it is.

Answers
2 The expression means that we often like and are interested in things that are far away or very different from our own culture without showing the same interest and respect in our own surroundings or culture.

Extra activity

Ask students to discuss the following questions about blog posts – either as a class or in small groups:
- What blogs do you read or have you read?

The Center Island Ferry offers an exceptional view of the Toronto skyline, including the impressive CN Tower.

Destination...here

Text about simple trips, not going abroad

A trip that doesn't involve packing for two weeks or finding your passport may not seem like the highlight *??* of your travel agenda, but it can be just as rewarding. *Meaning? Check later*

I live in Toronto, Canada's largest city and one of its most popular tourist destinations. And yet, when I'm looking for a way to spend my time off, more often than not I head out *verb? = 'go'?* of the city.

This year I'm determined to change that. Why is it I always feel the need to travel hundreds or thousands of miles to explore when I have so much to learn on my doorstep? ☺

Do you ... Want to try it too? Here are five tips to set about *= 'to start'* seeing your city through new eyes.

1 Take a historical tour.

Sure, you can tell a tourist the names of the buildings or tourist spots in your hometown, but do you know their history? Those hop-on, hop-off bus tours might be meant for tourists, but they're a great way to improve your local history knowledge. Plus, taking note of what visitors find interesting can be fascinating, allowing you to see what might at first seem uninteresting in a whole new light. If there is no tourist bus, try joining a free walking tour. It's a great way of not only discovering things you didn't know about your city, but also meeting new people.

2 Get a room.

Waking up in a hotel or bed and breakfast is a tried-and-tested way to set the mood for exploring.

If you live in a suburb, head into the city. If you live in the city, consider spending a weekend getting to know the nearest town. The added excitement of being away from home for the night will only add to the day's fun.

3 Set a date.

There are places I pass on a regular basis in Toronto. Every time, I promise myself that one day I'll check them out. Take it from me: it will never happen without a plan. So pull out your calendar, set a date and keep it.

4 Act like a tourist.

I'm not suggesting you stand in the middle of the street taking selfies, while the locals angrily try to get past, but do pop into the tourist information centre, look out for upcoming events and follow local websites to find out what's on.

5 Take something small and make it bigger.

Your daily wander around the block could turn into a walk around a new neighbourhood. Friday pizza night at home? Why not make it a mission to test out the newest pizzeria in town? You'll be surprised how simple adjustments to your everyday routines can broaden your experiences.

Discovering hidden places around you and being a tourist in your own city can not only be fun, but bearing in mind how much travelling can contribute to the climate emergency, it can also help save the planet. So, when planning your next holiday, start first by exploring your hometown!

EXPLORE MORE!

Search online for interesting things you can do in your town or region that you didn't know about or have never done.

37

- Which subjects do people often write blog posts about? (travel, food, parenting, etc.)
- What features of a blog post make it different to other types of text you might read? (It is usually written in an informal style; it is often written in the first person; it usually includes media such as photos, videos and audio material, etc.)

2

- Tell students to only look at the title of the blog post and avoid reading the rest of the text at this point.
- In pairs, students compare their ideas about the possible content of the blog post.

3

- Give students about a minute to read the blog post and try to understand what it is about.
- Students think about whether or not they have been persuaded by the blog post.
- Students compare and explain their answers in pairs.
- **Optional step** Ask students who were not persuaded by the blog post to suggest possible improvements to the post that would have made it more persuasive (for them).

VOCABULARY NOTES

rewarding /rɪˈwɔːdɪŋ/ = something that gives you pleasure or satisfaction

on one's doorstep /ɒn wʌnz ˈdɔːstep/ = close to home

check (something) *out* /ʧek aʊt/ = to explore/visit/go to see something

upcoming /ˌʌpˈkʌmɪŋ/ = something that is going to happen soon

adjustment /əˈʤʌstmənt/ = a small change made to achieve a desired outcome

4

- Students read the blog post again and look for information related to the statements so they can decide whether they are true or false.
- **Optional step** Challenge more confident students by asking them to correct the false statements.

5

- Check students understanding of 'annotate' (to add notes to a text to explain or highlight key details or points in it and 'active reading' (doing something while you are reading, such as annotating or making notes, which will enable you to better understand the text or find information that you need in the text more easily).
- Ask students to read the information in the Reading skill box. Ask, *What do you usually do when you are annotating texts?*
- Direct students to the annotations that have already been made on the blog post for them to use as a guide.
- Students annotate the rest of the blog post individually (either in their books or on a photocopy of the text) and then compare their annotations in pairs. Remind them that the aim is to highlight key information they can use to give their opinion about the post.

6

- In pairs, students take turns to give their answers to the questions. Tell students to use their annotations on the blog post to help them give supporting evidence.
- For Question 3: If both of the students in a pair do not understand a specific word or expression from the blog post, they could try to deduce its meaning from context, ask another pair, look up the meaning online, or ask you for help.
- **Optional step** In class, invite different students to say words or expressions from the text which were new for them and that they want to remember. Make a list of these words and expressions on the board for everyone to see.

Sample answers

4 Words/ expressions worth noting include: *travel agenda, tourist destinations, more often than not, on my doorstep, see (something) through new eyes, hop-on, hop-off bus, in a whole new light, not only … but also …, a tried-and-tested way, set the mood, will only add to …, Take it from me:…, taking selfies, upcoming events, find out what's on, wander around the block, test out, everyday routine, broaden your experience, bearing in mind, contribute to the climate emergency, save the planet, your hometown.*

Extra activity

Ask students to use new words and expressions from the blog post to write questions for a vocabulary quiz. For example, they could write sentence stems containing the new words: *Complete this sentence. The **highlight** of this week will definitely be ….* Students then form new pairs and take turns to ask and answer their vocabulary questions.

7

- Tell students to read the Critical thinking skill box and rank the tips in the blog post in pairs.
- Tell students that they will need to justify their ranking so they should keep this in mind as they are making their choices.
- Students then take turns to present and explain their ranking. Tell them to read the example explanation first so they have a model to follow.

Extra activity

Ask students to create a 'top five' list for another travel-related topic, such as the top five best things to do in their town/region/ country, the top five towns/cities/countries they have visited, or the top five most useful things to take on a camping trip or other type of holiday. Students could do this as a self-study task, and then form pairs and take turns to present their top five in their next lesson.

SPEAKING

8

- Put students into groups of four or five to complete the task.
- Give them 15–20 minutes to work together to design their holiday. Monitor students' discussions and check that they are including all of the necessary points in their plan. Encourage all group members to actively participate if this isn't already happening.

Extra activity

Students give a presentation of the holiday they designed in Exercise 8, either to the class or to another group. Encourage them to use visual aids, such as a poster with relevant pictures, photos and maps. Other students give feedback on how interesting the holiday would be and whether they would go on it.

EXPLORE MORE!

Suggest that students begin by looking at a website about their town or region, if there is one. Then, they could look for information on travel blogs. Events in their town or region or groups connected to it on social media could also be a useful source of information.

See **Workbook** pages 22–23 for extra practice.

LESSON GOALS

- **LISTENING AND GRAMMAR** The main aim is for students to listen to a story about a memorable travel experience and to review and practise using narrative tenses to tell stories about things that happened in the past.
- **PRONUNCIATION** A sub-aim is for students to practise pronouncing groups of two or more consonants (consonant clusters) so that they are able to clearly pronounce words that contain them.
- **SPEAKING** The speaking aim is for students to tell a story about a memorable journey or travel experience.

LISTENING AND GRAMMAR

1

- Give students about a minute to look at the photo.
- Students read the questions and think about their answers. Clarify that 'kind of place' in Question 1 refers to the purpose of the building where the people are (e.g. a café, a home, a shop, etc.)
- Students discuss the questions in pairs for about three minutes. Ask students to justify their answers.

Answers

1 a shop in a market, perhaps in a tourist destination
2 Sample answers: getting lost in the streets of an old city; buying something unusual, perhaps for a very low or high price; meeting someone

2 3.1

- Elicit that Andrej Gajić is one of the explorers that students watched at the start of this unit.
- Ask students to read the possible titles before they listen. Elicit or explain that the title 'The tourist trap' could refer either to a 'tourist trap' in the sense of a popular holiday destination, or a trap for tourists that could place them in danger if they fall into it.
- Play the audio and ask students to focus on understanding the gist of what happened to Andrej.

Extra activity

Ask students if they have ever had a similar travel experience to the one Andrej describes in the audio and that is depicted in the photo (i.e. making friends with and/or experiencing the hospitality of local people). If they have, ask them to describe this experience. If they haven't, ask them to say whether or not they would like to have an experience like this and what the benefits of this sort of experience could be.

3 3.1

- Students use what they can remember from the story and their understanding of past tenses to complete the sentences.
- This should be a revision exercise for students, but, if necessary, remind them to look for key words in the sentences that indicate the tense that is needed, for example: *ago* and *when* (past simple).
- Students complete the sentences and then listen to the audio again to check their answers.

4

- Tell students to answer the questions about what the past tenses from Exercise 3 are used for.
- **Optional step** Clarify that 'main event' in this context means the most important event being described or the event that the speaker or writer is choosing to focus on when telling a story.
- Students compare answers in pairs and then read the Grammar box to check their answers.

GRAMMAR NOTES

Past simple Students should be very familiar with this tense, but they may need to be reminded that 'have/has' isn't needed to form it (as may be the case in their first language equivalent tense) and that it is used for a single completed event in the past.

Past continuous It is also important to check that students are aware that the past continuous is typically used either for repeated activities or habits in the past or for ongoing past activities that were interrupted by a single event in the past.

Past perfect simple Students need to understand that the past perfect simple is almost always used in combination with the past simple. The past perfect simple is used for the first event that occurred chronologically and the past simple is used for the second event that occurred chronologically.

Past perfect continuous Students need to be able to differentiate between the past perfect simple and continuous tenses and this is especially important if one or both of these tenses don't exist in their first language. Make sure students are aware that the past perfect simple is typically used for one event or one action that occurred at one specific time in the past, whereas the continuous form is used for several events or an ongoing activity in the past.

For further information and practice, see **Grammar reference Unit 3B** on page 143 of the Student's Book.

5

- Direct students to the instruction and elicit that this story comes from the explorer, Ellie de Castro, who they watched earlier in this unit.
- Ask students to read the story all the way through first, then go back to the start of the story and complete the sentences.
- If students are unsure what the correct tense should be, tell them to read the Grammar box again and look for key words or expressions in the sentences, such as 'for the last few years' (past perfect continuous).

Extra activity

Elicit that the name of Andrej's story was 'New friends'. Ask students to think of a short title for Ellie's story that will get the reader's attention. They could work with a partner or in small groups to come up with title ideas and then decide on the best one.

6

- Students choose either Ellie or Andrej's story to retell.
- Tell students that the aim of the exercise is to include the key events in each story and to use past tenses accurately.
- Students work in pairs and take turns to retell their chosen story.
- **Optional step** If you have a mixed-level group, put a more confident student with a less confident one. The more confident student retells either Ellie or Andrej's story first and then the less confident student retells the same story. Alternatively, if students have a similar level, encourage each person in the pair to choose a different explorer.
- **Optional step** Ask students to listen carefully to their partner's retelling of the story and then give feedback on how accurately they used past tenses.

For additional practice, refer to the **Grammar activity** on page 249 of the Teacher's Book.

PRONUNCIATION

7 3.2

- Students read the Clear voice box. Elicit that a 'consonant' is a letter that isn't a vowel, i.e. every letter except for a, e, i, o and u.
- Students look at the six adverbs and identify the group or groups of consonants in each one. Ensure students are aware that there may be more than one group of consonants in some of the adverbs.
- Play the audio so students can listen and check their answers.
- Confirm answers as a class, if necessary.
- Give students the opportunity to practise saying the adverbs.

3B It's a long story!

LESSON GOALS
- Understand stories about memorable journeys
- Use narrative tenses to tell personal travel stories
- Pronounce groups of consonants correctly

Andrej Gajić with his friends in Hurghada, Egypt.

LISTENING AND GRAMMAR

1 Work in pairs. Look at the photo, which illustrates a travel story. Discuss the questions.

1 What kind of place does the photo show?
2 What do you think the story could be about?

NATIONAL GEOGRAPHIC EXPLORERS

2 3.1 Listen to Andrej Gajić talk about a memorable journey. Choose the best title for his story.

a A dangerous situation
b The tourist trap
c New friends (circled)
d Happy to be lost

3 3.1 Complete the sentences (1–5) with the correct form of the verbs in brackets, according to Andrej's account. Then listen again to check.

1 The story __happened__ (happen) eight years ago in Hurghada in Egypt.
2 Andrej __had been studying__ (study) sharks.
3 He __was walking__ (walk) from the hotel when he __saw__ (see) a small souvenir shop.
4 He was frightened because the men __had almost completely closed__ (close) the windows.
5 For the next two weeks, Andrej __visited__ (visit) them for some Egyptian tea.

4 Read the sentences in Exercise 3 again and answer the questions. Then read the Grammar box to check.

1 Which tense describes the main events in the story? past simple
2 Which tenses are used to refer to events that were in progress? past continuous, past perfect continuous
3 Which tense is used to refer to longer actions that were in progress before the main events? past perfect continuous
4 Which tense is used to emphasize that an action had finished before a main event? past perfect simple

GRAMMAR Narrative tenses

Past simple
Use for completed events in the past and the main events in stories.
*I **saw** a small souvenir shop selling papyrus.*

Past continuous
Use for events that were in progress at a specific moment in the past.
*I **was walking** from the hotel when …*

Past perfect simple
Use for events that happened before the main event and to emphasize the completion of activities.
*The salesman **had brought out** what looked like a wooden object.*

Past perfect continuous
Use for events that were in progress before the main event happened and to emphasize the continuation of activities.
***I'd been studying** the sharks, skates and rays.*

Go to page 143 for the Grammar reference.

38

PRONUNCIATION NOTES

Groups of two or more consonants used together in a word without any intervening vowel sounds are frequently referred to as 'consonant clusters'. Pronouncing consonant clusters may prove challenging for students whose first language does not include them, for example speakers of Arabic. Raising students' awareness of consonant clusters and giving them the opportunity to practise pronouncing them should make it easier for them to say them.

For additional practice, refer to the **Pronunciation activity** on page 270 of the Teacher's Book.

SPEAKING

8

- Students choose a title for their story or think of their own, then plan a scenario where something challenging, frightening, unusual or unexpected happens.

5 Complete Ellie de Castro's travel story with the correct form of the verbs in brackets. Sometimes more than one tense is possible.

> Two years ago, my parents and I went on a road trip to Kiangan, Philippines. I [1] had been going (go) there for the last few years for a project I [2] was working on (work on) and my parents [3] wanted (want) to see the place I [4] had been talking (talk) about so much. While my dad was stuffing our bags with snacks and supplies, my mum and I [5] raced (race) to the car. In our family, the first person to sit down gets to choose the music on the radio! We had been expecting the journey to take about seven hours, but we [6] had forgotten/forgot (forget) that it was the last weekend before Christmas. Everyone [7] was driving (drive) out of the city back to their homes. We got there after sunset – the drive [8] had taken/took (take) fourteen hours! The next day, we [9] went (go) to the Education Centre where I work. But as it was the Christmas season, no one was around! My parents were disappointed that they hadn't been able to meet the people I work with. On our last day, we [10] dropped by (drop by) the centre again and, this time, the place was full of people! My parents were excitedly toured around by one of my teachers and closest friends. While I sat [11] watching (watch) them, I was so happy to see my two homes – my parents and friends who mean so much to me – come together.

6 Work in pairs. Take turns to retell either Andrej or Ellie's stories from memory, paying careful attention to tenses.

PRONUNCIATION

7 3.2 Look at the Clear voice box. Underline the letters that make groups of consonants in the adverbs (1–6). Then listen to check. Practise saying the adverbs.

CLEAR VOICE

Pronouncing groups of two or more consonants

Some groups of consonants are more difficult to say than others, depending on …

- how many consonants are grouped.
- whether the consonant group exists in your language.
- how difficult it is for the mouth.

Practise saying the consonant groupings on their own as well as the whole words.

1 eventually	4 unexpectedly
2 surprisingly	5 fortunately
3 interestingly	6 accidentally

SPEAKING

8 You are going to tell a story about a memorable journey. Choose one of these story titles or use your own idea. Then plan your story by thinking about the questions (1–3).

A difficult choice A frightening moment
A helping hand Lost in the city Under the stars

1 What are the main events?
2 What background information would be useful for listeners to know?
3 What tenses will make the relationships between events clear?

9 Look at the Useful language box. Which of the expressions could you use to tell your story?

Useful language Telling personal stories

This happened to me when I was …
I was … *-ing* when …
All of a sudden, …
I felt so …
Fortunately, …
I ended up …

10 Work in groups. Take turns to tell your stories. Whose story was the funniest? Whose was the most dangerous?

EXPLORE MORE!

Search online for the funniest, strangest or most incredible travel story.

39

- Students can read the Grammar box again to remind themselves of how they can use each tense to describe specific events in the past or to describe the relationship between events.
- **Optional step** If students are unsure about how to respond to Question 3, suggest they make a list of the events in their story. They can then think about where the relationship between two or more events is important and what tense(s) they can use to show that relationship.

9

- Students read the Useful language box. Clarify that when the phrase 'I ended up …' is followed by a verb, this verb is always in the gerund or *-ing* form.
- Students refer back to the notes they made in Exercise 8 and choose appropriate expressions to use.

10

- Put students into groups of three or four to tell their stories.
- Allow students to refer to their notes to help them tell their story, if necessary, but ensure that they don't just read a story they have already written out loud. Encourage students to look at their notes as little as possible so they can tell their story more naturally.
- **Optional step** Challenge more confident students by asking them to also focus on using vocal variety, pauses and emphasis on certain words to make their stories more interesting to listen to.

Extra activity 1

In their groups from Exercise 10, students choose their favourite travel story and prepare a short roleplay of it. The groups can then act their stories out in front of another group or the class.

Extra activity 2

Students work individually or in pairs to turn their own story or their favourite story from Exercise 10 into a story board or comic. These could then be displayed around the classroom for other students to look at.

EXPLORE MORE!

Depending on students' social media use, they might find it easiest to use social media to search for travel stories, for example by looking at posts from travel bloggers on social media sites. If students do not use social media, they could go to the National Geographic website and look at the *Latest Stories* section of the site, or do a more open-ended web search for 'travel blog' or 'travel blogger'.

For additional practice, refer to the **Communication activity** on page 216 of the Teacher's Book.

See **Workbook** pages 24–25 for extra practice.

LESSON GOALS

- **LISTENING** A main aim is for students to listen to an extract from an audiobook and use visual information to help them understand its contents.
- **VOCABULARY** Another main aim is for students to practise using phrasal verbs and travel collocations with *go on* to talk about journeys and travel experiences.
- **SPEAKING** The speaking aim is for students to imagine they are going on a long journey and make plans for it.

SPEAKING

1

- Students read the definition of 'voyage'. Model and drill the pronunciation of 'voyage'.
- Students read the questions and use their general knowledge and personal opinions to answer them in pairs.

Sample answers

1 exploration, curiosity and a sense of adventure; to find wealth, e.g. gold; to start a new life elsewhere
2 starvation, drowning, illness at sea, getting lost, storms and other bad weather, war and fighting

Extra activity

Elicit feedback from the class on the reasons people went on voyages in the past and their dangers. Ask, *Do you think the reasons are persuasive enough to make it worth the risk? Why/Why not?* Put students into pairs or small groups and ask them to brainstorm the pros and cons of going on voyages one thousand or more years ago. Then ask them to evaluate and discuss whether the pros outweigh the cons or vice versa.

2

- **Optional step** Explain that Polynesia is a group of islands in the Pacific Ocean, located between and including Hawaii, New Zealand and Easter Island. Explain that the Polynesians travelled significant distances over the seas in canoes and they did this thousands of years ago. Also point out that the Lapita people, who are also mentioned on the map, were another group of people living on islands in the Pacific Ocean thousands of years ago.

3C Out of sight of land

LESSON GOALS
- Use visual information to help you listen
- Learn travel collocations with *go on*
- Talk about journeys

Built in 1975, the *Hōkūle'a* is our best guess at what a Polynesian ocean-going canoe looked like.

HOW DID THE POLYNESIANS MAKE IT SO FAR?

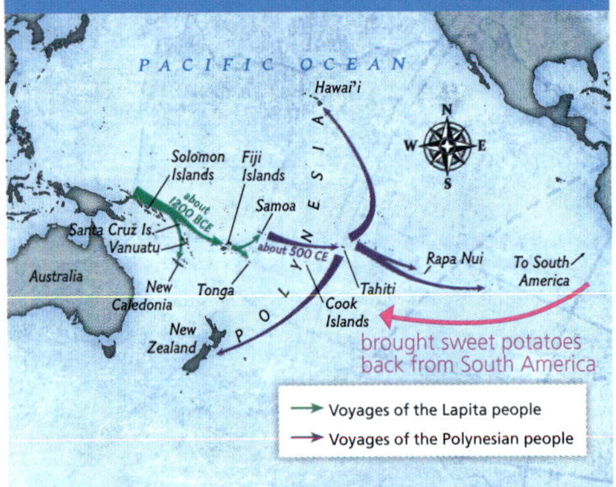

- twenty to thirty people on board
- no compasses or navigation tools – used the sun, moon and stars, and studied clouds, wave patterns, birds and fish to show them the way to land
- sang songs to help them remember the knowledge they needed
- took water and food with them and fished from canoes
- lightweight canoes for speed

SPEAKING

1 Work in pairs. Look at the definition and discuss the questions.

voyage (n) a very long journey, often by ship

1 Why did people go on voyages in the past?
2 What were some of the dangers of long voyages?
3 Would you like to go on a voyage? Where to?

2 Look at the map and read the text. Why do you think the Polynesian voyages were impressive?

LISTENING

3 Look at the Listening skill box. Then read the map carefully. Familiarize yourself with the key places and dates and consider the direction of the journey.

LISTENING SKILL
Using visual information to help you listen

When listening, we often have visual aids such as maps, diagrams and photos. Here are some techniques to use visual information effectively.
- Familiarize yourself with the visual information before you listen.
- Listen for keywords and numbers that match names, places or other information you can see.
- As you listen, point to the parts of the image that the speaker is talking about. Follow a route with your finger, for example.
- Make notes on the image or while listening.

40

- Students look at the map, read the text and think of a few reasons why the Polynesians' voyages were impressive.
- Students compare their reasons in pairs.

Sample answers

distances involved; long time ago so lack of technology; went to many islands; fast canoes; small crew; no navigation instruments

LISTENING

3

- Tell students to read the Listening skill box and then look carefully at the map. Point out that the map is an example of visual information.
- Tell students to concentrate on trying to understand the direction of the Lapita and Polynesian people's travel.

4 3.3

- **Optional step** If students are not able to write in their books, make photocopies of the map before the lesson and then distribute the copies to students.
- Elicit that the aim is to listen and identify a piece of information about the voyages that is *not* shown on the map.
- Play the audio so students can identify this piece of information. Ask them to add this information to the map.

4 3.3 Listen to an extract from an audiobook. Follow the tips from the Listening skill box. Add one additional piece of information you hear onto the map.

5 3.3 Listen again. Number the questions about the Polynesians in the order that they are answered.

a How did they do it? 6
b What did they take with them? 5
c When did they travel? 3
d Where did they come from? 2
e What was the furthest they travelled? 4
f Why are the journeys so amazing? 1

6 3.3 Work in pairs. Divide the questions from Exercise 5 between you. Listen again and take notes on the answers.

VOCABULARY

7 Complete the summary with the correct form of these verbs.

end go head make reach set steer stop turn

It was the Polynesians who 1 went on the greatest voyages by sea when they 2 ended up on some of the remotest islands on the planet. These were sailors used to island hopping, 3 stopping over for a while before carrying on. But around 1200 BCE, the Lapita 4 set off on a journey east. Some settled down in the Santa Cruz Islands, but others 5 headed for new undiscovered islands. They 6 made it as far as Tonga, where they stayed for a few hundred years. Eventually, the Polynesians 7 reached the Cook Islands; navigators used a combination of 'wayfinding' skills to 8 steer across the ocean. Much of the Pacific was within their reach in their fast canoes. If they needed to 9 turn back, they could just let the wind bring them home to safety.

Go to page 136 for the Vocabulary reference.

8 Read the Focus on box. Then discuss the difference in meaning, if any, between each pair of words and expressions in bold (1–5).

FOCUS ON Travel collocations with *go on*

Go on collocates with many expressions that describe: types of journey, e.g. *go on a cruise / bus tour*; travel for specific purposes, e.g. *go on a business trip / a language exchange / an expedition*; types of holiday, e.g. *a package holiday / a city break*.

Go to page 143 for the Focus on reference.

1 They're not here. They've gone on **holiday / vacation**.
2 When was the last time you went on a **journey / trip**?
3 When I was a student I went on several **exchanges / field trips** abroad.
4 Of those who went on the **expedition / voyage** to the South Pole, many lost their lives.
5 We're thinking of going on a **city break / package holiday** somewhere warm next month.

9 Work in pairs. Discuss at least three of the topics.

The last time you …

- set off on a journey and realized you'd forgotten something important.
- went on a long journey.
- couldn't make it to an appointment or meeting.
- had to turn back.
- stopped over somewhere interesting.
- ended up somewhere you weren't expecting.
- headed home in the dark.

SPEAKING

10 Work in pairs. Imagine you're going on a very long journey. Discuss the questions.

1 Where are you going and how will you get there?
2 You can only take two people with you. Who will you take? Why?
3 You can only take five things with you. What will you take? Why?
4 How will you cope with being away from home?

11 Work in groups of four. Take turns to tell each other about your journey. Which did you enjoy listening to the most?

EXPLORE MORE!

Search online for 'the voyages of the Vikings', 'the Ming treasure voyages' or another voyage you'd like to learn about.

41

- Students compare their additions to the map in pairs and then check answers in class.

VOCABULARY NOTES

navigator /ˈnævɪgeɪtə(r)/ = the person whose job it is to plan the direction a ship should travel

arguably /ˈɑːgjuəbli/ = a word that shows that what you are going to say is a matter of opinion

navigation /ˌnævɪˈgeɪʃ(ə)n/ = the process of finding out where you are and where you need to travel to reach your destination

settle /ˈsetl/ = to start living in a place on a permanent basis

remote /rɪˈməʊt/ = distant from other places

undiscovered /ˌʌndɪˈskʌvəd/ = something that nobody has seen or encountered before

5 3.3

- Ask students to read the questions and prepare to listen by briefly considering the type of information they would expect to hear in the answer to each question.
- Play the audio again so students can number the questions.

6 3.3

- In pairs, students divide the questions from Exercise 5 between them equally (three questions each).
- **Optional step** Suggest that less confident students divide the questions so that one student makes notes on the first, third and fifth questions that are answered in the audio and the other student takes the remaining questions. This will give students some time to look over, re-organize or add to their notes in between questions.
- Play the audio again so students can make notes on the answers to their three questions.
- **Optional step** If appropriate, encourage students to help their partner add to or correct their notes for the questions they did not focus on.

Answers

a they knew the position of the stars, how to interpret and use wind and wave direction; they also used the direction of bird flight, or the presence of leaves in the water
b fishing hooks and other useful tools, animals such as chickens and the plants they would need to farm
c they started in 1200 BCE and also made more voyages around 500 CE
d Papua New Guinea
e South America, 9,000 km away
f they travelled without any modern technology; they used wooden canoes; they made their voyages a very long time ago; they reached places very far away

VOCABULARY

7

- Tell students that most of the gaps in the text are followed by prepositions and therefore require a verb + preposition combination. Elicit that two gaps are not followed by a preposition, so these need to be filled in with verbs that are not followed by prepositions.

- Ask students to read the text all the way through first to get a general sense of it, then go back and identify the verbs and correct verb forms for each gap.
- Students compare answers in pairs.

For further information and practice, see **Vocabulary reference Unit 3** on page 136 of the Student's Book.

Extra activity

Ask students to use at least five of the phrasal verbs from Exercise 7 to write their own sentences. These could be sentences about their own travel experiences and/or sentences about any other experiences they have had or things they know about.

8

- Students read the Focus on box and the sentences and look closely at the pairs of words in bold.
- Students discuss their ideas in pairs. Check answers in class by inviting different students to explain the difference (or why there isn't a difference) between the words in each pair.

Answers

1 holiday is British English, vacation is American English; 2 a journey is just one part of a trip, i.e. the part when you are travelling from A to B, a trip includes the travel, and all the time you were there, i.e. the whole experience; 3 an exchange is an arrangement in which students from different countries stay with each other in their homes, a field trip is where students of a particular subject go to a place to study; 4 an expedition is a trip with a scientific or exploration purpose, a voyage is any long difficult journey, often by sea; 5 a city break is a short holiday in a city, a package holiday is organized by a company that arranges travel, accommodation, and other details for you.

For further information and practice, see **Focus on reference Unit 3C** on page 143 of the Student's Book.

Extra activity

Put students into pairs or small groups and ask them to discuss any experiences they have had of the different types of travel in Exercise 8 or, if they haven't experienced any, which they would most/least like to experience. Students could then discuss which types of travel experiences they think are the best or the most enjoyable by evaluating the pros and cons of each one and then reaching a consensus.

LANGUAGE NOTES

The combination *go on* + noun describes what you do when you leave home to take a specific type of holiday, trip or journey. When *go on* is used in this way, it is followed by *a/an* and then the appropriate noun, for example *go on a cruise*. *a/an* is omitted after *go on* in the example *go on holiday* because this expression refers to travel for pleasure in general, rather than a specific type of holiday, trip or journey.

9

- Tell students that the aim of this exercise is to use the vocabulary and collocations from Exercises 7 and 8.
- **Optional step** Ask students to briefly review the vocabulary and collocations. Then ask them to look at the situations and think about how they can use them when they talk about each of these.
- Give students ten minutes to discuss at least three of the topics. Ask students to give as much detail as they can and remind them to use the past tenses they have learned in this unit to talk about past events and the relationships between them.

For additional practice, refer to the **Vocabulary activity** on page 235 and the **Focus on activity** on page 250 of the Teacher's Book.

SPEAKING

10

- Students share their ideas for each of the questions and try to agree on their answers as a pair.
- Remind students to use the vocabulary and collocations from this lesson where possible.
- **Optional step** Fast finishers could also discuss the following questions about their journey. *Why are you going on the journey? What problems might you face on the way? How long do you think you will be away for? What will you do when you reach your destination?*

11

- Put two pairs who worked with each other in Exercise 10 into a group.
- Each pair then takes turns to tell the other pair about their very long journey in Exercise 10, explaining the decisions that they made. Students then give each other feedback on what they enjoyed about each other's presentations of their journey.

For additional practice, refer to the **Mediation activity** on page 285 of the Teacher's Book.

EXPLORE MORE!

Students can choose from the two suggestions given or choose another historical voyage they are interested in. Encourage students to look for online sources that are credible and easily accessible and, if possible, sources that include visual information about the voyages. Students could use the questions from Exercise 5 to make notes about the voyages they choose.

See **Workbook** pages 26–28 for extra practice.

LESSON GOALS

- **SPEAKING** This lesson integrates speaking and listening. Its main aim is to raise students' awareness of how to identify and fix misunderstandings in a conversation by simplifying, clarifying or re-organizing your original message. Students practise fixing misunderstandings and reflect on how they could have repaired past misunderstandings from their own lives based on what they have learned in the lesson.

SPEAKING

1

- Check students' understanding of 'misunderstanding' (a failure to understand something or someone correctly).
- Remind students that misunderstandings are a normal part of communication.
- Students think of one or two examples of misunderstandings they have had in the past and tell their partner: where they were, who they were talking to, who misunderstood what and what the consequences of the misunderstanding were.
- **Optional step** Invite a few students to share a story of a misunderstanding with the class, if they feel comfortable doing so.

2

- Students read the list of possible reasons for misunderstandings.
- Check understanding of 'rely on' (to be dependent on).
- In the same pairs, students decide on reasons for the misunderstandings they talked about in Exercise 1.
- Ask students to add at least one more reason for a misunderstanding to the list. Elicit the reasons students added in class.

Sample answers

Other reasons include: the message is indirect (e.g. 'That jacket is gorgeous' is an indirect way of saying 'I want that jacket for my birthday', but may be misunderstood); the message would be clearer if it was written down or shown visually (e.g. directions might be clearer with a map); the message is forgotten (e.g. because it was a long time ago, or the listener is forgetful); the message is ignored because it does not suit the listener's point of view (in arguments you may misunderstand the other person because you expect to disagree with them)

LISTENING

3 3.4

- Tell students to listen and identify the purpose or reason for each conversation. Play the audio.
- **Optional step** Pause the audio at the end of each conversation so that students can think about the purpose of that conversation and choose the correct option.

4 3.4

- Tell students to focus on the misunderstanding that occurs in each conversation and the reason for it.
- Refer students back to the list of reasons for misunderstandings in Exercise 2 and suggest they keep them in mind while they are listening.
- Play the audio again. Students write down the reason(s) for each misunderstanding.
- **Optional step** Ask students to reflect on the misunderstanding they told their partners about in Exercise 1 and decide how similar the reasons for this misunderstanding were to the reasons for the misunderstandings they heard in Conversations 1-3. They can then share their ideas with a partner.

Answers

Conversation 1: the message was disorganized; Conversation 2: the message was unnecessarily long and complicated; the message was disorganized; Conversation 3: the message relied on cultural information that the listener did not know

MY VOICE

COMMUNICATION SKILL NOTES

Fixing misunderstandings involves taking action to ensure that the two parties involved understand each other or that a relationship is restrengthened if a misunderstanding has caused any damage to it. It is a skill that helps students to understand others and be understood themselves, and will help them to build strong relationships with people they come into contact with.

It's important that students understand that misunderstandings are a natural part of communication and occur whether you're speaking your first language or a second/other language, regardless of proficiency. The lesson gives students practice of recognizing when a misunderstanding occurs, as well as offering strategies to help them repair a misunderstanding once it has happened (or to try to avoid it before it happens) as both a speaker and a listener.

5 3.2

- Tell students that the sentences they are going to complete summarize the video's contents. Suggest they make notes on key points in the video while watching, then complete the sentences afterwards.
- Students watch the video and complete the sentences.
- **Optional step** Confident students could also write any other information that they found particularly interesting or useful.

VOCABULARY NOTES

proficient / prəˈfɪʃ(ə)nt/ = very competent or skilled in doing something

signpost (n) /ˈsaɪnpəʊst/ = a word or phrase that shows what order a series of events or the steps in a process happen in

gesture (n) /ˈdʒestʃə(r)/ = a movement of a part of the body, usually the hands or head, that helps someone express an idea or feeling

6 3.5

- **Optional step** In class, elicit the reasons why it is important to fix misunderstandings when they arise. For example, from a practical point of view, it can help you complete a transaction or get information that you needed; from an interpersonal point of view, it ensures that your relationship with the other person isn't weakened or damaged due to the misunderstanding.
- Ask students to read the Communication skill box. Check students' understanding of 'clarify' (to make it clear exactly what you mean/meant); 'assume' (to think that something is/isn't true when you don't know this for sure) and '(to) signpost' (to use words to make it clear what order a series of events or the steps in a process happen in).
- Play the audio so students can listen and identify which of the strategies in the Communication skill box the speakers use.

Answers

Together, they start again from the beginning; identify the key information and repeat it back; check the listener has understood; summarize the instructions together; signpost the order clearly; the listener writes the directions down.

7

- Ask students to read the Useful language box. Elicit or explain that they have heard most of these phrases in the conversations they have listened to in this lesson.
- Students use words from the Useful language box to complete the four conversations.

3D Fixing misunderstandings

LESSON GOALS
- Identify misunderstandings in a conversation
- Learn three ways to fix misunderstandings
- Practise fixing misunderstandings and confirming understanding

SPEAKING

1 Work in pairs. Think of misunderstandings you have had with people, either in English, your first language or another language you know. What happened?

2 What were the reasons for the misunderstandings you described in Exercise 1? Choose from the list. What other reasons for misunderstandings can you think of?
- the message relied on cultural information that the listener didn't know
- the message used vocabulary that the listener didn't know
- the message was disorganized
- the speaker spoke too fast

LISTENING

3 3.4 Listen to three conversations where a misunderstanding occurs. In which conversation is the person …
 a giving a recommendation? 3
 b giving instructions? 1
 c discussing accommodation arrangements? 2

4 3.4 Listen to the conversations again. Choose the main reason(s) why the people in each conversation fail to understand each other from the list in Exercise 2.

MY VOICE

5 3.2 Watch the video about how misunderstandings occur. Complete each sentence with words from the video.
1 Messages need to be ___simple___, ___clear___ and ___organized___.
2 If a message is long and complicated, you could ask the speaker to ___summarize___ it.
3 Information that is specific to your ___culture/country___ can cause misunderstanding if you don't explain it.
4 If a message is disorganized, it might be necessary to ___start___ again.

6 3.5 Look at the Communication skill box. Then listen to a continuation of one of the conversations from Exercise 3. Which strategies do the speakers use to fix the misunderstanding?

COMMUNICATION SKILL
Fixing misunderstandings

Simplify
- The speaker can: identify the key information and repeat; check the listener has understood.
- The listener can ask for a summary.

Clarify
- The speaker can: assume cultural knowledge will not be known; explain anything unique to their culture or language.
- The listener can ask the speaker to explain.

Organize
- The speaker can: signpost the order clearly; write or draw the instructions.
- The listener can ask the speaker to start again.

7 Look at the Useful language box. Then complete the sentences (1–4) with appropriate language.

Useful language Fixing misunderstandings

Identifying misunderstandings
That isn't what I meant.
I'm getting mixed up.
That's the wrong way round.
I'm not following you.

Fixing misunderstandings
Let's start again from the beginning.
OK, to sum up, you need to …
So basically, you're saying …, right?
In other words, …
Shall I repeat it all back to you?

Confirming understanding
That makes sense.
Got it.
I see what you mean.

42

Extra activity

Put students into pairs and ask them to practise the conversations in Exercise 7. Tell them to imagine how the speakers would be feeling in these situations and try to convey this while they are speaking. Monitor students' conversations and ask pairs who sounded the most natural to read the conversations out loud in class again.

8

- Direct students to audioscript 3.4 on page 161 and ask them to read conversations 2 and 3.
- In pairs, students identify strategies from the Communication skill box that they could use to fix the misunderstanding in each situation.
- Students use the language in the Useful language box to write a continuation of the conversations.
- **Optional step** Less confident students could choose one of the conversations to continue.

1 A: Let's meet at eight.

B: Sorry, I'm getting ____mixed____ up. Are you ____saying____ eight in the morning?

2 A: So in other ____words____, I think we should look at train prices before we book a flight.

B: Yes, that makes ____sense____.

3 A: OK, if I've been ____following____ you correctly, this should be right now.

B: Let me see … No! You've got it the wrong way ____round____ still. This goes here, and that goes there.

4 A: Let me ____repeat____ it back to you. Out of the station, turn left. After 500 metres, second right into Broad Street.

B: You've ____got____ it!

8 Work in pairs. Look at audio script 3.4 on page 161. Continue conversations 2 and 3 from Exercise 3 so that the speakers fix the misunderstandings.

9 Work with another pair. Take turns to act out one of your conversations from Exercise 8. Which strategies did the other pair use to fix the misunderstanding?

SPEAKING

10 **OWN IT!** Think of a situation in the past where you had a misunderstanding. You can use the misunderstandings you thought of in Exercise 1, or choose a different one. In pairs, explain what happened and discuss how you could have communicated more clearly to fix the problem.

Sample answer
Conversation 2

D: You're right, I wasn't being very clear. Let me start again from scratch. I recently heard about a new kind of hotel that's cheaper, and they're cheaper because the rooms are very small.

C: Got it. But you said something about the location?

D: That's right. I think they're usually not in the city centre, so we need to decide: do we want a cheap hotel that's far from the centre, or a more expensive hotel in town?

C: I see what you mean. And that depends on how expensive the hotel is because we could catch a taxi or bus into town each day.

D: Exactly, so shall I find out if there's a hotel like that where we're going?

C: Good idea.

9

- Put pairs who worked together in Exercise 8 with another pair.
- Students take turns to act out the continuation of one of the conversations and identify the strategies for fixing misunderstandings that the other pair used.
- **Optional step** If it isn't clear to the other pair which strategies are being used, ask the pair to modify their conversation so that it is clear and then act it out again.

SPEAKING

10 OWN IT!

- Individually, students choose a misunderstanding they have experienced.
- Students take turns to talk about the misunderstanding, focusing on what they could have done to avoid it. Tell students to refer back to the strategies in the Communication skill box as they do this.
- **Optional step** Invite different students to summarize the misunderstanding they talked about and what they could have done to avoid it. Encourage other students in the class to comment on whether they think the students' suggested strategies would have worked, giving reasons for their choice.

For additional practice, refer to the **Communication activity** on page 217 of the Teacher's Book.

LESSON GOALS

- **WRITING** The aim of the lesson is to guide students to produce a blog post about a trip they have been on or a place they know well. The reading text provides a model. Students practise the writing skill of using descriptive language to engage the reader.

SPEAKING

1

- Students discuss the questions. Remind them to give examples of holidays from their own experience where appropriate.

Sample answers

3 advantages of a package tour: convenience, no hidden costs, companionship; advantages of travelling alone: can choose where you eat and stay, how long you stay in each place, etc., can save money by choosing cheap options

READING FOR WRITING

ABOUT THE TEXT

Santiago de Compostela is a city in the north-west of Spain. It is a popular destination for pilgrims who typically walk long distances along a network of walking routes known as the 'Way of St. James' (*Camino de Santiago* in Spanish) to reach the city. Most people spend several weeks walking to Santiago through the south of France and northern Spain, stopping off at hostels along the way.

2

- Students read the blog post quickly, looking for information about 'the end of the earth' and why it is important for the blogger's trip.

Answers

Finisterre: the furthest point west in Spain. It was the last part of the blogger's trip.

3

- Students read the information about the three travellers, then read the blog post again.
- Students identify which traveller is the most likely to be interested in the trip and compare their answers in pairs.

3E Getting away from the crowd

LESSON GOALS

- Use descriptive language to make writing more engaging
- Make recommendations and give advice about a place
- Write a blog post

SPEAKING

1 Work in pairs. Discuss the questions.

1 Which type of holiday would you prefer? Why?
 a visiting friends or relatives in another city
 b a camping holiday in the mountains
 c a trip to the beach
 d backpacking on your own or with a friend

2 What other types of holiday can you think of?
3 What are the advantages of …
 a going on a package tour with a group of other people?
 b travelling alone without a schedule?

Arriving at the end of the earth

Finally reached Santiago (read about my journey up through Spain here). From the bus station I headed to the flat where I was staying. A friendly welcome and just a five-minute walk from the old town. You could stay in a *pensión*, a small hotel, but a homestay is the perfect way to practise the language and at a reasonable price. What's more, my host, Señora Vásquez, made delicious *tarta de Santiago* – a local speciality cake with wonderful almond flavours. Definitely try one if you visit!

The town is soaked in history and architecture but, with only three days, I had to prioritize. Señora Vásquez had predictable advice: 'You must go on a guided tour,' and 'Take an umbrella.' However, I didn't want to be slowed down so I went on a walking tour of my own. And thankfully, no need for that umbrella, though you should be aware that it can really pour down here.

The highlight of the city for me had to be the stunning *Parque de Alameda*, where buskers played their guitars while I enjoyed the view. I'd visited Santiago's huge cathedral that morning but, even by 11 a.m., it was crammed with tourists. As with all tourist spots, I highly recommend you make it there as early as possible. I steered through the crowds into the narrow streets of the old town. I was exhausted when I got to the park.

On my last day I took a bus to Finisterre, which means 'the end of the earth', the furthest point west in Spain. Dark clouds moved in from the ocean as I stared towards America. Finisterre was a dramatic spot to say *adiós* to the country and the perfect place to end up after an amazing trip.

I'd love to hear about your trips that have concluded in dramatic or special places. Please leave a comment!

Sample answers

Natsuki. None of the activities the blogger describes cost much money. He doesn't want formal (organized) tours, neither does the blogger. Piotr is looking for a sunny destination, but the weather in Santiago is often wet. Karinna wants to learn about history and culture while the blogger recommends not being slowed down by a guided tour.

Extra activity

Put students into pairs or small groups to discuss what other types of person they think might be interested in the trip the writer describes, whether they are interested in doing it themselves and why or why not.

4

- Students read the Writing skill box and then read the three questions.
- Students make notes on their answers to the questions and then compare answers in class.

Answers

1 It refers to the reader ('you') as if they were in Santiago, e.g. 'You could stay in a pensión', 'you should be aware', etc. Also, it is full of recommendations and advice: 'a homestay is the perfect

READING FOR WRITING

2 Read the blog post on page 44. Where is 'the end of the earth' and why is it important in the blogger's trip?

3 Read the blog post again. Which of these three travellers, Piotr, Natsuki or Karinna, is the most likely to be interested in the trip the writer describes? Why?

Piotr is looking for a few days in the sun. He speaks Spanish fluently, so Spain is his preferred destination. He's never been to Santiago.

Natsuki enjoys meeting local people and getting to know a place informally. He wants to see as much of each place as he can, though he doesn't have much money.

Karinna wants to learn as much about Spanish culture and history as possible. She loves cooking and photography.

4 Look at the Writing skill box. Then follow the instructions (1–3).

WRITING SKILL

Engaging the reader in a blog post

- Personal blog posts may be about your life, but you should give readers a reason to read them. This may be to keep up to date with news, to get advice about something they are interested in doing or just for general interest.
- Use *you* to direct the message to the reader. Avoid formal language.
- Use descriptive language to make the writing more interesting. Use local words to give the reader a taste of the language and culture.
- End in an interesting way, e.g. by asking a question or inviting comments of a specific kind.

1 Find evidence in the blog post that the writer's intention is to give advice to readers who may want to go backpacking in Spain.
2 What Spanish words does the writer use to emphasize the culture of the place she's writing about?
3 What are readers invited to write about in the comments? Why does the writer ask for comments from readers?

5 Find descriptive words in the blog post that have the same meaning as these words.

1 full of soaked	4 big huge
2 rain pour down	5 full crammed
3 beautiful stunning	6 tired exhausted

WRITING TASK

6 You are going to write a blog post about a trip you have been on or a place you know well. Think about what kind of reader you want to interest and a reason they should read it. Share your ideas with a partner.

7 Look at the Useful language box. Write sentences using five of the expressions to include in your blog post.

Useful language Making recommendations

Recommending things to do
I'd highly recommend …
You really must visit …
… is the perfect way/place/spot to (relax)
… has so much to offer (travellers on a budget)
A highlight of the (city) for me was …

Warning and advising
You should be aware that …
Don't forget to …
It's important (not) to …

8 WRITE Write your blog post. Remember to follow the tips in the Writing skill box.

9 CHECK Use the checklist. I have …

- ☐ used descriptive language and local words to make my writing more interesting.
- ☐ used *you* to direct the message to the reader.
- ☐ used correct narrative tenses when describing events.
- ☐ used the Useful language to give advice and recommendations.
- ☐ ended the blog in an interesting way.

10 REVIEW Work in pairs. Read your partner's blog post. What was the most useful piece of advice? Which descriptive language engaged you in the post most?

Go to page 131 for the Reflect and review.

EXPLORE MORE!

Find a travel blog post about a place that interests you. Or start your own blog!

way to practise the language', 'I highly recommend you make it [to the cathedral] early', etc.
2 *pensión, tarta de Santiago, Parque de Alameda, adiós*
3 Trips they have been on that have finished in dramatic or special places. She asks for comments to engage readers.

5

- Elicit that the six words given are uninteresting and not very descriptive.
- Ask students to think of possible descriptive synonyms for each word.
- Students read the blog post again to check their predictions and find the relevant synonym for each word.

WRITING TASK

6

- Students choose a place to write about, preferably one they know well.
- Students choose a type of reader to interest and think of a reason why they would be interested in a blog post about their chosen place.
- If students are not sure about different types of reader, give some options, for example: young professionals, people with young families, retired people, etc.

7

- Students read the expressions in the Useful language box.
- Students work individually to write sentences using at least five expressions from the box.

Extra activity

Students decide on the order in which they would use these sentences in their blog post and use them to give their blog post its basic structure.

8 WRITE

- Refer students back to the Writing skill box before they begin writing.
- Students write the first draft of their blog posts.

9 CHECK

- Ask students to use the checklist and then make changes to their blog posts if necessary.

10 REVIEW

- Students exchange blog posts with their partner.
- Tell students to focus on answering the questions about their partner's blog post while they are reading it.
- Students give each other feedback on their blog posts.

EXPLORE MORE!

Suggest that students begin by choosing a place that interests them and then searching for the name of that place + *travel blog* online. Alternatively, a lot of travel bloggers have social media accounts. If students are interested in starting their own blog, direct them to a site where you can set up a blog for free, for example WordPress. Students could write a blog post about any place they have visited or that they know, using what they have learned in order to engage readers. Encourage students to share the link to it with other students who can then read and comment on it.

For **Unit 3 Reflect and review**, see Student's Book page 131.

See **Workbook** pages 28–29 for extra practice.

VIDEO 3.1

Andrej: *I love Istanbul. I've been there many times. But the real Istanbul is the Eminönü. I love it because when you go there, you really meet Turkish culture. Just taking five minutes to watch the people there, you can really see and feel what the Turkish culture is like.*

Ellie: *A pretty memorable trip for me was when I went to Ulaanbaatar in Mongolia a few years back. My dad had a work trip and my mom and I tagged along. We went at the start of winter and it was -20 degrees and snowing pretty much the whole time we were there! The whole trip opened my eyes to an environment that was so different from mine, and to people who had adapted to their environment in such unique ways.*

Andrej: *I went to Egypt two years ago. It's great for diving. The Red Sea is just incredible! But if you go to Egypt, you have to go to Giza to see the pyramids and the Egyptian Museum in Cairo is magic. I could spend five days inside. The Tutankhamun exhibit has hundreds of objects linked to the famous Egyptian Pharaoh. I could stare at the mask of Tutankhamun for hours.*

Ellie: *Another place that I love is the Dewil Valley in the Philippines, the site of my National Geographic project. The Dewil Valley landscape is made up of 250-million-year-old limestone towers and caves. I love the Dewil Valley because of how much fun I have there. Aside from the exciting archaeology my friends and I go on a lot of adventures – boating, snorkelling and rock climbing!*

Andrej: *OK, New York. If you ask me 'Where do you want to live?', even though I'm so fond of nature, I will say 'take me to New York'. Just being there, you get so much positive energy. So many fabulous places: the Brooklyn Bridge at the magic hour – in the evening, just before the sunset. It's absolutely astonishing. The sky is still blue and these buildings look like magic. I love Times Square. Oh, and the food! Pizza … Chinese restaurants …*

Ellie: *But my favourite place is the place where I grew up – the University of the Philippines Diliman campus, where both of my parents were professors. I have so many fond memories of growing up there. A place on campus that I am especially fond of is the corner café, because any time that my dad would be away for work, my mother would take me there to make me feel better that my dad was away! We started doing it when I was very young and we still do it together to this day.*

AUDIO 3.1

Andrej: *So, this happened eight years ago, in Hurghada, on the Egyptian coast. I was travelling as a part of my undergraduate studies. I'd been studying sharks, skates and rays and exploring places where young sharks might be born along the coast.*

On the first day, I was walking from the hotel when I saw a small souvenir shop selling papyrus – the paper that ancient Egyptians used to use. The moment I said 'Hello', the salesman asked me if I wanted to see some 'magic' papyrus - one that glows in the dark. Of course, I said 'yes' straight away. But at that moment, all of a sudden, three other guys appeared out of nowhere. They were carrying lots of old newspaper which they started to stick to the windows.

At that moment, I started to wonder what was going on! They had almost completely closed the windows and there was hardly any light in the room, and those three guys were blocking the front door. The salesman had brought out what looked like a wooden object. He put the object on the table, and started to unroll it. It was a huge roll of papyrus and it was shining in the dark. In English, he said, 'Look, papyrus that glows in the dark!'

Then they invited me to stay for dinner! And for a couple of hours, we communicated slowly, as they didn't know much English. And for the next two weeks, I visited them for some Egyptian tea or dinner. Today, eight years since that event, I am still in touch with Zizu and Nigm, the salesman and the shop owner. I'm looking forward to going back again to see the papyrus that glows in the dark.

AUDIO 3.2

1 eventually; 2 surprisingly; 3 interestingly; 4 unexpectedly; 5 fortunately; 6 accidentally

AUDIO 3.3

If you were asked to name a famous navigator – or ocean explorer – you might say Magellan, Zheng or Cook. You probably wouldn't think of, arguably, the most successful navigators in history: the ancient Polynesians.

Without a doubt, the Polynesian trips across the Pacific were the most incredible voyages, as these people settled in hundreds of islands over millions of square kilometres. Around three thousand years ago, Neolithic people with the simplest of canoes and no navigation equipment set off and eventually ended up on some of the remotest islands on the planet, hundreds, sometimes thousands of kilometres from anywhere else. People have compared their achievements to those of the Americans landing on the moon.

Who were they? People had been living on the islands around Papua New Guinea, as far west as the Solomon Islands, for as long as thirty thousand years. These were sailors used to island hopping, making stopovers before moving on to the next island, rarely sailing out of sight of land. But, around 1200 BCE, a people we now call the Lapita set off on a journey east. This meant losing sight of land for days at a time. Some settled down in the Santa Cruz Islands, but others carried on, heading for new undiscovered islands further and further east. They sailed against the wind, so if they missed their destination it was easy to turn back and come home. This way, they made it as far as Tonga, four thousand kilometres from Papua New Guinea.

They stayed on these islands for some time, part of a developing culture we know as Polynesia. But something prompted the Polynesians to climb on board their boats again, reaching the Cook Islands in about 500 CE. Then, the Polynesians set off on their most incredible voyages, north to Hawaii, east to Rapa Nui and south west to New Zealand. The distances involved are truly amazing. They even reached South America somewhere around what is now Ecuador, an incredible nine thousand kilometres from the Cook Islands.

The trick was to travel light. Their canoes were the fastest ocean-going vessels in the world, so they didn't need to carry so much water or food for the voyage because they were able to make great distances in a short period of time. However, they took things they would need in the new lands: fishing hooks and other useful tools, animals such as chickens and the plants they would need to farm. The sweet potato is originally from South America but is an important vegetable in Polynesian cooking. We know that Polynesians ate it before the Europeans arrived, and their word for it – kumara – is from an Ecuadorean language. In South America, they introduced the chicken to the people there and brought back with them the sweet potato.

So what was the secret of their success? How did a tiny civilization explore such a huge area of the Earth's surface? Like all sailors, they knew the position of the stars, of course, but they had other knowledge, such as how to interpret and use wind and wave direction. This complex skill, called 'wayfinding', was essential to the Lapita and Polynesians. Nearer their destination, they could use other signs in nature: the direction of bird flight, or the presence of leaves in the water, to find even the smallest of islands.

AUDIO 3.4

Conversation One

A: *So, you can make it to games night next Saturday then?*

B: *Definitely, it sounds like lots of fun. You need to tell me how to get to your house, though.*

A: *Of course. OK, so if you're coming by bus from the centre, you take the same bus as if you were heading for the airport, OK?*

B: *But that's direct to the airport.*

A: *No, not that one. The number 7 is the local bus and it stops near my place.*

B: *OK, and I catch that at the bus station …*

A: *Right. So just get on your normal bus and you'll end up at Kim Ma Station.*

B: *No, that takes me to Long Bien station, I think.*

A: *Oh, no. That's true. I'm getting mixed up. The Kim Ma is the one you need. So where are you setting off from? I thought you lived near the Night Market.*

B: *No, I'm near the Cho Hom.*

A: *Oh, I see. Right, so you need to change buses at the university.*

B: *Linh, wait! But if I'm going to the university, I might as well catch the number 13. I think you've got it the wrong way round.*

A: *Probably! Listen, I think we need to start again from scratch.*

Conversation Two

C: *I don't know where we can stay for the money we've got. Everywhere is so expensive.*

D: *It's funny you say that, because just the other day someone was telling me about these hostels, well, they're not really hostels at all, because you get your own room, like, er, you know, like … have you seen those weird places in airports that are sort of Japanese style, do you know what I mean?*

C: *Er, I'm not sure I follow.*

D: *Anyway, it's not important, just to say that these things are similar, quite small, but they're cheap. Although, now I come to think of it, if we're only there for a couple of days, do we really want to be on the outskirts, because I believe they're normally not centrally located, so we'd have to find our own way in. Hmm.*

C: *I didn't really understand much of that. These 'hostels', do you think we should ask about them, or not?*

D: *Of course! That's what I'm saying!*

Conversation Three

E: *I'm spending a few days in Poland next week – in Kraków. Have you got any recommendations for lunch?*

F: *You should go to a milk bar. It's where the locals go. Cheap and homemade.*

E: *Right. I was thinking more about food.*

F: *This is food. They're restaurants.*

E: *OK, but I don't really like milk. Is it more of a breakfast place, then?*

F: *Eh? What are you talking about? Listen, I don't know what you think milk bars are, but you've definitely got the wrong idea!*

E: *What are they, then?*

VIDEO 3.2

While you might be thinking that misunderstandings in English are more common if you don't speak English as your first language, they can also occur among very proficient English users.

Breakdowns in communication can happen because of different levels of English, but very often the problem concerns the message itself: how simple it is, how clear, and how well organized.

It is these three features of successful communication that we are going to look at.

A common error when communicating is, when you realize that your message is not getting across, to add more and more words, as if that will somehow help. Listeners in international communication situations need messages to be as simple as possible, so if you find yourself using a lot of words, ask yourself what the key information is that you are trying to communicate and summarize the message at the end.

Communication is a two-way process, of course and it's also the listener's responsibility to ask for things to be simplified when they need it.

It can be surprising to discover that someone you are speaking with doesn't know something you had assumed that everybody knew. But of course, in multilingual situations, we quickly realize that there is a lot of cultural knowledge that is unique to our culture and language. We therefore need to be careful when talking about things that only exist in our country. If we do want to include these things, we should explain them.

Many messages can be complicated because they describe steps in a process. For example, when giving directions, when learning new skills, or when doing something new on your computer. The message might be given very slowly, using easy-to-understand language, but if the order it's given in is not logical, the listener will have a much harder job following it.

To repair a misunderstanding due to a lack of organization, it's usually necessary to start again, from the beginning, and work carefully and logically to the end.

Notice the importance here of signposts. Words like 'First', 'After that', or 'Once you've done that, you need to …' are like signposts in that they tell the listener where the instructions are going.

It's important to be patient with the listener and, when instructions are very difficult, consider using non-verbal means of communicating, such as hand gestures, or writing things down. They say that a picture paints a thousand words, and it is sometimes just easier to send a photo or draw a diagram or a map. This may take longer, but it makes sure the message is clear!

AUDIO 3.5

B: *Linh, wait! But if I'm going to the university, I might as well catch the number 13. I think you've got it the wrong way round.*

A: *Probably! Listen, I think we need to start again from scratch. I'll have a think and get back to you in a minute, OK?*

B: *Ha ha. Good idea.*

....

B: *Hey!*

A: *Hi. OK, so it's really straightforward. Do you have a pen?*

B: *Yup.*

A: *So if we're starting from Cho Hom market, you can catch the number 23 bus that will take you all the way to Kim Ma bus station.*

B: *Right! That makes sense. I've never been on that bus, but I know where it stops at the market.*

A: *OK. Then, once you're at Kim Ma, ask for the number 7 bus. You need to get off at the park - Youth Park. That's about a ten-minute journey.*

B: *Is it obvious where I have to get off?*

A: *Just get off after you see the children's park on the left and a big supermarket on the right.*

B: *Park on the left and supermarket on the right. Got it.*

A: *After that, if you walk through the park you'll see my street on the other side. Dien Bien Phu Street. I'm number 160 - Apartment 3.*

B: *… Apartment 3.*

A: *Right. Do you want to repeat that all back to me?*

B: *Sure. OK. So, Cho Hom market. Number 23 bus to the station. Ask for the number 7 bus …*

UNIT 4

Reconnecting

Eritrean sisters are reunited after more than two decades.

UNIT GOALS

4A Reading, speaking

- summarize information from an article in a mind map; synthesize notes from a reading and a listening text; roleplay conversations about enjoying nature

4B Reading and grammar, pronunciation, speaking

- practise using reported speech to report conversations; change the stressed words in a sentence to give different information; roleplay a scenario about resolving a conflict

4C Listening and pronunciation, vocabulary, speaking

- practise listening to different accents; practise pronouncing a long and a short 'i' sound so the difference between them is clear; use phrasal verbs to talk about relationships; present the results of a questionnaire about personal relationships

4D Speaking, listening

- identify and understand turn-taking styles; understand how people adapt turn-taking styles; practise using and adapting a specific turn-taking style during a roleplay

4E Writing

- read a short story and identify the techniques used to make it entertaining; identify mood in a story; write a story with interesting descriptions and language that shows the mood

Photocopiable resources

Communication activities: pp. 218–219
Vocabulary activity: p. 236
Grammar activity: p. 251
Focus on … activity: p. 252
Pronunciation activity: p. 271
Mediation activity: p. 286

Workbook

Unit 4: pp. 30–37

ABOUT THE PHOTO

The photo shows two sisters from Eritrea meeting again after more than twenty years apart. Eritrea is a country located in the north-east of Africa. It has a multi-ethnic, multi-lingual population of six and a half million people. The country has a long coastline on the Red Sea. Due to conflict in the region many families have become separated with family members living abroad, like one of these sisters.

4

Reconnecting

GOALS

- Summarize and synthesize information from written and spoken sources
- Report what people say
- Discuss personal relationships
- Understand different accents
- Understand and adapt to different turn-taking styles
- Write a story

1 Work in pairs. Look at the photo and discuss the questions.

1 Why might the women have been apart?
2 How do you think they are feeling now?

WATCH

2 ▶ 4.1 Watch the video and answer the questions. Write Federico (F), Carolina (C) or both (B).

NATIONAL GEOGRAPHIC EXPLORERS

FEDERICO FANTI | CAROLINA CHONG MONTENEGRO

1 Who can't keep in touch with their family as much as they'd like to? B
2 Who always surprises their children when they come home? F
3 Who says they feel a strong connection to home? C

3 Make connections. Discuss the questions.

1 How do you (or would you) feel about being away from your family or friends for a long time?
2 What do you normally do when you come back home after being away?

1

- Tell students to look carefully at the unit title, the main photo and the caption.
- Check students' understanding of 'reconnect' (to create a relationship with someone again after having not been in contact with them for a period of time).
- In pairs, students discuss the questions. Ask them to justify their opinions with reference to what they can see in the photo and their own knowledge.

Extra activity

Put students into pairs and ask them to imagine what the two sisters said to each other just before or just after this photo was taken. Tell them to write a short dialogue and share it with another pair.

WATCH

2 ▶ 4.1

- Play the video and tell students to listen for language in it that paraphrases or is connected to the key words in the questions, for example: *keep in touch, surprise, strong connection with home.*
- Students make notes and then compare answers in pairs, before checking as a class.

Extra activity

In pairs, students discuss which of Federico or Carolina's experiences they, or people in their families have also had, for example: being clear with your family about when you can or cannot communicate with them; not being able to communicate with your family for several weeks; finding it difficult to communicate with your family due to a significant time zone difference, etc.

3

- Give students a minute to read the questions and think about their answers.
- Students discuss the questions. Remind students that they should try to connect with their partner by sharing personal experiences and feelings.
- Tell students that if they do not have experiences of being away from their friends and family for a long period of time, they should try to imagine what it would be like or use the experiences of people they know.

ABOUT THE EXPLORERS

FEDERICO FANTI is an Italian palaeontologist whose long-term goal is to investigate the fossil record to find out which forms of life succeed and why. Federico has conducted research in Mongolia's Nemegt Basin and led an international team that developed a method to prevent fossils from being sold illegally in the Gobi Desert. He is most well-known for discovering *Machimosaurus rex*, which is the largest sea-dwelling crocodile yet found, and he has also developed and presented a documentary, *The Dinosaur Hunter*, about the black market in dinosaur fossils.

CAROLINA CHONG MONTENEGRO is a marine fisheries ecologist focusing on rare and threatened species of groupers, which are large-mouthed, heavy-bodied fish. She was born in Ecuador, where her interest in fish began during family fishing trips. Carolina currently lives in Queensland, Australia where she continues to study small-scale fisheries in the Tropical Eastern Pacific and their impact on ecologically important and commercially exploited grouper species.

LESSON GOALS

- **READING** The main aim is for students to read an article and summarize the information in it. Students make notes on the article as well as a spoken source, then use their critical thinking skills to synthesize the information from both sets of notes and write a summary of it.
- **SPEAKING** The speaking aim is for students to talk about ways to connect with nature.

READING

ABOUT THE TEXT

The text type is a magazine article that describes ways in which people can stay healthy by reconnecting with nature. The article gives a general introduction to the benefits of reconnecting with nature and then goes into greater detail about four specific ways that people can do this. The writer uses the findings of research studies to support the arguments that he/she makes.

Many of the public health challenges we currently face, such as obesity and work-related stress or burnout, are connected with spending too much time indoors. Researchers in the areas of neuroscience and psychology now believe that spending time outside in nature has a noticeable positive effect on people's brain activity. Evidence suggests that it allows the brain's command centre (the prefrontal cortex) to relax and take a break, for example.

1

- **Optional step** Direct students to the lesson title and elicit that this expression is used to refer to spending time in nature and appreciating it. Ask, *Is there an expression in your first language that expresses the same idea? How would you translate it directly into English?*
- Give students about a minute to read the options and decide individually how enjoyable they think each option is.
- Students collaborate to create a ranking for their group. Remind them that they may have to make some compromises with other group members.

4A In touch with nature

LESSON GOALS

- Summarize an article
- Synthesize information from written and spoken sources
- Talk about ways to connect with nature

READING

1 Work in groups. Rank the ways of staying in touch with nature from the most to the least enjoyable.

a going for walks
b watching nature documentaries
c living in a house in a forest with no electricity or running water
d visiting wildlife parks
e taking part in a conservation project, e.g. planting trees
f going camping
g looking at pictures of nature

2 Read the article on page 49 quickly, scanning it for key words. Which ways of staying in touch with nature from Exercise 1 are mentioned? What other ways are mentioned?

3 Read the article again. Are the sentences true (T), false (F) or not given (NG)?

1 John Benedict lives in his car because he doesn't have enough money to pay the rent. F
2 Living close to nature isn't a completely new idea. T
3 People who live in the countryside have a lower risk of fifteen diseases. F
4 Walking in nature for at least five hours a month can lower your blood pressure. NG
5 Scientists also recommend that you stay at home and look at pictures of nature. NG
6 Most teenagers in the US spend time indoors rather than outdoors. T

4 Look at the Reading skill box. Then summarize the article in a mind map using these two main topics: ways of connecting with nature and benefits.

READING SKILL
Summarizing

You may find it helpful to summarize a text …
- to remember the main ideas better.
- to use the notes in your own text later.
- to retell to a friend.

One way to do this is by using a mind map. Remember to focus on the main ideas only and use short phrases.

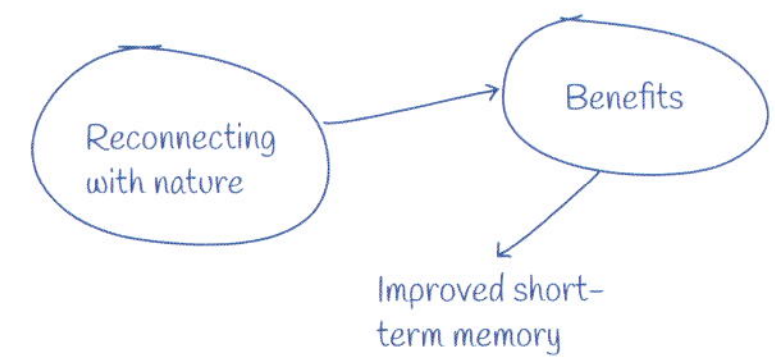

NATIONAL GEOGRAPHIC EXPLORER

5 4.1 Listen to Carolina Chong Montenegro talk about connecting with nature. Note down the main ideas she mentions.

6 Work in pairs. Compare your notes from Exercise 5 and answer the questions.

1 Which ideas and topics from the article does Carolina also mention?
2 What new things did you learn?

7 Look at the Critical thinking skill box. Then combine your notes on the article and the listening into a 50–100 word summary.

CRITICAL THINKING SKILL
Synthesizing information

Sometimes you need to synthesize information from various sources, combining the main ideas from each one. It involves thinking critically about what the most important information is and how the sources differ or are similar.
- Remember to include information from each source.
- Don't focus on too many details.
- Only mention the most important points.
- Organize the text logically (e.g. write about the similarities first, then the differences).

SPEAKING

8 Work in pairs. Go to page 155. Roleplay the two situations.

48

2

- Students scan the article for ways of connecting with nature. Then they identify the ways that are mentioned in Exercise 1 and those that aren't.
- Ask students to compare their answers in pairs.

Answers

Ways of staying in touch with nature that are mentioned in Exercise 1: going for walks, looking at pictures of nature
Other ways: moving closer to a park, listening to nature

3

- Students read the sentences and guess whether each one is true or false based on what they can remember from their first reading of the article.
- Students read the article again and write their answers.
- **Optional step** Ask students to correct the false statements.

People relax under the cherry blossoms in Sumida Park, Tokyo, Japan.

Stay healthy by reconnecting with nature

Can you imagine living a simple life close to nature? Can you imagine leaving most of what you own behind? It might seem impossible to many of us, but many people have done it and improved their mental and physical health in the process.

People like John Benedict, for example. He's been living out of his van for the last 25 years. Reducing his possessions to a minimum and only turning on his phone to listen to voicemail, Benedict is able to lead a very simple lifestyle that he says keeps him closer to nature and his community. And, as an added bonus, he's also saved a fair bit on the rent!

The idea of living a simple life in touch with nature might seem new to some, but many tribes around the world have lived lives free of most modern possessions for thousands of years. They not only live close to nature, but also feel a deep spiritual connection with it and the need to protect it.

> **... keeping in touch with nature can have enormous benefits for your body and mind.**

According to scientists, keeping in touch with nature can have enormous benefits for your body and mind. If you're a city resident, the good news is you don't need to necessarily leave your house and start living in a forest. Here are some easy research-based tips that can have big effects on your well-being.

1 Move closer to a park.
It seems that people who live within about half a mile of green space have a significantly lower risk of several diseases. Added bonus: you can easily go for a picnic or do some sport.

2 Go for a walk.
Even a short walk in a park or the countryside can make you feel less stressed and reduce your blood pressure. And a longer walk in a green area improves your short-term memory. Time to put those walking boots on!

3 Hang up a picture of nature at home.
Can't go for a walk every day? Don't panic! According to Korean scientists, just *looking* at nature images activates brain areas associated with caring for others. On the other hand, looking at urban landscapes can make you feel more anxious.

4 Listen to nature.
Ideally, while walking in the park or a forest. But if that's not possible, listening to the sounds of nature, such as bird calls or rain falling, while at home or work, can make you feel more relaxed. Something to consider when choosing the next playlist.

The scary thing is, though, that despite all these benefits that nature brings, it seems most of us are less and less in touch with nature. For example, it turns out American adults spend less time outdoors than they do inside their cars! And, believe it or not, only ten per cent of American teenagers spend time outside on a daily basis.

There's an ancient Korean saying, *Shin to bul ee* – your body and nature are one. It might be time we lived life with this in mind.

EXPLORE MORE!

Challenge yourself to reconnect with nature this month. Choose tips from the article or others you find online. Write a blog post or journal entry about your experience.

VOCABULARY NOTES

in the process /ɪn ðə ˈprəʊses/ = while doing something / during the course of something

a fair bit /ə feə bɪt/ = quite a lot / quite a large amount

resident /ˈrezɪd(ə)nt/ = a person who lives in a particular city or country

research-based /rɪˈsɜːʧ-beɪst/ = coming from the findings of research

4

- Ask students to read the information in the Reading skill box.
- Students already know the ways of connecting with nature mentioned in the article, but they may need to read the article again to remind themselves of their benefits.
- Students create their mind maps individually, using the example mind map to help them.

- **Optional step** Students compare their mind maps in pairs and explain the decisions they made and how their mind map effectively summarizes the information in the text.

Sample answers

Ways of connecting with nature:
- live closer to a green space
- go for a walk in the countryside
- look at pictures of nature
- listen to nature

Benefits:
- decreased risk of several diseases
- lowers blood pressure
- improves short-term memory
- makes you more caring
- relaxes you

Extra activity

Students expand their mind map. They can do this by including other ways of connecting with nature and possible benefits for each, and/or adding details of how they experience the benefit of each way of connecting with nature mentioned in the text.

5 4.1

- Tell students that they are now going to practise summarizing what they hear, rather than what they read. However, the same principles of identifying significant pieces of information and key words apply.
- Tell students that they will hear National Geographic explorer, Carolina Chong Montenegro, talking about the importance of spending time in nature. Play the audio so students can listen and write down the main ideas.

Sample answers

- Carolina enjoys spending time in nature – does activities, e.g. surfing, diving, hiking, listening to birds
- easy to forget our cities were once covered with trees
- staying in touch with nature helps us to stay mentally healthy – helps her feel more at peace and more aware of her surroundings
- interviewed a fisherman in a remote location in Colombia who felt he had everything he needed and didn't want to move to the city – he liked the peace of the sea and the jungle

Extra activity

Put students into pairs or small groups and ask them to discuss the pros and cons of living close to nature in a remote area, and of living in a big city. Ask them to make a list of these pros and cons for each place and use their lists to help them decide and discuss which place they would prefer to live in and why.

6

- Ask students to compare their ideas from Exercise 5 in pairs. Encourage them to help each other clarify any main ideas they did not fully understand or help each other complete their list of main ideas.
- **Optional step** Encourage students to give each other feedback on how well they summarized the main ideas in their notes.
- Students compare the points that Carolina made about the importance of reconnecting with nature with the points in the article and highlight any new information they learned from Carolina.

Answers

1 staying in touch with nature is necessary for a healthy mind; people living in remote areas; going walking in nature, listening to birds/sounds of nature
2 Sample answers: easy to forget cities were once covered with trees; other ways of being close to nature include going surfing, diving and being close to the ocean

7

- Students read the Critical thinking skill box. Remind them that they have to combine the information from the article and the listening coherently in their summary.
- Ask students to plan their summary before they begin writing it, for example, by making a list of the points they want to include and a few key words for each one.
- Students write their summaries individually.
- **Optional step** Students exchange the summaries they have written with a partner. They then use the checklist in the Critical thinking skill box to give their partner feedback on how effectively they have synthesized the information from the article and the listening.

Sample answers

While many people now do not spend enough time outside, scientists have shown that being in nature can have important benefits for our bodies and minds, for example lowering the risk of many diseases. Even a walk in the park or looking at pictures of nature will have beneficial effects. There are however traditional communities that have always lived close to nature. For example, in the Colombian region of Chocó, some people in remote fishing communities would never consider moving to a city.

SPEAKING

8

- Put students into new pairs.
- Direct them to the instructions for the roleplay on page 155 (page 205 of the Teacher's Book). Ask students to read them carefully and ask any questions students have.
- **Optional step** Briefly review language for making recommendations (e.g. *I'd recommend* verb + *-ing; It's a good idea to ...; I think you should ...*, etc.) and persuading people to do things (*If you try verb* + -ing, *you will/might ...; But what if you ...? Why don't you try ...?*) by eliciting example phrases from the class.
- Less confident students may need one or two minutes to make some notes to help them prepare for the roleplay, but check that they do not write out their part of the conversation in full and then just read it out loud.
- Give students five minutes to roleplay the two situations. Monitor students' roleplays, offering guidance where necessary.
- **Optional step** If time allows, ask students to switch roles and roleplay the two situations again.

Extra activity

Ask students to draft an email or a message to a friend to invite him/her to do a specific activity in nature with them. Students could re-use some of the language ideas they used in Exercise 8 to make this activity seem attractive to the recipient of the email or message. Students could show their first draft of the email or message to a partner who could tell them whether it would make them want to do the activity before they send it to the recipient.

EXPLORE MORE!

Tell students to be realistic in terms of what they will be able to do to connect with nature. Encourage students to try out ways of connecting with nature that will be enjoyable or meaningful for them. This may mean looking at possible options online (e.g. on the website of a nature conservation society or mental health organization), or asking friends and family members for suggestions.
Students are asked to write about their experiences in a journal entry or blog post. Suggest that students organize their texts by writing a paragraph about each of the activities they did, including what they did, why they chose the activity, where and when they did it and how it made them feel or what effects it had on their life.

See **Workbook** pages 30–31 for extra practice.

LESSON GOALS

- **GRAMMAR** The main aim is for students to review and practise using reported speech and reporting verbs.
- **PRONUNCIATION** A sub-aim is for students to practise using stress to emphasize different information in a sentence.
- **SPEAKING** The speaking aim is for students to practise resolving a conflict through a roleplay.

READING AND GRAMMAR

1

- **Optional step** Check students' understanding of 'reunited' (to be back together again after having been separated), 'lost touch with (someone)' (to not know where someone is or what they are doing because you haven't communicated with them for a long time) and 'get back in touch with (someone)' (to start communicating with someone after a period of no contact).
- Give students a minute to read the questions and think about their answers.
- Students discuss the questions in pairs. Ask them to explain their answers but remind them that they do not have to share any personal information they do not feel comfortable sharing.

2

- Tell students to only look at the headline of the text and the photo first. Suggest they cover up the rest of the text, if necessary.
- **Optional step** Quickly review language for speculating, for example, *It must/could/may/might be about …; It looks like it's about …; I imagine it's about …; I'd say there's a good chance it's about …*, etc.
- Students speculate about the story's contents in pairs and then read the article to check their answers.
- Elicit a summary of what the story is about.

Sample answer

It is a story about friends who reconnected after years of not speaking to each other, because one blamed the other for not receiving a wedding invitation, when in fact it got lost in the post.

3

- Draw students' attention to the fact that all the sentences in the exercise are examples of direct speech. Point out that italics is used for 'did' in sentence 6 to show that it's emphasized.
- Students use what they can remember from the article to guess who might have said each sentence.
- Students read the article again to check their answers. Tell them to look for words or phrases that are synonyms for or connected to the words or phrases given.
- Check answers as a class.

Answers

1 Maria and her partner or Maria's parents; 2 Maria; 3 Samira; 4 Samira; 5 Maria; 6 Maria; 7 postal service; 8 Maria and Samira

VOCABULARY NOTES

persuade /pə'sweɪd/ = to make someone change their opinion or decide to do/not to do something
deny /dɪ'naɪ/ = to say that you did not do something
claim (v) /kleɪm/ = to say that something is true
blame (v) /bleɪm/ = to say that someone is responsible for doing something

4

- **Optional step** Elicit or explain that a 'reporting verb' is a verb that is used to indicate what someone said (e.g. 'invite').
- Students identify the reporting verbs used in the parts of the article that refer to the sentences in Exercise 3.
- Students compare answers in pairs and help each other understand the meaning of any unfamiliar reporting verbs.

Answers

1 When Maria's family <u>invited</u> her friends to attend her wedding
2 need to <u>persuade</u> one of her closest friends, Samira, to come
3 She <u>admits</u> being confused
4 Samira <u>accused</u> Maria of forgetting her
5 Maria <u>denied</u> forgetting
6 and <u>claimed</u> to have sent the invitation with all the others
7 The postal service has <u>promised</u> to look into the situation
8 Maria and Samira <u>blame</u> the postal service for ending their relationship

GRAMMAR NOTES

Reported speech and reporting verbs

Some words and grammar features used in direct speech have to be changed to convert the sentence into reported speech. Present tenses change to past; present perfect and past tenses change to past perfect. The modal verbs *will, must, may* and *can* change to *would, had to, might* and *could* respectively. However, tense changes are not necessary if the statement being reported is still true, or if the reporting verb is in the present or present perfect tense.
Several different verb patterns can be used in reported speech. Students need to memorize which verb pattern is used with each reporting verb in order to use them accurately.

5

- Tell students that several different verb patterns are used after reporting verbs and students need to learn when to use these.
- Ask students to read the information about and examples of these different verb patterns in the Grammar box.

4B Reunited

LESSON GOALS
- Report what people say
- Use stress to highlight different information
- Resolve a conflict

READING AND GRAMMAR

1 **Work in pairs. Discuss the questions.**

1 Have you ever lost touch with an old friend or family member? Why?
2 Did you get back in touch with them? How?

2 **Look at the headline and photo of the news article. With your partner, discuss what you think the story might be about. Then read the article to check.**

3 **Which person from the article might have said these sentences? Read the article again to check.**

1 'We'd love it if you could come to the wedding.'
Maria and her partner or Maria's parents
2 'Come on, Samira, come to the wedding.'
3 'I have to say, I was very confused.'
4 'I think it was terrible you forgot me.'
5 'Of course I didn't forget you!'
6 'I *did* send you the invitation!'
7 'We'll definitely look into how the invitation got lost.'
8 'It's the postal service's fault we stopped talking to each other.'

4 **Find the parts of the article that refer to the sentences in Exercise 3. Underline the reporting verbs.**

When Maria's family invited her friends to attend her wedding ...

5 **Match these verbs with the correct verb pattern in the Grammar box on page 51. Use the news article to help you.**

admit blame claim deny invite persuade promise

Friends fall out over lost invitation

When Maria's family invited her friends to attend her wedding, Maria was sure she wouldn't need to persuade one of her closest friends, Samira, to come. After all, they had known each other for years. But the wedding came and went with no word from Samira. Meanwhile, Samira was waiting for her invitation. She admits being confused but said nothing, explaining that she didn't think it was correct to remind Maria to send her the invitation.

That was in 2015.

They met socially once afterwards and Samira accused Maria of forgetting her. Maria denied forgetting, of course, and claimed to have sent the invitation with all the others. But neither believed the other one and they gradually grew apart. Then, in August 2019, Maria got a message from Samira: 'Oh my goodness! You did send me an invite!' A photo showed the date of the letter: 10th January 2015. Somehow, it had got lost in the post. The postal service has promised to look into the situation. Maria and Samira blame the postal service for ending their relationship and say they can be friends again.

50

- Students use what they have learned from the Grammar box and the news article to deduce the correct verb pattern for each of the reporting verbs given.
- Students compare their answers in pairs and then check answers as a class.

Answers

verb + *to* + infinitive: claim to do/have done, promise to do; verb + object + *to* + infinitive: invite s.o. to do, persuade s.o. to do; verb + *-ing*: admit doing, deny doing; verb + object + preposition + *-ing*: blame s.o for doing

For further information and practice, see **Grammar reference Unit 4B** on page 144 of the Student's Book.

6

- Tell students to read the two conversations and complete the reports of the conversations with the correct reporting verbs and any other words they might need (e.g. prepositions).
- Refer students back to the Grammar box and their answers to Exercise 5 to find the correct verb patterns for each reporting verb.

Answers

1 He accused her of forgetting to call him. The woman denied it/forgetting to call him. The man apologized (for accusing her). He promised to make sure he charges his battery next time.
2 The brother invited his sister to go for a coffee on Saturday. At first, the sister refused to meet/see him because of his behaviour last time. But when he apologized (for his behaviour/behaving badly last time) and promised not to do it again, she agreed (to meet him).

Extra activity

Students work in pairs to imagine a situation where two people fall out with each other. Students tell the story about the falling out, taking turns to say a line at a time. They should use a different reporting verb in each line: *invite, persuade, admit, accuse, deny, claim, promise, blame*.

7

- Put students into small groups.
- Direct students to the instructions. Ask a stronger student to explain in his/her own words what they are supposed to do for the task.
- Students each choose a reporting verb from Exercises 5 or 6 and use it to write a sentence in direct speech. Then they take turns to say their sentence and the rest of the group writes it down as reported speech. Remind students not to say the reporting verb they chose.
- Students can use the information in the Grammar box to check if their reported speech sentences are correct.

Extra activity

Ask students to write a short news article or story that is similar to the model text and is either based on something that has really happened or on events that they have invented. Tell students to use at least four of the reporting verbs from Exercise 5 in their story. If students struggle to think of any ideas for their stories, you could give them the following to write about: A story where a man promises to give a shop assistant half the money if he wins the lottery. When he does actually win and does what he promises, his wife is not very happy that he has decided to share the money.

For additional practice, refer to the **Grammar activity** on page 251 of the Teacher's Book.

GRAMMAR Reported speech and reporting verbs

In reported speech, verb forms and reference words (e.g. time and place expressions) might change.

'Are you free tomorrow?' → Elyse asked her whether she was free the next day.

Some reporting verbs follow a specific pattern.

verb + *to* + infinitive

Maria agreed to meet Samira.

verb + object + *to* + infinitive

Maria asked her friends to celebrate.

verb + *-ing*

Samira recommended using online invitations.

verb + preposition + *-ing*

The post office apologized for losing it.

verb + object + preposition + *-ing*

Samira accused Maria of forgetting.

Go to page 144 for the Grammar reference.

6 Report the conversations (1–2) using the verbs in the correct space. You might need to add extra words.

1 Man: You forgot to call me to say you were going to be late!
Woman: That's not true. I did call, but your phone was off.
Man: Oh, you're right! I'm so sorry! I'll make sure I charge my battery next time.

accuse apologize deny promise

He ____________ to call him.
He accused her of forgetting to call him.
The woman ____________. The man ____________. He ____________ he charges his battery next time.

2 Brother: Would you like to go for a coffee on Saturday?
Sister: Not really, after how you behaved last time!
Brother: I'm really sorry … I won't do it again.
Sister: OK, fine. Let's meet up then.

agree apologize invite promise refuse

The brother ____________.
At first, the sister ____________ because of his behaviour last time. But when he ____________ and ____________, she ____________.

7 Work in groups. Follow the instructions.

1 Individually, choose one reporting verb from Exercise 5 or 6. Don't tell the rest of the group. Write a sentence that performs the verb's function.
accuse → 'Sung-Hyun, you lost my pencil!'

2 Take turns to say your sentence. The rest of the group writes it down as reported speech.
Eun accused Sung-Hyun of losing his pencil.

PRONUNCIATION

8 4.2 Look at the Clear voice box. Then listen to the same sentence said three times. Which of the underlined words is stressed each time?

She claimed to understand what I had said.

CLEAR VOICE
Using stress for emphasis (2)

Stressed words carry the most important meaning, such as new information.
If the meaning changes, different words are stressed.
*What did he do? → He **accused** me of lying.*
*What did he accuse you of? → He accused me of **lying**!*
*Who did he accuse of lying? → He accused **me** of lying!*

9 4.2 Listen again. Pay attention to the stress to work out the meaning of the sentences. Which sentence (a–c) would follow each one?

a … But I don't think she actually understood me. 3
b … I don't think she understood you, though. 1
c … But she was still confused by what I wrote. 2

SPEAKING

10 Work in groups of three. Go to page 155. Read your role cards. Then try to reach an agreement.

EXPLORE MORE!

Find and read an unusual story online of a pet or possession that got lost and was reunited with its owners.

51

PRONUNCIATION

8 4.2

- Ask students to read the Clear voice box to familiarize themselves with how a change in the word that is stressed in a sentence can change the meaning.
- Play the audio so students can listen and make a note of the word that is stressed each time the sentence is said.
- **Optional step** Confirm answers as a class by inviting students to say each version of the sentence with the stress used in the audio.

Answers
1 I, 2 said, 3 claimed

PRONUNCIATION NOTES

A speaker may decide to stress words that wouldn't usually be considered as key content words, such as grammatical words, in order to convey a particular meaning or emphasize a particular aspect of a sentence. If students are aware of the specific meaning that placing emphasis on a particular word conveys, they will be able to understand the speaker's overall message.

9 4.2

- Tell students to read the three sentences.
- Play the audio again so that students can match the stress used in each sentence with the possible following sentence for it.
- Students compare answers as a class.

For additional practice, refer to the **Pronunciation activity** on page 271 of the Teacher's Book.

Extra activity

Put students into pairs. Ask them to each write a sentence with one of the reporting verbs from this lesson in it. For example: *He didn't apologize to me for ruining my birthday party*. Tell students to choose three words in the sentence that could be stressed and think about the meaning that this emphasis would communicate. In their pairs, they then take turns to say their sentence three times with the stress on a different word each time. Their partner then responds appropriately based on what they think the meaning is (e.g. 'Oh no, that sounds awful.', 'That's good news.', etc.)

SPEAKING

10

- Put students into groups of three and direct them to their role cards on page 155 (page 205 in the Teacher's Book). Give students one or two minutes to read their role cards and make notes to prepare for the roleplay.
- Before they begin the roleplay, remind students that their aim is to reach an agreement in their group. That means they will need to use language for agreeing, disagreeing and conceding. Demonstrating empathy would also be useful in this activity and you could direct students to the Useful language in Lesson 1D to help them do this.
- **Optional step** Challenge more confident students by asking them to also focus on using stress for emphasis in order to make points in the discussion.

EXPLORE MORE!

Suggest that students look at the websites of more informal newspapers, local news websites or magazines and search for key words such as 'pet', 'lost', 'reunited' or 'prized possession'. These sources are more likely to include fun stories about everyday life than more formal newspapers.

See **Workbook** pages 32–33 for extra practice.

LESSON GOALS

- **LISTENING** A main aim is for students to listen to an interview with National Geographic explorer Federico Fanti and practise understanding different accents.
- **PRONUNCIATION** A sub-aim is for students to identify and practise pronouncing the difference in length between /iː/ and /ɪ/.
- **VOCABULARY** A further main aim is for students to review and practise using vocabulary about personal relationships and using transitive and intransitive phrasal verbs.
- **SPEAKING** The speaking aim is for students to discuss personal relationships.

SPEAKING

- Ask students to read the instructions and the example question and answer carefully. Check their understanding of 'get along well with (someone)' (to have a very friendly relationship with someone).
- Students write their lists of names individually.
- Students exchange their lists with a partner and ask and answer questions about their relationship with each person.

LISTENING AND PRONUNCIATION

2 4.3

- Tell students to look at the Listening skill box and then read the instructions and Federico's sentence.
- **Optional step** Elicit from students that, given what they have read in the Listening skill box, they can assume that Federico is likely to pronounce some of the words in a non-standard way because of his accent.
- Play the audio so students can listen and focus on how Federico pronounces the underlined words.
- **Optional step** Students compare how they think Federico said each of the words in pairs by trying to replicate how he said them.

4C Keeping in touch

LESSON GOALS
- Understand different accents
- Pronounce /iː/ and /ɪ/
- Discuss personal relationships
- Use phrasal verbs correctly

SPEAKING

1 Write the names of people in your life that match the descriptions (1–4). Exchange your list of names with a partner. Take turns to ask each other about the people on your list.

1 someone you have known for a long time
2 someone from your studies or work that you are glad to have met
3 someone you get along very well with
4 someone that you don't see often because they live far away

A: How long have you known Petra?
B: Only a few months, but she's someone I'm glad to know. She's a really close friend already.

LISTENING AND PRONUNCIATION

NATIONAL GEOGRAPHIC EXPLORER

2 4.3 Look at the Listening skill box. Then listen to a sentence from an interview with Federico Fanti, an Italian speaker of English. Listen to how he pronounces the underlined words.

I still get together with a couple of them from time to time. I mean, it helps working still in the same city I grew up in.

LISTENING SKILL
Understanding accents

When you listen to people speaking English, you will hear a wide variety of accents. It's helpful to practise listening to as many different accents as you can. Accents you are used to hearing are easier to understand, wherever they are from.

Federico Fanti with friends and colleagues in the Dolomites, Italy.

52

- Check answers as a class and introduce the term *long and short 'i' sounds*. Draw students' attention to the fact that although some words don't contain the letter 'i', like 'mean' and 'these', they contain an /i/ sound.

Answers
still /stɪl/, with /wɪd/, mean /mɪn/, city / siːti/, in /ɪn/

Extra activity

Find a video clip of a celebrity, sportsperson or other well-known person who speaks English but is not a first language user, for example the actor Javier Bardem. Play the video in class and encourage students to focus on understanding the gist of what the person is saying.
If internet connection is a problem in class, students could have a general discussion about which accents they are used to hearing and find easier to understand and any accents that they have struggled with because they are less familiar to them.
Outside of class, students find a video clip of a well-known person who speaks English with an accent that they are less familiar with and try to understand the gist of what they are saying.

3 Look at the Clear voice box. Practise saying the underlined words from Exercise 2, remembering the difference between long and short 'i'.

CLEAR VOICE

Pronouncing long and short 'i'

English has a long /iː/ as in *mean* and a short /ɪ/ as in *with*. Make sure that you make a difference in length between them. You may find it helpful to even exaggerate the long /iː/ slightly.

4 4.4 Listen to the interview with Federico. Who does he talk about?

a family members
b **old school friends** (circled)
c people he works with at the university now
d **people he has met when travelling for work** (circled)
e people he has met when travelling on holiday

5 4.4 Listen again. Choose the correct option to complete the sentences.

1 Federico **works** (circled) / *doesn't work* in the same city he grew up in.
2 He believes that the internet **has** (circled) / *hasn't* helped him keep in touch with friends.
3 Federico says it's important to have good relationships with people *at university* / **on a dig** (circled).
4 He *keeps* / **doesn't keep** (circled) in touch with most of the people he meets on digs.
5 He met his best friend in *Japan* / **Canada** (circled).
6 They last saw each other **two** (circled) / *ten* years ago.

VOCABULARY

6 Read the text. What relationships does the person mention?

I'm from Ghana, but now I'm part of a programme that helps migrants adapt to their lives in France. I've met a lot of fascinating people here. I [1]get along well with all of them, but with some you really [2]hit it off instantly. We try not to [3]lose touch with each other if they leave for another city, but it's difficult to [4]keep in close contact. Fortunately, some of us stay in the city and we try to [5]stick together, go out for a coffee once in a while to [6]catch up. I miss my friends and family back in Ghana and try to [7]keep in touch with them as much as possible. And whenever I go back, we [8]reconnect immediately.

7 Match the bold expressions in the questions (a–h) with the correct form of the underlined expressions in Exercise 6 (1–8).

a Which of your classmates do you **see, talk or write to outside class**? 7
b Which members of your family do you **see, talk or write to a lot**? 4
c Which people at work or at school do you **have a friendly relationship with**? 1
d Are you ever in situations where it's important to have friends so that you can **help and support each other**? 5
e Have you ever met someone and you **were very friendly with each other straight away**? 2
f Are there any friends that you have **stopped communicating with** who you'd like to see again? 3
g How often do you talk to your friends to **get their news and give them yours**? 6
h Who would you like to **meet and talk to again**? 8

Go to page 136 for the Vocabulary reference.

8 Read the Focus on box. Then write three other questions about relationships using expressions from Exercise 6. Make sure you use phrasal verbs correctly.

FOCUS ON Transitive and intransitive phrasal verbs

Some phrasal verbs can be both **transitive** (needing an object) or **intransitive** (not needing an object).
*I need to finally **catch up with** Rasman.* (Rasman is the object.)
*Rasman and I need to finally **catch up**.* (no object)
You can add *with* to many intransitive phrasal verbs to make them transitive.

Go to page 144 for the Focus on reference.

SPEAKING

9 Work in pairs. Use the questions from Exercises 7 and 8 to prepare a questionnaire about relationships. Follow the instructions.

1 Choose six questions to include.
2 Talk to as many people in the class as possible.
3 Prepare a two-minute presentation sharing the results with the class.

EXPLORE MORE!

Record yourself talking for one minute about someone special in your life or someone interesting that you have met.

3

- Tell students to read the information in the Clear voice box.
- **Optional step** Ask students to briefly practise saying 'mean' and 'with', exaggerating the length of the long 'i' sound in 'mean', so they can clearly hear the difference between the two sounds.
- Students use what they now know about long and short 'i' sounds to read the sentences from Exercise 2 out loud, concentrating on pronouncing those sounds clearly.
- **Optional step** Students say the sentences out loud to a partner who can then give them feedback on their pronunciation of the 'i' sounds. For more practice, ask students to say the following words and sentences: *live, leave; street; pretty; village; I live on a leafy street in a pretty village.*

4 4.4

- Tell students that they are now going to listen to the whole interview with Federico.
- Ask students to read the options. Then play the audio so they can make notes on the people Federico talks about.
- Students compare their answers in pairs and justify them by recounting details or examples from the interview.

VOCABULARY NOTES

dig /dɪɡ/ *(n)* = an archaeological excavation site, i.e. a place where soil and objects are being taken out of a place of historical interest

in the middle of nowhere /ɪn ðə 'mɪd(e)l ɒv 'nəʊweə(r)/ = describing a place that is far away from other towns and cities

by chance /baɪ ʧɑːns/ = describing something that just happened without anyone planning it or trying to make it happen

undergraduate /ˌʌndəgrædʒət/ = describing university studies and university students who have not yet completed a first or Bachelor's-level degree

5 4.4

- Ask students to read the sentences and guess the correct options using what they can remember from the first time they listened to the interview.
- Play the audio again so students can choose the correct options.

Extra activity

Students decide on the similarities and differences between their own relationships and Federico's and then tell a partner about these similarities and differences, bringing in examples from their own experiences.

VOCABULARY

6

- Ask students to read the text in order to get a general understanding of the writer's relationships.
- Tell students not to focus their attention on the meaning of the underlined phrases at this stage.

Answers

friends that he/she has made as part of the migrant programme, his/her family and friends back in Ghana

7

- Ask students to read the text from Exercise 6 again and then work in pairs to help each other deduce the meaning of the underlined expressions from the context in which they are used. Students have already encountered most of the expressions in this unit.
- Students match the underlined expressions from the text with the expressions in bold in the questions.
- **Optional step** Elicit or explain the differences between these two sets of expressions with similar meanings: 1) get along well / hit it off (the first expression refers to a good relationship, whereas the second expression refers to people establishing a good relationship when they meet each other for the first time); 2) stick together / catch up (the first expression means that people remain friends or continue to support each other over a long period of time, whereas the second expression refers to people talking or meeting up after not having seen each other for a while).

For further information and practice, see **Vocabulary reference Unit 4** on page 136 of the Student's Book.

8

- Students read the Focus on box and check their understanding of the difference between transitive and intransitive phrasal verbs.
- Individually, students write three questions about personal relationships using a different phrasal verb from Exercise 6 in each one.
- Students compare their questions in pairs and give each other feedback on whether they have used the phrasal verbs correctly in their questions.

Sample answers
Have you ever lost touch with a good friend? Why do you think some people hit it off immediately? What's the best way to keep in touch with friends and family you don't see every day?

Extra activity

Ask students to look at the underlined phrasal verbs in Exercise 6 and identify whether they are transitive or intransitive to confirm their understanding of the difference. Once they have identified this, ask students to write a new sentence for each phrasal verb, but converting the transitive to intransitive verbs and vice versa. They can use the context of the text in Exercise 6 or their own ideas. Direct students to the Focus on box for an example of how the same idea can be expressed with either a transitive or intransitive phrasal verb.

For further information and practice, see **Focus on reference Unit 4C** on page 144 of the Student's Book.

For additional practice, refer to the **Vocabulary activity** on page 236 and the **Focus on activity** on page 252 of the Teacher's Book.

SPEAKING

9

- Students work in pairs to choose six questions from Exercises 7 and 8 to include in their questionnaire.
- **Optional step** When students are selecting their questions, encourage them to consider which questions will generate the most interesting answers or which questions other members of the class will feel comfortable answering, i.e. because they are not too personal or intrusive.
- Give students ten to fifteen minutes to move around the classroom individually, asking other students their questions and making brief notes on the answers they receive.
- When their time is up, students sit back down with their partners and compare answers.
- Pairs then discuss and decide on the most important findings from their questionnaire and choose three or four interesting points to include in a presentation about their findings.
- Students give their presentations in class with their partners.
- **Optional step** If possible, students could create visual aids to accompany their presentation and show these to the audience.

EXPLORE MORE!

Students can use voice notes, a voice recording app or a voice messaging app to make the recording on their phones and then, if appropriate, share it with you and/or other students for feedback. Before they make the recording, tell students to plan the content and structure of their talk by making a plan with key words and phrases. Remind students that they will need to be selective about which information they include and present it in quite a succinct way, given the one-minute time limit.

For additional practice, refer to the **Communication activity** on page 218 of the Teacher's Book.

See **Workbook** pages 34–36 for extra practice.

LESSON GOALS

- **SPEAKING AND LISTENING** This lesson integrates speaking and listening. Its main aim is to raise students' awareness of three main turn-taking styles and to identify their own preferred style. Students learn language to help them participate more effectively in a discussion, including phrases to interrupt politely, deal with interruptions from others and to invite others to participate. Students then use what they have learned to practise adapting their turn-taking style to the turn-taking styles of the people they are talking to.

SPEAKING

1

- Check students' understanding of 'turn-taking' (a type of organization in conversation where one person speaks at a time).
- Students read the situations, using them to discuss the questions.
- **Optional step** Clarify that in question 3, 'kinds of people' could refer to people's age, the values their family has passed on to them (e.g. what it means to be polite or impolite) their personality type (e.g. introverted or extroverted), or the type of culture people come from.

Sample answers

3 People who would find quieter conversations more difficult include those who come from cultures where silence is seen as a sign of awkwardness and embarrassment; louder, extroverted people, and very busy or impatient people. People who might find noisier conversations difficult include: shy people, differently abled people (e.g. people with autism or speech impairments, people with hearing loss); people with lower levels of English than the others in the group; people who don't know the other members of the group so well.

LISTENING

2 4.5

- **Optional step** Tell students that: Conversation 1 takes place around a table at a friends' reunion; Conversation 2 takes place at a café; Conversation 3 takes place during an online video call.
- Play the audio so students can match the conversations to the situations in Exercise 1.
- Students discuss the questions in pairs.

Answers

Conversation 1 – c, Conversation 2 – a, Conversation 3 – b

3 4.5

- Direct students to the infographic. Explain that it compares communication styles to sports.
- **Optional step** Elicit or explain what the three sports in the infographic involve.
- Play the audio so students can match the conversations with the communication styles in the infographic.
- **Optional step** Ask students to give examples of things people said or did in the conversations to justify their choices.

Answers

Conversation 1 – rugby; Conversation 2 – bowling; Conversation 3 – basketball

COMMUNICATION SKILL NOTES

Everyone, consciously or not, has a preferred turn-taking style – i.e. how comfortable they are with interrupting people or being interrupted, whether they prefer faster- or slower-paced conversations, etc. This can be influenced by personality and various cultural factors as outlined in this lesson's video. The turn-taking style someone uses is often closely connected with their beliefs about what is rude or respectful behaviour and how you show the people you are talking to that you are interested in and engaged with the conversation.

By developing an awareness of their preferred style and that of the people they interact with, students will be better placed to understand why other people might communicate in a way that they are not used to and also be better able to adapt their own style to suit different situations.

Effective turn-taking is integral to collaboration. By knowing how to politely take the floor during a discussion, deal with interruptions and invite others to participate, students will be able to encourage fair and effective teamwork and decision-making.

VOCABULARY NOTES

bowling /ˈbəʊlɪŋ/ = a sport where participants roll a large, heavy ball down a bowling alley (a long, narrow strip of wooden flooring) with the aim of knocking down as many of the pins at the end of the alley as possible

basketball /ˈbɑːskɪtˌbɔːl/ = a team sport where two teams of five players play against each other on a basketball court. The aim is to get the ball to the other team's hoop and then score points by throwing it through the hoop. Basketball is particularly popular in the US, but it is also popular in other countries, including Argentina and the Philippines.

rugby /ˈrʌgbi/ = a team sport that is similar to American football. Two teams of fifteen players play against each other on a grass pitch outdoors. The aim is to carry an oval-shaped ball over the other team's goal line and force it to the ground to score points. Places where rugby is popular include the UK, Australasia, Argentina, South Africa, Ireland and France.

4D Understanding turn-taking styles

LESSON GOALS
- Understand the main turn-taking styles
- Adapt your style to communicate more effectively
- Participate and invite others to participate in a group discussion

SPEAKING

1 Work in pairs. Read the situations and discuss the questions (1–3).

a You're at a café with a friend you haven't seen for many years. There are pauses in between questions and answers from you and your friend.

b You're talking to your friends. You ask questions to invite each other to speak. You speak fairly fast but rarely interrupt each other.

c You're with some friends. They're speaking really fast. You're trying to participate, but they are interrupting each other and speaking loudly.

1 Who do you have similar styles of conversations with?
2 In which type of situations are you the most and the least comfortable? Why?
3 What kinds of people would find quieter conversations, like in the first scenario, more difficult? Who might find noisier conversations difficult?

LISTENING

2 4.5 Listen to three conversations. Match them with the situations in Exercise 1. Which group …

1 has the most similar conversation style to the one you normally use?
2 would you enjoy participating in the most?

3 4.5 Look at the infographic on page 55. Then listen again and match the conversations with the three turn-taking styles.

4 Work in pairs. Discuss the questions.

1 What do you know about the sports in the infographic?
2 How are the three turn-taking styles similar to bowling, basketball and rugby?
3 Which style is the most similar to your own?
4 Does your style sometimes change, depending on the situation?

54

4

- Give students a minute to read the questions and think about their answers.
- Students take turns to give their answers to the questions and react to their partner's answers.
- **Optional step** As a class, discuss how students' conversation styles might change in different situations and why.

Sample answers

2 Like bowling, the bowling style of communication involves waiting for the other person to finish their turn before having yours; there is time between bowls for the person to prepare their shot. Like basketball, the basketball style of communication involves a lot of quick 'passing' between speakers so that everyone is involved in the conversation, interruptions (like when the other team takes the ball) don't occur often; participating is valued highly. Like rugby, the rugby style of communication involves a fast pace, but with a lot of interruptions, with turns being 'tackled' from each other.
4 It might change depending on who you are talking to (someone younger or older, someone in a more or less senior position, how well you know them, etc.), where you are (in your own home you might be more dominant, for example), how you are feeling, etc.

Extra activity

Put students into pairs or small groups to brainstorm other sports or activities that each of the three communication styles in the infographic could be compared to. Ask them to come up with reasons why they have chosen these sports or activities and how they are similar to the communication styles.

MY VOICE

5 4.2

- Tell students not to write anything the first time they watch the video but to keep the questions in mind.
- Remind students to use the words and illustrations that appear on screen to help them understand the video's contents. Then play the video.
- Students discuss their ideas in pairs.

Extra activity

Ask students to reflect on their own turn-taking style and evaluate its advantages and disadvantages. They could do this by drawing a mind map with 'My turn-taking style' in the centre and lines going out from the centre with sub-headings such as 'My communication style helps me to …'; 'My turn-taking style makes it more difficult for me to …'; 'I can communicate well with people who …'; 'I can't always communicate well with people who …' When they have finished their mind map, students can explain it to their partner.

6

- Ask students to read the Communication skill box.
- Students consider and discuss the issues that could arise when two communicators with different styles talk to each other, then use the tips in the Communication skill box to think of advice they could give to the two communicators that would help them communicate more effectively.

Sample answers

1 speak more slowly; interrupt less; speak more quietly; pause more; invite them to participate

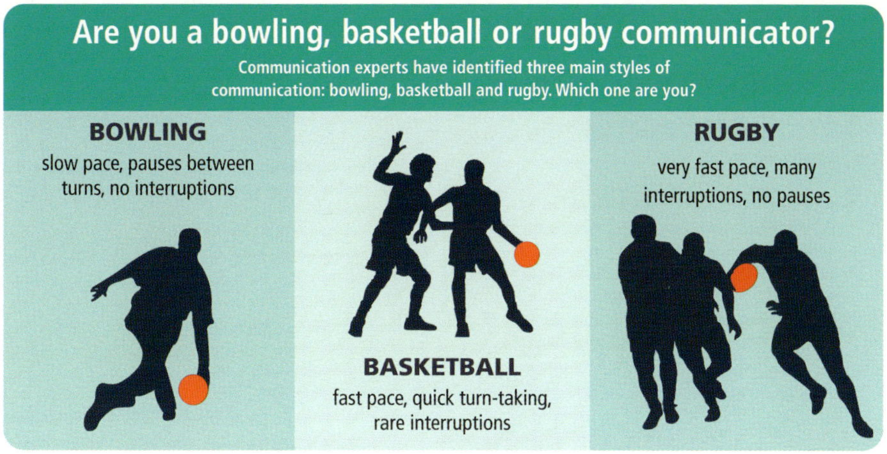

MY VOICE

5 ▶ 4.2 Watch the video and think about the questions. Then discuss your answers in pairs.

1 In your opinion, which are the most important factors that influence your turn-taking style?
2 What's the most important piece of advice for you to remember when speaking? Why?

6 Look at the Communication skill box. What advice would you give to …

1 a rugby-style communicator talking to a bowling-style communicator?
2 a bowling-style communicator talking to a basketball-style communicator?

COMMUNICATION SKILL
Adapting your turn-taking style

Naturally, you probably have one dominant turn-taking style, but sometimes you might need to choose a different one to communicate effectively. There are several things you can change.

- You can increase / decrease your dominance by speaking more slowly and quietly, or more quickly and loudly.
- You can give others a greater or lesser chance to speak in your place, by changing how often you interrupt or pause.
- You can help create a more even participation by inviting others to participate, asking not to be interrupted and asking for more time to speak.

7 🎧 4.6 Listen to one of the conversations from Exercise 2 again. This time, the speakers adapt their turn-taking style. How do they do this?

8 🎧 4.6 Look at the Useful language box. Which expressions did the speakers use in Exercise 7? Listen again to check.

Useful language Taking turns

Interrupting
I'd like to just add that …
I'm glad you brought that up because …
Can I just jump in there?

Dealing with interruptions
Sorry, can I just finish what I was saying?
As I was saying, …

Inviting others to participate
Tell me more about …
I've talked too much already. What did you want to say?

Buying yourself time to speak
So, let me see …
Where was I? Oh yes, …

SPEAKING

9 **OWN IT!** Work in groups of three. Go to page 155 and follow the instructions.

2 speak more quickly and loudly; ask to speak; ask not to be interrupted; pause less

7 🎧 4.6

- Tell students that they will hear the first conversation from Exercise 2 and the continuation of that conversation.
- Play the audio so students can listen and notice how the speakers adapt their turn-taking style. Tell students to think about interruptions, inviting participation and talking speed.
- Put students into pairs to share the ideas they came up with.

Answers

The speaker who is interrupted tries to take their turn and finish what they were saying. The speakers who interrupt invite the other person to participate. They also slow down and let the other person finish.

Extra activity

Ask students to discuss the following questions in pairs or small groups: *Can you think of a time when you changed (or should have changed) your conversation style in response to the other participants' needs? What did you do? Why? What impact did the change have?*

8 🎧 4.6

- Ask students to read the expressions in the Useful language box.
- Check students' understanding of the phrase 'to buy time' (to delay something so that you have more time).
- Students try to remember the expressions that were used in the conversation in Exercise 7.
- Play the audio again so students can listen and identify which expressions the speakers use.

Answers

Sorry, can I just finish what I was saying? / Sorry, we've talked too much already. / So, anyway, as I was saying …

SPEAKING

9 OWN IT!

- Put students into groups of three. Direct them to page 155 (page 205 in the Teacher's Book), assign roles and ask them to read the task instructions.
- You will need to prepare enough small pieces of paper to hand out one to each student. Write an equal number of turn-taking styles on each piece of paper: either Bo (bowling), Ba (basketball), or R (rugby). Explain to students what the letters mean and say that they must not tell anyone which turn-taking style they have. Shuffle the pieces of paper and hand them out.
- Tell students to use the expressions in the Useful language box during their conversations where appropriate.
- Monitor students' conversations to check that they have understood the task and adopted the turn-taking style they have been assigned.
- Stop students' first conversation after three minutes and ask them to discuss the questions.
- Students then choose another conversation topic. Elicit that this time, although they keep the same turn-taking style, they should try to adapt the style to ensure that everyone in the group is able to participate.
- Stop students' second conversation after three minutes and ask them to discuss the second set of questions.

For additional practice, refer to the **Communication activity** on page 219 of the Teacher's Book.

LESSON GOALS

- **WRITING** The aim of the lesson is to guide students to produce a story. The reading text provides a model. Students practise the writing skill of making a story more interesting by describing actions, using sentence length to indicate moods, and including direct speech.

SPEAKING

Extra activity

Elicit that a chance encounter is a meeting between two people that wasn't planned or expected. Put students into pairs or small groups and ask them to discuss these questions: *When was the last time you had a chance encounter with someone you know? Who did you encounter and what did you say to each other?*

1

- Direct students to the questions and remind them that a story can be any example of someone narrating a series of events in order to entertain people or to communicate a particular message.
- Students discuss the questions in pairs.

2

- Students look at the title of the story and the photo on page 56 and think about what the story could be about.
- Students write down their ideas and then compare them with a partner. Ask, *Who might the characters be? What might happen at the beginning, in the middle and at the end of the story?*

READING FOR WRITING

3

- Students read the story and compare it with their ideas from Exercise 2. In pairs, students identify similarities and differences between the two.

4

- Students read the story again and identify examples of the present tense and long and short sentences.
- Students discuss the answers to the questions in pairs.
- Students read the Writing skill box to check their answers.

4E A chance encounter

LESSON GOALS
- Use short and long sentences to express a different mood in a narrative
- Make a narrative more interesting by describing actions
- Write a story

SPEAKING

1 Work in pairs. Discuss the questions.

1 Do you read or listen to stories? What type of story do you like?
2 Do you tell stories to other people or know anyone who does? What kind of stories?
3 Do you think telling and listening to stories is a good way to connect with others? Why? / Why not?

2 You are going to read a story. Look at the title and photo. What do you think the story will be about?

READING FOR WRITING

3 Read the story. How is it similar to your ideas from Exercise 2? How is it different?

I couldn't believe my eyes!

It was just another grey and rainy Monday morning with no signs anywhere that it would be any different from all the other Monday mornings, nor that anything extraordinary was supposed to take place.

I had been living in Utrecht for two months. I was walking to work holding an umbrella in one hand and my breakfast in the other, which I hadn't eaten at home because of lack of time. 'That's a poor excuse', I told myself off.

Completely lost in thought, I suddenly felt something hit my forehead. Then I was on the ground. Everything went black. The next thing I remember is someone's concerned face above mine. 'It's OK. I'm fine', I mumbled with difficulty.

And then I realized whose face it was. 'Carlotta, is that you?', I yelled in disbelief. I jumped to my feet at once as if I'd never fallen down. We gave each other a big hug.

'What a coincidence!', I shouted, still shaking her hand. We hadn't seen each other in years and the last I heard was that Carlotta was living in Argentina.

'I moved here last week', she said, smiling at me. 'You clearly haven't changed – as clumsy as ever! You walked right into that lamppost!', she laughed. She offered to drive me to work. We spent the next half an hour rapidly exchanging news and agreed to meet at the weekend to catch up properly.

I really couldn't believe my eyes when I saw her that day. The world can be such a small place.

56

Answers

1 Present tense is used for presenting characters' thoughts and words directly. This makes the story feel more immediate.
2 The long sentences give the story a slower, more relaxed feeling. The shorter sentences are faster, more abrupt, and give a feeling of action.

5

- Ask students to identify the mood in each paragraph and check answers.
- Elicit that the first paragraph should contain long sentences and the second paragraph short sentences.
- Ask students to rewrite the sentences in each paragraph accordingly.

Sample answers

1 R: It was a sunny afternoon and while the birds were singing and the sun was slowly setting, I was jogging in the park, trying to leave the busy day behind me.
2 A: I was running. I held my phone in one hand trying to dial my son's number. I'd promised to pick him up from basketball practice. I knew I wouldn't make it on time. With the other hand I waved to stop a taxi. They were all busy.

4 Read the story again and answer the questions. Then look at the Writing skill box to check.

1 When is the present tense used?
2 The writer uses long and short sentences in different parts of the story. How does each sentence type affect the mood of the story?

WRITING SKILL
Making a story entertaining

In stories, longer sentences are often used for descriptions and to show a relaxed, slow mood. Short sentences, on the other hand, are used in action scenes to make them feel faster.

You can describe actions to make a story more interesting by using …

- adverbs, e.g. *happily, angrily, unexpectedly, silently*.
- prepositional phrases, e.g. *in anger, with effort*.
- gerunds, e.g. ***shaking** his head, **running** towards me*.

Stories use a variety of past tenses (see page 143 for reference), but present and future tenses are used to present characters' direct words and thoughts. This makes the story more immediate.

5 Look at the paragraphs (1–2). Which paragraph presents a relaxed (R) scene and which presents an action (A) scene? Change the length of the sentences to reflect what is happening.

1 It was a sunny afternoon. The birds were singing. The sun was slowly setting. I was jogging in the park. I tried to leave the busy day behind me.
2 While I was running, I held my phone in one hand trying to dial my son's number because I'd promised to pick him up from basketball practice and I knew I wouldn't make it on time; and with the other waving to stop a taxi, but they all seemed busy.

6 Rewrite the reported sentences as direct speech.

1 Alicia claimed she'd never seen that man before.
'I've never seen this man before', Alicia claimed.
2 My dad offered to drive us to the airport.
3 Widya reminded me to invite Miguel to the party.

7 Read the story again. Underline examples of the three ways of describing action: adverbs, prepositional phrases and gerunds.

Ex 6:
2 'I'll drive you to the airport,' my dad offered.
3 'Don't forget to invite Miguel to the party,' Widya reminded me.

8 Make the descriptions more interesting by adding these expressions.

in anger   in surprise   not moving   silently   terribly   with difficulty

1 I got up with difficulty. My back hurt me terribly. Too much exercise yesterday.
2 I opened my eyes in surprise and stood there not moving. I'd won first prize in the story competition!
3 My mum looked at me in anger while I stared silently at the floor. I'd broken her favourite vase.

WRITING TASK

9 **WRITE** Write a story based on either real or imaginary events. Follow the instructions.

1 Choose an option.
   a Work on your own. Write 200 to 250 words.
   b Work in pairs. Write 100 to 125 words each.
   c Work in groups of three. Take turns to begin, continue and end the story.
2 Choose a topic.
   a They thought they would never see each other again
   b A twin sister/brother I never knew I had
   c From enemy to best friend
   d Your own idea
3 Write your story. Use the Writing skill box to help you.

10 **CHECK** Use the checklist. I have …

- ☐ used longer sentences for descriptions of slow, relaxed events.
- ☐ used shorter sentences for action scenes.
- ☐ used adverbs, prepositional phrases and gerunds to describe actions.
- ☐ used present tenses for characters' thoughts and words.

11 **REVIEW** Exchange stories with another student or group. What's your favourite part of the story? Which sentences describe actions or a relaxed mood well?

Go to page 131 for the Reflect and review.

6

- Students rewrite the reported sentences as direct speech. Remind students to think about tense changes, i.e. from past perfect to past simple.
- Check answers as a class by inviting different students to read their sentences.
- **Optional step** Extend this activity by either giving further examples of direct speech and asking students to convert them into reported speech or getting students to do this.

7

- Students scan the story for examples of adverbs, prepositional phrases and gerunds. Students can refer to the Writing skill box to remind themselves of possible examples for each category.
- Put students into pairs to compare the words they found and then categorize them.

Answers

Adverbs: Completely, suddenly, at once, rapidly
Prepositional phrases: with difficulty, in disbelief
Gerunds: holding an umbrella, shaking her hand

8

- Students use the expressions to complete the descriptions and make them more interesting.
- To help them understand the context, tell students to pay attention to the gap's position in the sentence and the words that come before and after the gap.

Extra activity

Ask students to write a brief (three or four sentence) description of either their journey to class, or something they did yesterday or at the weekend, and to make their description as boring as they can. They should do this by not using adverbs, prepositional phrases or gerunds. Students then exchange their descriptions with a partner, who uses adverbs, prepositional phrases and gerunds to rewrite it so it sounds more interesting.

WRITING TASK

9 WRITE

- Ask students to read the instructions for the task and check they understand it.
- Ask students to also consider how they can make their story more interesting. Refer students to the Writing skill box for tips to help them to do this.
- Students write the first draft of their stories.

10 CHECK

- Ask students to use the checklist and then make changes to their story if necessary.

11 REVIEW

- Students exchange stories with another student or group.
- Tell students to focus on answering the questions about their partner's story while they are reading it.
- Students give each other feedback on their stories.

For additional practice, refer to the **Mediation activity** on page 286 of the Teacher's Book.

For **Unit 4 Reflect and review**, see Student's Book page 131.

See **Workbook** pages 36–37 for extra practice.

See **Workbook** pages 38–39 for Units 3 and 4 Review.

VIDEO 4.1

Federico: *Being a National Geographic explorer, I'm away from home quite often. And unfortunately I can't keep in touch with the family as much as I'd like to. So I try to be as clear as possible with them whether I'll be in touch or not. The worst was when I couldn't communicate with my family for 26 days! It was just horrible.*

But overall, I must admit you kind of get used to it. To being away, I mean. It's definitely easier for me as the traveller, and much more difficult for my kids and wife, but they have also got used to it to an extent. Not that they like it, though.

Interestingly, my wife and the school teachers claim that our kids behave differently when I'm away. My son, who is usually friendly and quiet becomes restless and sometimes behaves badly. My daughter, on the other hand, becomes quiet and shy.

Whenever I come back, I always try to surprise the kids. So they know I'm coming back, but they don't know exactly which day or what time of the day. They make me cry every time I get home as they are super happy to see me. I've also promised my family and myself that the next day is a day off from work, always. And I keep that promise.

Carolina: *One of the most challenging things I've done is moving farther and farther away from my family while I develop a career. I'm from Ecuador, I did my Masters in Germany but I conducted the research for it in Colombia. And now I'm living in Australia. That's fifteen hours of time difference! This means that sometimes I call my family in the morning and for them it's very late the night before. This makes catching up quite difficult. But somehow we stay in touch and I always call over the weekend.*

Fortunately, my family is very supportive. They say, 'you're getting all this education that you cannot get back home and you're training and you're learning'.

And even though I am very far away, I still feel a strong connection with home. I also like going back and reconnecting, not just with people I haven't seen, but also places. For example, I went back to my university after I'd been gone for ten years to talk to some professors. When I was walking through the halls of my university again, it felt very emotional.

AUDIO 4.1

Carolina: *I love nature and I try to be close to it whenever I get the opportunity. I like planning long weekend trips to the sea for surfing or diving. I also enjoy hiking in the woods, and listening to the birds in the trees.*

I believe that staying in touch with nature is essential to maintain a healthy state of mind. Many of us live in big cities, surrounded by cars, buildings, roads and noise. I guess often I forget that before all these buildings and roads, this place was once covered with trees, and instead of all the noise would be the sounds of the birds. Personally, when I go to the ocean or to the forest, I feel more at peace and aware of my surroundings.

While doing my research, I worked in one of the most remote places in Colombia. The Chocó region is a very tropical jungle next to the ocean. There, I interviewed lots of people in fishing communities and got the opportunity to hear about their stories and experiences. One fisherman once mentioned that his family wanted him to move to the city, far away from the place he knows and loves and he said, 'it might seem that I don't have much here, but I have everything I need and I love this place. Also, the city is too chaotic! I like the peace of the sea and jungle'. I will never forget that conversation.

AUDIO 4.2

*1 She claimed to understand what **I** had said.*

*2 She claimed to understand what I had **said**.*

*3 She **claimed** to understand what I had said.*

AUDIO 4.4

I = Interviewer, F = Federico Fanti

I: *So, do you still keep in touch with old school friends, Federico?*

F: *Yeah, there are a few of my friends I've never lost touch with. And we've always been there for one another.*

I: *And you still see them?*

F: *Yeah, I still get together with a couple of them from time to time. I mean, it helps working still in the same city I grew up in.*

I: *That's Bologna, in Italy?*

F: *Yeah. And there's people I hadn't heard from for years, but we've reconnected. It's not as difficult to do that any more, since Facebook and all of that. I am not a big fan of social media, so I use them to connect, but then I love to pick up the phone or use video calls to keep in touch. Many of my friends live on different continents, so I try to chat to them about once a month.*

I: *And what about work? I know you travel a lot for work. You must have made a lot of friendships along the way.*

F: *Absolutely! It's a part of the job I really love, meeting and working with new people, reconnecting with friends around the world. And when we're on a dig, it's essential to get along with everyone, you know, because you can be together for days or weeks at a time. Sometimes you have to work at relationships, you know scientists aren't always the easiest people! You don't want to fall out with anyone because you depend on them, and they depend on you.*

Since I travel a lot, I might lose touch with the people I meet on different trips. They may not use social media or pick up a phone, a farmer in the middle of nowhere, for example, but I know if I stepped into their front yard and knocked on the door, they'd probably start a barbecue! There are some people I get along very well with. It could be two years before I see or speak to them again, or it could be ten years, but we always go straight back to friendship again. It's very nice.

I: *Yeah, it must be nice going back to places you've been to before where you've made good friends. Is there anyone you've met in your work who you'd like to see more often?*

F: *Yeah, my best friend was born in Tokyo, Japan, and moved to Canada to become a dinosaur expert when he was young. We met by chance in Alberta, Canada, the first time I was there to complete my undergraduate studies. I was 22 and he was 17. When I was younger, I spent a lot of time in Alberta and we became really good friends. Then you get older and it's hard to be together – the last time we met in person was about two years ago! But we invite each other to dinosaur expeditions, we write research papers together and much more. We're not happy to live so far apart, but we know we can always count on each other.*

AUDIO 4.5

1

A: *It's been ages since I last saw you, so tell me what you're up to these …*

B: *Yeah, I'm curious as well, what's new?*

C: *Oh not much, you know, still got the same job …*

B: *That job in IT, if I remember …*

A: *It's a pretty good one, isn't it? Aren't you in charge of …?*

B: *You're the boss!*

C: *Ha ha, something like that …*

A: *Actually, that reminds me …*

B: *Oh, I know what you're going to say, it reminds you of …*

A: *… reminds me of Gabriela. Isn't she also working …*

C: *Who's Gabriela?*

2

D: *So, are you still a bookworm like you used to be when we were in school?*

E: *Yes. I still really like reading books.*

D: *I've never really got into reading to be honest. I only read them because we had to.*

E: *Yes, I remember. And not always, actually.*

D: *Yes, you're right.*

E: *Remember that time when you tried to copy the answers from me on a test? And the teacher caught you!*

D: *Of course! It's funny now, but it wasn't funny then. She told my parents and I got into big trouble!*

3

F: *Hey! It's so good to see the two of you!*

G: *You too! Look, Bee!*

H: *Hi Georgia!*

F: *Hey! Can you hear me OK?*

H: *Yeah, we can hear you just fine.*

G: *I love your earrings, Georgia.*

F: *Aww, thank you. They were a present from Ngozi. So tell me, how was your day?*

H: *It was really good. We learned some very interesting things at university.*

F: *Yeah, like what?*

G: *You'll love this! Tell her what you told me!*

H: *It's really amazing. So …*

VIDEO 4.2

How do you know when it's your turn to speak? If you think about this question, you'll realize that there is no easy answer and when we talk, we take turns without even thinking about it.

Right now, it's easy. It's my turn until I stop talking or until you stop the video! But in normal conversation there are many factors that determine whose turn it is, when we are allowed to interrupt and who speaks next.

For example, your personality can have an effect on how often you speak. Confident or louder people might speak more often.

If you're speaking a second or third language and are not very confident at speaking that language, you're likely to speak less often.

It's important to know that your first language identity is also a significant factor in turn-taking. People from certain language backgrounds might be happy to speak at the same time as other people. Meanwhile, people from other language backgrounds might prefer others to be quiet when they're taking their turn to speak.

Other factors might include: how old you are; whether you're a woman or a man; and even what kind of industry you work in.

So we all have a preferred turn-taking style, but we'll need to interact with people who communicate in different ways to us. This means that we might need to adapt our style to connect with the other person and communicate effectively. Otherwise, you might end up never being able to say a word, or dominating the conversation completely.

How can we do this? First of all, think about the pace, or how fast you speak. You might need to slow down or speed up to match how quickly the other person speaks.

Second, consider pauses and interruptions.

If you tend to pause a lot, but are speaking to 'rugby'-style communicators who are used to talking fast and interrupting a lot, you'll never be able to finish your sentence. You may need to tell them that you need space to speak.

On the other hand, if you're used to interrupting others frequently, be careful, because you might offend someone who prefers a slower pace of conversation. It might feel uncomfortable at first, but you will need to accept the silence and give them time to reflect.

And although you might personally value and expect active participation, others might need encouragement to take part.

Remember: no one style is better than another. If communication clearly isn't going well, it might be worth openly discussing the expectations you all have about what 'good communication' means and how these could be achieved together.

AUDIO 4.6

A: *It's been ages since I last saw you, so tell me what you're up to these …*

B: *Yeah, I'm curious as well, what's new?*

C: *Oh not much, you know, still got the same job …*

B: *That job in IT, if I remember …*

A: *It's a pretty good one isn't it? Aren't you in charge of …?*

B: *You're the boss!*

C: *Ha ha, something like that …*

A: *Actually, that reminds me …*

B: *Oh, I know what you're going to say, it reminds you of …*

A: *… reminds me of Gabriela. Isn't she also working …*

C: *Sorry, can I just finish what I was saying?*

A: *Oh, yeah, sure, of course.*

B: *Absolutely. Sorry, we've talked too much already.*

A: *So, tell us more about your work.*

C: *Thanks! So anyway, as I was saying, I've still got the same job, but now I'm working …*

UNIT 5

Healthy body, healthy mind

UNIT GOALS

5A Reading, speaking

- read an article to practise identifying cause and effect and distinguishing between cause and correlation; discuss ways of building a strong school community

5B Reading and grammar, pronunciation, speaking

- read and understand an infographic about sleep; listen to and practise understanding elision in connected speech; use conditionals to make sentences about consequences and use them to tell a story

5C Vocabulary, listening and grammar, speaking

- learn and practise using vocabulary for mental and physical health; listen for keywords in interviews to help understand the speakers' general meaning; use *I wish* and *If only* to talk about your dream job

5D Speaking, pronunciation, listening

- practise simplifying language to be better understood; practise making vowel sounds longer before voiced consonants to be understood more easily; practise helping other people understand each other

5E Writing

- use discourse markers and paragraphs when writing an essay; practise beginning an essay in an engaging way; write a 'for and against' essay

Photocopiable resources

Communication activities: pp. 220–221
Vocabulary activity: p. 237
Grammar activity: p. 253
Focus on … activity: p. 254
Pronunciation activity: p. 272
Mediation activity: p. 287

Workbook

Unit 5 pp. 40–47

ABOUT THE PHOTO

The photo shows people practising yoga together on a beach in Rizhao, China. This large-scale gathering reflects the popularity of taking part in sport and leisure activities in large groups outdoors in China. Yoga was first developed in India around 5,000 years ago and is believed to have originated as a method of preparing the body and mind for meditation. Today, yoga classes are offered all over the world.

1

- Tell students to look carefully at the photo and caption.
- Give students about a minute to think about their answers to the questions.
- In pairs, students discuss the questions. Ask them to justify their answers.

People practising yoga on the beach, Rizhao, China.

5 Healthy body, healthy mind

GOALS

- Identify and understand cause and effect in an article
- Talk about consequences using conditionals
- Discuss mental and physical health
- Listen for key words to understand general meaning
- Adapt language to be easier to understand
- Write a 'for and against' essay

1 Work in pairs. Discuss the questions.

1 Look at the photo. What are the people doing? Have you ever tried this type of exercise?
2 What do you do to stay healthy?
3 In what ways can physical exercise affect how you feel emotionally? Do you think how you feel emotionally can also affect your body? How?

WATCH ▶

2 ▶ 5.1 Watch the video. Answer the questions.

NATIONAL GEOGRAPHIC EXPLORERS

MARIA FADIMAN

ALEC JACOBSON

1 What does Maria do to help her relax?
2 What kinds of exercise does Alec enjoy?
3 In what ways are the body and the mind connected for Maria and Alec?

3 Make connections. Discuss the questions.

1 Do you enjoy the same activities as Maria and Alec?
2 What do you do when you feel stressed? How does it help?

59

Answers

1 They are practising yoga.
3 Sample answers: Exercise releases chemicals that make you happy; feeling physically healthy can allow you to do more activities; mental health issues, such as stress, are known to have negative physical effects too.

WATCH ▶

2 ▶ 5.1

- Tell students that they are going to hear Maria Fadiman and then Alec Jacobson. Students met Maria Fadiman in Unit 2.
- Ask students to read the questions.
- Play the video and tell students to listen for language that paraphrases or is connected to the key verbs in the questions, such as *relax*, *enjoy*, *connected*.
- Students make notes and then compare answers in pairs.

Answers

1 she runs or goes for a walk
2 outdoor activities that aren't competitive or team sports
3 Running helps Maria feel less stressed. Being active outdoors gives Alec a positive view of life and makes him feel part of nature.

Extra activity

Write Alec's sentence from the video on the board: *Keeping fit isn't an end in itself, it's a means of being part of nature and maintaining a positive attitude.* Ask students to discuss what Alec means in pairs (he means that keeping fit helps you to get outdoors and feel positive). They can then discuss whether or not they agree with Alec.

3

- Students discuss the questions in pairs.

Extra activity

Put students into small groups. Each student talks for one minute about one activity that they do to help them feel less stressed. After each student has talked about their activity, they ask the rest of the group if they would be willing to try their activity and if they think it would help them when they are stressed. Students try to persuade anyone who says they wouldn't do their activity to try it.

ABOUT THE EXPLORERS

MARIA FADIMAN is a conservationist and professor in the department of geosciences at Florida Atlantic University. She is American and lives in the US. She studies ethnobotany, which examines the relationship between people and plants. For more than 25 years, she has been working in the rainforests of Ecuador as well as in other countries such as Tanzania and Zimbabwe. Maria has been a TEDx speaker twice, where she talked about balance between humans and plants.

ALEC JACOBSON is a freelance photographer and writer from the US. Alec studied French and Anthropology at university before becoming a photographer. The main focus of his work is on human stories about natural resources and the environment. In 2015 and 2018, he received two grants from the National Geographic Society to record the effects of overfishing in Lake Victoria, the largest lake in Africa.

LESSON GOALS

- **READING** The main aim is for students to practise identifying and understanding cause and effect in an article and then use their critical thinking skills to distinguish between cause and correlation.
- **SPEAKING** The speaking aim is for students to discuss how to tackle loneliness in their school community.

READING

ABOUT THE TEXT

In recent years, there has been an increasing amount of public awareness about the damaging effects that loneliness can have on both our mental and physical health. Research shows that in 2018, more than nine million people in the UK were experiencing loneliness, which is around fifteen per cent of the country's population. This growing awareness has led to a growth in the number of initiatives designed to tackle loneliness and some governments have funded and supported such initiatives.

In the article, the writer introduces the topic of loneliness and its negative effects on people's health. Then the writer presents three innovative initiatives that are tackling the problem of loneliness: the HenPower project, the North London Cares charity and public gaming centres. The latter are businesses where people can come to play video games in a café-like environment. As people often play video games alone at home, the idea is to encourage these people to leave the house and spend time with other people at the public gaming centre.

1

- Direct students to the lesson title and elicit that the focus of this lesson is the topic of loneliness.
- Students read the questions and then collaborate with a partner to create a list of reasons why people might feel lonely and a list of things people could do to reduce loneliness.

5A You're not alone

LESSON GOALS

- Identify and understand cause and effect in an article
- Distinguish cause from correlation
- Discuss how to tackle loneliness

READING

1 Work in pairs. Discuss the questions.

1 What are some reasons why people might feel lonely?
2 What could people do to feel less lonely? Make a list of five things.

2 Read the article on page 61 quickly. Are any of your ideas from Exercise 1 mentioned? Which idea might be the most useful?

3 Complete the sentences with words from the article.

1 The article offers three __success stories__ showing how people are finding __solutions__ to the problem of loneliness.
2 Interacting with the animals brings __purpose__ to the lives of residents in homes for the elderly and gives them a chance to __connect__ with others.
3 Polly and Audrey don't find the difference in __age__ a problem because they have so much in __common__.
4 Gamers don't just know each other __online__; they get together __face-to-face__ in gaming centres too.

4 Match the beginnings of the sentences (1–5) with the endings (a–e).

1 Loneliness has a negative impact … a
2 It can also lead … c
3 The positive effects might not be due … e
4 Playing video games can result … d
5 Thanks to gaming centres, … b

a … on how people feel.
b … people can meet their online friends.
c … to poorer health.
d … in feeling more connected.
e … to the animals.

5 Read the sentences in Exercise 4 again. Underline the expressions that show cause and effect. Then look at the Reading skill box to check.

READING SKILL
Identifying and understanding cause and effect

There are a number of expressions that can help you identify and understand connections between effects and their causes.

To show effects: *have an impact/effect on, lead to, result in*

To show causes: *due to (the fact that), because (of), be caused by, one reason why is/was, thanks to*

6 Which part of the sentences in Exercise 4 is the cause (C)? Which is the effect (E)?

7 Work in pairs. Look at the Critical thinking skill box. Then read the article again and decide which sentences (1–3) show a correlation and which a probable cause.

CRITICAL THINKING SKILL
Distinguishing cause from correlation

Cause means that one event leads to another. Correlation means that two events happen at the same time but aren't necessarily caused by each other. To avoid confusing cause and correlation, ask:

How strong is the evidence that one thing causes the other?

What other possible causes could there be?

1 Looking after hens can have a positive impact on physical and mental health.
There's not much evidence for it in the article. Other causes might be …
2 Playing video games helps people make friends.
3 Older people in big cities feel isolated because they don't know their neighbours.

SPEAKING

8 Work in groups. Discuss ways to build your school community and avoid loneliness among the students. Use the questions to help you.

1 What are possible causes of loneliness?
2 What ideas for social activities might work in your school (e.g. coffee mornings, a film club)?
3 When and where would the activities be?

EXPLORE MORE!

Find out about projects that help tackle loneliness in your area and how you could take part.

Sample answers

1 They are living far from friends and family; they don't have many friends at work, school or university; they are in a foreign country and they don't speak the local language; they have recently split up from a partner; they find it difficult to get out to meet people.

2 Get to know your neighbours; get in touch with old friends and family; join a club; join a group that meets up to practise languages together; adopt a pet.

Extra activity

Conduct a class discussion on the reasons and possible solutions that students wrote on their lists. Try to reach a consensus about the five most common reasons for loneliness and the five best possible solutions. Students could also create a ranking of the possible solutions in terms of how effective they would be.

YOUR GOOD NEWS STORY OF THE DAY

Lonely people not so lonely any more

Loneliness can affect anyone and has a negative impact not only on how people feel, but it can also lead to poorer physical health. But it doesn't have to be that way! Organizations around the world are finding innovative ways to tackle the problem. Here are three success stories from around the world of people finding solutions for all ages.

(H)ENRICHING PEOPLE'S LIVES

Several projects in the UK, Australia and the Netherlands run by HenPower have been set up to tackle loneliness. Hens, female chickens, are brought to elderly homes, where the residents can feed them and look after them.

The interesting thing is that the positive effects might not be due to the animals themselves but because the project gives the residents a sense of purpose and allows them to connect with people around them while interacting with the animals.

Hen Roadshows bring the project into the community, with elderly volunteers, known as 'hensioners', sharing their knowledge with local schoolchildren and introducing them to their feathered friends.

One of the volunteers, 89-year-old Tommy Appleby, says: 'I wasn't sure about the hens at first, but when I think back now, I've never regretted it. I never miss a session. I've made some great friends through HenPower. What I like about it is that you're not entertained, you're involved.'

HenPower projects bring chickens to residents of homes for the elderly.

WHO CARES? YOUR NEIGHBOURS

North London Cares is a charity that has built a sense of community by bringing together young professionals and their older neighbours at regular social events and through one-to-one activities. They recognized that the rush and pace of the city can sometimes feel too much, and have helped many people who feel isolated. The group's founder, Alex Smith, says it's not just about befriending the older people, as the benefits are two-way, with the younger volunteers getting as much out of the interactions as the older participants.

Volunteer Polly says: 'I love visiting Audrey every week. We have a great, easy-going friendship. Just because there's an age gap doesn't mean we don't have lots in common. We both love the theatre and reading. We also listen to each other's problems (Audrey always has great advice) and most importantly we make each other laugh.'

REAL FRIENDS IN IMAGINARY WORLDS

Surprisingly, playing more video games can result in feeling more connected. So, if you're thinking 'Hold on, won't gaming in your bedroom make you even more lonely?', think again!

Playing more video games can actually result in feeling more connected. Some gamers don't feel accepted in the real world, so they look online where they can form friendships with like-minded people.

Thanks to gaming centres around the world, such as Frikiplaza in Mexico City, people can also meet their online friends face-to-face. Here, the isolation caused by feeling different from others disappears and they are safe to be themselves and feel accepted. Video games are just the starting point towards a sense of community and real-world relationships.

VOCABULARY NOTES

tackle /ˈtækl/ = to deal with or try to solve a problem

elderly home /ˈeld(ə)li həʊm/ = a place where older people live together and are cared for by staff

rush (n) /rʌʃ/ = a situation where people are moving towards a place quickly

founder /ˈfaʊndə(r)/ = a person who starts an organization or company

befriend /bɪˈfrend/ = to become friends

age gap /eɪdʒ gæp/ = a significant difference in the ages of two or more people

like-minded /ˈlaɪkˈmaɪndɪd/ = people with similar views and interests

2

- Students scan the text for reasons for loneliness and things that can be done to deal with loneliness.
- Students tick their reasons and solutions from Exercise 1 if they are mentioned in the article and make notes on any additional reasons or solutions from the text.
- Put students into pairs to review the ideas for reducing loneliness in their own list from Exercise 1 and the text, then decide which idea might be the most useful.

3

- Ask students to read the sentences and guess the missing words using their vocabulary knowledge and what they can remember from reading the article.
- Students skim the article to find the information they need to complete the sentences.

4

- Students match the sentence halves that summarize the content of the article.
- Advise students to think about which preposition can follow the word at the end of sentence halves 1–5 to help them complete the task.
- Students compare answers in pairs and then check answers as a class.
- **Optional step** Invite different students to read the completed sentences out loud in class.

5

- Direct students to the instructions and check understanding of 'expressions that show cause and effect' (words or phrases that are used to introduce either the reasons why things happen or the effects of things that happen).
- Students read the completed sentences from Exercise 4 again and identify the cause and effect expressions in them.
- Ask students to look at the Reading skill box and check their answers.

6

- Students look at the sentence halves in Exercise 4 and identify whether they contain a cause or an effect.
- Check answers in class and elicit that both the cause and the effect can either be in the first or the second half of a sentence. The order of the cause and effect in the sentence is determined by the expression used to connect them. For example, with expressions for an effect like 'lead to' the order is cause + effect, but with expressions for a cause, like 'due to', the sentence order is effect + cause.

Answers

(cause underlined, effect in italics)

1 Loneliness has a negative impact on *how people feel*.
2 It can also lead to *poorer health*.
3 *The positive effects* might not be due to the animals.
4 Playing video games can result in *feeling more connected*.
5 Thanks to gaming centres, *people can meet their online friends*.

Extra activity

Ask students to make a list of five things they have done so far today. These could be simple, everyday tasks like brushing their teeth. Students make notes on the reason why they did each activity (e.g. the fact that my teeth needed to be cleaned) and the effects of doing it (e.g. my teeth felt nice and clean). Then ask students to use the words and phrases in the Reading skill box to write a sentence about the cause and effect of each activity.

7

- Tell students to read the information in the Critical thinking skill box.
- Go through the first sentence in class. Identify the two events described in the sentence (1) looking after hens and (2) a positive impact on physical and mental health) and elicit that the article says that they happened at the same time.
- Students work in pairs to decide whether sentences 2 and 3 show a correlation or a probable cause.
- Check answers as a class.
- Students read the article again and answer the two questions in the Critical thinking skill box about each of the three sentences.

Sample answers

1 Correlation: The article says that the cause 'may not be due to the animals themselves', and therefore it's possible that any fun, communal activity would have the same positive effect.
2 Probable cause: Cause based on evidence of people playing online games at home, where you play with other people, and people who go to gaming centres. Allows people who struggle to fit in to 'form friendships with like-minded people'.
3 Probable cause: Effect may be caused by not knowing neighbours, although this is only one of many possible causes. Older people might not travel so far, so neighbours become increasingly significant in their lives.

SPEAKING

8

- Put students into small groups.
- Give students about ten minutes for their discussions.
- Tell students to refer back to their lists of possible reasons for loneliness and possible ways of reducing it from Exercise 1. These can form the basis for students' discussions, but remind them to adapt these ideas to fit with the specific context of building a school community.
- **Optional step** Students present their ideas. Have a class vote to decide on the best way of building a school community.

Extra activity

Tell students to imagine that they have read the article about loneliness in this lesson on a website that allows readers to leave comments. Ask them to write a comment to respond to the article, expressing their opinion about loneliness and the best ways to tackle it.

EXPLORE MORE!

Students can find information about local projects on social media, in posters or notices at local shopping centres or meeting places, or by talking to friends and family members who are familiar with the local area.

See **Workbook** pages 40–41 for extra practice.

LESSON GOALS

- **GRAMMAR** The main aim is for students to practise using conditionals to talk about present and future consequences of actions in the present as well as imaginary situations in the past and their consequences.
- **PRONUNCIATION** A sub-aim is for students to practise understanding elision in connected speech.
- **SPEAKING** The speaking aim is for students to practise using conditionals to create stories about consequences.

READING AND GRAMMAR

1

- Give students a minute to read the questions and think about their answers.
- Students discuss the questions in pairs for about three minutes. Ask students to give explanations and examples to support their answers.

2

- Students scan the infographic for the answers to items 1 and 2.
- Students decide which piece of information is important to them personally.

Answers

1 electric lights, distractions such as TV, LED and blue-light screens
2 take a warm bath or shower before bed, try the 4, 7, 8 breathing technique, squeeze and relax your muscles

VOCABULARY NOTES

retina /'retɪnə/ = a layer of cells sensitive to light at the back of the eyeball

optic nerve /'ɒptɪk nɜːv/ = a band of cells that sends impulses to the brain from the retina of the eye

artificially /ˌɑːtɪ'fɪʃ(ə)li/ = something that is made by humans rather than occurring naturally

tighten /'taɪt(e)n/ = the action you do to make the parts of something come closer together

3

- Ask students to look at the sentence halves. Elicit that 'unless' (in option a) means 'if not'.
- Students use what they can remember from reading the infographic to match the sentence halves.
- Students read the infographic again to check their answers.

4

- Elicit that the sentences that students completed in Exercise 3 are conditional sentences, or *if*-sentences.
- Ask students to read the questions. Check students' understanding of the word 'imaginary' (not real, existing only in the imagination).
- Tell students to use the overall meaning or context of the sentences in Exercise 3 as well as the grammatical words used in them (e.g. *will probably*) to match the sentences to the questions.
- Students compare answers in pairs and then check answers by reading the Grammar box.

Answers

1 Sentence 3: present tenses in both clauses.
2 Sentence 4: present tense in *if* clause, *will* in the main clause.
3 Sentences 1 and 2. Sentence 2 is talking about the past.

GRAMMAR NOTES

Conditionals

The most frequent mistake that students make with the conditional sentences is using the words *will/won't* and *would/wouldn't* in the *if*-clause of the sentence, particularly if this is possible in students' first language. For example:

If the eye won't receive enough blue light, the brain will find it difficult to wake up.

There may also be a reluctance to use the past simple in the *if*-clause of second conditional sentence (e.g. *If I had a million dollars, I would ...*) as this may seem counter intuitive when you are talking about present or future situations.

For further information and practice, see **Grammar reference Unit 5B** on page 145 of the Student's Book.

5

- Tell students to use the verb form in the complete clause and the type of situation the sentence describes (e.g. possible future situations) to help them choose the correct options.
- Students complete the sentences.
- Check answers as a class.

Extra activity 1

If students need more practise with the second conditional, play a game of *What would you do if ... ?* in pairs or groups. Write the following scenarios on the board and ask students to discuss what they would do in each one:

- *the person you live with did not do any housework*
- *you lost all of the notes you had spent weeks writing*
- *you got really nervous during a job interview*

Extra activity 2

If students need more practise with the third conditional, play a game of *What would you have done if … ?* in pairs or groups. Write the following scenarios on the board and ask students to discuss what they would do in each one:

- *it had rained while you were travelling home yesterday*
- *you'd woken up ten minutes late this morning*
- *you'd found a large amount of money while out walking last night*

For additional practice, refer to the **Grammar activity** on page 253 of the Teacher's Book.

PRONUNCIATION

6 5.1

- Tell students to read the information in the Clear voice box. Note that the main aim of this section is to develop students' receptive skills. The subsequent activities focus on listening rather than on producing this pronunciation feature themselves.
- Elicit that 'elision' is the term used for the 'squeezing' together of multiple words in fast speech that they have just read about.
- Students listen to a sentence where elision is used so they can hear what it sounds like. The specific section of the sentence where elision is used is then repeated twice so students can focus on trying to understand it.
- **Optional step** Ask students to say the sentence without elision.

5B The secrets of sleep

LESSON GOALS
- Read and understand an infographic about how to get a better night's sleep
- Talk about consequences using conditionals
- Understand elision in connected speech

READING AND GRAMMAR

1 Work in pairs. Discuss the questions.
1. How much sleep do you typically get each night? Do you think you get enough sleep?
2. What's the best night's sleep you've ever had?

2 Look at the infographic. Find …
1. three reasons we are not sleeping enough.
2. three tricks to help you get to sleep.
3. one piece of information that is important to you personally. Why?

3 Match the beginnings of the sentences (1–4) with the endings (a–d). Then look at the infographic again to check.

1 If we didn't have electric lights d	a … unless you have enough melatonin.
2 If I'd read my book instead of my e-reader, … c	b … you'll probably sleep better.
3 It can be hard to get to sleep … a	c … I would have been able to sleep.
4 If you have a shower every night at the same time, … b	d … we would have to go to bed earlier.

What makes us sleepy?

retina
Cells in the eye respond to blue light and set our body's internal clock, in time with day and night.

pineal gland
As blue light decreases, the brain releases melatonin, which tells the body to prepare for sleep.

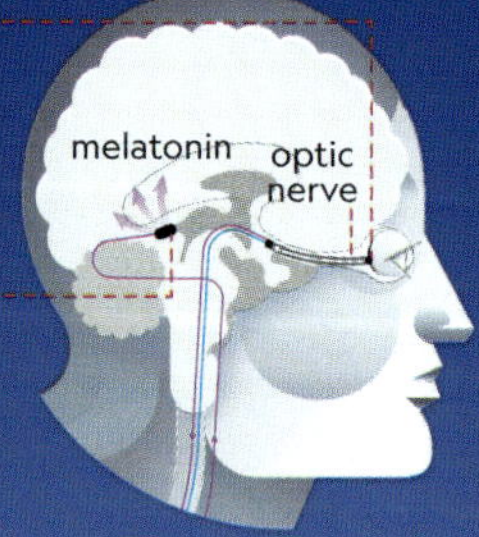

Not getting enough sleep?

We are sleeping two hours fewer each night than people did one hundred years ago. Why?
- electric light artificially extends the day
- all-night television and other distractions
- LED and blue-light screens (mobile phones, tablets)

Sleeping tips and tricks

Take a warm bath or shower before bed
The change in temperature when you step back into the cooler air helps prepare your body for sleep more quickly.

The 4, 7, 8 breathing technique
- Breathe in through your nose while counting to four.
- Hold your breath for a count of seven.
- Breathe out through your mouth for a count of eight.
- Repeat four times.

Squeeze and relax your muscles
Starting from your head down to your toes, tighten each muscle for five seconds and then relax it.

Sleep delay at night

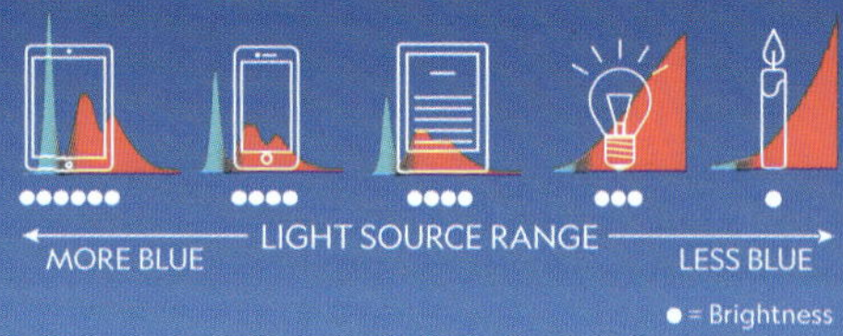

62

PRONUNCIATION NOTES

Elision

Tell students that it is common for first language users of English to use elision in casual conversation. It is therefore useful to be aware of the existence of elision and the effects it typically has on the speakers' pronunciation. However, students do not have to use elision themselves and, in fact, using it might make it more difficult for the people they communicate with to understand them.

Elision is used in many different languages, so students may also use it when they are speaking their first language. Ask students if elision is used in their first language and if they can think of any examples of it.

There are no rules about when to use elision in English, but the following types of words are often partially 'squeezed out' when words are 'squeezed' together in elision:

- auxiliary verbs – for example, *would have* is elided to *'d've*
- articles – for example, *I want an apple* is elided to *I want'n'apple*
- possessive pronouns – for example, the /h/ in *his* is elided in *he passed his exam*
- conjunctions – for example, *fish and chips* is elided to *fish 'n' chips*

7 5.2

- Play the audio so students can listen and complete the sentences with the elided words. Tell students that they can use contractions, such *as 'd* for *would*.
- Students compare answers in pairs. Then they practise saying the two sentences fast and with elision, then slowly and clearly. They tell their partner which version sounds better to them and which version they would find easier to pronounce.

4 Look at the sentences in Exercise 3 again and answer the questions (1–3). Then read the Grammar box to check your answers.

1 Which sentence describes a situation that is generally true? What verb form is used in each clause?
2 Which sentence describes a possible future situation? What verb forms are used?
3 Which sentences describe imaginary situations? Which of these is referring to the past?

GRAMMAR Conditionals

Present verb forms

Use **zero conditional** sentences to describe situations that are generally true.

If the eye doesn't receive enough blue light, the brain finds it difficult to wake up.

Use **first conditional** sentences to describe possible future situations.

You won't feel sleepy unless you turn off the light.

Past verb forms

Use **second conditional** sentences to describe imaginary present or future situations and their consequences.

Would we have more time if we didn't sleep?

Use **third conditional** sentences to describe imaginary situations in the past and their consequences.

He wouldn't have seen the sunrise if he hadn't woken up early.

Go to page 145 for the Grammar reference.

5 Choose the correct option to complete the sentences.

1 I'd be less grumpy if I *can* / *could* get more sleep!
2 I would *have stayed* / *stay* up late if I'd started watching that film.
3 I think if I *didn't try* / *hadn't tried* the 4, 7, 8 technique, I'd still be having sleep problems.
4 I'd never sleep on a long flight *if* / *unless* I didn't have my travel pillow.
5 You'll feel better if you *have* / *had* a nap.
6 It can be easy to feel stressed about not falling asleep *if* / *unless* you hide your clock!
7 If you *use* / *will use* a device with a lot of blue light at night, it *may* / *would* be harder to sleep.
8 If you *had* / *have* to look at your phone for long periods, you *can* / *will* use the 'Eye comfort' setting.

PRONUNCIATION

6 5.1 Look at the Clear voice box and listen to the example sentence.

CLEAR VOICE

Understanding elision in connected speech

In fast speech, multiple words are often 'squeezed' together so that it is difficult to hear them.

I'd've seen him yesterday if he'd come to work.

In this example, it's difficult to hear the first three words. Notice how the past participle *seen* helps you understand.

7 5.2 Listen and complete the sentences. Then practise saying the sentences fast like the speakers, then slowly and clearly. Which way do you prefer?

1 She'd have been fine if she'd managed to sleep on the train.
2 We'd have slept a lot more comfortably last night if the bed had been a bit bigger.

SPEAKING

8 Work in groups of three or four. Play 'Consequences'. Use these sentence beginnings and see how many sentences you can make. Each new sentence should follow on from the previous one.

1 If I hadn't forgotten to set my alarm, …
2 If I hadn't fallen asleep on the train, …
3 If it had been raining when I woke up this morning, …

A: If I hadn't forgotten to set my alarm last night, I wouldn't have got up so late.

B: If I hadn't got up so late, I …

9 Tell your 'consequences' as stories to the rest of the class. Which story is the longest? Which is the funniest?

I forgot to set my alarm, so I got up late and missed my train. That meant that I didn't get to the park on time and missed meeting my boyfriend …

EXPLORE MORE!

Search online for 'ways to improve your sleep'. Challenge yourself to get a better night's sleep by following some of the suggestions.

63

Extra activity

Say these sentences in class, using elision as shown. Tell students to listen and write the sentences they hear. Ask students to check answers in pairs and then confirm in class.

- *He passed his /passedis/ exam.*
- *I'd like fish and chips /fish 'n' chips/ for dinner.*
- *I'd have /I'd've/ done that for you if you'd have /you'd've/ asked me.*
- *It would have been /wouldabeen/ easier if I'd been prepared.*

For additional practice, refer to the **Pronunciation activity** on page 272 of the Teacher's Book.

SPEAKING

8

- Demonstrate how to play the game with two or three stronger students. For example, you say: *If I hadn't forgotten to set my alarm last night, I wouldn't have got up so late.* The first student says: *If I hadn't got up so late, I would have caught the bus to work.* Then the second student says: *If I had caught the bus to work, I would have got to work on time.* Then the third student: *If I had got to work on time, my boss would not have been angry with me.*
- **Optional step** The game can be adapted so that students pass round a piece of paper and take turns to write their consequences on it and continue the story.
- Put students into small groups. Tell them that the aim of this game is for students to work together to make conditional sentences to form a story.
- Students come up with their possible endings for each of the three stems. Tell students to refer back to the Grammar box to help them choose the correct verb forms if they need to.
- Encourage students to make their stories funny or entertaining if possible.
- Monitor students, offering corrections and feedback on their use of conditionals, where appropriate.

Sample answers

Suggested chain for first sentence: If I hadn't forgotten to set my alarm last night, I wouldn't have got up so late. If I hadn't got up so late, I would have caught the bus. If I'd caught the bus, I wouldn't have had to flag down a taxi. If I hadn't flagged down a taxi, I wouldn't have had to stand by the road in the rain. If I hadn't stood by the road, I wouldn't have been splashed by a passing car. If I hadn't been splashed by a car, I wouldn't have arrived at work in wet clothes. If I hadn't been in wet clothes, I wouldn't have caught a cold.

9

- Students take turns in their group to read their stories from Exercise 8.
- The rest of the class can give feedback on how entertaining and how long the stories were.
- **Optional step** Ask the class to vote on the best story.

EXPLORE MORE!

Suggest that students be selective with the tips they choose to put into practice, for example by only taking tips from websites they know or believe to be reputable and credible sources that do not have an explicit commercial motivation. Encourage students to think realistically in terms of the number and type of tips they are going to try.

For additional practice, refer to the **Communication activity** on page 220 of the Teacher's Book.

See **Workbook** pages 42–43 for extra practice.

LESSON GOALS

- **VOCABULARY** The main aim is for students to practise using vocabulary for talking about mental and physical health.
- **LISTENING** A further main aim is for students to listen to National Geographic explorers talking about mental and physical health and listen for keywords to understand the speakers' general meaning.
- **GRAMMAR** A sub-aim is for students to use *I wish* and *If only* to talk about things they would like to be true.

VOCABULARY

1

- Ask students to look at the photos carefully and identify the job (or type of job) they can see in each one.
- Students match the descriptions to the jobs and give reasons or examples to justify their choices. Encourage students to give examples from their experience, or the experience of people they know.
- **Optional step** Conduct a class discussion on how students would describe each job and try to reach a general consensus.

Sample answers
1 can be physically exhausting: B, C, D
2 are emotionally stressful: A, B
3 involve working nights: C, D
4 are dangerous: B
5 have stressful working conditions: B, C, D

Extra activity

Ask students to work with their partner to think of other jobs that would fit descriptions 1–5 in Exercise 1. After thinking about possible negative aspects of the jobs A–D (and the others that they have brainstormed), ask students to think of possible positive aspects for some or all of the jobs.

2

- Elicit that physical problems are problems with your body and mental problems are problems with your emotional well-being.

5C Fit for the job

LESSON GOALS
- Discuss mental and physical health
- Listen for keywords to understand general meaning
- Talk about things you'd like to be true using *I wish* and *If only*

A
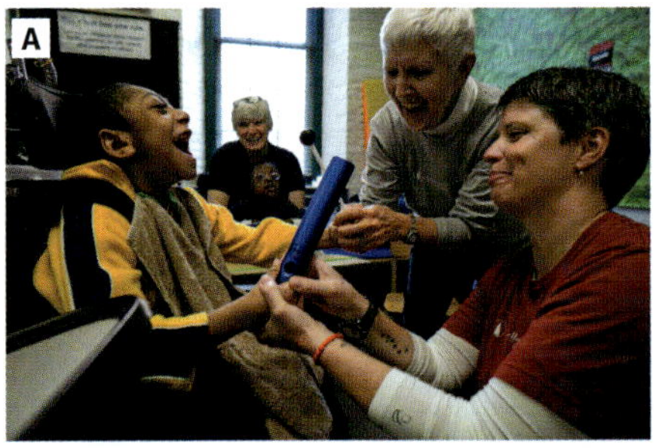

C

B

D

VOCABULARY

1 Work in pairs. Look at the photos. Which jobs …
1 can be physically exhausting?
2 are emotionally stressful?
3 involve working nights?
4 are dangerous?
5 have stressful working conditions?

2 Read the sentences. Are the problems described mainly physical (P) or mental (M)? What jobs do you think they might be talking about?
1 Those in competitive professions may find it hard to **cope with** the stress; many complain of **burn-out** at a young age.
2 My **symptoms** include feeling cold and a headache. I think I'm **coming down with** the flu. I probably got it from a customer.
3 Many workers suffer from **anxiety** and **depression**, just like their patients.
4 I have to **stay in shape**. If I wasn't, with all this physical work, I'd be **at risk** of serious injury.
5 This shift feels long. I haven't been able to **take a nap** yet. But there's no point **feeling sorry for yourself**. You just have to get on.
6 Normally it's me who covers classes when colleagues **call in sick**, but I'm off work at the moment. It's taking me ages to **get over** this cough.

3 Write five pieces of health advice using some of the phrases from Exercise 2. Then share your advice with a partner.
If you're coming down with a sore throat, you should drink hot water with honey and lemon.

Go to page 137 for the Vocabulary reference.

64

- Students read the sentences and then discuss and decide together whether they describe physical or mental problems, and identify the job(s) being described in each case. If students do not understand the meaning of any expressions in the problems, encourage them to deduce the meaning of the expression from the context it is used in.
- Check answers as a class.

Answers
1 M (e.g. high-powered city jobs, such as finance and law)
2 P (e.g. a shop assistant in a busy shop or a waiter)
3 M (e.g. social work, terminal patient care, other caring professions, especially involving mental health problems)
4 P (e.g. construction worker, tree surgeon, stunt performer)
5 P (shift work, e.g. nurse, doctor, taxi driver)
6 P (e.g. teacher)

3

- Ask students to read the sentences from Exercise 2 again and focus on the expressions in bold.
- Students can either write advice for the problems described in Exercise 2 – which may be a slightly easier option – or

LISTENING AND GRAMMAR

NATIONAL GEOGRAPHIC EXPLORERS

4 5.3 Look at the Listening skill box. Then listen to interviews with Alec Jacobson and Maria Fadiman. Answer the questions (1–3).

LISTENING SKILL
Listening for keywords to understand the general meaning

Listen for keywords related to the subject to help you work out the general meaning. Make sure you have heard at least two or three keywords to confirm your ideas. These might be …

- related by topic, e.g. *symptoms, sweaty, call in sick*.
- synonyms, e.g. *recover, get over it, get better*.

The keywords above suggest someone is ill and needs the day off to get better.

Be careful, you will hear some words that aren't important but could make you misunderstand.

A: *How are you feeling today?* B: *I'm* ***coping****,* but I've been ***better****, to be honest.*

In this example, Speaker B is saying that they feel ill, but Speaker A could misunderstand because they use positive words like *coping* and *better*.

1 Who discusses ways they look after their mental health at work?
2 Who talks about how they stay physically fit?
3 What words did you hear to help you decide the answers to questions 1 and 2?

5 5.3 Listen to the interviews again. Complete the notes with one to three words in each space.

Alec – likes running, cycling, [1]________ and skiing. Says you should do exercise that [2]________ e.g. enjoys running in the [3]________ but not interested in running on [4]________. At work, Alec doesn't have much [5]________ to look after himself, but he's learned that if you're [6]________, you can't tell the story.

Maria – finds not being able to express herself when she's abroad very [7]________. One way she copes is by [8]________, which helps her see the problem from [9]________. Writes letters to [10]________. Meditation is hard for her, but she enjoys [11]________.

6 Work in pairs. Discuss the questions.

1 Alec talks about having to balance work and relaxation. What advice would you give him?
2 Maria talks about the stress of using a foreign language. Do you ever feel the same way? Do you think her tips could work for you?

7 Read the sentences and answer the questions (1–2). Then read the Focus on box to check.

Alec: *I just wish I was able to sleep.*
Maria: *If only I'd discovered yoga before.*

1 Is Alec talking about the past or present? Is he able to sleep?
2 Is Maria talking about the past or present? When did she discover yoga?

FOCUS ON *I wish …* and *If only …*

Use *I wish …* or *If only …* to talk about something now or in the past that you want to be true.

I love my job, but ***I wish*** *it* ***wasn't*** *so stressful.*
If only I'd taken *a nap earlier.*

Use the past simple to talk about imaginary situations in the present. Use the past perfect to talk about imaginary situations in the past.

Go to page 146 for the Focus on reference.

8 Complete the second sentence in each pair to express disappointment about the information in the first sentence.

1 He went out in the rain and now he has a cold.
He wishes he hadn't gone out in the rain.
2 I can't go to my gym anymore because my ex-girlfriend has joined! If only ________.
3 I want to lose weight, but I can't stop eating biscuits in the evenings! I wish ________.

9 Imagine you are the people in the photos in Exercise 1. Write sentences with *If only* and *I wish* about how they feel about their jobs.
'I wish there were fewer patients!'

SPEAKING

10 Imagine you can have any job (real or invented). What would you choose to ensure you were the healthiest and happiest you could be? Share your idea with a partner.
I'd be a writer and work on a private island. I'd walk along the beach to think of ideas!

choose other examples of mental or physical problems if they prefer.

- Tell students to use at least one of the expressions in bold in each of their pieces of advice.
- Students share their advice with a partner.
- **Optional step** Students give their partner feedback on how useful their advice is and whether or not they have used the expressions accurately.

For further information and practice, see **Vocabulary reference Unit 5** on page 137 of the Student's Book.

For additional practice, refer to the **Vocabulary activity** on page 237 of the Teacher's Book.

LISTENING AND GRAMMAR

4 5.3

- Direct students to the Listening skill box. Tell students that the strategy it describes is useful when you are listening to people who are speaking very quickly, quietly or if the subject being discussed is particularly complicated.
- Ask students to read the questions before they listen.
- Play the audio so students can identify what each speaker talks about and make notes on the key words connected to each of the topics.
- Students share the key words they noted down with a partner.

Answers

1 (and 3) Maria talks about mental health (cope, frustrating, suffering from stress, stop feeling sorry for myself, get it out of my system, relax, anxiety, yoga, mind in a calm place); 2 (and 3) Alec talks about physical fitness (stay in shape, cycle, running, skiing, running machine, sleeping, taking a nap, call in sick)

VOCABULARY NOTES

(do something for something's) sake /seɪk/ = for this reason or purpose

get (something) out of (your) system /get 'sʌmθɪŋ aʊt ɒv jɔː 'sɪstəm/ = to get rid of a strong feeling or need to do something

meditate /'medɪteɪt/ = to make your mind empty of thoughts in order to relax

5 5.3

- Before they listen again, ask students to read both sets of notes and guess the missing words or phrases.
- Tell students that the words they need to complete the sentences are the key words they listened out for the first time they heard the interviews.
- Play the audio again so students can complete the notes.
- Students compare their answers in pairs before checking answers as a class.

Answers

1 (rock) climbing; 2 makes you happy / you like; 3 mountains; 4 (a) (running) machine(s); 5 time; 6 not healthy / unhealthy; 7 frustrating / exhausting / stressful; 8 writing; 9 the outside; 10 (her) family; 11 yoga

6

- Students read the questions and take a minute to think about their responses individually before discussing the questions in pairs.

Extra activity

Students choose one of the questions from Exercise 6 and use the advice they came up with to create a poster to present to another group or display in the classroom. Alternatively, they could use their advice to write a short blog post or advice column. Encourage students to create, find or plan visuals to accompany their poster or blog post. For both options, ask students to include some of the new vocabulary they have learned in this lesson.

7

- Ask students to read the sentences and try to remember the context in which they were used in the interviews.
- Ask students to answer the questions about the sentences without looking at the Focus on box yet.
- Students compare their answers in pairs and then read the Focus on box to check their answers.

Answers

1 Alec is talking about the present. He isn't able to sleep when he's on the road.
2 Maria is talking about the past. She wishes that she'd discovered yoga sooner.

For further information and practice, see **Focus on reference Unit 5C** on page 146 of the Student's Book.

8

- Tell students that they are now going to practise using *I wish* ... and *If only* ... in context.
- Ask students to read the first sentence and complete the second sentence so that it expresses disappointment. Students can refer back to the information in the Focus on box while doing this, if necessary.

Sample answers

1 (given); 2 If only my ex-girlfriend hadn't joined my gym! / If only I could still go to my gym!; 3 I wish I could stop eating biscuits in the evening.

GRAMMAR NOTES

I wish ... / If only ...

Students need to be aware that *I wish* ... and *If only* ... are only used to talk about imaginary situations. When they are using *I wish* ... and *If only* ... students need to know whether they are talking about an imaginary situation in the present or in the past because this will determine which tense they need to use. Students might find it confusing that the past simple is used to talk about imaginary present situations, for example, *I wish I had a more interesting job*. Remind students that past tenses are often used for imaginary situations and their consequences in English, for example the second conditional which is used to describe imaginary present or future situations and their consequences and where the past simple is used in the *if*-clause.

9

- Students look at the photos in Exercise 1 again and imagine what the people in them might wish for or what regrets they might have.
- Ask students to write at least one sentence with *I wish* ... or *If only* ... for each photo. Encourage them to also use the expressions they have learned (i.e. the expressions in bold in Exercise 2) where appropriate to consolidate their understanding of them.
- **Optional step** Less confident students could do this activity in pairs.

Sample answers

A: If only I had more time to spend helping each child.
B: I wish it wasn't so cold today!
C: I wish there were fewer patients! (given)
D: If only the shifts were shorter.

For additional practice, refer to the **Focus on activity** on page 254 of the Teacher's Book.

SPEAKING

10

- Students choose a job that they would really like to do. If they choose 'writer', they should not use the same context used in the model answer.
- Give students about two minutes to think about and make notes on what they would do to ensure they remain healthy and happy. Remind students to consider both their physical and mental health.
- Students share their ideas in pairs, using the model answer as a guide to help them.
- **Optional step** Students draw or find images to illustrate the job they chose in Exercise 10 and use these to present their ideal job in pairs or in a group.

Extra activity

Students expand on their ideas about their dream job in Exercise 10 by making sentences with *I wish* ... and *If only* .... Write on the board or say the following example:

- Student's original idea (the idea is given in Exercise 10): *I'd be a writer and work on a private island. I'd walk along the beach to think of ideas!*
- Can be expanded on by making this sentence with *If only* ...: *If only I was rich and could buy my own island!*
- Can also be expanded further by making this sentence with *I wish* ...: *I wish I'd studied creative writing!*

See **Workbook** pages 44–46 for extra practice.

LESSON GOALS

- **SPEAKING** This lesson integrates speaking and listening. Its main aim is to raise students' awareness of how they can adapt their language to be more easily understood, particularly when speaking with people who have a lower level of English competence. Students are given strategies to help them simplify their own language, as well as to recognize problems of understanding between other people and help resolve the issue. The lesson ends with a roleplay where students take turns to practise helping two speakers understand each other.

LISTENING

1

- Ask students to read the questions and give them about a minute to think about their answers.
- Encourage students to consider how easy they think it is for other people to understand them when they speak their first language or other languages. For example, do they speak very quickly or use a lot of idioms? Remind students that 'being easy to understand' does not mean not making any mistakes when they speak in a language that is not their first language or having an accent like a first language user would have.
- Students discuss the questions in pairs.

2 5.4

- Play the audio so students can make notes on questions 1 and 2.
- Students compare their answers to questions 1 and 2 in pairs, then discuss question 3 with their partner.

Answers

1 A doctor is talking to her patient. The doctor is asking questions, but the patient is having difficulty understanding.
2 The patient understands some of what the doctor says, but only by guessing (when she tells her 'I have this pain in my foot') or after repeated attempts at asking. The reason is that the doctor uses fast, complicated English that the patient doesn't understand.

VOCABULARY NOTES

precise /prɪ'saɪs/ = exact, specific

elaborate (v) /ɪ'læbəreɪt/ = to give more detailed information about something

acute /ə'kjuːt/ = serious, extreme

ache /eɪk/ = a continuous feeling of low-level pain

flesh out (the details) /flɛʃ aʊt/ = to give more information about something

pinpoint /'pɪnpɔɪnt/ = to identify a specific thing or place

whereabouts /'weərəbaʊts/ = in roughly which place/area

Extra activity

Encourage students to view misunderstandings as a common and normal part of international communication by telling an anecdote about a misunderstanding that you have experienced. Invite different students to share anecdotes of situations where they have experienced a misunderstanding.

3

- Ask students to use their experience of communicating in another language and their general knowledge of communication to think of suggestions for avoiding the specific misunderstanding they heard in the audio.
- Students share and discuss their ideas in pairs.
- **Optional step** Write students' tips for avoiding misunderstandings on the board.

MY VOICE

COMMUNICATION SKILL NOTES

At Upper Intermediate level, students will naturally be keen to demonstrate how much English they have learned. However, they should also remember that they are likely to come into contact with people who have a lower level of English than them. Making sure that the person you are talking to understands what you are saying is the most important part of communication. In English, their first language and any other languages they know, being able to adapt what they are saying to be more easily understood by their listener is a key skill for students to develop.
The lesson gives students advice on how to simplify their vocabulary, sentence structure and pronunciation to be more accessible to someone who may otherwise struggle to understand them. The lesson will also help students develop their mediation skills by helping them recognize problems of understanding between other people. They will practise acting as an intermediary by simplifying and explaining the message that someone is trying to communicate.

4 5.2

- Before students watch the video, have a general discussion of their answers to the questions without looking at the Communication skill box.
- Play the video and ask students to make notes on the answers to the questions.
- **Optional step** Ask students to consider and share with their partner whether the contents of the video changed their original answers to the questions and, if so, how.

Answers

1 Because your level of English may be higher than the other person; because you have specialist knowledge that needs simplifying; because your English is a different variety and has some different vocabulary

2 You can avoid: above-level words, informal language such as phrasal verbs, overly complicated structures; you can slow down and use fewer words; you can be patient and give more time to listen to the listener and how they respond to you
3 You can help others communicate by listening to the message and simplifying it for the listener.

5

- Ask students to read the Communication skill box and check their answers to Exercise 4.

6

- Ask students to read the situations.
- Students use their experience of communicating in English and their knowledge of English vocabulary to identify expressions that might be difficult for a listener to understand (if their first language is not English). Remind students that they learned the expressions *take a nap* and *come down with (something)* in Lesson 5C.
- Using the first section of the model answer for item 1 to help them, students work in pairs to rewrite the situations so that they are easier to understand.

Answers

Underlined phrases likely to be misunderstood. Suggested rephrases: 1 OK, so whereabouts in the US are you heading to? → She wants to know where in the US you are going? 2 You sound like you're coming down with a cold. Do you want to leave early? → He says he thinks you're starting to have a cold. 3 I'm exhausted after that meal! Need to take a nap if you don't mind. → She says she's very tired, and she needs a short sleep. Is that OK? 4 The problem is the very long sentence structure → Can you please do the presentation instead of me?

PRONUNCIATION

7 5.5

- Ask students to read the information in the Clear voice box.
- Tell students that they will hear sentences that include one of the two words in each pair.
- Play the audio so students can underline the words they hear.

5D Being understood

LESSON GOALS
- Adapt language to be easier to understand
- Make vowel sounds longer before voiced consonants
- Help others be understood

LISTENING

1 Work in pairs. Discuss the questions.
1 Do you think you are easy to understand in English? What about when you speak your first language? Why?
2 Who do you find difficult to understand? Why?
3 How do you feel when you can't understand someone? What about when someone can't understand you?
4 What do you do, or could you do, in these situations?

2 5.4 Listen to the conversation. Then answer the questions.
1 Who is speaking? What problem does the second speaker have?
2 Do the speakers understand each other? Why? / Why not?
3 Have you ever been in a similar situation? What happened?

3 Work in pairs. How could both speakers in Exercise 2 have made the communication easier to understand?

66

8

- Students take turns to read the sentences in Exercise 7 to their partner, saying one of the words in italics in each sentence.
- Ask students to follow the advice in the Clear voice box to make the vowel sound in their word longer if it finishes with a voiced consonant, so it is easier for their partner to understand it.

See **Workbook** page 47 (Pronunciation) for extra practice.

LISTENING

9 5.6

- **Optional step** Before students listen to the audio, ask them to brainstorm – either individually or in pairs – what the nurse might do to help the patient understand what the doctor says. Tell them to use what they have learned so far in this lesson and their experience of communicating in different languages to help them do this. They could also predict which of the doctor's words the nurse might simplify for the patient, and how they might do this.

MY VOICE ▶

4 ▶ 5.2 Watch the video about adapting your English. Answer the questions.

1 Why is it sometimes necessary to adapt the way you speak English?
2 What are the main ways that you can adapt your English?
3 How can you help others to be better understood?

5 Look at the Communication skill box and check your answers to Exercise 4.

COMMUNICATION SKILL
Adapting your English to be understood

Simplify your language
- Avoid informal or complex vocabulary, complicated structures, long sentences.
- Speak slowly and clearly, using fewer words.

Listen to the listener!
Be patient and allow them to express themselves – if they are trying to tell you something, it is probably important!

Recognize problems of understanding between others
As a strong communicator, you are able to 'translate' complicated messages and simplify them for others.

Adapt to other languages
If you speak other languages, you may be able to switch to another language the other person knows to explain or to translate a word.

6 Work in pairs. Read the situations. Which expressions might be difficult for the listener to understand? Write a clearer version for them.

1 A passport control officer says to a visiting tourist: 'OK, so whereabouts in the US are you heading to?'
She wants to know where ...
2 In class the teacher says to a student: 'You sound like you're coming down with a cold. Do you want to leave early?'
3 After dinner, to the host: 'I'm exhausted after that meal! Need to take a nap if you don't mind.'
4 To a colleague in an office abroad: 'Something I've been meaning to ask you but, you know, just kind of wasn't sure whether you'd be up for it, is if there might be any chance you could potentially do this presentation instead of me.'

PRONUNCIATION

7 5.5 Look at the Clear voice box. Then listen to the sentences (1–5). Underline the word you hear.

CLEAR VOICE
Making vowels longer before voiced consonants

Some words, such as *back* and *bag*, may sound very similar. To pronounce the difference between them clearly, make the vowel longer when it is followed by a voiced consonant (b, g, d, v). This also lets you pronounce the final consonant more easily and helps you avoid being misunderstood.

1 It's my <u>back</u> / *bag*!
2 Is that your <u>food</u> / *foot*?
3 He *hid* / <u>hit</u> it with his hat.
4 Do you have it <u>saved</u> / *safe*?
5 Take a *seed* / <u>seat</u>.

8 Work in pairs. Take turns to practise saying the sentences in Exercise 7. Decide which word your partner is saying.

LISTENING

9 5.6 Listen to a continuation of the conversation from Exercise 2. How does the nurse help the patient understand what the doctor says?

10 5.6 Listen to the conversation again. Write down what the nurse says to explain the doctor's words (1–5). What word from another language does he use?

1 elaborate on the type of pain
2 an acute pain
3 pinpoint whereabouts in the foot precisely
4 experiences the pain
5 get it X-rayed ASAP

SPEAKING

11 **OWN IT!** Work in groups of three. Look at the role cards on page 156. Act out the roleplay three times, changing roles each time.

67

- Play the audio so students can listen and identify what the nurse does.
- Check answers as a class.

Answers
The nurse simplifies what the doctor is saying so that the patient can understand.

10 5.6
- Ask students to read the list of expressions the doctor uses and try to remember how the nurse simplified them from the first time they listened.
- Play the audio again so students can write down the simplified versions of the things the doctor says and the word from another language that the nurse uses.

Answers
1 tell the doctor what pain you feel
2 sudden, quick pain
3 where in your foot
4 have the pain
5 take a picture of your foot now
The nurse uses the Spanish word *agudo*.

Extra activity
Ask students to discuss – either in pairs or in small groups – the differences they notice between the language the nurse uses and the language the doctor uses, for example, the length of the words they use, the verb tenses they use, whether they use more formal vocabulary (e.g. 'precisely') or simpler vocabulary (e.g. 'take a picture').

SPEAKING

11 OWN IT!
- Put students into groups of three and direct them to the role cards on page 156 (page 205 in the Teacher's Book). Give students one or two minutes to read their role cards and check the meaning of any new words in the box.
- **Optional step** Before students begin the roleplay, brainstorm some phrases that the nurse could use to identify a misunderstanding, fix a misunderstanding and confirm understanding, and also phrases that the patient could use to show he/she does not understand. If students need a reminder of possible phrases, refer them back to the Useful language box in Lesson 3D. Write the phrases (e.g. *in other words*, *I'm not following*, *that makes sense*) on the board and elicit which person in the roleplay might need to use each phrase.
- Brainstorm some synonyms to the words in the box that the nurse could use to simplify them when she is talking to the patient.
- Students act out the roleplay three times, changing roles each time.

Extra activity
In pairs or small groups, students discuss any situations where they have had to act as an intermediary between two (or more) people where one party struggled to understand the other. Ask them to describe: the situation, what the problem was, what they did to help, how comfortable they felt being the person solving the problem (i.e. were they happy to do it or did they feel awkward) and why, and how they would feel in that situation now after having done this lesson. If students have had no experience of this, ask them to brainstorm situations where this could happen and how comfortable they would feel acting as an intermediary having completed this lesson.

For additional practice, refer to the **Communication activity** on page 221 of the Teacher's Book.

LESSON GOALS

- **WRITING** The aim of the lesson is to guide students to produce a 'for and against' essay with an engaging introduction. The reading text provides a model. Students practise using discourse markers to create a coherent essay.

SPEAKING

ABOUT THE PHOTO

The Rijksmuseum in Amsterdam has a collection of paintings by the Dutch artist Rembrandt (1606–1669). The painting in the photo is Rembrandt's work *The Night Watch*. This photo went viral. People felt it reflected the problems caused by teenagers having constant access to the internet. However, the fact that the pupils are working in groups suggests that they were in fact working collaboratively on a school task.

1

- Ask students to look at the photo and read the comments.
- In pairs, students decide which comment they agree with and why.

READING FOR WRITING

2

- Briefly explain that this is a title for an opinion essay, which is an essay where you are given a statement and you express whether you agree or disagree with it and why.
- Students discuss the questions with a partner.

Sample answers

1 Phones provide a quick way to find information; they help us keep in touch with people; they help us learn important skills such as online communication and critical thinking
2 They distract us from work and other areas of life; they discourage physical activity; they give young people constant, largely unsupervised access to the internet where they can be bullied, access inappropriate content, etc.

5E A matter of public health

LESSON GOALS
- Use discourse markers to organize your ideas
- Write an engaging essay introduction
- Write a 'for and against' essay

Students at the Rijksmuseum, Amsterdam.

SPEAKING

1 Work in pairs. Look at the photo and read the social media comments. Which comment do you agree with?

> **Chris Itchingham**
> @ChrisItchingham
>
> I'm not surprised this photo of #Rembrandt's #NightWatch has gone viral. It's the perfect image to explain the problems of our time.
>
> **Marky Mark Maker**
> @MarkyMarkMaker
>
> Replying to @ChrisItchingham
>
> It's quite clear it's a school trip and these kids are all doing schoolwork, looking up info on their phones.

READING FOR WRITING

2 Read the essay title and discuss the questions.

There should be a minimum age limit on mobile phones so that young people do not suffer the dangers of owning them.

1 What are the benefits of owning a mobile phone?
2 What are the dangers?
3 Do you think young people are particularly at risk from these dangers? Why? / Why not?
4 Do you agree that there should be a minimum age limit on mobile phones? Why? / Why not?

3 Read the essay on page 69. Answer the questions.

1 Are any of your ideas from Exercise 2 mentioned?
2 What is the writer's overall opinion: are they for or against the statement in the essay title?

4 Look at the Writing skill box. Then underline all the discourse markers you can find in the essay. Match them with the categories in the Writing skill box.

68

3

- Students scan the essay for their ideas from Exercise 2.
- Students then read the essay to get a general idea of the writer's opinion and discuss what they have found in pairs.

Answers

2 The writer disagrees with the statement.

4

- Students read the Writing skill box and complete the tasks.

Answers

(introduce supporting ideas) – What is more… Moreover, In addition, … as well as…; (introduce reasons) – because of, on the one hand, since; (indicate opposing ideas) – however, Although, On the other hand, … Nevertheless,; (conclude) – To sum up, …

Extra activity

Tell students to look at the essay again and identify the purpose of each paragraph (i.e. to introduce the essay, to present the dangers, to present the benefits, to conclude the essay).

WRITING SKILL
Using discourse markers

In an essay, make sure you guide the reader through your arguments with discourse markers …

- to introduce more supporting ideas. *In addition, … , Furthermore, … , as well as, … , Secondly, …*
- to introduce reasons. *because … , due to …*
- to indicate opposing ideas. *However, … , On the other hand, …*
- to conclude. *In conclusion … , On the whole … , Personally, I believe that …*

WRITING TASK

5 Choose one of the essay titles (1–3). Make a list of reasons for and against the statement and decide which side you agree with. Then discuss with a partner. Can you add any other reasons?

1 Schools should teach students how to look after their mental health.
2 Vegetarianism is a healthier diet, so governments should tax meat.
3 Employers should provide space for workers to do exercise.

6 Look at the Useful language box. Match the expressions for essay introductions with the categories (1–4). Which expression could you use in your introduction?

Useful language Essay introductions

Many people think that …
It is commonly believed that …
There is no doubt that …
It is certainly true that …
Recently, there has been greater awareness of …
Is it the case that …?

1 State a fact about the topic.
2 State a common opinion about the topic.
3 Ask a question about the topic.
4 Describe changes that make the topic relevant.

7 WRITE Write your essay. Use the Writing skill box and Useful language to help you.

8 CHECK Use the checklist. I have …

- ☐ divided the essay into at least four paragraphs.
- ☐ begun the essay in an engaging way.
- ☐ used discourse markers to help the reader follow the argument.
- ☐ clearly stated my opinion in the conclusion.

9 REVIEW Exchange essays with a partner. Use the checklist in Exercise 8 to review their writing. What other arguments for and against the statement could they have mentioned?

Go to page 132 for the Reflect and review.

Mobile phones have become an essential tool for people of all ages. Over the last fifteen years, however, we have become more aware of the dangers of mobile phones. These include time wasting, addiction and poor sleep quality because of using phones too much. The question is whether people are right to be worried that young people are at risk.

On the one hand, it's true that some young people are suffering more than ever from anxiety and depression. Problems like loneliness and lack of sleep are also increasing amongst teenagers. What is more, young people are undoubtedly spending less time keeping fit outdoors if they are on their devices. Although it is true mobile phones distract us all from essential routines such as work, sleep and exercise, it may be that young people are simply less able to control their behaviour. If this is the case, it could be argued that they are at greater risk from the dangers of mobile phones.

On the other hand, we must recognize the usefulness of these devices for teenagers, who use them for study purposes. Moreover, it is not clear whether problems such as anxiety are due to mobile phone use or other reasons. In addition, since teenagers are not the only group suffering from mental disorders, we might, in fact, need to limit everyone from using these devices.

To sum up, stopping young people from owning mobile phones may not be the answer. Instead, we need to educate everyone – young people and adults – about the harm that mobile technology can cause, as well as teach people how to cope with mental health problems. Nevertheless, decisions about letting each teenager use a mobile phone should remain with their parents.

WRITING TASK

5

- Encourage students to choose an essay title related to a topic that they are interested in and, if possible, have some prior knowledge of.
- Give students about five minutes to think about and make a list of arguments for and against and decide which side they agree with.
- Students discuss their reasons with a partner and try to add other reasons.

Sample answers

1 FOR – increase in mental health issues, especially in young people; good mental health helps students study better
AGAINST – it should be the responsibility of parents, not schools; mental health is a complex issue, so difficult to train teachers to teach it well
2 FOR – eating meat not good for the environment; eating meat can lead to high blood pressure and heart disease
AGAINST – people should have a choice about what to eat; tax can have the greatest impact on the poor
3 FOR – convenient for employees (don't have to go somewhere else to exercise); good way to clear mind and be more productive/creative afterwards
AGAINST – cost for the employer; additional space for the facilities needed

6

- Students match the expressions in the Useful language box with the categories and then check answers in pairs.
- Students decide which expression they could use in their essay introduction.

Answers

1 There is no doubt that … It is certainly true that …
2 Many people think that … It is commonly believed that …
3 Is it the case that … ?
4 Recently, there has been greater awareness of …

7 WRITE

- Ask students to concentrate on how they can divide the content of their essay into paragraphs and use discourse markers to guide the reader through them.
- Students write the first draft of their essays.

8 CHECK

- Ask students use the checklist and then make changes to their essays if necessary.

9 REVIEW

- Students exchange essays with a partner. Ensure students work with a different partner to the one they made a list of arguments with in Exercise 5.
- Students read each other's essays and use the checklist from Exercise 8 to review them.
- Students then read their partner's essay again and focus on identifying the arguments their partner made in the essay.
- Students give each other feedback on their essays and suggest other arguments their partner could have made.

For additional practice, refer to the **Mediation activity** on page 287 of the Teacher's Book.

For **Unit 5 Reflect and review**, see Student's Book page 132.

See **Workbook** page 47 for extra practice.

VIDEO 5.1

Maria: *I'm pretty healthy, I think. I like going for a run. I know a lot of people do running to stay in shape, but for me it's not just about physical fitness – it's also about clearing my mind. When I'm feeling stressed out, going for a run really helps. Or if I don't have time to do that, even a short walk helps. Doing exercise in the morning helps me prepare for the day. It gives me an energy boost. So yeah, your body, what you do with it, can definitely influence your mind and how you feel.*

Alec: *I really love being outdoors, so anything that gets me into a forest or up a mountain is great. That's why I love my job so much. And yes, I'm quite sporty, but my favourite exercise has to be something outdoors. I'm not into team sports or competitive sports. I'd rather go for a run in the hills! Keeping fit isn't an end in itself, it's a means of being part of nature and maintaining a positive attitude.*

AUDIO 5.1

I'd've seen him yesterday if he'd come to work.

'I'd've seen … I'd've seen'

AUDIO 5.2

1 She'd've been fine if she'd managed to sleep on the train.

2 We'd've slept a lot more comfortably last night if the bed'd been a bit bigger.

AUDIO 5.3

Alec Jacobson

Interviewer: *So Alec, what do you do to stay in shape?*

Alec: *I run, road cycle, mountain bike and do some rock climbing and skiing. There's a lot of pressure for people to go to a gym, but I think just find whatever it is you like to do and do that. I don't like running for running's sake, but I like to run in the mountains a lot, where I don't see anybody else for hours. If only a running machine is available, that doesn't make me as happy.*

Interviewer: *I know you're out on the road a lot and you're very busy. How do you manage not to burn out when you're working?*

Alec: *Well, a big challenge is having a limited amount of time. And so I feel like I should be out taking photos or interviewing all the time. It's really easy to get into the habit of working too much and not sleeping enough. But I'm learning to recognize when to push and when to stop. I just wish I was able to sleep when I'm on the road, but I've never been able to take naps in cars or planes or whatever. Years ago, I did a class for journalists. And one of the tips was: if you are not healthy, you can't tell the story. So if you don't get sleep, the next day you can't get the story you need to tell. It's not like you can call in sick, you know?*

Maria Fadiman

Interviewer: *How do you cope with being away from home for long periods?*

Maria: *When I'm in a place where I don't speak the language, there are times when everything is just so different, I feel like I can't express myself. And it's so frustrating when I just want to be able to say what I want to say. And I want to understand everyone else. And I'm trying so hard to do the right thing and to be respectful and not mess up. And it's just so exhausting … I'm basically suffering from stress. And so a way that I learned to cope with this was through writing.*

Interviewer: *Really? How does writing help?*

Maria: *When I'm writing, I can see it from the outside for just a moment, so I can stop feeling sorry for myself. And it also lets me say exactly what I want to say. Sometimes I just want to shout 'Leave me alone!' which I would never say out loud, but I can write it in big, angry capitals. And that way I get it out of my system. And by talking about it in letters to my family, it also helps me understand where I am better and that lets me just kind of relax a little bit.*

Interviewer: *And is there anything else that you do to reduce the anxiety?*

Maria: *People have suggested I meditate, and I have tried it, but it's hard for me. But yoga is something I've added into my life. And that is huge for me. I walk out of there with my mind in a calm space. That is not usually how I am, my mind just jumps around. If only I'd discovered it before!*

AUDIO 5.4

Doctor: *How can I help you?*

Patient: *Ehm, I have this pain in my foot.*

Doctor: *OK, I was wondering if you could perhaps be slightly more precise than that.*

Patient: *…*

Doctor: *Could you maybe elaborate a little bit more as to specifically what kind of pain you're experiencing? Is the pain acute, or more of an ache?*

Patient: *You mean how the pain feels?*

Doctor: *Yes, exactly, if you could be a bit more specific, that would be great. Is it very acute for example?*

Patient: *Ehm, I'm not sure to be honest …*

Doctor: *Well, you'll need to definitely flesh out the details here for me if I'm to help you. If not the type of pain, do you mind perhaps pinpointing for me precisely whereabouts in your foot you're feeling the pain?*

Patient: *Ehm …*

VIDEO 5.2

I'm sure you've been in situations where you just couldn't understand what someone was saying or when they couldn't understand you. And in a world where more and more people use English, the chances of misunderstanding become even higher.

Interestingly, it is often advanced speakers who might be difficult to understand, especially if they don't know how to be clear to lower level speakers. Being a stronger speaker of English yourself, you might speak to people whose English is on a lower level than yours. So, in order to be understood, you may need to adapt the way you speak.

Often, it's not how you are speaking but what you're saying. We all speak regional varieties of English – Singaporean English, American English and so on. We need to be aware that some ways of speaking, like informal words, don't travel very far, so we might need to use language that is more familiar globally.

There can also be a lot of specialized vocabulary that is used when the subject is complex, such as at the doctor's and in professions like information technology and the academic world.

Let's look at an example of the kind of language to avoid and how to do it. In the audio you heard, the doctor said this: '... you'll need to definitely flesh out the details here for me if I'm to help you. If not the type of pain, do you mind perhaps pinpointing for me precisely whereabouts in your foot you're feeling the pain?'

We can see here that some informal words, especially phrasal verbs, can cause problems. 'Flesh out' means 'give details'. The doctor would be easier to understand if she just said 'You need to give me details'.

Notice the long, indirect structure too. The doctor says 'do you mind perhaps …?', but she could have simply said: 'Where in your foot is the pain?'

So the advice here is this: keep it short and direct.

It is also important to adapt your pronunciation. The doctor speaks very quickly. This makes it more difficult for the patient to understand.

Now let's listen to how much time the doctor gives to the patient.

***Doctor:** Is it very acute, for example?*

***Patient:** Ehm, I'm not sure, to be honest.*

***Doctor:** Well, you'll need to definitely flesh out the details here for me.*

Communication is a two-way process, so another key to being understood is to give your listener a chance to respond, to show if they understand, and to explain what they don't understand. Without this information you won't know how to clarify.

There are times when your ability to communicate clearly will be useful for other people. Imagine you go to the doctor with an elderly relative whose hearing is not so good, or who gets confused. Your job is to listen to the doctor and pass that information to your relative in a way that is easier for them to understand.

The key is to think about the listener and what information they really need. You may need to simplify words and explain concepts for them too.

In the end, adapting your English in order to be understood is about recognizing communication difficulties and responding to them, whether it is you or others who need to get the ideas across.

AUDIO 5.5

1 It's my back!

2 Is that your food?

3 He hit it with his hat.

4 Do you have it saved?

5 Take a seat.

AUDIO 5.6

***Doctor:** So good that you're here, Zhang. I've been trying to explain to the patient that I need her to elaborate on the type of pain she's feeling, but we don't seem to be getting anywhere …*

***Nurse:** Would you like me to help?*

***Doctor:** Yes, please.*

***Nurse:** Hello, can you tell the doctor what pain you feel in your foot?*

***Patient:** Oh, OK, sure. Ehm, it's strong when I walk.*

***Doctor:** Can you ask her if it's an acute pain?*

***Nurse:** Is it a very sudden, quick pain?*

***Patient:** I think it is very quick. When I put my foot down, I can feel it suddenly. And then it quickly goes.*

***Nurse:** If I remember right from my Spanish classes, the pain is agudo, right?*

***Patient:** Sí, it's agudo!*

***Doctor:** OK, so it's an acute pain. Can you ask her to pinpoint whereabouts in the foot precisely she experiences the pain?*

***Nurse:** The doctor wants to know where in your foot you have the pain.*

***Patient:** It's right here, at the bottom, close to my toes.*

***Doctor:** OK, we might need to get it X-rayed ASAP to get a better idea of what's going on.*

***Nurse:** We will need to take a picture of your foot now. We want to know what the problem is.*

***Patient:** Sure.*

UNIT 6

Breaking news

UNIT GOALS

6A Reading, speaking

- read an article about fake online content and practise identifying unsupported claims; learn strategies for fact-checking information online; verbally spread news around the class

6B Listening and grammar, pronunciation, speaking

- listen to and understand a news bulletin; practise using passive structures to report events in the news; practise pronouncing consonant groups in past participles; prepare and give a two-minute radio news bulletin

6C Listening, vocabulary, pronunciation, grammar, speaking

- learn collocations for talking about the news; listen to National Geographic explorers talking about how they get their news and practise understanding catenation in connected speech; practise pronouncing long vowel sounds; practise using the structure *the* + comparative ..., *the* + comparative; roleplay a meeting between the editors of a newspaper

6D Speaking and listening

- learn about influencing and different influencing styles; practise influencing other students during a roleplay about proposing ideas for a group project

6E Writing

- learn to recognize formal and informal article styles; use appropriate language for different article styles; write a news article

Astronauts Christina Koch and Jessica Meir replace a broken machine during a seven-hour spacewalk, 18th October 2019.

70

Photocopiable resources

Communication activities: pp. 222–223
Vocabulary activity: p. 238
Grammar activity: p. 255
Focus on ... activity: p. 256
Pronunciation activity: p. 273
Mediation activity: p. 288

Workbook

Unit 6 pp. 48–55

ABOUT THE PHOTO

The photo shows two astronauts at the International Space Station (ISS) during a seven-hour spacewalk in 2019. This spacewalk made headlines because it was the first ever spacewalk where both of the astronauts involved – electrical engineer Christina Koch and marine biologist Jessica Meir – were female.

6

Breaking news

GOALS

- Identify unsupported claims in an article
- Report news using passive structures
- Understand catenation in connected speech
- Talk about the news
- Practise influencing others
- Write a news article

1 Work in pairs. Discuss the questions.

1. Look at the photo. What news story do you think it shows?
2. What have been some of the biggest news stories for you personally? Why were they important?
3. If you could interview one of the people in these stories, what would you ask them?

WATCH

2 ▶ 6.1 Watch the video. Answer the questions.

NATIONAL GEOGRAPHIC EXPLORERS

1. What sort of news do Afroz and Imogen normally find the most interesting?
2. Which two stories does Afroz mention? How did they make him feel?
3. Why did Imogen enjoy following the London Summer Olympic Games in 2012?

3 Make connections. What sort of news do you find the most interesting? What sort do you dislike? Why?

71

1

- Tell students to look carefully at the photo and caption, then read the questions.
- Give students about a minute to think about their answers to the questions.
- In pairs, students discuss the questions. Ask them to justify their answers with either evidence from what they can see in the photo or reasons or short anecdotes from their own experience.

Extra activity

Ask students to think about three recent news stories and rank them according to importance (in their opinion). Then put them into pairs to share and give reasons for their choices. Ask students to discuss how we decide whether a news story is or is not important.

WATCH

2 ▶ 6.1

- Tell students that they are going to hear two National Geographic explorers talking about the type of news they find interesting. Ask students to briefly brainstorm the types of news stories that the explorers might mention, for example: science stories, political stories, sports stories, arts and culture stories, etc.
- Ask students to read the questions.
- Play the video and tell students to listen for the stories the explorers mention and their reactions to them.
- Students make notes, then compare answers in pairs before checking as a class.

Answers

1. Afroz: scientific and political; Imogen: conservation news, celebrity gossip, but almost never reads about sport
2. A hospital built by Imran Khan filled him with hope. He also mentions the Apollo moon landing which fascinated him.
3. The whole nation came together and it was all really positive.

3

- Give students about a minute to think about the questions. Encourage them to consider the types of stories they brainstormed in Exercise 2 and the types of stories that the explorers mentioned.
- Students discuss the questions in pairs.

ABOUT THE EXPLORERS

AFROZ SHAH is a geologist based in Brunei. His work involves mapping earthquake-causing fault lines in India, Pakistan, Borneo and New Guinea. While out in the field, he collects evidence of past earthquakes and then uses this to develop maps of where future earthquakes are likely to occur. Afroz works closely with local authorities and communities in the areas where he conducts his research.

IMOGEN NAPPER is a marine scientist from the UK. Her research focuses on plastic pollution in the marine environment. Her work has helped influence the ban of microplastics in cosmetics internationally, where she found up to 3 million plastic beads could be in one facial scrub. Imogen has recently been testing technology to capture the tiny microplastic fibres that are released when modern clothes are washed.

6A The camera never lies

LESSON GOALS
- Identify unsupported claims in an article
- Learn how to fact-check online information
- Discuss how reliable online media is

READING

1 Work in pairs. Look at the title of the article and the photos on page 73. Discuss the questions.
1 What do you think the article is about?
2 How might the photos show things that aren't true or real?

2 Read the article quickly to check if your answers to Exercise 1 were correct.

3 Read the article again. Answer the questions.
1 Why is the advice 'You can't trust everything you read' not enough these days?
2 In what ways is the 'deep fake' of Dalí different from a video of him from when he was alive?
3 Why are beautiful fake images on social media especially dangerous to young people?
4 Why can't 'the truth compete with lies'?
5 What's wrong with some food 'hacks'?
6 What is the main aim of the article: to describe, entertain or teach? How do you know?

4 Look at the Reading skill box. Then read the article again and identify any claims the writer makes without supporting evidence.

READING SKILL
Identifying unsupported claims

In articles where writers report facts, they should support any claims with evidence. A common way of providing this online is to include links to other websites that provide the relevant evidence, such as scientific papers and studies.

To identify unsupported claims, look for clear statements of fact that are not accompanied by facts and figures.

5 For each unsupported claim you identified in Exercise 4, think about what sort of information you could include a hyperlink to.

6 Work in pairs. Discuss the questions.
1 Do you think you would normally be able to notice faked images or videos?
2 Do you think it's OK to edit photos to make your life seem better than it is? Why? / Why not?

7 Work in pairs. Look at the Critical thinking skill box. Discuss how you might fact-check the story of the shark mentioned in the article. Then do the same for the headlines (a–c).

CRITICAL THINKING SKILL
Fact-checking online information

Here are some strategies to avoid being tricked by fake news!
- **Check that the source is reliable.** Do other articles on the website look suspicious? Do fact-checking websites tell you that you can trust this website?
- **Check that the information is supported by evidence.** Does it have a list of references? Does it have hyperlinks and do they link to reliable sources?
- **Check to see if anyone else has investigated the story.** What hits do I get when I search the keywords + *fake*?

a **By 2050 there will be more plastic in the oceans than fish**
b **30-year old man ordered to move out of his parents' house**
c **Chicago the most dangerous city in the US**

SPEAKING

8 You are going to spread news around the class. Follow the steps.
1 Think of two pieces of news (one true, one fake) about yourself or something you did.
I scored three goals in a football match on Sunday.
2 Talk to three other students in the class and share your news. Ask each other questions to work out how reliable the information might be.
What football team do you play for?
3 Work in pairs. Share the news you heard. Decide which is true and which is fake.
4 Share your ideas with the class and see if you were right.

EXPLORE MORE!
Search online for 'how to spot fake images with reverse image search' to learn how to fact-check images for yourself.

72

LESSON GOALS

- **READING** The main aim is for students to practise identifying unsupported claims in an article and then use their critical thinking skills to discuss how to fact-check online information.
- **SPEAKING** A sub-aim is for students to verbally spread information around the class and try to work out whether or not a story is real.

READING

ABOUT THE TEXT

In this article, the writer focuses on three ways in which media can be manipulated or 'faked'. The article mentions 'deep fakes', which refers to anything from state-of-the-art modified versions of videos generated by artificial intelligence to any image or video that seems fraudulent. However, to create a 'deep fake' video of a person, you would first need to expose a neural network to many hours of real video footage of the person and then combine this 'trained' network with computer graphics to superimpose a copy of the person onto a different actor in the video.

1

- Direct students to the article title and elicit the contrast between the first part of the title ('The camera never lies', that says that photographs always show things or people exactly as they are) and the second part of the title ('except when it does'), that suggests that some photographs do not actually do this.
- **Optional step** Ask students whether or not they believe that the statement 'The camera never lies' is still true today. Elicit possible reasons why a camera might be able to 'lie' and write these on the board, for example: because photos can be digitally altered.
- Students discuss the questions in pairs.

Sample answers
2 Photo A: this photo has been changed – the photo of the shark may be taken from another photo; Photo B: sometimes, what is shown as 'food' is not real food at all; Photo C: Photos can be changed using software like Photoshop. Dalí wasn't alive when mobile phones were invented, so this photo must have been changed.

2

- Students read the article quickly to check their answers from Exercise 1.
- Students compare answers in pairs.

VOCABULARY NOTES

be dedicated (to) /biː 'dedɪkeɪtɪd/ = to be exclusively focused on

recreated /'riːkrieɪtɪd/ = copied

open the doors to (something) /'əʊpən ðə dɔːz tuː/ = to make it possible for other people to begin doing an activity

hack /hæk/ (n) = a way of doing something easily

inedible /ɪn'edəbl/ = describing something that you cannot eat

clickbait /'klɪkbeɪt/ = an article that has been created to make people want to click on and read it, usually because its headline or photo is surprising or shocking

misuse /ˌmɪs'juːs/ = to use something for a purpose that it was not designed for and should not be used for

The camera NEVER lies

(except when it does)

A

B

C

'You can't trust everything you read.' Well, now it seems we can't trust anything we *see*, either. A lot of online content has been shown not to be genuine, from product reviews on shopping websites to incorrect science. And images, in particular, can have a powerful effect on what we believe.

Deep fakes

At The Dalí, a museum dedicated to the artist's life and work, visitors watch an on-screen Salvador Dalí telling them about his life, even though he died more than thirty years ago. He even takes a selfie of himself with his visitors on his phone!

The creators used artificial intelligence to 'learn' how he moved and talked. This isn't an old video; it's Dalí recreated – his face skilfully controlled for a lifelike result. While 'deep fake' videos like this can be used to teach and entertain, the technology opens the doors to less honest uses. For example, damaging the reputation of celebrities by making it look like they've done or said things that they haven't.

Photoshopped fakes

It's easier to alter still images. We do it every time we add filters to photos on social media. But fake photos can distort people's view of reality in serious ways. According to a study by YMCA, almost two thirds of the surveyed teenagers felt pressure to look a certain way because of the images on social media. That study also revealed that Instagram influencers with their 'perfect' lifestyles had the biggest impact on teenagers' self-esteem.

What's more, fakes often go viral more often than photos that haven't been altered and may get shared millions of times. A faked photo of a shark swimming up a flooded road goes viral every time there is a hurricane in the US. Online, the truth just can't compete with lies.

Fake bakes

A popular type of YouTube video is food 'hacks', videos of people making attractive-looking food in a few quick and easy steps. These clips get millions of hits, generating big money for the makers. But are these recipes too good to be true? It turns out many of them are. When people try to recreate the dishes, they end up inedible. This may not seem serious but, when videos suggest using dangerous chemicals on strawberries to make them white, we have to worry about the spread of misinformation. So why make a video showing a recipe that doesn't work? The simple answer is money; 'clickbait' videos like these generate millions by grabbing our attention.

So what can we do to protect ourselves from believing misleading images? We can use fact-checking websites, such as Snopes.com, to find out how reliable a news source is. We can also fact-check photos using 'reverse image searches'. These let you see where else the image exists on the web. If it's being used in a variety of stories, there's a good chance it's being misused here. The more you ask yourself about the truth of information you meet, the better you will be at spotting it.

73

Extra activity

Write on the board or say the following words: *alter*, *distort*, *fact-check* (verb), *fake*, *genuine*, *misinformation*, *misleading*, *source* (noun). Put students into pairs and ask them to discuss and decide whether the words are connected to information or images that are real (R), false (F) or both (B). Tell them to look up any words that they do not already know in a dictionary.

3

- Students read the article to find the information they need to answer the questions and then make notes on their answers.
- Students compare their answers in pairs and then check answers as a class.
- **Optional step** Students discuss whether they agree or disagree with the article's main ideas (i.e. that a lot of online content has been modified, we cannot trust anything we see online and that the faking of images and video content always has a negative impact).

Answers

1 because now you can't trust what you see either as there are so many fake images online
2 he never said the words he says in the video; he never had a mobile phone
3 they unfairly suggest people's lives and looks aren't good enough and damage their confidence
4 fakes often go viral more often than photos that haven't been manipulated
5 they are inedible
6 to teach – it ends with advice on what to do to protect ourselves from believing fake images

4

- Ask students to look at the Reading skill box to distinguish between supported and unsupported claims.
- Students read the article again to identify claims that the writer makes and identify the unsupported claims.
- Ask students to work in pairs to summarize the unsupported claims and write down the line(s) of the text where they are made.

Sample answers

incorrect science (line 4); powerful effect (line 5); they've done or said things that they haven't (line 16); more often (line 26); people try to recreate the dishes (line 38); dangerous chemicals on strawberries (line 41)

5

- **Optional step** As a class, brainstorm examples of information that can be used to support claims in factual articles, for example: videos, the findings of scientific studies, statistics, reports, news articles, etc.
- In pairs, students discuss the types of information that could be used to support each unsupported claim they identified in Exercise 4.
- Check answers as a class.

Sample answers

incorrect science (a study about the spread of bad science on social media);
powerful effect (scientific research showing the difference in effect between words and images on what we believe);
they've done or said things that they haven't (a news article about a celebrity deep fake or an article describing the potential threat of this happening in more detail);
more often (a report about how fakes go viral more often than genuine photos);
people try to recreate the dishes (a YouTube video showing people trying to recreate dishes);
dangerous chemicals on strawberries (a YouTube video where this happens – it's bleach)

6

- Tell students to use their experience (e.g. of looking at images or videos online, or seeing edited photos posted on social media) to help them answer the questions.
- Students discuss the questions in pairs.
- **Optional step** If it is possible, ask them to support the statements they make in their discussion by finding and showing their partner online photos or videos.

Extra activity

Ask students to discuss the following questions in pairs or groups:

- Why do you think people try to make their lives seem better than it really is on social media?
- What kind of impact can this have on other social media users viewing the photos or videos?
- Do you think that there is anything that people shouldn't share photos or videos of on social media?

7

- Direct students to the instructions and check their understanding of 'fact-check' (to find out if there is evidence to support a claim).
- Tell students to look at the Critical thinking skill box.
- Students discuss the most appropriate ways to fact-check the story about the shark in the article and the stories in the three headlines. Encourage them to think about specific methods for each story.
- Ask students to share and explain their answers in class.

Sample answers

Fact-check the shark story by: using a reverse image search (mentioned in the main article) to see where else the photo exists on the internet; look for evidence that the shark was there, such as other photos of the incident or reports that sharks swim inland; search for 'shark swimming in flooded road + fake' to check whether anyone has already investigated the story.

a: once the news article has been found, check to see what 'more' means, whether 2050 is the correct date they are estimating, what kind of plastic the article is talking about, etc.

b: find out what 'ordered' means in this context and who ordered him

c: find out what 'the most dangerous' means and what statistics have been used to calculate this

(Note: a and b are true, c is fake)

Extra activity

Ask students to choose one of the three headlines (a–c) from Exercise 7 and fact-check it online, using the strategies that they came up with. Students could then present their conclusions about whether or not the headline is accurate and the reasons why to a partner or in a group.

SPEAKING

8

- Go through the instructions and elicit the steps students have to complete.
- Students think of one real piece of news about themselves or something they did and make up an additional piece that is fake news. Tell students to ensure their fake news sounds plausible.
- **Optional step** As a class, students brainstorm the types of things they could ask questions about to fact-check another student's news. For example, where they were when the incident happened or who they were with.
- Students tell their news stories to three other students. These three other students then ask questions to fact-check the stories.
- Students tell their partner what stories they heard and the answers other students gave to their questions about the news stories. They then discuss whether they think each story was true or fake and why.
- Students share their ideas in class. Confirm whether they correctly identified which news stories were true.

EXPLORE MORE!

Refer students to lines 53–58 of the article to remind themselves of what a 'reverse image search' is and ask students to do an online search for the term. This will generate millions of search results, so students will need to decide which results link to credible and reliable webpages. Tell students to look at the information on a few different webpages and make notes on the key things they learn about how to fact-check images. Students could then follow-up this task by either writing an explanation of how to do a reverse image search or verbally sharing what they have learned with a partner or in a small group.

See **Workbook** pages 48–49 for extra practice.

LESSON GOALS

- **GRAMMAR** The main aim is for students to practise using passive structures to report the news.
- **LISTENING** A sub-aim is for students to listen and understand a news bulletin.
- **PRONUNCIATION** A further sub-aim is for students to practise pronouncing consonant groups in past participles.

LISTENING AND GRAMMAR

1

- Give students a minute to read the lesson title and the questions in Exercise 1 and think about their answers.
- Students discuss the questions in pairs for about three minutes. Ask students to give explanations in Exercise 1 and examples to support their answers.

2 6.1

- Play the audio and ask students to listen for words connected to each of the topics in the stories.
- Students match the stories with the topics, then decide which news story they are the most interested in.
- Students compare their answers and tell each other which story they are the most interested in finding out more about and why.

VOCABULARY NOTES

carbon neutral / 'kɑːbən 'njuːtrəl/ = balancing the carbon dioxide that is produced by removing it from the environment, for example by planting trees

environmentalist /ɪnˌvaɪrən'mentəlɪst/ = a person who works to protect the environment

blockbuster / 'blɒkbʌstə(r)/ = a film that is typically expensive to make and that becomes extremely commercially successful

bankruptcy / 'bæŋkrʌptsi/ = a state in which a person or organization has so little money that they are no longer able to pay their debts

3 6.1

- Tell students to read the sentences and use context and what they remember from Exercise 2 to predict which verb fits in each gap.
- Students listen to the audio again and complete the sentences. Remind them to use the correct form of each verb.
- Check answers as a class. Invite different students to read a sentence out loud.

4

- Elicit that the verb forms that students added to the sentences in Exercise 3 are examples of passive structures.
- Ask students to read and answer the questions, then read the Grammar box to check their answers.

Answers

1 *be* + past participle
2 passives in sentences 2, 6 and 7 are followed by *that* + clause (notice that *that* is optional); passives in sentences 3, 4 and 5 are followed by *to* + infinitive
3 When the passive begins with *it*, it will be followed by (*that*) + clause

GRAMMAR NOTES

Passive structures

Form

- Students need to be aware that when modal verbs (e.g. *must*, *mustn't*, *should*, *shouldn't*, *might*, *may*) and semi-modal verbs (e.g. *have to*, *ought to*, *need to*) are followed by a passive structure, the following structure is used: modal/ semi-modal verb + *be* + past participle. For example: *The cake needs to be put in the oven for 70 minutes.*
- Draw students' attention to the use of passive structures after a personal pronoun (*I*, *we*, etc.) which is sometimes called the personal passive. For example: *I **was visited** by a few colleagues of mine.*; *We **were taken** to the office by the receptionist.*

Common mistakes

- Using the past simple form of the verb rather than the past participle in a passive structure.
- Not using the correct auxiliary verb. For example: *The scientists **were** awarded the prize*, not *The scientists **was** awarded the prize.*
- Passive structures cannot be used with transitive verbs. For example, *She died* NOT *She was died*.
- Passive structures cannot be used with verbs that describe states. For example, you cannot say: *It is seemed to be an interesting story.*

For further information and practice, see **Grammar reference Unit 6B** on page 146 of the Student's Book.

5

- Tell students that the sentences are real news items.
- Go through the first sentence in class. Elicit that 'recently' after the gap indicates that the verb needs to be used in the present perfect simple form of the passive, which is 'have been banned'.
- Students complete the remaining sentences with the correct passive form of the verbs in brackets. Ask them to use the information in the Grammar box to check they have used the correct passive structure.

- [pair icon] Students discuss whether they remember reading or hearing about any of these news items and what their reaction to them was.

Answers
1 have been banned; 2 is thought; 3 is rumoured; 4 will have been launched/are going to be launched/will be launched; 5 is expected; 6 is said; 7 was awarded/has been awarded; 8 was reported

6 [audio 6.2]

- Ask students to read the whole text. Elicit that whenever the word 'people' is used in the active structure, the structure *it* + *be* + past participle + (*that*) + clause is used in its passive equivalent.
- **Optional step** Go through the first item in class. Elicit that the same verb in bold (*choose*) and the same tense (past perfect simple) need to be used in the passive structure. Elicit that the past perfect form of the passive is *had been* + past participle, so the correct answer is: *had been chosen*.
- Students convert the active structures into passive structures. Less confident students could do this in pairs.
- Play the audio so students can listen and check their answers.

Answers
1 he had been chosen
2 The prize is thought to be
3 It is awarded
4 Mr Tabichi was congratulated by the judges
5 His students' scores are said to/It is said that his students' scores
6 Mr Tabichi is also admired
7 He is reported to be

Extra activity

Ask students to use passive structures to write a brief report of something that has happened to them recently that also uses active structures and includes information about what people thought/believed/expected about the scenario. Students then give their text to a partner who reads it and gives them feedback on whether they have used passive structures accurately and in the appropriate places.

For additional practice, refer to the **Grammar activity** on page 255 of the Teacher's Book.

6B In the headlines

LESSON GOALS
- Understand a news bulletin
- Report news using passive structures
- Pronounce consonant groups in past participles clearly

LISTENING AND GRAMMAR

1 Work in pairs. Discuss the questions.
1 How often do you listen to news bulletins on the radio or on TV?
2 What other ways do you use to keep in touch with what's going on?

2 [audio 6.1] Listen to a news bulletin. Match the stories (1–3) with the topics (a–c). Which story would you most like to learn more about?

Story 1 c — a entertainment
Story 2 a — b sport
Story 3 b — c environment

3 [audio 6.1] Listen to the news bulletin again. Complete the sentences with these verbs in the correct form.

believe hope reveal say suggest think understand

1 The plan to become carbon neutral within two years _was revealed_ today by the Costa Rican government.
2 …, as it _is hoped_ it will lead other nations to take similar action.
3 The plan _is thought_ to be an important step in the global fight against climate change.
4 … which _is said_ to have made 2.79 billion dollars from cinema ticket sales.
5 Marvel _was believed_ to be close to bankruptcy.
6 However, it ________ that the shoes he was wearing gave him an unfair advantage. has been suggested
7 It _is understood_ that the World Athletics committee might ban their use in the Olympics.

In 2019, Eliud Kipchoge became the first athlete to run a marathon in under two hours.

74

PRONUNCIATION

7 [audio 6.3]

- Ask students to read the words and identify the consonants in each word.
- Play the audio so students can underline the consonant groups that are said together. Tell students that there may be more than one consonant group in each word.
- [pair icon] Students compare answers in pairs.

PRONUNCIATION NOTES

Pronouncing consonant groups
Remind students that they have previously listened to and practised consonant groups in adverbs in Lesson 3B. Tell students that it is particularly important to clearly pronounce consonant groups at the end of past participle verb forms because this can help the listener differentiate between present and past participles.

4 Look at the sentences in Exercise 3. Answer the questions. Then read the Grammar box to check.

1 How are passive structures typically formed?
2 What structure follows the passive in sentences 2, 6 and 7? What about sentences 3, 4 and 5?
3 When are these two different structures used?

GRAMMAR Passive structures

News reports often use passive structures to emphasize the action, when the person or thing that did the action is unknown, unimportant or obvious. In general, you form the passive voice using ***be* + past participle**.

*This decision **was praised** by environmentalists.* **(passive)** vs *Environmentalists **praised** the decision.* **(active)**

News reports often use …

- **subject + *be* + past participle + *to* + infinitive.**

*The plan **is thought/said/reported/understood/ believed to be** an important step …*

- ***it* + *be* + past participle + (*that*) + clause.**

*… but **it is understood/thought/hoped/said (that)** the World Athletics committee might ban their use in the Olympics.*

Go to page 146 for the Grammar reference.

5 Complete the sentences with the correct form of the words in brackets. In pairs, discuss if you've seen these news items.

1 Single-use plastic bags ________ recently by several countries, including France, China and Botswana. (ban)
2 It ________ that thousands of social media accounts were hacked in a cyberattack. (think)
3 Belgian singer Stromae ________ to be planning a return to the stage after several years of 'retirement'. (rumour)
4 Commercial flights to the Moon ________ before 2030, say the experts. (launch)
5 Meat grown in a lab ________ to become part of our daily diet in the next decade. (expect)
6 It ________ that, in some countries, sales of electric vehicles will soon overtake those of traditional cars. (say)
7 Olga Tokarczuk ________ the Nobel Prize in Literature, becoming the fifth Polish person to win. (award)
8 It ________ earlier this week that the economic growth in the EU is slowing down. (report)

6 6.2 Read the news report. Replace the phrases in bold with passive structures. Then listen to check.

Crowds gathered to welcome Peter Tabichi as he returned from Dubai, where [1]**they had chosen him** for the 'best teacher in the world' award. [2]**People think the prize is** one of the most important in the world. [3]**They award it** for exceptional teaching achievements. [4]**The judges congratulated Mr Tabichi** on his passion and for inspiring girls to study science. [5]**People say his students' scores** have improved dramatically since he started working at the school, and some have won international awards. [6]**People also admire Mr Tabichi** for his charity. He gives away almost all of his salary every year to help children from poorer families. [7]**There are reports that he is also planning to** donate the one-million-dollar prize he received.

PRONUNCIATION

7 6.3 Listen to the words. Underline any consonant groups (two or more consonant sounds together, e.g. *suggested*) you hear.

a expected
b believed
c praised
d observed
e hoped
f introduced

8 Look at the Clear voice box. Then practise saying the words from Exercise 7.

CLEAR VOICE
Pronouncing consonant groups

Many past participles have consonant groups at the end (hoped), some also at the beginning (praised) or in the middle (expected). To be easy to understand, it is important to pronounce all consonants in the group.

SPEAKING

9 Work in pairs. Follow the instructions to prepare a two-minute radio news bulletin.

1 Find at least three news stories that interest you.
2 Take notes on the important facts of the stories.
3 Use your notes to write a news bulletin. Remember to use passive structures.
4 Practise giving the news in pairs.
5 Work with another pair. Present your news bulletins.

EXPLORE MORE!

Search online for one of the news stories mentioned in this lesson. What extra information did you learn?

75

Common problems

- Consonant cluster reduction: Leaving one of the consonants in the group out.
- Adding another consonant between two of the consonants.
- Changing the order of the consonant sounds.

8

- Tell students to read the Clear voice box.
- Put students into pairs to practise saying the words from Exercise 7.
- **Optional step** Write short sentences that include each of the verbs from Exercise 7 on the board, for example: *I expected to get a good grade for that subject.* In their pairs, ask students to practise saying the sentences out loud, ensuring they pronounce the consonant group in the verbs correctly.

SPEAKING

9

- Put students into new pairs.
- **Optional step** Bring in some English print newspapers for students to find stories in if they cannot look online.
- Go through the steps involved in the task to check students understand what they have to do.
- When they are looking for news stories, encourage students to choose ones from credible sources. The stories could be either local news stories or national or global stories.
- Give students sufficient time to prepare and practise their news bulletin.
- Students take turns to present their news bulletin to another pair.

Extra activity

Find a radio news bulletin in English online, for example BBC News (news from the UK) or National Public Radio (news from the US). Play it in class and ask students to identify the topics of the news stories in the bulletin and make a note of any key words, phrases or details that they hear. Students could also reflect on how easy they found it to follow the news bulletin. If students found it challenging to understand the bulletin, ask them to reflect on what exactly the challenges were and how they could overcome them. If you ask students to do this as a self-study task, either find and assign them a specific news bulletin or ask them to find one online themselves.

EXPLORE MORE!

Students choose one of the news stories from Exercises 2, 5 or 6. Students select information from one or more credible online source for their story and make notes on any extra information they find about it. Students could select the most interesting or relevant extra information they found and use this to create a more detailed summary of the story.

For additional practice, refer to the **Communication activity** on page 222 of the Teacher's Book.

See **Workbook** pages 50–51 for extra practice.

LESSON GOALS

- **LISTENING** A main aim is for students to practise listening to people talking about the news and understand catenation in connected speech.
- **VOCABULARY** A further main aim is for students to learn and practise using collocations for talking about the news.
- **GRAMMAR** A further main aim is for students to learn and practise using the structure: *the* + comparative …, *the* + comparative …
- **PRONUNCIATION** A sub-aim is for students to practise pronouncing long vowels.
- **SPEAKING** The speaking aim is for students to roleplay an editorial meeting for a news site.

SPEAKING

1

- Give students a minute to read the questions and look at the infographic.
- Students discuss the questions in pairs for about five minutes. Ask students to give explanations and examples to support their answers to the second question.

LISTENING

2 6.4

- Remind students that they listened to Afroz Shah and Imogen Napper talking about what sort of news they follow at the start of this unit.
- Play the audio and ask students to listen and complete the sentences.

3 6.5

- **Optional step** Ask students to think about and discuss with a partner what differences they expect to hear between the slow and fast versions of the phrases.
- Play the audio and ask students to notice how the pronunciation changes when the phrases are said quickly and then more slowly. Ask students to think about which version they found easier to understand and why that is.

6C Have you heard the news?

LESSON GOALS
- Understand catenation in connected speech
- Talk about the news
- Pronounce long vowels clearly
- Talk about effects using *the … the …*

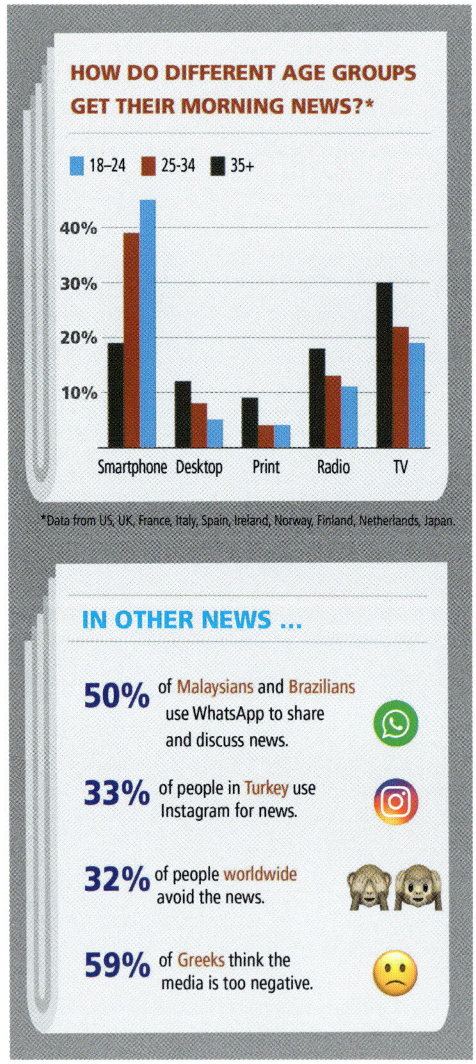

SPEAKING

1 Work in pairs. Look at the infographic and discuss the questions.

1 Which information in the infographic matches your own news habits and those of people you know?
2 Which of these topics do you think are the most important to people of different age groups?

celebrities and entertainment   economics   environment   health and fitness   local news   politics   science   sport

LISTENING

NATIONAL GEOGRAPHIC EXPLORERS

2 6.4 You are going to hear Imogen Napper and Afroz Shah talk about how they get their news. First, listen to the extracts and write down what you hear.

1 I _get a lot of_ my news from social media.
2 The five-minute news bulletins give me _an idea of_ what today's top stories are.
3 For example, I often _read online_ newspapers and magazines.

3 6.5 Listen to the phrases from Exercise 2 said fast and then more slowly. How does the pronunciation change? Look at the Listening skill box to check. When said fast, some words are connected and sound like one word.

LISTENING SKILL
Understanding connected speech: catenation

In connected speech, words often come together and sound like one word. When one word ends with a consonant sound (e.g. /z/, /t/, /p/) and the next word starts with a vowel (e.g. /ɒ/, /ɪ/, /ə/), the final consonant attaches to the vowel of the next word, e.g. *an idea* → *a nidea* /naɪˈdɪə/. This is called catenation.

4 6.6 Listen to Imogen and Afroz. What are their main sources of news? Whose habits and opinions are most similar to your own?
Imogen: social media, podcasts, radio, TV; Afroz: online newspapers and magazines

76

- Ask students to read the Listening skill box to find out more about how words can sound different when they are said quickly.
- **Optional step** Ask students to think about whether catenation is also used in their first language and if they can think of and share any specific examples of it.

4 6.6

- Play the audio so students can make notes on the news sources for each explorer.
- Ask students to tell a partner which explorer's opinions and habits are closest to their own. Encourage them to give examples to support their statements.

Extra activity

Ask students to use what they have learned about their partner's news preferences and opinions to recommend a podcast, radio, TV show, online newspaper or magazine that they either think their partner will like or that they think their partner should listen to/watch/read because it is completely different to what they usually listen to/watch/read.

5 6.6 Listen again. Are the sentences true (T), false (F) or not mentioned (NM)?

1 Imogen listens to podcasts when driving. F
2 Imogen doesn't read newspapers. NM
3 Afroz tends to read more serious articles. T
4 Imogen says some stories are reported many times to provide an in-depth analysis. NM
5 Afroz has a negative opinion of some news sources because they don't report news accurately. T
6 Afroz's work on earthquakes was not presented accurately by the media. F

VOCABULARY

6 Complete the collocations with these words. Some words may be used twice.

foreign in-depth make objective sensational skim over tabloid the news top

1 report the news
2 today's top story
3 skim over / make the headlines
4 sensational headlines
5 a(n) tabloid / foreign journalist
6 the tabloid press
7 a(n) in-depth / objective article

7 Complete the sentences with words from Exercise 6.

1 I only watch the first few minutes of the news, just to get the top stories.
2 Can a newspaper owned by a billionaire be objective about taxes on the rich?
3 I didn't read it properly, I just skimmed over it.
4 The tabloid press spend too long on silly stories about the private lives of celebrities.
5 When scientific research is reported, they often distort the information to make it more sensational.
6 Because podcasts are longer, they can offer in-depth interviews with interesting guests.

Go to page 137 for the Vocabulary reference.

PRONUNCIATION

8 6.7 Listen to the words. Which ones have a long vowel?

argument journalist misleading news objective report skim story

9 Look at the Clear voice box to check your answers to Exercise 8. Then practise saying the words, making sure the vowel is long.

CLEAR VOICE
Pronouncing long vowels

English has five long vowels. It's important to pronounce these as long. This will help the listener hear the difference with short vowels (e.g. *reach vs rich*).

/ɜː/ *journalist, world* /ɑː/ *argument, article*
/iː/ *misleading, piece* /ɔː/ *report, story*
/uː/ *news, choose*

GRAMMAR

10 Read the Focus on box. Then put the words in order to make sentences (1–4). You will need to add *the*.

FOCUS ON *the … the …*

Use ***the* + comparative …, *the* + comparative …** to show that one thing depends on another.
Comparative adjectives: ***The longer*** *the article is,* ***the fewer*** *readers it will have.*
Adverbs: ***The more*** *you get your information from different sources,* ***the more*** *objectively you'll see the news.*

Go to page 147 for the Focus on reference.

1 include / more / on the website / our audience / videos / we / will be / younger
The more we include videos on the website, the younger our audience will be.
2 to get / less likely / older / you are / your news online / you are
3 became / he / interesting / less / more / spoke / the interview
4 become / better / can / more / practise / you / you

SPEAKING

11 Work in groups. You're in charge of editing a news site. Follow the instructions.

1 Decide who your main readers are (e.g. people under 35, businesspeople).
2 Which news topics (e.g. politics, celebrities, sports) do you think you would need to report most in order to interest your readers? Why? Give examples of recent stories.

EXPLORE MORE!

Find an English language news source that you like. Challenge yourself to read an article every day for a week.

77

VOCABULARY NOTES

exaggeration /ɪɡˌzædʒəˈreɪʃ(ə)n/ = a statement that presents something as being better or worse than it actually is

commercialize /kəˈmɜːʃəlaɪz/ = to manage an activity in order to maximize profits

media outlet /ˈmiːdiə ˈaʊtlet/ = a platform that provides information and/or entertainment (e.g. a newspaper, TV channel, etc.)

5 6.6

- Students read the sentences first and guess whether each one is true, false or not mentioned based on what they can remember from the first time they listened.
- Play the audio again. Ask students to listen for key words connected to each sentence.

VOCABULARY

6

- Tell students that they are going to complete collocations about the news.
- Ask students to look at the type of word that comes before each gap (e.g. a verb or an article) and to use this to help them identify the missing word.
- Students complete the collocations, then check answers as a class.
- **Optional step** Model and drill the pronunciation of any words that students find difficult to say.

7

- Tell students that they are now going to practise using the collocations from Exercise 6.
- Students complete the sentences, then compare their answers in pairs.

For further information and practice, see **Vocabulary reference Unit 6** on page 137 of the Student's Book.

Extra activity

Ask students to write a paragraph about their preferences and opinions about the news using five or six of the collocations they have learned.

For additional practice, refer to the **Vocabulary activity** on page 238 of the Teacher's Book.

PRONUNCIATION

8 6.7

- Direct students to the instruction.
- Play the audio and ask students to identify which words have long vowels. Tell them not to look at the Clear voice box while they are doing this.

PRONUNCIATION NOTES

Long vowels

The 'length' of a vowel is measured by the amount of time that the speaker says the vowel sound for.
The length of a vowel sound in an English word is typically determined by the letter directly after it. For example, vowel sounds are longer when they come before voiced consonants, so the 'a' in *bad* /bæd/ is a long vowel sound because it comes before the voiced consonant 'd'. Vowel sounds are also long if they are followed by the letter 'e'. Compare: *not* and *note*; *cub* and *cube*.

9

- Ask students to look at the Clear voice box and check their answers to Exercise 8.
- Put students into pairs to practise saying the words with long vowel sounds in the Clear voice box.

For additional practice, refer to the **Pronunciation activity** on page 273 of the Teacher's Book.

GRAMMAR

10

- Ask students to read the Focus on box. Ask, *Have you read or used the structure* the + *comparative* ..., the + *comparative before?*
- **Optional step** Go through the first sentence to show students how to complete this exercise. Elicit that the two words that could come after 'the' in the sentence are 'more' and 'younger'. 'The more' needs to be followed by a verb phrase (*we include*) and 'the younger' by a noun phrase (*our audience*). The structure of the sentence, therefore, needs to be: *The more we include ..., the younger our audience ....* Also, draw students' attention to the word order in the second half of the sentence with the verb form at the end: *the younger our audience will be*.
- Students make sentences with the words given, referring back to the Focus on box where necessary.

Answers

1 The more we include videos on the website, the younger our audience will be.
2 The older you are, the less likely you are to get your news online.
3 The more he spoke, the less interesting the interview became.
4 The more you practise, the better you can become.

For further information and practice, see **Focus on reference Unit 6C** on page 147 of the Student's Book.

Extra activity

Write these two sentence stems on the board:
1 The more I watch the news, ...
2 The more I read the news in English, ...
Ask students to complete the sentences with their own ideas and then share them with a partner.

Sample answers: 1 The more I watch the news, the more I worry about what is happening in the world. 2 The more I read the news in English, the more vocabulary I learn.

GRAMMAR NOTES

the ... the ...
Equivalent structures to express a proportionate relationship between two factors exist in several languages, so find out whether this is the case for your students' first language(s) and what the equivalent structure would be.
Students are likely to make mistakes with word order in this structure, for example: *The more a news story is sensational, the more I like it. (The more sensational a news story is, the more I like it).*

For additional practice, refer to the **Focus on activity** on page 256 of the Teacher's Book.

SPEAKING

11

- Put students into small groups and go through the instructions for the task.
- Give students about ten minutes to brainstorm possible target groups. Students agree on one and then brainstorm news topics they think this group would be interested in and give reasons for their choices.
- **Optional step** Ask students to do some online research to find out what types of news stories the target group they have chosen are usually interested in.
- Give students another ten minutes to think of recent news stories they can provide as examples of the news topics they have chosen. If possible, allow students to go online to find details about these stories.

Extra activity

In their groups from Exercise 11, students prepare a presentation of the results of their editorial meeting. Ask them to include the following in their presentations:

- the target group
- which types of news stories they think this group is interested in and why
- specific recent stories that they think the group would be interested in

Students give their presentations. If possible, ask them to use visual aids in their presentations, for example photos or headlines from the stories in a poster or on slides.

EXPLORE MORE!

Ask students to search online for 'news in English' to find news sources in English. Remind students that a 'news source' could be the online version of a newspaper, a news website or news blog. Students could do one or more of the following after reading each article:

- write a summary of the story
- write words or expressions from the article that were new for them and their definitions
- write how they felt while or after reading, for example: *I thought the article would be difficult to read because it had a long headline, but I actually really enjoyed reading it.*

For additional practice, refer to the **Communication activity** on page 223 and the **Mediation activity** on page 288 of the Teacher's Book.

See **Workbook** pages 51–54 for extra practice.

LESSON GOALS

- **SPEAKING** This lesson integrates speaking, reading and listening. Its main aim is to introduce students to three different influencing styles (inspiring, convincing and negotiating) and language that can be used with each style. Students then practise using the different styles to 'sell' their ideas during a group discussion.

SPEAKING AND LISTENING

1

- **Optional step** Ask students to look at the title of the story and the accompanying picture. Ask *Have you ever heard or read this story? What is it about?*
- Direct students to the instructions and check understanding of 'influencing styles' (a way of doing or saying something that changes other people's thoughts, feelings or behaviour).
- Students read the story to identify its main message and then think about the link between the story and influencing styles.

Sample answers

The story shows that sometimes, when you try to push people too hard because you want them to do something, it's less likely to work than with a more gentle approach to influencing, like the Sun's. The Sun's approach was to change the man's mind, not to force him.

2 6.8

- Play the audio and ask students to listen and think about what each of the three speakers are doing to try to persuade each other.
- Students make notes on their answers to questions 1 and 2, then think about their answer to question 3.
- Students compare their answers to questions 1 and 2 in pairs and then discuss question 3.

MY VOICE

COMMUNICATION SKILL NOTES

Influencing styles

This skill will help students influence other people so that they will support and accept their ideas during collaborative tasks or when decisions need to be made.

Successful influencing is usually achieved through a combination of inspiring other people, negotiating with other people and convincing people to believe that what you are saying is true. Developing an awareness of different styles will, therefore, give students the flexibility to use the appropriate style for the person they are talking to or the situation they are in. It will also help them mediate discussions or facilitate group decisions where different styles need to be used in the same situation.

Influencing skills are useful in almost any situation where you need to collaborate with other people (e.g. while completing group project work), you want other people to accept or agree with a proposal of yours (e.g. when you have a solution for a problem you and other people are experiencing), or make a group decision (e.g. deciding where to go on holiday with friends or family).

In the workplace, you need to use influencing skills when you are leading a team of any kind, encouraging other people to embrace a change in your organization, deciding on the best course of action in a project team, pitching a strategy to a client or trying to convince a customer to agree to something.

3 6.2

- Tell students that they are going to watch a video that gives information about three different influencing styles.
- Play the video and ask students to put the questions in order and make notes on their answers to the questions.
- Students compare their ordering and answers in pairs.

Answers

1 c (in situations when we want to help other people see our way of thinking and persuade them to change their minds)
2 b (inspiring, negotiating, convincing)
3 a (you can use one or more, depending on what works best in the situation and for you)

VOCABULARY NOTES

fable /ˈfeɪbl/ = a story that is intended to teach a lesson

appeal to (something/someone) /əˈpiːl tuː/ = to do something to make people react positively

logical reasoning /ˈlɒdʒɪk(ə)l ˈriːz(ə)nɪŋ/ = using the available facts or evidence to reach a conclusion

4 6.2

- Ask students to focus on the three different influencing styles and their key features when they watch the video again.
- **Optional step** As an alternative to notes, students could put the information about the influencing styles into a mind map with three branches.
- Play the video again.
- **Optional step** Ask students to use their notes to summarize the three different influencing styles with a partner.
- Tell students to look at the Communication skill box to check their answers.

Sample answers

inspiring style – show people how your ideas benefit them; appeal to emotions; believe in your idea but be careful because you might appear unprofessional or inappropriate in certain situations

convincing style – use information, statistics or other facts; helps build trust and convince people
negotiating style – listening to other people; trying to find a middle ground; taking other people's opinions into account; helps build relationships

Extra activity

In pairs, ask students to think about which influencing style they would usually use and talk about any specific examples of using it that they can remember. They could then think about and discuss the possible advantages and disadvantages of each influencing style.

5

- Ask students to read the situations and then go through the first one in class. Elicit things you could do or say that would quickly have an influence on someone, for example presenting facts and showing your confidence by talking about something with great enthusiasm.
- Ask students to decide which influencing style(s) would work best for the remaining three situations.
- **Optional step** Students compare their ideas with another pair.

Sample answers

1 convincing – facts could help you quickly influence the other person; inspiring – conveying enthusiasm and confidence might also be a quick way of influencing someone
2 inspiring – you need to appeal to their feeling and emotions, sounding convinced yourself can also help; negotiating - your idea may benefit from another person's input; convincing – if you have any facts and numbers to back up what you're saying, that might help them believe you
3 negotiating – you probably need to establish a stronger relationship first, discover what the other person thinks, etc.
4 negotiating – you might actually need input from the other person for your idea, so this style might be the most appropriate

6

- Without looking at the Useful language box, ask students to read audioscript 6.8 and underline the expressions the speakers use to influence each other.

6D Influencing styles

LESSON GOALS
- Understand three different influencing styles
- Practise influencing others
- Propose an idea for a class project

SPEAKING AND LISTENING

1 Read the story. What lesson does it teach? How does it relate to the topic of influencing styles?

The North Wind and the Sun

The North Wind and the Sun were arguing about which of them was the strongest, when a traveller came along wrapped in a warm coat. They agreed that the one who succeeded in making the traveller take his coat off would be considered the strongest. First, the North Wind blew as hard as he could, but the more he blew, the more tightly the traveller pulled his coat around him. Then the Sun shone warmly. Immediately, the traveller took off his coat. So, the North Wind had to admit that the Sun was the stronger of the two.

2 6.8 **Listen to three friends talking about a trip they're planning. Then answer the questions in pairs.**

1 Which of the speakers sounds more like the North Wind from the story?
2 Which speaker's influencing style would work best on you? Why?
3 Which speaker's style do you think is most like your own?

1 The second speaker, Fuad, is most like the wind, pushing the hardest for going to Marrakesh.

MY VOICE

3 6.2 **Watch the video. Put the questions in the order that they are answered. Then discuss the answers with a partner.**

a Should you use more than one influencing style?
b What three influencing styles are mentioned?
c When are influencing skills useful?

4 6.2 **Watch the video again. Take notes about each influencing style. Then look at the Communication skill box to check.**

78

- Tell students to match the speakers to the three influencing styles based on the expressions each speaker uses, then to look at the Useful language box to check their answers.

Answers

Speaker 1 (negotiating style) says: *would you be willing to consider another city instead?; It might be a good compromise. What do you think?; I can see where you're coming from; I understand this is a big thing; how about this?*
Speaker 2 (inspiring style) says: *Just think how much you'd regret missing the chance to see Marrakesh; Just picture this …; I'm just so excited about …*
Speaker 3 (convincing style) says: *I've read that …; I've also heard from friends that …*

Extra activity

Tell students to imagine that they are planning a holiday with friends or family. Ask students to each think of a place they would like to go to and how they can influence their friends to agree with their proposal for the holiday. Students then use the expressions in the Useful language box to write sentences to try to influence their friends. Tell students to choose two or three real-life friends and imagine what the best influencing style to use with each of these friends would be.

COMMUNICATION SKILL
Influencing styles

Here are three approaches you can use to influence people. You may use more than one approach at once, or different approaches in different situations.

Inspiring style
Communicate your idea with enthusiasm and confidence so that others feel it too. Make it clear how your idea will benefit them.

Negotiating style
Develop relationships with others by listening carefully to their opinions and taking their feelings and opinions into account.

Convincing style
Use evidence, reasoning and common sense to convince people that your idea is a good one.

5 **Work in pairs. Imagine you are part of a team working on a project. You want to persuade other people about an idea of yours. Which influencing style(s) might work best in the situations (1–4)? Why?**

1 You need a decision quickly. You only need them to agree to this one idea, not to show long-term commitment. They are normally open to ideas.
2 Your idea is quite unusual, so it would be good to have another person's opinion.
3 You've only spoken to the other people a few times. You're not sure how much they like you.
4 Your idea is not fully developed and you're not 100% convinced yourself yet.

6 **Look at audioscript 6.8 on page 165. Underline the expressions the speakers use to influence each other. Then match them with the three styles. Look at the Useful language box to check.**

Useful language Influencing people

Inspiring
Just imagine/picture this …
Wouldn't it be amazing if …
I know how much you love …

Negotiating
I can see where you're coming from.
Would you be willing to consider …?
How about this?

Convincing
According to …
I've read/heard that …
The reason I say that is because …

SPEAKING

7 **OWN IT!** **Imagine you are going to do a class project in groups to produce a five-minute audio or video programme for other learners of English. It should both entertain them and help them improve their English.**

Individually, look at the ideas in the table and decide which you think your group should produce.

Media type	Programme type
• radio show • podcast • TV programme • online vlog • Facebook/Instagram stories	• news programme • entertainment news • mini drama • a guide to a place • documentary • chat show • your own idea

I think a podcast that tells other English learners about the local area is the best idea. Podcasts are really popular these days and you can listen to them everywhere …

8 **Plan how you are going to persuade the other members of your group to make the programme you want. You can choose one influencing style or a mix of styles. Use these questions and the Useful language to help you.**

Convincing style:
What information, such as facts and statistics, could you mention to support your idea? For example, check how many daily listeners a radio show has.

Negotiating style:
What do you think the other people in your group might suggest? What reasons might they give? Consider their opinions and show curiosity by asking questions.

Inspiring style:
How can you show others your enthusiasm for your idea (e.g. by sounding enthusiastic, using emotional language)? How will your idea benefit the rest of the group?

9 **Work in groups. Take turns to make your proposal. Use influencing skills to 'sell' your idea and listen to other team members. As a group, decide which idea you will use.**

EXPLORE MORE!

Observe how others around you try to influence each other. Which styles do they use? How successful are they?

79

SPEAKING

7 OWN IT!

- Direct students to the table and check their understanding of 'vlog' (a blog that consists of a series of video posts).
- Ask students to read the items in the table and individually decide which media type and which programme type they think would be best for the project.
- Tell students to write down their choices and the reason(s) for them as in the example sentences given.

8

- Ask students to review the three influencing styles and decide which style or combination of styles would be the most effective for them. Tell them to consider the situation (a class project with other students) and the media type and programme type they have chosen.
- Tell students to use the questions and Useful language to prepare to present a proposal to other students in the next exercise.
- **Optional step** Students could go online to find facts or other evidence to support their claims.

9

- Find out which ideas students chose in Exercise 7 (i.e. which media and programme type) and try to ensure students who chose different media and programme types work together.
- Put students into small groups.
- Students take turns to present their proposals. Encourage them to react to and, if appropriate, question the claims other students make after the presentation of each proposal.
- Students then have to reach a consensus on which idea to choose for their project. This will involve asking other group members for their opinions, reacting to their opinions and, most likely, negotiating with them.
- **Optional step** Students stay in the same groups. Ask them to reflect on the following questions and then share their answers in their groups: *What was it that convinced you to agree with the specific proposal that your group agreed on? What influencing style did the person who presented the proposal use?*

Extra activity

Ask students to work in their groups from Exercise 9 and use the idea they chose to produce a five-minute audio or video programme for other learners of English, using their mobile devices or computers. If it is not possible for students to actually produce a programme, they could make a detailed plan for how they would do it.

EXPLORE MORE!

Ask students to brainstorm situations in their everyday life when people around them try to influence each other. Encourage them to think about specific situations where people are making decisions, working on something collaboratively or where a person/group is making a proposal to another person/group. Ask students to be aware of when these situations arise over the course of a week or two and tell them to notice the influencing style or styles that the influencer uses and how successfully he/she does this. Students could make notes on what they notice and then either present this to other students in class or write a summary of what happened in each situation.

LESSON GOALS

- **WRITING** The aim of the lesson is to guide students to produce a news article. The reading text provides a model. Students learn to recognize formal and informal news article styles and practise using sensational language and careful and objective language as appropriate for each style.

SPEAKING

1

- Check students' understanding of 'plummet' (to decrease by a large amount in a short time).
- Students work in pairs to discuss the questions.

READING FOR WRITING

2

- Ask students to read the headlines of the two news articles. Ask, *Do the headlines claim that El Dorado has been found?*
- Tell students to read the two news articles and identify whether or not they conclude that El Dorado has been found.
- Students compare answers in pairs and use evidence from the articles to justify their choices.
- Elicit that the first article makes the story sound more sensational than it actually is and it probably is not actually El Dorado that has been found.

3

- Tell students that they are now going to focus on the types of language and information included in the two news articles.
- Students read the articles again and make notes on their answers.

4

- Ask students to look at the Writing skill box and check their answers to Exercise 3. Also, remind students that it is important to be consistent when they are writing an article by using the same style throughout.
- Elicit that article A is written in a more informal style and article B is written in a more formal style.

6E Same news, different style

LESSON GOALS
- Recognize formal and informal article styles
- Use sensational or objective language as appropriate
- Write a news article

SPEAKING

1 Work in pairs. Discuss the questions.

1 Do you ever read news articles? Do you prefer a more formal or informal style? Why?

2 Which headline do you think comes from a more formal article and which from a more informal article? Which would you be more likely to read?

a Airlines slash fares as passenger demand plummets

b Airlines reduce fares due to lower passenger demand

READING FOR WRITING

2 Read the two articles. Do you believe El Dorado has been found? Why? / Why not?

A woman reading a newspaper at a kiosk in Kathmandu, Nepal.

A

'City Of Gold' El Dorado Finally Found

The golden city, or El Dorado, was first described by Spanish and Portuguese conquistadores. This mysterious city was widely thought to be only the stuff of legends. But it looks like it's finally been found.

Recent satellite images reveal huge man-made buildings right in the middle of the Brazilian Amazon. 'When I saw them, I knew this has got to be El Dorado', we were told by Joao Felix, a local enthusiast.

This discovery promises mountains of gold for those adventurous enough to get it. But to reach the golden city, you'll have to battle mosquitos, survive 40°C heat and avoid deadly animals such as jaguars.

Not that it scares people like Joao. He's determined to get there, no matter the cost, and despite repeated warnings from authorities that it's too dangerous. 'The government and the scientists don't want us to find the gold, but we will!'

B

Ancient City Found In The Amazon

For decades, archaeologists have said that no great civilizations existed in the Amazon. However, a recent discovery is putting this view into question, suggesting large cities connected by a vast network of roads and canals did exist.

According to the researchers who found it, the newly discovered city was likely home to approximately sixty thousand people. Even more impressively, it seems to have been part of a vast 250-kilometre-wide network of cities, possibly built by the same civilization.

Since such enormous size and advanced engineering was thought to be impossible in the Amazon, the archaeologists were surprised by their findings. Nevertheless, it is rather unlikely to be the famous city of gold, El Dorado, which adventurers have been looking for since the 1500s but that researchers now agree is a myth.

- Students discuss which style they prefer, giving reasons to justify their choice.

Extra activity

Ask students to search for a current news story online and try to find an article about it that is written in an informal style and an article about it that is written in a formal style. Alternatively, you could find two articles yourself before the lesson, for use in class. Ask students to read the two articles and answer the questions from Exercise 3 about it.

5

- Remind students that they learned the word 'sensational' in Lesson 6C. Elicit that sensational language is used in news articles written in an informal style.
- Students identify the words that make the sentence sensational and compare their answers in pairs.
- Students scan article A for other examples of sensational language, then compare their answers in pairs again.

3 Read the articles again. Which article (A or B) …

1 focuses more on facts? B
2 presents personal stories? A
3 uses longer sentences? B
4 uses more formal language? B
5 is more careful and objective? B
6 uses more sensational language? A

4 Look at the Writing skill box to check your answers to Exercise 3. Which article style do you prefer? Why?

WRITING SKILL
Choosing your writing style

The style and tone that you choose when writing will affect the story being told and the way the reader reacts to it.

Some articles follow a more informal style. They use shorter sentences and paragraphs. Vocabulary is more sensational. They focus more on personal stories and opinions and are often more subjective.

Other articles are more formal. The sentences and paragraphs are longer. Vocabulary is more formal. They focus more on objective facts and research.

5 Look at the sentence below. Which words make it sound more sensational? Find other examples of sensational language in article A.

This discovery promises mountains of gold for those adventurous enough to get it.

6 Make the sentences (1–4) more sensational by replacing the words in bold with the correct form of the words in the box.

chase incredible smash thugs

1 He **kicked** the ball into the net. smashed
2 The **criminals** were finally caught by police. thugs
3 She will continue to **go after** her dream. chase
4 Her **unusual** story might inspire many others. incredible

7 Which sentence (1 or 2) sounds more objective?

1 According to researchers, it is rather unlikely to be the famous city of gold, El Dorado.
2 Local enthusiasts are certain they have finally found the long-lost city of gold, El Dorado.

8 Look at the Useful language box. Rewrite the sentences (1–4) so that they sound more objective. Use at least two 'careful' expressions in each sentence.

Useful language Being careful and objective

Verbs
About sixty thousand people **seem to** have lived there. The findings **suggest that** …

Modal verbs
Scientists **might/could/may** soon discover …

Adverbs
This city was **probably/possibly** built by …; **Practically/Virtually** all scientists agree …; We still know **relatively** little …

Adjectives
It is **likely/possible/probable** that …

Sample answers

1 Everyone is able to learn a foreign language to a high level. Practically everyone seems to be able
2 No one owns an electric car these days. Practically no one owns / seems to own
3 This shows stories about an ancient city in the Amazon were true. This (might) suggest, probably true
4 Climate change is the cause of the recent heatwaves. seems to be, likely/possible/probable cause

WRITING TASK

9 WRITE Write a news article of at least 200 words.

Decide whether you will write in a formal or informal style. Then choose a news topic that interests you. You can choose a current story or choose one of the headlines (1–3) to write about.

1 City plans to be carbon neutral by 2050.
2 Fans devastated as singer cancels tour.
3 Tourists left stranded after airline goes bankrupt.

10 CHECK Use the checklist. I have …

☐ included a headline.
☐ used passive structures.
☐ used careful and objective language (formal).
☐ used sensational language (informal).
☐ used long or short sentences as appropriate for the style I chose.

11 REVIEW Exchange articles with a partner. Answer the questions.

1 Which style did your partner choose? How do you know?
2 What is the most interesting part of the article?

Go to page 132 for the Reflect and review.

81

6

- Ask students to read the words in the box and the sentences. Check understanding of 'smash' (to make something move into something else quickly and with great force) and 'thug' (a violent person who breaks the law).
- Students replace the words in bold in the sentences with words from the box.
- Check answers as a class.

7

- Remind students that they learned the word 'objective' in Lesson 6C.
- Ask students to read the two sentences and decide which one is more objective and why.
- **Optional step** Ask students to identify other examples of sentences that present information objectively in Article B.
- Elicit the specific words, expressions and structures in the sentence that make it sound more objective.

Answers

Sentence 1: because of words 'according to researchers', 'rather', 'unlikely' and impersonal structure 'it is + *adjective*'

8

- Ask students to look at the Useful language box. Check they are aware that these expressions would usually be used in formal articles.
- Students rewrite the sentences and then compare answers in pairs.

WRITING TASK

9 WRITE

- Ask students to read the instructions for the task.
- If students choose a current story instead of using one of the headlines given, allow them some time to either search for news stories online or look in print newspapers.
- Ask students to concentrate on using appropriate language for the style or tone they have chosen for their article. Refer students back to the Writing skill box to help them do this.
- Students write the first draft of their news articles.

Extra activity

Ask students to rewrite the article, or part of the article, that they wrote in Exercise 9 in the opposite style, i.e. changing it from formal to informal or informal to formal.

10 CHECK

- Ask students to use the checklist and then make changes to their news article if necessary.

11 REVIEW

- Students exchange news articles with a partner. They read each other's articles and use the checklist from Exercise 10 to review them.
- Students read their partner's article again and focus on identifying the writer's style and whether he/she has consistently used either a formal or informal style in their text.
- Students give each other feedback on their news articles.

For **Unit 6 Reflect and review**, see Student's Book page 132.

See **Workbook** pages 54–55 for extra practice.

See **Workbook** pages 56–57 for Units 5 and 6 Review.

VIDEO 6.1

Afroz: *I like all news related to science and I keep a close watch on the political landscape of the world. I'm particularly keen on scientific discoveries that make life comfortable for all of us on the planet Earth.*

Imogen: *Due to the nature of my research, I follow conservation news closely. I am also weirdly into tabloid news. I always joke if I could remember scientific facts like I could celebrity gossip, I would be a genius! For example, I love news on the British royal family! On the other hand, I barely read the sports pages.*

Afroz: *One story that has had a huge impact on me was when I first came to know that Imran Khan, one of my favourite cricket players and a politician in Pakistan, had built a cancer hospital for the poor. He had lost his own mother to the same illness despite spending millions on her treatment. This news is refreshing and fills me with hope. It is said to be the first cancer facility in Pakistan that provides free health care to the poor.*

I was also fascinated by the Apollo 11 moon landing. Especially the satellite image that shows Earth rise from the moon. It shows our home planet as a bright blue marble in the darkness of space. It's one of the most fascinating images to have remained with me because it shows all of us as one family.

Imogen: *Stories that have had the biggest impact on me personally are stories where I know the news affects me or the people that I know. A story that immediately comes to my head is hearing about the snow warnings when I was travelling to school when I was younger. My dad and I would be listening closely to the radio to see if the school would be shut down and we would get a snow day. And even though I mentioned I'm not so much into sports news, a news story that I loved following was the London Olympic games in 2012. The whole nation came together to support Great Britain. Watching the events was often really stressful, and we found ourselves supporting athletes in sports that I hadn't even heard of before. Everyone was talking about it and it felt so positive.*

AUDIO 6.1

The plan to become carbon neutral within two years was revealed today by the Costa Rican government. This decision was praised by environmentalists around the world as it is hoped it will lead other nations to take similar action. The plan is thought to be an important step in the global fight against climate change. If successful, Costa Rica would become the first carbon neutral country in the world.

After a decade as the world's biggest-selling film, Avatar *has lost its record. It has been beaten by the superhero blockbuster* Avengers: Endgame *which is said to have made 2.79 billion dollars from cinema ticket sales. That's one hundred thousand dollars more than* Avatar*. This is quite an incredible achievement considering that, back in 1996, Marvel was believed to be close to bankruptcy.*

In sports, Eliud Kipchoge has made history after achieving what had been thought to be impossible – running a marathon in under two hours. However, it has been suggested that the shoes he was wearing gave him an unfair advantage. The shoes were designed to allow long-distance runners to run up to four per cent faster, but it is understood that the World Athletics committee might ban their use in the Olympics.

AUDIO 6.2

Crowds gathered to welcome Peter Tabichi as he returned from Dubai, where he had been chosen for the best teacher in the world award. The prize is thought to be one of the most important in the world. It is awarded for exceptional teaching achievements. Mr Tabichi was congratulated by the judges on his passion and for inspiring girls to study science. His students' scores are said to have improved dramatically since he started working at the school, and some have won international awards. Mr Tabichi is also admired for his charity. He gives away almost all of his salary every year to help children from poorer families. He is reported to be planning to also donate the one-million-dollar prize he received.

AUDIO 6.4

1 I get a lot of my news from social media.

2 The five-minute news bulletins give me an idea of what today's top stories are.

3 For example, I often read online newspapers and magazines.

AUDIO 6.5

1 get a lot of

2 an idea of

3 read online

AUDIO 6.6

Interviewer: *Where do you typically get your news from?*

Imogen: *I get a lot of my news from social media, like Twitter. This is normally what I see when I wake up and go on my phone. But I also listen to podcasts to learn about stories and news more in-depth. When I'm driving in my car, or working from home, I always have the radio on. The five-minute news bulletins give me an idea of what today's top stories are. And I watch the television to get foreign news, but I only watch this if I know something significant is happening.*

Afroz: *I mainly get my news from the internet. But the sources vary a lot. For example, I often read online newspapers and magazines, such as New York Times, Kashmir Observer or Scientific American. I will often skim over the headlines first, before choosing the story that interests me. I definitely prefer news sources that provide more in-depth articles. There are many news reporting sources which I completely avoid, such as tabloid press, because of a lack of honesty and often exaggerations that are filled with lies. I don't want to name such sources but there are many around!*

Interviewer: *Have you ever stopped following the news?*

Imogen: *Sometimes it just seems like a certain news story is on the front page of every newspaper and the headline of every news channel for weeks! You automatically start to ignore it because it isn't new anymore. Because you are so bored of it, you stop reading news stories in depth, you just skim over them. I even remember a radio host once saying 'I bet you are all bored to hear more about this news story again, but here are the latest updates.'*

Interviewer: *What problems do you see with how the news is reported?*

Afroz: *Because news has been largely commercialized these days, there is too much focus on certain types of news. In order to make the headlines, the news often has to be very sensational. I feel it's not about objective news reporting anymore but about clickbait articles with attention-grabbing pictures. It is entirely on the readers to separate real from fake news.*

Interviewer: *Has your work ever been reported by the media?*

Imogen: *Since starting my PhD in 2015, there has been a huge amount of interest with plastic pollution in the ocean. This interest has grown and grown and resulted in some of my research making the headlines in the UK. I was really excited but also really nervous. I didn't want to say the wrong thing!*

Afroz: *Yes, my work on earthquakes has been published by various media outlets. At first, I was slightly worried that the media might try to make the research sound more sensational. But I was really happy because the way it was reported was accurate and objective.*

AUDIO 6.8

A: *OK, so from what I can hear there are two possible cities, right? Fez or Marrakesh? What are we thinking at the moment? Fuad?*

B: *I say we go to Marrakesh. I think we'd struggle to find a better option.*

C: *I'm with you on that. I've read that it's been voted one of the top five cities to visit.*

A: *It is brilliant, but as I've already been there, would you be willing to consider another city instead?*

B: *You haven't been there for ten years! I'm sure lots has changed since then …*

C: *… Well, I've also heard from friends that Fez is supposed to be fantastic.*

A: *I'd be up for that. It might be a good compromise. What do you think?*

B: *Just think how much you'd regret missing the chance to see Marrakesh! Just picture this: the Bahia Palace with its beautiful decorations and peaceful gardens, the Jemaa el-Fna market; I know how much you love historical architecture. I'm just so excited about it all!*

A: *I can see where you're coming from and I understand this is a big thing when you've had Marrakesh on your mind for so long, so how about this: we go to Fez, but Albert and I will let you decide which places to visit for the first two days?*

C: *Er, yeah, I'd be happy with that, I think … Hey, I just looked at flights to Fez – they're half the price of those to Marrakesh!*

B: *What?! That can't be right. Let me see that. Are you sure that's the cheapest flight you can find? …*

VIDEO 6.2

We often find ourselves in situations when we want to help other people see our way of thinking and persuade them to change their mind. Perhaps you need to convince your teacher to give you more time for a homework assignment, for example, or you want your boss to agree to a new project. This skill of influencing is useful in many situations. Some might choose to use a lot of arguments and talk a lot when trying to influence others. That's very similar to the old Greek fable where the North Wind tries to make a traveller take his coat off to prove he's stronger than the Sun. So the Wind blows and blows, but the traveller just wraps up. On the other hand, some might choose to listen more and build relationships. They might be less direct in their influencing, like the Sun.

What influencing styles are there? Let's look at three different types.

Are you excited about your idea? Are you confident about it? Maybe you can use your excitement and confidence to inspire others to feel the same way. To inspire people, you need to show them how your idea benefits them. You need to appeal to their emotions and above all, believe in your idea. The more you believe in it, the more others will believe in it too! Be careful, however, that your excitement and enthusiasm doesn't come across as unprofessional or inappropriate in certain situations.

Another option is to use evidence and logic. Perhaps you have information that shows your idea is a good one. Do you have statistics or other facts that prove that what you say is true? Using data and logical reasoning is another way to build trust. If you have evidence to support your ideas, people are more likely to be convinced. But remember, complicated logical arguments, or lots of numbers and data can confuse people or be too detailed and they might lose interest in what you're saying.

The third style is about listening to other people's ideas and trying to find a middle ground, a compromise. Taking others' opinions into account can ensure everyone feels listened to. It's about building relationships, which are key to any successful communication.

To sum up, it's important to realize there is no one best style. Different approaches are useful in different situations, depending on who we're talking to. One idea to help you expand your influencing skills is to identify the style you use most often, the one that is easiest for you and try to adopt one of the other styles sometimes, to practise alternative ways to persuade people of your ideas.

UNIT 7

Shared spaces

UNIT GOALS

7A Reading, speaking

- read an article to practise dealing with unknown words in texts and use critical thinking skills to analyse solutions to problems presented in the article; discuss problems involving humans and animals sharing space

7B Reading and grammar, pronunciation, speaking

- read about and discuss space-saving solutions in different cities around the world; learn and practise using causative verbs to make suggestions for solutions to problems; practise stressing the correct syllable in multiple-syllable verbs

7C Listening, vocabulary, pronunciation, speaking

- listen to an interview with a National Geographic explorer and identify and understand figurative language; learn and practise collocations for describing places; practise pronouncing /b/, /v/ and /w/ clearly

7D Speaking, listening and grammar

- learn and practise using structures for complaining; practise dealing with difficult conversations sensitively and use language that softens the message; roleplay a conversation where people explain problems to each other

7E Writing

- practise using informal language and writing style in social media posts; write and respond to social media posts

A fish market on the Galápagos Islands is popular with the local human and sea lion population.

Photocopiable resources

Communication activities: pp. 224–225
Vocabulary activity: p. 239
Grammar activity: p. 257
Focus on … activity: p. 258
Pronunciation activity: p. 274
Mediation activity: p. 289

Workbook

Unit 7 pp. 58–65

ABOUT THE PHOTO

The photo shows a scene at a fish market in the Galápagos Islands, Ecuador. Several men are preparing fish to be sold. A sea lion is standing up on its rear fins and peering into the crates of fish. The men appear to be completely tolerant of the sea lion's presence.

The Galápagos Islands are known for being very biologically diverse. Some species are unique to the islands and are also known for their lack of fear of the humans they co-exist with. Sea lions can be found napping on public benches or begging for food on the beaches. The Galápagos sea lion is the smallest species of sea lion

7 Shared spaces

GOALS

- Deal with unknown words in an article
- Use causative verbs to talk about solutions to problems
- Identify figurative language when listening
- Describe places
- Explain a problem without offending others
- Write and respond to social media posts

1 Work in pairs. Look at the photo and discuss the questions.

1 What is happening in the photo?
2 Why do you think the people tolerate the animals in this place? Why do you think the animals tolerate the people?
3 What animals do you share space with in your home, your neighbourhood or your country?

WATCH

2 ▶ 7.1 Watch the video. Match the sentences with the correct explorer, Abby (A) or Robbie (R).

NATIONAL GEOGRAPHIC EXPLORERS

ABBY MCBRIDE ROBBIE SHONE

1 Sharing space with other people can be difficult. R
2 Sharing space with a big animal can be dangerous. A
3 What seemed like a mistake was actually a very good idea. R
4 Sharing space means being aware of how much we need, and how much we can harm, each other. A

3 Make connections. Do you remember any funny or interesting stories about when you've shared spaces with other people or animals?

83

(weighing a maximum of 250 kilograms) but some species can be much larger and heavier, for example the New Zealand sea lion (mentioned in Abby McBride's story in Exercise 2).

Extra activity

Direct students to the title of this unit and give them two minutes to write anything that comes to mind when they hear the expression 'shared spaces'. They could write notes, draw a mind-map or record their thoughts in any other way they wish. When their time is up, ask students to share their ideas in pairs or small groups.

1

- Tell students to look carefully at the photo and the caption, then read the questions.
- Check students' understanding of 'tolerate' (to accept someone or something else's behaviour even though it might have a negative impact on you) and then give students about a minute to think about their answers.
- In pairs, students discuss the questions.

Extra activity

Ask students to imagine they are observing the scene in the photo in person. Students prepare a description of the scene and share it with a partner.
Alternatively, ask students to imagine what each person (and animal) in the photo is saying or thinking and, if permitted, add speech or thought bubbles to the page.

WATCH

2 ▶ 7.1

- Tell students that they are going to hear two National Geographic explorers talking about sharing space.
- Ask students to read the sentences.
- **Optional step** Ask students to brainstorm situations where sharing space could be 1) difficult; 2) dangerous; 3) a good idea.
- Play the video and tell students to listen for the opinions the explorers give about sharing space.
- Students write their answers and then compare answers in pairs before checking as a class.

3

- Give students about a minute to think of any funny or interesting stories related to the question.
- **Optional step** If students cannot think of anything suitable, they could talk about something that happened to someone they know or something they have read about in the newspaper.
- Students share one or more anecdotes with their partner.

ABOUT THE EXPLORERS

ABBY MCBRIDE is a sketch biologist from the US. She travels all over the world to draw wildlife and create multimedia stories about science and conservation. Abby has spent time in New Zealand observing the country's endangered seabirds and reporting on efforts to reverse the damage done to their populations and habitats. **ROBBIE SHONE** is a cave explorer and visual storyteller. Originally from the UK, he is now based in Austria. He has photographed caves in some of the most remote parts of the world.

LESSON GOALS

- **READING** The main aim is for students to practise dealing with unknown words in an article about problems and solutions and then use their critical thinking skills to analyse solutions to problems.
- **SPEAKING** The speaking aim is for students to discuss problems in their country between humans and animals.

READING

ABOUT THE TEXT

In this article, the author writes about the successful co-existence of elephants in the Gorongosa National Park in Mozambique and local communities nearby. The Gorongosa National Park covers an area of around 4,000 square kilometres in central Mozambique. The national park provides a home to a large range of wildlife. However, the number of large mammals in the park fell by as much as 95 per cent during the long civil conflict in Mozambique at the end of the 20th century. Conservation efforts are now being made to increase the number of large mammals again, for example through the Elephant Ecology Project. The aim of this project is to make the co-existence of people and elephants sustainable by researching elephant behaviour and the ecology of the park and then using this knowledge to find ways that elephants and people can adapt to live alongside each other.

1

- Ask students to use their general knowledge to think about the possible effects of large creatures like elephants and humans living close to one another.
- Students discuss the question in pairs.
- Ask students to share their ideas.

Sample answers

People: crops get destroyed, property might be damaged, people might be harmed or killed if they get too close
Elephants: they lack space and the food they need, they might get shot or injured by humans defending their property

7A Sharing space with animals

LESSON GOALS
- Deal with unknown words in an article
- Analyse solutions to problems
- Discuss spaces shared between humans and animals

READING

1 **Work in pairs. What problems might happen when elephants and people live close to one another?**

Elephants don't have enough space. They might destroy people's homes.

2 **Read the article on page 85. What problem caused by people and elephants sharing space is mentioned? What solution to this problem has been used?**

3 **Look at the Reading skill box and discuss the questions (1–2).**

READING SKILL
Dealing with unknown words

When reading a text, you will find words you don't know. Looking them up in a dictionary can sometimes be impractical and slow down your reading. So, instead, you can also …
- **check the context:** e.g. after *rebounded* in paragraph 1, it says *from one hundred to over seven hundred*, so *rebound* probably means *go up again*.
- **compare the new word with words from your first language:** e.g. *voracious* in paragraph 2 has similar words in French (*vorace*), Spanish and Portuguese (*voraz*), Romanian (*vorace*).
- **look at how the word is formed:** e.g. you may not know *protection* in paragraph 2, but you understand *to protect* and know that *-ion* is used to make nouns.
- **use the visuals:** e.g. in paragraph 7, *suspend the beehives from poles* might be difficult to understand, but the photo can help you.

1 Which tips in the Reading skill box have you used before? How effective were they?
2 Which tips would you like to try?

4 **Find at least five words in the article that you don't know. Use the tips in the Reading skill box to work out their meaning. Then share with a partner.**

5 **Read the article again. Which of the ideas are mentioned?**

1 Increasing elephant populations have caused difficulties for the local people.
2 Farmers used to shoot the elephants that destroyed their fields.
3 Bees are small but strong fighters.
4 The best place for a bee to sting an elephant is on its ears.
5 *Piri-piri* is a chilli that can be used to scare elephants away.
6 The bee and chilli fence has more than one benefit for local communities.

6 **Work in pairs. Look at the Critical thinking skill box. Then analyse the bee and chilli fence solution from the article by discussing the questions in the box.**

CRITICAL THINKING SKILL
Analysing solutions to problems

When analysing proposed solutions to a problem, ask yourself questions to evaluate how effective the solution might be. For example:
- What effects (positive and negative) can it have on those involved?
- How practical is it?
- How much will it cost (e.g. materials, staff)?
- What training or skills might be needed?

7 **Analyse two different solutions to the problem in the article, using the questions from Exercise 6. Do they seem more or less effective than the bee and chilli fence solution?**

Solution 1: Moving the elephants to a new region.
Solution 2: Compensating (paying) farmers for the loss of money caused by elephants eating their corn.

SPEAKING

8 **Work in pairs. Do you know of any problems caused by people and animals sharing space in your country? Discuss the questions.**

1 Are the problems in cities or the countryside?
2 What problems do the animals cause humans? What problems do humans cause the animals?
3 Have you heard about any possible solutions?

EXPLORE MORE!
Search online for other unusual ways animals and humans interact. You can use these key words to help you: 'wild boars + Rome'; 'butterfly wings + waterproof raincoats'.

84

2

- Ask students to read the article and find a problem caused by elephants and people living close to each other and a solution for this problem.
- **Optional step** Tell students that there will be several unknown words in the article, but they should ignore these and concentrate on identifying and understanding the key information about the problem and solution.

Answers

Problem: elephants eating farmers' crops;
Solution: building a fence of bees/beehives, covering ropes in chilli peppers/*piri-piri*

VOCABULARY NOTES

voracious /və'reɪʃəs/ = having a large appetite, especially for food

livelihood /'laɪvlihʊd/ = a job or other source of income that provides the money you need to cover your living costs

sting /stɪŋ/ = an insect or plant pushing a sharp part of its body into the body of a person or animal

defence system /dɪ'fens 'sɪstəm/ = a method or mechanism that protects something or someone from danger, harm or theft

'BEE' ware of the fence!

Over the last two decades, elephant numbers in Gorongosa National Park in Mozambique have rebounded, from just one hundred to over seven hundred. While this has been a great success story from an environmental point of view, it has also created challenges for the local communities living around the park. It's a challenge that the Elephant Ecology team at Gorongosa have been trying to tackle.

Elephants are voracious eaters. They spend over half the day eating and an adult will easily eat four hundred kilograms of food a day. So, a field full of corn is quite a tasty temptation. For the local farmers then, the elephants are not animals in need of protection, but pests that destroy their only means of making money. It's important to protect both the elephants and the people's livelihood by considering and balancing their separate needs.

How? By building a natural fence to block the elephants' path. A fence made of bees.

Three hundred times smaller than the African elephant, the bee seems a rather unlikely candidate to stop a hungry elephant from having a farmer's crops for lunch. But don't let its size fool you. Bees can be fierce fighters.

While elephants have quite a thick skin, the bees know where to sting to force an elephant to move away. They'll attack the skin around the eyes, for example. You might be a big elephant, but you certainly don't want to make these bees angry.

The Gorongosa team added another ingredient to make their fence elephant-proof: the chilli pepper, or *piri-piri* as it's called in Mozambique. While typically used to give a spicy kick to local food, chillies can also be a fantastic defence system against elephants. Apparently, these giants don't like spicy food.

So how do you create a *piri-piri* bee fence? The recipe is simple. Take a few beehives and link them with a rope covered in chilli powder. Then suspend the beehives from poles.

The first thing that happens when an elephant tries to enter a field is that they smell the *piri-piri*. They'll very likely leave the fence, and the field on the other side of it, alone. If they don't, the bees buzz into action. When an elephant touches the rope, it shakes the beehive and the bees fly out in their hundreds, stinging the elephants and scaring them away.

These natural fences not only help the locals keep their farms safe from elephants, they also provide them with an additional income. Farmers can now collect and sell the honey that the bees produce. It's a win-win situation. This helps encourage the locals to protect rather than harm the elephants.

This is just one example of how cooperation between humans and nature can help solve the key challenges of sharing the same environment. People need employment, schools, food. Elephants, on the other hand, need an enormous amount of space and food to be able to survive. But these needs do not have to be in opposition. By learning how to share space together in a smart way, both humans and animals can thrive.

Fences with beehives and chilli powder keep elephants away from farms.

85

buzz /bʌz/ = to make a low, continuous humming sound

thrive /θraɪv/ = to become very successful or grow or reproduce quickly

3

- Tell students to look at the Reading skill box. Check they understand what each of the tips involve.
- **Optional step** Students could write down a paraphrased version of each tip in their notebooks to consolidate their understanding and give them something to refer back to.
- Students discuss the questions in pairs. Encourage them to share examples of situations where they have used the tips and explain why they would like to try any of the tips.

4

- Students scan the article for words they do not know the meaning of.
- Students use the tip(s) from Exercise 3 to deduce the meaning of these words.
- Students share the words they have chosen and what they think they mean. Where possible, students give each other feedback on whether they have correctly worked out the words' meanings.
- **Optional step** Students look up the meaning of the words they chose in a dictionary to check they correctly guessed its meaning.

Extra activity

Ask students to search online or go through books or newspapers that are available to them in class to find an article in English on a topic that interests them. Students then read the article and use the strategies they have learned to work out the meaning of any unknown words.

5

- Tell students to read the article again to identify which of the ideas (1–6) are mentioned.

Extra activity

Ask students to search for information about Gorongosa National Park in Mozambique. They could begin with an article about it on the National Geographic website. Tell them to find out about what events or trends in Mozambique have caused problems for the national park and its animal inhabitants over the last fifty years and the solutions that the park employees have used to try to increase the number of mammals in the park. Students can make notes on the information they find out and then compare their notes with a partner.

6

- Tell students to look at the Critical thinking skill box.
- Students discuss the questions in the Critical thinking skill box in relation to the solution of building fences with beehives and chilli powder.
- **Optional step** Ask students to write their answers to the questions in note form so they can then present and compare their ideas with another pair.

Sample answers

- What effects (positive and negative) can it have on those involved? – elephants will get stung by bees, which can be painful (negative); elephants will have to find something different to eat (negative); elephants will stay away from human settlements (positive); farmers' crops will not be destroyed (positive); locals can make money from selling honey (positive)
- How practical is it? – very practical as uses local materials at low cost and doesn't harm the animals unless they cannot find alternative food
- How much will it cost? – it seems very cheap; both *piri piri* and bees are easily and cheaply available locally; not many materials needed – some rope, poles and wood for beehives; in fact, thanks to the honey, it might actually generate income
- What training or skills might be needed? – not much: local people need to understand why it's effective and how to build the fences; this should be fairly easy to explain

7

- Tell students they are now going to apply what they have learned about analysing solutions to two other possible solutions to the problem with the elephants.
- Ask students to write answers to the questions in the Critical thinking skill box for each of the solutions. They then use their answers to compare the effectiveness of these two solutions with the bee and chilli fence solution.
- Students share their analyses of Solutions 1 and 2 in pairs and explain to their partner why they think these two solutions are more or less effective than the bee and chilli fence solution.

Sample answers

- Solution 1: What effects (positive and negative) can it have on those involved? – animals taken away from their natural habitat (negative); may be that new location is a national park with more space and therefore better for the animals (positive); farmers won't have elephants stealing their crops (positive)
  How practical is it? – very impractical – moving hundreds of elephants is a very difficult task (needs big truck, lifting equipment, vets, etc)
  How much will it cost? – likely to be very expensive (lots of transportation and professionals needed)
  What training or skills might be needed? – it's not something that the local population can do on their own, would need specialists
- Solution 2: What effects (positive and negative) can it have on those involved? – local people get compensation (positive); elephants continue eating corn (negative)
  How practical is it – impractical as doesn't really solve the problem at hand; humans and elephants will still continue having the same problems
  How much will it cost? – depending on the compensation, it could end up being very expensive. Farmers need to claim compensation, which might be difficult if they can't read or write. Some farmers may cheat and ask for too much compensation.
  What training or skills might be needed? – would need farming experts to evaluate how much each farmer has lost and how much that is worth

SPEAKING

8

- Put students into pairs to brainstorm the problems and discuss the questions.
- **Optional step** If students are not aware of any problems caused by humans and animals sharing space in their country, ask them to choose an animal that is found there and search online for the name of this animal + 'humans/living with humans' to get some ideas for the problems that face it and possibly also solutions for those problems.
- **Optional step** Monitor students' discussions and make a note of any interesting ideas or interesting examples of language that they use, and then share these in class afterwards.

Extra activity

In the same pairs they were in for Exercise 8, ask students to choose two of the solutions for a problem that they thought of in that exercise. Tell students to use the questions in the Critical thinking skill box to analyse each solution and evaluate which would be the most effective. They could then use their notes to prepare a description of the situation, the problem and possible or actual solutions to the problem.

EXPLORE MORE!

Ask students to think of any interesting examples of interaction between animals and humans (past or present) that they have heard or read about. They can then search online for the key terms for that story, like 'wild boars + Rome'. If students cannot think of any examples themselves, they can use one of the two search terms given. Once they have found (more) information about the example they have chosen, ask students to make notes on the most important points.

See **Workbook** pages 58–59 for extra practice.

LESSON GOALS

- **GRAMMAR** The main aim is for students to practise using structures with causative verbs to talk about solutions to problems.
- **READING** A sub-aim is for students to read a text about space-saving solutions in different cities around the world.
- **PRONUNCIATION** A further sub-aim is for students to practise placing stress on the correct syllable in multiple-syllable words.
- **SPEAKING** The speaking aim is to work in a group to suggest space-saving solutions.

READING AND GRAMMAR

1

- **Optional step** Direct students to the title of this lesson. Ask, *What do you do to 'save space' at home?* For example, putting a suitcase on top of a wardrobe.
- Ask students to read the questions, then look at the text and photos and note down their answers to the questions.
- Students discuss the questions in pairs for about three minutes.

Sample answers

Bangkok railway market: advantages – makes use of all available space, popular with tourists; disadvantages – dangerous, stall owners have to pack up stalls when the train comes through
Paris rooftop garden: advantages – provides fresh fruit and vegetables, allows for green spaces in a city; disadvantages – can't grow very much, might be limited to what you can grow
Caracas cable cars: advantages – good view of the city, reduces pollution; disadvantages – not good for people who are scared of heights, might be expensive
Shipping container housing: advantages – cheap accommodation, don't need lots of space, good for the environment; disadvantages – might be small and cramped, could be cold
Bangkok football pitches: advantages – people can play football, players may develop special skills; disadvantages – football pitch is smaller, harder to play on

VOCABULARY NOTES

stall (stɔːl) = a stand, table or area in a market from which people sell goods

shipping container /ˈʃɪpɪŋ kənˈteɪnə(r)/ = a large metal box which is used to transport goods on ships

ingenious /ɪnˈʤiːniəs/ = extremely clever and (usually) innovative

commuter /kəˈmjuːtə(r)/ = a person who travels from one place to another every day to go to work

2

- Tell students to read the Grammar box. Elicit that the 'object' is the person/people/thing(s) that are having something done to them.
- Students scan the text for examples of each structure.
- **Optional step** Students could do this collaboratively in pairs or small groups by sharing the structures between them.
- Check answers as a class.

For further information and practice, see **Grammar reference Unit 7B** on page 148 of the Student's Book.

Answers

verb + object + *to* + infinitive
allowing them to do just that, enables hundreds of students to live, permit footballers to play, encourage more people to farm
verb + object + infinitive (without *to*)
let trains get through, let the train pass, makes you feel
verb + object + from + *-ing*
has saved universities from having to buy, prevents commuters from getting stuck in traffic

GRAMMAR NOTES

Causative verbs

Form

Notice that the verb *help* is most commonly followed by the infinitive, but it may also be followed by the infinitive without *to* (more common in informal English).

Meaning

Allow and *permit* have the same meaning as *let*, but they are more formal.
The verb *make* can be either used as a synonym for *force*, e.g.: *My mother made me tidy my room yesterday*, or to describe an involuntary effect that something you experienced has on your thoughts and feelings, e.g.: *The film made me feel very emotional*.

3

- Ask students to look at the questions. Check students' understanding of 'force' (to give people no choice but to do something) and 'allow' (to say that it is OK for people to do something and that there will be no negative consequences).
- Students complete the task with the verbs from Exercise 2.
- Students compare their answers in pairs.

4 7.1

- Ask students to read the list of topics. Check their understanding of 'possessions' (things that people own).

- Play the audio so students can note down the topics that the explorers talk about.
- Students compare answers in pairs.

Answers

1 Abby - feels crowded; 2 Robbie - kitchen and office; 3 Abby - her car; 4 Robbie - trains and buses 5 Robbie - kitchen cupboard

5 7.1

- Go through the first item with students. Elicit that there is an object after the gap (*me*) and then the infinitive without *to* form of a verb (*feel*). Ask students to consider which causative verbs can be used in the structure verb + object + infinitive without *to* and which of these would fit with the meaning of 'feel'. Elicit that the correct answer is *make*.
- Students complete the remaining sentences with the correct form of the verbs in the box.
- **Optional step** Students complete the sentences in pairs.
- Play the audio again so students can check their answers.

Answers

1 make; 2 save (stop, prevent also possible); 3 forces (requires, encourages also possible); 4 encourages (forces, requires also possible); 5 lets; 6 prevents (stops also possible); 7 enabled (allowed, permitted also possible); 8 permits (allows, enables also possible)

6

- **Optional step** Ask students to read the sentence stems and elicit the verb forms that need to follow each one, e.g. 1) *encouraged me* + *to* + infinitive; 2) *stopped me from* verb *-ing*, etc.
- Students complete the sentences with their own experiences. If students do not feel comfortable sharing personal information, they could make up information instead.
- Students share their sentences with a partner, who gives them feedback on whether they have used the correct structures.

Extra activity

Students write two or three sentences about an object or an experience that includes a causative verb but use 'it' instead of the name of the thing or experience. Put students into pairs to take turns to read their sentence out loud while their partner guesses the thing or experience that the sentence refers to by asking additional questions with a yes/no answer. You could demonstrate the task with the example of a microwave and say the sentence: *It allows me to make food hot quickly. It enables me to save space in the kitchen because I don't need an oven.*

For additional practice, refer to the **Grammar activity** on page 257 of the Teacher's Book.

7B It helps you save space

LESSON GOALS
- Read about and discuss space-saving solutions in cities
- Use causative verbs to talk about solutions to problems
- Stress the correct syllable in verbs

READING AND GRAMMAR

1 Work in pairs. Look at the text and photos and discuss the questions.

1 What are the advantages and disadvantages to each space-saving solution?
2 Could any of the solutions work in your town or city? Why?
3 Which of the solutions would you be happy to use or experience?

2 Read the Grammar box. Find verbs in the text that match each pattern in the box.

GRAMMAR Causative verbs

Causative verbs describe different ways to affect the actions of someone or something.

verb + object + *to* + infinitive
*House prices **forced us to move** away even though we loved the area.*

verb + object + infinitive (without *to*)
*There are a number of great ideas to **help you save** space if you have a small apartment.*

verb + object + *from* + *–ing*
*We have a really small apartment, but that doesn't **stop us from having** visitors because we have a sofa bed in the living room.*

Go to page 148 for the Grammar reference.

3 Which of the verbs from the text describe ways of …

1 forcing someone to do something?
force, require, make
2 allowing someone to do something?
allow, permit, let
3 stopping someone from doing something?
stop, save, prevent

NATIONAL GEOGRAPHIC EXPLORERS

4 7.1 Listen to Robbie Shone and Abby McBride talk about the spaces they live in. Which topics does each person talk about?

1 city living
2 their home
3 unusual spaces they've lived in
4 getting around town
5 space-saving possessions

5 7.1 Complete the sentences (1–8) with the correct form of these verbs. Sometimes more than one answer is possible. Then listen to Robbie and Abby again to check.

advise allow enable encourage force help
let make permit prevent require save stop

In this Bangkok food market, stall owners are required to move out of the way to let trains get through! Shoppers must stand to one side to let the train pass.

86

PRONUNCIATION

7 7.2

- Play the audio. Students listen and identify the stressed syllable in the words in Exercise 5.
- Students compare answers in pairs.

PRONUNCIATION NOTES

Stressing multiple-syllable words
Accurate syllable stress is particularly important with examples where the same word can be used as a verb and a noun, for example: noun: *permit* / verb: *permit*.

1 A: I don't spend much time in cities because they always __________ me feel crowded.
2 R: Tunnels __________ us from having to make long journeys around the mountains.
3 A: There is usually some sort of space limitation that __________ me to make adjustments …
4 A: The lack of personal space __________ me to spend time outdoors by myself.
5 R: Gina's office is at the university, so that __________ me use the home office.
6 A: Travelling so much __________ me from having too many possessions.
7 A: It __________ me to keep everything I needed with me all the time!
8 R: It __________ us to store all our pots and pans without taking up much space.

6 Complete the sentences so that they are true for you. Then share them with a partner.
1 My [parents/partner/friend] encouraged me …
2 My [parents/teacher/job] sometimes stopped me from …
3 [My/My sister's/My friend's teacher] helped …
4 I'd like a job where the boss lets me …

PRONUNCIATION

7 7.2 Listen to the verbs from Exercise 5 that have more than one syllable. Where is the stress in all of them? *on the second syllable*

8 Look at the Clear voice box to check your answer to Exercise 7. Then practise saying the verbs.

CLEAR VOICE
Stressing multi-syllable verbs

The stress on most verbs with two or more syllables falls on the second syllable: ad**vise**, al**low**, en**a**ble. Notice that the vowel in the unstressed syllable will often be shorter, so placing the stress correctly can help you pronounce the difference between long and short vowels.

SPEAKING

9 Work in groups. Choose one of the situations below. Suggest solutions using the Useful language box. Look for ideas online to help you.

A Your school is planning to convert one of the classrooms into a library. However, it is a very small room. Suggest ways to fit everything in the room, while giving students enough space to study in.
You could build shelves into the walls. This would save you from having big bookcases.

B Your friend has just bought a studio apartment. It is only 25 m². Help them decide how to fit all their belongings into such a small space, while at the same time making it practical and comfortable.
A foldable sofa bed would help you save space.

Useful language Solving problems
It deals with the problem/issue of …
It stops/saves you from having to …
It means you don't have to …
It allows more people to …

Paris has one of the largest urban farms in Europe … on a roof! The increasing demand for fresh food in cities will only encourage more people to farm on their rooftops.

In various cities, including Glasgow, Amsterdam and Johannesburg, architects have converted shipping containers into university housing. This has saved universities from having to buy big areas of land. This ingenious solution enables hundreds of students to live close to university.

A public system of cable cars above Caracas prevents commuters from getting stuck in traffic. A journey to the office makes you feel as if you're on a skiing trip!

Where do you fit a football pitch among the skyscrapers? People in Bangkok found a perfect solution allowing them to do just that. Strange-shaped pitches permit footballers to play their favourite game.

Common problems

- Students stress the stressed syllable too little so that the stress is not clear or exaggerate the stress on the stressed syllable so that it sounds unnatural.
- A different stress pattern is used for multiple-syllable words in students' first language or a different stress pattern is used for similar-sounding words in students' first language. This might make students automatically revert to the stress pattern from their first language.

8

- Tell students to read the Clear voice box and check their answer to Exercise 7.
- Put students into pairs to practise saying the verbs from Exercise 7 with the correct stress pattern.

Extra activity

Remind students that stress is placed on the second syllable of most verbs with two or more syllables. Then tell them that stress is placed on the first syllable of most nouns. Write these words that can be both verbs and nouns on the board: permit, progress, record, present.

Model the pronunciation of each word as both a noun and a verb. Then ask students to practise saying the words as verbs (i.e. with the stress on the second syllable) and as nouns (i.e. with the stress on the first syllable). In pairs, students take turns to say the words as either a verb or a noun to their partner, who identifies whether the word is a noun or a verb.

SPEAKING

9

- Put students into small groups.
- Go through the steps involved in the task and the situations. Elicit search terms that students could use to find possible solutions for each situation online. For example, A: 'space-saving solutions book shelves'; B: 'space-saving solutions studio apartment'.
- Students choose a situation and brainstorm solutions for it. Encourage them to think of ideas on their own before going online to search for more.
- Students reach a consensus on which solutions they think are the most useful for their situation and use the language in the Useful language box to present the solutions in their group. Tell students to also think of reasons why their solutions would be effective.

Sample answers
A Self-study centre: use wall space with lots of shelves – allow the library to have lots of books without taking up space; have desks that fold down from the wall; students bring their own devices.
B Studio apartment: a sofa bed will let them have friends to stay; replace the bath with a shower; a foldable table will allow them to put it away when not using it.

Extra activity

Ask students to present their solutions in class. They could do this as if they were pitching or selling the solutions to a group of people who have the power to make decisions in each of the situations. The group then votes on whose ideas are the most practical and whose ideas are the most imaginative.

See **Workbook** pages 60–62 for extra practice.

LESSON GOALS

- **LISTENING** A main aim is for students to listen to an interview with a National Geographic explorer and practise identifying the meaning of the figurative language the speaker uses.
- **VOCABULARY** A further main aim is for students to learn and practise using adjectives to describe places.
- **PRONUNCIATION** A sub-aim is for students to practise pronouncing /b/, /v/ and /w/ sounds.

LISTENING

1

- Give students a minute to look at the photo and read the questions. Elicit or explain that Georgia is a country in south-eastern Europe.
- Check students' understanding of 'confined' (limited in terms of space).
- Students discuss the questions in pairs for about three minutes.

2 7.3

- **Optional step** Remind students that they have previously listened to Robbie Shone talking about different spaces he has been in. Elicit that Robbie specializes in taking photos of caves.
- Ask students to read the list of topics. Elicit that part of the Veryovkina cave system can be seen in the photo and elicit or explain the meaning of 'get away from it all' (to do something completely different in a different place).
- Play the audio and ask students to make notes about each topic.
- Give students a minute to prepare a summary of what Robbie said, using their notes. They can then either take turns to summarize what he said, or collaborate with their partner to produce a summary.

Sample answers

1 Robbie's work – expert in 'extreme underground exploration', been to world's longest and deepest caves; photographer; can be frightening and challenging

2 the Veryovkina cave system – in Georgia, two km deep; four days to go down, day ten or eleven, a flood of water; water started rising, had to climb through the waterfall; been back to complete the assignment

3 his home life – likes sitting with cat and drinking coffee; beautiful view of mountains

4 how he 'gets away from it all' – his home in a small village with surrounding mountains

7C Confined spaces

LESSON GOALS
- Identify figurative language when listening
- Describe places
- Pronounce /b/, /v/ and /w/ clearly

Robbie's team begin their journey into the lowest levels of Veryovkina, Georgia.

LISTENING

1 Work in pairs. Discuss the questions.

1 How would you feel about exploring a cave like the one in the photo?
2 Are you claustrophobic? (Do you have a fear of small spaces?) Do you know anyone who is?

NATIONAL GEOGRAPHIC EXPLORER

2 7.3 **Listen to an interview with Robbie Shone. Make notes about the topics (1–4). Then work in pairs and summarize what Robbie said.**

1 Robbie's work
2 the 'Veryovkina' cave system
3 his home life
4 how he 'gets away from it all'

3 7.3 **Listen again. Choose the correct option to complete the sentences.**

1 Robbie is a …
   a writer.
   b painter.
   c photographer.
2 The interviewer …
   a enjoys caving.
   b thinks the caves are amazing.
   c has visited Veryovkina.
3 The water …
   a was black.
   b came from above them.
   c hit them hard.
4 They had to …
   a climb through the waterfall.
   b leave their equipment.
   c swim to safety.
5 Robbie …
   a thinks about home a lot when he's away.
   b likes Italian coffee.
   c lives in a busy city.

4 7.3 **Look at the Listening skill box. Then listen to the first part of the interview again. Complete the figurative language (1–4) with one word.**

LISTENING SKILL
Identifying figurative language

Figurative language is language used, not with its basic meaning, but with a more imaginative meaning. For example, *to see the light* can mean *to understand*, which has nothing to do with actual seeing or light.
- If you hear a word that seems unlikely in the context, don't focus too much on specific words. Try to guess what the speaker probably means in the context.
- Imagine the pictures that figurative language creates. If someone tells you they were *on the edge of their seat* when they watched a film, the image should help you understand that they were nervous and excited.
- Learn commonly used figurative language. This includes idioms, phrasal verbs and metaphors.

88

VOCABULARY NOTES

out-of-the-way /ˈaʊtəvðəˈweɪ/ = remote, difficult to reach

hairy /ˈheəri/ = scary because you faced a threat of danger

deafening /ˈdefnɪŋ/ = extremely loud

caving /ˈkeɪvɪŋ/ = the activity of exploring caves

Meaning	Figurative language
1 describe	_paint_ a picture
2 scares me a lot	frightens the _life_ out of me
3 not everyone likes it	it's not everybody's _thing_
4 it's never easy	it's never a _walk_ in the park

5 7.3 Work in pairs. Listen to the last part of the interview again. What do you think the figurative language means?

1 You've got to **get back on the horse**.
2 Don't you ever feel the need for your **creature comforts**?
3 When the end is **in sight**, I start to think about home.
4 The mountains are **my escape**.

6 Work in pairs. How comfortable would you feel in each of these confined or busy spaces?

- a busy train carriage or bus
- a concert or football match
- a famous tourist site with crowds of sightseers
- a small tent
- a lift full of people

VOCABULARY

7 What words and expressions can describe caves, like the one shown in the photo? Use a dictionary to help you.

absolutely stunning breathtaking cold and damp cramped densely crowded elegantly decorated light and airy narrow sheltered spacious vast warm and cosy

8 Complete each sentence with two nouns. Notice the common adjective-noun collocations.

car cave flat rooms sight spot streets tent tourists view weather windows

1 I can't wait to get inside, out of this **cold, damp** _weather_ and back to my **cosy** _flat_.
2 The charming **narrow** _streets_ of the old town are **densely crowded** with _tourists_.
3 On the first night we slept in the _car_, which was **a bit cramped**, so we bought a four-man _tent_, which was more **spacious**.
4 Look! The _view_ from the top is **absolutely stunning**! But it's so windy. Let's find a **sheltered** _spot_ to eat our sandwiches.
5 Suddenly, the passage opened out into a bigger space. Their torches revealed a **vast** _cave_. The _sight_ was **breathtaking**.
6 The _rooms_ are **elegantly decorated**, with large _windows_ that give them a **light and airy** feel.

9 7.4 Listen and check your answers to Exercise 8.

Go to page 138 for the Vocabulary reference.

PRONUNCIATION

10 7.5 Look at the Clear voice box and listen to the words (1–4). Then practise saying the sounds in pairs. Take turns to say one of the words. Your partner decides what word you have said.

CLEAR VOICE
Pronouncing /b/, /v/ and /w/

To pronounce the /b/ sound (e.g. *Robbie*), use both of your lips. For /v/ (e.g. *vast*), put your lower lip on your upper teeth. To say /w/ (e.g. *warm*), keep your lips slightly apart and rounded. It's important to pronounce these three sounds correctly to be easily understood.

1 best	vest	west
2 bee	V	we
3 bet	vet	wet
4 bent	vent	went

SPEAKING

11 Work in pairs. Take turns to describe some of these places.

- your favourite room
- a great view near you
- a good place for a picnic
- a popular area in your town
- the cosiest place you can think of

EXPLORE MORE!
Find out more about Robbie Shone online, and choose a photo of his that you like.

89

3 7.3

- **Optional step** Ask students to read the sentences and predict the answers based on what they can remember from their first listening of the interview.
- Play the audio and ask students to listen and complete the sentences.
- Check answers as a class.

4 7.3

- Tell students to read the Listening skill box to find out what figurative language is and how it is used.
- Play the audio until 00:53. Ask students to listen for the meanings of the figurative language so they can complete the four expressions.
- Ask students to compare their answers in pairs and then check answers as a class.

5 7.3

- Ask students to read the sentences and familiarize themselves with the expressions in bold before they listen.
- Play the audio from 01:56 onwards. Ask students to listen for the expressions and use the context to work out their meaning. They can make notes while they are listening and write their definitions afterwards.
- Ask students to compare answers in pairs. Check students have the correct definitions for the expressions as a class.

Answers
1 do something again that you tried before but failed at or had difficulty with
2 things that make life comfortable
3 going to happen soon
4 something that allows you to forget about normal life and its worries

Extra activity

Put students into pairs and ask them to think of two or three examples of figurative language from their first language. These should be expressions like the ones they have looked at in Exercises 4 and 5. If students have a partner with the same first language, they could come up with expressions with the same meanings as the expressions in Exercises 4 and 5 in their shared first language. If students have a partner with a different first language, they could translate the expressions from their first language into English, if possible, and explain how the expressions are usually used.

6

- Ask students to read the list of places individually and think about how they would feel in each of them.
- Students discuss how they would feel if they found themselves in each of the places and give reasons for their reactions.
- **Optional step** Encourage students to make comparisons between how they would feel in two or more of the places, for example: *I would feel a lot more uncomfortable in a lift full of people than in a small tent, because at least you can easily get out of the tent if you want to.*

VOCABULARY

7

- Ask students to look at the photo of the cave on page 88 again.
- Tell students to read the word box and work with a partner to explain the meanings of unknown words and expressions to each other or help each other work them out. They can then use a dictionary to look up the meaning of any other words.

- **Optional step** When looking up words in a dictionary, remind students to check for context as some words, like *sheltered*, have multiple meanings.
- Students decide which words and expressions could be used to describe a cave and then compare and explain their answers in pairs.

Sample answers
To describe the beauty of a large cave: absolutely stunning, breathtaking, spacious, vast; to describe a small, narrow cave or passage: cold and damp, cramped, narrow; to describe a small cave to escape a storm: sheltered

Extra activity

Put students into pairs and ask them to play a word association game to check their understanding of the adjectives in Exercise 7. One student chooses a word or expression from the word box at random and says it. Their partner then says the first noun that comes into their heads that could follow it. Monitor students to check that they are saying words connected to each other and provide clarification of the meaning of words if necessary.

8

- **Optional step** Tell students to begin by reading the sentences. They can then focus on the adjectives in bold and speculate about which words (or types of words, e.g. words for places where people live: *cosy*) could follow them.
- Students complete the sentences with the correct nouns.

9 7.4

- Play the audio so students can listen and check their answers to Exercise 8.

For further information and practice, see **Vocabulary reference Unit 7** on page 138 of the Student's Book.

For additional practice, refer to the **Vocabulary activity** on page 239 of the Teacher's Book.

PRONUNCIATION

10 7.5

- Tell students to look at the Clear voice box and the list of words they are going to hear.
- Play the audio so students can listen to the three sets of words and focus on the differences in how the speaker pronounces the /b/, /v/ and /w/ sounds in each one.
- Ask students to follow the instructions in the Clear voice box and practise saying the words. Students take turns to say one of the words and their partner identifies which word was said.

PRONUNCIATION NOTES

Pronouncing /b/, /v/ and /w/
Common problems

- In some languages, for example German, Russian, Hindi and Urdu, there is no phonological distinction between a /v/ and a /w/ sound. Students who are first language users of these languages therefore need to concentrate on differentiating between these two sounds as well as pronouncing them correctly.
- In some other languages, for example Spanish, no distinction is made between the /b/ and /v/ sound so again, users of these languages will need to concentrate on listening for and producing the two sounds differently.

Practising the pronunciation of /b/, /v/ and /w/ sounds
When students pronounce the /w/ sound, their mouth will need to be rounded, whereas /b/ and /v/ are pronounced by releasing closed lips. If students find it difficult to differentiate between and pronounce the /b/, /v/ and /w/ sounds, suggest that they take a piece of paper and put it in front of their mouths (about ten centimetres away). They then alternately say a word starting with /b/ and a word starting with /v/ or /w/. They should notice that the paper moves slightly when they say the /b/ word and they will feel a vibration on their lips when they pronounce the /v/ word. Model this for students and ask them to focus on the shape of your mouth when saying each word.

For additional practice, refer to the **Pronunciation activity** on page 274 of the Teacher's Book.

SPEAKING

11

- Put students into pairs and ask them to each choose at least three of the places on the list.
- Tell students to list suitable adjectives and adjective-noun collocations to describe each place. Encourage them to use as many of the adjectives from Exercise 8 as they can.
- Students then take turns to describe one of the places they chose. They could then give each other feedback on whether they used appropriate adjectives in their descriptions.
- Monitor students as they are talking and make a note of any examples of good or interesting sentences that students say and then share these in class.

Extra activity

Ask students to choose a photograph of a place that interests them. Students then use the adjectives and adjective-noun collocations they have learned to write a description of their photo.

For additional practice, refer to the **Communication activity** on page 224 of the Teacher's Book.

EXPLORE MORE!

Suggest that students begin their online search with Robbie Shone's personal website. There they can find more information about him, view his photography portfolio and also click on links to other examples of his work online. Also suggest that students search for 'Robbie Shone + National Geographic' where they will find an article and photographs of the Veryovkina cave system in Georgia featured in this lesson.

See **Workbook** pages 62–63 for extra practice.

LESSON GOALS

- **GRAMMAR** The main aim is for students to learn and practise useful structures for complaining, including: *so* + adjective and *such a* + noun, the present continuous with *always* and *I wish …* and *If only …*
- **SPEAKING** A further main aim is to introduce students to ways of explaining a problem that encourage a change in behaviour without offending people, as well as language that they can use to soften the message. Students participate in a roleplay to practise explaining a problem with someone's behaviour without offending them.

SPEAKING

1

- Ask students to read the questions and give them about one minute to think about their answers.
- Students discuss question 1 in pairs.
- Put students into groups. For question 2, if students have never had a flatmate, ask them to think about anyone they have lived with. Check their understanding of 'insist' (to very firmly say that someone should do something or something should happen) and 'pile' (several things that lie on top of each other).
- Students rank the habits in their groups.

LISTENING AND GRAMMAR

2 7.6

- Ask students to read the instructions. Elicit that a 'nightmare flatmate' is a flatmate who is extremely difficult to live with.
- Play the audio and ask students to listen to get a general understanding of what the speaker's flatmate has done that is annoying. They could make notes on the key points.
- Students discuss and explain their answers in pairs. Encourage them to mention examples from the conversation.

3 7.6

- Ask students to read the sentences and use the context to guess what the missing words could be.
- Play the audio and ask students to listen for the sentences so they can complete them with the missing words.
- Students compare their answers in pairs.
- Tell students to read the Focus on box to learn about the structures they completed and see more examples. Remind students that they learned how to use *I wish … / If only …* in Lesson 5C.

For further information and practice, see **Focus on reference Unit 7D** on page 148 of the Student's Book.

4

- Direct students to the instructions and check they have understood that the sentence they complete needs to have the same meaning as the first sentence and that they need to write four words including the word in bold.
- Students complete the sentences. Tell them to refer back to the Focus on box if they need to.
- Check answers by inviting different students to read their completed sentences out loud.
- **Optional step** Tell students that this task is similar to the task in Part 4 of the Reading and Use of English paper in the Cambridge First and Advanced exams.

Answers

1 wish they would throw; 2 such difficult exam questions; 3 wish my brother wouldn't; 4 flatmate is so lazy; 5 is always leaving lights

Extra activity

Ask students to rewrite the completed sentences from Exercise 3 with a different structure from the Focus on box that conveys the same meaning. Go through the first item with students as an example. Elicit that it contains the structure *so* + adjective and that this could be changed to use the structure *such* + a noun (*He's just such a messy person*), present continuous with *always* (*He's always making a mess*) or a structure with *I wish/If only …* (*I wish he would tidy up after himself*; *If only he didn't make a mess*). Ask students to rewrite the remaining sentences.

5

- Tell students to brainstorm the annoying habits of people they know, or people in general.
- Direct students to the model answer and elicit that it includes the present continuous with *always* structure.
- Ask students to write five sentences about different annoying habits using the structures in the Focus on box.

6

- Students read their sentences to each other in pairs and discuss the questions.

Extra activity

Put students into pairs or small groups and ask them to brainstorm common mistakes that people make when they complain about things, for example: asking very direct and confrontational questions such as *What is wrong with you?* or focusing on the problem without suggesting possible solutions.

For additional practice, refer to the **Focus on activity** on page 258 of the Teacher's Book.

MY VOICE ▶

COMMUNICATION SKILL NOTES

Dealing with difficult conversations

This lesson provides students with guidance on how to talk to someone about a problem they have with that person's behaviour, without damaging their relationship with that person. It is particularly important in intercultural communication as students from one culture may find that their way of raising a problem (that they consider perfectly acceptable, and even polite) is unacceptable and offensive for someone from a culture where a softer communication style is expected. Softening the message helps reduce or prevent conflict in such a situation. When students are dealing with difficult situations, it is important that they separate the problem from the person who they see as being responsible for it and instead focus on convincing the other person to change their behaviour by explaining the specific impact it is having on them.

7 ▶ 7.2

- Tell students that they are going to watch a video that gives some tips for encouraging people to change their behaviour when it is annoying you.
- Play the video and ask students to make notes on the advice they hear.
- Students think back to the flatmate's problems in Exercise 2 or read the audioscript if they need reminding of the conversation.
- Students write two pieces of advice for the flatmate in the conversation.
- Students compare their advice in pairs.

Answers

The advice given in the video: consider the context - how well you know the other person, how normally they react to feedback; manage your own negative emotions (i.e. don't get angry); focus on explaining your observations, be specific and avoid generalizations and exaggerations; explain why the change in behaviour is important for you and/or why it could benefit you both and improve your relationship; describe your feelings rather than acting them out; ask for a change rather than telling them to change

7D Difficult conversations

LESSON GOALS
- Practise complaining
- Explain a problem without offending others
- Use language that softens the message

SPEAKING

1 Work in groups. Discuss the questions.

1 Have you ever lived with someone in the same house or flat? What did you like and dislike about it?
2 Rank how annoying these habits would be in a flatmate. Give reasons.
   a Insists on thoroughly cleaning the flat twice a week.
   b Leaves a pile of dirty dishes in the sink.
   c Listens to very loud music until late in the evening.
   d Often invites friends round and has parties.
   e Spends most of the time in their room and rarely talks to you.

LISTENING AND GRAMMAR

2 7.6 Listen to someone complaining about a flatmate. Do you agree that the person they're talking about is a nightmare flatmate? Why? / Why not?

3 7.6 Listen to the conversation again. Complete the complaints with one or two words. Then read the Focus on box to learn about useful structures for complaining.

1 He's just ___so___ messy.
2 For example, he's ___always leaving___ dirty dishes in the sink for days!
3 I wish he ___would wash___ them at least once a day.
4 He's also ___such___ a party animal.
5 ___If only___ he had people over once a week, but it's like three or four nights a week!

FOCUS ON Useful structures for complaining

Use **so + adjective** and **such a + noun** to complain about things that annoy or upset you.
*He's **so messy**.*
*His room is **such a mess**.*
Use the **present continuous with *always*** to emphasize that something happens all the time.
*She**'s always listening** to loud music in the middle of the night.*
Use ***I wish/If only* + past simple** and ***I wish/If only* + *would* + infinitive** to say that you want something to be different.
***If only he looked after** his money better!*
***I wish he would wash** the dishes!*

Go to page 148 for the Focus on reference.

90

VOCABULARY NOTES

offence /ə'fens/ = a feeling of anger or annoyance caused by an insult or disrespectful behaviour

constructive /kən'strʌktɪv/ = something that has a helpful purpose

exaggeration /ɪɡˌzædʒə'reɪʃ(ə)n/ = talking about something in a way that makes it sound better or worse than it really is

generalization /ˌdʒen(ə)r(ə)laɪ'zeɪʃ(ə)n/ = a general statement applied to a group of people or things

8

- Tell students to look at the Communication skill box.
- Students use their awareness of how they usually interact with other people (specifically: how well they can describe problems without emotion, express what is important to them, describe their feelings and ask someone to do something for them) to answer the question.
- Students discuss the question in pairs, giving examples from their own experiences of talking to people in difficult situations.

4 Look at the first sentence in each pair. Complete the second sentence so it has the same meaning. Use four words, including the word in bold and the structures from the Focus on box.

1 It's annoying that they don't throw their litter away.
I ________ their litter away. **would**
2 Those exam questions were so difficult.
Those were ________. **such**
3 My brother makes such a mess.
I ________ make such a mess in our room. **wouldn't**
4 She's such a lazy flatmate.
My ________ **flatmate**
5 He never switches lights off.
He ________ on. **leaving**

5 Think about people who have habits that annoy you. Write five sentences complaining about them. You do not need to mention who they are.
I have a friend who's always looking at his phone when we're together. It's so rude!

6 Work in pairs. Share your sentences from Exercise 5 and answer the questions.
1 Which habits are the most annoying? Why?
2 Do you usually talk about problems with the people who are upsetting you?
3 What can happen if you don't talk to them?

MY VOICE

7 7.2 Watch the video. How can the person from Exercise 2 encourage their flatmate to change their behaviour? Write at least two pieces of advice, using tips from the video. Look at audioscript 7.6 on page 167 if you need to.

8 Work in pairs. Look at the Communication skill box. How easy is this advice for you to follow?

COMMUNICATION SKILL
Dealing with difficult conversations

If you are trying to encourage someone to change their behaviour, try to …
1 describe the problem from your point of view as an observation, not an emotion, e.g. *I notice that* … Don't exaggerate, e.g. *You never* …
2 explain why the issue is important to you, e.g. *It means that I can't* …
3 describe your feelings without acting them out, e.g. *It upsets me when* …
4 request a change, e.g. *Would you be willing to* …

9 7.7 Listen and complete the words in each sentence. Then match the phrases with similar expressions in the Useful language box.
1 Could I **m**ake a **s**uggestion? Why **d**on't we write a 'to do' list together?
2 I **u**nderstand that you want to relax in the evening, but so do I.
3 I'm **s**ure you won't **m**ind me **a**sking this, but do you have some headphones you could use?
4 It's just that if you were **a**ble to avoid messaging me when I'm at work, I could reply sooner.

Useful language Softening the message
I hope you don't mind me saying this, but … 3
I appreciate that you want to … but I … 2
I'd really appreciate it if you could … 4
It's just that if you could … that would allow me to … 4
Can I suggest something? How about …? 1

10 Work in pairs. Think about the people you complained about in Exercise 5. How could you explain the problem without offending them? Use the tips in the Communication skill box and the Useful language to help you.

SPEAKING

11 **OWN IT!** Work in pairs. Imagine you are flatmates or neighbours. Follow the instructions.
1 In pairs, decide on two annoying behaviours each of you has that makes living together or next to one another difficult.
2 Individually, use the tips in the Communication skill box to decide how to explain the problems to your partner without offending them.
3 Discuss the annoying behaviours together. Try to find a solution.

12 Act out the conversation in front of another pair. How well did the other pair give feedback? What could they have done better?

91

9 7.7

- Direct students to the sentences. Elicit that they are things people could say in difficult situations.
- Play the audio. Students listen and write the missing words.
- Tell students to look at the Useful language box. Elicit or explain that when you 'soften' your language, you usually speak in a more indirect way to show your respect for and understanding of the other person's feelings.
- Students match the phrases with the expressions in the Useful language box.
- Check answers as a class.

Extra activity

On the board, write examples of complaints that might upset the person they are directed at, e.g. You never ever do the dishes! Just turn the music down, OK? I know you like playing video games, but the noise is too much.
Ask students to use the language in the Useful language box and any other language they know to rewrite the sentences, so they are softer.

10

- Direct students to the instruction. Check their understanding of 'offend' (make someone else feel angry or hurt).
- Refer students back to the sentences they wrote in Exercise 5. Ask students to work in pairs to prepare something they could say to each of the people about their annoying habits. Encourage them to refer back to the tips in the Communication skill box and the expressions in the Useful language box.
- Students take turns to explain the problem without offending the person.

SPEAKING

11 OWN IT!

- Put students into pairs and read the three steps to complete the task.
- Students decide on two annoying behaviours each of them has that makes them a difficult flatmate or neighbour.
- Students work individually to decide how to explain the problems to their partner without offending them. Remind students to refer back to the tips in the Communication skill box.
- In their pairs, students roleplay a conversation between two flatmates or neighbours to discuss the annoying behaviours their characters have. Alternatively, students could discuss how they could talk to a flatmate or neighbour about each of the annoying behaviours. Remind students that they should try to find a solution to the problems in both cases.

12

- Put each pair from Exercise 11 together with another pair.
- The two pairs take turns to act out their conversation or explain their ideas from Exercise 11. Tell students that while one pair is acting out their conversation, the other pair needs to listen and make notes to give the other pair feedback on how effectively they dealt with the difficult situation.

For additional practice, refer to the **Communication activity** on page 225 and the **Mediation activity** on page 289 of the Teacher's Book.

LESSON GOALS

- **WRITING** The aim of the lesson is to guide students to produce three social media posts for other classmates to respond to. The reading text provides a model. Students practise converting neutral language into informal and abbreviated language and then using informal language in their own posts.

SPEAKING

1

- Ask students to look at the infographic about social media use and then read the questions.
- Students discuss the questions in pairs.

READING FOR WRITING

2

- Ask students to match the posts with the types of content and personality type.
- Students compare answers in pairs and use evidence from the posts and the infographic to justify their choices.

Answers

Dani is a 'Comic', content = photos and videos; Juana is a 'Share-it-all', content = status update of what they are doing; Kaish is probably a 'Thinker', content = photos and videos, news items

Extra activity

Ask students to brainstorm things that they find annoying or dislike about social media posts, for example: people boasting. They could then use the structures for complaining from the *Focus on* box in 7D to write one-sentence messages to the people who exhibit these annoying behaviours. Then students could brainstorm things that they like about social media or the positive effects that it can have on people's lives.

3

- Put students into small groups to discuss the questions.

4

- Before students look at the Writing skill box, check their understanding of 'omit' (to leave out or not include) and 'a ton of' (a lot of).

7E Social media sharing

LESSON GOALS
- Omit pronouns and auxiliaries to make writing more informal
- Use informal quantifiers, expressions and phrasal verbs
- Write and respond to social media posts

SPEAKING

1 Work in pairs. Look at the infographic and discuss the questions.

1 Which social media platforms do you use? If you don't use any, why not?
2 What content would you be most and least likely to share on social media? Why?
3 Which type of social media person are you? Are you sometimes a different type depending on what and why you share? Why?

READING FOR WRITING

2 Read the three social media posts on page 93. Match them with a type of content and a personality type from the infographic. Explain your choices to your partner.

3 Work in a group. Discuss the questions.

1 Which of the social media posts would you be most likely to read in real life?
2 What comment would you leave below each post?

4 Look at the Writing skill box. Find two examples of each type of informal language in the social media posts and comments.

WRITING SKILL
Informal language in social media posts

When writing on social media, we tend to be more informal. Some common examples are ...

Omitting pronouns and auxiliary verbs
~~Have you~~ *Ever seen a bear doing yoga?*
Informal quantifiers
*after **a bit of** a nap*
*got **a ton of** comments*
Phrasal verbs
*She**'s** quite **into** yoga*
*What have you **been up to**?*
Informal expressions
*I might **give it a shot** myself!*
*You'd love it! It's **right up your street**.*

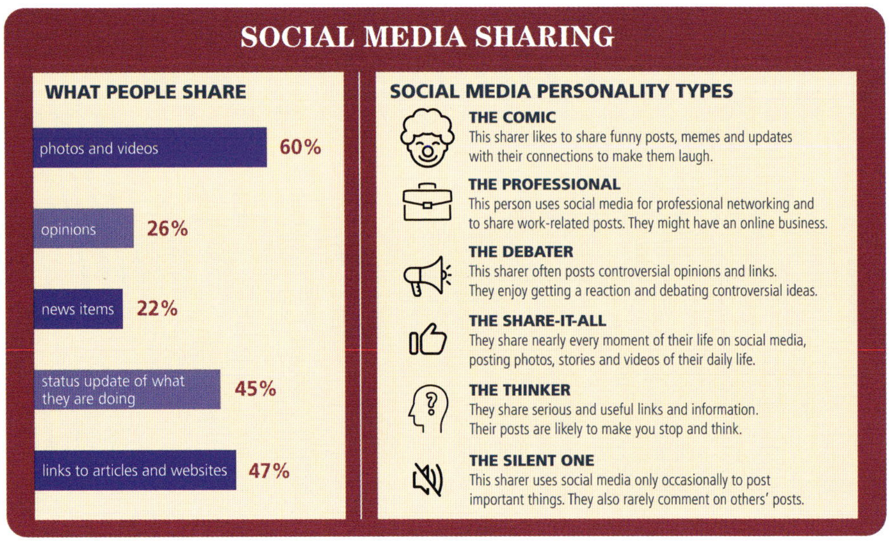

92

- Ask students to read the examples in the Writing skill box and deduce the meaning of the phrasal verbs and informal expressions, such as 'give it a shot' (try to do something), from the context.
- Students read the posts again and identify two examples of each type of informal language mentioned in the box.

Sample answers

Omitting pronouns and auxiliary verbs: (It's) pretty cool, right?!; (Do you have) any advice?; (I've) just got back; (It) would be great to have some ...
Informal quantifiers: a ton of dirty dishes; a million times; loads of them
Phrasal verbs: get down to; piled up; deal with; puts it off; come up with
Informal expressions: talk behind people's backs; I've seriously had it! a fab weekend; wait for this; How about ... ?

5

- **Optional step** Go through the first item in class. Elicit that the pronoun 'I've' is omitted and 'a large amount of' can be replaced by a more informal equivalent expression (e.g. *a ton of*).
- Students rewrite the sentences by changing or omitting the words in bold.
- Students share their sentences with a

Dani
2 hrs ago
Ever seen a bear doing yoga? Pretty cool, right?! Santra is a bear in Ahtari Zoo, Finland and she's quite into yoga. Apparently, she'll get down to her fifteen-minute yoga routine every day after a bit of a nap. I might give it a shot myself!

Anya That's class! Love it!

Juana
1 hr ago
I don't normally talk behind people's backs on social media, but I've seriously had it! My flatmate is so messy! He never tidies up. There's a ton of dirty dishes piled up in his bedroom. I really don't know how to deal with it. I've told him a million times to clean up. He's always promising he will but then just puts it off and off forever! Any advice? What should I do?

Jacob Why don't you just talk to him? It means you don't have to live in a messy flat!

Kaish
4 hrs ago
Just got back from a fab weekend trip to Berlin, and the city is full of moss! They've been putting up benches with a wall of moss behind them all over the city. There are loads of them everywhere. But wait for this – apparently one bench like that cleans as much air as a small forest. Could we get something like this in our city too? What do you all think?

Amit Wow! That's so cool. Would be great to have some moss benches here! How about we come up with an online petition and share it on social media?

5 Change the expressions in bold to make them more informal. Use the Writing skill box and social media posts to help you.
1 **I've just** got back from the city. There's **a large amount of** air pollution there.
2 I think I'll **try yoga. I've never** done it, but it looks fun.
3 The benches can be **installed** in **many** different places.
4 **Have you got** any thoughts on this? **I would** love to hear your opinion.
5 **I really** hate people who always **postpone** things.

WRITING TASK

6 **WRITE** Write three social media posts. Use your own ideas or choose from the table. Write about 200 words in total and leave room for comments underneath. Find or describe any photos or links you would like to include with your post.

Things you've read about	Personal stories	Recommendations
• interesting articles • funny stories • important news	• places you've visited or things you've done • frustrations and complaints	• a film / book / video game you'd recommend • a product you bought and liked

7 **CHECK** Use the checklist. I have ...
☐ written posts that are engaging and/or useful to other people
☐ used informal quantifiers.
☐ replaced formal verbs with phrasal verbs.
☐ omitted unnecessary pronouns and auxiliary verbs.

8 **REVIEW** Stick your posts up around the classroom. Walk around the room and read your classmates' posts. Leave a comment below at least two of the posts.

SPEAKING

9 Discuss the questions as a class.
1 Which post did you find the most interesting?
2 What new information about your classmates did you learn from their posts?
3 Based on the posts, what sort of social media personality from the infographic are your classmates?

Go to page 133 for the Reflect and review.

EXPLORE MORE!
Find examples of social media posts that sparked your attention recently. Which could you reshare on your social media?

partner.

Sample answers
1 Just got back … a load of/a ton of
2 give yoga a shot, Never done it before
3 put up, loads of/tons of
4 (Got) Any thoughts, Would love,
5 Really hate, put things off

WRITING TASK

6 WRITE

- Ask students to read the instructions for the task and the table.
- Students write the first draft of their three posts, concentrating on using informal language. Ask them to write each post on a different piece of paper.
- Tell students to also search online for links or photos they could include in the posts they have written. Alternatively, if this is not possible, they could think of ideas for suitable links or photos and write descriptions of them.

Extra activity

On the board, write a list of abbreviations that people often use in social media posts (without their meanings), for example:
- idk (I don't know)
- imo (in my opinion)
- DM (direct message) / PM (private message)

Ask students to guess the meanings of the abbreviations.

7 CHECK

- Ask students to use the checklist and then make changes to their posts if necessary.

8 REVIEW

- Before the lesson, ensure you have enough tape or another adhesive to stick students' posts on the classroom walls.
- Ask students to put each of their three posts in a different part of the room.
- Students walk around and choose at least two posts to leave a comment on. They could either write their comment on the piece of paper itself or stick a post-it note with their comment to the bottom of it.
- Circulate while students are doing this to check that every student receives at least one comment from another student.

SPEAKING

9

- Ask students to read the questions and think about their answers individually.
- As a class, invite different students to give their answers to the questions.
- **Optional step** Encourage students to react to other students' comments.

EXPLORE MORE!

Ask students to find social media posts they remember finding interesting recently by searching for the user who posted them or a hashtag that could have been used in them. Students brainstorm the criteria they could use to decide whether to share a social media post. For example: It will be interesting for at least some of my followers; It will help my followers work towards an aim they want to achieve (e.g. improving their English). Students then use these criteria to decide which posts to share.

For **Unit 7 Reflect and review**, see Student's Book page 133.

See **Workbook** pages 64–65 for extra practice.

VIDEO 7.1

Abby: *We all depend on others to live and be happy, whether in a human community or as part of the wider planet. But I think it's also important to be aware of the harm you can do to other humans and to the wildlife which is sharing your space. A lot of wildlife suffers from the effects of our actions. Really, the whole world is a shared space, so our effects on others end up coming around to affect us too.*

Robbie: *A shared space might not suit everyone, but you have to make the best of it. Sharing spaces in different environments offers different challenges and it is important to compromise with one another. This might mean not getting everything you want, as we all need to benefit from the space we're sharing.*

Abby: *I was once on a sub-Antarctic island, counting penguins, when an endangered New Zealand sea lion approached. He checked me out for a minute and then roared and threw his huge body at me. I jumped out of the way and ran. I looked back once and saw that he was chasing after me down the beach, which was a terrifying sight. Then I got to a marshy area that slowed me down. The sea lion caught up and I had no choice but to turn around and try shouting. That actually made him stop for a second and hesitate. I kept yelling at him, trying to work out how I was going to escape from this situation, until another male sea lion approached and they started fighting with each other. I took the opportunity to get out of their space as quickly as possible.*

Robbie: *In 2014, I worked on a magazine story for National Geographic in Uzbekistan. The leader of the expedition put me and two American guys in one tent, but he gave us only two sleeping bags. So three people and two bags. We thought, well, there's three of us, you know, so who's not going to get a sleeping bag? And that's when the expedition leader pointed out that if you zip the bags together you can make one big shared bag. But it was still a real squeeze to get three people inside these two sleeping bags zipped together. And I'd never met these guys before this trip. But of course, it actually made perfect sense. We only had to carry two sleeping bags down to camp. Plus, the warmth from our bodies soon filled the smaller space inside the two bags rather than three. Yes, it was cosy, but I was glad of it – the cave was really cold!*

AUDIO 7.1

Abby: *I don't spend much time in cities because they always make me feel crowded. I think it's a big challenge to have such a small amount of space for a large number of people.*

Robbie: *I don't own a car. I use the train and buses when I'm here in Innsbruck. The public transport links are great. There are also a lot of road and rail tunnels through the mountains. This saves us from having to make long journeys around the mountains.*

Abby: *My living situation varies a lot. I don't own my own house, so there is usually some sort of space limitation that forces me to make adjustments. For example, if I'm staying with a friend for a few days, I might live out of my backpack. When I'm sharing a home with other people, the lack of personal space encourages me to spend time outdoors by myself.*

Robbie: *At home, I share my space with Gina, my fiancée, and our two cats, Zirby and Sakai. Fortunately, Gina and I have similar tastes and requirements. Her office is at the university, so that lets me use the home office. In the kitchen, we have a really neat corner cupboard that turns around, which permits us to store all our pots and pans without taking up much space.*

Abby: *Travelling so much prevents me from having too many possessions. I enjoyed living out of a car – a station wagon – for a year in New Zealand, because it enabled me to keep everything I needed with me all the time! Since I usually live out of a backpack, a car is more than enough space to keep things.*

AUDIO 7.2

advise, allow, enable, encourage, permit, prevent, require

AUDIO 7.3

Interviewer: *Robbie Shone is an expert in 'extreme underground exploration'. He's been to some of the most out-of-the way places on the planet, including the world's longest and deepest caves. As a photographer, it's his job to tell the story through pictures. Robbie hello and thanks for talking to us today.*

Robbie: *A pleasure.*

Interviewer: *Robbie, hopefully you can paint a picture for us of what it's like to visit these extraordinary sites. Just thinking about them frightens the life out of me.*

Robbie: *Ha! It's not everybody's thing!*

Interviewer: *Do you ever get claustrophobia?*

Robbie: *Not exactly, but I've been very frightened. My job takes me to some of the most challenging caves in the world. It's never a walk in the park! Sometimes, when you're in a narrow passage or there's water around, it can get a bit hairy.*

Interviewer: *Have you had any really scary moments?*

Robbie: *A couple of years ago we were in Abkhazia, Georgia on an expedition to explore an incredibly deep cave system called 'Veryovkina'. It's the deepest known cave in the world. It's at least two kilometres underground. It took four days to get to the bottom where we camped. Then on day ten or eleven, we heard what sounded like a huge train coming down through the cave. Suddenly, a huge wall of water fell from the black hole in the roof above us. It was deafening. Luckily, the water just missed us but the waterfall was right in the path of our way out. We waited to see how it would develop. After a few hours, everything changed as the water started rising fast. We had no time, so we quickly put our equipment on and one by one began climbing the ropes. It was hard to breathe as we were right in the middle of the waterfall. When the last person left the camp, it was already under water. That was very scary.*

Interviewer: *Have you been back there?*

Robbie: *I have actually, the following year. Like they say, you've got to get back on the horse. The main reason was to complete the assignment and photograph the upper half of the cave. But also to get over the fear.*

Interviewer: *Don't you ever feel the need for your creature comforts, something a little cosier for a change?*

Robbie: *When I'm away I don't tend to think about creature comforts because it's a distraction, but towards the end of an expedition, when the end is in sight, I start to think about home. I think about having a nice Italian coffee with my cat sat on my lap. I think about the beautiful view of the mountains from the balcony. I think about some good food and my comfortable bed.*

Interviewer: *And when you're not caving, do you ever feel the need to just get away from it all?*

Robbie: *Well, it can be a bit strange going from living with nature on an expedition to being back on the busy streets in cities where everyone is rushing past you. On the journey home, I like to sit near the window so that I can look out and forget that I'm* *on a busy plane, or a train. But my village only has a population of about 2,500 people, so home and its surroundings, the mountains, are my escape from my busy life.*

AUDIO 7.4

1 Brrr! I can't wait to get inside, out of this cold, damp weather and back to my cosy flat.

2 The charming narrow streets of the old town are densely crowded with tourists. It's a good idea to get here early to beat the crowds.

3 ***A:*** *Where did you sleep?*

B: *On the first night we slept in the car.*

A: *Urgh!*

B: *Yeah! Which was a bit cramped, so we bought a four-man tent, which was more spacious.*

A: *Rather you than me!*

4 ***A:*** *Look! The view from the top is absolutely stunning!*

B: *Wow!*

A: *But it's so windy! Let's find a sheltered spot to eat our sandwiches.*

B: *Good idea.*

5 Suddenly, the passage opened out into a bigger space. Their torches revealed a vast cave. The sight was breathtaking.

6 The rooms are elegantly decorated, with large windows that give them a light and airy feel.

AUDIO 7.6

A: *So, I've heard you've got a new flatmate? How is he?*

B: *Oh, don't even get me started …*

A: *Now I really want to know!*

B: *He's just so messy. You wouldn't believe it!*

A: *But you're not too organized around the house either …*

B: *I know, but this is a different level, I'm telling you. For example, he's always leaving dirty dishes in the sink for days!*

A: *Ugh, that's disgusting!*

B: *I know! I wish he would wash them at least once a day.*

A: *Yeah, I mean, it only takes like five minutes, doesn't it?*

B: *Exactly! He's also such a party animal. I mean, I don't mind a house party every now and again but it's a bit too much now. If only he had people over once a week, but it's like three or four nights a week!*

A: *Wow, that is a bit too much!*

B: *I know, right?*

A: *So what are you going to do?*

B: *I'm not sure to be honest. What would you do?*

A: *Umm, I'm not sure, but I might …*

VIDEO 7.2

Most of us will have shared a flat or a house with someone. Whether you live with parents, brothers and sisters, friends, or partners, it can be tough living with another person. Naturally, conflicts might happen, and you'll need to resolve them. Of course, we live alongside many people as well as flatmates – neighbours, work colleagues, fellow club members and, yes, classmates!

Before we look at the skills needed to successfully encourage the people around us to change their behaviour, without causing offence, it's important to consider the context: How well do you know the other person? What's your relationship with them? How does this person normally react to feedback? Do they prefer direct feedback or less direct encouragement?

Whatever the situation, we should focus on achieving the goal of the conversation and keep things constructive. That means not being too personal or emotional. So to start with, we need to manage our own negative emotions. Getting angry will not help and might result in an angry response from the other person, rather than getting us the change we want.

A good way to start the discussion is to focus on your observations and the facts of the situation. When you do this, make sure you avoid exaggerations and generalizations … and try to be specific.

The next step is to explain why the issue is important to you and how, by talking about the problem together, it can benefit both of you and make your relationship better. You could say for example, 'I can see why you enjoy inviting people round, and I like it too, but from my point of view, it's making it hard for me to get enough sleep.'

Your emotions are still important, but try to explain how you feel rather than acting your emotions out (for example, by getting angry). So instead of 'Why do you always wait so long to do the washing up?!', you could say: 'I feel really annoyed when I see the dirty dishes in the sink'.

Finally, you're ready to request the change. Remember, you're asking them to change, not telling them! Exactly what you say will depend a lot on how well you know them, of course, but it needs to clearly put the next step in their hands. The main idea here is to not let your anger, your disappointment and your frustration take control. If you can stay calm, you have a much better chance of coming away from the discussion with agreement and a stronger, happier relationship.

AUDIO 7.7

1 Could I make a suggestion? Why don't we write a 'to do' list together?

2 I understand that you want to relax in the evening, but so do I.

3 I'm sure you won't mind me asking this, but do you have some headphones you could use?

4 It's just that if you were able to avoid messaging me when I'm at work, I could reply sooner.

UNIT 8

Incredible technology

UNIT GOALS

8A Reading, speaking

- read an article to practise recognizing synonyms and antonyms and use critical thinking skills to examine the writer's assumptions; predict the most needed and most exciting inventions of the future

8B Reading and grammar, pronunciation, speaking

- read about ancient inventions we use today and practise using structures for speculating about the past; practise understanding the pronunciation of the weak form of *have*; discuss the possible use of inventions from the past

8C Vocabulary and listening, pronunciation, speaking

- learn and practise using vocabulary to talk about technology; expand vocabulary by forming nouns, verbs and adjectives in the same word family; practise understanding prepositions in connected speech; practise pronouncing the long and short 'o'

8D Speaking

- discuss how people communicate online; talk about what online etiquette is and how to follow it to communicate more effectively; create and present a poster about online etiquette

8E Writing

- practise using multi-word adjectives; express opinions about products; write a review for a gadget or other tech product

Photocopiable resources

Communication activities: pp. 226–227
Vocabulary activity: p. 240
Grammar activity: p. 259
Focus on … activity: p. 260
Pronunciation activity: p. 275
Mediation activity: p. 290

Workbook

Unit 8 pp. 66–73

ABOUT THE PHOTO

The photo shows a child's birthday celebration which includes making a group video call with two other relatives. The photo reflects the increasing frequency with which video conferencing technology is used to share special moments.

1

- Tell students to look at the photo and caption and read the questions.
- In pairs, students discuss the questions. For the second question, ask students to brainstorm the negative effects of technology and then think of

A family share a birthday celebration via live stream in Barcelona, Spain.

8

Incredible technology

GOALS

- Recognize synonyms and antonyms in an article
- Speculate about the past using modal verbs
- Talk about gadgets and technology
- Understand prepositions in connected speech
- Understand and discuss online etiquette
- Write a product review

1 Work in pairs. Discuss the questions.

1 Look at the photo. How are the people using technology?
2 The photo shows a positive side to technology; what photos would you suggest to show the negative sides to technology?

WATCH ▶

2 ▶ 8.1 Watch the video. Make notes about …

1 whether Nora and Francisco think of themselves as 'techie' people and why.
2 one important piece of technology in their lives and why they like it.
3 any worries that they have about technology.

NATIONAL GEOGRAPHIC EXPLORERS

NORA SHAWKI | FRANCISCO ESTRADA-BELLI

3 Make connections. Discuss the questions.

1 Are you a 'techie' (someone who likes tech) or a technophobe (someone who dislikes tech)?
2 What piece of technology are you particularly glad you have? Why?

95

photos that could be used to represent some of these effects. Ask students to justify their answers.

Sample answers

1 The people are using technology to talk to their relatives during a birthday party so they can share the experience of celebrating with them.
2 Photo of bored-looking child indoors, watching videos on a phone; an adult looking at their phone or laptop late at night; e-waste clearly left to pollute rather than be recycled

WATCH ▶

2 ▶ 8.1

- Tell students that they are going to hear two National Geographic explorers talking about technology.
- Check students' understanding of the term 'a techie person' (someone who uses a lot of technology, enjoys and/or is good at using technology).
- Play the video and tell students that the explorers will take turns to talk about each of the three topics.
- Students make notes and then compare answers in pairs.

Answers

1 Both think of themselves as techie people. Nora's friends go to her for help, and Francisco's friends and family know he is good with technology.
2 Nora: the Notes app on her phone. She uses it to write lists and positive thoughts. Francisco: his smartphone. He does most things related to work on it.
3 Nora worries that people, especially young people, need technology too much and don't read and learn enough because they play too many games on their devices. Francisco isn't worried about technology and sees how much it helps scientists like him.

Extra activity

Ask students to brainstorm the specific characteristics of a 'techie' person, i.e. what type of technology this person uses, what types of things they can do with it, the person's feelings about technology, what job they might do, and so on.

3

- Students discuss the questions in pairs. Encourage them to compare and contrast their experiences with those of the explorers, where appropriate.

Extra activity

Students choose two pieces of technology: one that they would never give up and one that they could easily live without. Students describe each piece of technology to a partner and explain why they need or do not need it.

ABOUT THE EXPLORERS

NORA SHAWKI is an Egyptian archaeologist who excavates ancient sites in the Nile Delta and Northern Sudan. The focus of her research is on Late Period settlements and she is specifically using material culture and religion to better understand the impact of royal policy on non-elite Egyptians.

FRANCISCO ESTRADA-BELLI is an Italian archaeologist, based in the US. His research focuses on Maya civilizations in Guatemala. He is the co-founder of the Maya Archaeology Initiative, a non-profit organization that supports heritage conservation in Guatemala's Maya Biosphere Reserve.

8A Impossible tech

LESSON GOALS
- Recognize synonyms and antonyms in an article
- Examine the writer's assumptions behind an article
- Talk about science fiction and technology

SPEAKING AND LISTENING

1 Work in pairs. Have you ever watched science-fiction films or read science-fiction books?

NATIONAL GEOGRAPHIC EXPLORERS

2 8.1 Listen to Nora Shawki and Francisco Estrada-Belli. Answer the questions.

1 What is one aspect of sci fi that each explorer likes? What annoys Francisco?
2 Do you agree with their opinions? Why? / Why not?

READING

3 Work in pairs. Which sci-fi technology in the box have you heard of? Which do you think are impossible? Which might be possible …

1 in the next few decades? invisibility
2 within a hundred years? lightsabers
3 in several hundred years? teleportation
4 in thousands of years from now? faster than light travel

faster than light travel   invisibility   lightsabers
teleportation (instant transport across space and distance)

4 Read the article on page 97. Were your predictions in Exercise 3 right?

5 Look at the Reading skill box. Then scan the article to find a close synonym or an antonym of the words (a–h) in the same paragraph.

READING SKILL
Recognizing synonyms and antonyms

Writers often use synonyms (words/phrases with the same meaning) and antonyms (words/phrases with opposite meanings) to avoid repeating words. Recognizing them can help you guess the meaning of unknown words. Understanding one word can help you understand its synonym or antonym.

Synonyms:	Antonyms:
a change [l. 9]	f possible [l. 22]
b hot gas [l. 23]	g appear [l. 42]
c power source [l. 31]	h stretch [l. 53]
d breaks the rules [l. 49]	
e make a hole [l. 56]	

6 Read the article again. Answer the questions.

1 Why would flying an invisible spaceship be difficult?
2 Why shouldn't we get too excited about lightsabers yet?
3 When does teleportation happen naturally?
4 How might we be able to travel faster than light?

7 Look at the Critical thinking skill box. Then decide which of the assumptions (a–c) you think the writer is making in the article. Find sentences that support your ideas.

CRITICAL THINKING SKILL
Examining writer assumptions behind texts

Assumptions are ideas you accept as true without evidence. Texts contain unwritten assumptions based on what writers think they know about their readers, such as: 'This will be interesting to readers', and 'Readers will know what I'm talking about'. There are often assumptions about specific topics too, even if there is no evidence.

Thinking about the assumptions a writer has made can help you understand why they've chosen to write the text, and to consider how useful, relevant and interesting it is to its readers.

a Readers enjoy thinking about sci-fi inventions.
b It is the responsibility of science to try to make fictional inventions become reality.
c Technological advances mean that everything we think of as impossible now will become reality in the future.

8 What other assumptions can you identify? Do you think the assumptions the writer has made are fair and correct? Why? / Why not?

SPEAKING

9 Work in groups. What do you think are the three most needed and the three most exciting tech inventions of the future? Use the suggestions below or your own ideas.

alternatives to plastics   clean energy sources
cure for cancer   intelligent robots   self-driving cars
space travel   teleportation   time travel

EXPLORE MORE!

Search online for 'da Vinci's inventions'. Watch one of the suggested videos. Are they similar to any current technology?

96

LESSON GOALS

- **READING** The main aim is for students to practise recognizing synonyms and antonyms in an article and then use their critical thinking skills to examine the writer's assumptions behind the text.
- **SPEAKING** The speaking aim is for students to discuss and reach a consensus on what the three most needed and the three most exciting tech inventions of the future will be.

SPEAKING AND LISTENING

1

- Check students' understanding of 'science-fiction' or 'sci-fi' (a type or genre of books, films and TV shows about an imagined future, often in space or on another planet and often involving some advanced future form of technology).
- Students tell each other which science-fiction films or books they have seen or read.

Extra activity

Show students a clip from a science-fiction film or TV programme in English, for example *Star Wars*, *Star Trek*, *Doctor Who* or *Guardians of the Galaxy*. If it is not possible to play or share a video clip, show a few photos from films or TV programmes where technology can be seen. Ask students to note down what technology they see and any vocabulary related to technology they hear or think of based on what they see. They could then discuss how likely they think it is that this technology will actually be invented.

2 8.1

- Play the audio and ask students to listen and make notes to help them answer question 1.
- Students compare their answers to question 1 and discuss the second question.
- **Optional step** On the board, write the word 'pseudo-archaeology', and elicit the words Francisco used to describe it (i.e. 'not real at all', 'weird theories'). Elicit or explain that the prefix 'pseudo' is used to describe something that is presented as one thing, e.g. a scientific fact, but is not accurate, genuine or based on reliable evidence.

Answers

1 Nora: opens up your imagination and helps us understand ourselves, mixes reality with imagination; Francisco: sci-fi based on real science, like *The Martian*. He is annoyed by pseudo-archaeology, that can be damaging to his work.

Extra activity

Write the following sentence fragments from the audio on the board with the prepositions omitted:

- I'm obsessed (with) sci-fi
- I used to be fascinated (by) it
- it is based (on) real science

Ask students to complete the fragments. Then ask them to use some of the verb/noun-preposition combinations to write sentences about books, TV programmes and films.

The SCIENCE of the IMPOSSIBLE

Can you make a spaceship invisible? What about building a *Star Wars* lightsaber? In his book, *Physics of the Impossible*, physicist Michio Kaku uses the latest advances in science to explain how sci-fi technology could actually work in the near future.

Invisibility

There are spaceships in *Star Trek* that can disappear. This sci-fi technology is slowly becoming reality. In 2007, scientists managed to create flat materials that became invisible in red and blue light by manipulating their structures to change how they reflected light waves. The next challenge is to make 3D objects disappear, but this should be possible in the next ten to twenty years. However, some scientists point to an obvious issue with travelling in an invisible spaceship: because all visible light from the outside would be reflected without ever getting inside the ship, the crew wouldn't be able to see what's outside the spaceship without making it visible first!

Lightsabers

Star Wars' iconic lightsabers have become part of pop culture. Although initially experts were quick to laugh them off as unrealistic, new advances in physics show that they are technically possible. What you need is some plasma, or an incredibly hot gas (25,000°C), and an empty tube with small holes along it. The plasma flows into the lightsaber and then out through the holes, creating a current of hot gas that can cut through steel. If you're already getting excited at the possibility of becoming a Jedi, there's a bit of a problem, unfortunately. To create plasma, you'd need a very powerful energy supply. So, unless you'd want to stay constantly plugged in to a power source, running around with a lightsaber isn't possible yet. Still, it might be within a hundred years.

Teleportation

Teleportation, or instantly sending objects or people across vast distances, has fascinated humans from *Arabian Nights*, through to *Sherlock Holmes*, to modern sci fi. This technology could change our civilization and would forever alter the transport system. While it sounds like the stuff of science fiction, teleportation already happens naturally, with atoms vanishing and appearing in a completely different place. Currently, scientists can teleport atoms and photons (units of light). Within the next few decades, they might be able to teleport DNA. Developing technology that allows teleporting a whole human body might take several centuries, though.

Faster than light travel

Faster than light travel breaks the rules of Einstein's theory of relativity. So how does the Millennium Falcon from *Star Wars* do this? There are two possibilities that do not violate Einstein's theory. Option one: bend spacetime. If you could stretch the space behind you and contract the space in front of you, you could get to even the most distant stars almost instantly. Option two: rip spacetime to make a hole that connects two distant parts of the universe (often referred to as a *wormhole*). The problem is you would need an almost unimaginable amount of energy to do either of the two. So faster than light travel is possible, but it might only become reality thousands of years from now.

Just a hundred years ago your smartphone would have been considered an impossible sci-fi technology. Similarly, the potential day-to-day tech from 2120 might seem like impossible sci-fi gadgets to us.

97

READING

ABOUT THE TEXT

This is an article about a book entitled *Physics of the Impossible* by theoretical physicist Michio Kaku. The writer presents Kaku's opinion on the likelihood of science-fiction technology becoming a reality. The text includes the following examples from popular culture:

- *Star Trek* is a film and television series franchise in which people travel around and explore space in the near future. The writers imagine the technology that people might have in the future, for example, teleportation.
- *Star Wars* is a film and television series franchise about the adventures of characters a long time ago in a galaxy far away. Some of the characters use lightsabers, which are swords whose blades are a powerful laser.
- *One Thousand and One Arabian Nights* (*Arabian Nights* in the text) is a collection of Middle Eastern folk tales, believed to have originated in the ninth or tenth centuries.
- *Sherlock Holmes* is an eccentric detective character created by the English author Arthur Conan Doyle at the end of the 19th century. The books have inspired many films and TV series.

The text also refers to German-American physicist Albert Einstein's theory of relativity, developed in the early twentieth century. The essential idea is that gravity is a curving or warping of space. The more massive an object, the more it warps the space around it.

3

- Go through the examples of sci-fi technology in the word box and elicit or explain what each of them involves (*faster than light travel* = travelling at a speed faster than the speed of light, which is 299,792,458 metres a second).
- **Optional step** Briefly review language for speculating, e.g. *I would imagine that …; It seems (highly/very) likely that …; … will probably …* etc. Ask students to use the expressions in their discussions.
- In pairs, students discuss when, if at all, they think each technology might be possible.
- Ask students to share their ideas and have a class vote on when each technology might be possible.

4

- Students scan the text for the examples of technology listed in the word box in Exercise 3 and find information about when they might be possible.
- Students compare answers in pairs.

VOCABULARY NOTES

light wave /laɪt weɪv/ = light that moves through the air or through an object

iconic /aɪˈkɒnɪk/ = very famous or popular

laugh (something) off /lɑːf ˈsʌmθɪŋ ɒf/ = to make yourself laugh about something to make it seem less important or serious

instantly /ˈɪnstəntli/ = immediately

vast /vɑːst/ = extremely large or covering a very large area

civilization /ˌsɪv(ə)laɪˈzeɪʃ(ə)n/ = complex human society

DNA /diː-en-eɪ/ = an acid in the chromosomes of living things that determines the specific structure and functions of every cell and carries genetic information

5

- Tell students to look at the Reading skill box.
- Students scan the text for synonyms or antonyms of the words (a–h).
- **Optional step** Students collaborate with a partner to identify the correct synonyms or antonyms.
- Check answers as a class.

Answers

a manipulate, b plasma, c energy supply, d violates, e rip, f unrealistic, h vanish, i contract

Extra activity

Give students some additional practice with identifying synonyms and antonyms. Choose six to eight words from the article that have a synonym or antonym and write these on the board. Give students two minutes to think of a synonym or antonym (or both) for each word.
Example words and answers:
advances (l. 2) (syn: discoveries, inventions)
creating (l. 26) (syn: making, ant: destroying)
powerful (l. 30) (syn: very strong, ant: weak)
instantly (l. 35) (syn: immediately; ant: slowly)
vast (l. 36) (syn: huge, massive; ant: tiny)
distant (l. 55) (syn: far away, ant: close)

6

- Tell students they are going to focus on finding specific information in the article.
- Students read the article again and answer the questions.
- Students compare their answers in pairs.

Answers

1 You wouldn't be able to see outside.
2 Making them requires a very large amount of energy.
3 Atoms naturally vanish and reappear.
4 Stretch and contract space time or rip it to create a wormhole.

7

- Tell students to look at the Critical thinking skill box.
- Students then read the list of assumptions and think about what they could expect to find in the article if each one is true.
- Students work in pairs to find information that shows whether the writer makes or doesn't make each assumption. They can then write down key sentences to support their answers.

Answers

a Yes, for example: 'If you're already getting excited at the possibility of becoming a Jedi ...'; questions that assume readers are interested in and have knowledge of sci-fi inventions, for example: What about building a *Star Wars* lightsaber?', '… how does the Millennium Falcon from *Star Wars* do this?'
b No, he assumes they will, but not that they have to for any reason
c Yes, for example: '… how sci-fi technology could actually work in the near future … … sci-fi technology is slowly becoming reality … The next challenge is to make 3D objects disappear but this should be possible in the next ten to twenty years … … Developing technology that allows teleporting a whole human body might take several centuries, though.'

8

- Ask students to re-read the article and identify other assumptions that the writer makes and write down sentences or parts of sentences that support their ideas.
- Students discuss their ideas in pairs.
- **Optional step** If students are struggling to identify other assumptions, tell them to focus on things such as the writer's beliefs about what the reader is familiar with, what technology people are interested in now and what they will be interested in in the future, etc.
- Invite students to share the assumptions they identified, and whether they think they are fair and correct.

Sample answers

Readers have seen the relevant sci-fi movies (*Star Wars*, *Star Trek*, etc.), and know what is meant by these inventions.; The enormous amount of money that will be needed to develop these technologies will be available.; The problems he mentions about each technology will be overcome eventually.; People will still be interested in these technologies hundreds of years from now.

SPEAKING

9

- Put students into groups. Go through the inventions in the word box and elicit or explain what each invention is.
- Students brainstorm ideas and then discuss which inventions they want to choose and why so that they can reach a consensus. Remind students to think of reasons to justify their choices.
- **Optional step** Ask each group to present their chosen inventions and explain their choices. They can then have a class vote on the three most needed and three most exciting tech inventions of the future.

EXPLORE MORE!

Students should find a wide range of videos about Leonardo da Vinci's inventions online. Ask them to use their knowledge of reliable sources to identify a video that provides accurate and useful information. Tell students that many of da Vinci's inventions are believed to have been earlier – or, in fact, the first – versions of technology we use today, most famously aeroplanes. Suggest that students focus on finding out more about one of da Vinci's inventions that is similar to a piece of technology we use today and make notes on the most important information they find. They could then use their notes to share what they found out in groups.

See **Workbook** pages 66–68 for extra practice.

LESSON GOALS

- **GRAMMAR** The main aim is for students to practise using structures for speculating about the past.
- **READING** A sub-aim is for students to read and understand a text about ancient inventions we use now.
- **PRONUNCIATION** A further sub-aim is for students to understand the weak form of *have*.
- **SPEAKING** The speaking aim is to speculate about inventions from the past.

READING AND GRAMMAR

1

- Direct students to the list of innovations and elicit or explain each one. Tell students not to look at or read the text about inventions while they are doing this.
- Ask students to use the phrase 'might have been invented' when they are speculating about each innovation.
- Students discuss their ideas in pairs. Elicit students' ideas and write them on the board.
- **Optional step** Draw a timeline on the board from 10,000 years ago until now. Ask students to guess when each innovation was invented and add these to the timeline.

ABOUT THE TEXT

The Pantheon is located in Rome, Italy and is a former Ancient Roman temple. The main part of the building is covered by a concrete dome with an open hole in the middle that is almost 2,000 years old, but is still the largest unreinforced concrete dome in the world. The height of the dome and its diameter are both 43 metres.
The term 'Indus Valley' refers to what is widely regarded as the world's first urban civilization. This civilization existed from 3300 BCE to 1300 BCE and was located in what is now northern India and Pakistan.

2

- Students read the text and check their predictions from Exercise 1.
- Students discuss which information they find the most surprising and why.

Answers

Make-up: more than 6,000 years ago in Egypt
Brain surgery: more than 8,000 years ago in France
Concrete: over 2,000 years ago in Rome (Italy)
Water system: more than 4,000 years ago in the Indus Valley (now Northern India and Pakistan)

3

- Students read the text again and determine how true sentences 1–7 are.
- Ask students to compare their answers in pairs and then check answers as a class.

4

- Ask students to scan the text for structures with modal verbs.
- Tell students to find the sentences in the text that helped them decide on their answers in Exercise 3, then use the context of those sentences to match the modal verb structures with their meanings.
- Students read the Grammar box to check their answers.

Answers

1 must have; 2 may/might have; 3 can't/couldn't have; 4 shouldn't have

GRAMMAR NOTES

Speculating about the past

Form

Students need to remember to always use 'have' rather than 'has' in this structure, even when it refers to a third person singular. They also need to ensure that they are using the past participle form of the verb rather than the past simple form and remember that these two verb forms will be different with irregular verbs.

Meaning

Check students are aware that the structure modal verb + *have* + past participle can only be used to speculate about what happened in the past. It is typically used in situations where we can see the effects of something that happened in the past today, but we are not sure exactly what happened or why.

For further information and practice, see **Grammar reference Unit 8B** on page 149 of the Student's Book.

5

- Go through the first item with the class. Elicit that the context of the sentence tells you that it describes something that was certainly not true (i.e. 'pottery or metal didn't exist'). Elicit the modal verb structure from the Grammar box that you use to say something is certainly not true, i.e. *can't/couldn't have (been)*.
- Students complete the remaining sentences. Ask them to use the Grammar box to check that they have chosen the correct modal verbs.

8B It must have been invented by ...

LESSON GOALS
- Speculate about the past
- Understand the weak pronunciation of *have*
- Talk about inventions from the past

READING AND GRAMMAR

1 Work in pairs. When and where do you think these innovations might have been invented?

brain surgery concrete eye make-up water sanitation systems

❖ Ancient inventions ❖

Thousands of years ago people invented many things that we now think of as 'modern'. Here are some of the most surprising ancient inventions.

Make-up We all know ancient Egyptians for their incredible architecture, but they also may have been the first to use make-up, more than 6,000 years ago. Their art also shows it must have been worn both by men and women.

Brain surgery Brain surgery has been practised for more than 8,000 years, and some of the earliest evidence comes from France. Even though our ancestors couldn't have known about bacteria, and perhaps shouldn't have performed these surgeries, many patients did survive and get better.

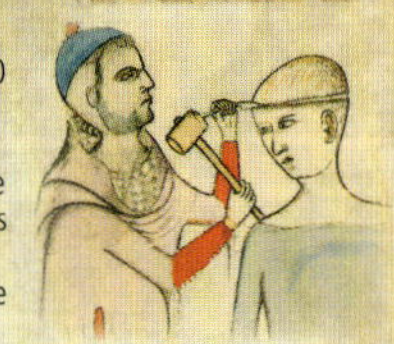

Concrete Over 2,000 years ago the Romans invented concrete. While scientists say it can't have been as good as modern concrete, it must have still been very strong as two thousand years later it still supports one of the largest domes in the world: the Pantheon.

Water system The first system for managing and cleaning dirty water in a city was invented 4,000 years ago in the Indus valley. It might have kept the city and the population safe from dangerous diseases.

2 Read the text about ancient inventions. How close were your predictions in Exercise 1? Which information did you find the most surprising?

3 Read the text again. How certain is it that the sentences are true? Write certainly true (CT), possibly true (PT) or certainly not true (NT).

1 Egyptians invented make-up. PT
2 Both men and women in ancient Egypt wore make-up. CT
3 Our ancestors knew about bacteria. NT
4 It was a bad idea to perform brain surgery. PT
5 Roman concrete was as good as modern concrete. NT
6 Roman concrete was very strong. CT
7 The people in the Indus valley were safe from dangerous diseases. PT

4 Find the sentences in the text that told you the answers to Exercise 3. Match the modal structures with their meaning (1–4). Then read the Grammar box to check.

1 It's very probable or certain that something happened.
2 It's quite possible that something happened.
3 It's impossible that something happened.
4 It was wrong to do something.

GRAMMAR Speculating about the past

You can talk about possibility and certainty in the past using the structure: **modal verb + *have* + past participle**.

- Use ***must have*** if it's very probable or certain that something happened.
  *Some of these operations **must have been** successful.*
- Use ***may have*** or ***might have*** if it's possible that something happened.
  *Egyptians **may/might have been** the first to use make-up.*
- Use ***can't/couldn't have*** if it's impossible that something happened.
  *Roman concrete **can't have been** as strong as modern concrete.*
- Use ***should/shouldn't have*** to talk about mistakes or express criticism.
  *They **shouldn't have been** doing surgery then.*

Go to page 149 for the Grammar reference.

Extra activity

Before the lesson, find three or four contrasting images for the following terms: 'celebration' or 'victory', 'disappointment' and 'surprise'. Show the photos to students and ask them to choose one for each search term that they find interesting. They then work in pairs to speculate about what happened before each of the photos was taken, using language for speculating about the past.

6 8.2

- Elicit that Nora Shawki is one of the National Geographic explorers that students watched in the video at the start of this unit. Remind students that Nora is an Egyptian archaeologist.
- Play the audio and ask students to decide whether the sentences are certainly true, possibly true or certainly not true. They can then use this information to complete the sentences.

Answers

1 may/might have used, 2 must have been, 3 can't have spoken, 4 may/might have made, 5 must have been

For additional practice, refer to the **Grammar activity** on page 259 of the Teacher's Book.

PRONUNCIATION

7 8.3

- Play the audio so students can check their answers to Exercise 6 and notice how the speaker pronounces *have*.
- Tell students to look at the Clear voice box. Remind students that the main aim of this section is to develop students' receptive skills. The subsequent activities focus on listening rather than on producing this pronunciation feature themselves.
- In class, elicit that the speaker reduces *have* to its weak form /əv/.

PRONUNCIATION NOTES

Understanding the weak form of *have*

First language users of English often pronounce all auxiliary verbs (including *have*) as weak forms. English speakers who are not first language users of English will usually voice the word *have* as a stronger form. It may be the case that auxiliary verbs are pronounced as strong forms in their first language.

A common mistake (even with some first language speakers of English) is to confuse *have* with *of* in phrases such as 'couldn't have' /ˈkʊdnt əv/.

Tell students that they can either pronounce *have* as a weak form or a strong form, depending on what they feel the most comfortable with. However, they should be aware that English speakers who are not first language users of English will usually find it easier to understand them if they pronounce *have* as a strong form.

8 8.4

- Play the audio and ask students to write the sentences they hear. See audio script on page 162 for answers.
- Elicit that students first heard a speaker who is using English as a second or other language saying the full form of *have* (sentence 1). They then hear a first language user of English saying the weak form of *have* (sentence 2). In sentence 3, the first speaker uses the weak form and the second speaker uses the full form of *have*. Check that students are aware that both types of English users may use either full or weak forms.

5 Choose the correct option to complete the sentences.

1 A million years ago, pottery and metal didn't exist, so people *can't* / *may* have boiled water in pots.
2 Archaeologists found rocks that have been heated up many times in fires. They aren't certain, but some claim these rocks *might* / *must* have been used to boil water.
3 Wild sheep are less aggressive than cows or pigs. They *may* / *can't* have been the first animals to be domesticated for farming.
4 Trepanning, a type of brain surgery, was a dangerous operation. It *can't* / *must* have killed more people than it saved.
5 In the 1970s, Joey Mellen made a hole in his own head and ended up in hospital. He *shouldn't* / *can't* have tried to trepan himself!
6 The ancient Maya *might* / *couldn't* have been the first to invent chocolate, although Aztec and Toltec civilizations are also likely candidates.

NATIONAL GEOGRAPHIC EXPLORER

6 8.2 **Listen to Nora Shawki talking about important innovations in ancient Egypt. Complete the sentences using an appropriate modal verb and the verb in brackets.**

1 The Egyptians ________ (use) papyrus for many other things we don't know about.
2 It ________ (be) very exciting to read hieroglyphics for the first time in centuries.
3 They ________ (speak) without vowel sounds even though they only wrote the consonants.
4 They ________ (make) bread in a similar way to how we make it today.
5 This type of pottery ________ (be) very important to ancient Egyptians.

PRONUNCIATION

7 8.3 **Listen and check your answers to Exercise 6. How does the speaker pronounce *have*? Look at the Clear voice box to check.**

the speaker pronounces it as 'ev'

CLEAR VOICE

Understanding the weak form of *have*

In past modal structures *have* is usually unstressed, and some speakers reduce it to its weak form /əv/, making it harder to hear. To be easily understood, it can be better to pronounce the full form /hæv/.

8 8.4 **Listen and write the sentences you hear.**

SPEAKING

9 **Work in groups. Look at the photos of inventions from the past. For each invention, discuss the questions.**

1 What might it have been used for?
2 When and where might it have been invented?
3 How do you think it might have worked?

It can't have been invented in Europe. I think it could have been somewhere in China, because …

99

Extra activity

Put students into pairs. Ask each student to write four sentences that include the structure modal verb + *have* + past participle. Students then take turns to read their sentences aloud to their partner. Tell them to use the weak form of *have* in two of the sentences and the full form of *have* in the other two sentences. Students then identify the sentences in which their partner used the weak and full forms.

SPEAKING

9

- Put students into groups of three or four.
- Go through the task and ask students to read the example.
- Students brainstorm possible answers for each invention in their groups and reach a consensus.
- Encourage students to use structures for speculating about the past in the discussion.

Answers

1 Han era seismoscope: invented in 132 CE in China; it was used to detect earthquakes; it's possible the Chinese knew that earthquakes produced vibrations in the soil even hundreds of kilometres away, so by detecting these small vibrations, they could say that an earthquake happened somewhere; it had a simple design: an urn with a pendulum, when the device detected vibration, it dropped a ball from the mouth of a metal dragon into a metal frog, making a loud sound.
2 Chimu phone: made about 1,200–1,400 years ago in what is now Peru by the ancient Chimu people; it might have been used to listen in on other people's conversations or to communicate over several hundred metres without shouting; it had a simple design: two receivers are connected via a cotton line that carries voice vibrations from the speaker to the listener.

Extra activity

Extend Exercise 9 by finding a photo online of another ancient invention called the Baghdad Battery. Ask students to look at the photo and discuss their answers to questions 1 and 2 in Exercise 9, using structures for speculating about the past.

Answers

1 The Baghdad Battery is believed to have been used either: a) for electroplating (using electricity to put a layer of metal onto an object) or electrotherapy (using electricity as a medical treatment) or b) as a storage vessel for sacred documents.
2 It was invented in Baghdad, Iraq some time between 150 BCE and 650 CE.

For additional practice, refer to the **Communication activity** on page 226 of the Teacher's Book.

See **Workbook** pages 68–69 for extra practice.

8C Two sides to tech

LESSON GOALS
- Talk about gadgets and technology
- Form nouns, verbs and adjectives in word families
- Understand prepositions in connected speech
- Pronounce long and short 'o' sounds clearly

Francisco Estrada-Belli and his team use technology called LIDAR to find Maya ruins in the Guatemalan jungle.

VOCABULARY AND LISTENING

1 Work in pairs. Look at the technology in the box and discuss the questions.

driverless vehicles   electric scooters   self-service checkouts   sharing apps (e.g. Uber, Airbnb)   video conferencing

1 What are the advantages of each technology: to the company? to workers? to customers?
2 What disadvantages can you think of?
3 Which technology have you used or experienced yourself? Why did you use it?

NATIONAL GEOGRAPHIC EXPLORER

2 8.5 **Listen to Francisco Estrada-Belli talk about technology in his work. What advantages and disadvantages does he mention about ...**

1 LIDAR?
2 his smartphone?

3 8.5 **Listen again. Complete each sentence with one word.**

1 Remote sensing uses a number of devices to find ancient remains.
2 LIDAR is really innovative but it's not very user-friendly. You need a lot of training because it's so sophisticated.
3 Francisco couldn't work without his smartphone because it is so handy. It's a pocket-sized collection of gadgets: G.P.S., compass, flashlight, camera and notepad.
4 But on the flip side, it's not waterproof, so it might get wet and damaged.

4 **Match the words (1–10) with the definitions (a–j).**

1 gadget a
2 handy i
3 innovative f
4 outdated h
5 perform e
6 pocket-sized c
7 recharge d
8 sophisticated b
9 user-friendly j
10 waterproof g

a a small machine with a particular purpose
b advanced in design so it can do complex things
c small enough to carry in your pocket
d fill something with electricity so it keeps working
e complete an action or job, especially a difficult one
f using new and different ideas and methods
g not allowing water to enter it
h old and no longer as good as more modern things
i useful
j simple for people to use

100

LESSON GOALS

- **VOCABULARY** A main aim is for students to learn and practise using vocabulary for gadgets and technology and to practise expanding their vocabulary by identifying the other nouns, verbs or adjectives in the same word family.
- **LISTENING** A further main aim is for students to listen to and understand a radio phone-in about a new sharing app and practise understanding prepositions in connected speech.
- **PRONUNCIATION** A sub-aim is for students to practise pronouncing the long and short 'o' sounds.
- **SPEAKING** The speaking aim is to discuss whether the internet has had more of a positive or negative impact on people's lives.

VOCABULARY AND LISTENING

1

- Ask students to read the examples of technology in the box. Briefly elicit or explain what each one is.
- Ask students to read the questions and discuss them together.

Sample answers

1 driverless vehicles: companies don't have to pay drivers, customers may be safer?; electric scooters: fast, quiet, cheap and clean way to get around town; self-service checkouts: company doesn't have to employ so many staff, customers don't have to queue so often; sharing apps: company makes money for a purely administrative role, without needing to own taxis, hotels, etc., workers can make money from their own flat, house, car, customers get cheaper accommodation and taxi service; video conferencing: more frequent communication between offices without money or time spent travelling, workers don't have to travel for work, students can learn at home
2 disadvantages may include: less personal customer service, e.g. self-service checkouts, driverless vehicles; greater unemployment if jobs are automated or made unprofessional, e.g. driverless vehicles, sharing apps; poor safety, e.g. driverless vehicles, electric scooters

2 8.5

- Direct students to the photo and its caption. Remind students that Francisco appeared in the video at the start of this unit. Elicit that he is an archaeologist who studies the Maya civilization in Guatemala. Explain that this civilization existed between about 600 BCE and 1546 CE.
- Play the audio and ask students to listen and make notes about the advantages and disadvantages of each technology.
- Ask students to compare their answers in pairs.

Answers

1 see hidden buildings and other structures; accurately map location; very sophisticated, not user-friendly, expensive
2 small portable device, replaces other gadgets; not waterproof, always available

5 Write sentences using the words from Exercise 4 to describe …

1 the technology you often use.
2 the technology in Exercise 1.

Go to page 138 for the Vocabulary reference.

6 Which words from Exercise 4 (1–10) are in the same word families as the bold words (a–c)? Are they nouns, verbs or adjectives? Read the Focus on box to check.

a a computer with high **performance** n., perform (v.)
b the latest **innovations** n., innovative (adj.)
c **rechargeable** batteries adj., recharge (v.)

FOCUS ON Forming nouns, verbs and adjectives

You can expand your vocabulary by exploring the word families of words you are learning.
Notice some common suffixes that are typically added to words to create different parts of speech.
Nouns: -ion, -ment, -ity, -e/ance, -ness
complicated → complication, achieve → achievement, complex – complexity, silent → silence, happy → happiness
Adjectives: -al, -ical, -able, -ous, -ive
universe → universal, technology → technological, afford → affordable, danger → dangerous, act → active
Verbs: -ate, -ize, -ify, -en
active → activate, memory → memorize, simple → simplify, strength → strengthen

Go to page 149 for the Focus on reference.

7 Complete the sentences, using suffixes to change the words in the box to the correct part of speech. Then use a dictionary to check.

invent memory sense

1 The Chinese are typically credited with the invention of paper.
2 This app saves you from having to memorize all your passwords.
3 The alarm is sensitive to movement and beeps as soon as someone enters the room.

LISTENING

8 8.6 You are going to listen to a radio phone-in about a new sharing app. First, look at the Listening skill box. Then listen to three extracts and complete the sentences (1–3).

LISTENING SKILL
Understanding prepositions in connected speech

In connected speech, prepositions might not be heard clearly. They will often be connected to the words next to them, so *for example* might sound like /frəˈzɑːmpl/. Note that speaking like this might make you *less* easy to understand.

1 We've had them ________.
2 MyCarYourCar is revolutionizing ________.
3 That way they share the cost ________.

9 8.7 Listen to the phone-in. Match the statements (1–5) with the person who said them: the host, Marsha, Yuki or Jens.

1 One benefit of carpooling is the interesting conversations you can have. Jens
2 Carpooling is cheaper than the alternatives. Marsha
3 Carpooling isn't the most environmentally-friendly way of travelling. host
4 Personal safety is an issue when carpooling. Yuki
5 There is an important difference between carpooling and hitchhiking. Marsha

PRONUNCIATION

10 8.8 Look at the Clear voice box and listen to the words (1–6). Do they have a short or long 'o' sound? Practise saying the words.

CLEAR VOICE
Pronouncing long and short 'o'

In English there are two different 'o' sounds: a short one /ɒ/ (usually spelled 'o') and a long one /ɔː/. (often spelled as 'au' or 'or').

1 automatic	3 laptop	5 pocket-sized
2 complex	4 performance	6 waterproof

SPEAKING

11 Work in groups of three. Read the statement and discuss whether you agree or not, and why.

The internet has damaged our personal and professional lives more than it has helped them.

101

5

- Ask students to think about a few types of technology that they use and choose a few (different) types of technology from the box in Exercise 1.
- Ask students to use as many words from Exercise 4 in their sentences as they can.
- Students share their sentences with a partner.

For further information and practice, see **Vocabulary reference Unit 8** on page 138 of the Student's Book.

Extra activity

Put students into pairs and ask them to brainstorm other items, i.e. not types of technology, which they could use adjectives from Exercise 4 to describe. Tell them to think of at least two nouns for each adjective. They could then use some of these adjective-noun combinations to write sentences about things they own or things they have experienced.

6

- Direct students to the instruction and check their understanding of the term 'word family' (a group of words of different parts of speech that all have the same stem).
- Ask students to match the words in bold with the words in Exercise 4 that are in the same word family. Tell them to identify the part of speech for each of the six words.
- Tell students to read the Focus on box and check their answers. Tell them to pay attention to the common suffixes for each part of speech.

For further information and practice, see **Focus on reference Unit 8C** on page 149 of the Student's Book.

VOCABULARY NOTES

map /mæp/ = to make a map of a specific area

line of work /laɪn əv wɜːk/ = a type of work or job

compass /ˈkʌmpəs/ = a device that is used to show directions and navigate

on the flip side /ɒn ðə flɪp saɪd/ = an expression used to show the contrast between the previous statement and the statement that it introduces

3 8.5

- Play the audio again and ask students to listen for the key words at the start of each sentence so they can write the missing words.
- Invite different students to read the completed sentences.

4

- Students match the words with their meanings.
- Check answers as a class.

FOCUS ON NOTES

When students are recording vocabulary, encourage them to think about what other words in the same word family could be, using the suffixes from the Focus on box to help them. They can record words from the same word family together, which should help them expand their vocabulary more quickly. Understanding how verbs, nouns and adjectives from the same word family are formed should also help students better understand unfamiliar words. If they already know one word from a word family, this will help them understand the meaning of an unfamiliar word from that word family.

7

- Ask students to begin by reading the sentences and using the word that comes before each gap to decide whether the missing word is a noun, verb or adjective.
- Students then choose the word from the box for each gap and decide on the correct suffix.
- Students compare their answers in pairs and then use a dictionary to check their answers. Notice that in item 2, the suffix *-ise* could be used instead of *-ize* in British English.

Extra activity

In pairs, students look back at the article in Lesson 8A. Tell them to find five words in the article that belong to a word family, i.e. words that have a verb, noun and/or adjective form, and then write a word family for each word. For example, the verb *create* is used in line 29 of the article: the noun form of *create* is *creation* and the adjective form is *creative*.

For additional practice, refer to the **Vocabulary activity** on page 240 and the **Focus on activity** on page 260 of the Teacher's Book.

LISTENING

8 8.6

- Direct students to the instruction and elicit what a 'radio phone-in' is (a radio show where listeners call the radio station and give their opinion about a particular topic on air). Explain that the topic of the phone-in is a ride-sharing, or carpooling, app, which you can use to find someone near you who is driving to the place you want to go to so you can ride with them in their car. This is different from ride-hailing apps, which are taxi services.
- Tell students to look at the Listening skill box.
- Play the audio and ask students to complete the sentences.
- Students compare their answers in pairs.

Answers

1 for a number of years now; 2 the way we travel from town to town; 3 of the petrol

9 8.7

- Ask students to read the statements. Check their understanding of 'hitchhiking' (travelling by asking strangers if you can travel with them).
- Play the audio so students can match the statements with the speakers.

Extra activity

Ask students to work in pairs to discuss which speaker they most agree with and whether they would be willing to try carpooling. Encourage them to think about examples they could use to support their point of view.

PRONUNCIATION

10 8.8

- Ask students to look at the Clear voice box.
- Play the audio so students can listen to the words and identify whether they hear a short or long 'o' sound.
- Check that students understand the underlined vowel is not always stressed. When drilling, check that you stress the correct syllables: auto**ma**tic; **lap**top.
- Ask students to practise pronouncing the words with the correct 'o' sound with a partner.

Answers

Short 'o' sound: complex, laptop, pocket-sized; Long 'o' sound: automatic, performance, waterproof

PRONUNCIATION NOTES

Pronouncing long and short 'o'

The long 'o' sound is pronounced with rounded lips and it exists in most languages. The dipthong /əʊ/ is often considered the long 'o' sound because it is represented by the letter 'o' (e.g. home /həʊm/). However, the phonemic symbol for the long 'o' sound is actually /ɔː/ which may be represented by the letter 'o' (e.g. *door* /dɔː/) but doesn't have to be. Exceptions include *caught* /kɔːt/ and *waterproof* /ˈwɔːtəpruːf/.
The short 'o' (as in *long and lot)*, is less frequently used and is pronounced with the mouth open and with the tongue low and relaxed.

For additional practice, refer to the **Pronunciation activity** on page 275 of the Teacher's Book.

SPEAKING

11

- Ask students to read the statement. Elicit that it is asking whether the internet has had more of a positive or negative impact on people's lives.
- Students decide whether they agree with the statement or not and think of arguments and examples to support their opinion.
- Put students into groups of three to discuss the statement.

Extra activity

Ask students to write an outline for a 'for and against' essay for the statement in Exercise 11. Tell them to use ideas from the discussion. If students need to be reminded of how to structure a 'for and against' essay, refer them back to Lesson 5E. Once students have planned their essays, ask them to write the introduction for it.

For additional practice, refer to the **Communication activity** on page 227 and the **Mediation activity** on page 290 of the Teacher's Book.

See **Workbook** pages 70–72 for extra practice.

LESSON GOALS

- **SPEAKING** This lesson integrates speaking, reading and listening. Its main aim is for students to discuss their approach to online communication and consider how to follow online etiquette to ensure clear, appropriate communication in different situations online. Students then use what they have learned to create a poster about online etiquette.

SPEAKING

1

- Ask students to read the questions and think about their answers and reasons or examples to support them.
- Students discuss the questions in pairs.

2

- Ask students to read the definition of 'netiquette'. Ask, *What is etiquette and what contexts have you heard it used in? Have you ever heard the term 'netiquette'? If you have, what context was it used in and what 'netiquette' rules did you learn?*
- Ask students to brainstorm 'netiquette' rules with their partner. Tell them to consider all aspects of online communication, including emails, messaging, video conference calls and social media.

Sample answers

In video conference calls, mute your microphone if you are not involved in the conversation to avoid background noise. In emails, make hyperlinks active so that the reader can click to access the web page. Don't 'reply all' in emails unless the reply is relevant to everyone. Don't use large groups such as WhatsApp groups if the message is only relevant to one person in that group. When sending emails to large groups of people, use the BCC function to avoid sharing people's email addresses.

3

- Ask students to read the instructions. Ask students what they understand by being 'most or least relaxed about netiquette' (being relaxed about netiquette means not seeing it as important or necessary).
- Students complete the quiz on page 103 and then look at the answer key on page 156 (page 205 of the Teacher's Book).
- Put students into groups to compare their answers and decide who is the most and least relaxed about 'netiquette'.

Extra activity

Ask students to share in class how relaxed they are about netiquette: very relaxed, quite relaxed, not very relaxed, not relaxed at all. Together, draw a conclusion about how relaxed the class as a whole is about netiquette. Then put students into pairs or small groups and ask them to discuss reasons why people might be more or less relaxed about netiquette (e.g. their age, their job, the type of company they work for, what they have been taught at school or university, etc.)

4

- Put students into pairs and ask them to read the questions.
- If students are unsure about how online behaviour can influence relationships, ask them to consider situations where they have been offended or confused by online communication and what that made them think about the other person. Then ask them to consider situations where people's online communication made a positive impression on them and consider whether this was because the other person followed 'netiquette' rules.
- Students discuss the questions in pairs. Encourage them to share anecdotes and evidence from their own experiences of communicating online.

MY VOICE

COMMUNICATION SKILL NOTES

Communicating online

The ability to communicate clearly and effectively online is extremely important in the modern world. Students should already be familiar with how to communicate online appropriately in their first language culture, in their school or workplace/industry and among people in their age group, but they need to be aware that people from other cultures, and in different workplaces/industries and age groups will have different perceptions of what constitutes appropriate online communication. For example, it may be appropriate to use emoticons in communication within students' school or workplace context and among people in their age group, but using emoticons may appear inappropriate and even disrespectful to people from other contexts and age groups. Striking the right tone in online communication in a second or other language usually takes time and practice. If students get reactions from the people they communicate with that suggest they have got something wrong, they need to respond by modifying how they communicate in future. They also need to avoid making assumptions about people who write to them because they communicate in a different style.

5 ▶ 8.2

- Ask students to read the questions.
- Play the video and ask students to make notes on the online rules and behaviours mentioned in it. Check students' understanding of the term 'to tag someone' (to include a link to

someone else's social media profile in a social media post), that was used in the video.

- Students then refer back to the rules they wrote in Exercise 2 and the behaviours from the quiz so they can answer the questions.
- Students compare their answers in pairs.
- Elicit feedback from the class on the rules and behaviours mentioned in the video.
- **Optional step** Ask students if they disagreed with any of the advice given in the video and to explain why.

Answers

2 Mentioned in the quiz: posting an embarrassing photo of someone you know, using abbreviations; 3 Other behaviours: how emotions can be misinterpreted, using emojis/emoticons, posting something that could be offensive or hurtful, how levels of formality can be misinterpreted

6 ▶ 8.2

- Ask students to read the questions. Tell them to focus on the key ideas that they need to listen for (e.g. emojis, abbreviations).
- Play the video again so students can make notes on their answers.
- Students compare their answers in pairs and then check answers as a class.

Answers

1 We can't hear the person's voice or see them, so it's difficult to judge their emotions.
2 They can help explain our emotions.
3 Not everyone might be familiar with what an abbreviation stands for.
4 It's important to check that the people involved are happy for you to share a photo or post on social media to avoid upsetting or annoying them.

Extra activity

If you feel this task would be appropriate for your class, ask students to think of a story they have heard in the news or on social media where a well-known person has embarrassed themselves or accidentally offended people through a social media post. Students describe what happened and explain why the social media post caused embarrassment or offence (e.g. if the person shared too much information or presented the post in an inappropriate style).

8D Communicating online

LESSON GOALS
- Discuss online communication habits
- Understand and discuss online etiquette
- Create a poster about online etiquette

SPEAKING

1 Work in pairs. Discuss the questions.

1 How often do you communicate with others online? Who do you typically chat with?
2 Which do you prefer: messaging, calling or video calling? Why?
3 Do you think we will soon communicate with others more online than face-to-face? Would this be something positive or negative? Why?
4 What problems can occur when people communicate online? Why?

2 Look at the definition. What examples of 'netiquette' rules can you think of?

> netiquette /ˈnetɪket/
> rules about acceptable behaviour on the internet
> *It's considered bad netiquette to use all capital letters in emails.*

3 Do the quiz on page 103. Then go to page 156 to see the answers. Share your answers in groups. Who is the most and least relaxed about 'netiquette'?

4 Work in pairs. Do you think any of the behaviours in the quiz can help to build a relationship with the other person? Could any of the behaviours damage the relationship?

MY VOICE ▶

5 ▶ 8.2 Watch the video about online etiquette. Answer the questions.

1 Are any of the rules you listed in Exercise 2 mentioned?
2 Which behaviours from the quiz are discussed?
3 Which other behaviours are discussed?

6 ▶ 8.2 Watch the video again. Answer the questions.

1 Why can emotions be interpreted differently in online communication?
2 How can emojis be helpful?
3 Why can abbreviations cause problems in online communication?
4 Why should you be careful when posting photos on social media?

7 Look at the Communication skill box and discuss the questions (1–2).

> **COMMUNICATION SKILL**
> **Communicating online**
> - Consider how the emotions behind your words or emojis can be interpreted differently. It's important to make sure that your meaning is clear. Ask the other person for clarification if you're not sure how to interpret their message.
> - Avoid using too many abbreviations; not everyone will be familiar with them.
> - Be careful what you share and who with – you don't want to offend or upset others.
> - Try to read other people's messages with an open mind rather than assuming they're being rude or unfriendly.

1 Do you think these rules are universal or do they depend on the person and context? Why?
2 Have you ever had any misunderstandings when talking to someone online? What happened? How could the misunderstanding have been avoided?

8 Look at the messages and situations. How appropriate is each message? Why? Rewrite any that you think aren't appropriate.

1 WhatsApp message to a good friend: I was wondering if you had time to meet later today.
2 First message to someone you have only just met: It was meeting you yesterday
3 Email to your teacher: Thx 4 checkin my homework
4 Post on your professional social media profile: I wanted to share with you some of the BIGGEST lessons in marketing I've learned.

SPEAKING

9 OWN IT! Work in groups. Create a poster about online etiquette. Follow the instructions.

1 Include the online etiquette rules that are the most important to you. They can be rules from the Communication skill box or your own ideas.
2 Add specific examples, stories or pictures that illustrate the rules.
3 Present your poster to another group. Did you choose similar rules?

102

7

- Ask students to look at the Communication skill box and read the questions. Check understanding of 'universal' (always true; can be applied to every situation).
- Students discuss the questions in pairs, giving examples of misunderstandings that they or people they know have experienced when communicating online.

8

- Ask students to read the situations and the messages. Remind them that the appropriateness of the messages largely depends on the person it was sent to or the context in which it was written.
- Students use their awareness of the rules for communicating online to decide on the appropriateness of each message and rewrite the ones they think are inappropriate to make them appropriate.
- Students compare their answers in pairs and justify their answers.

QUIZ

How seriously do you take netiquette? Take this quiz to find out.

How often do you do each of the following?

1 Reply to an email a week later.
Never Rarely Sometimes Often Always

2 Use abbreviations such as LOL or BTW.
Never Rarely Sometimes Often Always

3 Write using capital letters only.
Never Rarely Sometimes Often Always

4 Use emoticons in work emails.
Never Rarely Sometimes Often Always

5 Post an embarrassing photo of someone you know.
Never Rarely Sometimes Often Always

6 Write as you speak, e.g. *coz, gonna.*
Never Rarely Sometimes Often Always

7 Send emails with no subject line.
Never Rarely Sometimes Often Always

8 Add people you've never met or don't know as friends on Facebook.
Never Rarely Sometimes Often Always

Score

Never – 1 point, Rarely – 2 points, Sometimes – 3 points, Often – 4 points, Always – 5 points

103

Answers

1 Could potentially be too formal, but it might depend on how the two friends communicate. Potential change to less formal, e.g. Got time to meet up later?
2 Could potentially be too informal unless a great rapport was established in that first meeting; the kiss could be inappropriate; potential change: delete the current emojis and say 'It was great meeting you yesterday 😊'
3 Likely too informal; avoid abbreviations and emojis and writing as you speak ('checkin'); potential change: Thank you very much for checking my homework.
4 Seems fine; capital letters for emphasis are unlikely to be seen as shouting but could consider dropping them.

SPEAKING

9 OWN IT!

- Put students into groups of three or four and go through the three steps involved in the task. Assign roles within each group (e.g. making a list of rules to include during students' discussion; thinking of examples, stories and pictures to use on the poster; planning the presentation of the poster) or ask students to do this themselves in order to ensure everyone participates.
- Students discuss in their groups and reach a consensus on the most important online etiquette rules. They can then use their own knowledge to come up with examples or stories for each rule or, if possible, search for these online.
- **Optional step** Students could draw pictures or find and print photos to illustrate the information on their posters. They should think about how they can organize the text and pictures so that their poster both presents information clearly and looks visually appealing.
- Students prepare a presentation of their poster, ensuring that everyone in the group says something. The groups take turns to present their posters to another group.

Extra activity

After their presentations, students could all put up their posters around the classroom. Two students from each group stand next to their poster while the other student from their group walks around the classroom, looking at the other posters. Tell students to choose one or two of the posters that they did not see in Exercise 9 and ask the students who produced it a few questions to either clarify information or learn more.

LESSON GOALS

- **WRITING** The aim of the lesson is to guide students to write a product review for a gadget or other tech product that they own or have used. The reading texts provide a model. Students practise the writing skill of using multi-word adjectives to write more economically and practise expressing positive and negative opinions about a product.

SPEAKING

1

- Ask students to look at the photos and captions, focussing on the useful features of each product and the type of situations they would be useful in.
- Students discuss the questions in pairs.

Sample answers

a waterproof speaker: to use it on a beach or camping holiday or to listen to music while they are outdoors

b sports video camera: to film yourself or other people doing sports

c instant camera: to take photos at a party or event that you can then give to the guests, to be able to instantly see what something looks like when you are working on creative projects

d solar-powered power pack: to use while you are staying outdoors for a longer period of time, for example on a camping holiday, and you need power for light or to use electric devices

2

- Check students' understanding of 'criteria' (standards by which you decide on or deal with something).
- Students decide on their ranking for the criteria.
- Put students into pairs and ask them to explain their ranking to each other. They then discuss which other factors they take into account when deciding which products to buy.

8E Five-star gadgets

LESSON GOALS
- Use multi-word adjectives to describe gadgets
- Give opinions about gadgets and other products
- Write a product review

a waterproof speaker

b sports video camera

c instant camera

d solar-powered power pack

SPEAKING

1 Work in pairs. Look at the photos. Why might someone buy each product?

2 When you buy a new gadget, what helps you decide which one to choose? Put the criteria (a–h) in order from 1 (the most important) to 8 (the least important). What other criteria might you take into account?

a appearance and size
b availability near you
c brand
d impact on the environment
e other people's opinions
f performance and special features
g user-friendliness
h value for money

READING FOR WRITING

3 Read the three reviews. What kind of gadget is each one reviewing? How many stars out of five do you think each reviewer gave the product?

Shavi wireless/waterproof speaker; 3 or 4 stars

Misleading info but decent sound

This would be the ideal choice if you're looking for a small but powerful device to travel with. The design is clean and simple, but the fact that it's waterproof makes it the perfect companion for outdoor activities like camping. Plus it doubles up as a power charger for other devices, which saves space. On the flip side, another review claimed it has a long-lasting, 24-hour battery life, but they must have been talking about a different model because the most it's lasted for me was about 10 hours. Luckily, the recharge time is surprisingly quick. The only other downside is that there's no volume button. All in all, not bad.

Petra instant camera; 2 or 3 stars

OK for kids, not so much for adults

Needed a cheap and cheerful one quickly for a friend's wedding but couldn't find anything locally so had to buy online. Fortunately, it arrived in good time. Clear and easy-to-use on-screen buttons makes editing straightforward. That, and the fun choice of colours (comes in blue, pink, or red) makes me think it's really for kids. Picture quality OK in good light, but the flash isn't strong enough for indoor photography. Also, the print quality is a lot worse than I expected, though I got some acceptable results in black and white. The other major drawback is the poor Bluetooth connection - you need to be very close to your phone to send photos. They should have included a USB cable.

Otto smartphone; 4 or 5 stars

Great value for money

This make is well-known as high-end (they say the camera is a must if you enjoy photography) so I thought the C14 was out of my price range until I looked at second-hand offers. What a great deal! Plus it's better for the planet. Just a few minor scratches on the screen and the battery is perhaps not as long-lasting as it was when new. Really, I couldn't have got a better phone for the price.

104

READING FOR WRITING

3

- Ask students to read the reviews and look for key words that indicate the product and how many stars the reviewer could have given it.
- Students compare their ideas in pairs.

4

- Students read the reviews again and identify which of the criteria listed in Exercise 2 is mentioned in each review.
- Students compare their answers in pairs.

Answers

Shavi: a,f, e; Petra: b, g, a, f; Otto: c, d, f, h

Extra activity

Find or ask students to find a real review of a gadget in English online. Students read the review and identify the criteria from Exercise 2 that the writer has included. They can then search for evidence in the review that reflects the number of stars given.

5

- Ask students to look at the Writing skill box.

4 Read the reviews again. Which of the criteria listed in Exercise 2 does each one mention?

5 Look at the Writing skill box. Then find at least five compound adjectives and three adjective pairs in the reviews.

WRITING SKILL
Multi-word adjectives

Compound adjectives allow you to write more economically. They are made of more than one word and are usually joined by a hyphen.

This handy feature saves space. It combines two functions in one. ➔ *This handy,* ***space-saving*** *feature combines two functions in one.*

It comes with a guarantee of two years. ➔ *It comes with a* ***two-year*** *guarantee.*

Some adjectives are often seen together in **adjective pairs**, joined by *and*.

The app is free and, though it's quite ***rough and ready****, it works well.*

The order of the adjectives in these expressions is fixed, i.e. not ~~ready and rough~~.

6 Put the words in order to complete the sentences. You may need to add hyphens.

1 This operating system starts very quickly and … a / and / clean / has / interface / simple.
2 No other model can compete ... its / minute / recharge / thirty / time / with.
3 I recommend this running machine if you're looking for … and / cheap / cheerful / something.
4 Talkback was the only … and / easy / free / to / use ... video conferencing platform that we found.
5 You can sing along to each song … by / lyrics / on / reading / screen / the.
6 The controls are multi-coloured, but the problem is that the manual … and / black / in / is / printed / white.
7 It's known as … a / brand / end / high …, but you can find bargains if you search online.
8 The plastic cover provides … and / lasting / long / protection / strength … for the watch screen.

1 has a clean and simple interface
2 with its thirty-minute recharge time
3 something cheap and cheerful
4 free and easy-to-use
5 by reading the on-screen lyrics
6 is printed in black and white
7 a high-end brand
8 strength and long-lasting protection

7 Look at the expressions in the Useful language box. Are you more likely to hear positive or negative comments with each expression? Which could be used with both positive and negative comments?

Useful language Product reviews

This is the ideal option if you're looking for … positive
… makes the perfect choice for … positive
On the flip side, … both
Another downside is that … negative
All in all, … both
A minor drawback is … negative
You could do a lot worse than … positive
… is a must. positive
… within your price range. positive

WRITING TASK

8 You are going to write a review for a gadget or other tech product that you own or have used. Write five sentences to include in your review, using expressions from the Useful language box.

9 **WRITE** Decide how many stars out of five you will give the product. Then write the review.

10 **CHECK** Use the checklist. I have …

☐ included several criteria from the list in Exercise 2.
☐ said what type of person would enjoy or benefit from the product.
☐ described both the positive and negative aspects of the product.
☐ used multi-word adjectives to make my writing economical.

11 **REVIEW** Exchange reviews with a partner. Did they include everything in the checklist in Exercise 10? Does their review reflect the number of stars they have given their product?

Go to page 133 for the Reflect and review.

EXPLORE MORE!

Find out what percentage of online reviews are fake, i.e. written by companies to make customers buy their products.

- Students scan the reviews for compound adjectives and adjective pairs.

Answers

Compound adjectives: long-lasting, 24-hour, easy-to-use, on-screen, (waterproof and straightforward are also compound adjectives written as one word), high-end, second-hand, long-lasting. Adjective pairs: clean and simple, cheap and cheerful, black and white.

6

- Go through the first item together. Elicit that the two adjectives given are 'clean' and 'simple' and ask students which order they would be used in: 'clean' first and then 'simple' – this is a fixed pair; the adjective with fewer syllables usually comes first. Elicit that the complete phrase is 'has a clean and simple interface'.
- Students complete the remaining sentences by putting the words in order, adding hyphens where necessary.

7

- Ask students to look at the Useful language box. They can mark any expressions they already know as either positive or negative and then try to guess the meaning of new expressions based on the words they contain. For example, 'down' in 'downside' suggests that this is part of a negative expression.
- Students compare their answers in pairs.

WRITING TASK

8

- Students choose a gadget or other tech product to write their review about.
- Students brainstorm the good and bad points of their product and then use the phrases in the Useful language box to write five sentences for a product review.

9 WRITE

- Ask students to decide how many stars out of five they will give their product.
- Remind students to use appropriate multi-word adjectives in their review.
- Students write the first draft of their review.

10 CHECK

- Ask students to use the checklist and then make changes to their reviews if necessary.

11 REVIEW

- Students exchange reviews with a partner.
- Students read each other's reviews and use the checklist from Exercise 10 to review them.
- Students then read their partner's review again and focus on whether it reflects the number of stars they have given their product.
- Students give each other feedback on their reviews.

EXPLORE MORE!

Students search online for 'fake online reviews' or a similar term to find statistics about the percentage that are fake. Encourage students to look at several reliable online sources for statistics.

For **Unit 8 Reflect and review**, see Student's Book page 133.

See **Workbook** pages 72–73 for extra practice.

See **Workbook** pages 74–75 for Units 7 and 8 Review.

VIDEO 8.1

Nora: *I definitely think of myself as a techie person. My father was a tech geek, so growing up I was exposed to the latest technology; I even used to get excited when we got the latest 'Britannica Encyclopaedia' CD-ROMs every year. Now, I'm usually the person my friends come to if they have a problem with equipment, or if they want to know which latest gadget they should buy. I also use a lot of technology in my fieldwork while digging – it helps a lot in terms of speed and efficiency.*

Francisco: *My friends and family see me working with tech all the time. They know that's my area of expertise. So yes, I do have that reputation as being 'techie' among family and friends.*

Nora: *The one app on my iPhone that I really can't live without is the 'Notes' app. It's so basic, but I use it the most out of any other app. I love to write lists, so I am constantly adding notes or reminders; but also positive thoughts that help me when I'm having bad days.*

Francisco: *My smartphone. I got my first smartphone as soon as they came out, I think it was 2008 or 2009. It was before anyone else I knew got one. I do almost everything related to my work with it. It is like a small laptop that I carry in my pocket.*

Nora: *I'm worried that technology takes over people's lives where they get to a point where they can't manage without it. Especially the younger generation. They are so obsessed with the screens and all these apps. People should learn to have a balance. Instead of playing games all day on our phones or computers, we should also take time to do some reading, to learn.*

Francisco: *I'm not worried about technology. We need it to benefit science. We archaeologists really benefit from a technology that can show us where all the Mayan archaeological sites are hidden under the forest.*

AUDIO 8.1

Nora: *I'm obsessed with sci-fi as a genre. I used to be fascinated by it as a kid. I love that science fiction opens up your imagination. It makes you think and question certain realities. And it helps us try to understand ourselves as human beings more thoroughly.*

Francisco: *I like the science fiction that is based on real science. I really enjoyed the film* The Martian. *I like the way the main character used his science background to solve challenges that at first seemed impossible to overcome, to survive all by himself on a distant planet and without communication.*

Nora: *I think sci-fi films mix reality with a little bit of imagination about science and technology. For example,* Back to the Future *focuses on real life events but uses time travel. I loved that movie because of the time travel aspect of it. I was always fascinated by going backwards and forwards into different times. We don't have time travel technology yet, but it might be a possibility in the future, you never know!*

Francisco: *I don't enjoy pseudo-archaeology, you know when it's not real at all, when they invent all these strange theories about who built the pyramids and stuff like that. It affects my work as an archaeologist because, you know, people start believing these weird theories, so it kind of puts the scientific work we do in danger.*

AUDIO 8.2

Papyrus

Nora: *Papyrus was the ancient form of paper, made from the papyrus plant. Sometimes, if we're lucky, we find tightly rolled sheets of papyrus in scrolls – this was one of the earliest forms of a book! We know they used papyrus for writing, but they also used it for making sandals to wear, baskets to keep things in and even rope to be used as a tool. Who knows what else they used it for? Papyrus is amazing because of what's written on it as well. They tell us amazing stories about Ancient Egypt.*

Hieroglyphics

Hieroglyphics are fascinating. They look like shapes. For centuries no one knew how to read them – that information was lost. I'm sure it was very exciting when the first people learned how to read them again. But we actually don't know what they sounded like in real life! This ancient Egyptian language does not have any vowels. You can't imagine a language without vowels, so there were definitely vowel sounds, they just didn't write them.

Pottery

We find many clay pots all over sites in Egypt. They were used to hold many things and are the equivalent of our plastic nowadays. We also find many bread moulds which they used to bake bread, so it's possible they made bread in a similar way to how we make it today. There's no doubt pottery was very important to ancient Egyptians because they often had their best types of ceramic buried with them in their tombs!

AUDIO 8.3

1 The Egyptians may have used papyrus for many other things we don't know about.

2 It must have been very exciting to read hieroglyphics for the first time in centuries.

3 They can't have spoken without vowel sounds even though they only wrote the consonants.

4 They may have made bread in a similar way to how we make it today.

5 This type of pottery must have been very important to ancient Egyptians.

AUDIO 8.4

1 He must have said something.

2 They can't have gone.

3 You shouldn't have done that!

4 It may have just been me.

AUDIO 8.5

Francisco: *I'm an archaeologist. I study the Maya civilization – the people who lived in what is now southern Mexico, Guatemala and further south, in Central America. I specialize in 'remote sensing', which is about being able to find things from high up, in planes and satellites. This uses a number of devices to find ancient remains – buildings and other structures – that might be on the surface or buried under the ground.*

One new advanced technology, called LIDAR, is a measuring tool that allows you to map very accurately what is hiding below all those trees in the jungle. We use LIDAR to discover huge cities, roads, a whole landscape showing how people had once lived. Can you imagine ever doing this on foot? So LIDAR is really innovative and it has advanced the field enormously already. However, it's not very user-friendly; you need a lot of training because it's so sophisticated. Plus, it's very expensive.

There are a number of other gadgets that I use regularly in my line of work. But the one I really couldn't work without, because it's so handy, is my smartphone. I use my smartphone pretty much as a pocket-sized collection of gadgets that I had to carry separately before: G.P.S., compass, flashlight, camera and notepad.

But on the flip side, it's not waterproof, and there are a lot of places where it might get wet and damaged. The other problem is that it is always available and sometimes I forget to stop working, even to eat!

AUDIO 8.6

1 We've had them for a number of years now.

2 MyCarYourCar is revolutionizing the way we travel from town to town.

3 That way they share the cost of the petrol.

AUDIO 8.7

Host: *Today, we're talking about sharing apps. We've had them for a number of years now, and they've completely transformed the way we do business. I'm joined by Marsha Brewer, spokesperson for MyCarYourCar. Marsha, how does the app work?*

Marsha: *Well, MyCarYourCar is revolutionizing the way we travel from town to town. It's handy and user-friendly. If you're travelling, you could catch an expensive train or a slow bus. With MyCarYourCar you can get the speed of driving for less than the cost of a bus. We put drivers going on a particular journey together with passengers who want to go on the same journey. That way they share the cost of the petrol and keep each other company at the same time.*

Host: *OK, great! Let's open up the phone lines and find out what you have to say. Let's hear from Yuki.*

Yuki: *Hi. I think this sounds like a good idea, but I'd be worried about the people I travel with.*

Host: *So you've never used a carpooling service?*

Yuki: *No, but when I was younger in Japan I once hitchhiked across the country with a friend. But I wouldn't hitch on my own, and I guess carpooling is like hitching. I don't think I would feel relaxed getting into a stranger's car. And not just because I'm a woman, but also just the idea of spending hours in a car with someone you don't like.*

Marsha: *Except in the case of hitching you have no control over who your driver is, whereas with MyCarYourCar you can choose your driver. It's a common feeling you're expressing Yuki, but with MyCarYourCar you can read about and talk to the driver before you book. Most importantly, you can see what previous passengers thought about them. This ratings system makes sure the driver is trustworthy. And for women there's Women's Club - only female drivers and passengers.*

Yuki: *Well that's reassuring, definitely. But I'm still not sure if I could trust the ratings. It must be possible to get a good rating by behaving well for a few journeys, but that doesn't mean you will always be well-behaved.*

Host: *True. Thanks very much for your call, Yuki. Now let's speak to Jens.*

Jens: *Hello, I use MyCarYourCar a lot as a passenger, and I am very keen on it. For me, it's just so easy and I enjoy the interaction with my fellow passengers. And it's good for the planet, reducing the number of cars on the road. It feels good to be part of the solution, you know.*

Host: *Is that true I wonder? What about taking the train? Isn't that cleaner than travelling by road?*

Jens: *I read that if you're sharing cars, so instead of one person there are three or four people, and with cars being more efficient, more of them electric and so on, then I don't think there's much difference.*

Marsha: *That's true and, to be honest, we don't need to justify it by comparing it with trains. What about driving on your own, or flying for that matter? There's no doubt MyCarYourCar is a green choice.*

Host: *OK. And I think we'll take a break …*

VIDEO 8.2

More and more of us communicate with each other online. So here are a few tips to help you ensure that your online communication goes smoothly.

When communicating online, you can't see or hear the person you're talking to, so it's much more difficult to guess their emotions. Aysha's words 'That's great' are clear. But her emotions? She could be genuinely happy Nadia had a good time. But there are no emojis, so is Aysha feeling angry she couldn't make it to the party? Because Aysha and Nadia can't see or hear each other, the real feelings behind the words are much more difficult to guess. Think how your words might be interpreted and consider adding an emoji to the words, so it's clear what you're feeling. Note, however, that in more formal settings emoticons might not be appropriate. And if you've just a received a message like the one from Aysha, ask the person to clarify what they mean if you're unsure.

On the one hand, abbreviations allow you to communicate more quickly. But they only work if the other person is familiar with them. For example, the other person may not know what 'PM me' means. It would be clearer to say 'Send me a private message'. Think about whether the person you're speaking with will know what you mean. And if not, explain the abbreviation.

Another common netiquette rule is to be careful what you share and who with. Imagine you've just come back from a day out with a group of friends and their children. You took lots of photos and want to share some to show everyone what a nice day you had. You post some group photos of all the children playing together. However, you receive messages from some of your friends who are angry that photos of their children have been put on a public site. So before posting something, consider what you share. If in doubt, check that the other people involved are happy for something to be posted.

Finally, try to always read other people's messages with positive intentions. For example, if you are used to using formal greetings with colleagues at work, you may be shocked if a new colleague uses informal greetings and emojis in their messages.

However, rather than feeling offended and assuming that the other person is being rude or disrespectful, think about the possible positive reasons behind their message. They may be being informal to try to build a relationship with you. Equally, if someone's message is more formal than you would expect, consider that this might be their way of showing respect towards you, rather than a sign of unfriendliness.

UNIT 9

Against all odds

Chris Moon competes in the 135-mile ultra-marathon race in Death Valley National Park, US.

106

UNIT GOALS

9A Reading, speaking

- read an article and make inferences about the writer's opinions, then use critical thinking skills to practise considering the perspective of other readers of a text; share a personal success story with group members

9B Reading and grammar, pronunciation, writing and speaking

- practise talking about the future; learn when to use short and long pauses while speaking; write an email to your future self about your hopes for the future and discuss the email with a partner

9C Listening, vocabulary, pronunciation, speaking

- listen to a National Geographic explorer tell two anecdotes and recognize words and expressions that introduce contrasting ideas; learn verb-noun collocations for talking about challenges, successes and failures; practise pronouncing /ʃ/, /ʒ/,/tʃ/ and /dʒ/

9D Speaking

- learn about and practise direct and indirect communication styles and how to adapt your style; learn how to ask for clarification

9E Writing

- practise explaining your suitability for a job; learn how to write about specific examples of skills and experience; write a job application email

Photocopiable resources

Communication activities: pp. 228–229
Vocabulary activity: p. 241
Grammar activity: p. 261
Focus on … activity: p. 262
Pronunciation activity: p. 276
Mediation activity: p. 291

Workbook

Unit 9 pp. 76–83

ABOUT THE PHOTO

The photo shows Chris Moon competing in a 135-mile ultra-marathon race in Death Valley National Park, US. An 'ultra-marathon' is significantly longer than a standard 26-mile marathon and Death Valley is one of the hottest places on Earth, making running long distances there particularly challenging. For Chris Moon, the challenge was even greater because he was injured in a landmine explosion that resulted in the loss of two limbs. However, within a year of leaving hospital, Chris ran the London Marathon to raise money for charity and has continued to compete in marathons.

9
Against all odds

GOALS

- Make inferences about a writer's opinion
- Talk about future plans, goals and hopes
- Discuss challenges, successes and failures
- Understand contrasts when listening
- Adapt to direct and indirect communication styles
- Write a job application email

1 Work in pairs. Discuss the questions.

1 Look at the photo and caption. What makes the person's success special?
2 Which of these things mean success for you? Put them in order from the most to the least important.

the ability to help others   the chance to travel
dealing with difficult challenges   enormous wealth
inner peace and happiness   a lot of friends
a loving family   a rewarding career

WATCH

2 ▶ 9.1 Watch the video. Which of the things in Exercise 1 matter the most to Robbie and Paola? What else matters to them?

NATIONAL GEOGRAPHIC EXPLORERS

ROBBIE SHONE   PAOLA RODRÍGUEZ

3 Make connections. Write a one-sentence answer to the question *What does success mean for you?*

4 Share your sentence with your classmates. Whose sentences express similar ideas? Whose are similar to Robbie's or Paola's?

107

1

- Tell students to look carefully at the photo and the caption, then read the questions and phrases in the box.
- Check students' understanding of 'rewarding' (describing something that gives you a feeling of satisfaction).
- Students discuss the questions in pairs. Ask them to justify their answers.

Answers

1 He competed in a challenging race, with the additional challenge of being a double amputee.

Extra activity

Ask students to discuss the following questions about success in small groups:

- Is success sweeter when you have had to overcome difficulties to achieve it?
- What factors influence how we choose to define success? (e.g. our family background, our beliefs, etc.)
- Which factors or experiences have influenced your definition of success?

WATCH

2 ▶ 9.1

- **Optional step** Remind students that Robbie Shone was featured in Unit 7.
- Play the video so students can make notes on the things that matter to each explorer.
- Students compare answers in pairs.

Answers

Robbie – inner peace and happiness ('Success is just being happy, being content with yourself ...'); a rewarding career ('being able to do the job I love.'); a loving family and a lot of friends ('other aspects are friends and family and your partner.'); knowing 'what type of person' he is.
Paola – a loving family ('knowing that my family is fine ...'); a rewarding career ('my everyday happiness is my research work'); developing yourself in some way ('to evolve, to go further') and realizing 'that we do not need to be recognized for our success'.

3

- Tell students to use their ideas about what success means to them from Exercise 1 and any other ideas that the video gave them to decide on their definition of success.

4

- Invite students to share the sentences they wrote in Exercise 3.
- Ask other students to comment on which students' ideas are similar to each other and which students have ideas similar to Robbie's or Paola's.

ABOUT THE EXPLORERS

ROBBIE SHONE is a cave explorer and visual storyteller. Originally from the UK, he is now based in Austria. He has spent around twenty years photographing caves in some of the most remote parts of the world and his work has appeared in a wide range of international publications, including National Geographic magazine.
PAOLA RODRÍGUEZ is an associate professor and researcher at the University of Guadalajara, Mexico. She researches the ecology of tropical corals in the Central Mexican Pacific. She is working with other Mexican researchers to forecast how corals will be affected by global climate change and devise solutions for their conservation.

LESSON GOALS

- **READING** The main aim is for students to read an article and practise making inferences about the writer's opinion and then use their critical thinking skills to consider other people's perspectives on a text.
- **SPEAKING** The speaking aim is for students to form groups and each talk about a success they have achieved in their lives.

READING

ABOUT THE TEXT

The text is a collection of four short biographies of people who have overcome difficulties to achieve something significant in their chosen area: science, film, business or sport.

- **Marie Skłodowska Curie** (1867–1934) was a Polish-born physicist and chemist who developed the theory of radioactivity and practical medical applications of it. She was the first person and the only woman to win the Nobel Prize twice.
- **Bong Joon-ho** (b. 1969) is a South Korean film director, producer and screenwriter who is best-known for his 2019 Academy Award winning film *Parasite*.
- **Hamdi Ulukaya** (b. 1972) is a Kurdish billionaire and philanthropist who is based in the US. He is best-known as founder and chairman of Chobani, which is the best-selling strained yoghurt brand in the US.
- **Terezinha Guilhermina** (b. 1978) is a visually impaired Paralympic athlete from Brazil who competes in sprint events. She won two Paralympic gold medals at the London 2012 Games.

1

- Ask students to choose someone to talk about. Remind them that this does not have to be a well-known or famous person, it could be someone they know personally or someone who is not famous whose story they have heard.
- Give students one or two minutes to brainstorm the person's achievements and the difficulties they overcame.

9A Paths to success

LESSON GOALS
- Make inferences about a writer's opinion
- Consider perspectives of other readers
- Talk about a personal success

READING

1 Think of someone you know or have heard about who has succeeded despite facing challenges. What did they achieve? What problems did they have? Tell a partner.

2 Work in pairs. Read the four mini biographies on page 109 and discuss the questions.

1 Name a key skill or talent each person has.
2 Name a challenge each person has faced.
3 Whose story sounds the most inspiring? Why?

3 What do the collocations in bold mean? Use the biographies and a dictionary to help you.

1 still **faced** serious **challenges**
2 **experienced personal tragedies**
3 **refused** to **give up**
4 challenges that **stand in her way**
5 started from **modest beginnings**
6 **donates** millions **to good causes**

4 Read the biographies again. Then close your books. In pairs, summarize what you remember about each person.

5 Look at the Reading skill box. What do the extracts (1–4) suggest about the writer's opinions of the things or people in brackets?

READING SKILL
Making inferences about a writer's opinion

A writer may clearly state their opinion or leave it open to the reader to interpret. Look for how the writer supports their point of view.
- Do particular words and expressions they use suggest a particular opinion?
- What information did they include and leave out?

1 Guilhermina gets stronger by meeting challenges that stand in her way. (Terezinha Guilhermina)
The writer thinks Terezinha is a great athlete because she has the right attitude.
2 ... he pays his employees well and donates millions to good causes. (Hamdi Ulukaya)
3 However, initially, the Nobel committee did not even nominate her because she was a woman! (the people on the committee)
4 In fact, it was the first non-English-speaking film to win Best Film after almost 100 years of the Academy Awards. (the Academy)

6 Look at the Critical thinking skill box. Then discuss the questions (1–4) in pairs.

CRITICAL THINKING SKILL
Recognizing other perspectives

When we read a text, we are likely to have an immediate reaction to it. However, other readers might react differently. This can depend on where we come from, our beliefs and values, our knowledge of the world, etc. Trying to understand how others might react to a text can help you see the information in a new light and question your initial reaction.

1 What might other businesspeople think about Hamdi's modest start in life or his generosity?
They might admire him because he did it all himself without family help.
2 What might Polish people think of Maria and her achievements? Would this be any different from someone who is not Polish?
3 What might other visually-impaired people think of Terezinha's achievements?
4 What might those who booed *Okja* at the Cannes Film Festival think of that reaction now that Joon-ho has won an Oscar?

SPEAKING

7 Choose one success in your life, big or small. You can choose from the ideas below or use your own idea. Answer the questions (1–3) to organize your ideas. Then share your story in groups.

winning a prize   passing a very difficult exam
getting a job you really wanted

1 Why was the achievement important?
2 Did you face any difficulties? How did you overcome these?
3 How did you feel after achieving your goal?

EXPLORE MORE!
Search online for the people mentioned in the article. What's the most interesting thing you learned about them?

108

- Ask students to use their notes or ideas to tell their partner about their chosen person.
- **Optional step** Encourage students to ask their partner follow-up questions to find out more information about the person he/she talked about.

Extra activity

Write on the board or dictate the following quotes about success:

- 'Success is stumbling from failure to failure with no loss of enthusiasm.' – Winston Churchill (Former British Prime Minister)
- 'Fall seven times and stand up eight' – Japanese proverb
- 'I never dreamed about success, I worked for it.' – Estée Lauder (American businesswoman who founded the Estée Lauder cosmetics company)
- 'Success is liking yourself, liking what you do, and liking how you do it.' – Maya Angelou (American poet, writer and civil rights activist)

Ask students to read the quotes and decide which one they most agree with or which one is closest to their own opinion. They can then share their choices and the reasons for them in pairs or small groups.

There are many paths that lead to success, but for some their roads are longer than others. Here are four inspiring stories of people who've managed to succeed despite difficulties.

Maria Skłodowska Curie, SCIENTIST

Maria Salomea Skłodowska was born in 1867 in Warsaw, Poland which, at that time, was part of the Russian empire. People were not allowed to study in Polish, and women could not enrol in universities at all. This meant Skłodowska had to study at the Flying University, a secret organization. Despite these difficulties, and having almost no money, she later continued her education in Paris, France.

In 1903 she was awarded the Nobel Prize in Physics. However, initially, the Nobel committee did not even nominate her because she was a woman! Even after winning her second Nobel Prize, she still faced serious challenges and experienced personal tragedies, such as the death of her husband, Pierre, in 1906. Best known by her French name, Marie Curie, she is now one of the most famous and inspiring figures in scientific history.

Bong Joon-ho, FILMMAKER

Bong Joon-ho made history as the first South Korean director to win an Oscar for his film *Parasite*. In fact, it was the first non-English-speaking film to win Best Film after almost one hundred years of the Academy Awards. Even though he seemed calm on the outside when receiving the award, he's actually suffered from anxiety all his life. 'I have severe anxiety … to the point where it would be impossible for me to have a social life. But thanks to filmmaking, I've been able to survive', he told *Vanity Fair*.

He's also struggled as a director. His first film, *Barking Dogs Never Bite*, didn't make much money and his film *Okja* was booed at the Cannes Film Festival! Still, he refused to give up.

Terezinha Guilhermina, ATHLETE

Terezinha Guilhermina, a Brazilian athlete, won gold in the 100m and 200m at the 2012 Paralympic Games in London. She was born with an eye disorder that causes visual impairment, so athletes in her category run with a guide to help them.

Aged 22, Guilhermina realized she wanted to be an athlete but, in order to compete, proper running shoes were necessary – a luxury that she couldn't afford. It was only when her sister gave her a pair that she could join the running club. Guilhermina gets stronger by meeting challenges that stand in her way. 'People that don't have anything can make it,' she says. 'I have never accepted how little I had.'

Hamdi Ulukaya, BUSINESSMAN

Ulukaya's company, Chobani, makes the best-selling Greek-style yoghurt in the US, but he started from modest beginnings. His family were sheep farmers in Turkey. He moved to the US in 1994, where he learned English and, after a number of jobs, eventually started manufacturing yoghurt.

The first two years he made very little money and he says that these were the most challenging years of his life. He has since transformed the business into an international empire. Famous for his generosity, he pays his employees well and donates millions to good causes. In 2016, he shared the ownership of the company with his staff to say thank you. 'There are a lot of important things in business, but people come first.'

109

VOCABULARY NOTES

path /pɑːθ/ = a series of things you have to do or experience in order to achieve something

empire /ˈempaɪə/ = a group of states that are ruled over by another state

initially /ɪˈnɪʃəli/ = happening first; at the start

figure /ˈfɪgə/ = a person who is well-known or important in some way

boo /buː/ = to shout the word 'boo' to indicate that you dislike or are dissatisfied with a performance

visual impairment /ˈvɪʒuəl ɪmˈpeəmənt/ = a decrease in the ability to see, to the extent that it causes difficulties in operating in daily life

2

- Put students into pairs. Direct students to the questions. Point out that in question 1, students are looking for the general area in which each person has achieved things.
- Ask them to focus on getting a good general understanding of each person's key skill or achievement and their difficulties while they are reading.
- Students can work together to make notes and answer questions 1 and 2, then think individually about their answer to question 3, coming up with reasons to justify their answer.
- Students then compare and discuss their answers for question 3.

Answers

1 Skłodowska Curie – scientific invention; Bong – directing films; Guilhermina – running; Ulukaya – entrepreneurship

2 Skłodowska Curie – sexism / language barriers; Bong – anxiety / financial issues; Guilhermina – visual impairment / little money; Ulukaya – little money

3

- Ask students to read the list of collocations and identify any they know the meaning of.
- Ask students to scan the text to locate the collocations that they do not know the meaning of. Tell students that the collocations appear in the same order in the text as they do on the list. Encourage students to try to deduce each collocation's meaning from the context in which it is used.
- Students can use a dictionary to help them identify the meaning of unfamiliar collocations if they are not able to deduce them from the context.
- Students compare their answers in pairs and then check answers as a class. Invite different students to say their definitions in class.

Answers

1 lived through difficulties; 2 lived through terrible events such as deaths of loved ones; 3 stop doing something; 4 stop someone from progressing; 5 grow up in a family without much money; 6 give money to charities and people who need it

Extra activity

Ask students to think about the people who inspire them or their definition of an inspirational person. They could discuss these ideas in pairs. Tell students to use at least three of the collocations from Exercise 3 to write sentences explaining their ideas. They could do this individually or in pairs if their ideas are similar.

4

- Students read the biographies again. Tell them to notice the most important points about each of the people so they can include these in their summaries.
- **Optional step** Ask students to try to include the collocations from Exercise 3 in their summaries.
- In pairs, students work together to summarize each of the biographies.

5

- Ask students to read the Reading skill box and check their understanding of 'inference' (a conclusion that someone draws based on the evidence available to them). Elicit or explain that when you make an inference about a writer's opinion, you use the evidence of what they have written to draw a conclusion about it.
- Go through the first extract in class. Ask students to identify the key phrases which show the writer's opinion (e.g. 'gets stronger' and 'meeting challenges'). Elicit what each of the phrases tell you about the writer's opinion of Terezinha (e.g. 'gets stronger' = she is a strong or great athlete, 'meeting challenges' = she has a good attitude / she can rise to challenges).
- Students collaborate with a partner to identify the writer's opinions.
- Check answers as a class.

Sample answers

1 The writer thinks Terezinha is a great athlete because she has the right attitude.
2 The writer sees Hamdi as very generous and someone who cares about other people.
3 The writer is suggesting that the people on the Nobel committee at that time were prejudiced against women.
4 The writer thinks it's strange and perhaps inappropriate that it took the Academy almost 100 years to choose a non-English-speaking film as Best Film.

6

- Direct students to the Critical thinking skill box. Check students' understanding of 'other perspectives' (what other people think or feel about something).
- In pairs, students read the questions and the example answer and brainstorm how each group of people might feel about each person's achievements.
- Students come up with a sentence to summarize their answer to each question.

Sample answers

1 They might admire him because he did it all himself without family help; similar businessmen might be inspired by him. Employers might be interested in whether paying his staff so well has made him more successful or less so. They may not like the idea that his actions suggest employees should expect more.
2 It's likely that Polish people might feel prouder of Maria than non-Poles; they might have a stronger positive and more emotional reaction to her achievements.
3 Some are likely to be inspired by her, or proud but there may be others who don't like feeling inadequate because they haven't had the same level of success as she has.
4 Perhaps they now feel bad they booed the film and didn't appreciate it.

Extra activity

Ask students to individually decide which of the four people from the text they personally find the most inspiring and why. Also ask students to consider what effect their personal perspective and experiences have had on their choice, for example whether they think their choice was influenced by the part of the world they come from, their personal or professional interests or their gender. Put students into pairs or small groups to share their choice and the factors that they believe had an influence on this choice.

SPEAKING

7

- Ask students to choose a success that they have had in their lives. Remind them that this can be a smaller-scale success, such as the examples in the box or passing their driving test, for example. The type of achievement itself is not important but rather what they can say about it.
- Students make notes on their answers to the questions.
- **Optional step** Remind students to try to use vocabulary that they have learned in this lesson, especially the collocations from Exercise 3.
- Ask students to prepare to share their success story.
- Put students into groups of four or five. Students take turns to share their story with the rest of the group.
- **Optional step** If possible and if students feel comfortable doing so, they could show the rest of their group photos to illustrate their success story while they are talking. For example, a photo of them after they had just passed their driving test or a photo of them with their first car.

EXPLORE MORE!

When they are searching for information online, tell students to select reliable sources, for example the person's personal website or information provided by well-known educational publications or institutions, such as Britannica.com.
Students can also do a search for videos with 'Bong Joon-ho', 'Terezinha Guilhermina' and 'Hamdi Ulukaya' and will find interviews with all three of them in which they talk about their work and their beliefs or opinions. While they are doing their research, ask them to make notes on new things they learn about each person. They could then select the most interesting thing about each person and share it with a partner or in a group in class.

See **Workbook** pages 76–77 for extra practice.

LESSON GOALS

- **GRAMMAR** The main aim is for students to learn and practise using structures for talking about future plans, goals and hopes.
- **PRONUNCIATION** A sub-aim is for students to learn when to use short and long pauses.
- **SPEAKING** The speaking aim is to discuss emails students have written to their future self.

READING AND GRAMMAR

1

- Give students a few minutes to think about what they would like to achieve personally and professionally in each time period.
- Students discuss what they would like to achieve and why.

2

- **Optional step** Explain that emails to your future self are emails that you schedule to be sent to your email address at a time in the future. The usual reason is to share information about the present that you want to remember or to remind yourself of a goal you had intended to achieve by a specific time.
- Ask students to read the emails and get a general feel for the characteristics of each writer.
- Tell students to read all three emails again to identify the purpose that all the writers have in common.

Sample answers

1 A student – probably late teens or early twenties, ambitious, optimistic and excited about life; B older person, hard on themselves, someone who has big regrets; C any age, unhappy with their fitness levels, possibly suffering from low self-esteem

VOCABULARY NOTES

put your mind to something /pʊt jɔː maɪnd tuː ˈsʌmθɪŋ/ = to decide to do something and be determined to achieve it

3

- Ask students to read the emails again and underline the expressions in each of them.
- Ask students to compare their answers in pairs and then check answers as a class.

Answers

1 A graduated: 'you will have just graduated I'; B apologized to his family: 'you'll have apologized to the family'; C joined the gym: 'you should have joined the gym'
2 A 'you should be making some money'; B 'there's a photo … you might be needing to see'; C 'you won't still be sitting on that sofa'

4

- Ask students to read the list of functions and check their understanding of the term 'in progress' (describing something that has started but hasn't yet finished).
- Tell students to look at the sentences they underlined in Exercise 3 again and discuss which function each one has.
- Students read the Grammar box to check their answers.

Answers

a 'You won't still be sitting on that sofa.'; b 'you will have just graduated'; c 'you should have joined the gym'; 'you should be making some money'; 'there's a photo … you might be needing to see'

GRAMMAR NOTES

Talking about the future

The future continuous

The most important point that students need to remember is the idea of two events happening at the same time in the future: one of which is 'in progress' (i.e. it has already started to happen) when the other one occurs. The future continuous tense is used for the event that the speaker wants to focus on rather than the 'in progress', or 'background event'. Sometimes, one of the events is already known and then it is usually not mentioned, for example you can use the future continuous to say: *Will you be bringing a guest?* when the 'in progress' event is a known event, such as a wedding.

The future perfect

It is important that students understand that this tense is only used to say what you expect to happen in the future. The tense is usually used with either: *by/before* + future time point with the future perfect to show the time before which the action will be completed, or *in* + time period (e.g. five years) to show the time period over which the action will be completed. Students need to ensure that they use the past participle rather than the past simple form of the verb, and these two verb forms will be different with irregular verbs.

For further information and practice, see **Grammar reference Unit 9B** on page 150 of the Student's Book.

5

- Go through the first item with students. Elicit that the structure *should have* + past participle is needed at the start of the sentence. Then elicit the complete sentence.
- Students form sentences for the remaining items. Ask them to use the information in the Grammar box to check their sentences.
- Students check answers in pairs.

Answers
1 I should have finished university in two years.
2 I might be living in another country next year.
3 My best friend will have started her online business by the end of this year.
4 I will be travelling around Asia next summer.

Extra activity

Ask students to change the words in the future perfect sentences from Exercise 5 so that they are true for them. Go through sentence 1 (*I should have finished university in two years*) with the class as an example to help them do this.

6

- Direct students to Paola's email. Check their understanding of *cliché* (a phrase, opinion or scenario that is used too much and is not original).
- Ask students to read the email and identify Paola's hopes and plans. They can then read the email again to identify which hopes and plans she sounds the most confident about.
- Ask students to discuss their ideas in pairs and then invite different students to share their answers with the class.

Answers
Paola is the most confident she will have done well at work. Her plans are to go to Europe for her 41st birthday. She is quite confident that she will go to London, Madrid and Paris. She plans to NOT take a selfie at the Eiffel Tower (but she thinks she might anyway).

7

- Ask students to read Paola's email again and underline the phrases that refer to the future. Remind students that these might not necessarily contain *will*.
- Students decide which expressions describe plans and which describe predictions. Encourage them to use the context in which they are used in the email to help them.
- Tell students to look at the Useful language box to check their answers. Elicit or explain that 'I'm bound to' is used to say that something will definitely happen in the future.

Answers
plans: 'I'm determined to'; predictions: 'I have no doubt', 'It's likely that', 'there's a fifty-fifty chance that', 'you are bound to'

9B Emails to my future self

LESSON GOALS
- Talk about future plans, goals and hopes
- Write about your hopes for the future
- Practise pausing when reading out loud

READING AND GRAMMAR

1 **Work in pairs. Tell your partner what you would like to achieve personally and professionally …**
1 this year.
2 in a few years' time.
3 by 2050.

2 **Read three emails written by people to their future self (A–C). Discuss the questions.**
1 What do you imagine the writers are like? (age, personality)
2 Which of these reasons for writing do all the emails have in common?
a to check they are happy
b to express hope for the future
c to give their future self some inspiration

3 **Read the emails again and answer the questions. Underline the expressions in each email that helped you answer them.**
1 What one big change does each writer expect to have happened?
2 What does each writer expect they'll be doing in the future?

4 **Match the sentences you found in Exercise 3 with the functions (a–c). Then read the Grammar box to check.**
a an action that will be in progress at a particular time in the future
b an action that will be complete before a particular time in the future
c an action the writer is less certain will happen

GRAMMAR Talking about the future

Use the **future continuous** to predict things in progress at a particular time in the future.
*You **won't** still **be sitting** on that sofa.*

Use the **future perfect** to refer to actions that will be complete before a particular time in the future.
*When you read this, you **will have just graduated**.*

Use ***should*** and ***might*** instead of ***will*** to show you are less certain that something will happen.
*You **should be making** some money.*
*There's a photo you **might be needing** to see.*

Go to page 150 for the Grammar reference.

A

Dear Future Me,

If I know you – and I think I do ;) – when you read this you will have just graduated. Yay! And you should be making some money! But I'm determined to make things perfect, so if I haven't already … go and find Karsten and ask him out!

Old Me
Sent to nine months in the future

B

Dear Kris,

Confused? It's likely you've forgotten you sent this email to yourself, so if you've still got that copy of *War and Peace* on the bookshelf, go take a look – there's a photo in it you might be needing to see about now. Anyway, sincerely hoping that by now you'll have done what I can't right now and apologized to the family for what you did. If not, I'll be disappointed. Take care,

Kris
Sent to five years in the future

C

Hey FutureMe,

If I've stuck to my plan, you won't still be sitting on that sofa and you should have joined the gym! If you haven't, this is the reminder that you need! A voice from the past. Now is the time to get moving.

Remember that you can do anything you put your mind to. I just thought that you needed to hear that today.

Love,

Me
Sent to one year in the future

5 **Use the words to form sentences.**
1 I / should / finish / university / in two years.
2 I / might / live / another country / next year.
3 My best friend / will / start / her online business / by the end of this year.
4 I / will / travel / around Asia / next summer.

110

For additional practice, refer to the **Grammar activity** on page 261 and the **Communication activity** on page 228 of the Teacher's Book.

PRONUNCIATION

8 9.1

- Students look at the Clear voice box.
- Play the audio so students can notice the difference between short and long pauses in speech.
- Suggest that students read Paola's email from Exercise 6 out loud to help them decide where the pauses would be.

PRONUNCIATION NOTES

Pausing

The best way for students to raise their awareness of how to divide their speech into chunks (i.e. a subject, verbs, object, adverbial or prepositional phrase or a clause) is to practise listening to speakers who are able to do this effectively and notice how they do it. TED Talks and news programmes can be useful for this purpose.

NATIONAL GEOGRAPHIC EXPLORER

6 Read Paola Rodríguez's email to her future self. What hopes and plans does she mention? Which does she sound the most confident about?

> Dear Future Pao,||
>
> You are a really determined person,||so I have no doubt|that you will have done very well at work,|so|let's not talk about that.||What I really want to know is,||how was your trip to Europe|for your 41st birthday?||It's likely|that your first stop was London|and specifically the London Eye.||Is the view as amazing as I picture it?||And please|tell me that you visited that café in Madrid –|I'm determined to have that amazing cup of coffee.||Also,|there's a fifty-fifty chance that you took a selfie at the Eiffel Tower –||yes,|the one you swore you weren't going to take|because it's such a cliché,|but you are bound to get really amazed and take it anyway.||
>
> So||… what's next?|Please tell me that it's a trip to Australia.||
>
> As always|keep going!||Hugs,|
>
> Present Pao
> Sent to three years in the future

7 Underline the phrases in Paola's email that talk about her future. Which ones describe plans? Which describe predictions? Look at the Useful language box to check your answers.

Useful language Talking about the future

Plans
I'm about to … ; I'm determined to …
I'm thinking of/considering *+-ing* …

Predictions
I'm bound to …
It's likely/unlikely that …
There's a good/fifty-fifty/slight chance …
I doubt that …

PRONUNCIATION

8 9.1 Look at the Clear voice box and listen to the example. Then divide Paola's text from Exercise 6 into short pauses (|) and long pauses (||).

CLEAR VOICE
Pausing

Pauses make what you are saying easier to understand. Short pauses (|) divide sentences into shorter sections, which are usually grammatical chunks. Typically, one word in each section will be stressed. Long pauses (||) divide longer clauses or whole sentences from each other.

It's important | to set goals | for ourselves, || but we are likely | to forget things sometimes. || It's useful | to remind ourselves | of these goals, || and writing future self emails | could be a good way | to do this.

9 9.2 Listen to Paola read her email to check your answers to Exercise 8.

WRITING AND SPEAKING

10 Write an email to your future self. Choose a reason for writing from Exercise 2. Use the Useful language box to help you express your plans and predictions.

11 Work in pairs. Read out your emails to each other. Think about where to pause. Ask your partner follow-up questions.

111

9 9.2

- Play the audio. Tell students to focus on where the short and long pauses are so they can check their answers to Exercise 8. It's worth noting that the length of pauses can be quite subjective and listeners may hear and process them differently.

Extra activity

Ask students to choose an audio script of a monologue from an explorer that was used in a previous unit. Tell students to read what the explorer said and use what they have learned about pauses to mark the long and short pauses. Students then listen to the audio recording and notice where the long and short pauses actually are so they can check their predictions.

For additional practice, refer to the **Pronunciation activity** on page 276 of the Teacher's Book.

WRITING AND SPEAKING

10

- Ask students to choose a reason for writing from Exercise 2 and plan what they would like to tell their future self.
- Students decide which expressions from the Useful language box to use in their email. Encourage them to use at least three of the expressions.
- Students write their email to their future self. Remind students to only include information that they feel comfortable sharing with other students.

11

- **Optional step** Ask students to think about where they should pause when they are reading their emails out loud and then practise reading their email out loud on their own.
- Put students into pairs and ask them to take turns to read their emails out loud.
- **Optional step** Encourage students to ask their partner follow-up questions to find out more about the things they wrote about in their email, for example: how they plan to achieve something they wrote about in their email or how long they think this will take.

For additional practice, refer to the **Communication activity** on page 229 of the Teacher's Book.

Extra activity

Write the following on the board:
Find someone who …

1 may have got their first job, or a new one, in the next two years.
2 hopes to be living in another country in five years' time.
3 should have retired by 2040.
4 might be doing more exercise soon.

Tell students that they are going to talk to people in the class to find someone who fits each description (1–4). Ask students to write one extra idea of their own related to future plans and goals that they can ask classmates about. Encourage students to ask follow-up questions and note down anything interesting that they learn about their classmates. At the end of the task, ask some of the students to share what they found out.

See **Workbook** pages 78–79 for extra practice.

LESSON GOALS

- **LISTENING** A main aim is for students to listen to anecdotes about incidents in someone's life and understand expressions for showing contrast.
- **VOCABULARY** A further main aim is for students to learn and practise using verb-noun collocations for talking about challenges, successes and failures.
- **PRONUNCIATION** A sub-aim is for students to practise pronouncing words with /ʃ/, /ʒ/,/tʃ/ and /dʒ/.
- **SPEAKING** The speaking aim is to play a storytelling game in groups.

SPEAKING

1

- Direct students to the quiz. Check their understanding of the idiomatic expression 'to kick yourself' (to feel frustrated with yourself because you have made a mistake or failed at something).
- Students read the scenarios and choose their answers. Check that students are aware that there are no 'right' or 'wrong' answers.
- Ask students to look at the analysis for their answers on page 156 (page 205 of the Teacher's Book).
- Put students into pairs to discuss how easy they find it to turn negative experiences into positive ones, bringing in examples of events from their own lives, where appropriate.

Extra activity

Ask students to write their own quiz question to find out how someone deals with negative experiences. Tell them to think of a situation where you can fail at something, face a challenge or experience something difficult. They then think of three options for how people could react in the situation, following the format of the quiz in Exercise 1: A) should be something unhelpful like worrying or feeling bad; B) should involve giving up; C) should be about asking for feedback or analyzing what went wrong. Once students have written their quiz questions, tell them to ask and answer them in pairs.

9C Learning from mistakes

LESSON GOALS
- Understand contrasts when listening
- Discuss challenges, successes and failures
- Learn verb-noun collocations
- Practise pronunciation of /ʃ/, /ʒ/, /tʃ/ and /dʒ/

SPEAKING

1 Do the quiz. Then look at the answers on page 156. How easy do you find turning negative experiences into positive ones?

NEGATIVE TO POSITIVE

How do you deal with negative experiences? We all have good and bad days, but do we all use the bad days to our advantage?

1 You've failed your driving test. Do you …
 A kick yourself and book more lessons?
 B quit now and accept that driving is just too hard?
 C learn how to cycle instead?

2 You lose a lot of money and time when your small business fails. Do you …
 A decide being a business owner is not for you, and get a job in a big company instead?
 B promise yourself that you'll never try anything difficult that you could fail at ever again?
 C analyse why it didn't succeed and build a better new business?

3 You're shy and public speaking makes you uncomfortable, but you have to give a presentation. Do you …
 A spend days worrying and losing sleep over it but do it anyway?
 B find a colleague who will do the presentation for you?
 C ask your friends to help you fight the fear?

LISTENING

NATIONAL GEOGRAPHIC EXPLORER

2 9.3 Listen to Robbie Shone telling two anecdotes about incidents in his life. Which anecdote, 1 or 2 …
 a resulted in Robbie learning something valuable about himself? 2
 b involved Robbie getting help from friends? 1
 c was the most difficult for Robbie? 2
 d ended with Robbie learning a practical lesson? 1

3 9.4 Look at the Listening skill box. Then listen and complete the extracts from the anecdotes.

LISTENING SKILL
Understanding contrasts

Certain words and expressions introduce contrasts. When you listen, try to be aware of these, so you know that you are about to hear a contrasting idea. Here are some common examples:
actually … ; or at least … ; but then again … ; despite the fact that … ; Even though … ; On the other hand, … ; Really, though, … ; That being said, …

1 To get out of the cave we all just simply jumped in the river. Despite the fact that it was quite safe, we still all needed buoyancy aids to help us float.
2 And what you thought was a failure at first, can actually make you better at what you do.

4 9.3 Listen to the interview again. Are the sentences true (T) or false (F)?
1 It wasn't easy getting out of the Clearwater cave. F
2 Robbie realized what the problem was before he opened the container. T
3 Robbie had to return to the UK because his expedition had ended. F
4 In the interview, the editor didn't like any of the photos Robbie showed her. F
5 After the interview, Robbie got a job painting bridges. F
6 Robbie is now glad that he had such a disappointing interview in Washington. T

112

LISTENING

2 9.3

- Remind students that they have previously watched National Geographic explorer Robbie Shone in the video at the start of this unit and in Unit 7.
- Ask students to read the instructions and the options. Check students' understanding of 'anecdote' (a short story about something that really happened) and 'incident' (an event / something that happened).
- **Optional step** In pairs, ask students to use what they already know about Robbie's job (he is a cave photographer) and how he lives his life (he spends a lot of time outdoors and travelling) to speculate about the lessons he might have learned, when he might have needed help and something he might have found difficult.
- Play the audio and ask students to listen and get a general idea of each anecdote so they can match a–d with the correct anecdote.
- Ask students to compare their notes in pairs.

5 Work in pairs. Answer the questions.

1 Which of the experiences Robbie talks about had the biggest effect on him?
2 Do you agree with Robbie that failing at something is a good way to learn? Why?
3 Have you ever experienced a similar setback or problem to Robbie? What happened?

VOCABULARY

6 Complete the sentences with these pairs of words. Which sentences describe successes? sentences 3, 5 and 6

achieved + objectives made + mess made + through overcame + issues struggling + understand tackle + problem

1 We need to tackle the main problem before it gets worse.
2 I'm struggling to understand this website. It shouldn't be this tricky to shop online!
3 It was a tough time , but we made it through.
4 Oh! I'm not getting anywhere with this tax form and I've made such a mess of it.
5 She eventually overcame her self-confidence issues and opened her first shop.
6 The project wasn't perfect, but it has achieved its main objectives.

Go to page 139 for the Vocabulary reference.

7 Read the Focus on box. Then find verbs in Exercise 6 that collocate with the expressions (1–5).

FOCUS ON Verb-noun collocations

It's useful to notice common combinations of words, or collocations. Different types of word collocate, e.g. *a tough time* and *tough competition* are **adjective-noun collocations**.
Another group to learn are **verb-noun collocations**. Recording words in the collocations you find them in can help you remember them.

Go to page 150 for the Focus on reference.

1 achieve your aims / your objectives / very little
2 make a mess / it through / a decision
3 overcome/tackle obstacles / difficulties / problems
4 struggle to understand / with the problem
5 tackle/overcome the crisis / issue / problem

PRONUNCIATION

8 Look at the Clear voice box. Then complete the table with the words (1-10), according to the consonant sounds they have in common. Underline the letters that produce the sound.

CLEAR VOICE
Saying /ʃ/, /ʒ/, /tʃ/ and /dʒ/

For clear pronunciation, it's important that you can say /ʃ/, /ʒ/, /tʃ/ and /dʒ/. Spelling patterns can help you know which sound to say.
/ʃ/ **ss** e.g. *mission*; **ti** e.g. *combination*; **ch** e.g. *machine*
/ʒ/ **si** e.g. *conclusion*; **ge** e.g. *beige*; **su** e.g. *measure*
/tʃ/ **tu** e.g. *future*; **ch** e.g. *challenge*
/dʒ/ **ge** e.g. *page*; **dge** e.g. *bridge*; **j** e.g. *object*

1 ambition
2 professional
3 achieve
4 issue
5 knowledge
6 manage
7 decision
8 objectives
9 project
10 vision

/ʃ/	/ʒ/	/tʃ/	/dʒ/
ambition, professional, issue	decision, vision	achieve	knowledge, manage, objectives, project

9 9.5 Listen to check your answers to Exercise 8. Then practise saying the words.

SPEAKING

10 Play 'Fortunately, … Unfortunately, …' in groups.

1 Take turns to tell a story, each person saying one sentence at a time.
2 Use one of these sentences to begin or your own idea.
I lost my mobile phone the other day. Fortunately, …
Some new neighbours moved in next door …
My football team won the match yesterday …
3 Sentences must alternate good and bad news.
I got a new job. → Unfortunately the pay wasn't very good. → Fortunately, they gave me a company car. → That being said, it was only a toy car. → However, my colleagues were really nice.
4 Decide together whether each sentence continues the story successfully. Players score a point for each successful new sentence.
5 Players can score an extra point if they successfully include words from today's lesson!

113

VOCABULARY NOTES

gush out /gʌʃ aʊt/ = to flow out of something very quickly

buoyancy aid /'bɔɪənsi eɪd/ = a type of life jacket that is commonly worn by people who do water sports

lump /lʌmp/ = a solid piece of something that often has a rounded shape

kick-start /kɪk-stɑːt/ = to make something start to happen or develop more quickly

abseiler /æb'seɪlə(r)/ = someone who goes down a rock face or other near-vertical surface with a double rope wrapped around their body and secured at the top of the rock face or other surface

3 9.4

- Ask students to look at the Listening skill box. Elicit which expressions for showing contrast they have heard before and which ones they have used.
- **Optional step** Elicit another expression for showing contrast which students learned in Lesson 8E with the word 'flip' in it (on the flip side).
- Ask students to read the sentences and then play the audio so they can listen for the expressions for contrast that Robbie uses.
- Check answers as a class by inviting two students to read the completed sentences out loud.

Extra activity

In pairs, tell students to brainstorm possible benefits of doing dangerous sports, like caving (e.g. it gets the adrenaline pumping, which makes you feel alive) and problems that it can cause (e.g. you could seriously injure, or even kill yourself). Then ask them to use their ideas to write two or three sentences contrasting a benefit with a problem, each of which uses a different expression from the Listening skill box.

4 9.3

- Ask students to the read the sentences before they listen.
- Play the audio again so students can decide if the sentences are true or false.
- Ask students to compare their answers in pairs and then check answers as a class.

5

- Give students about two minutes to read the questions and think about their answers. They could write down their ideas as preparation for discussing the questions.
- Students discuss the questions in pairs. Encourage them to justify their answers or opinions when answering questions 1 and 2 and tell a short anecdote, similar to the ones they heard Robbie tell, when answering question 3.
- **Optional step** Refer students to the audioscript for track 9.3 on page 169 to find the evidence that the second incident had the biggest effect on Robbie.

Answers

1 The second had the biggest effect ('… you're so much stronger because you're driven, it's the fire inside, it's huge. I certainly benefited so much …')

VOCABULARY

6

- Direct students to the instruction and pairs of words in the box. Elicit the meanings or ask students to look up any words they do not know.
- Ask students to use the context of the sentence(s) to deduce the collocation needed to complete them and then decide which sentences describe success.
- Students compare answers in pairs and then check answers as a class.

For further information and practice, see **Vocabulary reference Unit 9** on page 139 of the Student's Book.

7

- Ask students to read the information about verb-noun collocations in the Focus on box.
- Ask students to identify the verbs in the collocations in Exercise 6 and then decide which verb collocates with each set of expressions (1–5). Tell students that there may be more than one verb that could collocate with a set of nouns.
- Ask students to compare answers in pairs and then check answers as a class. Point out that either 'overcome' or 'tackle' could be used with Set 3, but 'overcome' would be used more frequently and that 'overcome' or 'tackle' could also both be used with Set 5, but 'tackle' would be used more frequently.

FOCUS ON NOTES

Verb-noun collocations

Students need to be aware that only certain adjectives or verbs can collocate with a given noun. Raise awareness of the fact that a certain collocation may be possible in students' first language but not possible in English.

Encouraging students to record collocations and their meaning, rather than just individual words and then trying to use these regularly in their writing or speaking is the best way to help students learn collocations.

For further information and practice, see **Focus on reference Unit 9C** on page 150 of the Student's Book.

Extra activity

Tell students that they are going to practise using the collocations in Exercises 6 and 7 by writing sentences about their own successes, failures and challenges. If students do not feel comfortable sharing personal experiences, they can write about someone else's experiences or make something up. Ask students to write sentences about the following:

- an objective they have achieved or would like to achieve in the future
- an issue they have overcome or are currently overcoming
- a problem in their lives that they have tackled or think they might need to tackle in the future
- something they have struggled or are currently struggling to understand (e.g. how to use a piece of technology)

For additional practice, refer to the **Vocabulary activity** on page 241 and the **Focus on activity** on page 262 of the Teacher's Book.

PRONUNCIATION

8

- Ask students to look at the Clear voice box and the list of words (1–10).
- Students put the words into the correct category according to the consonant sounds they contain and underline the letters in each word that produce the sound. Students could say the words out loud to help them identify the sound in each one.

9 9.5

- Play the audio so students can listen and check their answers to Exercise 8.
- Ask students to practise saying the words, focussing on pronouncing the consonant sounds clearly and accurately.

PRONUNCIATION NOTES

Saying /ʃ/, /ʒ/, /tʃ/ and /dʒ/

When students are listening to and practising saying these sounds, tell them that they could learn and practise using phonemic symbols while they are learning, but this is not essential. Encourage them to find a way to remember the sounds, such as connecting them with a letter combination and a word they are used in. For example: /ʃ/ = 'sh' → *issue*, /ʒ/ = 'zh' → *conclusion*, /tʃ/ = 'ch' → *challenge* and /dʒ/ = '-dge' → *page*. However, it is important to remember that the words in which these sounds are used usually do not contain the letter combination they have associated the sound with, for example 'issue' has a /ʃ/ or 'sh' sound but does not contain the letters 'sh'.

SPEAKING

10

- Explain that 'Fortunately, ... Unfortunately, ...' is a game that switches between good and bad news in a story, usually for comic effect.
- Go through the instructions. Check students understand that each player says one sentence of the story at a time and, after saying the first sentence to establish the context of the story, the subsequent sentence alternately starts with 'fortunately' or 'unfortunately'. Draw students' attention to point 5 in the instructions and ask them to think about how they can include the collocations from Exercise 7 or any other language from this lesson in their sentences.
- Put students into groups of four or five.
- Students take turns to say their sentences. While they are not speaking, they listen to the speaker and decide whether or not their sentence successfully continues the story.
- **Optional step** If students are not sure what kind of story to tell, suggest they use the topic of successes, failures, difficulties and overcoming difficulties. Encourage students to make their stories funny or entertaining if possible.

For addtional practice, refer to the **Mediation activity** on page 291 of the Teacher's Book.

See **Workbook** pages 80–81 for extra practice.

LESSON GOALS

- **SPEAKING** The main aim of this lesson is to introduce students to the concept of direct and indirect communication styles. Students learn how to adapt to styles that are more direct or indirect than their own preferred styles by using strategies such as asking for clarification.

SPEAKING

1

- Put students into pairs. Ask them to read the questions and look at the cartoon carefully.
- **Optional step** Direct students to the cartoon and ask two confident students to each read one of the captions in the speech bubbles. Saying them out loud should make the characteristics of the two communication styles clearer.
- Students discuss the questions, providing reasons or examples to support their answers.
- Check answers as a class to ensure students have correctly understood the difference between the direct and the indirect style. Check that they are aware that one style is not better than the other and issues can arise with both of them.

Answers

1 In the first, the language is unnecessarily polite and indirect. In that situation, a more efficient way of communicating is needed. The teacher is clearly busy and about to begin a class, so it would be quicker to ask 'Could I talk to you about my essay later, please?'. In the second, the teacher needs to respect the student's feelings and prepare him for the negative feedback with more indirect language.

2 b

Extra activity

Put students into pairs and ask them to brainstorm situations when it is acceptable, appropriate or necessary to use direct or indirect language, giving reasons for their choices. Encourage students to think not only about the person or people they're talking to, but also about the setting (for example, colleagues in a work meeting, someone you haven't met before, a group of friends, etc.). Make it clear that there are no right or wrong answers. Put two pairs together to present and compare their ideas, saying whether or not they agree with each other and why.

MY VOICE

COMMUNICATION SKILL NOTES

Adapting to direct and indirect communication styles

As cultural and social factors tend to have a significant impact on people's level of directness, students are likely to encounter a range of different styles when they communicate. Students need to keep in mind that there is a spectrum of directness from very direct to very indirect, with many variations in between. Some people may also be direct in some situations (e.g. with their family), but indirect in others (e.g. while talking to a customer at work).

In addition, students need to be aware that even if language is considered to have a neutral or inoffensive level of directness in their first language, the same approach might be perceived as too direct and even rude in English. First language users of English might have this perception, as well as some people who use English as a second or other language. The phrases in the Useful language box can help students explain their communication style to these people and avoid or limit these kinds of misunderstandings.

A lack of awareness of other people's communication style can cause tensions or misunderstandings between the people involved. By gaining an understanding of their own communication style and making an effort to identify other people's styles, students should be better able to adapt so that these issues are less likely to arise.

2 ▶ 9.2

- Tell students that they are going to find out more information about direct and indirect styles of communication and think about which style they use more often.
- Draw students' attention to the phrase 'use more often' in the question and elicit or explain that almost everybody uses a combination of direct and indirect styles, but they will usually use one more than the other.
- Play the video.
- **Optional step** Ask students to make notes on the key points for each communication style.
- Students tell a partner which communication style they use more often and give specific or general examples of things they say or do that demonstrate that they use this style more than the other.

VOCABULARY NOTES

preserve /prɪ'zɜːv/ = to keep something in its original or existing state

get to the point /get tuː ðə pɔɪnt/ = to say or write the main or most important thing you wanted to communicate

assume /ə'sjuːm/ = to believe that something is true without having any evidence that it is true

3 ▶ 9.2

- Tell students to read the sentences before they watch the video again.
- Play the video again so students can decide if the sentences are true or false.
- **Optional step** Tell students to correct the false sentences.
- Ask students to compare their answers in pairs and then check answers as a class.

Answers

1 T; 2 F – it's direct communicators who value efficiency; 3 T; 4 F – it's not the style but our assumptions about it that can create communication problems; 5 T

Extra activity

Ask students to think about which communication style they use more often, thinking about the following questions:

- What is more important to you: giving the facts or being polite?
- What do you think is the best way to solve problems: having a discussion where you say exactly how you feel or a discussion where the priority is to not offend or blame anyone?
- How do you perceive people who communicate directly and people who communicate indirectly?
- Do you start a conversation by bringing up the main point you need to talk about or do you make small talk or talk about other related topics first?
- Are there situations and contexts where you do not use the communication style that you usually use? What is different or special about these situations or contexts?

Put students into small groups to discuss their communication styles.

9D Adapting to direct and indirect styles

LESSON GOALS

- Understand the difference between direct and indirect communication
- Adapt to direct and indirect communication styles
- Ask for clarification

SPEAKING

1 **Work in pairs. Look at the cartoon and answer the questions.**

1 What's the problem with the language used in each situation?
2 What's the best caption for the cartoon?
  a Be as polite as possible at all times.
  b Understand when to use direct or indirect language.
  c Don't use a hundred words when one is enough.

MY VOICE ▶

2 ▶ 9.2 **Watch the video. Which style do you use more often?**

3 ▶ 9.2 **Watch the video again. Are the sentences true (T) or false (F)?**

1 Both direct and indirect communication styles can lead to better relationships.
2 People who are more indirect feel that being efficient when communicating is important.
3 The student talked about the situation rather than directly asking for paper from their classmate.
4 Using the wrong style can create problems.
5 It's important you recognize your and the other person's preferred style.

4 **Work in pairs. Read the situations (1–3). Decide if the speaker is being too indirect or direct. What do you think the indirect people are really saying? How could the direct person be perceived?**

1 A colleague explains to Marcus a project she wants to propose to the boss. It is very ambitious and will cost the company a lot of money. Marcus: 'Well ... it's a very *brave* proposal.'
2 Kareem is trying to finish his essay. It has to be given in tomorrow. His flatmate is practising for a speaking exam.
Kareem: 'Go upstairs, OK? I'm trying to concentrate here.'
3 Patri is going to a job interview. It's raining hard. Her friend has a car.
Patri: 'Isn't the weather horrible today! I hope my suit doesn't get wet.'

114

4

- Put students into pairs. Ask them to read the three situations and decide together first whether the speaker in each situation is being indirect or direct.
- Encourage students to be more specific in their descriptions of each style by saying 'a little direct/indirect', 'quite direct/indirect' or 'very direct/indirect' instead of just 'direct' or 'indirect'. This will help them decide whether a speaker is too indirect or direct.
- Students then discuss the questions about each situation. With situations 1 and 3, tell students to consider what each person is really thinking or wants, even if they are not (directly) communicating this and why other people might not be able to understand what they think or want.
- **Optional step** Ask students to discuss which example of communication from situations 1–3 is the most similar to their own communication style and, where appropriate, to talk about situations where they have said or done similar things.

Answers

1 quite indirect – Marcus thinks the proposal isn't a very good one, or not an appropriate one
2 direct – could be seen as rude
3 very indirect – she is asking for a lift

Extra activity

Ask students to think of a situation they, or someone they know, has experienced in real-life in which a misunderstanding or conflict occurred because someone communicated in an indirect or direct style. Put students into pairs and ask them to give some background information about

5 Look at the Communication skill box. In pairs, write a continuation of the conversations from Exercise 4 to show how the directness or indirectness could be dealt with effectively.

'Er, sorry, when you say 'brave', what do you mean?'
'Well, you've got some good ideas, but I think there are some issues with it. Let's talk it through together.'

COMMUNICATION SKILL
Adapting to direct and indirect communication styles

1 When communicating with someone who is being more indirect, use the background information to interpret their information, show curiosity and ask questions for clarification.
2 When communicating with someone who is being more direct, remember they are simply trying to be efficient and clear, not rude. If you need more context, don't be afraid to ask for it.
3 Consider the situation and the person you're speaking to and adapt your communication style as appropriate. Discuss your preferred communication style with the other person.

6 Look at the Useful language box. Answer the questions (1–2).

Useful language Adapting to different communication styles

Asking for clarification
I appreciate your honesty, but could you explain your reasons a bit more? 1a
What exactly do you mean by …? 1b
Why do you say that? 1a
Just to check I understand, do you mean …? 1a, 1b

Talking about different styles
I tend to get to the point quickly, so please ask me questions if anything is unclear. 2a
Sometimes I take a while to get to the point, so feel free to ask me to be more direct. 2b

1 Which expressions in the 'Asking for clarification' section could be used when speaking to someone who is: a) communicating directly?; b) communicating indirectly?
2 Which expressions in the 'Talking about different styles' section could be used if you are: a) a direct speaker?; b) an indirect speaker?

SPEAKING

7 Read the messages (1–3) that users of a study centre have sent in an online chat group. Match them with the comments (a–c).

STUDY GROUP

1 **PAT**
TO EVERYONE! Please don't use the study centre on Thursday from 4:30 – 5:30. I need it. (If I don't hear anything from you, I'll assume that's OK.)

2 **JI-SOO**
🙂 Let's all work together to keep the centre tidy! 🙂 I'm not sure we all are, are we?

3 **BLAS**
Do you like reading mysteries, fantasy and sci fi? There are some great books in English. Talking about the books we love is good English practice too! Why don't we do something like a club? I'd love to know what you think.

3 a 'He was talking about it the other day in the canteen. I love how excited he is about this idea of his, but I'm not exactly sure what it is!'
1 b 'She did the same thing last week. I was on the computer and she came in and asked me to leave. I don't think she can just use the room like that whenever she wants!'
2 c 'That's typical of him. He came in the other day and rushed around putting all the books back on the shelves. He wasn't very pleased!'

8 **OWN IT!** Imagine you are part of the online chat group in Exercise 7. Make notes for each question.
1 Which of the three situations would make you the most uncomfortable? Why?
2 How would you normally react in a situation like this? Do you think you might react differently, having learned about direct and indirect styles?
3 What message would you send in response? Use the Useful language to help you.

9 Work in pairs. Compare your different responses to each situation. If your responses are different, discuss why that is.

115

the situation they chose and report what was said. They can then explain what type of communication style the speaker has and the effect of using this style in that particular situation.

5
- Ask students to look at the Communication skill box.
- Put students into pairs. Ask students to read the situations in Exercise 4 again and consider together which tips in the Communication skill box could help them deal with each situation more effectively.
- Students work together to write the continuation of the conversations.
- **Optional step** Ask students to compare what they have written with another pair and give each other feedback on whether their sentences show that the speaker is adapting to the other person's style.

6
- Ask students to look at the Useful language box. Check their understanding of 'clarification' (the action of making something clearer and easier to understand).
- Students use their awareness of direct and indirect communication styles to determine which expressions could be used when speaking to someone communicating directly or indirectly.
- Students then decide which expression in the 'Talking about different styles' section could be used by a direct speaker and which could be used by an indirect speaker.
- Students compare their answers in pairs, justifying their choices.

SPEAKING

7
- Tell students that the three messages they are going to read are written by people with different communication styles.
- Students match the messages with the comments about their writers.
- Students compare their answers in pairs.

8 OWN IT!
- Ask students to read the questions and take a few minutes to read the online messages in Exercise 7 again, then think about and make notes on their answers to the questions.

9
- Put students into pairs and ask them to share and explain their answers to Exercise 8.
- If students have different responses to their partner, they should discuss why that is, referring to their knowledge of different communication styles.
- **Optional step** Encourage students to react to what their partner is saying by showing interest, asking a follow-up question or asking for clarification if something was unclear for them.

LESSON GOALS

- **WRITING** The aim of the lesson is to guide students to produce an email applying for a job. The reading text provides a model. Students learn how to write a job application email that explains why they are suitable for a job and provide specific examples of their skills and experience. They also learn useful expressions that they can use in the job application email to talk about their skills and experience, education, etc.

SPEAKING

1

- Ask students to read the questions and job adverts and give them about one or two minutes to think about their answers individually.
- Students discuss the questions in pairs.

READING FOR WRITING

2

- Clarify that in question 1, the requirements for a job would be considered 'fair' if they include qualifications and skills that are appropriate for the job's level of responsibility and typical salary.
- Ask students to read the job advert and the application email and make notes on their answers for the questions.
- Ask students to discuss and compare their answers in pairs.

Answers

1 Student's own answers, but requesting that the applicant is a woman, native speaker and educated to Master's degree level could be considered irrelevant to the person's ability to do the job successfully and therefore unfair/unnecessary; 2 Yes, apart from 'ability to solve unexpected problems'; 3 He always provides a specific example of how he gained a skill and uses phrases such as 'thanks to', 'with regards to', 'such as'.

9E I got the job!

LESSON GOALS
- Explain why you are suitable for a job
- Provide specific examples of your skills and experience
- Write a job application email

SPEAKING

1 Work in pairs. Look at the job adverts and discuss the questions.
1 Which of these jobs would you be interested in? Which would interest you least? Why?
2 Which do you think you might be good at? Why?

Professional sleeper
'El Descanso' hotel in Mexico is looking for a professional sleeper to test the quality of its beds.

Full-time Netflix watcher
Netflix is hiring people to watch content before it becomes publicly available.

Drying paint watcher
We will hire a part-time worker to watch how long it takes for our paint to dry.

Scuba diving pizza delivery person
Jules Undersea Lodge is looking for an experienced scuba diver to deliver pizza to its guests.

READING FOR WRITING

2 Read the hotel receptionist job advert and application email. Answer the questions.
1 Do all requirements for the job seem necessary or fair? Why? / Why not?
2 Does Alexander mention all the other requirements from the job advert in his email?
3 How does Alexander provide evidence for his skills and qualities?

116

HOTEL RECEPTIONIST

Seafront Hotel is looking for a female hotel receptionist to work either part- or full-time.

Requirements:
- minimum two years of experience in a similar position
- excellent communication skills
- ability to solve unexpected problems
- strong organizational skills
- native English speaker and fluent in at least one European language
- minimum Master's degree or certificate in hospitality preferred

APPLY NOW

3 Look at the Writing skill box. Which of the sentences (1–4) would be relevant in a job application for the hotel receptionist role?

WRITING SKILL
A job application email

When writing a job application email, it is important to mention all the key requirements listed in the job advert. You should also avoid including information that is not relevant to the position you are applying for. Finally, try to provide evidence and specific examples to prove you really have the necessary skills, experience or qualities.

1 I can communicate fluently in English.
2 I have previously worked as a chef in a restaurant.
3 I have developed my ability to communicate with people from different countries.
4 I am creative and able to solve unexpected problems quickly.

VOCABULARY NOTES

hospitality /ˌhɒspɪ'tæləti/ = the provision of food, drink and places to stay by hotels, restaurants and bars

approachable /ə'prəʊtʃəbl/ = friendly and easy to start a conversation with

proficient /prə'fɪʃ(ə)nt/ = highly skilled and very experienced

professional development /prə'feʃənl dɪ'veləpmənt/ = further training that people complete in order to be able to do their jobs more effectively

stand for /stænd fɔː/ = to support or represent a particular belief

(be) in line with /ɪn laɪn wɪð/ = to correspond with or be complimentary to

3

- Tell students to look at the Writing skill box.
- Ask students to read the sentences (1–4). Elicit or explain that you usually use the present perfect (e.g. *I have … worked*) to talk about your experience, *I can/am able to …* to talk about your skills and *I am …* to talk about your qualities.
- Students identify the appropriate sentences. Check answers as a class.

Dear Sir or Madam,

I am writing to apply for the position of hotel receptionist as advertised on your website.

As outlined in my CV, which I have attached, I have over three years' experience working as a hotel receptionist. During my BA degree in hospitality, I worked part-time at the Imperial Hotel in Berlin where I gained valuable experience. Since graduating, I have been working at the Riverside Hotel, Berlin, but I will be relocating to New York next month.

As far as my personality is concerned, I am friendly and approachable. I have always received high ratings in guest satisfaction surveys. Moreover, I am able to organize my daily tasks well to fulfil them on time, which is something my previous employers have positively commented on.

Thanks to my experience in the German hotel industry, I have also learned how to communicate effectively with international guests. While I am not a first language user of English, I am highly proficient in it. Having welcomed many international guests, I have developed a good working knowledge of French and Spanish, in addition to my first language (German).

With regards to my qualifications, I hold a BA degree in hospitality from SRH University Berlin. I am also about to complete a professional development course in international communication.

I would be very interested in joining your team at Seafront. The values your hotel stands for, such as an individual approach to guests and attention to detail, are very much in line with my own professional values. I hope you will consider me for the role.

Yours sincerely,

Alexander Müller

4 Read Alexander's application email again. Underline phrases that mean ...

1 got really good experience
2 since finishing university
3 moving to
4 about my personality
5 speak very well with
6 my French and Spanish aren't too bad
7 I'm now almost done with

5 Look at the Useful language box. Then write sentences about ...

1 your education.
2 the languages you speak.
3 your work experience and/or personal skills.

Useful language Job application emails

Previous experience
I have enclosed/attached my CV.
I gained valuable experience in ...
I work part-/full-time in/as a ...

Languages
I am (highly) proficient in ...
I have a good working knowledge of ...

Education
I hold a degree in ...
I completed a course in ...
I graduated in ...

Introducing a new topic
With regards to ...
As far as (my personality) is concerned ...

WRITING TASK

6 WRITE Write an email of 200-250 words applying for a job. You can choose to apply for ...

- the hotel receptionist job from Exercise 2.
- a job advert of your choice from the internet.

7 CHECK Use the checklist. I have ...

☐ included evidence and examples of skills / experience.
☐ only included information relevant to the job.
☐ used formal language.

8 REVIEW Work in pairs. Exchange job adverts and application letters. Decide if you would invite your partner to a job interview and give them feedback.

Go to page 134 for the Reflect and review.

EXPLORE MORE!

Search online for 'top tips for a job interview'. Which tips did you find the most useful?

4

- Ask students to read the items (1–7). Elicit that these are all informal expressions and, therefore would not be appropriate for a job application email where more formal language is expected.
- Tell students to scan the email for phrases that share the same meaning as items 1–7.
- Students compare their answers in pairs and then check answers as a class.

5

- Ask students to look at the Useful language box and check they understand the categories and expressions.
- Tell students to write at least two sentences for each category, using a different expression from the Useful language box in each.

WRITING TASK

6 WRITE

- Remind students to use the expressions from the Useful language for writing a job application email. They may be able to reuse the sentences they wrote in Exercise 5. Also ask students to refer back to the Writing skill box to remind them how to organize their email.
- Students write the first draft of their email.

7 CHECK

- Ask students to use the checklist and then make changes to their emails if necessary.

8 REVIEW

- Students exchange emails with a partner.
- Students read each other's emails and use the checklist from Exercise 7 to review them.
- Students then read their partner's email again and think about whether they would invite him/her to a job interview based on their email.
- Students give each other feedback on their emails, explain why they would or would not invite them to a job interview and offer one or two tips for improving their emails.

Extra activity

Ask students to brainstorm possible questions that could be asked in an interview for the job advert in this lesson and possible answers to these questions. Students roleplay the job interview once and then exchange roles.

EXPLORE MORE!

When they are gathering and recording the tips, tell students to try to find information about different aspects of job interviews, for example body language, using your voice, reacting to questions, gaining time to think before answering a difficult question, and presenting yourself in a positive light / turning negatives into positives. They could brainstorm these different aspects of interviewing for a job successfully and then look for tips for each one.

For **Unit 9 Reflect and review**, see Student's Book page 134.

See **Workbook** pages 82–83 for extra practice.

VIDEO 9.1

Robbie: *For me, success is not about your career or how much money you make. Success is just being happy, being content with yourself and how you've lived your life. You know, what type of person you are. I think that's success. But then happiness feeds off things, doesn't it? It evolves through other forms of being successful, like being able to do the job I love. And then other aspects are friends and family and your partner. But the principle is the same and I think that's the key to success. My ambitions have changed a lot over the years. Before I met my partner Gina, my ambitions were very single-minded and focused on me and what I wanted to do. But now it's difficult to think about my own ambitions without including Gina.*

Paola: *As I've got older, I've realized that success is not having something, or achieving a specific goal. It's not a degree or a prize. It is enjoying what you do – your work, your life. And, above all, always looking to evolve, to go further and share all these moments with the people you love. Moreover, I feel that success comes when we realize that we don't need to be recognized for our success. I am happier always knowing that my family is fine, being able to feel close to them despite the distance since I live in a different city. But above all my everyday happiness is my research work and having the time to dive! It doesn't matter how many times I dive on the same coral reef, there is always something different to see, to be amazed by and I forget about the rest of the world.*

AUDIO 9.3

Robbie Shone, cave photographer, describes two failures in his career that taught him valuable lessons, not just about his work but also about life in general.

1

In 2009, I was on an expedition exploring the caves in Mulu National Park, Borneo. I had been practising cave photography for about nine years by this point. During one trip, we were exploring a huge river cave called Clearwater. The cave has many entrances but we came out of the main one where the river gushes out. To get out of the cave we all just simply jumped in the river. Despite the fact that it was quite safe, we still all needed buoyancy aids to help us float. I carry my camera equipment in a waterproof container, so decided to use that as my buoyancy aid. The trip down the river was so much fun! At the end, we all climbed out of the water happy and excited.

However, when I picked up my camera case, it was unusually heavy. In my heart I knew what the problem was, though I really didn't want to believe it. I knelt down and opened the case and a flood of water gushed out. I picked up my camera but it was destroyed. I felt so bad. I had a lump in my throat. My expedition was over, or at least I thought it was. The expedition members all helped though. We made some phone calls and managed to get a new camera brought out from the UK. I was so thankful for having such good friends. Actually, I went on to take some of the best photos of my career at that point. The lesson to be learned – always travel with a second camera!

2

I think there's one incident which is huge for me. Even though it was painful, it really did help kick-start my career.

I was in Washington to show a National Geographic editor my work. I showed her a book of cave photos that I'd had printed especially. It was quite expensive for me at the time, but I thought the presentation was really important. However, the editor wasn't impressed at all. There was only one she liked and that was the last one.

I came away from the interview in tears. The feeling I had afterwards, I really thought my life was over. I had been working as a professional abseiler, painting bridges and insulating roofs in supermarkets. Whilst at work, I lived in a van. One week I only ate pepper sandwiches to save money. My parents wanted me to 'get a proper job'. But after that meeting, I felt like it had all been a complete waste of time.

But then, you come round and that's an incredible feeling when you convince yourself, no, I'm not going to quit. So I went away and practised. I was told to work with other photographers and learn from them. And what you thought was a failure at first can actually make you better at what you do. And you're so much stronger because you're driven, it's the fire inside, it's huge. I certainly benefited so much by what happened on that day.

AUDIO 9.4

1 To get out of the cave we all just simply jumped in the river. Despite the fact that it was quite safe, we still all needed buoyancy aids to help us float.

2 And what you thought was a failure at first can actually make you better at what you do.

AUDIO 9.5

/ʃ/ ambition, professional, issue

/ʒ/ decision, vision

/tʃ/ achieve

/dʒ/ knowledge, manage, objectives, project

VIDEO 9.2

We all communicate in our own way and no single way is better than another, but have you thought about the reasons behind these differences?

Some people feel it's more important to protect and preserve the listener's feelings, and this will naturally lead to a better, stronger, relationship. They tend to use the situation or the relationship with the listener to explain things. They will often first talk about the general situation and the context. They tend to speak around the point. They use an indirect style of communication.

Others value honesty and efficiency in their communication. This can also lead to better, stronger relationships. These people prefer to get straight to the point. They use a direct style of communication. But what happens when one style meets another?

Well, those who communicate more indirectly can sometimes see direct communicators as being insensitive or rude. Direct communicators get to the point quickly, which might surprise or confuse indirect people. They're also more likely to interrupt the other person. On the other hand, more direct people may see indirect communicators as boring, slow or even dishonest. The extra context may be seen as unnecessary and time-consuming. As you can see, it's not the style that's the problem here, it's what we assume about the other style when we come across it.

To be a good communicator, it's important to know your own style: do you get impatient with other people when they are talking about things you feel are not relevant to the conversation? Or do you feel hurt that others are insensitive for interrupting you or finishing your sentences?

The next is to know the sorts of contexts your preferences are stronger in. Perhaps you are more indirect when you need to ask for a day off at work and more direct when you're speaking to your friends, for instance. Professional, social and cultural factors all play a role here.

You also need to recognize whether the person you're speaking to prefers a more direct or indirect style. Listen to the way they're communicating: are they happy to chat about things that aren't one hundred per cent relevant to the reason for speaking, for example? Do you need to ask more questions to understand their point?

Don't judge the other person's style negatively. Remember that they're not trying to make you feel frustrated or confused on purpose. They simply communicate in a different way.

The final stage is to be clear and honest about your preferences and the reasons for them and start to find ways to communicate with other preferences in mind.

UNIT 10

A world of cultures

UNIT GOALS

10A Reading, speaking

- identify and understand examples of figurative language and use critical thinking skills to practise evaluating the relationship between a text and the media used to support it; talk about favourite music and its role in students' identity

10B Reading and grammar, pronunciation, speaking

- learn and practise using verb patterns with infinitive and *-ing*; listen to aspiration in sets of word pairs and practise using it; ask and answer questions about subcultures, groups and clubs

10C Listening, vocabulary, pronunciation, grammar, speaking

- listen to an interview with a National Geographic explorer and practise understanding ellipsis; learn and practise collocations about cultural identity; practise pronouncing the /th/ sound; practise using *the* to talk about groups of people or things

10D Writing and speaking

- write about and discuss the assumptions that people often make about a particular group; consider reasons for differences in behaviour; learn about how to deal with personal assumptions to avoid misunderstandings; discuss instances where misunderstandings can occur

10E Writing

- practise expressing numbers approximately; design and conduct a survey about cultural attractions, then write a report on its findings

Photocopiable resources

Communication activities: pp. 230–231
Vocabulary activity: p. 242
Grammar activity: p. 263
Focus on … activity: p. 264
Pronunciation activity: p. 277
Mediation activity: p. 292

Workbook

Unit 10 pp. 84–91

ABOUT THE PHOTO

The photo shows a group of children in India, probably playing a game that is known as 'Blind Man's Bluff' or 'Blind Man's Buff' in English. In the game, one player is blindfolded and has to try to 'catch' one of the other players by touching them. A version is known to have

Children playing in Haryana, India.

10

A world of cultures

GOALS

- Identify and understand figurative language in creative writing
- Learn verb patterns with infinitive and *-ing*
- Talk about your cultural identity
- Understand ellipsis in spoken language
- Learn to deal with assumptions to avoid misunderstandings
- Write a report about cultural attractions

1 Work in pairs. Discuss the questions.

1 Look at the photo. What game do you think the children are playing? Did you play a similar game as a child?
2 What other games do you think are played by children all over the world?
3 What other behaviours and customs do you think are universal around the world? Which do you think are different?

WATCH

2 ▶ 10.1 Watch the video. Answer the questions.

NATIONAL GEOGRAPHIC EXPLORERS

ALYEA PIERCE | LIA NAHOMI KAJIKI

1 What cultures do Alyea and Lia compare?
2 What similarities do they each notice?

3 Make connections. What do Alyea and Lia's stories have in common? Do you have any similar stories?

119

been played as early as two thousand years ago in Greece, but many versions of it exist around the world, such as *Kanamachi* ('blind fly') in Bangladesh and *gallina ciega* ('blind hen') in Spain.

1

- Ask students to look at the photo and caption. Tell students that this game is played all over the world.
- Direct students to the questions. For question 2, examples could include: *Hide and seek* (a game where one player hides and one or more other players try to find them) or *Keep away* (a game where two players throw a ball to each other while a third player in between them tries to intercept it).
- In pairs, students discuss questions 1 and 2 and brainstorm ideas for question 3. Ask them to give examples from their own experiences.

Extra activity

Ask students to think of a game that they played when they were children. Put students into groups and ask them to explain the objective and rules of the game. If other group members are not familiar with the game, encourage them to ask questions to clarify any details that are unclear to them.

WATCH

2 ▶ 10.1

- Tell students that they will hear Alyea speaking first and then Lia. Ask them to make notes on the similarities between the cultures the explorers mention.
- Play the video so students can make notes.
- Students compare answers in pairs.

Answers

1 Alyea compares poet cultures in New York and in Trinidad; Lia compares open markets in Europe and Brazil 2 the atmosphere and feelings in the markets were the same; Lia experienced the same joy; the atmosphere and snaps (finger clicking) were the same

3

- Ask students to look at the notes they made in Exercise 2 again. Then ask them to think about an experience of being in, or talking to someone from another culture but discovering something familiar or similar to their own culture.
- Students discuss the questions in pairs.

ABOUT THE EXPLORERS

ALYEA PIERCE is an author, educator, international speaker and performance poet from the US. As a storyteller, she aims to focus on stories that are not usually told. Alyea undertook a Fulbright-National Geographic Digital Storytelling project that examined the revitalization of oral storytelling and folktale traditions in Trinidad and Tobago through present-day spoken word and rhythm poetry.
LIA NAHOMI KAJIKI is a Brazilian ornithologist and PhD candidate at the University of Brasilia. She is interested in social networks and social behaviour among birds and how these drive the diversity of species.

LESSON GOALS

- **READING** The main aim is for students to read an example of creative writing, identify and understand the figurative language in it and then practise evaluating the relationship between a text and its supporting media.
- **SPEAKING** The speaking aim is for students to talk about their favourite types of music and the role the music has in their identity and culture.

10A A thousand rhythms

LESSON GOALS
- Identify and understand figurative language in creative writing
- Evaluate the relationship between a text and its supporting media
- Talk about your favourite music and its role in your identity and culture

SPEAKING

1 10.1 Listen to three short pieces of music. Discuss the questions with a partner.
1 Which piece of music did you like best? Why?
2 How did each piece make you feel?
3 How would you describe the music? Use these words and your own ideas.

cheerful mournful rapid rhythmic rich slow traditional

READING

2 Look at the title of the article on page 121. Which place do you think is 'the land of a thousand rhythms'? Quickly skim the article to check. Colombia

3 Read the article. Then discuss the questions.
1 What was the most interesting thing you learned from the article?
2 Which of the places the writer describes would you like to visit the most? Why?
3 What traditional music is there in your country? How is it similar or different to the music styles the writer describes?

4 Look at the Reading skill box. Then read the article again and find …
1 one simile (paragraph 2)
2 one metaphor (paragraph 4)
3 two examples of personification (paragraph 7 and 8)

READING SKILL
Identifying figurative language in creative writing

Figurative language is frequently found in creative writing, such as stories, poetry, articles and songs. It includes …
- similes – comparing two unrelated things using *as* or *like*: *The look in his eyes was like ice.*
- metaphors – saying one thing *is* another thing (no *as* or *like*): *During rush hour, the motorway is a giant car park.*
- personification – giving human qualities or feelings to something that isn't human: *My alarm clock yells at me every morning.*

5 Work in pairs. Discuss the questions.
1 What does the figurative language you identified in Exercise 4 mean? For example, in what way is San Basilio de Palenque similar to a greenhouse?
2 Why did the writer use this language in the article? What effect does it have on the reader?

6 Look at the Critical thinking skill box. Discuss the questions in the box, thinking about the photos, music and article from this lesson.

CRITICAL THINKING SKILL
Evaluating the relationship between text and supporting media

Understanding a text can sometimes be just one part of the whole story. The text might be accompanied by photos, graphs, maps, video or audio, which can help you understand the text. But they can also influence your opinion of the text or create an emotional reaction. Consider:
- What additional information do the photos or video/audio contain?
- How do these help you understand the text?
- How do they influence your reaction to the text?

SPEAKING

7 Take notes about your favourite types of music and why you enjoy them. Find examples of this music to play to your classmates. Consider these questions:
1 What do you like about these music types? How do they make you feel?
2 What has influenced this music? For example, traditional songs, other musical styles, a specific culture or group of people. Use the internet if you need to find this information.
3 Is this music popular among many people in your country? Is it popular among a specific age group?

8 Share your favourite music in groups of three. Play the music to your classmates.

EXPLORE MORE!
Choose a country you are interested in. Find and listen to three different music styles from there. Which did you like the most? Why?

120

SPEAKING

1 10.1
- Direct students to the questions and the words in the box. Check their understanding of 'mournful' (feeling or expressing great sadness) and 'rich' (deep, strong, warm and pleasant).
- Play the audio and ask students to focus on how each piece of music makes them feel and whether or not they like it.
- Students discuss the questions in pairs. Encourage them to explain why they liked or didn't like a particular piece of music and why they think the words they chose from the box describe it.
- **Optional step** Ask students to discuss these questions: *Was the music similar or different to the type of music you usually listen to? Would you consider listening to music like this from now on, if you do not already listen to it?*

READING

ABOUT THE TEXT

The text is an example of creative writing that presents facts about the writer's trip to Colombia and the country's music in the style of a travel narrative. In the first paragraph, the writer sets out his/her aim of bringing to the reader's attention the types of Colombian music that are not widely known to outsiders. The writer then goes on to describe three particular types of Colombian music.

Colombia is a country in north-western South America. Europeans first visited Colombia in 1499, and the Spanish started to settle there soon after. Many aspects of Colombia's culture, including its music, can be traced back to the collision between Spanish culture and the culture of the indigenous people of Colombia. Enslaved African people began to be brought to Colombia during the 16th century, mainly from West Africa, and added their own cultural influences to the mixture of Spanish and indigenous culture.

2
- **Optional step** Tell students that the three pieces of music they listened to in Exercise 1 are examples of the music they are now going to read about. They will read about the pieces of music in the same order that they heard them.
- **Optional step** Write the title of the article on the board so that students do not glance at the first paragraph and see the answer straight away.
- Ask students to use their knowledge of the world to predict which country could be 'the land of a thousand rhythms'.
- Students quickly scan the text and check their predictions.
- Check answers as a class.

Afro-Colombian singer La Burgos and her group Las Alegres Ambulancias.

So You Want to Explore the Land of a Thousand Rhythms?

For the past few weeks, I have been on a remarkable music exploration. Most people have probably heard of, and hopefully danced to, international hits by artists like Shakira and Carlos Vives. But fewer are familiar with other fascinating folk rhythms of Colombia that have been calculated at an incredible 1,025 different types.

Palenque: Afro-Colombian vibes

A visit to San Basilio de Palenque, considered the first free town in the Americas, is like a trip to a greenhouse. You'll be greeted by high temperatures, humidity and dusty streets. Maybe not much to this town after all? [para 2]

Wrong.

The strong and proud Afro-Colombian spirit in this town tells the story of human determination and is likely to touch your heart. Four hundred years ago, when ships transporting enslaved people arrived in Cartagena, many people escaped and settled in the remote and hard-to-access *palenques*, or tiny towns, where they would not be found. They'd brought with them from Africa the rhythmic music that I was now hearing everywhere: 15+ drum types played both at mournful funerals and cheerful celebrations. This music is a trip across time and space. [para 4]

Cali: More than just salsa

For those who love Latin American music, Cali – the Salsa capital of the world – needs no introduction. My first thought? I have arrived at the right place!

For the locals, or *caleños*, salsa is a native sound, a musical style to be proud of. The rich and rapid tunes are bound to make you dance all night (and day!) long. But Cali goes beyond salsa sounds.

Each year, rhythms such as *Currulao* or *Chirimia* dance in the air during Petronio Alvarez Music Festival. Artists such as Esteban Copete, grandson of the iconic Colombian composer after whom the festival takes its name, take these traditional local vibes a step further, mixing them with well-known international music styles, such as R&B, Bossa Nova and jazz. [para 7]

Los Llanos: Cowboy music

I finally arrived in *Los Llanos*, or flatlands, where life goes about its business slowly and unchanged over generations. The daily tasks are accompanied by an oral tradition known as *cantos de vaquería*. Cows are milked at dawn and the songs are adapted to rhyme with the name of each cow. Sometimes slow and sad, the songs are frequently improvised. [para 8]

Moving my feet to the rhythms, I thought about how *Los Llanos* preserve not only natural beauty, but also the voices and identity of those Colombian cowboys fighting hard to maintain ancestral knowledge and vanishing traditions.

The land of a thousand rhythms is a fascinating example of how the different people who have come to Colombia have brought their music with them, influencing and changing not only the local culture but global culture as well.

GLOSSARY:

ancestral (home/knowledge/traditions) – related to your relatives from a long time ago
improvised (music/performance/dance) – not prepared in advance

121

3

- Ask students to read the article and make notes about anything they find interesting about the places that the writer mentions.
- Ask students to also prepare to talk about traditional music in their country.
- **Optional step** Students could search online for information in English about their country's traditional music, to check facts or find the English words for specific terms they need to use to talk about it.
- Put students into pairs to discuss the questions. If the students in your class come from different countries, try to put students together with someone from a different country. If students are paired with someone from their own country, encourage them to think of something unique or interesting to say about their country's music for question 3.
- **Optional step** Invite different students to talk about the traditional music from their country.

VOCABULARY NOTES

vibe /vaɪb/ = an emotional reaction or atmosphere that something creates

enslaved /ɪn'sleɪvd/ = someone whose personal freedom has been taken away and who has been forced to work for no money

milk /mɪlk/ = to get milk from an animal using either your hands or a machine

Extra activity

Ask students to write a short text about a type of music that they know well, from anywhere in the world for people who are not familiar with it. Ask them to include some or all of the points below. They can use the internet to find additional information if needed.

- the story behind the music; how the music originally developed
- what this type of music sounds like and how it makes people feel when they hear it
- what makes this type of music different to others
- any music festivals or events where people play this type of music

When students have finished writing, ask them to exchange and discuss their texts in pairs, or invite different students to use their text to briefly present their type of music in class.

4

- Ask students to read the Reading skill box. Elicit a few additional examples of 'similes', 'metaphors' and 'personification' to check their understanding of these terms.
- Students look at the relevant paragraphs of the article and identify the examples of each type of figurative language.
- Ask students to compare their answers in pairs.

Answers

1 like a trip to a greenhouse
2 a trip across time and space
3 rhythms ... dance in the air; life goes about its business

5

- If students are unsure about the meaning of any of the figurative language they identified in Exercise 4, they can discuss it with their partner. Encourage them to use the context in which the examples are used in the text and their general knowledge to help them.
- Students discuss the reasons for using figurative language and its effect on the reader. Ask them to consider the effect that the figurative language had on their feelings about and interest in the text and how the experience of reading the text would have been different without it.
- Check answers by eliciting the meanings of the figurative language from Exercise 4 and inviting different students to share their reflections about figurative language.

Sample answers

1 like a trip to a greenhouse = trip to a very hot place (San Basilio de Palenque is like a trip to a greenhouse because the environments are similar, i.e, hot, sticky and humid); a trip across time and space = it makes you feel like you're in a different time and place; rhythms ... dance in the air = you can hear a lot of music; life goes about its business = life is or continues in a certain way

2 The figurative language makes the descriptions more interesting and colourful; it helps the reader feel, see or hear what the writer describes.

6

- Tell students to read the Critical thinking skill box.
- Students discuss their answers to the questions in pairs. Remind them to consider and bring all three elements into their discussion: music, photos and text.

Answers

The photo shows you the musical instruments and the people playing them. This is not mentioned in the text, so it expands what you read about. The music is mentioned and described in the text but listening to it can help you understand what the music actually sounds like. You can also decide whether you agree or disagree with the author's description of the music. Hearing the music can evoke emotions and feelings too.

Extra activity

Put students into pairs and ask each student to choose an article in Lesson A of previous units that interests them – good examples would be the texts in Lessons 2A, 6A, 7A and 9A. Alternatively, students could choose an online article they have read recently that is accompanied by either photos or video/audio material, or both. Students then take turns to ask and answer the questions in the Critical thinking skill box about the text and its supporting media.

SPEAKING

7

- Ask students to choose two or three types of music they like. This could be any type of music and does not have to be traditional music from their country.
- Students read the questions and make notes on their answers individually. Encourage them to use the internet to find additional information about or examples of the music types they have chosen.
- Tell students to prepare a brief presentation of their chosen types of music that incorporates their answers to the questions.
- Ask students to select at least one example of each of their favourite music types to share with other students in Exercise 8.
- **Optional step** If students are unable to use the internet in class, suggest that students answer questions 1 and 3 in class and then answer question 2 as a self-study task so that they can use the internet to find additional information about and examples of the music types they have chosen.

8

- Put students into groups of three (or four if you have an even number of students). Students take turns to present their favourite music types and use their chosen device to play the pieces of music they have selected.
- **Optional step** Encourage students to respond to their group members' presentations by saying what they think about their chosen music type(s) and how the music they heard makes them feel. They could also ask questions to find out more information about the types of music.

Extra activity

Ask students to choose one of the artists whose music another member of their group played in Exercise 8. Tell students to have a longer listen to this artist's music – if possible, in class, otherwise outside of class – and write down their initial thoughts about this artist's music. They could then share this with the person who chose the artist in Exercise 8.
The task could be expanded by asking students to write a full review of the artist's music outside of class, doing online research to find out more details or background information about the artist.

See **Workbook** pages 84–85 for extra practice.

LESSON GOALS

- **GRAMMAR** The main aim is for students to learn and practise using verb patterns with infinitive and *-ing*.
- **PRONUNCIATION** A sub-aim is for students to listen to words pronounced with an aspirated /p/, /k/ or /t/ sound and practise using aspiration to say these sounds.
- **SPEAKING** The speaking aim is to discuss subcultures and talk about groups and clubs students belong to or belonged to.

READING AND GRAMMAR

1

- Check students' understanding of 'subculture' (a group of people that share the same interests, enjoy the same activities or often enjoy dressing or behaving in the same way).
- Give students a few minutes to look at the illustrations in the article and guess each subculture.
- **Optional step** Students could work with a partner to identify the subcultures, or do this individually and then compare their answers in pairs.
- Check answers as a class. Elicit or explain that 'cos' in 'cosplayer' is short for 'costume'.

Extra activity

Assign a subculture from Exercise 1 to each student. Ensure that the subcultures are distributed among the students as evenly as possible. Tell students to do some online research to find more information about the key features of their assigned subculture (i.e. what its members do, how they dress, etc.) and when, where and how it developed. Students can then use their notes to present it to other students who have researched different subcultures.

2

- Put students into pairs to discuss which subcultures exist in their home country or culture.
- **Optional step** Students could also say which subcultures they think are the most dominant or popular and speculate about the reasons for this.

3

- Ask students to read the article and make notes on their answers to the questions.
- Ask students to discuss and justify their answers in pairs.

Answers

1 Subcultures develop when people who struggle to find a place in 'normal' society come together and form a group identity.

Extra activity

If students need extra support with the meaning of vocabulary in the text that may be new for them, write the following definitions and line numbers on the board. Ask students to find verbs in the text that match the definitions.

1 be likely (line 3: tend)
2 try hard to do something that is difficult (line 4: struggle)
3 be brave enough (line 6: dare)
4 to behave as if something is true when you know that it isn't (line 8: pretend)
5 change (line 13: adapt)

4

- Tell students to use what they can remember from the first time they read the article and their general knowledge to match the sentence halves.
- **Optional step** Less confident students could do this with a partner.
- Students read the article again to check their answers.

5

- Direct students to the instructions. Elicit that the 'infinitive' form of a verb is *to* + verb (e.g. *to appeal*) and that the *-ing* form of a verb is a verb with *-ing* at the end of it (e.g. *designing*).
- Students read the article again and look for examples of verbs that are followed by another verb, marking them according to whether the second verb is an infinitive or verb + *-ing*.
- Students read the Grammar box to check their answers.

GRAMMAR NOTES

Verb patterns with infinitive and *-ing*

Check that students are aware that patterns with infinitive and *-ing* are only relevant for instances where one verb directly follows another verb. The first verb in these two-verb combinations are usually verbs that describe thoughts or feelings (e.g. *can't stand*, *enjoy*, *expect*), or reporting verbs describing what someone said or did (e.g. *suggest*, *recommend*, *arrange*). There are no rules as such for whether a verb should be followed by an infinitive, *-ing* or *to* + *-ing*, so students will need to memorize these combinations. Using the verb combinations in writing or speaking is an excellent way of committing the patterns to memory.
Direct students to the second category in the Grammar box (verbs followed by *to* + *-ing*) and elicit or explain that *to* is typically followed by the present participle of the verb, but there are exceptions to this rule where *to* is followed by verb + *-ing*. The most common examples of these exceptions are *be / get used to* + verb + *-ing* and *look forward to* + verb + *-ing*.

For further information and practice, see **Grammar reference Unit 10B** on page 151 of the Student's Book.

6 10.2

- Remind students that Alyea is the explorer they saw in the video at the start of this unit. She comes from the US, but has worked in Trinidad and Tobago and has family there.

- Play the audio and ask students to make notes on the subculture Alyea describes.
- Ask students to complete the sentences that paraphrase what Alyea said.
- Ask students to compare their answers in pairs and then invite different students to share their answers in class.
- **Optional step** Find an example of steel pan music online and play it in class so students can hear how it sounds.

Extra activity

Put students into pairs. Ask each student to write five sentence beginnings for their partner to complete with information about himself/herself. Each sentence beginning must end with one of the verbs given as examples in the Grammar box, for example: *can't stand*, *recommend*, *look forward to*, *can't wait*, *expect*. Students then say each of their sentence beginnings, for example: *I really can't stand ...*, and their partner completes it with a sentence ending that starts with a verb in the correct form, for example, *I really can't stand ... cleaning the kitchen floor at home.*

For additional practice, refer to the **Grammar activity** on page 263 of the Teacher's Book.

10B Dare to express yourself

LESSON GOALS
- Learn verb patterns with infinitive and *-ing*
- Practise aspiration of voiceless consonants
- Talk about groups and clubs you belong to

READING AND GRAMMAR

1 Look at the illustrations (a–h). What subcultures can you identify? Match each one with its name.

cosplayer e gamer g geek b hippy a
influencer c rapper f steampunk d surfer h

2 Work in pairs. What subcultures do you know about in your country?

3 Read the article about subcultures. Answer the questions.
1 Why do subcultures develop?
2 What was your favourite fact about subcultures?
3 Which subcultures would be fun to be a part of?

4 Match the beginnings of the sentences (1–4) with the endings (a–d). Then read the article again to check.
1 Subcultures tend ... b
2 Sometimes the main culture adapts subculture fashion ... c
3 The internet makes ... d
4 Cosplayers often spend weeks ... a

a ... designing their costumes.
b ... to appeal to people who find it hard to fit in.
c ... to make it more appealing to the rest of society.
d ... finding people you identify with much easier.

5 Underline the verbs in the article that are followed by infinitives. Circle the verbs followed by a verb in the *-ing* form. Then read the Grammar box.

GRAMMAR Verb patterns with infinitive and *-ing*

Verbs followed by verb + *-ing*: *can't stand, carry on, enjoy, feel like, give up, keep, make recommend, remember, suggest*
*The internet **makes finding** your group much easier.*

Verbs followed by *to* + *-ing*: *be/get used to, look forward to*
*People **look forward to showing off** their costumes.*

Verbs followed by the infinitive with *to*: *afford, arrange, can't wait, dare, deserve, expect, forget, remember*
*People can **dare to express** themselves.*

Go to page 151 for the Grammar reference.

Why so many subcultures?

Subcultures are groups of people with interests, ways of behaving, etc. that are different to the rest of society. They tend to appeal to people who struggle to find their place in 'normal' society. Within the space of the group, people can dare to express themselves. From the outside it may appear as though members of a group are pretending to be something they are not, but the more likely truth is that subcultures allow people to be who they really are.

Members of a subculture may identify with exciting clothes or unusual music, but often the main culture will adapt these to make them more acceptable. This happened with hip hop and now its influence can be seen in everyday street fashion and pop music.

The internet makes finding your group much easier, but members of subcultures still love getting together. 130,000 cosplayers are expected to show up at the San Diego Comic Con each year, dressed as their favourite cartoon characters and superheroes. People look forward to showing off their costumes and some spend weeks designing them.

Many subcultures develop around a hobby or passion. Surfing and skateboarding are attractive because of the sport as much as the lifestyle and attitude. In a way, there are as many subcultures as there are interests!

EXPLORE MORE!
Search online for a subculture you've never heard of and watch a video online of members talking about it.

122

PRONUNCIATION

7 10.3
- Tell students to look at the Clear voice box.
- Tell students to put a hand in front of their mouth, say the words *pan*, *cot*, *tear* (/teə(r)/) and check if they can feel the burst of air on their hand.
- Play the audio so students can listen and identify which word in each pair has an aspirated /p/, /k/ and /t/ sound in it. Check that students are aware that air leaves the mouth when you say the /p/, /k/ and /t/ sound in both of the words in each pair, but they need to listen to the word where more air leaves the mouth.
- **Optional step** To help students feel the difference more clearly, ask them to hold a piece of paper in front of their mouths and aspirate the consonants. They should be able to see more movement in the paper when they do this.
- Ask students to compare their answers in pairs and then practise saying the words out loud.
- Check answers as a class by inviting different students to say the word in each pair that is aspirated or say the two words in each pair and demonstrate the difference between the pronunciation of the /p/, /k/ or /t/ sound in each one. Model and drill the pronunciation of any words where students struggle to aspirate the /p/, /k/ or /t/ sound.

PRONUNCIATION NOTES

Aspirating /p/, /k/ and /t/

Aspiration occurs in many different languages and dialects from all over the world, although the letters that it is used with vary.

In English, aspiration happens only when the /p/, /k/ or /t/ sound appears in a stressed syllable and is followed by a vowel. Remind students that a /k/ sound may not always be represented by a letter 'k', for example re**c**ommend (ˌrekəˈmend).

NATIONAL GEOGRAPHIC EXPLORER

6 10.2 Listen to Alyea Pierce talk about a subculture in Trinidad and Tobago. Then complete the sentences with the correct form of the verbs in brackets.

1 As soon as you arrive in Trinidad, you can't help noticing (notice) the humidity.
2 Alyea remembers seeing (see) very diverse people of different ages and races on the streets.
3 Alyea kept wondering (wonder) why some people had two sticks in their back pockets.
4 The local musicians, called pannists, tend to vary (vary) in age.
5 You can expect to recognize (recognize) pannists easily because of these metal sticks they carry.

Pannists in the Shell Invaders Steel Orchestra perform in Trinidad and Tobago.

PRONUNCIATION

7 10.3 Look at the Clear voice box and listen to the words. With which words (column A or B) does more air leave the mouth in the sounds /p/, /k/ and /t/ in bold? Practise saying the words.

CLEAR VOICE
Aspirating /p/, /k/ and /t/

Aspiration is the quick burst of air that comes out of your mouth when you say certain sounds. It occurs on sounds /p/, /k/ and /t/ in stressed syllables, when they are followed by a vowel, e.g. *tend* /tend/, *occur* /əˈkɜː/ but not *appreciate* /əˈpriːʃieɪt/. Put your hand in front of your mouth and say *pan, cot, tear*; you should feel a burst of air on your hand.

A	B
keep	re**c**ommend
pre**t**end	presen**t**
people	hi**pp**y
cosplay	expe**ct**

The four pairs show that the voiceless consonant is only aspirated if it is at the start of a stressed syllable.

SPEAKING

8 Use the words to form questions. Then write two of your own questions using verbs from Exercise 5.

1 which / subcultures / remember / see / when you were young?
2 what / look forward / do / after studies or work?
3 ever / feel like / join / clubs or groups? Which?
4 enjoy / dress up / in costumes?
5 which subcultures / you / struggle / understand? Why?

9 Work in pairs. Ask and answer the questions from Exercise 8.

10 Tell your partner about any groups or clubs you belong to or belonged to in the past. What attracted you to the group?

11 Share the information you learned about your partner with other classmates.

Ex 8
1 Which subcultures do you remember seeing when you were young?
2 What do you look forward to doing after your studies or work?
3 Do you ever feel like joining any clubs or groups? Which?
4 Do / Would you enjoy dressing up in costumes?
5 Which subcultures do you struggle to understand? Why?

123

For additional practice, refer to the **Pronunciation activity** on page 277 of the Teacher's Book.

SPEAKING

8

- Direct students to the words and elicit that each question will include a verb directly followed by another verb. Students will therefore have to decide whether the second verb should be in the infinitive, verb + *-ing* or *to* + *-ing* form.
- Students use the words to make questions. Tell them to look at the Grammar box again to check that the second verb in each question is in the correct form.
- Ask students to use their own ideas to write two more questions that include the verb patterns from Exercise 5.
- Ask students to compare their answers in pairs and then check answers as a class.

9

- Put students into pairs. Give them one or two minutes to think about their answers to the questions.
- Students take turns to ask and answer the questions in their pairs. Encourage students to explain their answers and, where appropriate, tell anecdotes about their experiences.
- Monitor students' conversations and make a note of any particularly good or interesting answers. Ask students to share these in class.

10

- Ask students to think about which groups and clubs they currently belong to or have belonged to in the past. Tell students that 'groups and clubs' can be understood as any collection of people who either belong to the same subculture or share the same interests or values.
- Students choose two or three interesting examples of groups and clubs they belong to or belonged to in the past and share these with their partner, explaining what attracted them to the group.
- Tell students to either memorize or make notes on what their partner tells them so they can use this information in Exercise 11.

11

- Put students into groups and ask them to take turns to talk about the groups or clubs that their partner from Exercise 10 mentioned. Alternatively, invite different students to talk about their partner from Exercise 10 in class.

For additional practice, refer to the **Communication activity** on page 230 of the Teacher's Book.

EXPLORE MORE!

Students look for information about other subcultures online. Students could do an open search 'List of subcultures' to identify a subculture they have never heard of. Alternatively, they could search for a specific subculture from a particular country or area of interest (e.g. a musical genre). Once students have identified the subculture, they do a video search so they can watch its members talking about it. Ask students to make notes on the key features of the subcultures and when, where and how it developed. They could then share what they learned in small groups.

See **Workbook** pages 86–87 for extra practice.

LESSON GOALS

- **LISTENING** A main aim is for students to listen to an interview with a National Geographic explorer and practise understanding the use of ellipsis.
- **VOCABULARY** A further main aim is for students to learn and practise using collocations for talking about identity and belonging to a group.
- **PRONUNCIATION** A sub-aim is for students to practise pronouncing /th/ clearly.
- **GRAMMAR** A further sub-aim is for students to learn and practise using *the* when talking about groups of people or things.
- **SPEAKING** The speaking aim is for students to talk about different cultural influences in their lives.

SPEAKING

1

- Give students time to read the infographic and think about their answers to the questions. Check their understanding of 'diverse' (consisting of people with many different ethnicities, nationalities, socio-economic backgrounds, etc.).
- Students discuss the questions in pairs, justifying and explaining their choices.
- **Optional step** Ask students if they have visited the countries in the infographic and whether they noticed any examples of the diversity described in the infographic while they were there.

Extra activity

Ask students to do some online research to find out how diverse their home town / city, region or country is. Suggest that they look for information about the different ethnic groups who live there, the different languages that are spoken, the number of residents who are foreigners, and so on. Students then use the information to produce a summary of what they found out. Alternatively, if students are not able to go online, they could have small group discussions about how diverse they think the place where they are currently living is and what places of interest you can visit there.

10C My different cultures

LESSON GOALS
- Understand ellipsis in spoken language
- Talk about your cultural identity
- Say /th/ clearly
- Understand when to use *the* when talking about groups of people or things

Lia Nahomi Kajiki practising kyūdō, Japanese archery.

SPEAKING

1 Look at the infographic. Discuss the questions.

1 How diverse is your city or town compared to the places in the infographic?
2 Which place(s) mentioned in the infographic would you like to visit? Why?

Some of the most diverse places on Earth

Bareilly, India There are over 40 festivals a year, each celebrating the different peoples that live there.

Brussels, Belgium Only about a third of 'Brusselians' are Belgian, so as well as Belgian waffles, you can try cuisine from all around the world.

Dubai, United Arab Emirates Meeting a local in this modern and diverse city can be a challenge when 86% of residents are foreigners.

São Paulo, Brazil Over 2.3 million immigrants from all over the world, including Portugal, Spain and Japan, arrived in São Paulo between 1870 and 2010.

Sydney, Australia With 250 languages spoken on its streets, it's one of the most linguistically diverse places in the world.

LISTENING

NATIONAL GEOGRAPHIC EXPLORER

2 10.4 Listen to Lia Nahomi Kajiki talk about her cultural roots. Does she feel Brazilian, Japanese or a bit of both? a bit of both, but mostly Brazilian

3 10.5 Listen to three short extracts from the interview. Which words are left out after the word in bold (1–3)? Why did the speaker leave them out? Look at the Listening skill box to check.

1 You're of a mixed Brazilian and Japanese background: which of the **two** do you feel you most fit in with?
2 I think **some don't**, especially my father, who was born in Japan.
3 One **thing** is football, especially during the World Cup!

LISTENING SKILL
Understanding ellipsis

In spoken conversation, not all words are said. This is usually because they were mentioned before and so the sentence can be understood without them. This is called ellipsis. The speaker might leave out ...

a noun phrase: *which of the two (backgrounds)*

a verb and object: *I think some don't (feel 75% Brazilian and 25% Japanese).*

part of the question (in your response): *One thing (that brings the nation together) is football.*

124

LISTENING

2 10.4

- Remind students that they watched National Geographic explorer Lia in the video at the start of this unit. Ask students to read the instructions and check their understanding of 'roots' in the context of culture or nationality/ethnicity (the place or culture that someone, or their parents or grandparents, etc. originally comes from and/or feels a connection to).
- Play the audio and ask students to listen and notice how Lia identifies herself.
- Ask students to compare answers in pairs and, if possible, give examples of things Lia said in the interview that support their answer.

VOCABULARY NOTES

archery /ˈɑːtʃəri/ = a sport that involves using a bow to shoot arrows at a target

indigenous /ɪnˈdɪdʒɪnəs/ = describing people, animals or plants that are native to a particular area

3 10.5

- Play the audio and ask students to listen for the sentences (1–3).

4 10.4 Listen to the full interview again. Are the sentences true (T) or false (F)?

1 It's easy for Lia to identify with one culture. F
2 Lia feels she fits in more with Brazilian culture. T
3 The way she expresses her opinion is influenced by her Japanese origins. T
4 Lia doesn't share the same values as the other people who practise kyūdō. F
5 Lia felt like an outsider when she was at school. F
6 Lia's father was raised in Japan. F
7 Many people in Brazil are of mixed cultural background. T
8 Lia likes that Brazil is so culturally diverse. T

VOCABULARY

5 Look at the sentences in Exercise 4 again. Underline the collocations that talk about identity and 'belonging' to a group.

6 Complete the sentences to make them true for you. Then share with a partner.

1 Generally speaking, I think / don't think I fit in well with ________.
2 I share the same values as ________. For example, we ________.
3 There are some aspects of my culture, such as ________, that I don't identify with.
4 One person I know / have heard about who comes from a mixed background is ________.
5 I live / don't live in a culturally diverse place. For example, ________.

Go to page 139 for the Vocabulary reference.

PRONUNCIATION

7 10.6 Listen to three different speakers. How does each speaker say the words *think* and *the*?

8 Look at the Clear voice box. Which pronunciation of *th* do you prefer? Why? Practise it with the sentences in Exercises 4 and 6.

CLEAR VOICE
Saying *th*

In standard British and American English, *th* is said with the tongue between your teeth: *think* /θɪŋk/ and *the* /ðə/. But many people say 'th' as /f/ and /v/, or /t/ and /d/. This change will not make your pronunciation less clear. However, avoid mixing different pronunciation.

GRAMMAR

9 Read the text. Can you guess which city from the infographic in Exercise 1 it's about? Brussels

> You can try dishes from all around the world there, but the dishes typical of this city are fries with mayonnaise, beef stew and waffles. Interestingly, most people there are foreigners, such as people from France, Romania or Morocco. The locals only make up about one third of the residents.

10 Look at the underlined plural nouns in Exercise 9. When is *the* used? When is *the* not used? Read the Focus on box to check.

FOCUS ON *the* **with groups of people and things**

With plural nouns, you typically don't need *the*.
You can try dishes from all around the world there.
However, if you're referring to a specific set of things or people, you do need to use *the*.
... but the dishes typical of this city are ...

Use *the* with *majority, some of, many of* and *none of*, e.g. *the majority of people, some of the people*. Don't use *the* with *most, some, many* or *no*, e.g. *most people*.

When referring to groups of people, always use *the* with an adjective (*the Japanese*), but not with plural nouns (*Brazilians, Australians*).

Go to page 152 for the Focus on reference.

11 Complete the sentences with *the* or *X* when no article is needed.

1 __The__ majority of people who live in my city have been here for __X__ generations.
2 It's nice how __X__ different cultures and languages mix together in New York.
3 Hospitality is typically important to both __X__ Brazilians and __the__ Japanese.

SPEAKING

12 Work in pairs. Talk about the different cultural influences in your life. Do you think they've influenced who you are? Use these topics and your own ideas.

books you read   films and series you watch   meeting people from other cultures   sports and hobbies   travelling   your family's origins

125

- Ask students to read the sentences again and consider which words could come after the words in bold. Tell them to use the information that comes before the words in bold to help them identify what could follow them.
- Ask students to think about why the speaker left these words out.
- **Optional step** Less confident students could work with a partner to complete the task.
- Ask students to compare answers in pairs, explaining to their partner how they decided what the omitted words were and why they think they were omitted.
- Tell students to look at the Listening skill box to confirm their answers.

Answers
1 (Japanese and Brazilian) backgrounds
2 members of my family, feel 75% Brazilian and 25% Japanese 3 that brings this diverse nation / us together

4 10.4

- Ask students to the read the sentences before they listen.
- Play the audio again so students can decide if the sentences are true or false.
- Ask students to compare their answers in pairs and then either check answers as a class or ask students to use the audioscript on page 170 to check their answers.

VOCABULARY

5

- Students read the sentences from Exercise 4 again and identify the collocations in each sentence.
- Check answers as a class and elicit the meanings of each collocation to check students' understanding of them.

Extra activity 1

Tell students to put the collocations from Exercise 4 into the correct category: How we're similar; How we differ; Where we're from. Tell them that one of the phrases can go in two categories.

Answers:
How we're similar: identify with, fit in (with), share the same values as
How we differ: felt like an outsider, mixed cultural background, culturally diverse
Where we're from: (Japanese) origins, raised in, mixed cultural background

Extra activity 2

Put students into pairs to practise the verb-preposition collocations they identified in Exercise 5 (*identify with; fit in with; influenced by; share the same values as; felt like an outsider, raised in*). One person in each pair says part of a collocation and the other says the complete phrase. For example:
Student A: *identify*
Student B: *identify to a culture?*
Student A: *Almost! It's 'identify with'.*

6

- Tell students that they are now going to practise using the collocations they identified in Exercise 5.
- Ask students to read the sentences and think about their own experiences and ideas. Check students are aware that where there are two options separated by a forward slash, they should delete one of the two options, according to what is appropriate for them.
- **Optional step** Tell students that if they do not feel comfortable with completing some of the sentences (e.g. 1, 2 and 3) with personal information, they can make up their answers instead.

- Ask students to read their completed sentences out loud to a partner.
- **Optional step** Students comment on and ask questions about each other's completed sentences. They could try to identify one thing they have in common and one thing that is different about the two of them.

For further information and practice, see **Vocabulary reference Unit 10** on page 139 of the Student's Book.

For additional practice, refer to the **Vocabulary activity** on page 242 of the Teacher's Book.

PRONUNCIATION

7 10.6

- Tell students that they are going to hear three different speakers say the word 'think' three times and the word 'the' three times. Ask students to notice differences in the way the speakers say them.
- Play the audio so students can listen and notice the differences.
- Ask students to compare answers in pairs and then check answers as a class by inviting different students to describe or verbally replicate the differences.
- Confirm that each of the speakers pronounced 'think' and 'the' differently. Check that students are aware that all of these variations are valid.

Answers
Speaker 1: /θɪŋk/ and /ðə/
Speaker 2: /tɪŋk/ and /də/
Speaker 3: /fɪŋk/ and /və/

8

- Explain that the /θ/ phonemic symbol is for the /th/ sound you hear in *think* and the /ð/ phonemic symbol is for the /th/ sound you hear in *the*.
- Ask students to look at the Clear voice box.
- Elicit that speaker 1 from Exercise 7 pronounced the *th* sound as it is said in standard British or American English /θɪŋk/, while speakers 2 and 3 used non-standard variations of the *th* sound.
- Ask students to decide which pronunciation of the *th* sound they prefer.
- Students practise saying sentences 3, 4, 6 and 8 in Exercise 4 and sentences 1 and 3 in Exercise 6 with a partner, using their preferred pronunciation for the *th* sound.

PRONUNCIATION NOTES

Saying *th*
The pronunciation of the *th* sound is challenging for many learners of English, with the exception of those who have a similar sound in their first language, notably speakers of European Spanish. It is important to make it clear to students that they will usually still be understood even if they do not pronounce the *th* sound as /θ/ (as in *think*) or /ð/ (as in *the*). You can point out that some first language users of English do not pronounce the *th* sound in this way. Some Irish speakers of English will typically use the /t/ sound instead of the /θ/ sound, for example. There are a small number of words where the use of either an /f/ or an /θ/ sound can make a difference to the meaning of a word, for example *fort* (fɔːt) and *thought* (θɔːt). However, generally the meaning of the word is clear from the context, even if a non-standard pronunciation of the *th* sound is used.

GRAMMAR

9

- Ask students to look at the infographic in Exercise 1 again to remind themselves of the places in it.
- Students read the text and use the information from the infographic to decide which place it describes.

10

- Ask students to look at the plural nouns that are underlined in the text in Exercise 9 and notice whether or not they are preceded by 'the'.
- Tell students to think about why 'the' is used in front of some of the underlined nouns, but not others.
- **Optional step** Ask students to discuss their ideas about why 'the' is used or not used in pairs.
- Ask students to read the information in the Focus on box to find out if their ideas are correct.

For further information and practice, see **Focus on reference Unit 10C** on page 152 of the Student's Book.

11

- Ask students to read the sentences and decide whether 'the' or no article should be used in the gaps.
- Tell students to refer to the information in the Focus on box if they are unsure whether an article should be used.
- Ask students to compare their answers in pairs.

For additional practice, refer to the **Focus on activity** on page 264 of the Teacher's Book.

SPEAKING

12

- Ask students to read the topics in the box and use some of them to brainstorm ideas about their cultural influences. Tell them to think of examples of each topic that has influenced them, for example a relative whose culture has had a big impact on them, a genre of book that plays a significant role in their lives, or a friend from another culture who has let them into that culture.
- Check that students are also aware that they can choose topics that are not in the box if they feel that these would be a better fit for their own cultural influences.
- Put students into pairs and ask them to talk about their cultural influences using the topics they have prepared.

See **Workbook** pages 88–90 for extra practice.

LESSON GOALS

- **SPEAKING** The main aim of this lesson is to introduce students to the false assumptions that people can make about those with different identities, backgrounds or behaviours and strategies for dealing with these assumptions. Students then use what they have learned to analyse and discuss a difference in viewpoint or misunderstanding that they have experienced. This skill will help them deal with assumptions that they may make or people may make about them.

WRITING AND SPEAKING

1

- Direct students to the example of a word cloud under the instructions.
- Ask students to use the categories given or brainstorm ideas about the different groups that they belong to and then decide which are very important, quite important and the least important to them.
- Students can draw their word clouds on paper with either pens or pencils. Remind them to draw the words so their size reflects the groups' importance to them, i.e. the most important groups appear the largest.
- **Optional step** If possible, students could use an online platform to create their word clouds. Searching online for 'word cloud generator' will produce results for websites where they can do this. Depending on which word cloud generator students decide to use, they may need to enter some words several times so they appear larger than others. For example, they could type the words for very important groups three times, the words for quite important groups twice and the words for the least important groups once.

2

- Direct students to the instructions and the table. Elicit or explain the meaning of 'assumption' (a belief you hold although you have no evidence to support it).
- Ask students to read the model answer to show them what they need to do.
- Students choose one of their groups from Exercise 1 and think of a false assumption people make about it and a fact that challenges that assumption.
- Students use the expressions in the table to write their sentences individually.

3

- Put students into groups of four or five. Ask them to share their sentences from Exercise 2 with each other.
- Students listen to their group members and comment on which of the false assumptions they have heard before.

Extra activity

Put students into pairs or small groups to discuss why they think we make assumptions about other people. For example, is it because this is part of human nature and just something that everybody does or is it because of specific experiences we have had? They can then also discuss the situations when they think people are the most likely to make assumptions, for example: when we meet someone for the first time or do not know them very well, or when their appearance or where they're from suggests that they are different to us (or the same as us).

4

- Tell students they are now going to identify false assumptions made in three different situations.
- Ask students to read the situations and think about what false assumption Vihaan, Marlies and Louis are making about other people's behaviour and what the actual reason for this behaviour could be.
- Students discuss their ideas in pairs.

Sample answers

1 Vihaan assumes the teacher is bored. Other possible reasons: she is concentrating on what Vihaan is saying; her understanding of a 'discussion' is that one person speaks while the other person listens with full concentration and then when the other person has clearly finished speaking, you take your turn to say something.

2 Marlies assumes that Gautam is paying because he thinks she doesn't have money to pay. Other possible reasons: he sees paying the whole bill as a friendly or romantic gesture; he does not place a lot of importance on who pays the bill and had simply offered to pay the bill without realizing the possible symbolism of this.

3 Louis thinks the other people are rude calling his baby fat. Other possible reasons: they believe that a fat baby is a healthy, happy baby and they are giving Louis' baby a compliment.

Extra activity

Put students into pairs or small groups. Ask them to discuss whether the false assumptions Vihaan, Marlies and Louis made are the types of assumptions that they would typically make and why or why not. Then they could discuss other possible scenarios where misunderstandings like the ones with Vihaan, Marlies and Louis could occur.

MY VOICE

COMMUNICATION SKILL NOTES

Dealing with assumptions

The making of assumptions is a normal feature of human behaviour. We are all influenced by our life experience and the ideas of what is or is not acceptable that have been instilled in us from a young age, so we might believe certain things to be true, even if we have no real evidence for this. Students may encounter false assumptions being made about them or make false assumptions about other people when they come into contact with people from different age groups, backgrounds, ethnic groups, genders, etc. In these situations, an awareness of whether you could be making a false assumption and how to avoid doing that and/or adapt your behaviour, can help students avoid conflict and tension and therefore build strong relationships with people from other backgrounds or with different points of view.

5 ▶ 10.2

- Tell students that they are going to find out more information about analysing assumptions and how to avoid letting them lead to misunderstandings with another person.
- Students read the five steps they are going to put in order.
- Play the video and ask students to number each step they hear and make notes on the key points that are mentioned about each step.
- Students share and compare their notes about each of the steps in pairs. They can add any important information from their partner's notes that they missed to their notes.

6 🎧 10.7

- Ask students to look at the advice in the Communication skill box.
- Tell students that they are going to hear Vihaan analysing what happened in situation 1 from Exercise 4 with a friend. Ask students to quickly read the situation again before they listen.
- Play the audio so students can identify which steps from the Communication skill box Vihaan and his friend follow when they are analysing the situation.
- Students discuss the steps that Vihaan and Amanda went through in pairs.

10D Dealing with assumptions

LESSON GOALS
- Talk about false assumptions
- Consider differences in behaviour and the reasons for them
- Learn to deal with assumptions to avoid misunderstandings

WRITING AND SPEAKING

1 Create a word cloud showing the different groups that you identify with. Use the size of the words to show which groups are the most important to you (biggest = most important).

Use these categories or your own ideas: age, ethnic group, interests, nationality, physical and mental ability, profession, gender.

WOMAN
STAR TREK FAN
PERSON WITH HEARING LOSS
YOUNG ADULT
MALAYSIAN
ENGINEERING STUDENT

2 Choose one of your groups from Exercise 1. Use one expression from the table to write about a false assumption that other people often make about that group. Then use one expression to challenge this assumption.

False assumptions about people	Challenging the assumption
Many people assume that …	In fact, …
People typically think/ believe that …	Even so, I think it's important to understand that …

Many people assume *people with hearing loss can't speak.* ***In fact****, that isn't true for most deaf and hard of hearing people. We can all communicate with hearing people, but we might need you to be patient.*

3 In groups, share what you have written. Which assumptions about your classmates' groups have you heard before?

4 Work in pairs. Read the three situations (1–3). What assumptions does each person make about the behaviour of the other person? What are other possible reasons for the other person's behaviour?

1 Vihaan is doing a PhD and visits his supervisor to discuss his research project. Whenever Vihaan begins talking about the project, the supervisor closes her eyes, as if she is asleep. When Vihaan finishes speaking, she opens her eyes and makes comments or asks a question. 'I don't know what's wrong with her. She falls asleep every time I speak. Am I just boring?'

2 Gautam and Marlies are having dinner together for the first time. At the end of the meal, the waiter puts the bill on the table. Gautam takes the bill and offers to pay for everything. Marlies looks offended and says: 'Why are you paying?! Do you think I can't pay for myself? I have money.'

3 Louis and his baby daughter are visiting a friend in another country. When they meet people in the street, many stop to admire his daughter and comment on how fat she is. Louis is offended: 'Do they not realize how rude that is?'

126

7

- Put students into pairs and ask them to read situations 2 and 3 from Exercise 4 again to remind themselves of the false assumptions that were made.
- Students brainstorm and make notes on Marlies and Louis' possible answers to the questions, using the prompts to help them.
- **Optional step** Less confident students could just analyse one of the situations.
- Monitor what students are saying and check that they are following the steps from the Communication skill box.

Sample answer

Marlies: 1 I'm surprised but also a bit offended and angry. 2 I'm assuming Gautam thinks I wouldn't be able to pay for the meal, that I don't have the money. 3 Perhaps Gautam offered to pay because he is trying to be polite and nice; maybe for him it's normal to pay the bill the first time he has dinner with someone. 4 I kind

MY VOICE

5 10.2 **Watch the video. Put the five steps for dealing with assumptions in the order they are mentioned. Then take notes to add more information about each step.**

a Make connections with the other person's behaviour. 4

b Consider what assumptions you are making about the other person. 2

c Be aware of your feelings. 1

d Analyse the reasons behind the other person's behaviour. 3

e Adapt your behaviour. 5

6 10.7 **Look at the Communication skill box. Then listen to Vihaan and a friend analysing his situation from Exercise 4. Which steps from the box do they follow?**

they follow all 5 steps in the order they appear in the box

COMMUNICATION SKILL

Dealing with assumptions

When people from different backgrounds communicate, they may make assumptions that get in the way of the communication process. To understand why a misunderstanding may have occurred, try these steps:

Be aware – How am I feeling? What was I expecting?

Don't judge – What assumptions am I making? Could my assumptions be wrong?

Analyse – Why is the other person doing/saying this?

Make connections – Do I relate to the other person's reasons? What behaviour of mine is similar to theirs?

Try to adapt – Can I live with their behaviour now that I understand it better? Is there anything I can do to adapt my behaviour to make the relationship work better?

7 **Work in pairs. Imagine you are Marlies and Louis from Exercise 4. Use the steps in the Communication skill box to deal with assumptions they made about the other people in the scenarios.**

Step 1: I'm feeling ...

Step 2: I'm assuming Gautam ...

Step 3: Perhaps Gautam offered to pay because ...

SPEAKING AND WRITING

8 **OWN IT!** **Look at the list of contexts where differences in viewpoint and misunderstandings can occur. Which ones have you experienced?**

- Between people from different generations, e.g. children and parents/grandparents.
  When I was younger, we would never dare talk back to our parents.
- Between people from different countries, e.g. in tourist areas or in international business situations.
  I don't get why they smile so much in a serious situation. It feels really fake.
- Between people from different regions of the same country, e.g. a company where people from different regions work together.
  It's so annoying they never seem to say what they think; where I come from we just speak our minds.
- Between people from different subcultures, e.g. football fans, book lovers, rock fans.
  They're all just so violent and unpleasant; it's scary.
- Between people from different professions, e.g. teachers, plumbers, doctors.
  He lost me after the first sentence – all those medical terms.

9 **Work in pairs or on your own. Discuss or make notes about one of your experiences from Exercise 8, explaining what happened and what the misunderstanding was. Then answer the questions.**

1 How did you feel in that situation?

2 What assumptions did you make about the other person? Do you think they made any about you?

3 What might have been the real reasons for the behaviour?

4 How could you or the other person have adapted your behaviour to avoid misunderstanding?

10 **Share your experiences in groups or work individually and write a short summary of the situation.**

127

of get that; when meeting someone for the first time I also try to be as polite and nice as possible. 5 I can certainly live with Gautam paying for the meal; but perhaps next time I can offer to pay, or we can split the bill; it would also be good to discuss why splitting the bill is important for me. Louis: 1 I'm offended because people are saying my baby is fat. I want them to compliment her. 2 I'm assuming that 'fat' isn't a compliment when maybe it is. 3 Surely people wouldn't be negative about a baby, so I must be wrong. 4 Yes, I remember calling a friend's baby 'chubby' but I meant that he was looking really healthy. 5 I can live with the fact that people think my daughter looks healthy and I will ask a friend if my initial assumption was wrong.

SPEAKING AND WRITING

8 OWN IT!

- Ask students to read the list of contexts and the example misunderstandings.
- Ask students to identify which types of misunderstandings or differences in viewpoint they have experienced.

9

- Students decide if they are going to work individually or in pairs. Some students may prefer to write down their answers if they don't feel comfortable discussing the topic.
- **Optional step** Less confident students might benefit from working individually so they can take some time to think about and make notes about the situation. More confident students should be able to talk about the situation they chose in a more spontaneous way with a partner.
- Students talk about or make notes about their chosen situation, then do the same for questions 1–4.

10

- If students are keen to practise verbally summarizing their answers from Exercise 9, put them into groups to do this. If students will benefit more from practising writing a summary of their answers, they can do this individually instead.
- **Optional step** Instead of writing a summary, students could write a dialogue based on the experiences they discussed in Exercise 8. Monitor students while they are talking or writing to check that they have analysed the situation and come up with a way of avoiding the misunderstanding and that they are communicating clearly and accurately.

Extra activity

Put students into pairs. Ask them to prepare a roleplay based on one of the situations they talked about or summarized in Exercise 10. In the roleplay, students take on the roles of the two people involved in the situation. They roleplay the situation in which the difference in viewpoint or misunderstanding occurred, and then roleplay what the speakers could have said or done to adapt to their partner's behaviour and avoid a misunderstanding.

For additional practice, refer to the **Communication activity** on page 231 of the Teacher's Book.

LESSON GOALS

- **WRITING** The aim of the lesson is to guide students to produce a report summarizing information they have collected from a survey about cultural attractions. The reading text provides a model. Students practise the writing skill of expressing numbers approximately.

SPEAKING

1

- Tell students to read the list of places in the box and choose the ones that they would most like to visit or experience.
- In pairs, students say which things they would like to experience and why.

Extra activity

Ask students to think of an example of one of the items from the box that they have experienced. In pairs or groups, students describe the place, event or food. They can mention whether or not they would recommend visiting or trying it, giving reasons for their answers.

READING FOR WRITING

2

- Ask students to read the report to find the answers to the questions.
- Check answers as a class.

Answers

1 an online survey of local residents
2 architecture and historical buildings, museums, markets, festivals and events, sports events, typical food, art and entertainment

3

- Ask students to read the text again.
- Students complete each heading with one word.

4

- Tell students to read the relative clauses, notice whether they refer to a place, a thing or people and then notice or highlight key words in them.
- Students match the relative clauses to the correct gaps.
- Students compare their answers in pairs and then check answers as a class.

10E Cultural highlights

LESSON GOALS

- Express numbers approximately (e.g. *just under a third*)
- Design and carry out a survey
- Write a report about cultural attractions

SPEAKING

1 Work in pairs. Which aspects of cultural interest would you make sure you experienced on a trip to a new region? Why?

architecture and historical buildings
art and entertainment festivals and events
markets and shops museums music and dance
sport venues theatres theme parks typical food

READING FOR WRITING

2 Read the report and answer the questions.

1 Where does the information for the report come from?
2 Which aspects of cultural interest does it mention?

3 Read the report again. Complete the headings (1–4) with one word.

Recommendations for cultural highlights of the Muscat region

The aim of this report is to recommend places and activities of cultural interest in the Muscat region in Oman. It is based on feedback from local residents, who responded to an online survey.

The top (1) sites/destinations/attractions

The vast majority of respondents agreed that the most important cultural destination is the Grand Mosque, (a) ____1____. Over half of those questioned also mentioned the Natural History Museum and the Mutrah Souq market (b) ____2____. A small number said that the Sultan's Palace is the best place to visit.

Festivals and other (2) events/celebrations

Oman has a rich cultural heritage in terms of celebrations and events. As might be expected, the event that most respondents mentioned is the Muscat Festival, (c) ____5____, although the annual highlight for a large number of people (d) ____6____ is the cycling race *Tour of Oman*, which goes through Muscat.

Local (3) food/dishes/cuisine

By far the largest percentage of those surveyed stated that rice and curry should be the defining food of the region, (e) ____4____. Several people mentioned *Kabsa* – made with rice, meat and spices – as the national dish, though there was disagreement here. There was also little agreement as to which is the best restaurant in the capital although a few chose *Bait Al Luban* to represent the most typical cuisine.

Regional (4) arts/entertainment

Unsurprisingly, the most popular choice for an entertainment venue was the Royal Opera House, even though the building has only been open for about ten years. Of the works of art on public display in the city, respondents identified the National Museum as the best location for learning about Oman's artistic heritage, (f) ____3____.

Port Sultan Qaboos waterfront in Muscat, Oman.

128

5

- Ask students to read the questions and the example answers to clarify what types of words they need to look for.
- Students scan the report for the relevant nouns, phrases and verbs.

Answers

1 respondents, those questioned, those surveyed, people, a few, a small number
2 mentioned, said, stated, chose, identified

6

- Students look at the Writing skill box.
- Students match the expressions from the box with the percentages (1–6) and then compare their answers in pairs.
- Students scan the report for other ways to express numbers approximately.

Answers

1 Only a tiny percentage ...; 2 A small number; 3 One in four; 4 Roughly a third; 5 Just under half ...; 6 The vast majority ...
Other expressions used: over half, most respondents, a large number of people, by far the largest percentage, several people, a few

4 Choose from the relative clauses (1–6) the one that best fits each space in the report (a–f).

1 whose five towers overlook the city
2 where you can buy souvenirs and gifts
3 which includes beautiful jewellery, traditional costumes and musical instruments
4 which is situated on the Indian Ocean and is influenced by Indian and African cuisine
5 which takes place over a month in January and features fireworks, dancing and crafts
6 who enjoy sport

5 Work in pairs. Answer the questions.

1 In what different ways does the writer of the report refer to the people who took part in the survey? *local residents, …*
2 What different verbs are used to report what the people in the survey said? *agreed, …*

6 Look at the Writing skill box. Which expressions in the box could be used instead of the percentages (1–6)? What other ways of summarizing the survey results can you find in the report?

WRITING SKILL
Expressing numbers approximately

Reports summarize large amounts of information, often statistics, so that readers don't have to read long, boring documents full of numbers. To make them easier to read, they can also describe the statistics with vague language, e.g. 72% = *most*. Here are some other useful expressions.

The vast majority of (the respondents) …
Roughly a third (suggested) …
One in four (people said) …
Just under half of (those questioned) …
A small number of (people) …
Only a tiny percentage …

1 2%	4 34%
2 8%	5 48%
3 25%	6 93%

7 Look at the charts from a class survey. Write five sentences describing the statistics shown, using words and expressions from the Writing skill box.
As might be expected, the vast majority of those questioned preferred going to the cinema.

Class survey: Evening entertainment preferences

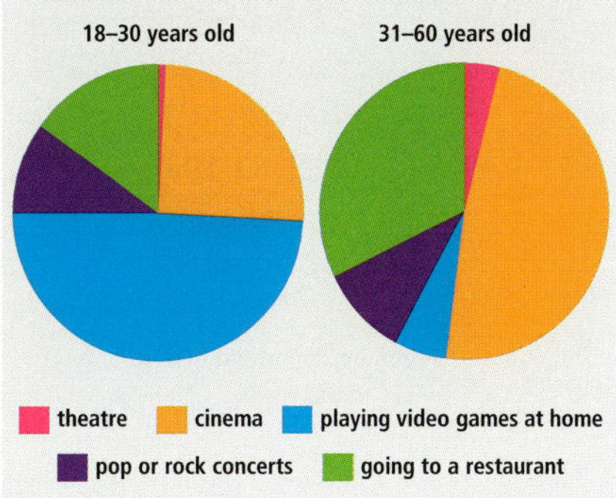

WRITING TASK

8 Work in pairs. Design a survey to ask other classmates about your city or region. Decide whether you will ask about cultural highlights in general or focus on one aspect of culture (e.g. music, food). Write five questions.
Which of the following attractions would you most recommend tourists visit: the City Museum, the castle, …?

9 Carry out your survey. Divide the work between you and your partner. Speak to as many classmates as possible. Then share your results with your partner.

10 **WRITE** Write a report summarizing the information you have collected. Divide your survey results into sections with headings. Make sure you include an introduction.

11 **CHECK** Use the checklist. I have …

- ☐ included a report title and several sections with short, clear headings.
- ☐ written an introduction explaining the purpose of the report.
- ☐ used a variety of ways of referring to the respondents to avoid repetition.
- ☐ given a clear idea of the information without boring the reader with statistics.

12 **REVIEW** Read a classmate's report. Give feedback using the checklist in Exercise 11 to help you. Which information in the report did you find the most surprising?

Go to page 134 for the Reflect and review.

EXPLORE MORE!

Find out more about a place or event of cultural interest near you. Record a two-minute mini-presentation (audio or video) about it.

129

7

- Ask students to look at the two charts and check that they understand what each one shows.
- **Optional step** Draw students' attention to the expression 'As might be expected' in the model sentence. Brainstorm other language that students could use to comment on the survey results, for example adverbs such as: *interestingly, (un) surprisingly, unexpectedly*.
- Ask students to identify five pieces of information that the charts show and use phrases from the Writing skill box to write sentences about them.
- Students share their sentences in pairs.

Sample answers

Only a tiny percentage of respondents in both age groups enjoy going to the theatre. / Just under half of respondents aged 31 or over regularly go to the cinema.

WRITING TASK

8

- Students decide together which option to choose for their survey.
- Ask students to think about what they would like to find out and write five survey questions.

9

- Give students fifteen minutes to carry out their survey.
- Students ask their questions. Tell them that each student in a pair should talk to different people.
- Remind students that they will need to write down their answers.

10 WRITE

- Tell students to start by calculating the number of people who gave each possible answer for every question.
- Students plan their report, using the text about Muscat as a model.
- Encourage students to use the language for expressing numbers approximately that they have learned.
- Students write the first draft of their report.

11 CHECK

- Students use the checklist and make changes to their reports if necessary.

12 REVIEW

- Students exchange reports with a new partner.
- Students read their partner's report and use the checklist from Exercise 11 to review it.
- Students give each other feedback on their reports, and tell their partner what information surprised them and why.

For additional practice, refer to the **Mediation activity** on page 292 of the Teacher's Book.

EXPLORE MORE!

Students find information online about the place or event they have chosen or talk to people they know who are familiar with it. Students can use the video function on the camera on their smartphone or a voice recording app to record their presentation.

For **Unit 10 Reflect and review**, see Student's Book page 134.

See **Workbook** pages 90–91 for extra practice.

See **Workbook** pages 92–93 for Units 9 and 10 Review.

VIDEO 10.1

Alyea: *While in Trinidad and Tobago, I was asked to be a judge for their annual poetry competition. As I entered the venue, I looked around and saw local artists' paintings along the walls reflecting black people and black culture. Young men and women with large curly hair, dreads, or a beautiful scarf covering their hair were sharing poems, stories and positive thoughts about the competition that evening; while others practised their poems alone in corners.*

I moved to the back of the building where the judges sat and finally reached the stage, the single microphone standing in front of a sea of chairs. As we began to start, I thought this poetry competition would have to be different from the ones in New York City. I expected a different performance style from the poets; I expected a different behaviour from the audience. But as it started … the cheers, the love, and most importantly, the snaps went through the crowds. You see, during poetry performances, the audience typically 'snap' their fingers instead of clapping. I turned around, shocked, and remembered, this is poet culture. Why would it be extremely different in Trinidad and Tobago from New York City? What was I expecting? Because at the end of the day, the snaps is what it means to be a part of a creative and powerful community. The snaps are a universal language of love.

Lia: *In 2014 I went backpacking through Europe and I experienced a wide range of different cultures. Something I particularly wanted to experience was a European open market, and I got the opportunity in many of the countries I visited. I am crazy about open markets in Brazil: I love the fuss, all the colours, the smells, tasting things for free, bargaining and chit-chatting with sellers, observing and learning different techniques the elderly use to check if a fruit is good or not. So when I was travelling through Europe, I wondered if the open markets would be very different from the ones we have here. Would they be equally busy? Would they sell similar products? Would the sellers and buyers behave in similar ways?*

I visited open markets in France, Germany, England, the Netherlands, Finland and Sweden. To my astonishment, I felt the same joy I usually feel when visiting open markets in Brazil! The food and fruits were different but the feeling and the atmosphere was identical. People were visiting the markets with their families, there were kids running and playing around, and the smells of fresh fruits, vegetables and food blended in a way I recognized.

AUDIO 10.2

Alyea: *I remember visiting Trinidad and Tobago for the first time. It was the month of August, which is hurricane season in the Caribbean. The first thing you'll notice is the humidity. And then you'll notice the heat. As my uncle gave us a tour of the country, we saw young people, older people, people of all races and religions, but there was one particular type of people that stood out most to me. As we were walking through the streets of Port of Spain, I kept seeing young people with two sticks in their back pockets. Quite curious about these people and the sticks, I turned to my uncle, and he said, 'They are called pannists. And those are their steel pan sticks. You usually always know a steel pan player because they get used to carrying those sticks everywhere with them.' So a pannist uses the metal sticks and pans like drums and drummer sticks to create music. Typically, steel pan musicians tend to range in age. In a traditional Caribbean band you can find a player as young as in their early teens and as old as 85. As a past musician myself, I always appreciate the fact that when you meet a pannist, visit their home, or even travel in their car, you will find some reminder of their instrument. From the music playing out of their speakers, the variety of sticks depending on what kind of sound they want the pan to make, the pan itself, the stand, or even just the case, pan is a way of life.*

AUDIO 10.4

Interviewer: *Hi, Lia, I want to start by talking about your cultural roots. You're of a mixed Brazilian and Japanese background: which of the two do you feel you most fit in with?*

Lia: *Sometimes, I'm not sure which. It can be very difficult to identify with one. Although I feel much more familiarity with Brazilian culture, sometimes I'm not sure how I fit in. I'm a bit lost in this mix of things, because I also feel that I sometimes behave much more like a Japanese or, you know, have a way of thinking that's more Japanese. I'd say I share some of the same typical values as the Japanese. So, yeah, I think that I'm now like seventy, maybe seventy-five, per cent Brazilian and twenty-five per cent Japanese.*

Interviewer: *That's fascinating! What about the rest of your family? Do you think they feel similar to you? Seventy-five per cent Brazilian and twenty-five per cent Japanese?*

Lia: *I think some don't, especially my father, who was born in Japan. I think he feels more the opposite to me because he grew up talking in Japanese with his family. So even though he was raised in Brazil and went to Brazilian schools, he felt a little bit like an outsider being Japanese in a Brazilian school. Now, he sees himself as Brazilian, but he always watches Japanese TV channels and he's always following the news about Japan. So I think sometimes he doesn't feel like he fits in.*

Interviewer: *You also mentioned you sometimes 'behave like a Japanese'. What does behaving like a Japanese mean to you?*

Lia: *I feel the way I express my opinion in public has been influenced by my Japanese origins. Japanese are usually very cautious in how they express themselves, and the whole culture reflects it – the language, poetry style, painting styles, etc. When I have to express my opinion, I only do it when I feel I will contribute to the conversation.*

Interviewer: *You also practise kyūdō, which is Japanese archery, right?*

Lia: *Yes. I feel it makes me feel reconnected with my Japanese origins and I feel the practice changes my perspective on the world and myself. I also love kyūdō because the people who practise it share the same values and goals in this martial art and in their lives: the 'shin-zen-bi', which means truth-goodness-beauty.*

Interviewer: *Coming back to your seventy-five per cent of culture, what does it mean for you to be Brazilian? What makes you feel like a Brazilian?*

Lia: *This is a very difficult question! Brazil is very diverse culturally. People in Brazil come from very mixed backgrounds because of our history of colonization and immigration. The South has a lot of European influence in their food, architecture, music. On the other hand, the North still keeps its indigenous roots, while the Northeast its African roots. I feel this is really beautiful and that we should celebrate this diversity.*

Interviewer: *Absolutely! But tell me, what brings such a diverse nation together?*

Lia: *One thing is football, especially during the World Cup! For me, to be a Brazilian is also to know how to enjoy life. And we all share a sense of hospitality, even with strangers and foreigners.*

AUDIO 10.5

1 Interviewer: *Hi, Lia, I want to start by talking about your cultural roots. You're of a mixed Brazilian and Japanese background: which of the two do you feel you most fit in with?*

2 Interviewer: *That's fascinating! What about the rest of your family? Do you think they feel similar to you? Seventy-five per cent Brazilian and twenty-five per cent Japanese?*

Lia: *I think some don't, especially my father, who was born in Japan.*

3 Interviewer: *Absolutely! But tell me, what brings such a diverse nation together?*

Lia: *One thing is football, especially during the World Cup!*

VIDEO 10.2

Every time communication takes place there is a chance that people interacting will not understand each other fully. There are many possible reasons, but often misunderstandings occur because the people involved make assumptions about each other which turn out to be wrong.

We might make false assumptions because of cultural differences, such as differences in social group, age, nationality, professional experience and so on. For example, different generations, nationalities or social groups may have different ideas about the roles of men and women in relationships or how people should behave in groups.

In situations where people behave differently to how you'd expect and there's a misunderstanding, there are steps you can take to try to work out what the problem is.

The first step is about recognizing how you're feeling.

Ask yourself: 'What was I expecting? How is the situation making me feel?' Increasing our awareness in this way will help us in the following steps.

Try to stop yourself from jumping to conclusions.

Say to yourself: 'What assumptions do I have that might affect how well I understand the other person?' It's important to prevent any assumptions from affecting your judgement.

Next, consider the reasons for their behaviour.

Ask yourself why the other person might be behaving this way, and what you could do to find out more. An easy way to find out is to ask the other person directly, but make sure you do so politely. You could end up offending them if your questioning is too direct or seems aggressive. Also, try to assume the other person means well, that they have positive intentions and do not mean to offend you or make you angry.

Try to relate to the other person.

You may find that although their behaviour is very different from yours on the surface, there are things you do that aren't very different. It can be very useful to find similarities to help you understand the other person's words or actions.

Finally, you might decide to change the way you behave in the situation now that you understand the other person better.

Really, this can be summed up easily. Understanding others is an active process that requires you to put yourself in their position and see things from their point of view.

AUDIO 10.7

Amanda: *How was the meeting with the supervisor? Same?*

Vihaan: *Yeah! She just closes her eyes as soon as I start talking! It's really weird! I'm worried that she doesn't like me, or I'm just boring her stupid!*

Amanda: *You're not boring, Vihaan. And there's no way she doesn't like you. Everyone likes you!*

Vihaan: *That's really nice of you! But, I don't know, I was expecting her to show a bit more interest in my work.*

Amanda: *You said before that she does make comments … ?*

Vihaan: *That's the weird thing. She asks questions and I do find what she says useful. So maybe she isn't bored! Maybe I'm just assuming that, but I could be wrong.*

Amanda: *Right. I mean, being bored isn't the only reason she'd close her eyes.*

Vihaan: *I guess. Perhaps she needs to close her eyes for some reason to concentrate on what I'm saying better?*

Amanda: *Well, you do talk very fast.*

Vihaan: *Do I? I do, don't I? Oh my goodness, maybe that's why! My dad closes his eyes sometimes when I'm talking to him.*

Amanda: *Ha ha! I do it when I'm concentrating on music.*

Vihaan: *Actually, I block my ears when I'm reading in a noisy place, and this is similar, I guess.*

Amanda: *I've seen you do that! Well, there you go. It's probably just her way of listening properly. Making sure she gets every word.*

Vihaan: *Yeah, maybe you're right. Next time I won't worry so much. Maybe I should slow down a bit too.*

Amanda: *That might help.*

Vocabulary reference

UNIT 1

astonished (adj) /ə'stɒnɪʃt/ *I was astonished when I heard the news. It was just so unexpected.*

concerned (adj) /kən'sɜːnd/ *I'm concerned about tomorrow's exam. I think it's going to be difficult.*

furious (adj) /'fjʊərɪəs/ *I can't believe you borrowed my car without asking. I'm absolutely furious!*

impatient (adj) /ɪm'peɪʃnt/ *What a great programme! I'm so impatient to see the next series.*

motivated (adj) /'məʊtɪveɪtɪd/ *Since she's such a good teacher, everyone in the class feels motivated.*

optimistic (adj) /ˌɒptɪ'mɪstɪk/ *I'm optimistic we'll have good weather for our bike ride next Saturday.*

petrified (adj) /'petrɪfaɪd/ *I don't think I would watch that film again. It left me feeling absolutely petrified.*

relieved (adj) /rɪ'liːvd/ *Thank goodness you're OK! I don't think I've ever been so relieved!*

thrilled (adj) /θrɪld/ *We're thrilled to announce that we're getting married!*

1 Choose the correct option to complete the sentences.

1 I hope Anka gets here soon. I'm starting to feel *impatient / thrilled*.
2 She always feels things will work out, maybe because she's quite *astonished / optimistic*.
3 I'm *concerned / motivated* about Paul. I haven't heard from him recently.
4 Jed was *impatient / astonished* when he heard the news. He wasn't expecting it at all.
5 I feel *petrified / relieved* now I've heard from you. I was starting to worry.
6 My children have such great teachers. They make them feel really *furious / motivated*.
7 That ride was so scary. We felt absolutely *petrified / relieved*.
8 Congratulations on your promotion! I'm *concerned / thrilled* for you.
9 Farah looks *optimistic / furious*. I wonder what made her so angry?

2 Write three questions, using adjectives from the word list. Then work in pairs. Ask and answer your questions.

Have you ever read a book that left you completely astonished? What was it about?

UNIT 2

bring up (phr v) /brɪŋ 'ʌp/ *I'm not sure why you brought that up. It was really rude.*

come up (phr v) /kʌm 'ʌp/ *A number of interesting topics came up in the discussion.*

come up with (phr v) /kʌm 'ʌp wɪð/ *If we all work together, I'm sure we can come up with a solution.*

get across (phr v) /get ə'krɒs/ *Lukas is very confident, so it's easy for him to get his ideas across.*

make up (phr v) /meɪk 'ʌp/ *Every time my sister is late, she makes up a different excuse.*

pick up (phr v) /pɪk 'ʌp/ *Lin is great at languages. She picks them up so easily!*

point out (phr v) /pɔɪnt 'aʊt/ *I'd like to point out that this isn't the first time it's happened.*

read up on (phr v) /riːd 'ʌp ɒn/ *I spent the weekend reading up on linguistics.*

1 Match the beginnings of the sentences (1–8) with the endings (a–h).

1 I'm sorry to bring this up, but
2 Laura spent six weeks in Rome,
3 Hardly anything interesting came up,
4 I'm having trouble coming up with
5 As soon as the teacher pointed out
6 To prepare for our exam, you should
7 I find it hard to get my ideas across,
8 Whenever Hiba misses a deadline,

a even though we talked for two whole hours.
b read up on phrasal verbs.
c ideas about what to do next weekend.
d she makes up a crazy excuse.
e I'm disappointed you can't come to my party.
f maybe because I'm quite shy.
g our mistake, everything made more sense.
h but she didn't pick up much Italian.

2 Complete the sentences with your own ideas. Then compare with a partner.

1 In our next class, something that might come up is …
2 I wish someone could come up with a solution for …
3 The language I would most like to pick up is …
4 I would like to read up on …

135

Vocabulary reference

UNIT 3

end up (phr v) /end 'ʌp/ *After a series of wrong turns, I ended up completely lost.*

go on (phr v) /gəʊ 'ɒn/ *Next month, I'm going on a trip to Paris.*

head back (phr) /hed 'bæk/ *It looks like it's going to rain. Maybe we should head back.*

make it (phr) /'meɪk ɪt/ *It's quite late already. Will you make it to school on time?*

reach (v) /riːtʃ/ *Everyone was happy when we reached the top of the mountain.*

set off (phr v) /set 'ɒf/ *What time do you think we should set off?*

steer (v) /stɪə(r)/ *Expert sailors can steer any kind of boat.*

stop over (phr v) /stɒp 'əʊvə(r)/ *It was late when we finished dinner, so I stopped over at my sister's house.*

turn back (phr v) /tɜːn 'bæk/ *I forgot my keys. I'll have to turn back.*

1 Complete the conversation with the correct form of the words or phrases from the word list.

Charlie: What time shall we [1] ____________ tomorrow?
Victor: Maybe eight o'clock? That way we can [2] ____________ Bristol before lunch.
Charlie: OK. I hope we don't [3] ____________ getting lost, like last time.
Victor: I don't think we will. I think it was because Ana wanted to [4] ____________ at that hotel the night before.
Charlie: That trip was a bit stressful. Remember when we had to [5] ____________ when she forgot her phone? It was nearly midnight by the time we [6] ____________ there.
Victor: We should [7] ____________ another trip with Ana sometime though. She's a lot of fun!

2 Write a short story using the prompt or your own idea. Try to use at least five verbs or phrasal verbs you have learned in this unit.

With only £100 in my pocket, I wasn't sure how far I would get. I was hoping to reach Paris, or maybe …

UNIT 4

catch up (phr v) /kætʃ 'ʌp/ *We should meet soon. We haven't caught up in a long time.*

get along with (phr v) /get ə'lɒŋ wɪð/ *Paul is very friendly. It's no surprise that he gets along with everyone.*

hit it off (phr) /hɪt ɪt 'ɒf/ *Samer and I have a similar sense of humour. Maybe that's why we hit it off.*

keep in close contact (phr) /kiːp ɪn kləʊs 'kɒntækt/ *My cousins and I keep in very close contact. We speak to each other every day.*

keep in touch with (phr) /kiːp ɪn 'tʌtʃ wɪð/ *Thanks to technology, there are lots of great ways you can keep in touch with friends.*

lose touch with (phr) /luːz 'tʌtʃ wɪð/ *I'm not sure what happened to Lizzy. I lost touch with her a few years ago.*

reconnect (v) /riːkə'nekt/ *I'm so happy that we've reconnected after all this time!*

stick together (phr v) /stɪk tə'geðə(r)/ *It's important that we stick together, especially at a time like this.*

1 Complete the sentences with the correct form of the words or phrases from the word list.

1 I've been so happy ever since we ____________. Let's not lose touch again!
2 We should get together soon. It's been ages since we ____________.
3 I ____________ Janet several years ago. I don't know how to contact her.
4 Even though we live in different cities, we ____________ contact.
5 I'm not very good at ____________, but email does make it easier.
6 At difficult moments, it's important for families to ____________.
7 My classmates and I ____________ right away. It'll be sad when the course ends.
8 I don't really ____________ my brother. We always argue.

2 Work in pairs. Discuss the questions.

1 When you catch up with friends, what do you tend to speak about?
2 Do you ever keep in touch with people by writing emails?
3 Why do people sometimes lose touch?
4 In what circumstances is it important to stick together?
5 Which family members do you get along with best?
6 Do you keep in close contact with any old school friends?

136

UNIT 5

anxiety (n) /æŋ'zaɪəti/ *Losing your job can cause feelings of anxiety.*

at risk (phr) /ət 'rɪsk/ *Many children are at risk of developing a technology addiction.*

burnout (n) /'bɜːnaʊt/ *Towards the end of his career, my father suffered from burnout.*

call in sick (phr) /kɔːl ɪn 'sɪk/ *Kyle called in sick today.*

come down with (phr v) /kʌm 'daʊn wɪð/ *Last week I came down with a terrible cold.*

cope with (phr) /'kəʊp wɪð/ *My sister is very good at coping with stress.*

depression (n) /dɪ'preʃən/ *Nearly three million people suffer from depression every year.*

feel sorry for yourself (phr) /fiːl 'sɒri fə(r) jə(r)'self/ *I decided to stop feeling sorry for myself and try to fix the problem instead.*

get over (phr v) /get 'əʊvə(r)/ *How long did it take you to get over your injury?*

symptom (n) /'sɪmptəm/ *The doctor asked me about my symptoms.*

stay in shape (phr) /steɪ ɪn 'ʃeɪp/ *Jogging is an excellent way to stay in shape.*

take a nap (phr) /teɪk ə 'næp/ *I sometimes take a short nap after lunch.*

1 Complete the text with the correct form of the words and phrases from the word list.

Have you ever experienced burnout? You're not alone. These days, more and more people suffer from high levels of [1] ____________ and stress. [2] ____________ these emotions is not an easy task. Contrary to popular belief, most people can't just [3] '____________ it'.

Common [4] ____________ of burnout include low motivation and tiredness. [5] ____________ a cold is also quite normal. If you believe you may be [6] ____________ of burnout, try not to [7] ____________ yourself. Instead, make self-care a priority. [8] ____________ if you feel tired, or consider [9] ____________. Regular exercise is also very important, as [10] ____________ can give you energy and improve your mood.

2 Read the message. Write a short response, using the word list to help you.

> I was worried when I didn't see you in the office today. I just wanted to check that you were OK. Are you sick? Is there anything I can do to help?

UNIT 6

in-depth (adj) /ɪn 'depθ/ *The analysis was very in-depth. The reporter included a lot of relevant details.*

make the headlines (phr) /meɪk ðə 'hedlaɪnz/ *We don't know why yesterday's fire didn't make the headlines.*

objective (adj) /əb'dʒektɪv/ *When carrying out serious research, it's better to read objective sources.*

report (v) /rɪ'pɔːt/ *The journalists looked visibly upset as they reported yesterday's events.*

sensational (adj) /sen'seɪʃənl/ *I don't like that newspaper because the articles are too sensational. When I read a newspaper, what I want is facts.*

skim over (phr) /skɪm 'əʊvə/ *In the mornings, I skim over the headlines as I drink my coffee.*

tabloid (adj) /'tæblɔɪd/ *My sister sometimes reads tabloid newspapers because she loves celebrity gossip.*

the press (n) /ðə pres/ *In my opinion, the scandal should have received more coverage in the press.*

top story (n) /tɒp 'stɔːri/ *I can't believe you don't know about this. It was the top story for most of last year!*

1 Complete the conversation with words from the word list.

Marcos: The news these days is so depressing. Some days I can't even bring myself to [1] ____________ the headlines.
Anne: I know what you mean. If the [2] ____________ isn't some scandal, it's something else equally upsetting, like a disaster of some kind.
Marcos: And do you feel like the coverage that [3] ____________ gives to a lot of things isn't as [4] ____________ as it used to be? Even the major papers don't go into much detail.
Anne: Yeah, I agree. And not only that, but the way that journalists [5] ____________ things is getting to be more and more biased. They only tell one side of the story. I prefer to read [6] ____________ articles if I can.
Marcos: Yeah, that's definitely a problem. A similar issue is that some news is just too [7] ____________. When I check out the news, I don't want to read about drama. I just want facts, you know?
Anne: Do you ever read the [8] ____________ news? Like, celebrity gossip and stuff?
Marcos: Only articles about my favourite actor!

2 Write a description of a news article you have read recently. Use the word list to help you.

137

Vocabulary reference

UNIT 7

absolutely stunning (phr) /ˈæbsəluːtli ˈstʌnɪŋ/ *The sunrise was absolutely stunning this morning.*

breathtaking (adj) /ˈbreθteɪkɪŋ/ *At the top of the mountain, the view was simply breathtaking.*

cold and damp (phr) /kəʊld ənd dæmp/ *I hate it when the weather is cold and damp.*

cramped (adj) /kræmpt/ *It was very cramped inside the cave. I couldn't wait to get back outside.*

densely crowded (phr) /ˈdensli ˈkraʊdɪd/ *In summertime, some national parks become densely crowded.*

elegantly decorated (phr) /ˈelɪgəntli ˈdekəreɪtɪd/ *The hotel was elegantly decorated with beautiful artwork.*

light and airy (phr) /laɪt ənd ˈeəri/ *The building was light and airy, with large windows and high ceilings.*

narrow (adj) /ˈnærəʊ/ *The corridor was so narrow that we had to walk one by one.*

sheltered (adj) /ˈʃeltəd/ *We hardly noticed the wind because the beach was sheltered by the cliffs above.*

spacious (adj) /ˈspeɪʃəs/ *The student centre is very spacious. There's lots of room to study or meet friends.*

vast (adj) /vɑːst/ *On our visit to the Amazon rainforest, I was impressed by how incredibly vast it is.*

warm and cosy (phr) /wɔːm ənd ˈkəʊzi/ *The log fire makes the living room really warm and cosy.*

1 **Choose the correct options to complete the advert.**

Tired of riding [1]*densely crowded / sheltered* commuter trains? Want to get away from the [2]*vast / cold and damp* winter weather? Why not book a short break at the Astoria Hotel?

Surrounded by [3]*densely crowded / breathtaking* views, you can spend the day exploring our [4]*absolutely stunning / narrow* countryside or the town's [5]*cold and damp / narrow* cobblestone lanes before coming back to our [6]*cramped / warm and cosy* fireside lounge. All of our rooms are [7]*sheltered / elegantly decorated* and have a [8]*narrow / spacious* en suite bathroom.

We're also accepting bookings for events in our [9]*cramped / light and airy* garden room.

2 **Read the message. Write a reply using at least five words from the word list.**

I know you are on holiday, but I really miss you! I thought I would check in and see how you were getting on. How was your trip? And how is the hotel? Have you taken any photos?

UNIT 8

gadget (n) /ˈgædʒɪt/ *My brother's room is full of gadgets. He loves to take them apart and then put them back together again.*

handy (adj) /ˈhændi/ *I find it handy to wear a watch because sometimes my mobile phone is in my bag.*

innovative (adj) /ˈɪnəvətɪv/ *The researchers use quite innovative methods in their investigations.*

outdated (adj) /aʊtˈdeɪtɪd/ *I can't believe you still use a fax machine! They are completely outdated.*

perform (v) /pəˈfɔːm/ *The new technology isn't performing quite as well as we had hoped.*

pocket-sized (adj) /ˈpɒkɪt saɪzd/ *Larger phones are more popular, but I prefer to have one that is pocket-sized.*

recharge (v) /riːˈtʃɑːdʒ/ *I need to recharge my phone before we go out for the evening.*

sophisticated (adj) /səˈfɪstɪkeɪtɪd/ *Modern technology is becoming more and more sophisticated. Just look at what simple phones can do these days!*

user-friendly (adj) /juːzə ˈfrendli/ *My new PC is so user-friendly. It's much simpler to use than my old one.*

waterproof (adj) /ˈwɔːtəpruːf/ *Most tablets aren't waterproof, so be careful not to get yours wet.*

1 **Choose the correct option to complete the sentences.**

1 My new laptop has lots of *innovative / outdated* features that I want to try out.
2 Excuse me, would it be alright to *perform / recharge* my phone here?
3 Today, architects use *sophisticated / waterproof* applications to plan their projects.
4 Photo editing apps are really *pocket-sized / handy*. I need to download one.
5 My hard drive is *sophisticated / pocket-sized*. But even though it's small, it has loads of memory.
6 My sister redesigned my website. Now it's much more *outdated / user-friendly*.
7 I accidentally put my phone in the washing machine. I hope it's *handy / waterproof*.
8 My family often gets lost. I'm not sure our GPS always *performs / recharges* properly.
9 I can't believe you still have an mp3 player. What an *innovative / outdated* gadget!

2 **Work in pairs. What are your two favourite gadgets or apps? Why?**

138

UNIT 9

achieve objectives (phr) /əˈtʃiːv əbˈdʒektɪvz/ *If you want to achieve your objectives, you have to work at them every day.*

make a mess (phr) /meɪk ə mes/ *It's the first time I've been given so much responsibility. I'm worried I'll make a mess of everything!*

make it through (phr) /meɪk ɪt ˈθruː/ *My colleagues and I have no idea how we'll make it through this week. We have so much to do.*

overcome an issue (phr) /əʊvəˈkʌm ən ˈɪʃuː/ *The company had to overcome a number of issues when they decided to expand.*

struggle to understand (phr) /ˈstrʌgl tuː ˌʌndə(r)ˈstænd/ *It was easy for me to read and write in French, but I struggled to understand when I spoke to people.*

tackle a problem (phr) /ˈtækl ə ˈprɒbləm/ *In order to tackle your problems, it's important to stay positive.*

1 **Complete the sentences with the correct form of words from the word list.**

1 Come on guys, keep your spirits up! I know we can ______________ the presentation!
2 Unless I make a timetable, I find it hard to ______________.
3 I'm ______________ to understand this maths problem. Would you be able to help me?
4 My manager is very confident. She says we can ______________ any issue.
5 It's better to ______________ straight away. It will only get worse otherwise.
6 I made such ______________ of that exam. I'm going to have to take it again.

2 **Work in pairs. Discuss the questions.**

1 What objectives would you like to achieve this year? How will you do this?
2 What is something that you have struggled to understand or learn? Were you able to do it in the end?
3 What should you do in order to stay positive when you're tackling a problem?
4 When you make it through a difficult time, how do you like to celebrate?

UNIT 10

culturally diverse (adj) /ˈkʌltʃərəli daɪˈvɜːs/ *I love living in New York because it's very culturally diverse.*

cultural background (n) /ˈkʌltʃərəl ˈbækgraʊnd/ *My best friend has a mixed cultural background. She is half Spanish and half Vietnamese.*

feel like an outsider (phr) /fiːl laɪk æn aʊtˈsaɪdə/ *It can be upsetting to feel like an outsider, but these experiences can also help us grow.*

fit in (phr v) /fɪt ɪn/ *I am quite different from my brothers and sisters. For some reason I just don't fit in.*

identify with (v) /aɪˈdentɪfaɪ wɪð/ *I'm half French and half Italian, but I identify more with the French.*

influenced by (v) /ˈɪnfluənst baɪ/ *Teenagers tend to be influenced by their peers.*

origins (n) /ˈɒrɪdʒɪnz/ *As an adult, I've begun to take a greater interest in my family history and our origins.*

raised in (v) /reɪzd ɪn/ *I was raised in a big city, but I'd like to bring up my children in the countryside.*

share values (v) /ʃeə ˈvæljuːz/ *My friends and I share the same values, so we rarely have disagreements.*

1 **Match the beginnings of the sentences (1–8) with the endings (a–h).**

1 My husband and I don't …
2 As a nurse, the people I most identify with …
3 People who live abroad often …
4 Children who are raised in …
5 My choice of profession was definitely …
6 In our globalized world, more and more …
7 My partner and I both have …
8 Many teenagers go through …

a feel like outsiders in their new communities at first.
b mixed cultural backgrounds.
c influenced by my parents' opinions.
d are other medical professionals.
e a stage where they feel as though they don't fit in.
f share the same values as most of our neighbours.
g people are growing up in culturally diverse places.
h the countryside often have a lot of freedom.

2 **Complete the sentences with your own ideas. Then compare with a partner.**

1 Someone I was really influenced by is …
2 If you don't fit in, you might …
3 My family were raised in …
4 One advantage of living in a culturally diverse place is …
5 It's important to know about your origins because …

139

Grammar reference

UNIT 1

1B Grammar: Forming questions

Most questions are formed with auxiliary verb + subject + main verb. In the present and past simple, where there is no auxiliary verb, add *do/does* or *did*.

***Do** you **want** a coffee?*
***Can** you **help** me with my homework?*

It's also possible to use a question word with this structure.

***What do** you **want** for lunch?*

Negative questions

You usually use negative questions when you expect your listener to agree, or in order to express surprise or annoyance.

To form a negative question, use auxiliary verb + *not* + subject + main verb.

***Isn't** this food amazing?* (expecting to agree)
***Didn't** you **like** the book?* (surprise)

It's also possible to use a question word with this structure.

***Why don't** you **want** to come with me?*

Short questions

Use short questions to express surprise or interest, or to encourage the other speaker to continue.

To form a short question, use auxiliary verb (+ *not*) + subject.

A: Paula complained about quite a few things in today's meeting.
*B: **Did she**? Like what?*

A: Jad hasn't been to any lectures this week.
*B: **Hasn't he**? Why not?*

Subject questions

You use subject questions to find out more information about a subject, e.g. a person or thing that is performing an action.

To form a subject question, use *Who / What* + verb + object. Do not use an auxiliary verb with subject questions because *who* or *what* is the subject of the question.

***Who** went with you?*
***What** helps you study?*

Indirect questions

You use indirect questions when you want to be more polite.

To form an indirect question, use subject + verb within part of a longer sentence. Unlike other types of questions, there is no inversion of subject and verb.

*Could you tell me where **the bus stop is**?*
(NOT ~~Could you tell me where is the bus stop?~~)

You often use indirect questions with a set phrase, e.g. *Could you tell me … ? Do you happen to know … ? Would you mind letting me know … ? Do you have any idea … ?*

You can also form indirect questions as statements, using a set phrase, e.g. *I'd like to know … What I am asking is …* The structure is also subject + verb. You can use *if* or *whether* after the set phrase.

***I'd like to know if tomorrow is** a holiday.*

Question tags

Question tags are short phrases that you add to the end of a statement.

Use them to:

- check information. When you do this, you use a rising intonation in the tag question.
- ask the listener to agree. When you do this, you use a falling intonation.

Form tag questions with auxiliary verb + pronoun. If the statement is positive, add a negative question tag and if the statement is negative, add a positive question tag. If the statement includes a proper noun, replace it with a pronoun in the question tag.

*We are going for dinner on Friday, **aren't we**?*
*You don't study at the university, **do you**?*
*Nada isn't coming later, **is she**?*

1 **Find and correct the mistakes in the questions.**

1 Could you tell me when does the meeting start?
2 She was very surprised, was she?
3 Haven't gone we there before?
4 I'd like to know where is the bank?
5 A: I think my sister looks a bit tired.
B: You do?
6 Who did came with you to the restaurant?

2 **Complete the conversations with these words. There is one option you do not need.**

are you how much is would you mind	did you why didn't	does it will take	have you wouldn't you

A

Harry: I thought that exhibition was fantastic. [1]______________ enjoy it?
Lucinda: I did, yes. But [2]______________ say it was a bit expensive?
Harry: Hmm … perhaps. I think our ticket lets us in to some other events, though.
Lucinda: [3]______________?

B

Omar: [4]______________ listened to the new Radio 5 podcast?
Lidia: No, I don't think so.
Omar: It has some great tips about meditation.
Lidia: How interesting. You're not normally interested in that, [5]______________?

140

C

Passenger: Excuse me. [6]______________ the fare to Green Park?
Bus driver: It's £3.20.
Passenger: And [7]______________ letting me know how long the journey [8]______________?
Bus driver: We should be there in about 25 minutes, sir.

1C Focus on: Adverbs of degree

Adverbs of degree go before an adjective to change its strength. Compare:

I am happy.
*I am **very** happy.*
*Gary felt **a bit** frustrated.*
*Gary felt **really** frustrated.*

Some adverbs of degree make adjectives stronger, and some adverbs make them weaker.

Adverbs that make a word stronger		Adverbs that make a word weaker	
absolutely completely extremely really	totally tremendously very	a bit a little fairly pretty	relatively slightly somewhat

The word *quite* can make words stronger or weaker.

*I made it **quite** clear that I don't want to talk about it any more.* (stronger = absolutely/completely clear)
*Our teacher is **quite** sure the exam is on Thursday, but she is going to double check.* (weaker = fairly sure, but not completely sure)

1 **Choose the correct adverb of degree to complete the sentences.**

1 I'm *absolutely / fairly* certain. There is no doubt in my mind.
2 Luke is *extremely / a bit* tired because he skipped his afternoon nap.
3 I can't concentrate on my work because I'm *really / slightly* hungry. I have to get something to eat!
4 It was a *relatively / tremendously* good film. I think everyone should see it.
5 Julia was *a little / totally* amazed by the spectacular mountain scenery.
6 Amir felt *very / somewhat* stressed that his bus arrived five minutes late, but he knew he'd still get to work on time.

2 **Read the sentences. Decide whether *quite* makes the adjective stronger or weaker.**

1 You're quite right. I should never have doubted you.
2 Leticia must have been quite upset. I had never seen her cry before.
3 Our dog is quite energetic, but nothing compared to how she used to be.

UNIT 2

2B Grammar: Present tenses

Present simple

Use the present simple to describe present habits, actions that happen regularly and facts or things that are always true.

***I wake up** at seven o'clock every day.*
***I don't watch** films very often.*
***Do you take** the number 5 train to work?*

Present continuous

Use the present continuous to describe things that are happening in the present moment (right now) or things that are happening around the present moment (not exactly now).

***I'm walking** around the museum just now.*
*You **aren't cooking** dinner.*
***Is** John **working** today?*

Present perfect simple

Use the present perfect simple to describe the present results of past actions when the time is not specified. You often use it to describe life experiences, changes that have happened over a period of time and accomplishments.

To form the present perfect simple, use *have/has* + past participle.

*Sally **has finished** her project.*

You can also use it with state verbs (e.g. *have, be, know, love*) to describe a situation that began in the past but is still true in the present.

*I **have** always **wanted** to take piano lessons.*

Use it when you want to specify how many times an action has happened.

*My boss **has had** three cups of coffee today.*

Present perfect continuous

Use the present perfect continuous to describe actions that began in the past, are still in progress and are likely to continue in the future.

To form the present perfect continuous, use *have/has* + *been* + verb + *-ing*.

*Maya **has been learning** Japanese since she was at school.*
*We**'ve been going** to that restaurant for years.*

The present perfect continuous emphasizes the length of time that has passed since the action started (the action may or may not be finished), while the present perfect simple emphasizes the completion of the action.

*We **have been studying** for hours!*

You don't usually use state verbs (*have, be, know,* etc.) in the present perfect continuous.

141

Grammar reference

1 **Choose the correct option to complete the sentences.**

1. In general, my sister *picks up / is picking up* languages easily.
2. We *are reading up / have been reading up* on the Renaissance recently.
3. *I have been / I'm studying* French at the moment. I have a big exam next week.
4. Thank you, but I don't want any coffee. I *have had / have been having* two cups already.
5. They *don't come up / haven't come up* with an idea yet.
6. I don't think *we've made / we make* many mistakes, but let's double check.

2 **Complete the diary entry with the correct form of the verbs in brackets.**

It [1] ______________ (be) two weeks since I arrived in New York for my language course. I [2] ______________ (enjoy) life in the city a lot. I have a small room in a student residence. Every day, I [3] ______________ (have) breakfast with my classmates at a local café. In the afternoon we explore the city. I [4] ______________ (visit) the Empire State Building and the Statue of Liberty. I [5] ______________ (miss) home quite a lot since I got here. But at the same time, I [6] ______________ (have) lots of things to keep me busy. I [7] ______________ (study) for my exam at the moment and [8] ______________ (spend) a lot of time practising writing in English.

2C Focus on: Separable and inseparable phrasal verbs

Most phrasal verbs are **separable**: the object can come before or after the preposition.

*Please can you **turn off the lights** before you leave?*
*Sorry, I forgot to **turn the lights off**.*

However, if the object is a pronoun, it must come before the preposition.

*I remembered to **turn them off**.*
NOT ~~I remembered to turn off them.~~

Some phrasal verbs are **inseparable**: the object always comes after the preposition, even if the object is a pronoun.

*We'll have to **come up with** a solution.*
NOT ~~We'll have to come up a solution with.~~

Phrasal verbs can be put into the following categories:

Two-part verbs (separable)	Two-part verbs (inseparable)	Three-part verbs (inseparable)
bring up	take after	come up with
look up	look after	get away with
make up	get over	look up to
pick up	look for	put up with
point out	go over	read up on

Verbs in the first category are always separable when the object is a pronoun.

*I'll **pick you up** at five.*
NOT ~~I'll pick up you at five.~~

They tend not to be separable when the object is a longer word or noun phrase.

*I **picked up** quite a lot of Japanese when I visited Tokyo last year.*
NOT ~~I picked quite a lot of Japanese up when I visited Tokyo last year.~~

When the object is a short word or phrase, separating the verb is optional.

*Did you **pick up** any French in Paris?*
*Did you **pick** any French **up** in Paris?*

A small number of phrasal verbs must always be separated, e.g. *get across* and *call back*.

*Marika didn't **call** Peter **back**.* NOT ~~Marika didn't call back Peter.~~

Three-part verbs (verbs with two particles) are always inseparable.

*I need to **read up on** phrasal verbs.* NOT ~~I need to read up phrasal verbs on.~~

1 **Choose the correct option (a or b) to complete the sentences.**

1. I really appreciate you …
   a pointing that out.
   b pointing out that.
2. It's a good idea to use a dictionary to …
   a look the spelling and definitions of new words up.
   b look up the spelling and definitions of new words.
3. I sometimes find it difficult to …
   a get across my point.
   b get my point across.
4. I don't have anyone to …
   a look the children after this evening.
   b look after the children this evening.
5. If you don't know the answer, just …
   a make it up.
   b make up it.
6. John really …
   a looks up to his dad.
   b looks up his dad to.

142

UNIT 3

3B Grammar: Narrative tenses

Past simple

Use the past simple to describe consecutive events that started and finished in the past, or the main events of a story.

*I **had** a great time in Paris. I **visited** the Louvre and **went** to the Eiffel Tower. I **bought** a lot of souvenirs.*

You often use it to describe important events in someone's life.

*Leonardo da Vinci **was born** in 1452. He **became** famous for his art and creative inventions.*

Past continuous

Use the past continuous to describe background events, or to give the background to the main story.

To form the past continuous, use *was/were* + verb + *-ing*.

*Susannah **was feeling** happy as she made her way to the bus stop, as it had been a great day.*

You also use it to describe longer actions or events that were in progress when something else occurred.

*I **was looking** for a place to have lunch, when suddenly I realized that my phone had disappeared.*

Past perfect simple

Use the past perfect simple to describe events or actions that happened before the main event.

To form the past perfect simple, use *had* + past participle.

*She **had visited** the city before.*

You can use it to emphasize that events or actions have been completed.

*We **had** already **decided** to go on a trip, but we weren't sure which country we wanted to visit.*

Past perfect continuous

Use the past perfect continuous to describe longer events or actions that were in progress in the past, either before or up to the main event.

To form the past perfect continuous, use *had been* + verb + *-ing*

*We**'d been expecting** the train journey to be long, but we didn't know it would be so uncomfortable.*

You can use it to emphasize the duration of an activity.

*They **had been working** all night long.*

1 **Choose the correct options to complete the text.**

Ever since I was a child, I [1] *was dreaming / had dreamed* of visiting Granada. I [2] *wanted / was wanting* to explore the narrow winding streets of the Albaicín, just as my mother [3] *had done / was doing* when she was in her twenties. After my plane [4] *landed / had been landing* in Madrid, I [5] *had / was having* to take a five-hour bus ride through the dusty Spanish countryside. The trip [6] *has been made / was made* longer by frequent stops in small villages that [7] *had been lying / lay* hidden amongst miles of olive groves for centuries. Eventually, we [8] *had reached / reached* my destination. As my bus [9] *had been pulling / was pulling* into the city, I caught a glimpse of the sun setting over the Sierra Nevada. I [10] *had arrived / was arriving.*

2 **Complete the sentences with the correct narrative tense.**

1. We ______________ (walk) to the train station when we ______________ (come across) an old antiques market.
2. More than two hundred people ______________ (stop by) the visitor centre yesterday. Perhaps one of them ______________ (find) Divya's mobile phone.
3. Beatrice ______________ (look forward to) her trip for months, so she ______________ (feel) very upset when the airline cancelled her flight.
4. After I ______________ (become) interested in archaeology, I ______________ (decide) to visit Pompeii.

3C Focus on: Travel collocations with *go on*

You form many travel collocations by combining *go on* with words or expressions to do with travel.

Some describe different types of journey:

go on a cruise
go on a bus tour
go on a voyage

Some describe different types of holiday:

go on a package holiday
go on a city break
go on a safari
go on a guided tour
go on a ski holiday
go on a backpacking trip

Some describe travel for specific purposes:

go on a business trip
go on a language exchange
go on a scientific expedition

1 **Complete the sentences with the correct form of the expressions from the list above.**

1. If I had the chance to ______________, I'm not sure I would take it. I'd feel frightened to be so close to so many wild animals.
2. Lucy doesn't usually ______________, because she prefers to be more independent when she travels.
3. We're ______________ next month. We know it'll be hard, but we're excited about improving our Portuguese.
4. A team of researchers is ______________ to Antarctica. The trip has taken months of hard work and planning.
5. Next month, I'm ______________ to Singapore. I'm quite nervous, as I'm new to the company.
6. My aunt ______________ around the Mediterranean. She stopped in Mallorca, Sicily and many other islands.

143

Grammar reference

UNIT 4

4B Grammar: Reported speech and reporting verbs

Reporting verbs describe what someone else said or did. When you use reporting verbs, verb forms and reference words (pronouns, time and place expressions, etc.) tend to change.

*Hannah: 'I'm going to help you tomorrow.' → Hannah said that **she** was going to help **me** the **next day**.*

Many reporting verbs follow a specific pattern.

verb + *to* + infinitive	agree, offer, promise, threaten *They **agreed to help.***
verb + object + *to* + infinitive	advise, ask, convince, invite, order, remind, warn *I **advised him to study** hard.*
verb + *-ing* form	recommend, remember, suggest *She **recommended arriving** early.*
verb + preposition + *-ing* form	admit, apologize, confess, insist *He **apologized for hurting** her feelings.*
verb + object + preposition + *-ing* form	accuse, blame, praise *She **accused me of lying.***

In negative sentences, use the negative infinitive or *-ing* form.

*She **accused me of not telling** the truth.*
*They **agreed not to get** in the way.*

Some verbs, e.g. *accept, complain* and *explain* follow the structure verb + *that* + clause.

*Vincent **explained that** he didn't know where the hotel was.*

Some verbs in the table above can also follow this structure, e.g. *admit, agree* and *promise*.

*He **admitted that** he forgot to buy the tickets.*

1 **Rewrite the sentences using the correct reported speech pattern.**

1. Adam: 'I'm going to come tomorrow.'
   Adam said that
   ______________________________.
2. Ben: 'My sister was feeling tired.'
   Ben mentioned that
   ______________________________.
3. Zack: 'I've been feeling ill.'
   Zack complained that
   ______________________________.
4. Silvia: 'We should go for dinner next week.'
   Silvia suggested that ______________________________.

2 **Complete the sentences with the correct form of the verbs in brackets.**

1. Dania agreed ______________ (help) me with the project.
2. My aunt blamed me ______________ (break) the vase.
3. She accused me ______________ (forget) her birthday.
4. My wife and I offered ______________ (come) early.
5. David admitted ______________ (make) a mistake.
6. We apologized ______________ (be) late.
7. She reminded me ______________ (arrive) on time.
8. My boss recommended ______________ (ask) lots of questions.

4C Focus on: Transitive and intransitive phrasal verbs

Transitive verbs require an object. Intransitive verbs do not require an object.

Many phrasal verbs can be both transitive and intransitive. You can add *with* to many intransitive phrasal verbs to make them transitive. Compare the following examples:

*My family and I **get along**.*

This sentence does not have an object. *Get along* is being used intransitively.

*I **get along with** my family.*

In this sentence, *my family* is the object. *Get along* is being used transitively.

1 **Underline the phrasal verbs in the sentences. Then write T if the verbs are being used transitively or I if they are being used intransitively.**

1. Technology makes it much easier for friends to keep in touch. ______
2. I had a great time catching up with my sister last weekend. ______

2 **Rewrite the sentences so that the phrasal verb is transitive.**

1. We should catch up sometime.
   I'd love to catch up with you sometime.
2. Do you and Lei keep in touch?
   Do you ______________________________?
3. My best friend and I hit it off right away.
   I ______________________________.
4. I felt very sad when my cousin and I lost touch.
   When I ______________________________.
5. My cousins and I keep in close contact.
   I ______________________________.

144

UNIT 5

5B Grammar: Conditionals

Zero conditional

Use the zero conditional to describe facts, or things that are generally true.

The form is *If / When* + present simple, … present simple. You can also use the present continuous or present perfect.

***If** you **heat** water to 100°C, it **boils**.*
***When** plants **don't get** enough water, they **die**.*
***If** you **are** constantly **feeling** tired, you **are** probably **not sleeping** enough.*
***If** you **haven't seen** the Eiffel Tower, you **haven't seen** the most famous landmark in Paris!*

You can change the order of the clauses so the main clause comes first. When the *if* clause comes first, you must use a comma to separate the two clauses. When the main clause comes first, you don't use a comma.

*I **have** an allergic reaction **if** I **eat** peanuts.*

First conditional

Use the first conditional to describe possible future situations.

The form is *If* + present simple, … *will / won't* + infinitive.

You can also use the present continuous or present perfect in the *if* clause. You can use other future forms in the main clause, e.g. *going to*, future perfect or future continuous.

You can change the order of the clauses so the main clause comes first.

***If** it**'s** sunny, we**'ll go** to the park.*
*You **won't be** able to sleep **if** you **have** another coffee.*
***If** you**'re** still **studying**, **I'm going to go** to the party without you.*
***If** you **haven't finished** the assignment by tomorrow, you**'re going** to regret it.*

Most first conditional sentences use *if*, but you can sometimes use other words, e.g. *unless, as long as* and *provided that*. You use *unless* to say *if not*.

***Unless** the meeting **is** cancelled, we **won't be** able to come to the lunch.*

(= If the meeting isn't cancelled, we won't be able to come to the lunch.)

***As long as** I **have** enough money, **I'll buy** some new clothes.*
***Provided that** we **leave** right now, I'm sure **we won't** miss the train.*

Second conditional

Use the second conditional to describe the consequences of an unreal or imaginary situation in the present or future.

The form is *If* + past simple or past continuous, … *would / wouldn't* + infinitive.

You can change the order of the clauses so the main clause comes first.

***If** I **had** more money, I **would buy** a nicer phone.*
*They **would understand if** they **were** in my situation.*
***If** you **were coming down with** a cold, you **would be** coughing and sneezing.*

In second conditional sentences, you can use *might / might not* and *could / couldn't* instead of *would / wouldn't*.

*She **could get** higher marks **if** she **tried** harder.*

Third conditional

Use the third conditional to describe the consequences of an unreal or imaginary situation in the past. Common consequences include wishes and regrets.

The form is *If* + past perfect or past perfect continuous, … *would / wouldn't have* + past participle.

You can change the order of the clauses so the main clause comes first.

***If** I **had woken up** earlier, I **would have arrived** on time.*
*You **wouldn't have got** a low mark **if** you **had studied** more.*
*Ahmed **would have come** to dinner if he **hadn't been playing** basketball.*

In third conditional sentences, you can use *might / might not have* and *could / couldn't have* instead of *would / wouldn't have*.

*I **might not have been** upset **if** you **had talked** to me first.*

1 **Decide whether the sentences are zero, first, second or third conditional. Write 0, 1, 2 or 3.**

1. If you have time later, will you give me a call?
2. If you feel ill, you shouldn't go to work.
3. If Lauren had a fever, she would take some ibuprofen.
4. You would have more energy if you exercised more.
5. If I hadn't been so tired, I would have come with you.
6. You'll miss your train if you don't hurry up.

2 **Complete the conversation with the correct form of the verbs in brackets.**

Andrew: Are you coming to the cinema later?
Bella: I don't think so. If I [1] ______________ (have) more time I [2] ______________ (come). But I'm a bit stressed about my new project at work.
Andrew: Is there anything I can do to help?
Bella: Maybe … you know a bit about web design, right?
Andrew: I enrolled on a course last year. If I [3] ______________ (manage) to finish, I'm sure I [4] ______________ (learn) quite a lot. But I dropped out halfway through.
Bella: That's a shame.
Andrew: If you tell your boss you need a bit more time, I'm sure you [5] ______________ (feel) better.
Bella: Yeah, that's a good idea. If I [6] ______________ (take) a break, that [7] ______________ (help) too.

145

Grammar reference

5C Focus on: *I wish* … and *If only* …

You can use *I wish* … and *If only* … to describe things that you want to be true.

Use *I wish / If only* + past simple to talk about a situation in the present or future.

__I wish__ I was going on holiday this year.
__If only I could__ remember his name.

Use *I wish / If only* + past perfect to talk about a situation in the past that you want to be different.

__I wish I had stayed__ at home today.
__If only__ she __hadn't sprained__ her ankle.

You can use *were* rather than *was* with *I, he, she* or *it* to sound more formal.

__I wish I were__ feeling better.

1 **Match the beginnings of the sentences (1–6) with the endings (a–f).**

1 I hate being ill. I wish …
2 I was hoping to go to the park. If only …
3 Our basketball tournament is next week. If only …
4 Wei is absolutely exhausted. She wishes …
5 Daniel feels a bit unwell. If only …
6 We have an important meeting. I wish …

a she could have a nap.
b he could stay at home.
c the weather was nicer.
d you hadn't called in sick.
e I hadn't broken my ankle.
f I didn't have this dreadful cold.

2 **Complete the sentences with the correct form of the verb in brackets.**

1 Jackie wishes she ______________ (have) more free time.
2 I wish I ______________ (know) how to play the piano.
3 If only you ______________ (go) to sleep earlier last night.
4 I wish I ______________ (not have) to take the train.
5 If only Isaac ______________ (not forget) his phone.
6 Robin wishes he ______________ (train) more. He might have won the race.

UNIT 6

6B Grammar: Passive structures

Use the passive to place emphasis on the action that is being performed, rather than on the person or thing that is performing the action. You can also use it when the person or thing that did the action is unknown, unimportant or obvious. It is commonly used in news reports.

If you want to mention the person or thing performing the action, you can introduce it with the preposition *by*.

Form the passive with *be* + past participle. However, the form of *be* changes according to the verb tense being used.

Present simple	*Many decisions **are made** every day.*
Present continuous	*Important steps **are being taken.***
Present perfect	*Three men **have been** arrested.*
Future with *will*	*Several key ideas **will be presented.***
Future with *going to*	*The best proposals **are going to be discussed.***
Past simple	*A lot of questions **were brought up.***
Past continuous	*The president **was being questioned.***
Past perfect	*Many ideas **had been put** forward.*

There are also infinitive (with and without *to*) and *-ing* forms of the passive.

*She didn't expect **to be praised** so much.*
*My article might **be published!***
*I enjoy **being photographed.***

Passive reporting verbs

You can use passive verbs to report beliefs, opinions and rumours, especially in news reports. Verbs that are commonly used include *think, say, report, understand, believe, hope* and *recommend.*

It + *be* + past participle + (*that*) + clause	***It is hoped that** the situation will soon improve.* ***It is said** we may never know the answer.*

You can report events in the passive using a subject instead of *it*. You don't usually use the verbs *recommend* and *hope* in this pattern.

To report a past action in the present perfect or past simple with this pattern, use a perfect infinitive (infinitive with *have* + past participle).

146

To report an action in the future or in progress now with this pattern, use a continuous infinitive (*be* + *-ing*).

subject + *be* + past participle + *to* + infinitive	*The person responsible **is thought to be** in France.* *The fire **is believed to have begun** sometime last night.* *Real Madrid are said **to be looking** for a new manager.*

1 **Complete the sentences with these phrases.**

are being	been spent	is believed to
is going	understood to	will be presented

1 Jenny Wiles ______________ be one of the best athletes of her generation.
2 The awards ______________ at Hippodrome Centre on 22nd September.
3 A lot of money has ______________ on this year's publicity campaign.
4 Generally speaking, bankers are ______________ earn high salaries.
5 The government's decision ______________ to be announced this afternoon.
6 Some questions ______________ raised about the company's approach.

2 **Look at the first sentence in each pair. Complete the second sentence so that it has the same meaning.**

1 We discussed a number of important issues at the meeting.
At the meeting, ______________.
2 Many people hoped that the problem would be resolved.
______________ would be resolved.
3 People believe that Jaime Vega is the best person to lead the company.
______________ to lead the company.
4 An author has written an important book on the subject.
An important book ______________.
5 The recommendation is to arrive at 5 p.m.
______________ we arrive at 5 p.m.
6 Someone is going to answer all of our questions soon.
All of our questions ______________ soon.

6C Focus on: *the* … *the* …

Use *the* … *the* … to describe the relationship between two things. It shows the effect that one thing has on another. You can use it with verbs, nouns, adjectives and adverbs.

Notice that each sentence has two clauses with *the* and each clause can use *the* in a different structure.

the + comparative adjective / adverb + subject + verb	***The older my students are**, the more they know.* ***The more clearly you explain** this, the better I'll understand.*
the + *more / less* + subject + verb	***The less I sleep**, the worse I feel.*
the + *more / less / fewer* + noun + subject + verb	***The more friends I have**, the happier I am.*

1 **Complete the sentences with these words.**

the better	the more	the more loudly
the older	the sooner	

1 ______________ you go to sleep, the more energy you'll have tomorrow.
2 The more homework my children get, ______________ they learn.
3 The less time I spend on social media, ______________ I tend to feel.
4 ______________ Roberto sings, the angrier his neighbours become.
5 ______________ Janet gets, the more her parents worry about her.

2 **Find and correct the mistakes in the sentences.**

1 The less I study, the more free time have for my hobbies.
2 The fewest pets people have, the cheaper it is for them.
3 The more quickly we drive, soon we'll get to the airport.
4 The time you can spend relaxing on holiday, the better you will feel.
5 The darker my bedroom is, the more easy I get to sleep.

147

Grammar reference

UNIT 7

7B Grammar: Causative verbs

Use causative verbs to indicate the different ways that the actions of someone or something can be affected.

Verb + object + *to* + infinitive

With this pattern, use *allow* and *permit* to describe allowing someone to do something or giving permission, *enable* to describe how something is made possible, *encourage* to describe motivating someone to do something, and *force* for obligation (when you must do something).

*The airline **permitted us to fly** with two pieces of luggage.*
*They **require us to arrive** at 5 p.m.*

Verb + object + infinitive (without *to*)

With this pattern, use *help* to describe giving assistance to allow something to happen, *let* to describe allowing something to happen or giving permission and *make* for obligation (when you must do something).

*My mum **is letting me go** to the cinema tonight.*

Verb + object + (*from*) + *-ing*

With this pattern, use *prevent, save* and *stop* to describe stopping something from happening.

*My work might **prevent me from attending** this weekend's event.*

1 **Choose the correct option to complete the sentences.**

1 I'm sorry, but I can't *allow / let* you to say that kind of thing.
2 We *advised / made* clients to think carefully about their business strategy.
3 My students *are encouraging / are helping* me see many things differently.
4 Proper rest *forces / prevents* people from getting ill.
5 I'm afraid we *can't let / can't permit* you board the train without a ticket.
6 Going to pick up supplies now *will enable / will save* us from having to go later.

2 **Complete the paragraph with the correct form of the verbs in brackets.**

A few years ago, I decided to begin cycling to work. This change to my lifestyle has made me [1]______________ (become) a healthier and happier person. It's enabled me [2]______________ (include) exercise as part of my daily routine and has helped me [3]______________ (save) money. It requires me [4]______________ (leave) home a little earlier. However, it stops me [5]______________ (feel) stressed about finding a seat on the metro and prevents me [6]______________ (worry) about missing my train. Recently, I've encouraged a few friends [7]______________ (begin) cycling to work as well. Of course, I'd never force anyone [8]______________ (give up) public transport in favour of a bike, but I'd advise anyone who is looking for a lifestyle change [9]______________ (try out) cycling!

7D Focus on: Useful structures for complaining

***so* + adjective or *such (a)* + adjective + noun**

Use these structures to put emphasis on something that has annoyed or upset you.

*It's **so annoying** when you do that!*
*I had **such a** bad day – you just wouldn't believe it.*
*We had **such** terrible weather on our holiday.*

Present continuous with *always*

Use this structure to communicate that something happens all the time.

*You**'re always interrupting** me when I talk!*
*She**'s always turning up** late.*

***I wish / If only* + past simple or *I wish / If only* + *would* + infinitive**

Use these structures to say that you want something to be different or true.

__I wish__ I __didn't have to come in__ early.
__If only__ you __would listen__ to me once in a while!

1 **Match the beginnings of the sentences (1–6) with the endings (a–f).**

1 I thought the meal last night was so …
2 I don't like to fight, but John is always …
3 That was so embarrassing. If only …
4 Last night, Miguel was in such …
5 He's a bit lazy. I wish he …
6 I don't believe you. You're always …

a you would try to be a bit more polite next time.
b a bad mood that he refused to speak to me.
c making up lies and excuses.
d expensive! I don't think we'll eat there again.
e took on a bit more responsibility sometimes.
f starting arguments about the silliest things.

2 **Put the words in order to make sentences. For each sentence, one word will not be used.**

1 find / such / frustrating / I / so / long queues
2 she / only / harder / would / if / work / will
3 bad / too / Henry / in / such / is / a / mood
4 the / I / weather / is / wish / better / was
5 always / my / telling / boss / such / me / is / off

148

UNIT 8

8B Grammar: Speculating about the past

To talk about possibility and certainty in the past, use modal verbs together with *have* + past participle.

Use *must have* + past participle to say that it is very probable or certain that something happened.

*My laptop doesn't seem to be working. I **must have** accidentally **downloaded** a virus.*

Use *may have / might have / could have* + past participle to say it is possible that something happened. Similarly, use *may not have / might not have* + past participle to say it is possible that something didn't happen.

*Jenny isn't at her desk. She **might have gone** to lunch.*
*Alicia **might not have read** the email because she's not normally late.*

Use *can't have / couldn't have* + past participle to say you are almost sure that something didn't happen, or that it is impossible that something happened.

*It **can't have been** easy to live without the internet.*
*Carlos **couldn't have forgotten**. I reminded him yesterday!*

Use *should have / shouldn't have* + past participle to talk about mistakes or express criticism or regret.

*I **should have woken up** earlier this morning.*
*You **shouldn't have spent** so much money.*

1 **Choose the correct meaning (a or b) for each sentence.**

1 Thousands of workers must have been needed to construct the temple.
a Thousands of workers were probably necessary to build the temple.
b Thousands of workers participated in the construction of the temple.
2 It can't have been easy to be a nineteenth-century scientist.
a Perhaps it wasn't easy to work as a scientist in the nineteenth century.
b There is no way it was easy to work as a nineteenth-century scientist.
3 The developers shouldn't have forgotten to double-check their work.
a Not double-checking their work was the wrong thing to do.
b The developers didn't forget to double-check their work.
4 This tool might have been used for cutting vegetables.
a It's possible this tool was used for cutting vegetables.
b This tool was definitely used for cutting vegetables.

2 **Complete the sentences with the correct modal verb. Sometimes more than one answer is possible.**

1 Inventing the first computer ______________ have been difficult. I wouldn't know where to begin!
2 This pottery ______________ have originated in Chile, but I'm not sure. Maybe an archaeologist would know.
3 We ______________ have worked harder, to get better results. For our next project, let's dedicate a bit more time.
4 Vaccines are so complicated. The researchers ______________ have found it very easy to develop this one.
5 She's not answering her phone, so she ______________ have left the office already.
6 You ______________ have done that. It wasn't very safe.

8C Focus on: Forming nouns, verbs and adjectives

The list below shows nouns, verbs and adjectives that you form with common suffixes. Studying these patterns is a useful way to expand your vocabulary because you can learn new words by exploring the word families of words you already know.

*Annie **persuaded (v)** me to come to the cinema. She is a very **persuasive (adj)** person.*
*The speaker gave a very **motivational (adj)** speech. It gave me the **motivation (n)** I needed to try something new.*

Nouns

-ion: *create → creation, innovate → innovation, invent → invention, accuse → accusation*
-ment: *enjoy → enjoyment, achieve → achievement*
-ity: *possible → possibility, responsible → responsibility*
-e/ance: *depend → independence, perform → performance*
-ness: *weak → weakness, happy → happiness*

Adjectives

-al: *tradition → traditional, universe → universal, critic → critical*
-ical: *economy → economical, history → historical*
-able: *afford → affordable, enjoy → enjoyable, memory → memorable, recharge → rechargeable*
-ous: *mystery → mysterious, anxiety → anxious*
-ive: *attract → attractive, create → creative, invent → inventive*

Verbs

-ate: *graduation → graduate, motive → motivate*
-ize: *critic → criticize, empathy → empathize, memory → memorize, apology → apologize*
-ify: *simple → simplify*
-en: *weak → weaken, strength → strengthen*

149

Grammar reference

1 Choose the correct option to complete the sentences.

1 I'm sorry, but that is a complete *impossible / impossibility*.
2 Winning first prize at the science fair was far from her only *accomplishment / accomplish*.
3 I think you're being far too *critic / critical*.
4 The governor has issued a *statement / state* about her plans for next year.
5 Our holiday last year was incredibly *memory / memorable*.

2 Complete the announcement with the correct form of the words in brackets.

Develop a [1] ______________ (create) mobile phone app and win $5,000!

Are you into programming? Do you believe in the endless [2] ______________ (possible) of technology? If so, this [3] ______________ (compete) may be for you. We are seeking interesting phone apps that meet the following criteria:

- [4] ______________ (origin) concept with an [5] ______________ (attract) design
- Useful and [6] ______________ (afford) for students
- Easily [7] ______________ (download) over our networks

[8] ______________ (add) information can be found at the IT Department. All [9] ______________ (submit) must be received by 31st October.

UNIT 9

9B Grammar: Talking about the future

Future continuous (subject + *will* + *be* + *-ing*)

Use the future continuous to describe or make predictions about events or actions that will be in progress at a particular time in the future. You can also use it to ask questions about plans at a particular time in the future.

*This time next week, **they'll be skiing** in the Pyrenees.*
*We **won't be going away** this summer.*
***Will** you **be starting** university in September?*

Future perfect (subject + *will* + *have* + past participle)

Use the future perfect to refer to actions that will be completed by a particular time in the future. You can often use it with a time expression such as *in two weeks, in two weeks' time* or *by that time*.

*In a week's time, Teriha **will have arrived** back home.*
*Unfortunately, I **won't have finished** my book until next year.*
***Will** you **have reached** the restaurant by that time?*

***Should* and *might* to talk about the future**

Use *should* and *might* instead of *will* to show that you are less certain about something. *Should* expresses a higher degree of certainty than *might*.

*The plane **should be taking off** in the next half hour.*
*I **might have moved** into my new apartment by then.*

1 Complete the sentences with these phrases.

'll be might have should will have won't

1 By December, it's almost certain that Paolo ______________ finished his second novel.
2 On Saturday, I ______________ tidying up the house. It's a total mess.
3 By 2023, I ______________ have finished my degree.
4 We ______________ be travelling this summer because we have too much work to do.
5 We ______________ discovered a cure by the end of the decade, but it's not certain.

2 Complete the email with the correct future form of the verbs in brackets. Sometimes more than one answer is possible.

Dear students,

We're sure you are looking forward to your first term at university. By this time next week, you [1] ______________ (arrive) and, hopefully, [2] ______________ (chat) with new friends as you unpack. You [3] ______________ (think of) some questions. So, the purpose of this email is to clarify a few last-minute details.

On Saturday, a member of staff will meet you at Harrington Gate to show you to your accommodation. You [4] ______________ (receive) an email with information about transport options already. If you have not received this message by Friday, please contact us.

On Sunday morning, during breakfast at Avery Hall, administrators [5] ______________ (explain) the timetable for our induction week. As preparation, we've requested that you submit a short statement describing your hobbies and interests. Ideally, you [6] ______________ (submit) this statement by Thursday.

9C Focus on: Verb-noun collocations

A collocation is a group of words that often go together. It is important to use the correct collocation because mistakes with collocations can make your speech sound unnatural. Here are some collocations for five common verbs.

achieve	your aims your objectives a goal very little
make	a mess of something it through a decision a choice
overcome	difficulties obstacles problems objections
struggle	to understand something for survival with the problem
tackle	a crisis an issue a problem

1 Match the beginnings of the sentences (1–6) with the endings (a–f).

1 If you're struggling …
2 Even if you make …
3 Most people tackle …
4 In order to achieve …
5 Some kinds of difficulties …
6 I couldn't have made …

a problems at some point in their life.
b cannot be overcome, no matter how hard you try.
c a mess of something, you shouldn't give up.
d it through without the help of my friends and family.
e your objectives, you should make a plan and stick to it.
f to understand something, ask someone for help.

2 Complete the sentences using the correct form of the verbs. One verb will be used twice.

achieve make overcome struggle tackle

1 The main objective I want to ______________ this year is learning to drive.
2 It's easier to ______________ obstacles with the help of supportive friends.
3 Last month was tough, but we somehow ______________ it through.
4 Many species around the world are ______________ for survival.
5 The crisis we are ______________ is unlike any other I've known.
6 If you ______________ a mess of something, you should admit it.

UNIT 10

10B Grammar: Verb patterns with infinitive and *-ing*

When one verb follows another, the form of the second verb depends on the first verb.

Verbs followed by verb + *-ing*

Use this pattern with certain verbs and phrases including *enjoy, feel like, can't stand, carry on, give up, hate, keep, love, recommend* and *suggest*. You also use it with *remember* (in the sense of thinking about the past).

*As I child, I used to **enjoy swimming**.*
*We **can't stand hiking** in rainy weather.*

Verbs followed by *to* + *-ing*

You usually use an infinitive after *to*. However, in certain cases you use *-ing*. This is because the *-ing* form of the verb acts like a noun. Use this structure with the verbs *be used to, get used to* and *look forward to*.

***I'm not used to living** in such a hot country.*
*She's **looking forward to travelling** abroad.*

Verbs followed by infinitive with *to*

Use this pattern with certain verbs and phrases, including *afford, arrange, can't wait, dare, deserve* and *expect*. You also use it with *remember* (in the sense of thinking about something you need to do).

*I can't **afford to buy** a new car.*
*Let's **arrange to have** dinner next week.*

Verbs followed by infinitive without *to*

This pattern is typical of causative verbs such as *let* and *make* (see Unit 7). You also use this pattern after modal verbs.

*We **make our children tidy** their rooms.*

1 Complete the sentences with the correct form of the verbs in brackets.

1 We really enjoyed ______________ (listen) to the music at last night's festival.
2 This year, I can't afford ______________ (go) anywhere on holiday.
3 Are you looking forward to ______________ (attend) the conference?
4 I'm finding it hard to get used to ______________ (wake up) early.
5 I'm always happy when my flatmate remembers ______________ (clean) the bathroom.
6 We've arranged ______________ (spend) Saturday morning with my cousins.
7 Can you help ______________ (tidy up) the flat, please?

Grammar reference

2 Find and correct the mistakes in the sentences.

1 What do you feel like to do this evening?
2 I think the students deserve winning a prize.
3 We are looking forward to go scuba diving.
4 We remember to travel to the Caribbean as children.
5 My younger sister always makes me to laugh.

10C Focus on: *the* with groups of people and things

To describe groups of people and things, use *the* in the following contexts:

- to describe a specific set of things and people.
  *At this hotel, **the staff** are so hardworking.*
- before the word *majority*, and after the words *some of, many of* and *none of*.
  *The festival was attended by **the majority** of the town's residents.*
  ***Many of the** students are bilingual.*
- when referring to groups of people using the adjective form of the nationality.
  ***The French** are known for their food.*

You don't need *the* in these contexts:

- to describe plural nouns when you are speaking in general.
  ***Spices** are an important part of many cuisines.*
- with the words *most, some, many* and *no*.
  ***Many** cultures have festivals in the springtime.*
  ***Some** countries have several national languages.*
- when referring to groups of people using the plural noun form of the nationality.
  ***Canadians** often enjoy watching ice hockey.*

1 Choose the correct option to complete the sentences.

1 *The most / Most* bilingual people find speaking more than one language incredibly useful.
2 Perhaps due to their diet, *the Japanese / Japanese* have a long life expectancy.
3 The internet has made it easier for *the many / many* subcultures to develop and grow.
4 *The tapas / Tapas* are small savoury dishes that are served as a snack.
5 At last night's show, *the dancers / dancers* gave an excellent performance.
6 Independence Day is celebrated by *the Colombians / Colombians* on 20th July.

2 Read the paragraph. Find and correct eight mistakes related to *the*.

Living in a diverse community is very important to me, perhaps because I've lived in the many multicultural cities throughout my life. My parents were the diplomats and as a result we travelled all over the world. I loved majority of the places we lived, although I found the climate in some of warmer countries hard to adapt to. On the other hand, in every country I met the incredible people and got to experience the culture in a unique way. Now, as an adult, I live in the East End of London. For me, the East End is a perfect fit because it reminds me of my travels. I love hearing dozens of the different languages as I walk through streets, and doing the shopping at family-owned corner shops is just the best. I buy my vegetables at an Indian grocery shop and owners are teaching me short phrases in their language.

Irregular verbs

INFINITIVE	PAST SIMPLE	PAST PARTICIPLE
be	was / were	been
beat	beat	beaten
become	became	become
begin	began	begun
bite	bit	bitten
blow	blew	blown
break	broke	broken
bring	brought	brought
build	built	built
burn	burned / burnt	burned / burnt
buy	bought	bought
catch	caught	caught
choose	chose	chosen
come	came	come
cost	cost	cost
cut	cut	cut
deal	dealt	dealt
dig	dug	dug
do	did	done
dream	dreamed / dreamt	dreamed / dreamt
drink	drank	drunk
drive	drove	driven
eat	ate	eaten
fall	fell	fallen
feel	felt	felt
fight	fought	fought

INFINITIVE	PAST SIMPLE	PAST PARTICIPLE
find	found	found
fly	flew	flown
forget	forgot	forgotten
forgive	forgave	forgiven
freeze	froze	frozen
get	got	got
give	gave	given
go	went	gone
grow	grew	grown
have	had	had
hear	heard	heard
hide	hid	hidden
hit	hit	hit
hold	held	held
hurt	hurt	hurt
keep	kept	kept
know	knew	known
lay	laid	laid
lead	led	led
leave	left	left
learn	learned / learnt	learned / learnt
lend	lent	lent
let	let	let
lie	lay	lain
lose	lost	lost
make	made	made

Irregular verbs

INFINITIVE	PAST SIMPLE	PAST PARTICIPLE
mean	meant	meant
meet	met	met
pay	paid	paid
put	put	put
read	read	read
ride	rode	ridden
ring	rang	rung
rise	rose	risen
run	ran	run
say	said	said
see	saw	seen
sell	sold	sold
send	sent	sent
set	set	set
shake	shook	shaken
shine	shone	shone
shoot	shot	shot
show	showed	shown
shut	shut	shut
sing	sang	sung
sit	sat	sat
sleep	slept	slept
smell	smelled / smelt	smelled / smelt
speak	spoke	spoken
spell	spelled / spelt	spelled / spelt

INFINITIVE	PAST SIMPLE	PAST PARTICIPLE
spend	spent	spent
spoil	spoiled / spoilt	spoiled / spoilt
spread	spread	spread
stand	stood	stood
steal	stole	stolen
stick	stuck	stuck
swear	swore	sworn
swim	swam	swum
take	took	taken
teach	taught	taught
tell	told	told
think	thought	thought
throw	threw	thrown
understand	understood	understood
wake	woke	woken
wear	wore	worn
win	won	won
write	wrote	written

Extra speaking tasks

PAGE 48, 4A, EXERCISE 8

SITUATION 1

Student A

You have recently moved to this neighbourhood. You'd like to learn about ways of enjoying nature in the local area.

Student B

You enjoy being outdoors. Recommend to Student A what they can do in the local area to stay close to nature.

SITUATION 2

Student A

You would like to do something outside with Student B, who isn't very keen. Persuade them.

Student B

You don't really like outdoor activities. You prefer staying indoors reading a book or watching a film. Student A will try to persuade you to spend time outside with them this weekend.

PAGE 51, 4B, EXERCISE 10

Student A

You and B are brothers/sisters. When your parents died, they left the family bakery to you both to share the profits equally. You think B is lazy and takes advantage of your work, so you have decided that you should receive most of the profits. You are so angry with B that you don't speak to her/him at all. Your friend C wants to help you and B end the arguments and reach an agreement. Tell C what the problems are. Use reporting verbs when possible.

My sister/brother promised to do more work, but she/he never does.

Student B

You and A are brothers/sisters. When your parents died, they left the family bakery to you both to share the profits equally. You think A is very bossy. She/he also makes you do extra work, while she/he sits in the office and does nothing. You are so angry with A that you don't speak to her/him at all. Your friend C wants to help you and A end the arguments and reach an agreement. Tell C what the problems are. Use reporting verbs when possible.

My sister/brother accuses me of being lazy, but actually it's her/him that doesn't do any work.

Student C

You are a good friend of A and B. They are brothers/sisters. They inherited the family bakery and were supposed to share the profits equally. However, they have been arguing about many things and don't talk to each other at all, so you've decided to help them. Listen to A and B to find out why they are unhappy. Report what each one says to the other and try to help them reach an agreement that they are both happy with.

Your brother/sister says you promised to help out more. Maybe you could take turns to run the bakery at the weekend?

PAGE 55, 4D, EXERCISE 9

1 Choose one of these topics to discuss.

Interesting places you've been to
Keeping in touch with friends
Is having a foreign accent OK?
The best way to keep in touch with friends long distance

2 Your teacher will assign you one of the three turn-taking styles (rugby, bowling, basketball) to use during the discussion. Don't tell your partners which you have.

3 Have a conversation about the topic, using your assigned turn-taking style.

4 After three minutes, stop the conversation and discuss the questions:
- Which turn-taking style did each person have?
- How do you know this?

5 Choose a different topic and have another conversation. Keep the same turn-taking style you were assigned. This time, however, adapt your style during the conversation in order to ensure fair participation.

6 After three minutes, stop the conversation and discuss the questions:
- How did each person adapt their communication style?
- What went well?
- What could you do better next time?

Extra speaking tasks

PAGE 67, 5D, EXERCISE 11

Student A

You're the doctor. Speak as fast as you can. Choose at least three of the words in the box to use in a conversation with the patient. Check the meaning of any new words before you begin.

acute pain	do an X-ray
anxiety	elaborate on
appropriate treatment	mental health
come down with (a cold/ the flu)	physical wellbeing
cope with	symptoms

Student B

You're the patient. You have a lower level of English. Think of a problem you have. The doctor will speak very fast and might use words you will find difficult to understand.

Student C

You're the nurse. Help the patient communicate with the doctor by adapting the language. The doctor might use some of the words in the box. Think how you could explain them to the patient so that they understand. Check the meaning of any new words before you begin.

acute pain	do an X-ray
anxiety	elaborate on
appropriate treatment	mental health
come down with (a cold/ the flu)	physical wellbeing
cope with	symptoms

PAGE 102, 8D, EXERCISE 3

1-15 Points

You're quite strict about your online etiquette. You try to maintain some level of formality and pay attention to how you communicate online.

16-25 Points

You're somewhere in the middle. You might sometimes break a few online etiquette rules, but you also follow quite a few.

26-40 Points

You're very relaxed about your online etiquette. You think online communication should be informal and prefer not to follow formal rules.

PAGE 112, 9C, EXERCISE 1

Mostly As

You make life difficult for yourself sometimes but try not to give up. Try to remember that things may not be as bad as they seem.

Mostly Bs

Taking the easy option isn't always the best option in the long run. If you face the problem, you may discover a new talent or opportunity!

Mostly Cs

You are good at taking advantage of bad situations. You know how to turn negatives into positives.

Vocabulary and Grammar reference Answer key

VOCABULARY REFERENCE

UNIT 1 **1** 1 impatient 2 optimistic 3 concerned 4 astonished 5 relieved 6 motivated 7 petrified 8 thrilled 9 furious

UNIT 2 **1** 1 e 2 h 3 a 4 c 5 g 6 b 7 f 8 d

UNIT 3 **1** 1 set off / head back 2 reach 3 end up 4 stop over 5 turn back / head back 6 made it 7 go on

UNIT 4 **1** 1 reconnected 2 caught up 3 lost touch with 4 keep in close 5 keeping in touch 6 stick together 7 hit it off 8 get along with

UNIT 5 **1** 1 anxiety 2 Coping with 3 get over 4 symptoms 5 Coming down with 6 at risk 7 feel sorry for 8 Take a nap 9 calling in sick 10 staying in shape

UNIT 6 **1** 1 skim over 2 top story 3 the press 4 in-depth 5 report 6 objective 7 sensational 8 tabloid

UNIT 7 **1** 1 densely crowded 2 cold and damp 3 breathtaking 4 absolutely stunning 5 narrow 6 warm and cosy 7 elegantly decorated 8 spacious 9 light and airy

UNIT 8 **1** 1 innovative 2 recharge 3 sophisticated 4 handy 5 pocket-sized 6 user-friendly 7 waterproof 8 performs 9 outdated

UNIT 9 **1** 1 make it through 2 achieve (my) objectives 3 struggling 4 overcome/tackle 5 tackle the problem/issue 6 a mess

UNIT 10 **1** 1 f 2 d 3 a 4 h 5 c 6 g 7 b 8 e

GRAMMAR REFERENCE

1B GRAMMAR: FORMING QUESTIONS **1** 1 Could you tell me **when the meeting starts**? 2 She was very surprised, **wasn't she**? 3 **Haven't we gone** there before? 4 I'd like to know **where the bank is**. 5 A: I think my sister looks a bit tired. B: **Do you**? 6 **Who came** with you to the restaurant?
2 1 Did you 2 wouldn't you 3 Does it 4 Have you 5 are you 6 How much is 7 would you mind 8 will take

1C FOCUS ON: ADVERBS OF DEGREE **1** 1 absolutely 2 a bit 3 really 4 tremendously 5 totally 6 somewhat **2** 1 stronger 2 stronger 3 weaker

2B GRAMMAR: PRESENT TENSES **1** 1 picks up 2 have been reading up 3 I'm studying 4 have had 5 haven't come up 6 we've made **2** 1 has been 2 'm enjoying / 've / have been enjoying 3 have 4 've / have visited 5 've / have been missing 6 have 7 'm / am studying 8 spending / am spending

2C FOCUS ON: SEPARABLE AND INSEPARABLE PHRASAL VERBS **1** 1 a 2 b 3 b 4 b 5 a 6 a

3B GRAMMAR: NARRATIVE TENSES **1** 1 had dreamed 2 wanted 3 had done 4 landed 5 had 6 was made 7 had been lying 8 reached 9 was pulling 10 had arrived **2** 1 were walking; came across 2 stopped by; had found 3 had been looking forward to; felt 4 became; decided

3C FOCUS ON: COLLOCATIONS WITH *GO ON* **1** 1 go on a safari 2 go on package holidays 3 going on a language exchange 4 going on a scientific expedition 5 going on a business trip 6 went on a cruise

4B GRAMMAR: REPORTED SPEECH AND REPORTING VERBS **1** 1 he was going to come the next day 2 his sister had been feeling tired 3 he had been feeling ill 4 we / they should go for dinner the following week **2** 1 to help 2 for breaking 3 of forgetting 4 to come 5 to making 6 for being 7 to arrive 8 asking

4C FOCUS ON: TRANSITIVE AND INTRANSITIVE PHRASAL VERBS **1** 1 keep in touch (I) 2 catching up with (T) **2** 1 catch up with you sometime 2 keep in touch with Lei 3 hit it off with my best friend right away 4 lost touch with my cousin, I felt very sad 5 keep in close contact with my cousins

5B GRAMMAR: CONDITIONALS **1** 1 first 2 zero 3 second 4 second 5 third 6 first **2** 1 had 2 would come 3 had managed 4 would have learnt / learned 5 'll / will feel 6 take 7 will help

5C FOCUS ON: *I WISH* … AND *IF ONLY* … **1** 1 f 2 c 3 e 4 a 5 b 6 d **2** 1 had 2 knew 3 had gone 4 didn't have 5 hadn't forgotten 6 had trained

6B GRAMMAR PASSIVE STRUCTURES **1** 1 is believed to 2 will be presented 3 been spent 4 understood to 5 is going 6 are being **2** 1 a number of important issues were discussed 2 It was hoped that the problem 3 Jaime Vega is believed to be the best person / It is believed that Jaime Vega is the best person 4 has been written on the subject 5 It is recommended (that) 6 are going to be answered / will be answered

6C FOCUS ON: *THE* … *THE* … **1** 1 The sooner 2 the more 3 the better 4 The more loudly 5 The older **2** 1 The less I study, the more free time **I have** for my hobbies. 2 The **fewer** pets people have, the cheaper it is for them. 3 The more quickly we drive, **the sooner** we'll get to the airport. 4 **The more time** you can spend relaxing on holiday, the better you will feel. 5 The darker my bedroom is, **the more easily** I get to sleep.

7B GRAMMAR: CAUSATIVE VERBS **1** 1 allow 2 advised 3 are helping 4 prevents 5 can't let 6 will save **2** 1 become 2 to include 3 (to) save 4 to leave 5 (from) feeling 6 (from) worrying 7 to begin 8 to give up 9 to try out

7D FOCUS ON: USEFUL STRUCTURES FOR COMPLAINING **1** 1 d 2 f 3 a 4 b 5 e 6 c **2** 1 I find long queues so frustrating. Not used: such 2 If only she would work harder. Not used: will 3 Henry is in such a bad mood. Not used: too 4 I wish the weather was better. Not used: is 5 My boss is always telling me off. Not used: such

8B GRAMMAR: SPECULATING ABOUT THE PAST **1** 1 a 2 b 3 a 4 a **2** 1 must 2 might/may/could 3 should 4 can't/couldn't 5 must 6 shouldn't

8C FOCUS ON: FORMING NOUNS, VERBS AND ADJECTIVES **1** 1 impossibility 2 accomplishment 3 critical 4 statement 5 memorable **2** 1 creative 2 possibilities 3 competition 4 Original 5 attractive 6 affordable 7 downloadable 8 Additional 9 submissions

9B GRAMMAR: TALKING ABOUT THE FUTURE **1** 1 will have 2 'll be 3 should 4 won't 5 might have **2** 1 will have arrived 2 will be chatting 3 might have thought of 4 should have received / will have received 5 will be explaining 6 should have submitted / will have submitted

9C FOCUS ON: VERB-NOUN COLLOCATIONS **1** 1 f 2 c 3 a 4 e 5 b 6 d **2** 1 achieve 2 overcome 3 made 4 struggling 5 tackling 6 make

10B GRAMMAR: VERB PATTERNS WITH INFINITIVE AND *-ING*
1 1 listening 2 to go 3 attending 4 waking up 5 to clean 6 to spend 7 (to) tidy up **2** 1 What do you feel like **doing** this evening? 2 I think the students deserve **to win** a prize. 3 We are looking forward **to going** scuba diving. 4 We remember **travelling** to the Caribbean as children. 5 My younger sister always makes me **laugh**.

10C FOCUS ON: *THE* WITH GROUPS OF PEOPLE AND THINGS **1** 1 Most 2 the Japanese 3 many 4 Tapas 5 the dancers 6 Colombians **2** Living in a diverse community is very important to me, perhaps because I've lived in [1]**many multicultural cities** throughout my life. My parents were [2]**diplomats** and as a result we travelled all over the world. I loved [3]**the majority of** the places we lived, although I found the climate in some of [4]**the warmer countries** hard to adapt to. On the other hand, in every country I met [5]**incredible people** and got to experience the culture in a unique way. Now, as an adult, I live in the East End of London. For me, the East End is a perfect fit because it reminds me of my travels. I love hearing dozens of [6]**different languages** as I walk through [7]**the streets**, and doing the shopping at family-owned corner shops is just the best. I buy my vegetables at an Indian grocery store and [8]**the owners** are teaching me short phrases in their language.

Photocopiable resources Introduction

On the following pages you will find a variety of photocopiable worksheets to complement your lessons using *Voices* Upper Intermediate Student's Book.

Communication activities (pp. 212–231). There are two communication activities for each unit. Teacher's notes and answer keys can be found on pages 207–211.

Vocabulary activities (pp. 233–242). There is one vocabulary activity for each unit. Answer keys can be found on page 232.

Grammar and Focus on activities (pp. 245–264). There is one grammar activity and one 'Focus on …' activity for each unit. Answer keys can be found on pages 243–244.

Pronunciation activities (pp. 268–277). There is one pronunciation activity for each unit. Teacher's notes and answer keys can be found on pages 265–267.

Mediation activities (pp. 283–292). There is one mediation activity for each unit. Teacher's notes and answer keys can be found on pages 278–282, as well as a guide to mediation and a correlation of the activities to CEFR descriptors.

Communication activities Teacher's notes

UNIT 1 Communication 1 What makes you laugh or cry?

Aim: to practise question forms

When to use: after Exercise 9 in Lesson 1B

Procedure: Put students in groups of four (Students A, B, C and D). Give each student a card so that students in each group each have a different set of questions. Give students a few minutes to prepare questions and ask about vocabulary. Tell Student A to interview B, and tell Student C to interview D. Then D interviews A, and B interviews C. In feedback, students tell their group what they found out about the student they interviewed.

UNIT 1 Communication 2 What happened to you?

Aim: to practise emotions vocabulary

When to use: after Exercise 14 in Lesson 1C

Procedure: Put students in small groups. Cut out the talking point cards. Give each group one set of cards and place them face down in a pile. Students take turns to pick a card. They must talk for one minute without stopping or changing the subject. If they talk for one minute, they win the card. If they don't, it goes back to the bottom of the pile. The next student turns over a card and talks. The winner is the player to win the most cards.

UNIT 2 Communication 1 Find someone who …

Aim: to practise present forms

When to use: after Exercise 9 in Lesson 2B

Procedure: Give one worksheet to each student. Give students time to prepare questions. Then ask them to stand up, walk around and ask questions to as many fellow students as they can in ten minutes. Encourage students to ask *Who*, *What*, *When*, *Where* and *Why* questions to get extra information. At the end, students sit down and tell the class what interesting information they found.

Alternatively, make the activity competitive by telling students to try to be the first to get a different name in answer to each question, and one piece of extra information for each situation.

UNIT 2 Communication 2 Special French words

Aim: to practise talking about first language identity

When to use: after Exercise 11 in Lesson 2D

Procedure: Put students in groups of three to six. Cut out the six words and definitions and ask students to deal them out in their groups.

Explain that English has a lot of French expressions. Ask students if they can think of any. Then say, *You are going to discuss six French expressions used in English.*

Write the questions below on the board. Ask students to discuss each expression using these questions.

1 How would you say this in your first language?
2 How might you use this word in conversation?
3 What word or phrase from your language would you teach English speakers to use in this situation?

Students take turns to read out a phrase and definition. Students then discuss each phrase in their groups. Encourage students to talk about their first language identity, using some of the language below. If there are any L1 French speakers in your class, encourage them to tell the rest of their group if the expressions have the same literal meaning in French and if they would use them in the same way in French.

How do you say that in [Russian]?

It sounds a bit like […].

We have a similar expression that translates as …

I'm sure we have a phrase in […]. It's on the tip of my tongue!

Follow up by asking students to think of an expression from their first language that they think could be adopted by English speakers. Tell them to think of a way of using it in an English sentence.

UNIT 3 Communication 1 Important moments

Aim: to practise narrative sentences

When to use: after Exercise 10 in Lesson 3B

Procedure: Put students in groups of four. Cut out the situations and give a set to each group. Ask students to choose one of the six situations. Give them a few minutes to prepare a true story based on the situation and the questions. When students are ready, they place their card on the table and tell their story. Other students can ask questions to check details or ask for further information. Once students have all told a story, they can choose a different situation and tell a new story.

You could introduce an element of competition by asking students to choose to prepare either a true story from their lives or a false story they have made up. Once everybody has told their story, students must decide who was telling the truth and who had made up their story.

UNIT 3 Communication 2 It's another way to say …

Aim: to practise clarifying meaning and simplifying language

When to use: after Exercise 10 in Lesson 3D

Procedure: Put students in groups of four. Then ask each group to form two pairs. Cut out the idioms and give five at random to each pair. Tell pairs to look at their idioms and research their meanings using dictionaries or the internet – or by checking with you.

Give each group the list of conversation starters. One student reads out the first conversation starter. Pairs look at their idioms and decide if they have an idiom that is a suitable response to the conversation starter. For example: *1 Susie drove all the way to the airport to pick us up and take us home – and we didn't land until 2 a.m. SHE HAS A HEART OF GOLD.* They place the idiom down and read it out. Students must then clarify its meaning. Encourage students to use useful language when doing this: *Do you see what I mean? It's another way of saying …; What I mean is …; In other words, …; It basically means …*

The other members of the group should confirm their understanding of the phrase. Encourage students to use useful language such as: *So you're saying … ?; That makes sense.; Got it!*

Students move on to the next conversation starter. Once students have matched an idiom to each conversation starter, and clarified its meaning, the activity is over. In feedback, check whether students have matched their idioms correctly. Pairs get a point for each idiom matched correctly.

Answers (and possible clarifications):

1 SHE HAS A HEART OF GOLD. (She's very kind and thoughtful.)
2 EVERYBODY WILL BE UP IN ARMS. (Everybody will be angry and complaining.) [i.e. waving their arms in the air]
3 DON'T BITE MY HEAD OFF! (Don't criticize so aggressively.)
4 YOU'VE HIT THE NAIL ON THE HEAD. (I agree with you completely.)
5 I'M A MAN/WOMAN OF MY WORD. (I always keep a promise.)
6 I'LL PULL SOME STRINGS. (I will talk to people in power that I know in order to get things done.)
7 IT'S NOT ALL IT'S CRACKED UP TO BE. (It isn't as good as it seems – it's disappointing.) [here, 'crack up' means 'talk up']
8 ONCE IN A BLUE MOON. (very, very rarely) [i.e. like the occurrence of a blue moon]
9 I'M BURNING THE CANDLE AT BOTH ENDS. (I'm working from very early in the morning to very late at night.)
10 IT WENT DOWN LIKE A LEAD BALLOON. (It was not popular or successful.) [i.e. a balloon made of lead would fall down because it's very heavy]

UNIT 4 Communication 1 Keeping in touch

Aim: to describe friendship groups using relationships vocabulary

When to use: after Exercise 9 in Lesson 4C

Procedure: Give one worksheet to each student. Ask students to read the key carefully and to look at the example. Then draw your friendship circle on the board, e.g. Draw an oval. Next, draw a short straight line from the oval with the word *Dan* at the end, and say, *This is Dan. He's my best friend from school. We hit it off the moment we met and we get along well – he supports me a lot.* Mention and draw one or two other people at the end of lines that match the worksheet key. Once students have the idea, ask them to draw friendship circles with at least five people mentioned.

When students are ready, put them in pairs or small groups. Students describe the people in their friendship circle in any order (but avoid doing it in the same order as the key). Other students listen and draw what they think their classmate's friendship circle looks like. At the end, students compare their friendship circles.

UNIT 4 Communication 2 Speaking hats

Aim: to practise taking turns in a debate

When to use: after Exercise 9 in Lesson 4D

Procedure: Tell the class they are going to play roles in a debate. Put students in groups of four. Cut out a set of four speaking hat cards for each group and place them so everybody in the group can read them. Ask students to decide as a group who will take each card. Once everybody has selected a card, tell them to read it carefully so that they are sure exactly what their role is.

Hand out the debate topics to the student in each group who is the Blue Hat. Tell Blue Hats to choose a topic to debate and to introduce it. The rest of the group must join in the debate playing the role of their 'Hat'. Blue Hats may wind up any debate and move on to a new topic whenever they think the debate has run its course.

There are alternative ways to do this activity. You could hand out 'hats' randomly and tell students to keep their identity secret. At the end of the debate, let students read about all four hats and decide which person in their group was wearing which hat. Another idea is to ask students to change hats when they switch from one debate to another, or to change hats halfway through a debate.

Remind students of turn-taking language to use in a debate:

Sorry, can I just finish what I was saying?

I'm glad you brought it up because …

I'd like to just add that …

Can I just jump in there?

As I was saying, …

I've talked too much already. What did you want to say?

NB This idea is an adaptation of Edward de Bono's *Six Thinking Hats*.

UNIT 5 Communication 1 What would you have done?

Aim: to practise the third conditional

When to use: after Exercise 9 in Lesson 5B

Procedure: Put students in pairs or small groups. One worksheet per pair or group. Ask students to fold the worksheet along the line so they can't see the bottom half of the sheet.

Students read the situations and discuss what they would have done in each situation. Set a ten minute time limit, but extend if students get into the activity. Monitor the class to ensure students are using the third conditional in their answers e.g. *If I was Brad, I would have …* Once students have read and discussed all the situations, ask them to unfold the *Were they right?* section. Students read and check their answers. In feedback, find out which group would have done the right thing most often.

UNIT 5 Communication 2 Can you explain that more simply?

Aim: to practise adapting and simplifying English

When to use: after Exercise 11 in Lesson 5D

Procedure: Put students in pairs or small groups. Give out one worksheet per pair or group. Ask students to cut out each box and place them face down in a pile. Students turn over a 'message' and think of how to express it in simpler language. Tell students to look up the meaning of any words they don't know using dictionaries or the internet – or by checking with you. At the end, ask different groups to give their simplified version of each message, and see which groups have the best simplified versions.

Sample answers

1 Take the medicine three times a day after meals.
2 The course will start two weeks late.
3 Apply for your free gift in the next ten days.
4 Can you return my magazine, please?
5 Connect cables A, B and C to ports A, B and C.
6 The sky was blue and the sun was shining.
7 The library will be open from Monday to Friday.
8 Can I have a lift? I'm tired.
9 Please read the college regulations in the leaflet we sent.

UNIT 6 Communication 1 Hold the front page

Aim: to practise writing and comparing news articles using passive forms

When to use: after Exercise 9 in Lesson 6B

Procedure: Put students in pairs and give one worksheet to each pair. Ask students to read the headlines and decide which they think would be the most interesting story to write. Once students have chosen a headline, tell them to write their story. Tell them to make it really exciting and sensational because they want their story to be the lead story in the *Daily News*. Remind them that they should use passive structures. Check that students have selected a range of headlines, and that not too many pairs are doing the same story. Alternatively, you could choose to allocate headlines randomly to ensure the class write about all the stories.

When students have written their stories, put pairs together to make groups of four. Tell these new groups that they are *Daily News* editors. It is their job to read the stories and decide which one to make the lead story in their newspaper. Pass the news stories round from group to group. Students read the stories, discuss them and choose one to make their lead story.

UNIT 6 Communication 2 The bigger, the better

Aim: to speculate about quotations using *the … the …*

When to use: After Exercise 11 in Lesson 6C

Procedure: Put students into groups of three to five. Hand out one worksheet per student. Ask students to read the two halves of the famous quotes and match them. Let students work individually before comparing in their groups. Go through the answers in feedback. Note that some alternative answers are possible (e.g. *The more I learn about people, the more I want you.* makes for a good quote). Praise good alternatives but check that students have got the right quotes.

Ask groups to read about the eight famous people. Then ask them to discuss which person they think said each quote and why.

Answers

1 h The better the actor I am acting with, the better my performance gets. (Ali Fazal)
2 d The greater the obstacle, the more glory in overcoming it. (Molière)
3 e The older you get, the less people remember what you did before. (Sue Barker)
4 f The more I know, the more I realize I know nothing. (Socrates)
5 a The more I learn about people, the more I like my dog. (Mark Twain)
6 c The more I see you, the more I want you. (Chris Montez)
7 g The bigger they are, the harder they fall. (Bob Fitzsimmons)
8 b The harder I work, the luckier I get. (Samuel Goldwyn)

UNIT 7 Communication 1 The perfect home

Aim: to practise describing places

When to use: after Exercise 11 in Lesson 7C

Procedure: Divide your class into two halves. Tell one half they are estate agents. Tell the other half they are customers. Then tell estate agents to get in pairs, and customers to get in pairs. Hand out an estate agent card to each pair of estate agents. Hand out an equal number of A or B cards. Hand out one of the role cards to each pair of customers. Tell estate agents to think about the headings on their cards and to make notes. Tell customers to add more detail about what they want from a property.

After five minutes, tell customers to stand up, visit estate agents and describe what they are looking for in a property and why. Estate agents must try to sell them one of their properties. Ask students to visit at least three different estate agents before they decide what to buy. At the end, ask the customers to say which properties they are going to buy and from which estate agents.

UNIT 7 Communication 2 Mighty moaners and careful critics

Aim: to practise structures for complaining and ways of softening the message when criticizing or asking people to do something differently

When to use: after Exercise 12 in Lesson 7D

Procedure: Put students in groups of four or five. Hand out one worksheet per group. Ask students to place a token on START. Students take turns to throw a dice and move round the board. When they land on a square, they must obey the instruction. They must speak for as long as they can, either moaning or requesting a change of behaviour without offending. The winner is the first student to reach FINISH.

To slow students down, tell them they can move one space if they throw 1 or 4, two places if they throw 2 or 5, and three places if they throw 3 or 6.

To make the activity more demanding, set a thirty second minimum time during which students must moan or criticize. If they run out of things to say before thirty seconds are up, they must go back one space.

Remind students of useful language:

Complaining:

He's / She's so / such a …

If only / I wish + past simple

If only / I wish + would + infinitive

He's/She's always + -ing

Softening the message:

I hope you don't mind me saying this, but …

I appreciate that you want to … but I …

I'd really appreciate it if you could …

It's just that if you could … that would allow me to …

Can I suggest something? How about …?

UNIT 8 Communication 1 What could have happened?

Aim: to practise *must/could/might/may/can't have*

When to use: after Exercise 9 in Lesson 8B

Procedure: Put students in small groups. Give each group a worksheet. Ask one student to read out the introduction to their group. In feedback, ask a few questions to check understanding, then ask students to speculate about what might have happened. Elicit a few ideas.

Ask students in their groups to take turns to read out a clue from the list 1–16. After a clue is read out, the group must speculate about what may have happened. They can revise previous opinions and add new possibilities. Once groups have read out and discussed each clue, they must present their idea about what may have happened to Briggs and his crew.

Note: Nobody knows what happened to the *Mary Celeste*. It remains a mystery. Some suggestions include: a pirate attack (though nothing was taken), an abandonment of the ship because they thought the barrels could explode, an insurance scam that went wrong, the crew panicked in bad weather and got into the lifeboat, Briggs went mad and killed everybody. In truth, though, it's still a mystery.

UNIT 8 Communication 2 Which new gadget?

Aim: to practise describing gadgets

When to use: after Exercise 11 in Lesson 8C

Procedure: Put the class in groups of three. Give each group a worksheet. Tell each group that they are an electronics company with four new gadgets to sell in their showroom. They have ten minutes to prepare to sell the four gadgets on their worksheet.

Tell groups to begin by thinking of a company name that will attract customers. Then ask them to prepare notes on each of their four gadgets. Tell them to think of and note down an appealing name for their product, and to think of realistic but appealing ways of describing the basic features of each product. If students are not very 'techy', they can write 'Excellent' or 'better than standard smartphones', etc. Tell them to invent special features that they think might help sell the product. Encourage students to use some of the vocabulary from Unit 8:

device innovative handy outdated performance
pocket-sized recharge revolutionize sophisticated
user-friendly waterproof

Once groups have prepared ideas, ask each group to choose one member to play a customer. That student then moves to the next group. Groups have to present their four products to the customer. After five minutes, ask customers to move to the next group. After five more minutes, ask customers to move on once more.

Once customers have visited three electronics companies, they must decide which gadgets to buy. Ask customers to say which smartphone, TV, headphones and laptop they wish to buy. Find out which electronics company has sold the most items.

UNIT 9 Communication 1 New job, new future

Aim: to practise future forms including future continuous and future perfect

When to use: after Exercise 7 in Lesson 9B

Procedure: Put students in small groups. Give each group one set of question cards and one set of role cards, face down in separate piles.

One student in each group turns over a role card, reads it and keeps it secret. They must now answer questions from their group without revealing their job or using any of the words on the card.

The group turn over a question card and ask the student with the role card to answer. They can ask two or three follow up questions. Then the group turn over and ask a second question. After turning over and asking five questions (plus follow up questions) the group must guess the job of the student with the role card.

A new student selects a role card. The group shuffles the question cards and starts asking questions again.

UNIT 9 Communication 2 25 years from now

Aim: to practise future predictions

When to use: after Exercise 11 in Lesson 9B

Procedure: Put students in small groups. Hand out one worksheet to each group and ask them to cut out the squares. Ask groups to place the statements in a pile face down. Alternatively, students need not cut out the cards – they could just work from the worksheet.

Write these two questions on the board:

Do you think it will have happened 25 years from now?

Do you think it will be a good thing or not?

Ask a student to turn over a card and read out the statement. The group has three minutes to discuss the topic using the questions on the board before moving on to another question. At the end of the activity, have a general whole class feedback and find out which predictions groups agree with.

UNIT 10 Communication 1 Are you classic or modern?

Aim: to use verb + *-ing* or infinitive to guess what type of people we are

When to use: after Exercise 11 in Lesson 10B

Procedure: Put students in pairs. Hand out an A card to Student A in each pair and a B card to Student B. Give students a few minutes to complete their questions using the correct form of the verbs in brackets.

Write the following 'types' on the board:

classic modern

Define the words and ask students to think of what someone with a classic style or personality and what someone with a modern style or personality might wear, enjoy doing, etc. Ask students to say which label they think applies to them.

Students take turns to interview each other using the questions they prepared. At the end, ask students to say whether (based on the answers to their questions) they think their partner is classic or modern.

Answers: A: 1 wearing 2 to read 3 to have 4 watching 5 doing 6 listening/to listen 7 to buy 8 doing 9 to go 10 doing

B: 1 reading 2 wearing/to wear 3 to do 4 to do 5 seeing 6 doing 7 to listen 8 to live 9 to watch 10 to doing

UNIT 10 Communication 2 Assumptions

Aim: to discuss how we make assumptions about people

When to use: after Exercise 10 in Lesson 10D

Procedure: Put students in pairs. In order to make this activity work well, encourage students to sit with partners that they do not know all that well. Hand out one worksheet to each student. Tell students to fold along the line so that they can't see the discussion questions.

Ask students to answer the twelve questions about their partner and to make brief notes. Tell them to guess or make assumptions in order to answer the questions. When students have completed their notes, ask them to interview their partner to find out if their guesses were correct. Have a brief feedback session and find out which students made good guesses about their partner.

Follow up by asking students to unfold the discussion questions and discuss them with a partner. You could turn this into a whole class discussion about the assumptions we make about each other.

1 Communication 1 What makes you laugh or cry?

HUMOUR

Ask your partner questions to find out …

1 … what makes them laugh.

2 … which TV comedies they watch.

3 … which comedians are popular in their country and why.

4 … whether they think laughter is the best medicine.

5 … if they think they have a good sense of humour.

SADNESS

Ask your partner questions to find out …

1 … what makes them cry.

2 … whether they get upset when watching certain films, and which ones.

3 … what they do when they're feeling down.

4 … if they think it is good to feel sad sometimes.

5 … how they are feeling now.

ANGER

Ask your partner questions to find out …

1 … what really annoys them.

2 … what they do when they feel annoyed.

3 … how often they lose their temper.

4 … when they last strongly disagreed with someone.

5 … if they think they get too annoyed sometimes.

HAPPINESS

Ask your partner questions to find out …

1 … what makes them happy in daily life.

2 … whether they feel happy right now – and if so, why.

3 … how they cheer themselves up when they are down.

4 … when the happiest time of their life was.

5 … what time of year is the happiest time for them.

Communication 2 What happened to you?

a time when you cried	the most amazing place you have been to	a person currently in the public eye who annoys you
what motivates you to learn English	why you are in this class	what you are feeling optimistic about
an act of kindness you have received	an issue or cause that you feel strongly about	the things that scare you
a day when everything went wrong	the best book or film you have seen	a person currently in the public eye who you admire
a time when you felt relieved	a sports event that means a lot to you	a time when you felt scared or even petrified
the best holiday you have ever had	a time when you were so angry you lost your temper	your pet hates (small things you really dislike)

Communication 1 Find someone who …

Find someone who …

1 … speaks more than two languages.

2 … is doing evening classes in something other than languages.

3 … has lived in a country where English is the first language.

4 … has been studying English for more than ten years.

5 … has made friends with someone who speaks English as their first language.

6 … is using technology to improve their English.

7 … has read a classic novel in English.

8 … knows three synonyms for 'angry' in English.

9 … has been studying English every day this week.

10 … hasn't done their homework yet.

AU FAIT /ˌəʊ ˈfeɪ/

This means that you are familiar with a situation – you know what to do.

English speakers might say: *I've lived here a while, so I'm au fait with how people do things.*

SAVOIR-FAIRE /ˌsævwɑː(r) ˈfeə(r)/

This means that you know how to behave in social situations.

English speakers might say: *Jack embarrassed himself at the dinner party – he displayed a lack of savoir-faire.*

BRIC-À-BRAC /ˈbrɪkəˌbræk/

Objects and ornaments of little value that we keep about our houses.

English speakers might say: *Aunt Helen's house was full of bric-à-brac.*

DE RIGUEUR /də rɪˈgɜː(r)/

This describes something that is required or expected of you.

English speakers might say: *At the annual company dinner, a shirt and tie is de rigueur.*

DÉJÀ VU /ˌdeɪʒɑː ˈvuː/

This describes the feeling that you have already visited a place or experienced something before.

English speakers might say: *When we arrived at the old house, I had a real sense of déjà vu – perhaps I had visited this place when I was a child.*

FAIT ACCOMPLI /ˌfeɪt əˈkɒmpliː/

This describes a situation when something has already happened, and so it can't be changed.

English speakers might say: *My brother had sold the house before we got back to England. It was a fait accompli. There was nothing we could do.*

Communication 1 Important moments

AN INTERVIEW

Think of an important interview you have had.

- *What was it for?*
- *How were you feeling?*
- *What had you done to prepare?*
- *What questions did they ask?*
- *How did you answer them?*
- *Was it successful? Why? / Why not?*

A MISUNDERSTANDING

Think of a time when there was a misunderstanding between you and another person (e.g. on holiday, in a hotel, taxi or restaurant).

- *Where were you and who were you talking to?*
- *What was the misunderstanding?*
- *Why did it happen?*
- *What happened in the end? Did you sort out the misunderstanding? If so, how?*

A VICTORY

Think of something you have won in your life (e.g. a competition, or a sports or arts event).

- *What event did you win?*
- *What did you have to do to win?*
- *How did you feel when you won?*
- *Were you expecting to win?*
- *Did you get a prize?*
- *What did you do after winning?*
- *Had you won anything before that? If so, what?*

A LOSS

Think of a time when you lost something.

- *What did you lose?*
- *Where did you lose it?*
- *What had you been doing before you lost it?*
- *What were you doing when you lost it?*
- *Did you find it again?*
- *What happened as a result of losing it?*

AN ACCIDENT ON HOLIDAY

Think of a time when things went wrong on holiday or during a trip, e.g. an injury.

- *What was the accident?*
- *What were you doing when it happened?*
- *Where were you and how did it happen?*
- *Whose fault was it?*
- *How did you feel?*
- *How did you fix the problem or get better?*

A SOUVENIR

Think of a trip or holiday when you bought a souvenir.

- *What was the souvenir?*
- *Where did you buy it and why?*
- *What were you doing when you bought it?*
- *How did you feel?*
- *How did you get it back home?*
- *Where is it now and why?*

3 Communication 2 It's another way to say …

CONVERSATION STARTERS

1 Susie drove all the way to the airport to pick us up and take us home – and we didn't land until 2 a.m.

2 The hotel manager has asked all the staff to work extra hours on Saturday.

3 I can't believe you've left the passports at home! You're hopeless!

4 The problem with this country is that nobody wants to work hard.

5 Thanks for coming all this way – I know you promised, but I didn't know if you would come.

6 I'm getting no help with my passport application. You work for the foreign office – can you help me?

7 Most people say the museum is great, but I hear you didn't enjoy it as much as you expected.

8 Now that you have children, do you get a chance to go away by yourself?

9 You look tired – do you have a lot of work on at the moment?

10 Did everybody like your presentation about ways to improve the company?

YOU'VE HIT THE NAIL ON THE HEAD.	I'LL PULL SOME STRINGS.
DON'T BITE MY HEAD OFF!	IT'S NOT ALL IT'S CRACKED UP TO BE.
I'M A MAN/WOMAN OF MY WORD.	ONCE IN A BLUE MOON.
SHE HAS A HEART OF GOLD.	I'M BURNING THE CANDLE AT BOTH ENDS.
EVERYBODY WILL BE UP IN ARMS.	IT WENT DOWN LIKE A LEAD BALLOON.

UNIT
4 Communication 1 Keeping in touch

Look at the example friendship circle. Then look at the instructions below and complete your own friendship circle.

- Write your name in the middle of the large circle.
- Use lines from the key. Write the names of people at the end of each line.
- Use at least one example of each line.
- The shorter the line the closer that person is to you.

KEY

•••••••••• = acquaintance or colleague that you don't know well but get on well with

———— = close friend that you get along with and see often

～～～ = good friend that you keep in touch with but don't see often

– – – – = close family member that you are in close contact with

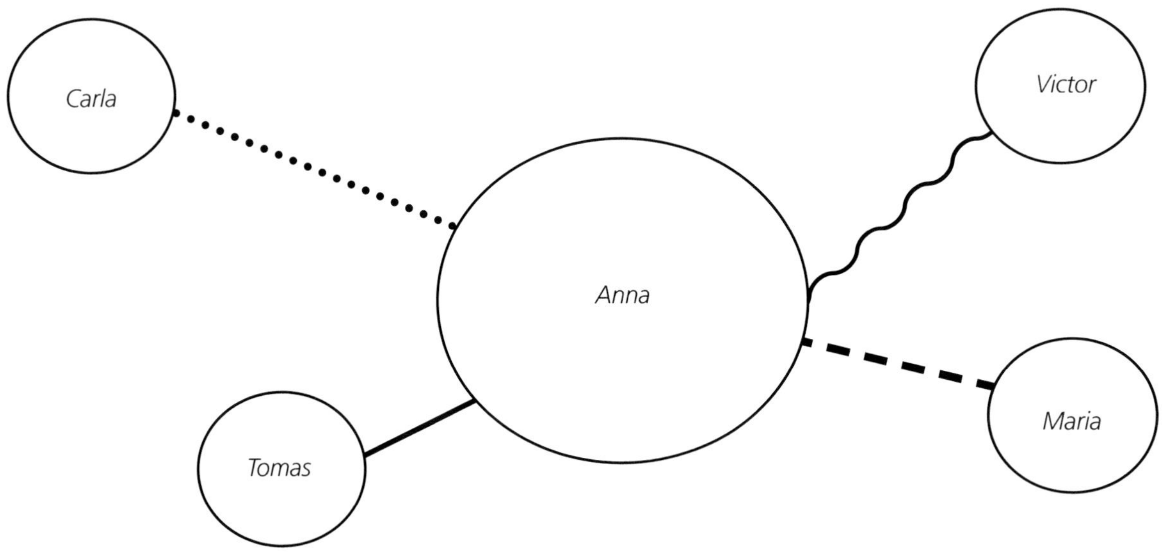

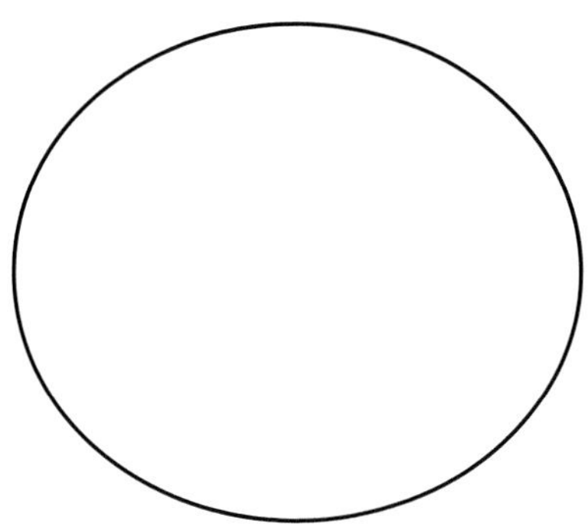

UNIT

4 Communication 2 Speaking hats

DEBATE TOPICS

We should reduce the voting age to fifteen.
We should increase tax for people who go on a plane more than twice a year.
We should stop testing products on animals.
We should make all cars electric.
University education should be free for everybody.

BLACK HAT

You are wearing a black hat. You ask questions about everything and focus on problems in a pessimistic and critical way. Others may think you are negative but it is important that somebody asks the difficult questions, right?

YELLOW HAT

You are wearing a yellow hat. You are always optimistic and see the positives. Perhaps you are able to see more positives than anyone else! It's good to make the world a better place, right?

WHITE HAT

You are wearing a white hat. To your mind, facts are important. People should not be emotional in a discussion. They should look at the data and nothing else. You should listen to your head not your heart, right?

BLUE HAT

You are wearing a blue hat. This means that you are in charge of the discussion. It is your job to make sure that everybody speaks, nobody dominates, and that all opinions are heard. It is also your job to make sure a final decision is reached. You're the boss, right?

UNIT

5 Communication 1 What would you have done?

1 During a cycling trip in Canada, Brad cycled round a bend in the road, and there, in front of him, was a grizzly bear. He jumped off his bike and climbed a nearby tree as fast as he could. Was he right? What would you have done?

2 While swimming off the coast of New South Wales, Harsith spotted the fin of a great white shark. He turned to face it, made a fist, and punched the shark in the eyeball. Was he right? What would you have done?

3 While walking in the cloud forest of Costa Rica, Sofia suddenly felt a pain in her leg. She looked down and saw a snake slithering away. Quick as a flash, she bit into the mark on her leg and tried to suck the poison out. Was she right? What would you have done?

4 Lucas was walking across a field full of cows when he suddenly realized the cows were coming towards him and getting very close. He stretched out his arms and said, 'Go on! Go away!' and pushed the nearest one away firmly. Was he right? What would you have done?

5 Dani was caught in a riptide while swimming off the Florida coast. Instead of taking her into shore, it was carrying her out to sea. Being a good swimmer, Dani turned and swam towards the shore, determined to get back to safety. Was she right? What would you have done?

6 During a fire festival event, a spark hit Omer, and he suddenly realized his clothes were on fire. He fell to the ground immediately and rolled over and over. Was he right? What would you have done?

Were they right?

1 Oops. Bad move, Brad. Bears are amazing tree climbers, so Brad was in big trouble. If he had stopped, slowly got off his bike, and laid down on the ground, the bear would probably have ignored him. If he had turned and walked away slowly, he would probably have been OK too. But if he had run, the bear would definitely have chased him.

2 Good move, Harsith. The eyes are just about the only part of the shark that is sensitive. If he hadn't hit the shark in the eye, it probably wouldn't have swum away. Mind you, Harsith would have had to have been very calm and very lucky.

3 Bad move, Sofia. Trying to suck out the poison wouldn't have made it worse, but, despite what you see in the movies, it wouldn't have worked. It would have been better to wash the bite with soap and wrap it tightly to slow the poison down while seeking medical help. You must keep the bite mark lower than the level of your heart.

4 Lucas knows his stuff. Cows can be aggressive, especially when they have calves, but if you make yourself as large as possible by stretching out your arms and waving, they will move away. If you move slowly but assertively, and don't run or look them in the eye, they will move on. If you have a dog with you, you're in trouble – they don't like dogs so get out of the field if they start to get jumpy!

5 Dani was wrong. Most deaths in riptides are caused by swimmers exhausting themselves trying to swim against the tide. If she had avoided panicking and just floated with the tide, while signalling she was in danger by raising her arms and shouting, she would have been OK. Riptides will eventually stop after a while, and a strong swimmer, having saved energy for the swim back to shore, would have no problems getting to safety.

6 Good move, Omer. That probably saved his life. To put out burning clothing, stop, drop and roll. Don't panic or run. Fall flat to the ground, cover your face with your hands, and try to smother the flames by rolling over and over. If you are calm enough to pay attention to what's burning, you'll be able to put out the flames quicker.

Communication 2 Can you explain that more simply?

Read the messages and express them in language that is more easily understood.

1 Take three doses of the medicine daily immediately after, but not during, any meals you may have.	2 The start of your course will be subject to a delay of two weeks from the date you expected to start the course.	3 If you wish to claim your free gift, ensure that you act promptly to avoid disappointment as the period during which the offer is in place expires in ten days.
4 So sorry to bother you, but I wonder whether you could possibly consider returning that magazine I believe I loaned you two weeks ago.	5 In a three-step process, connect cables (labelled A, B and C) in the relevant ports, each of which is labelled with the corresponding letters.	6 Far above, the sky was of a perfect and splendid shade of wonderful azure – and the pure, round sun was held aloft like a great bright lollipop.
7 With the exception of weekends (Saturdays and Sundays), access to the library will be available to the public on days except for those mentioned.	8 Any chance of a seat in your car on the way home? I'm absolutely exhausted to be honest, and the idea of hanging around the bus stop for an hour doesn't appeal.	9 It is essential that candidates make themselves familiar with the details of the college regulations as laid out in the leaflet provided by post.

Daily News

1

CELEBRITY COUPLE ANNOUNCE SPLIT

Who? When? Why?

What are the consequences?

2

TOP FOOTBALLER BANNED

Who? Banned from what? Why?

What are the consequences?

3

NATIONAL AIRLINE GOES BUST

Which one? Why?

What are the consequences?

4

GORILLA RECAPTURED

Where? By who? Why was the gorilla free?

What are the consequences?

5

STUDENTS RESCUED FROM FLOODED SCHOOL

Where? When? How?

What are the consequences?

6

MISSING DIAMONDS FOUND

Where? Why were they missing?

What are the consequences?

7

NEW CAKE INVENTED

What sort? Who by?

What are the consequences?

8

12-YEAR-OLD WINS

Wins what? Where? How?

What are the consequences?

UNIT

6 Communication 2 The bigger, the better

A Match the two halves of the famous quotes.

1 The better the actor I am acting with, **a** the more I like my dog.

2 The greater the obstacle, **b** the luckier I get.

3 The older you get, **c** the more I want you.

4 The more I know, **d** the more glory in overcoming it.

5 The more I learn about people, **e** the less people remember what you did before.

6 The more I see you, **f** the more I realize I know nothing.

7 The bigger they are, **g** the harder they fall.

8 The harder I work, **h** the better my performance gets.

B Who said it? Read about the famous people and decide who said each quote.

1 **Bob Fitzsimmons** (1863 – 1917) was a British professional boxer who won the world heavyweight championship in 1897. He is considered to have one of the strongest punches in boxing history.

2 **Samuel Goldwyn** (1879 – 1974) was a Polish-American film producer who founded a studio in Hollywood and produced some of the most iconic films of the 1930s and 1940s. He was famous for always being at his desk, and never taking a day off.

3 **Ali Fazal** (born 1986) is an Indian actor and model. He made his screen debut with a small role in the English language film *The Other End of the Line* before appearing in the American television miniseries *Bollywood Hero*.

4 **Socrates** (470 – 399 BC) was a Greek philosopher from Athens who is considered one of the founders of Western philosophy. His Socratic Method involves imagining that you know nothing at all, then asking questions to search for the truth.

5 **Mark Twain** (1835 – 1910) was an American writer and lecturer whose novels include *The Adventures of Tom Sawyer* (1876) and its sequel, *The Adventures of Huckleberry Finn* (1884). He is famous for his clever, witty humour.

6 **Sue Barker** (born 1956) is a British tennis player who retired in 1984 and is now more famous as a TV presenter than a sportswoman. She won the French Open title in 1976.

7 **Chris Montez** (born 1943) is an American guitarist and vocalist, who had hits with 'Let's Dance' and 'Call Me' in the 1960s. He has recorded in pop and Latin styles.

8 **Molière** (1622 – 1673) was a French playwright, actor and poet, and one of the greatest writers in the French language. His famous plays include *The School for Wives, Amphitryon* and *Don Juan*.

UNIT
7 Communication 1 The perfect home

ESTATE AGENT A

Location:
Price:
Unique selling points:

Would suit:

Location:
Price:
Unique selling points:

Would suit:

Location:
Price:
Unique selling points:

Would suit:

ESTATE AGENT B

Location:
Price:
Unique selling points:

Would suit:

Location:
Price:
Unique selling points:

Would suit:

Location:
Price:
Unique selling points:

Would suit:

A

You are writers seeking peace and quiet in order to finish your novels.

B

You are celebrities looking for a place to rent between filming movies. You want to invite your famous friends over but want to be well away from the press.

C

You are artists who love dramatic scenes. You and your three children need light and space.

D

You are fed up with the modern world. You have no money and want to live off the land in isolation without spending anything.

Communication 2 Mighty moaners and careful critics

START

Your new flatmate is the worst! Moan about all the things she does wrong!

One of your classmates has been using your books and pens without asking. Ask him or her to stop.

This country is getting worse. Moan about all the things that are wrong.

GO BACK TWO SPACES

One of your classmates talks too much in class. Ask him or her to stop.

One of your national sports teams is hopeless. Moan about it.

One of your classmates is often late. Ask him or her to be on time.

MISS A GO

Your family have annoying habits. Moan about them.

One of your classmates keeps checking their phone. Ask him or her to stop.

You get too much homework. Moan about it.

One of your classmates is copying your homework. Ask him or her to stop.

GO BACK TWO SPACES

FINISH

INSTRUCTIONS

1 Each player places a token (e.g. a small coin) on START.

2 The first player throws the dice and moves their token.

3 When a player lands on a square, they should follow the instruction and speak for as long as they can.

4 Play moves on to the next player. The winner is the first to reach FINISH.

They're so rubbish! If only they would win one match!

I'd really appreciate it if you could talk less in class. It's just that I find it hard to concentrate.

UNIT
8 Communication 1 What could have happened?

The Story of the *Mary Celeste*

On 7th November 1872, the 282-ton sailing ship *Mary Celeste* set sail from New York Harbour on its way to Genoa, Italy. On board were the ship's captain, Benjamin Briggs, his wife, Sarah, and their two-year-old daughter, Sophia, along with eight crew members. Less than a month later, on 4th December, a passing British ship called *Dei Gratia* spotted the *Mary Celeste* at full sail and adrift about four hundred miles east of the Azores, with nobody on board ...

Clues

1 There was a little over a metre of water in the hold but not enough to sink the ship.

2 One of the lifeboats was missing.

3 There was no significant damage to the ship.

4 The ship was still loaded with six months' worth of food and water.

5 The *Mary Celeste* was originally called the *Amazon*, but its name was changed after its first captain died on board.

6 The crew of the *Dei Gratia* were paid insurance for rescuing the *Mary Celeste* and bringing it to port.

7 There were barrels of flammable liquid that could easily explode in the hold of the *Mary Celeste*. Nine of the barrels were empty when the ship was found.

8 In the last entry in his logbook, Captain Briggs records that he has just seen the island of Santa Maria in the Atlantic. However, it is a long way from the ship.

9 The *Dei Gratia* was a much slower ship than the *Mary Celeste* and left New York eight days after the *Mary Celeste* had sailed.

10 The captain's personal possessions were still on the ship and some of them were valuable.

11 Briggs was an experienced captain.

12 The weather in the North Atlantic can be very unpredictable.

13 Some say that Captain Briggs was very good friends with Captain Morehouse, the captain of the *Dei Gratia*.

14 The *Mary Celeste* was found five hundred kilometres from where it was located by the last entry in its logbook.

15 The missing lifeboat has never been found.

16 Briggs, his family and his crew were never seen again.

UNIT

8 Communication 2 Which new gadget?

Company name: ____________________________

Name:

Release date:

Basic features:

Size:

Screen size:

Battery life:

Camera:

Special features:

*
*
*

Price:

Name:

Release date:

Basic features:

Size:

Screen quality:

Sound quality:

Special features:

*
*
*

Price:

Name:

Release date:

Basic features:

Size:

Comfort:

Battery life:

Special features:

*
*
*

Price:

Name:

Release date:

Basic features:

Size:

Screen quality:

Sound quality:

Special features:

*
*
*

Price:

UNIT

9 Communication 1 New job, new future

What will you be doing this time tomorrow?	How are you going to spend the summer?	How will your life be different in three years' time?	Where will you be this time next week?	What will you have achieved by the end of this decade?
What will you be doing when you're in your 70s?	How much money do you think you'll earn this year?	What are you doing this weekend?	At what age will you retire?	Where will you be living five years from now?

ARCHAEOLOGIST **Do not use these words:** archaeology archaeologist	**OLYMPIC ATHLETE** **Do not use these words:** Olympics medal athlete/athletics	**VETERINARY SURGEON** **Do not use these words:** operation surgeon vet/veterinary	**OPERA SINGER** **Do not use these words:** sing/singer opera/opera house	**CHILDREN'S AUTHOR** **Do not use these words:** write book author
FILM STAR **Do not use these words:** act star film/movie	**ASTRONAUT** **Do not use these words:** space astronaut	**POLAR EXPLORER** **Do not use these words:** polar explore/explorer North Pole South Pole	**WILDLIFE PHOTOGRAPHER** **Do not use these words:** camera photograph/ photographer	**ZOOKEEPER** **Do not use these words:** zoo/zookeeper animal

Communication 2 25 years from now

Nobody will be reading newspapers (on paper) anymore.	All cars will be driverless.	The official retirement age will have been raised to 80.
More than 50% of people will be working from home.	Computer-animated actors will have replaced human actors in most action films.	We will be doing all our shopping online.
Lions and tigers will have died out in the wild.	Fast food will be illegal.	There won't be any bookshops.
We won't be walking around with smartphones anymore.	Notes and coins will be a thing of the past.	Sportspeople will no longer represent national teams at the Olympics.

UNIT
10 Communication 1 Are you classic or modern?

STUDENT A

1 What clothes do you enjoy ______________? (wear)

2 Would you prefer ______________ an e-book or a real book? (read)

3 What job do you expect ______________ five years from now? (have)

4 Which TV programmes do you recommend ______________? (watch)

5 What do you remember ______________ on your first holiday without your parents? (do)

6 Is there any type of music you can't stand ______________ to? If so, what? (listen)

7 If you could afford ______________ any car in the world, which one would you buy? (buy)

8 What are you looking forward to ______________ in the summer? (do)

9 Where do you tend ______________ on a night out? (go)

10 What do you usually feel like ______________ after class? (do)

STUDENT B

1 What magazines do you enjoy ______________? (read)

2 Do you prefer ______________ smart shoes or trainers? (wear)

3 What do you often forget ______________ in the morning? (do)

4 Is there anything you'd like to learn ______________? (do)

5 Is there a film you would suggest ______________ at the cinema? If so, which one? (see)

6 What do you most feel like ______________ on a summer's day? (do)

7 Given a choice, would you choose ______________ to music digitally or on records? (listen)

8 If you could afford ______________ anywhere in the world, where would you live? (live)

9 Which new TV series can't you wait ______________? (watch)

10 What are you looking forward ______________ at the weekend? (do)

UNIT
10 Communication 2 Assumptions

Look at the questions below. Before asking your partner, predict and write what you think their answers will be. When you have finished, interview your partner and check if your predictions were right.

1 Do they prefer tea or coffee?

2 What is their favourite genre of film?

3 What sport do they like watching on TV?

4 What is their favourite colour?

5 What time do they usually get up in the morning?

6 What type of restaurant would they prefer to go to?

7 Do they like dancing?

8 What music do they listen to at home?

9 What is their hobby?

10 Who is their hero?

11 What do they wear at the weekend?

12 Where would they like to go on holiday?

---

1 How many questions did you get right? Why do you think you did so well or so badly?

2 Which of the following assumptions about your partner affected your choice of answers? In what way did they affect your choices?

- nationality
- gender
- age
- what you know of their personality
- what you know of their life experience

3 Were any of your answers affected by social conventions or by your own preferences?

Vocabulary activities Answer key

UNIT 1 Dramatic stories in 22 words

A **Sample answers** 1 absolutely petrified 2 relatively optimistic 3 slightly impatient/annoyed 4 absolutely furious 5 a little concerned 6 really thrilled / very excited 7 tremendously relieved 8 really motivated

UNIT 2 Phrasal verbs: communication quiz

A 1 come up 2 get across 3 pick up 4 point (it) out 5 come up with 6 made up 7 read up on 8 bring up

UNIT 3 A holiday disaster

A A made B ended C go D turn E set F headed G steered H reached

B 1C 2E 3A 4F 5G 6B 7H 8D

UNIT 4 My relationships

Students' own answers

UNIT 5 Mental and physical health

A She should take a nap. She's coming down with the flu. She should call in sick. She can't cope with anxiety/(the) stress/depression/burnout. She's suffering from anxiety/burnout/the flu/stress. She shouldn't feel sorry for herself. She'll soon get over the flu. She should stay in shape.

B 1 She has the flu or a cold. She looks like she's feeling sorry for herself. She should call in sick and take a nap.

2 He's suffering from stress/depression/anxiety/burnout. Stress/Depression/Anxiety/Burnout is difficult to cope with. He should talk to a doctor or a specialist.

UNIT 6 News crossword

A **Down** 1 report 2 sensational 4 in-depth **Across** 2 skim 3 foreign 5 tabloid 6 objective 7 headlines 8 journalist

UNIT 7 Describing places

A

1 light and airy, breathtaking, vast
2 cramped, narrow, absolutely stunning
3 sheltered, cold and damp, warm and cosy
4 spacious, elegantly decorated, warm and cosy
5 densely crowded, cramped, narrow

UNIT 8 Describing technology

A 1 user-friendly 2 pocket-sized (picture B) 3 waterproof (picture C) 4 sophisticated 5 outdated (picture A) 6 innovative 7 handy

UNIT 9 Successes and failures

A 1 achieved 2 make 3 struggle / am struggling 4 tackle 5 make 6 overcoming

UNIT 10 Belonging

A 1 diverse 2 origins 3 identify 4 share 5 raised 6 outsider 7 influenced 8 fit

UNIT

1 Vocabulary Dramatic stories in 22 words

A Complete the sentences with an adverb and an adjective.

1 It was my turn to jump. I edged towards the plane's wide open door and checked my parachute. I felt ______________.

2 After losing the first ten matches of the season, our team started improving. Now, we felt ______________ about winning some games.

3 The speaker went on and on. People wanted to go home – you could see on their faces they were feeling ______________.

4 I was reversing my car into the parking space, when *CRUNCH*! I could see the car's owner approaching in my mirror. He was ______________.

5 Martina said she'd be back by 10 p.m. It was 10.30. We felt ______________, but decided not to ring her yet.

6 They announced that my daughter's favourite pop star was coming to her school on Friday to present prizes. She was ______________.

7 It was midnight when Martina walked through the door. She said her car had broken down. We felt ______________. Thank goodness.

8 Our boss told us she was proud of our team and mentioned us all by name. Everybody clapped. I felt ______________.

B Write your own dramatic stories in 22 words.

1 ______________________________

____

I felt completely petrified.

2 ______________________________

____

I was really astonished.

3 ______________________________

____

We felt totally relieved.

4 ______________________________

____

I was absolutely furious.

C Work in pairs. Take turns to share your stories.

UNIT

2 Vocabulary Phrasal verbs: communication quiz

A Complete the sentences with phrasal verbs. Use the correct form of the verbs provided and the correct particles.

1 When chatting with your friends, what subjects tend to ________________? COME

2 When talking in English, what techniques can you use to ________________ what you are trying to say if you can't think of the right words? GET

3 Do you ________________ new expressions in English quickly and easily? If so, what's your secret? PICK

4 If you are talking to a friend in English, and they make a mistake, would you ________________ it ________________? Why / Why not? POINT

5 In English conversation classes, do you find it easy to ________________ things to say? Why? / Why not? COME

6 Have you ever ________________ a new word in English, either accidentally or on purpose? What was the word? MAKE

7 Do you ________________ areas of grammar that you don't understand very well? READ

8 Are there any topics you would never ________________ in an English conversation class? BRING

B Discuss the questions with your partner. In what ways are you similar or different?

UNIT
3 Vocabulary A holiday disaster

A Complete the sentences from a holiday story. Use the correct form of the verbs in the word box.

end	go	head	make	reach	set	steer	turn

A We only ______________ it as far as the end of our road, however, when we realized we had forgotten our passports.

B We ______________ up crashing into a tree but, luckily, we weren't hurt and the car wasn't badly damaged.

C Last December, my brother and I tried to ______________ on holiday to Bolivia.

D We had to ______________ back and drive home, feeling very miserable. We had missed out on a very special holiday.

E We ______________ off for the airport at six in the morning.

F We went back home and picked up the passports, then ______________ for the airport as fast as we could.

G Unfortunately, however, my brother was driving too fast, lost control, and ______________ the car off the road.

H We got the car back on the road and continued our journey. But when we ______________ the airport, we were too late – we had missed our plane.

B Order the sentences in A to tell the story.

1 ___C___ 2 ________ 3 ________ 4 ________ 5 ________ 6 ________ 7 ________ 8 ________

C Write about a trip that went wrong in your life.

Once, I went on …
Unfortunately, …
I ended up …

____

____

____

____

____

____

UNIT

4 Vocabulary My relationships

A Complete the sentences with the name of a person in your life.

1. In my family, I get along really well with ______________________.
2. When I first met ______________________, we hit it off immediately.
3. I use the internet to keep in touch with ______________________.
4. Of all the old friends I never see, I'd really like to catch up with ______________________.
5. I wish I hadn't lost touch with ______________________.
6. From my school days, I keep in close contact with ______________________.
7. I don't see ______________________ very often, but when I do, we reconnect straightaway.
8. ______________________ and I tend to stick together.

B Talk to a partner about the people in your life. Ask questions using *Who, Why, How, What, When* and *Where*.

C Write about a person in your life and how you keep in touch. Use vocabulary from the lesson.

____

____

____

____

5 Vocabulary Mental and physical health

A Make sentences connected with mental and physical health using the words in the table.

She should take		burnout
She's coming down	from	a nap
She should call	in	sick
She can't cope	with	the flu
She's suffering	-	shape
She shouldn't feel sorry	for	anxiety
She'll soon get	over	(the) stress
She should stay		depression
		herself

B Use the phrases from A and your own ideas to describe and advise the people in the two photos.

He/She might be suffering from … He/She should …

1

2

C Write about when you were last ill. Use the questions to help you.

What were your symptoms?
How did you feel?
What did you do?

UNIT

6 Vocabulary News crossword

A Look at the sentences. Complete the crossword with the missing words.

Down

1 Our website aims to *report* local news stories that local people will be interested in.

2 This magazine publishes ________ stories about the private lives of celebrities – it just wants to shock and surprise people!

4 After the release of her new film, the director gave ________-________ interviews to a number of magazines. She answered a wide range of questions about her life and career.

Across

2 I never read the news in detail – I just ________ over the main stories.

3 The chairman of the company answered questions from reporters in his own country but refused to answer questions from the ________ press because he felt he was being misrepresented abroad.

5 He works on a ________ – a newspaper that publishes stories about celebrities and isn't very serious about major events.

6 I listen to the news on the radio – I think it is ________ – it is neutral and doesn't take one side or the other.

7 The incident was so serious it made the ________ around the world.

8 My brother works as a ________ for a leading newspaper.

B Write crossword clues for the words below.

article ____

press ____

UNIT 7 Vocabulary Describing places

A Complete the sentences with three of the words or phrases. There is one word or phrase you don't need.

1 light and airy sheltered breathtaking vast

It was a ______________ room with ______________ views over the ______________, empty landscape.

2 absolutely stunning cramped warm and cosy narrow

We could barely move our legs in the ______________ seats and the aisle was so ______________ two people couldn't walk past each other. The views over the coastline, however, were ______________.

3 warm and cosy densely crowded sheltered cold and damp

On the way down, it began to rain heavily, so we found a ______________ spot away from the rain and put up the tent. It was ______________ outside but so ______________ inside the small tent that we fell asleep.

4 elegantly decorated cramped warm and cosy spacious

We stayed in a wonderful, ______________ apartment – so much larger than we expected. The living room was ______________ in a traditional style and the fire in the open fireplace made it feel ______________.

5 cramped sheltered narrow densely crowded

At 8 a.m., it was ______________ and there were no free seats. It felt really ______________ standing among so many people in the ______________ carriage.

B Write a description of the photo. Use words and phrases from Exercise A.

____
____
____
____
____
____
____
____
____
____
____

Vocabulary Describing technology

A Write the adjective that best matches the description. Then match the three pictures with one of the adjectives.

1 Everyone will find this machine easy to operate!

u____________________________

2 It is so small you can take it with you anywhere even if you don't have a bag.

p____________________________

3 If you leave it in the rain, or drop it in the pool, no problem – it won't be damaged!

w____________________________

4 It uses advanced technology and can perform very complicated tasks.

s____________________________

5 It is already old-fashioned – there are newer models available that have more modern functions.

o____________________________

6 It is a product that is modern and original and features new technologies.

i____________________________

7 It is incredibly useful – you can use it often and for many purposes.

h____________________________

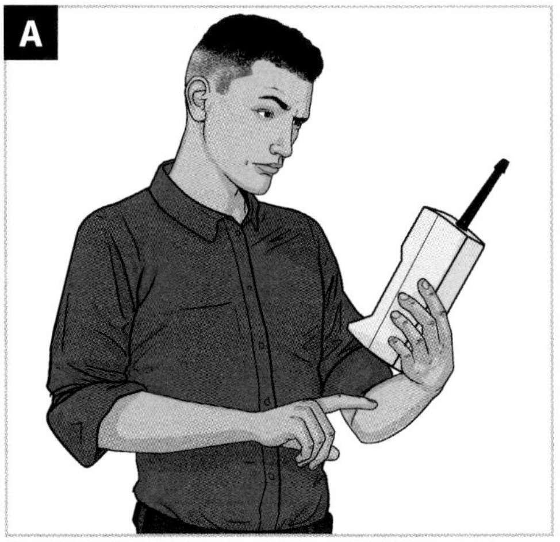

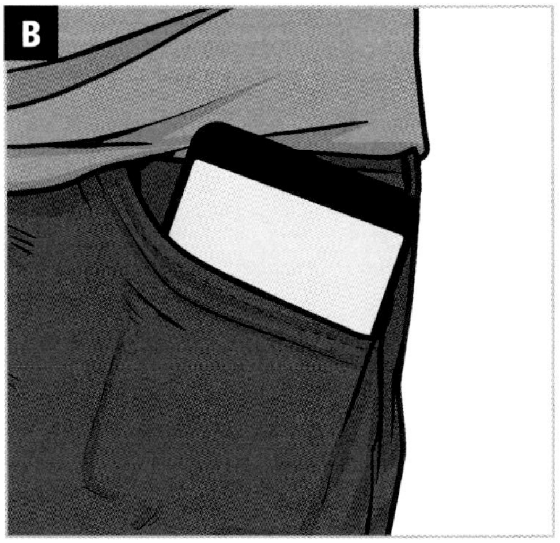

B Write descriptions for objects you own using some of the adjectives from Exercise A and the words in the word box.

gadget	perform	recharge

____

____

____

____

____

____

____

UNIT

9 Vocabulary Successes and failures

A Complete the sentences with the correct form of the verbs in the word box.

achieve   make (x2)   overcome   struggle   tackle

1 This year, I have mostly ______________ my objectives and aims.

If true: What are they? How did you do it?

If false: What objectives and aims are outstanding? Why?

2 I feel as though I ______________ a mess of things sometimes.

If true: What examples can you give? How does this make you feel? What could you do about it?

3 There are a number of things I ______________ to understand.

If true: What are they? What effect does this have on you? What do you do about it?

4 I have managed to ______________ all my problems head on this year.

If true: What examples of problems can you give? How have you dealt with them?

If false: What would you do differently?

5 I am good at helping people stay positive and helping them ______________ it through difficult times.

If true: What examples can you give?

6 I am good at ______________ issues I face in life.

If true: What is your secret?

If false: Why not?

B Work in pairs. Decide if the statements are true for you or not. Discuss the questions.

C Write about what objectives you have achieved and what difficulties you have overcome in the last few months.

____

____

____

____

____

____

____

____

____

UNIT
10 Vocabulary Belonging

A Complete the statements using the words in the word box.

diverse	fit	identify	influenced	origins	outsider	raised	share

1 People from a culturally ______________ country generally have a richer, more exciting arts scene.

2 Everybody should find out about their ______________. It is only by knowing where our ancestors came from that we can get a true sense of ourselves.

3 If you ______________ with more than one culture, it becomes harder to fit in with people around you.

4 People can only really get on if they ______________ the same values.

5 People who have been ______________ in one country but live in another are more objective about what is good or bad about a country's culture or lifestyle.

6 The best way to avoid feeling like an ______________ in a new country is to accept and embrace its culture.

7 We are all heavily ______________ by the culture in which we have grown up – it is rare that people reject that culture and embrace a different culture.

8 We ______________ in best with people who have the same cultural references as us: people who have seen the same TV programmes, have visited the same places, and can remember the same recent historical events.

B Work in pairs. Discuss the statements in Exercise A. Which do you agree with?

C Write about your cultural background.

I was raised in …
I share the same values as …
I fit in best with …
I identify with …

Grammar and Focus on activities Answer key

UNIT 1 Grammar Forming questions

A 1 Did you, they are 2 helped you, do you 3 Don't you 4 I am / we are 5 don't you, do you 6 she had, Does she

UNIT 1 Focus on … Adverbs of degree

A 1 absolutely 2 slightly 3 tremendously 4 completely / totally 5 relatively 6 totally / completely

B Sample answers

1 really annoyed / a bit frustrated 2 absolutely furious / extremely disappointed

UNIT 2 Grammar Present tenses

A 1 are, feeling 2 have, been sitting 3 Do, want 4 have, been studying 5 do, find 6 are, trying 7 Do, see 8 have, practised / have, been practising 9 Has, improved 10 are, thinking 11 Are, wondering 12 Have, had

UNIT 2 Focus on … Separable and inseparable phrasal verbs

A
1 ✗ getting them across
2 ✓
3 ✗ comes over every afternoon
4 ✗ bring it up
5 ✗ pick up a friend of mine from English class
6 ✓
7 ✗ run into Maria
8 ✓
9 ✗ make up very funny stories
10 ✗ takes after his dad
11 ✓
12 ✗ read up on the life of Napoleon

UNIT 3 Grammar Narrative tenses

A
1 was riding
2 found
3 had dropped
4 decided
5 was putting
6 began
7 didn't know
8 didn't want
9 was stealing / had stolen
10 was planning / (had) planned / had been planning
11 took
12 gave
13 was still ringing
14 answered
15 did you lose

UNIT 3 Focus on … Travel collocations with *go on*

A 1 c 2 h 3 a 4 d 5 f 6 b 7 e 8 g

UNIT 4 Grammar Reported speech and reporting verbs

A a to send b booking c to come d to help e of ignoring f for not inviting g taking h to reduce

B 1 b 2 e 3 a 4 f 5 h 6 c 7 d 8 g

UNIT 4 Focus on … Transitive and intransitive phrasal verbs

A
1 keep in touch with
2 keep in contact with
3 lose touch / contact
4 get on
5 hit it off with
6 catch up

UNIT 5 Grammar Conditionals

A
1 was/were, would drop, would go, would plan, would stay
2 'd bring, 'd change, wouldn't change
3 had chosen, had started
4 Would you describe, didn't feel, would have left, wouldn't say
5 asked, 'd say, 'd tell, 'd claim
6 was/were

UNIT 5 Focus on … *I wish* … and *If only* …

A
1 didn't eat
2 lived / was living
3 had joined
4 worked / was or were working
5 had learned
6 weren't
7 hadn't wasted
8 knew
9 drank
10 enjoyed

UNIT 6 Grammar Passive structures

A
1 was elected
2 have been rescued
3 was sent
4 were asked
5 has been found
6 are being told
7 is understood
8 will be closed / is going to be closed
9 was presented
10 will be held / is going to be held
11 is hoped
12 will be reduced

UNIT 6 Focus on … *the* … *the* …

A
1 The wealthier people are, the more (money) they want.
2 The older people are, the better they get at listening.
3 The more open-minded you are (when you read the news), the greater your understanding of the world (is / will be).
4 The higher you aim, the better you will do in life.
5 The earlier you go to bed, the happier you will feel.
6 The less biased our newspaper, the better we (it) serve(s) the public.
7 The more alarms you (can) install, the safer you will feel.
8 The harder people work, the more likely they are to get a promotion.

Grammar and Focus on activities Answer key

UNIT 7 Grammar Causative verbs

A 1 to pack 2 (to) know 3 to take 4 to start 5 damaging 6 relax 7 to think 8 wasting 9 feel 10 spending

UNIT 7 Focus on ... Useful structures for complaining

A 1 so annoying, such stupid things
2 always making, would turn
3 always complaining, would concentrate
4 such a thoughtless flatmate, would wash
5 always staring, would switch
6 so rude, would think
7 such a poor worker, always leaving
8 so lazy, would get

UNIT 8 Grammar Speculating about the past

A 2 I must have forgotten to close it ...
3 We should have turned left ...
4 She must have eaten ...
5 She can't have known ...
6 He must have worked really hard.
7 You shouldn't have thrown the receipt away.
8 They might not have bought a ticket.
9 I might have switched my phone off.
10 She can't have gone far.

UNIT 8 Focus on ... Forming nouns, verbs and adjectives

A 1 technological 2 revolutionized 3 achievements 4 historical 5 affordable 6 creative 7 enjoyable 8 anxiety 9 strengthened 10 possibilities 11 attractive

UNIT 9 Grammar Talking about the future

A 2 (will/won't/might/should) be sitting, (will/won't/might/should) be doing
3 (will/won't/might/should) have done
4 (will/won't/might/should) have played
5 (will/won't/might/should) be sleeping
6 (will/won't/might/should) have spent
7 (will/won't/might/should) be living
8 (will/won't/might/should) be visiting / will have visited
9 (will/won't/might/should) have completed
10 (will/won't/might/should) be watching
11 (will/won't/might/should) have improved

UNIT 9 Focus on ... Verb-noun collocations

A 1 a 2 c 3 c 4 a 5 c 6 c 7 b 8 b

UNIT 10 Grammar Verb patterns with infinitive and *-ing*

A 1 to speak 2 wearing 3 drinking 4 to go 5 to bring 6 getting 7 learning 8 to do 9 going 10 making 11 living 12 shouting

UNIT 10 Focus on ... *the* with groups of people and things

A 1 The 2 the 3 the 4 – 5 – 6 The 7 the 8 – 9 – , – 10 the

UNIT 1 Grammar Forming questions

A Complete the conversations with two words in each space.

1

A: I saw another group of hikers walking through your garden this morning, Mrs Patel.

B: Really? ______________? I'd like to know who ______________. Then I'd call the police and give them their names. My garden is private property, you know.

A: Yes, I know. It must be really annoying.

2

A: I've just put up a shelf on the wall.

B: Really. Who ______________?

A: Nobody helped me! Why ______________ think I needed help?!

3

A: I just eat them raw – like this.

B: No way! ______________ cook them?

A: No … watch.

B: Uggh. That's disgusting!

4

A: Could you tell me where ______________ on this map?

B: You're here. Not far from the train station.

5

A: Hey, Marta. You speak French, ______________?

B: Yes. A bit. Why ______________ ask?

A: Well, I've got a French guy on the phone and he doesn't speak much English. Could you help me?

6

A: Sara left the meeting early again.

B: I know. Do you think ______________ a headache? She tends to have really bad headaches.

A: ______________? I didn't know that. Yes. Perhaps that was why.

B Practise the conversations with a partner.

C Write your own short conversation using one of the sentence starters below. Use two or three different types of question.

1 I've just seen Ruben cycling home on your bike …

2 Could you move your car? It's blocking the view from my window …

3 Sasha isn't at school today …

4 I don't like ice cream …

UNIT

1 Focus on . . . Adverbs of degree

A Choose the best adverbs of degree for the responses.

slightly *absolutely* *tremendously*

1

A: How would you feel if you were in a deep, dark forest all alone?

B: Me? Oh, I'd be ______________ petrified! I hate the dark!

2

A: How would you feel if you were in a short queue inside a shop?

B: I guess I'd be ______________ impatient, but, hopefully, the queue would soon start moving.

3

A: How would you feel if you were worried about being very ill, but your doctor told you it was only a minor problem?

B: Obviously, I'd be ______________ relieved. There's nothing worse than fearing bad news.

relatively *totally* *completely*

4

A: How would you feel if you had just finished a marathon?

B: Naturally, I'd be ______________ exhausted! It's a long way!

5

A: How would you feel if you got a C (but not an A) in your test?

B: I'd be ______________ pleased. It's not great, but it's not bad either.

6

A: How would you feel if your teacher wore a hat in class?

B: I'd be ______________ surprised! My teacher never wears a hat!

B Write your own response. Use an adverb and an appropriate adjective.

1

A: How would you feel if it started to rain on the way home?

B: ____

2

A: How would you feel if your national football team lost 10-0!?

B: ____

C Compare your responses with a partner. Explain your choice of adverbs and adjectives. Then practise the conversations.

UNIT
2 Grammar Present tenses

A Complete the questions. Use the verbs in brackets in the correct present form.

1 How __________ you __________ (feel) right now?

2 How long __________ you __________ (sit) here?

3 __________ you __________ (want) to stand up and walk around?

4 How long __________ you __________ (study) English?

5 What __________ you __________ (find) difficult about the language?

6 Why __________ more and more people__________ (try) to learn English these days?

7 __________ you __________ (see) why I'm asking all these questions?

8 In which situations __________ you __________ (practise) your English recently?

9 __________ your English __________ (improve) in recent weeks? If so, in what ways?

10 What __________ you __________ (think) about right now?

11 __________ you __________ (wonder) why I keep asking all these questions?

12 __________ you ever __________ (have) to answer so many questions in your life before?

B Use the questions to interview your partner.

C Write three more questions to ask your partner using different present tenses.

____

____

____

____

UNIT

2 Focus on . . . Separable and inseparable phrasal verbs

A Write a ✔ (for correct) or a ✗ (for incorrect) next to the phrasal verbs. Correct the incorrect phrases.

1 The book is full of ideas and the author does a great job of **getting across them** ____________________ in simple language.

2 I've completely **run out of ideas** ____________________! What will I talk about in my presentation?

3 I am so tired of putting up with my roommate's sister! She **comes every afternoon over** ____________________ and she's so loud!

4 You know that you and your brother always disagree about politics. Why do you have to **bring up it** ____________________ every time you see him?

5 Can I use the car? I need to **pick a friend of mine from English class up** ____________________ this afternoon.

6 It's terribly cold outside. Please **put your coat on** ____________________ before you go out.

7 I always **run Maria into** ____________________ at the market. We always stop for a chat.

8 Anna won a free trip to the coast, but she **turned it down** ____________________ because she has an English exam that week.

9 The children in my class **make lots of very funny stories up** ____________________ when we have story time!

10 Jack **takes his dad after** ____________________. They have the same interests and both love learning new languages.

11 I'm **looking for my Spanish dictionary** ____________________. Have you seen it?

12 We had to **read up the life of Napoleon on** ____________________ for our history class.

B Compare answers with a partner.

Grammar Narrative tenses

A Complete the story with the verbs in brackets in the correct past form.

The phone in the road

While I [1] ______________ (ride) to college on my bike the other day, I [2] ______________ (find) a phone lying on the ground. Clearly, somebody [3] ______________ (drop) it.

I [4] ______________ (decide) to pick it up and take it into college with me. However, as I [5] ______________ (put) it in my bag, it [6] ______________ (begin) to ring. I [7] ______________ (not know) what to do.

I [8] ______________ (not want) the person on the other end to think that I [9] ______________ (steal) it, and [10] ______________ (plan) to keep it for myself.

In the end, I [11] ______________ (take) it to the reception desk at college and [12] ______________ (give) it to the receptionist. It [13] ______________ (still / ring), and we both wondered what to do.

In the end, the receptionist [14] ______________ (answer) the phone.

'Hello,' said a voice.

'Hi,' said the receptionist. 'We think we have your phone. How [15] ______________ (you / lose) it?'

'Well, now,' said the voice. 'There's a funny story …'

B Write an ending to the story.

____

____

____

____

____

____

____

____

____

____

____

____

UNIT

3 Focus on … Travel collocations with *go on*

A Match the beginnings of the sentences (1–8) with the endings (a–h).

1 Recently, we went on a city break …
2 Jo went on a business trip …
3 Harry went on a package holiday …
4 They went on a voyage …
5 José and Clara went on a cruise …
6 Stefano went on a field trip …
7 Noriko went on a language exchange …
8 They went on an expedition …

a … to Majorca in Spain – two weeks in a hotel, with meals included.
b … to study bees. The team collected a lot of data.
c … to Prague for three days and saw all the interesting sights.
d … across the South Atlantic in a small yacht. It was very dangerous.
e … to the US to improve her English.
f … in the Caribbean Sea. They visited a lot of beautiful islands and ate delicious food on the ship.
g … to a remote part of the Amazon rainforest that had never been visited before.
h … to London to meet clients and sell products.

B Write down three journeys or trips you have been on. Then exchange sentences with a partner. Ask each other questions about each experience.

I went on ______________________ to ______________________.

I went on ______________________ to ______________________.

I went on ______________________ to ______________________.

UNIT

4 Grammar Reported speech and reporting verbs

A Complete the sentences with the correct form of the verbs in brackets. Add any prepositions necessary.

a Don't worry. She's promised ________________ (send) us the money.

b Sure. She has recommended ________________ (book) tickets in advance.

c Yeah. I persuaded him ________________ (come). He needs to meet some new people!

d Yeah. She's asked us ________________ (help) her move her furniture.

e Yeah. He has accused us ________________ (ignore) his emails.

f I know. She's apologized ________________ (not invite) you.

g Yes. He's denied ________________ (take) it. He says it wasn't him.

h Yeah. He's agreed ________________ (reduce) the price.

B Match these questions and sentences to the responses in A to make short conversations. Practise the conversations with a partner.

1 Are you still on for going to the cinema with Ameera at the weekend?

2 Do you know why Dan seemed angry with us?

3 Sylvia still hasn't paid for the course.

4 I'm upset that Daria went away for the weekend without asking me to come.

5 Have you spoken to Mateo about buying his car?

6 Did you tell Steven about the party?

7 Is Yuzu still moving house at the weekend?

8 I saw Tom walking home with my bag. Have you asked him why?

C Write what you have done in the past week.

I offered … *I promised …* *I apologized …* *I agreed …* *I asked …* *I invited …*

____

____

____

____

____

____

____

____

____

____

____

UNIT

4 Focus on . . . Transitive and intransitive phrasal verbs

A Complete the text with transitive or intransitive phrasal verbs using the verbs in brackets.

How to [1] ______________ (keep / touch) friends

Method 1: Find time to make that phone call. It's the best way to [2] ______________ (keep / contact) the people you love.

Method 2: Use text. Keep an ongoing chat for updates about each other's lives. That way you and your friends won't [3] ______________ (lose).

Method 3: Write an email. I share my news with my cousin via email each week. We [4] ______________ (get) really well.

Method 4: Use social media. When you meet someone new, and you [5] ______________ (hit) that person straightaway, you can tag them on social media to let them know you found something they might like. And, of course, social media is a great way to reconnect with old friends and [6] ______________ (catch).

B Write five sentences about how you keep in touch with people. Use phrasal verbs in each sentence.

____

____

____

____

____

C Share your sentences with a partner.

Grammar Conditionals

A Complete the sentences with the correct conditional forms. Then choose the best option (A, B or C) for you.

What kind of employee or student are you?

1 What would you do if it _______________ (be) six o'clock on Friday and you still hadn't finished an important project or assignment?

A I _______________ (drop) everything and go home.

B I _______________ (go) home, but I _______________ (plan) to finish first thing on Monday.

C I _______________ (stay) at work or in college until everything was finished.

2 What would you change about your work or study environment if you could?

A I _______________ (bring) in the decorators and change everything.

B I _______________ (change) a few things, but basically it's a good place to be.

C I _______________ (not change) a thing – it's great.

3 Do you think you are in the right profession or on the right course?

A Not at all – I wish I _______________ (choose) something different.

B It is for now, but who knows what I'll be doing ten years from now.

C Definitely! If only I _______________ (start) earlier!

4 _______________ (you / describe) your job or course as stressful?

A Definitely – I wish I _______________ (not feel) stressed all the time.

B Not particularly. I _______________ (leave) the job or course long ago if it had been stressful.

C No. I _______________ (not say) it was stressful at all.

5 How would your work colleagues or fellow students describe you if we _______________ (ask) them?

A They _______________ (say) I wasn't very focused on my work.

B They _______________ (tell) you I was a good worker or student but with other interests.

C They _______________ (claim) I was the company's hardest worker.

6 Do you wish your job or course _______________ (be) more interesting?

A Yes – I get quite bored sometimes.

B Not really – it has its good points and bad points.

C I couldn't ask for a more interesting job/course.

B Add up your scores then find out what kind of employee or student you are. Compare scores with a partner. Do you agree with the results?

A answers = 3 points B answers = 2 points C answers = 1 point

Score 6 to 8 – You are a great employee or student. You are hard-working, enthusiastic and love your job or course.

Score 9 to 11 – You are a good employee or student. Your job or course isn't perfect, but you like it a lot and you work hard.

Score 12 to 15 – You are a typical employee or student. Your job or course isn't perfect. It has its good and bad points, and if you get the chance, you might change job or course one day.

Score 16 to 18 – You are an unhappy employee or student. You wish you were doing something else.

UNIT

5 Focus on … *I wish* … and *If only* …

A Complete the wishes and regrets. Use the past simple or past perfect.

Ravi

I wish I [1]________________ (not eat) so much chocolate every day. It really isn't good for me!

Olga

I wish I [2]________________ (live) in a warmer country. I'd spend a lot more time outdoors.

Anna

If only I [3]________________ (join) a gym sooner. Imagine how fit I would be now!

Joseph

I wish I [4]________________ (work) shorter hours! I could do so much more sport in my free time!

Paola

I wish I [5]________________ (learn) to play tennis well when I was younger – I'd love to join a club and keep fit that way.

Dani

If only my friends [6]________________ (not be) so lazy. I'd be fitter and healthier if I didn't have such lazy friends!

Abigail

I wish I [7]________________ (not waste) so much time on video games when I was young.

Andrea

I wish I [8]________________ (know) what to eat! When I'm shopping, I never know which foods are healthy and which aren't!

Toshiko

If only I [9]________________ (drink) less coffee! I love coffee – it's impossible to cut down!

Matteo

I wish I [10]________________ (enjoy) doing exercise. Truth is, I find it so boring.

B Are any of the sentences in A true for you? Write three of your own wishes using *I wish* and *If only*.

____

____

UNIT

6 Grammar Passive structures

A Read the headlines and complete the opening lines of the newspaper stories with passive forms.

NEWS Home World Business Politics Environment Sport Entertainment Weather

Mayor elected for second term

Last Thursday, a horse 1 ______________ (elect) to serve as the city's mayor for a second term.

Seabirds rescued

In the last few days, hundreds of seabirds 2 ______________ (rescue) by volunteers on local beaches.

Homeowners must paint doors blue

In a leaflet that 3 ______________ (send) to households across the region last week, homeowners 4 ______________ (ask) to paint their front doors blue.

Dinosaur egg found

An undamaged dinosaur egg 5 ______________ (find) inside an extinct volcano.

Students to retake exams

Right now, students across the country 6 ______________ (tell) to retake exams because the results of exams they took in May have been lost.

National Theatre to close

It 7 ______________ (understand) that the National Theatre 8 ______________ (close) over the course of the next two weekends for repairs.

Actor wins award

Last night, in a glittering ceremony, actor Giuseppe Rossi 9 ______________ (present) with a lifetime achievement award.

Match date changed

The cup final between City and United 10 ______________ (hold) at midday on 6th June.

Initiative to reduce crime

It 11 ______________ (hope) that crime 12 ______________ (reduce) as a result of a new crime initiative the police are planning to reveal next month.

B Choose a story from Exercise A and write the complete article, adding extra details.

____

____

____

UNIT
6 Focus on ... *the ... the ...*

A Rewrite the sentences using *the ... the ...*

1 People who are wealthy always want more money.

The ______________________________.

2 People get better at listening as they get older.

The ______________________________.

3 Be open-minded when you read the news and you will have a greater understanding of the world.

The ______________________________.

4 Aim high and do well in life!

The ______________________________.

5 If you go to bed early, you will feel happy.

The ______________________________.

6 By not being biased, our newspaper serves the public.

The ______________________________.

7 Install as many alarms as you can in order to feel as safe as possible.

The ______________________________.

8 People who work hard are the most likely to get a promotion.

The ______________________________.

B Work in pairs. Which sentences do you think are generally true? Are there any you don't agree with? Why?

C Rewrite any of the sentences you disagreed with to make them true in your opinion.

____

____

____

____

____

____

____

Grammar Causative verbs

A Write the correct form of the verbs in brackets.

Top tips for moving house

1 Collecting large cardboard boxes in the weeks before you move enables you ________________ (pack) easily and quickly.

2 Writing the names of rooms in your new house on cardboard boxes helps you and the removal company ________________ (know) exactly where to take the boxes.

3 Getting up really early on house-moving day allows you ________________ (take) your time and not get stressed.

4 Moving house easily and painlessly requires you ________________ (start) planning weeks in advance.

5 Wrapping breakable items in bubble wrap prevents you from ________________ (damage) important or valuable objects.

6 Hiring a professional removal company lets you ________________ (relax).

7 Writing a list of all your belongings before you start to pack forces you ________________ (think) about exactly what you need to do.

8 Throwing away stuff you don't need in your new house saves you from ________________ (waste) time because you won't pack or transport it.

9 Playing classical music while packing makes you ________________ (feel) happy and in control.

10 Hiring your own van and getting friends to help stops you from ________________ (spend) lots of money on expensive removal company fees.

B Choose your top five tips from Exercise A and order them from 1 to 5. Then add an extra tip of your own.

C Share your ideas from Exercise B with a partner.

UNIT

7 Focus on . . . Useful structures for complaining

A Complete the sentences. Use the words in brackets and at least one of the words in the word box.

always	so	such	would

1 My brother is ________________ (annoying)! He says ________________ (stupid things) all the time!

2 My neighbour is ________________ (making) a noise. I wish she ________________ (turn) down her music.

3 One of my colleagues at work is ________________ (complaining) about everybody else. I wish he ________________ (concentrate) on his own work.

4 Jerome is ________________ (a thoughtless flatmate). I wish he ________________ (wash) the dishes at least once a week!

5 Olga's behaviour in class is inappropriate. She is ________________ (staring) at her phone. If only she ________________ (switch) it off and pay attention to the teacher!

6 Sylvia is ________ (rude)! The way she talks to me and other colleagues is upsetting. I wish she ________________ (think) about other people's feelings.

7 Lionel is ________ (a poor worker) – he's ________________ (leaving) his desk to chat with his friends. Other colleagues have to do his work for him.

8 Jack's ________________ (lazy). If only he ________________ (get) up before midday once in a while.

B Work in pairs. Practise reading the sentences out loud.

C Change the information in two or three sentences in Exercise A to make them true for you or people you know.

____

____

____

____

UNIT

8 Grammar Speculating about the past

A Rewrite the sections in bold in the conversations. Use *might (not) have, must have, can't have* or *should(n't) have* + past participle.

1
A Why is there so much traffic today?
B I'm not sure. **Perhaps there was an accident.**
There might have been an accident .

2
A The front door's open!
B Sorry. **I obviously forgot to close it.**
____
when we left home this morning.

3
A We're lost.
B I know. **We needed to turn left** back there.
____
when we passed the petrol station.

4
A There isn't any chocolate.
B My flatmate loves chocolate. **I'm sure she ate** it all.
____
the whole bar!

5
A Agnes didn't send me a birthday card.
B Oh dear. **I'm sure she didn't know**.
____
that it was your birthday.

6
A My brother passed his exams.
B That's great! **I'm sure he worked really hard**.
____

7
A The kettle isn't working.
B Well, you can't return it to the shop. **You made the mistake of throwing the receipt away**.
____

8
A Marco and Cristina weren't at the concert.
B Oh. OK. **Perhaps they didn't buy a ticket**.
____

9
A Every time I call you, it goes straight to voicemail.
B Oh, sorry. **Perhaps I switched my phone off**.
____

10
A Have you seen the cat?
B No, but don't worry. She's always wandering off. **I'm sure she hasn't gone far.**
____

B Practise the rewritten conversations in Exercise A with a partner.

C Write two two-line conversations. Use *might (not) have, must have, can't have* or *should(n't) have* + past participle. Then practise them with your partner.

____
____
____
____
____
____

UNIT

8 Focus on … Forming nouns, verbs and adjectives

A Complete the text by changing the words in brackets to the correct part of speech (noun, verb or adjective).

OUR DIGITAL REVOLUTION

There's no question that the [1]________________ (technology) breakthroughs of the first two decades of the 21st century have [2]________________ (revolution) people's day-to-day lives. Arguably, the scientific [3]________________ (ACHIEVE) of this short period have been greater than in any other [4]________________ (history) period. TV, radio, paperback novels, landline telephones, and letter writing have been replaced by [5]________________ (afford) digital devices our grandparents barely dreamed of. It has been a [6]________________ (create) era, and one that has made life more [7]________________ (enjoy) for many. Of course, rapid change has its downsides. Being constantly connected can cause [8]________________ (anxious) for some people, and it has, arguably, [9]________________ (strength) the ability of big businesses to interfere in our lives. Overall, however, the [10]________________ (possible) that these new technologies bring are incredibly [11]________________ (attract). We are lucky to live in such exciting times.

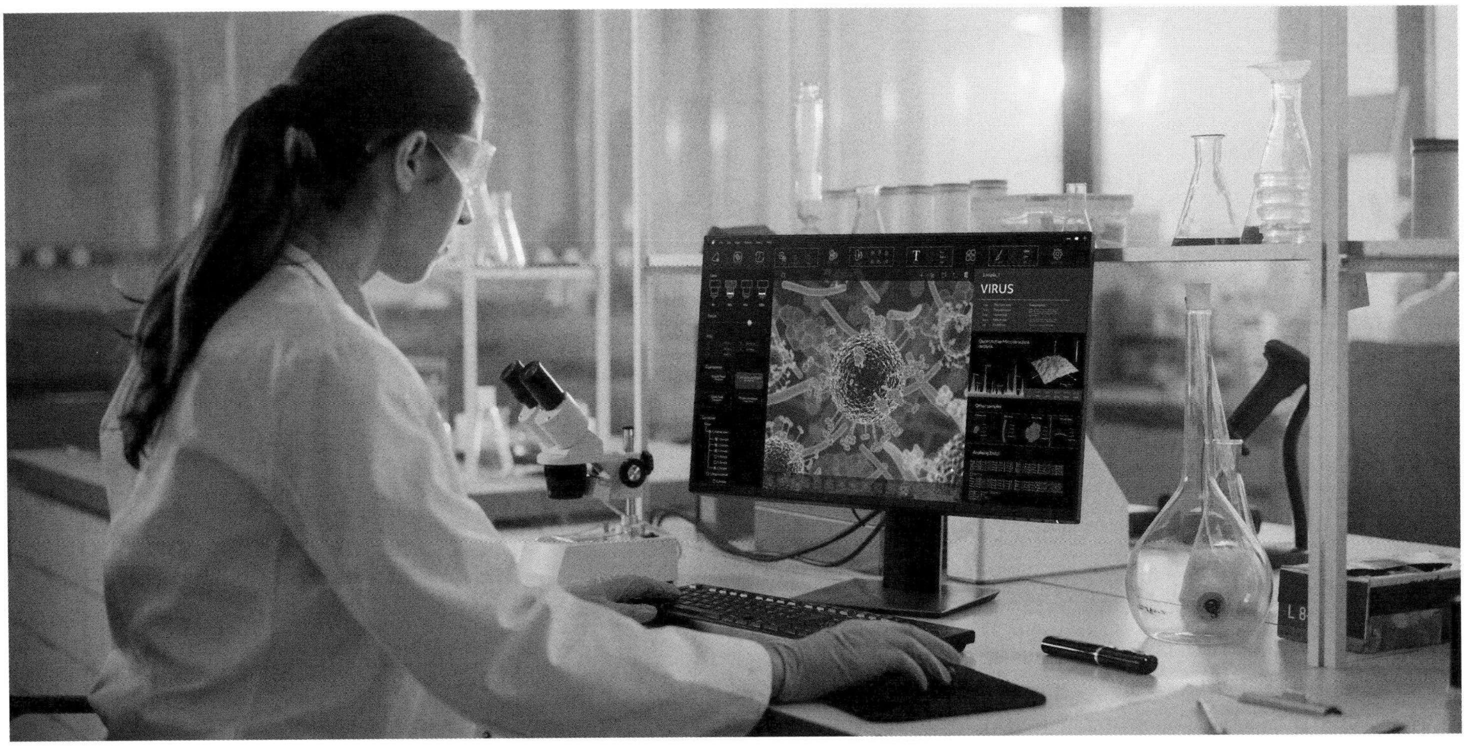

B Work in pairs. Practise reading the text in Exercise A out loud.

C Do you agree with the argument in the text? Why? / Why not? Discuss with your partner.

UNIT

9 Grammar Talking about the future

A **Complete the sentences with the correct form of the future continuous or future perfect. Make the sentences true for you by using *might, should* or *will/won't* and the verbs in brackets.**

1 By midnight tonight, I *won't have played* (play) football.

2 This time next week, I ______________ (sit) in this same room. I ______________ (do) the same thing.

3 I ______________ (do) this week's homework by Saturday afternoon.

4 By the end of the weekend, I ______________ (play) a team sport.

5 At midnight tonight, I ______________ (sleep).

6 By the end of the month, I ______________ (spend) a lot of money.

7 This time next year, I ______________ (live) in this country.

8 On Sunday afternoon, I ______________ (visit) a place I have never been to before.

9 By the end of this year, I ______________ (complete) all my studies.

10 At nine o'clock on Saturday evening, I ______________ (watch) a film.

11 I ______________ (improve) my English by the end of this month.

B **Compare your sentences from Exercise A with a partner. Explain why your sentences are positive or negative.**

C **Write about what you will …**

… be doing at this time tomorrow.

… have done by the end of the week.

____

____

____

____

UNIT

9 Focus on . . . Verb-noun collocations

A Choose the correct verbs to complete the sentences.

1 I'm ________ to understand this question. Can you help me?

a struggling

b overcoming

c tackling

2 If you really believe in yourself, you'll ________ your aims.

a make

b overcome

c achieve

3 Take the time you need to ________ the right decision.

a struggle

b overcome

c make

4 We have a number of issues to ________, but I'm sure we can deal with all of them.

a tackle

b make

c achieve

5 We had to ________ for survival out there and I'm so glad we are here now.

a tackle

b overcome

c struggle

6 We spent a lot of time and money on the project, but ________ very little.

a overcame

b tackled

c achieved

7 To get where I am today, I had to ________ many difficulties and obstacles.

a struggle

b overcome

c make

8 By the end of this year, we will have to ________ a choice that will affect the rest of our lives.

a achieve

b make

c overcome

B Compare your answers to Exercise A with a partner. Then discuss who might say each sentence and in what situation.

UNIT 10 Grammar Verb patterns with infinitive and *-ing*

A Complete the sentences with the correct form of the verbs.

1	I learned ______________ Spanish when I was at school.	SPEAK
2	I enjoy ______________ smart clothes.	WEAR
3	I want to give up ______________ coffee.	DRINK
4	I can't wait ______________ away this summer.	GO
5	I forgot ______________ something important to class.	BRING
6	I can't stand ______________ up early.	GET
7	I'd like to carry on ______________ English forever.	LEARN
8	I expect ______________ well at work or in school this year.	DO
9	I remember ______________ to pre-school when I was very young.	GO
10	I keep ______________ the same grammar mistakes.	MAKE
11	I get used to ______________ in a new place very quickly.	LIVE
12	I feel like ______________ out loud.	SHOUT

B Work in pairs. Discuss the sentences in Exercise A. Are they true or false for you? Ask follow-up questions using *what*, *when*, *where*, *why* and *how*.

C Write about you.

1 I'd like to give up ______________.

2 I enjoy ______________, but I can't stand ______________.

3 Most days, I often forget ______________ and never remember ______________.

4 I'm looking forward to ______________.

5 I remember ______________ when I was young.

6 I'm finding it hard to get used to ______________.

UNIT
10 Focus on … *the* with groups of people and things

A Complete the sentences with *the* or – (no *the*). Then discuss the sentences with a partner. Are they true or false?

1 __________ majority of Arabic speakers are in Africa.

2 English is just one of __________ official languages of South Africa. There are ten others!

3 None of __________ countries in South America have English as a first or official language.

4 Most __________ Chinese people speak Cantonese, not Mandarin.

5 Since 2015, __________ Maori speakers in New Zealand have grown in number.

6 __________ Welsh live in Wales, which is part of the UK. They all speak fluent English, but for the majority of them, their first language is Welsh.

7 Almost all of __________ people in New York speak English as a first language.

8 At the height of the summer season, __________ locals make up about one third of the population of Venice.

9 __________ Pakistanis and __________ Bangladeshis speak the same first language.

10 Some of __________ islands in the Caribbean have Dutch as an official language.

B Check your ideas in the key at the bottom of the page.

Key:

1 TRUE (62% are in Africa.)
2 TRUE (The other ten are: Ndebele, Pedi, Sotho, Swati, Tsonga, Tswana, Venda, Xhosa, Zulu and Afrikaans.)
3 FALSE (It is an official language in Guyana.)
4 FALSE (Mandarin is often placed first in lists of languages by number of native speakers – with nearly a billion speakers.)
5 TRUE
6 FALSE (Welsh is an official language, but only spoken by about 30% of the country.)
7 FALSE (65% speak English as a first language, but over 20% speak Spanish as their first language.)
8 TRUE
9 FALSE (Most Pakistanis speak Urdu, most Bangladeshis speak Bengali.)
10 TRUE (On Aruba, Bonaire, Curaçao and Sint Maarten, Dutch is the official language but spoken as a first language by only 7% to 8% of the population.)

Pronunciation activities Teacher's notes

UNIT 1 Long and short vowel sounds

Aim: to practise short vowels (/ɪ/, /e/, /ɒ/) in contrast to long vowels and diphthongs (/iː/ /ɔː/ /aɪ/ /eɪ/)

When to use: after Exercise 8 in Lesson 1C

Procedure: Put students in groups of three. Place the dominoes in a pile face down, and deal them out so each student in the group has five cards. Place the remaining cards face down in a pile on the table.

The first student places any card from their hand on the table. Students must then take turns to play cards, matching the underlined sounds. Students can match a card to the right or left, or above or below any card so long as any words that match share the same underlined sound.

If a student can't make a match, they must miss a go and pick up a card. If a student makes a wrong match, they also miss a go and pick up a card from the pile. If there are no cards left in the pile, they just miss a go.The winner is the first student to use all their cards.

UNIT 2 Understanding weak forms in questions

Aim: to practise understanding weak forms of auxiliary verbs, and linking and word boundaries in continuous speech

When to use: after Exercise 6 in Lesson 2B

Procedure: Put students in pairs. Give one worksheet per student. Individually, students study and practise the weak and strong sounds and practise saying the questions with clear, natural stress. Ask students to think about whether they want to use the weak or the strong forms in their questions.

When students are ready, they take turns to dictate their questions to their partner. To do this, ask Student A to read question 1. Student B listens then writes what they hear. Student A then reads the question again. Student B checks their answer. Once students have dictated all questions, let them share worksheets and compare answers. Students interview each other using the dictated questions.

Answers:

A

1 How many languages do you speak? /də jə/ or /duː juː/
2 How long have you been studying English? /əv jə bɪn / or /hæv juː biːn /
3 Have you ever studied English abroad? /əv jə/ or /hæv juː/
4 What aspects of pronunciation do you find hard? /də jə/ or /duː juː/
5 What's your favourite word in English? / jə/ or /jɔː/

B

1 What's the most interesting place you have been to? /jəv bɪn / or /juː hæv biːn /
2 Have you ever worked abroad? /əv jə/ or /hæv juː/
3 What countries would you like to live in? /jə/ or /juː/
4 What's the best thing about living in your town? /jə/ or /jɔː/
5 How long have you lived at your current address? /əv jə/ or /hæv juː/

UNIT 3 Wordbuilding with groups of consonants

Aim: to practise consonant clusters in long adjectives and adverbs with suffixes and prefixes

When to use: after Exercise 7 in Lesson 3B

Procedure: Put students in groups of three or four. Place the set of eight core words face up on the table for each group.

If your students are unfamiliar with phonemic symbols, read out the words in the list, pointing out the consonant clusters and the pronunciation of new symbols.

Cut out the phoneme cards showing prefixes and suffixes and place them in a pile face down. Shuffle them, then deal them out so each student in the group has five cards. Place the remaining cards face down in a pile on the table.

Then read out the sounds on the cards. If students need help remembering what sound each card represents, write them out on the board with example words:

/ʌn/ - <u>un</u>helpful	/dɪs/ - <u>dis</u>appoint	/ɪd/ - expect<u>ed</u>
/li/ - friend<u>ly</u>	/ɪŋ/ - interest<u>ing</u>	/əl/ - accident<u>al</u>

Students must place suffixes or prefixes before or after core words to make adjectives or adverbs. Each time they place a suffix or prefix, they must pronounce the new word accurately. So, Student A might start by placing ɪŋ after 'ɪntrəst, and saying 'ɪntrəstɪŋ. Student B could add ʌn to make ʌnɪntrəstɪŋ, or could add a suffix or prefix to another word: əl to æksɪdənt, for example. Students can also remove a card already played (e.g. ɪŋ) and replace it with a card in their hand (e.g. ɪd). If students can't go, they miss a turn and exchange any card in their hand for one in the pile. The winner is the first student to play all their cards.

Sample answers

1 interest: interesting, interestingly, disinterest, interested, uninterested
'ɪntrəst(ɪŋ / ɪŋ li) / (ʌn / dɪs)'ɪntrəst(ɪd)
2 fortunate: unfortunate, unfortunately, fortunately
(ʌn) 'fɔːtʃənət (li)
3 expect: expected, unexpected, unexpectedly
(ʌn) ɪk'spekt (ɪd)(li)
4 surprise: surprising, unsurprising, surprisingly, unsurprisingly
(ʌn) sə'praɪz (ɪŋ) (li)
5 eventual: eventually
ɪ'ventʃuəl (li)
6 accident: accidental, accidentally
ˌæksɪ'dent (əl)(li) (note that the ə in 'accident' changes to e)
7 appoint: disappoint, disappointing, disappointed, disappointedly
(dɪs) ə'pɔɪnt (ɪŋ) (li) / (ɪd) (li)
8 courage: discourage, discouraging, discouragingly
(dɪs) 'kʌrɪdʒ (ɪŋ) (li)

UNIT 4 Using stress to change the meaning

Aim: to practise emphatic stress

When to use: after Exercise 9 in Lesson 4B

Procedure: Put students in pairs and give out one worksheet per student. Start by reading out the first sentence 'Sylvie asked me to buy flowers' with different emphatic stress and asking students to say which question is being answered. Put students in pairs. They take turns to say a sentence. Their partner must guess which question they are answering.

UNIT 5 Connected speech dictation

Aim: to practise hearing squeezed words in connected speech

When to use: after Exercise 7 in Lesson 5B

Procedure: Give out one worksheet per student. Students read the talk and guess which words are missing. Read out the talk. Pronounce missing words clearly but naturally. Students listen and write missing words. Pause after each paragraph to give students time to catch up. Read out the talk again. This time don't pause – just read naturally to the end. Students check answers in pairs, then turn over the text at the foldline to compare and check answers.

UNIT 6 Long vowels /ɜː/, /iː/, /uː/, /ɔː/ and /ɑː/

Aim: to practise long vowel sounds: /ɜː/, /iː/, /uː/, /ɔː/ and /ɑː/

When to use: after Exercise 9 in Lesson 6C

Procedure: Put students in groups of three or four. Cut out the cards and give one set to each group. Tell them to mix up all the words and place them face down on the table in order to play pelmanism.

One student should begin by turning over two cards and reading out each word on the cards. If the long vowel sounds are the same, the student takes the cards and keeps them, then has another go. If they are different, the student turns the cards face down. Then it is the next student's turn to turn over two cards. Check that students are clear that only the long vowel sounds need match (not the consonants) – so *dark* can go with *guard* or *army*, not just *shark*.

The aim of the game is to turn over and match as many pairs as possible. To do this, players must pay close attention and remember where different cards are.

The winner is the player with the most pairs of cards at the end.

UNIT 7 Tongue twisters with /b/, /v/ and /w/

Aim: to practise /b/, /v/ and /w/

When to use: after Exercise 10 in Lesson 7C

Procedure: Put students in pairs and give out one worksheet to each pair. Give students time to practise saying their tongue twisters.

Students take turns to read out a tongue twister and match it with the patterns provided on their worksheet.

Answers:

A

a VBVW [4]	b WBVW [1]	c WVBW [2]	d BVWV [8]
e BBWV [6/7]	f WBVV [5]	g BBWV [7/6]	h WVVW [3]

B

a BVWW [5]	b WBWW [3/6]	c WVBB [8]	d BVBB [1]
e WBWW [6/3]	f VWWB [4]	g WBWV [2]	h WVBW [7]

UNIT 8 Long and short vowel sounds

Aim: to practise long and short vowel sounds

When to use: after Exercise 10 in Lesson 8C

Procedure: Start by writing the following short vowel sounds and words on the board and pronouncing them: /ɒ/ (*complex*), /æ/ (*hat*), /e/ (*bread*), /ɪ/ (*ship*), /ʊ/ (*wood*) and /ʌ/ (*cup*). Then the following long vowel sounds: /ɔː/ (*poor*), /ɑː/ (*car*), /iː/ (*sleep*), /uː/ (*boot*) and /ɜː/ (*word*). Check understanding by saying the following short words and asking students to say which sound they contain: *top, sit, son, farm, turn, born* (Answers: /ɒ/, /ɪ/, /ʌ/, /ɑː/, /ɜː/, /ɔː/). Put students in pairs. Give each pair a worksheet. Go through Challenge 1 as a class.

Challenge 1 (example)

Tell students they have to go from *smash* (in the top line) to *lorry* (in the bottom line), but they can only 'step' on words that have at least one short vowel sound (NB if a word has both a short and a long vowel sound, it is OK to 'step' on that). They can move vertically, horizontally or diagonally across the board. Answers: *smash – missing – cross – trip – foghorn – spilt – international – spirit – brush – truck – lorry*.

Challenge 2

Pairs find a route from *people* in the first column to *stew* in the last column. This time, they can only 'step' on words with at least one long vowel sound. Once students have found a route ask them to read it out. (Possible answer: *<u>peo</u>ple – pret<u>e</u>nd –sm<u>oo</u>th – c<u>or</u>ner – <u>aw</u>esome – tr<u>u</u>th – sh<u>oe</u>s – st<u>ew</u>*).

Challenge 3

Pairs find a route from *pocket* in the first column to *pump* in the last column.They can only step on words that have the short vowel sounds /ɒ/, /æ/, /ʌ/, /ʊ/ or /e/. (Answer: *pocket – pushing – calculate – second – cough – truck – brush – pump*).

Once students understand the game, ask them to work in pairs to challenge each other to find routes across the board. Encourage students to say each word they 'step' on to show the vowel sounds they contain.

Here are some possible challenges students can set:

1 You must go from *organize* to *poor* while only stepping on words that have a long vowel sound.
2 You must go from the top of the board to the bottom, from *impossible* to *left*, while only stepping on words that have a short vowel sound.

Encourage students to say each word they 'step' on to show the vowel sounds they contain.

UNIT 9 Pausing

Aim: to practise pausing when reading out a text

When to use: after Exercise 9 in Lesson 9B

Procedure: Put students in pairs and give out one worksheet to each pair. Each pair of students chooses one of the texts to work on. Ensure that students choose each of the cities in more or less equal numbers.

Ask students in pairs to mark pauses in their text, using | for a short pause, and || for a long pause. Once students have marked up their text, ask them to practise reading the text out loud.

Once pairs are happy that they are reading their text accurately, mix pairs in your class so that a pair who prepared the Bogotá text are with a pair who prepared the Seoul text. Students in each group of four take turns to read out their text. Listeners comment on and correct their performance.

Answers:

Bogotá

The city of Bogotá | is one of the most beautiful cities | in South America ||. It is situated | in the centre of Colombia | and is surrounded by high mountains ||. It is |, of course |, the capital city |, and is the largest |, most crowded |, and most exciting city | in the country ||.

Bogotá has a lot of large shopping malls, || as well as fine restaurants | and exciting nightclubs. || However |, there are plenty of quieter, | attractive areas |, where people live and work |, and the city is home | to many students | because of its excellent universities ||.

Visitors to the city | can find plenty of interesting attractions | in the historical centre ||, where there are elegant eighteenth-century buildings |, including the Colón Theatre | and the old neighbourhood of La Candelaria ||.

Seoul

The city of Seoul | in South Korea | is one of the world's largest | and most important cities ||. It is both | the capital of South Korea | and the centre | of its economic and cultural life ||. It is situated | in the north of the country |, near the west coast |, on the Han River ||.

Seoul is a very safe | and friendly place | to live and work ||, but it is also very crowded |, and never seems to sleep ||. The city has amazing new buildings |, built of steel and glass |, as well as many notable landmarks |, including royal palaces | and traditional houses ||. Visitors | can see ancient buildings | in the narrow streets of Namsangol Hanok Village | in the heart of the city ||.

Many tourists to Seoul | come for the shopping | and the food ||. There are numerous huge shopping malls | selling fashionable clothes | and accessories ||. In the heart of the city |, it is easy to find | great eating experiences |, from street takeaways |, selling incredibly tasty food |, to top class, | five star restaurants ||.

UNIT 10 Aspirating /p/, /k/ and /t/

Aim: to practise recognizing aspiration in /p/, /t/ and /k/ when followed by a stressed vowel

When to use: after Exercise 7 in Lesson 10B

Procedure: Put students into pairs and give out one worksheet per student. Ask pairs to work together to look at the supermarket items below the foldline and find the eight items to write on Kate's shopping list. Tell them that only food items with an aspirated /k/ can go on Kate's list. Once students have completed this list, ask them to do the same for Tom's list (items with an aspirated /t/) and Pat's list (items with an aspirated /p/).

When students have finished, read out each word on the list below the foldline so that students can listen to see if the sounds are aspirated, and check their lists.

At the end reveal the answers and discuss why other words in the list did not contain aspirated sounds and why.

Answers:

Kate's list: /k/ ketchup, coffee, cake, cornflakes, cabbage, kale, ice cream cones, cookies

Tom's list: /t/ tea, potatoes, tights, towels, tinned apricots, tangerines, toast, turmeric

Pat's list: /p/ pastries, pills, peas, paracetamol, pepper, peaches, pasta, pies

UNIT

1 Pronunciation Long and short vowel sounds

DELIGHTED HOT WORRIED IMPATIENT	AFRAID ASTONISHED OPTIMISTIC EXCITED	THRILLED RELIEVED EXHAUSTED PETRIFIED	PLEASED DISAPPOINTED PATIENT LOGICAL
EMOTIONAL REASONABLE UNPLEASANT LIKEABLE	STRESSFUL STRANGE TALKATIVE SHOCKED	PLEASANT POSITIVE DANGEROUS AFRAID	INTELLIGENT DIFFICULT MOTIVATED EXCITED
SENSITIVE BRAVE MEAN STYLISH	UPSET IMAGINATIVE WEAK SHY	EASY WORN OUT NEGATIVE PLAYFUL	SIMPLE BORING FRIENDLY SURPRISED
POOR STRONG ARTISTIC CREATIVE	SILLY SENSIBLE INFORMAL TERRIFIED	TERRIBLE AMAZING BORED PEACEFUL	INTERESTING LAZY UPSET WEAK
POLITE NAUGHTY PRETTY PESSIMISTIC	PLEASED POSITIVE NEGATIVE MOTIVATED	WORRYING SELFISH EXHAUSTED CONFIDENT	DELIGHTED LAZY SHOCKED TALKATIVE

UNIT

2 Pronunciation Understanding weak forms in questions

STUDENT A

A Study and practise the weak and strong forms of the words in the table.

	Weak form	Strong form
do	də	duː
have	əv	hæv
you	jə	juː
your	jə	jɔː
been	bɪn	biːn

B Say the questions to your partner using weak or strong forms of *do, have, you, your* and *been*. Write the questions your partner says.

1 How many languages do you speak?
2 How long have you been studying English?
3 Have you ever studied English abroad?
4 What countries would you like to live in?
5 What's your favourite word in English?

1 ______________________________

2 ______________________________

3 ______________________________

4 ______________________________

5 ______________________________

C Take turns to ask questions and give true answers.

STUDENT B

A Study and practise the weak and strong forms of the words in the table.

	Weak form	Strong form
do	də	duː
have	əv	hæv
you	jə	juː
your	jə	jɔː
been	bɪn	biːn

B Say the questions to your partner using weak or strong forms of *do, have, you, your* and *been*. Write the questions your partner says.

1 What's the most interesting place you have been to?
2 Have you ever worked abroad?
3 What aspects of pronunciation do you find hard?
4 What's the best thing about living in your town?
5 How long have you lived at your current address?

1 ______________________________

2 ______________________________

3 ______________________________

4 ______________________________

5 ______________________________

C Take turns to ask questions and give true answers.

UNIT

3 Pronunciation Wordbuilding with groups of consonants

ˈ**ɪntr**əst 1 interest	ˈfɔː**tʃ**ənət 2 fortunate	**ɪk**ˈ**sp**ekt 3 expect	səˈ**pr**aɪz 4 surprise
ɪˈve**ntʃ**uəl 5 eventual	ˌæ**ks**ɪˈdənt 6 accident	əˈpɔɪ**nt** 7 appoint	ˈkʌrɪ**dʒ** 8 courage

ʌn	dɪs	**ɪ**d	li	**ɪ**ŋ
ɪd	**ɪ**ŋ	ʌn	li	dɪs
ɪŋ	**ɪ**d	li	li	ʌn
ɪŋ	əl	ʌn	dɪs	əl
ʌn	**ɪ**ŋ	li	ʌn	li

UNIT

4 Pronunciation Using stress to change the meaning

A **Practise reading out the sentences in different ways. Change the emphatic stress so that they answer different questions (a–d).**

1 Sylvie asked me to buy flowers.

- **a** Who asked you to buy flowers?
- **b** What did Sylvie do?
- **c** What did Sylvie ask you to do?
- **d** What did Sylvie ask you to buy?

2 Tom apologized for losing the tickets.

- **a** Who apologized?
- **b** What did Tom do?
- **c** What did Tom apologize for?
- **d** What did Tom apologize for losing?

3 Danny blamed me for getting lost.

- **a** What did Danny do?
- **b** Who blamed you?
- **c** Who did Danny blame?
- **d** What did Danny blame you for?

4 Ameera recommended buying a computer online.

- **a** What did Ameera do?
- **b** Who recommended buying a computer online?
- **c** Where did Ameera recommend buying a computer?
- **d** What did Ameera recommend buying online?

5 Sajid agreed to pay for the meal.

- **a** Who agreed to pay for the meal?
- **b** What did Sajid do?
- **c** What did Sajid agree to do?
- **d** What did Sajid agree to pay for?

6 Ronan accused Sam of copying his homework.

- **a** Who accused Sam?
- **b** What did Ronan do?
- **c** Who did Ronan accuse?
- **d** What did Ronan accuse Sam of?

B **Read out the sentences in A to your partner in any order. Change the emphatic stress each time. Your partner should decide which question (a–d) you are answering.**

5 Pronunciation Connected speech dictation

A Read the text. There are three missing words and contractions in each space. Guess what they are.

B Listen to your teacher read the talk in full. Complete the text with the missing words and contractions.

In today's talk, I [1] ________________ talk about some of the strategies I use [2] ________________ extra hour or two's sleep each day. In my current job, I [3] ________________ a lot of speeches and presentations, so [4] ________________ best and brightest is important to me. Believe me, I [5] ________________ to give up my job long ago if I [6] ________________ to maximize my sleep.

I [7] ________________ morning person and I often have a hard time falling asleep the night before an important presentation.

So, what [8] ________________ to get those hours of sleep in?

Firstly, I work out how much sleep I'm going to need each night to function properly the next day. So, I [9] ________________ bed at ten if I have to [10] ________________ six, or eleven if my day [11] ________________ seven. Secondly, I engage in a relaxing activity before bedtime, so I [12] ________________ bit of yoga, for example. I avoid watching TV and I turn the lights down, or even [13] ________________.

It all sounds simple, but it's something [14] ________________ thought of doing a few years ago [15] ________________ staying up late night after night.

Answers

In today's talk, I [1]**'m going to** talk about some of the strategies I use [2]**to get an** extra hour or two's sleep each day. In my current job, I [3]**have to make** a lot of speeches and presentations, so [4]**being at my** best and brightest is important to me. Believe me, I [5]**would have had** to give up my job long ago if I [6]**had been unable** to maximize my sleep.

I [7]**'m not a** morning person and I often have a hard time falling asleep the night before an important presentation. So, what [8]**do I do** to get those hours of sleep in?

Firstly, I work out how much sleep I'm going to need each night to function properly the next day. So, I [9]**'ll get into** bed at ten if I have to [10]**be up at** six, or eleven if my day [11]**doesn't start until** seven. Secondly, I engage in a relaxing activity before bedtime, so I [12]**'ll do a** bit of yoga, for example. I avoid watching TV and I turn the lights down, or even [13]**switch them off**.

It all sounds simple, but it's something [14]**I wouldn't have** thought of doing a few years ago [15]**when I was** staying up late night after night.

Pronunciation Long vowels /ɜː/, /iː/, /uː/, /ɑː/ and /ɔː/

first	world	journal	fur	heard
murder	piece	freeze	sheep	tea
mean	leaf	view	screw	balloon
tune	queue	lose	large	guard
shark	dark	army	garage	form
war	awful	floor	more	roar

7 Pronunciation Tongue twisters with /b/, /v/ and /w/

STUDENT A

A Read out the tongue twisters. Your partner must match with the correct pattern of words beginning with the sounds /w/, /v/ and /b/. Give the example first to get your partner started.

We're very worried about Bruna. *WVWB*

1 Western beaches are very wet.
2 Why do vegetables from Borneo weigh so much?
3 Winter in Vladivostok has violent winds.
4 Vera's best vest is in the wash.
5 Where do Briony and Victor play volleyball?
6 Billy lives in a big, white van.
7 Our buses are black and white vehicles.
8 Broken vases are without value.

B Listen to your partner. Match their tongue twisters to the patterns below.

a BVWW ☐ **e** WBWW ☐
b WBWW ☐ **f** VWWB ☐
c WVBB ☐ **g** WBWV ☐
d BVBB ☐ **h** WVBW ☐

STUDENT B

A Listen to your partner. Match their tongue twisters to the patterns below.

a VBVW ☐ **e** BBWV ☐
b WBVW ☐ **f** WBVV ☐
c WVBW ☐ **g** BBWV ☐
d BVWV ☐ **h** WVVW ☐

B Read out the tongue twisters. Your partner must match with the correct pattern of words beginning with the sounds /w/, /v/ and /b/.

1 Bermuda and Saint Vincent have the best beaches.
2 Why are Belgian watermelons so vast?
3 Why don't bus conductors work on Wednesdays?
4 Valentina wears white blouses.
5 I'd be very worried if I were you.
6 Wild Bill's Wild West Show.
7 Which villages are best or worst?
8 We'll vote for Bob Brown.

UNIT
8 Pronunciation Long and short vowel sounds

Can you get through the maze by stepping on words that contain particular short or long vowel sounds?

/ɒ/ /æ/ /e/ /ɪ/ /ʊ/ /ʌ/ /ɔː/ /ɑː/ /iː/ /uː/ /ɜː/

organize	impossible	card	user	smash	produce	spoon	loser
complex	surprising	pepper	pearl	creepy	missing	mister	screen
waterproof	recharge	tune	four-sided	engineer	army	cross	grew
keyboard	automatic	disturbance	large	drawing	tomato	shoes	trip
laptop	return	detour	mean	splendid	truth	foghorn	stew
people	pretend	beloved	corner	awesome	spilt	underarm	steam
pocket	student	smooth	minute	partner	eagle	international	grasp
awful	pushing	start	second	sneeze	floor	spirit	hurt
represent	heart	calculate	neat	cough	remove	brush	pump
music	teeth	hat	drifting	roof	truck	broom	morning
burning	harmful	bus stop	left	riverside	lorry	winner	poor

UNIT

9 Pronunciation Pausing

Bogotá

The city of Bogotá is one of the most beautiful cities in South America. It is situated in the centre of Colombia and is surrounded by high mountains. It is, of course, the capital city, and is the largest, most crowded, and most exciting city in the country.

Bogotá has a lot of large shopping malls, as well as fine restaurants and exciting nightclubs. However, there are plenty of quieter, attractive areas, where people live and work, and the city is home to many students because of its excellent universities.

Visitors to the city can find plenty of interesting attractions in the historical centre, where there are elegant buildings, including the Colón Theatre and the old neighbourhood of La Candelaria.

Seoul

The city of Seoul in South Korea is one of the world's largest and most important cities. It is both the capital of South Korea, and the centre of its economic and cultural life. It is situated in the north of the country, near the west coast, on the Han River.

Seoul is a very safe and friendly place to live and work, but it is also very crowded, and never seems to sleep. The city has amazing new buildings, built of steel and glass, as well as many notable landmarks, including royal palaces and traditional houses. Visitors can see ancient buildings in the narrow streets of Namsangol Hanok Village in the heart of the city.

Many tourists to Seoul come for the shopping and the food. There are numerous huge shopping malls selling fashionable clothes and accessories. In the heart of the city, it is easy to find great eating experiences, from street takeaways selling incredibly tasty food, to top class, five star restaurants.

Pronunciation Aspirating /p/, /k/ and /t/

Kate's shopping list

____________	____________	____________	____________
____________	____________	____________	____________

Tom's shopping list

____________	____________	____________	____________
____________	____________	____________	____________

Pat's shopping list

____________	____________	____________	____________
____________	____________	____________	____________

- -

raspberries	aspirin	ketchup	tea	tomatoes	biscuits
potatoes	coffee	crisps	cake	lettuce	asparagus
plums	pastries	cornflakes	pills	peas	tights
strawberries	paracetamol	chips	cabbage	kale	ice cream cones
salt	pepper	prawns	fruit	vegetables	chicken
towels	tinned apricots	peaches	cookies	shrimps	pasta
spaghetti	pies	tangerines	toast	octopus	turmeric

Index of mediation activities

Activity	Page	Mediation Type	Links with CEFR Descriptor (B2):
1 The dinner party	283	Mediating concepts in spoken English	**Facilitating collaborative interaction with peers:** Can help define goals for teamwork and compare options for how to achieve them. Can refocus a discussion by suggesting what to consider next and how to proceed. Can ask questions to stimulate discussion on how to organize collaborative work. Can act as rapporteur in a group discussion, noting ideas and decisions, discussing these with the group and later giving a summary of the group's view(s).
2 Talking about bilingualism	284	Mediating concepts in written English	**Processing text in writing:** Can summarize in writing (in Language B) the information and arguments contained in texts (in Language A) on subjects of general or personal interest.
3 Desert island adventure	285	Mediating concepts in spoken English	**Encouraging conceptual talk:** Can encourage members of a group to describe and elaborate on their thinking. Can encourage members of a group to build on one another's information and ideas to come up with a concept or solution. Can formulate questions and feedback to encourage people to expand on their thinking and justify or clarify their opinions. Can build on people's ideas and link them into coherent lines of thinking. Can ask people to explain how an idea fits with the main topic under discussion.
4 A gripping story	286	Mediating a text in spoken English	**Expressing a personal response to creative texts:** Can give a clear presentation of their reactions to a work, developing their ideas and supporting them with examples and arguments. Can describe their emotional response to a work and elaborate on the way in which it has evoked this response. Can express in some detail their reactions to the form of expression, style and content of a work, explaining what they appreciated and why.
5 A debate about meat-eating	287	Mediating communication in spoken English	**Facilitating pluricultural space:** Can encourage a shared communication culture by expressing understanding and appreciation of different ideas, feelings and viewpoints, and inviting participants to contribute and react to each other's ideas. Can work collaboratively with people who have different cultural orientations, discussing similarities and differences in views and perspectives. Can, in intercultural encounters, demonstrate appreciation of perspectives other than that of their own worldview, and express themselves in a way appropriate to the context.

Activity	Page	Mediation Type	Links with CEFR Descriptor (B2):
6 Ecology news	288	Simplifying a text in written English	**Streamlining a text:** Can simplify a source text by excluding non-relevant or repetitive information and taking into consideration the intended audience. Can edit a source text by deleting the parts that do not add new information that is relevant for a given audience in order to make the significant content more accessible for them.
7 Housemates	289	Mediating concepts in spoken English	**Collaborating to construct meaning:** Can further develop other people's ideas and opinions. Can present their ideas in a group and pose questions that invite reactions from other group members' perspectives. Can consider two different sides of an issue, giving arguments for and against, and propose a solution or compromise.
8 How to use old technology	290	Explaining a new concept in spoken English	**Breaking down complicated information:** Can make a complicated process easier to understand by breaking it down into a series of smaller steps.
9 Let's talk it through together	291	Mediating concepts in spoken English; Mediating communication in spoken English	**Facilitating collaborative interaction with peers:** Can, based on people's reactions, adjust the way they formulate questions and/or intervene in a group interaction. Can help define goals for teamwork and compare options for how to achieve them. Can refocus a discussion by suggesting what to consider next, and how to proceed. **Facilitating agreement:** Can elicit possible solutions from parties in disagreement in order to help them to reach consensus, formulating open-ended, neutral questions to minimize embarrassment or offence. Can help the parties in a disagreement better understand each other by restating and reframing their positions more clearly and by prioritizing needs and goals. Can, by asking questions, identify areas of common ground and invite each side to highlight possible solutions.
10 Where to go and what to see	292	Mediating a text in spoken English	**Explaining data in graphs, etc.:** Can interpret and describe reliably (in Language B) detailed information contained in complex diagrams, charts and other visually organised information (with text in Language A) on topics in their fields of interest.

Mediation activities

WHAT IS MEDIATION?

Mediation is when we use language to explain 'something' to someone who doesn't fully understand it without our help. This 'something' could be a text, a concept or another person or group of people.

1 Mediating a text

Sometimes, we may need to 'mediate' a text in order to convey the main points. Here are some of the things we can do to explain a text to someone who doesn't fully understand it:

- **a** Simplify, shorten or amplify – or 'process' – the text so that they understand it.
- **b** Relay specific information (i.e. the key points in the text), using clearer or simpler language, or a different language.
- **c** Interpret and explain information that contains visual data such as graphs.
- **d** Translate the text into a language the other person understands.
- **e** Take notes on the text (either a spoken text – a lecture, for example – or a longer written text) so that the other person can understand the notes.
- **f** Clearly express a personal response to – or an analysis or critique of – a creative text. This is, of course, more common at an upper secondary and university level and is closely connected to studying literature.

2 Mediating concepts

Language is a tool used to think about a subject and to talk about that thinking. To do this effectively, a mediator needs to be able to facilitate collaboration in a group (which establishes the right conditions for mediating concepts) and lead that group work (which allows the development and elaboration of ideas).

To facilitate collaboration and lead groupwork, we can do the following:

- **a** Ask students to practise groupwork skills such as inviting others to speak, asking and answering questions, giving reasons, making suggestions, defining goals, reformulating questions, highlighting issues, or summarizing main points.
- **b** Ask students to play the role of group leader, which involves giving instructions and checking understanding, monitoring the participation and understanding of others, re-orienting communication, and intervening and adapting their contribution according to the needs of others.

3 Mediating communication

There are many reasons why one person doesn't understand another. It could be that they don't speak the same language, or do speak it, but with different levels of proficiency, different accents or different cultural references. It could also be to do with age, background or beliefs.

To develop students' ability to mediate communication, we need to provide practice in the following areas:

- **a** Acting as an intermediary in informal situations – this could be translating a menu for someone from another country, or explaining something that may be culturally different, or summarizing information concisely.
- **b** Facilitating communication in delicate situations and disagreements – so, helping out when people disagree, establishing common ground, or trying to resolve disagreements.

The activities that follow bear the above in mind. In all these tasks, students are asked to explain, translate, reinterpret, simplify and make something clearer. Each activity practises a sub-skill identified in the Council of Europe (2020) *Common European Framework of Reference for Languages* (CEFR) - *Companion Volume with New Descriptors*. These are listed in the chart on the next page. There is one Mediation activity for each unit of the book. Suggestions for when to use each activity are included in the teacher's notes.

Mediation activities Teacher's notes

UNIT 1 The dinner party

Aim: to work as a group to decide where to sit guests at a wedding party dinner; to take an active part in a discussion, encourage other group members to take part and to reach an agreement as a group

When to use: at the end of the unit

Procedure: Put students in groups of four or five. Hand out one worksheet to each student. Students read the role cards and select a role. Make sure that the roles of organizer and note-taker (rapporteur) are clearly understood. The organizer is responsible for encouraging collaboration and ensuring the group reaches a consensus. The note-taker must note down the ideas and decisions and summarize these for the group. The other students will be 'team players'. They must all help compare options, encourage collaboration and reach a group consensus. Ask students to look at the table diagram and the six cards. Explain that students have to talk together to decide where to place each guest. Set a ten-minute time limit. At the end, ask note-takers to summarize their group's discussions for the class and present a suggested table plan.

Sample answers

There is no perfect solution. In the possible solution below, Marta is next to quiet people, and away from Charlie, while Serena has Ameera for gossip, and Cynthia has Lorenzo for a serious conversation. Charlie is at the end, so as not to dominate, but he would probably annoy Cynthia:

	LORENZO	CYNTHIA	
MARTA			CHARLIE
	SERENA	AMEERA	

Mediation activities Teacher's notes

UNIT 2 Talking about bilingualism

Aim: to identify and summarize the key points in an article about the benefits of bilingualism, considering which points are most relevant to the intended audience; to reach a consensus in pairs and then in groups about the most important points before presenting ideas to the class

When to use: after Exercise 10 in Lesson 2C

Procedure: Students read the instructions and the article and identify the key points most relevant to the friends mentioned in the instructions. Students summarize these key points and compare with a partner. In pairs, students then present the key points to another pair (the friends), explaining why they should speak to their child in both languages.

If your students speak the same L1, you could choose to do this task so that students translate the points in the English text and present them in their L1.

For additional practice, ask students to find an online article in their L1 on the benefits of bilingualism (or a new topic if preferred). Ask the students to identify the key points in the article and summarize them as bullet points in English. Students then present their summaries in English to their partner.

If students do not have access to the internet in class, set the research and summary writing as homework, and ask students to present their summaries in groups in the next lesson.

Sample answers

Key points to include:

- bilingualism is encouraged – 75% of people speak two languages or more
- social, psychological and lifestyle advantages
- can live and work in a wider variety of countries and cultures
- can meet people from a broader range of backgrounds and be culturally aware and more broad-minded
- view of the world is not limited to the media and culture of one language or one country
- health benefits: can concentrate, solve problems and focus, have better mental flexibility and a much greater ability to multitask

UNIT 3 Desert island adventure

Aim: to choose the six most important items in a desert island scenario; to present and justify ideas in a group and reach a group consensus

When to use: after Exercise 11 in Lesson 3C

Procedure: Hand out one worksheet to each student. Read out the situation with your class and check the meaning of the words in the items listed on the page. Once students have selected items, put students in groups of four or five to debate a list of six items. Students should ask each other to expand on, clarify and justify their ideas in order to help the group decide on the best solution.

Once students have decided, ask one spokesperson from each group to present their list to the class. As a follow up, ask students to think of and say what personal item they would choose to save from the yacht and why.

UNIT 4 A gripping story

Aim: to discuss personal responses to a story about a climbing accident; to discuss how the writer's use of language influences this response

When to use: after Exercise 11 in Lesson 4E

Procedure:

Hand out one worksheet to each student. Ask students to read the story for a general understanding first and answer the questions in Exercise A. Then put students in pairs or small groups. Students read the story again and work through the more detailed questions in Exercise B together. Students explain their interpretation of the creative language and style of the text and their emotional response to this as a reader.

Answers

A It is set in the mountains. One of the climbers falls and is left hanging from rope with a broken leg.

B

1 The author wants us to feel a and b.

a: defeated all attempts / I wondered whether I could truly trust him, not as a friend, but as a climber; b: so high and so impenetrably steep / defeated all attempts / the toughest of climbs

2 Dramatic language: swung, crashed, throbbing horribly, scream, clung

Metaphor: It felt as if it was on fire.

Sentences are short and simple but occasionally more dramatic: Before long, I was just hanging, still, in the silent, clear air …

Internal thoughts: A million thoughts raced around my head … I screamed against the mountain and against my fate.

3 Students' own ideas. Strongly implies that Marco will cut the rope: … holding his sharp, jagged mountain knife in his hands.

4 First person 'I' makes it feel very close and personal – you are with the climber and his thoughts.

UNIT 5 A debate about meat-eating

Aim: to debate the issue of meat-eating

When to use: after Exercise 9 in Lesson 5E

Procedure: Hand out one worksheet to each student. Ask students to discuss the questions in A in groups of four. Point out that 'culture' in question 2 could refer not just to different nationalities, but to different ages, backgrounds, etc.

Students read the two blog posts and answer question 1 in B. Have a brief open class feedback session to establish understanding and to find out whether students are broadly supportive of or against meat-eating. You will need to establish a difference of opinion in each group to make the debate work. This may mean asking students to change places so that there is at least one person in each group willing to argue on each side of the debate. Allow students to note down their own personal arguments before starting the debate. Students should use their mediation skills to show appreciation and understanding of other viewpoints and ideas, and respond appropriately to these during the debate.

Mediation activities Teacher's notes

UNIT 6 Ecology news

Aim: to simplify and shorten a scientific article to be more accessible to a chosen audience

When to use: after Exercise 11 in Lesson 6C

Procedure: Hand out one worksheet to each student. Ask students to read the text and discuss the question in A with a partner (see answers below).

Ask students to choose a target audience in pairs. (Alternatively, you may wish to assign each pair an audience.) Students work together to make a list of key points and to choose a title. Then ask students to prepare their streamlined article individually.

Ask students to pin their completed articles round the class so that students can read them. Encourage students to guess the intended audience of each article and give feedback on whether the retelling made the article more accessible for that audience.

As a follow-up task or homework, find online (or ask students to find) two or three articles that report the same news story but for different audiences (e.g. national/international, younger people/older people, people with a particular interest such as business or science). Students identify the differences in each one (e.g. tone, complexity, key points included) and consider how these reflect the needs of each audience.

Answers

Main argument: Insect numbers are declining due to human actions and measures must be taken to solve the problem.

Key points to include:

Insect numbers are falling by 2% per year (20% per decade)

Decline caused by: modern agriculture, deforestation, light pollution, urbanization and chemicals in the soil.

It is recommended that we: educate the public, ban pesticides, plant native plants to create better insect-friendly habitats, limit light pollution, and stop citizens and companies introducing products like detergents to the eco-system.

Students must also consider whether and how to include some of the shocking information (20% decrease; without insects there isn't enough food in the world) depending on their target audience.

UNIT 7 Housemates

Aim: to work as a group to decide on a new housemate; to propose a solution and to weigh up arguments for and against each suggested solution

When to use: after Exercise 12 in Lesson 7D

Procedure: Hand out one worksheet to each student. Ask students to work in groups of four. Students read the situation and the four descriptions of potential new housemates.

Ask students in each group to choose one of the four people. Make sure they each choose a different person. Give them three minutes to prepare the case for their person to move into the house.

Students make the case for the person they have chosen. Then they talk together to order the potential housemates from most to least desirable. By the end of the discussion, they must reach a consensus about who to invite to move into their house.

UNIT 8 How to use old technology

Aim: to break down into smaller steps a set of instructions on how to operate an old piece of technology, considering how to make them clear to the intended audience

When to use: after Exercise 11 in Lesson 8C

Procedure: Lead into this topic by asking: *Have you ever used a cassette player or record player? What do you do to operate it?* Pre-teach some key words: batteries, cable, the eject button (on a cassette player), the turntable, (cue) lever and arm (on a record player).

Hand out one worksheet to each student. Ask students to work in pairs. Tell half the pairs to read text A, and the other half to read text B. Students work in pairs to prepare a simpler, shorter set of operating instructions for a younger relative who is unfamiliar with the technology.

When students are ready, split pairs, so students from A pairs are now working with students from B pairs. Students take turns to explain how to operate their machines. The student listening is the 'younger relative'.

UNIT 9 Let's talk it through together

Aim: to discuss and come to an agreement on possible solutions for a failing business; to facilitate agreement between two parties

When to use: after Exercise 10 in Lesson 9C

Procedure: Hand out one worksheet to each student. Put students in groups of three and ask each group to decide on their role. Students read their rolecard, A, B or C. Have a brief class feedback session and establish that A thinks B is responsible for the failure, B thinks A is responsible and C must try to help solve the problem. A and B should express their views and justify their opinions, while also listening to each other and C. C must consider both sides and try to facilitate agreement between A and B.

Give students a few minutes to think of what they want to say in the meeting. You could remind students of language connected to adapting to communication styles: *I appreciate your honesty, but could you explain your reasons a bit more? Why do you say that? Just to check I understand, do you mean …?*

Set a ten minute time limit. Students hold a meeting and decide on a way forward. In feedback, ask Student Cs what they have all agreed to do.

UNIT 10 Where to go and what to see

Aim: to interpret and adapt an infographic about a city to prepare a presentation that encourages a particular type of tourist to visit

When to use: after Exercise 12 in Lesson 10E

Procedure: Hand out one worksheet to each student. Put students in groups of three or four. Half the groups are A and half are B.

Students work together to read and interpret the information in their infographics. They use the information to put together a presentation. Group A should prepare a presentation aimed at families with older children. Group B should prepare a presentation aimed at older couples looking to book a special holiday. Students should select and present the information that they think will be most appealing to their intended audience.

If you want to extend the activity, and students have internet access in class, they can look for additional information online in their L1 and then translate the information into English to include in their presentations.

Groups take turns to do their presentations. At the end, ask students which presentations they think would be the most persuasive and appealing for the intended audience and why.

UNIT

1 Mediation The dinner party

A Work in groups. Read the role cards. Decide who will be the 'organizer' and who will be the 'note-taker'. The other group members are 'team players'.

The organizer
You are in charge. Start the discussion and encourage everybody to take part and express their views. Make sure everybody agrees at the end.

The note-taker
You are in charge of noting ideas and decisions. Ask questions to make sure you know what everybody thinks. At the end, you will give a summary to the class of your group's discussion and the reasons for the group's decisions.

The team player
You are a team player in the discussion. Be sure to make your opinions and ideas clear to everybody, but listen to others and encourage them to speak too.

B You are organizing a wedding party dinner. Read about the guests. Then work as a group to decide on the best place to put each guest around the dinner table. Think about which guests will get on well.

Marta
Marta is a dancer. She loves talking about the arts, and will happily stand up and deliver a poem or start singing in the middle of a meal. Life is a performance and she loves being the star. She is outgoing and friendly, but gets bored very easily. People who talk too much get on her nerves.

Lorenzo
Lorenzo is naturally very shy and he finds it hard to think of things to say. He is a scientist and is working on a cure for tropical diseases. In his free time, he enjoys going to the theatre and the cinema. He is never impatient, never loses his temper, and is a very good listener. He can't stand being the centre of attention.

Ameera
Ameera is chatty and friendly and loves meeting new people. She loves finding out all about people – their likes and dislikes, their hobbies, their relationships – and is always asking a lot of questions. When she meets new people, she can't help gossiping either. Sometimes, she reveals secrets she shouldn't be telling people.

Charlie
Charlie is a lot of fun at a party. He always has a funny story to tell and he can make everybody laugh. He is very confident and talkative and has a loud voice. The thing about Charlie is that he doesn't talk to people – he talks to the room!

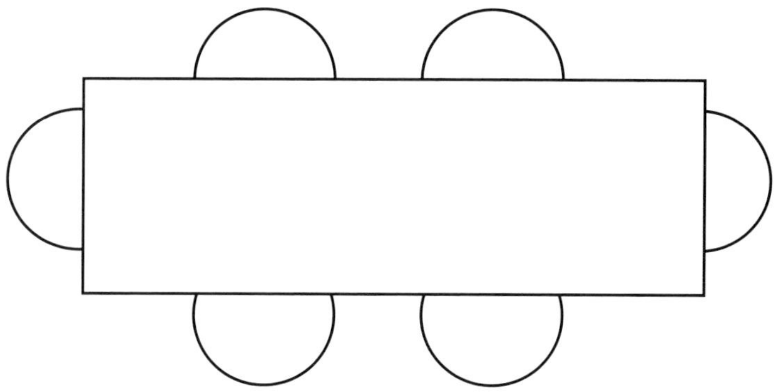

Serena
Serena does not know anybody at the party. She is Lorenzo's friend and she only came because he asked her. With her own friends, she is lively and chatty, but she is nervous with people she doesn't know. She doesn't want to let Lorenzo down by talking too much. She is an activist for an ecological organization, and interested in the environment, but she prefers to keep her views to herself when she's with strangers. She's happy to talk about herself though and hopes to find out more about Lorenzo's friends.

Cynthia
Cynthia is very strong-minded and very serious. She doesn't like talking about things that aren't important and prefers a good political discussion to a chat about fashion. She has very strong political views and can lose her temper when she's arguing. If you haven't got anything intelligent to say, then Cynthia really isn't interested. And she has never laughed at a joke!

UNIT

2 Mediation Talking about bilingualism

A Read the situation.

Your Spanish friends live in the UK and have just had a baby. They are not sure whether to speak to their child in Spanish as well as English. They have asked for your advice.

B Read the article. Identify the key points in the article that are most relevant to your friends and summarize them as bullet points.

C Compare your list of key points with a partner and agree on a combined list of key points.

D Present your key points to another pair. They are your Spanish friends. Use your key points to explain why they should speak to their child in Spanish and English.

The amazing benefits of being bilingual

We live in a world in which bilingualism is not only common but encouraged. As much as 75 per cent of the world's population speak at least two languages and many countries have more than one official national language. Being able to speak, read and write at least one international language, such as English, Mandarin Chinese, or Spanish, has become so important that school systems across the world are designed to teach these languages to a high level. And yet, many native English speakers continue to be monolingual. They are in the minority and are unquestionably missing out.

Multilingualism has been shown to have many social, psychological and lifestyle advantages. On a practical level, being fluent in more than one language enables the speaker to live and work in a wider variety of countries and cultures and to meet people from a broader range of backgrounds. In turn, this is likely to make multilingual speakers more culturally aware and more broad-minded.

Moreover, researchers are finding that there are an enormous number of health benefits from speaking more than one language. Bilingual speakers have a superior ability to concentrate, solve problems and focus, and they show a much greater ability to multitask. The fact that the brain has to work harder and be more flexible is beneficial when we get older too. In tests, bilingual speakers have been shown to recover faster from a stroke and there is evidence that it delays the onset of dementia.

Some argue that the human brain has developed to be multilingual. Early humans lived in small groups, so they probably had to speak different languages to communicate with other groups. In short, being multilingual is not new. It has always been more common than monolingualism. It is about time everybody learned a second language.

UNIT

3 Mediation Desert island adventure

A Read the situation.

You are on a yacht in the Caribbean Sea, but, unfortunately, the yacht has started to sink. Don't panic! You are close to a desert island with coconuts and fresh water and you can swim to shore. However, you only have time to save six items from the yacht before it disappears under the sea. Be careful – you may have to wait weeks before you are rescued from the island.

B Tick the six items you think you should save from the yacht. Prepare arguments to say why you think they are important.

a large glass bottle	sun cream	a sewing kit
a compass	a torch	a bottle of shampoo
a fishing net	some plasters	a long piece of rope
a beach towel	a bottle of aspirin	a watch
a pen	a box of matches	a pair of scissors
a knife	a box of cereal bars	some toilet roll
a wooden bowl	a pair of sunglasses	a book of short stories

C Work in groups. Agree on a list of six items to save. Be prepared to argue in favour of items you think are important. You will need to justify and elaborate on your thinking and build on other people's ideas. Ask questions to encourage the other members of the group to explain and justify their ideas.

D Present and explain your list to the class.

UNIT

4 Mediation A gripping story

A Read the story. Where is it set? What goes wrong?

The final ascent

One

Rising high above us, two spectacular and majestic mountains were visible, both so high and so impenetrably steep that few had even attempted to climb them. Tomorrow, we would attempt the east face of the highest mountain – the face that had filled my waking thoughts for so long and that had so far defeated all attempts. I turned off the stove and poured the hot water into two cups. As I turned to hand one of the cups to my old friend, Marco, I looked into his eyes. I got along really well with Marco and we had stuck together over many years. But this was the toughest of climbs and I wondered whether I could truly trust him, not as a friend, but as a climber.

Two

The rope broke loose, and I swung away from the mountainside, and then back towards it at great speed. My knee crashed into the rock. I felt bones breaking, but there was nothing I could do except hold on as tight as I could and hope that I would not fall hundreds of metres to my death. The rope swung back and to five or six more times but less violently now. Each time I headed towards the cliff face, I was able to place the foot of my good leg against the rock and ease myself away. Before long, I was just hanging, still, in the silent, clear air, my broken leg throbbing horribly. It felt as if it was on fire. A million thoughts raced around my head. I knew that, with my leg broken, I would not be able to climb up the mountain. I knew that breaking a leg at such altitude, and in such dangerous terrain, was a death sentence. I screamed against the mountain and against my fate. When I looked up, far above me, I could see Marco, firmly attached to the side of the mountain in all his climbing gear. He was looking back down towards me, but I could not see the expression on his face. The long rope that I clung to dropped directly below him. For a moment, I was blinded by the light of the sun that seemed to reflect down from his helmet. When I looked again, Marco appeared to be holding his sharp, jagged mountain knife in his hands.

B Read the story again. Discuss these questions in pairs or small groups.

Extract one

1 Which of these emotions does the author want the reader to feel?

a a feeling that something might go wrong
b a feeling that this is an incredibly difficult challenge
c a feeling that the two men trust each other very much

How does the writer convey these feelings to the reader?

Extract two

2 How does the writer convey the horror of the accident and the narrator's response? Think about the use of dramatic language, metaphor, sentence structure and the narrator's internal thoughts.

3 What do you think will happen next? How does the writer make us feel that something bad may happen?

Overall

4 The story is in the first person 'I'. What effect does this have?

5 How did you feel while reading the story? Was it exciting? Did you want to keep reading? Why? / Why not?

UNIT

5 Mediation A debate about meat-eating

A Work in groups of four. Discuss the questions below.

1 Do you eat meat? Why? / Why not? Is your choice personal, ethical or cultural?

2 In your culture, how do people feel about eating meat? Has there been a change in the culture? If so, why?

B You are going to debate the issue of meat-eating in your group. Follow the steps (1–3).

1 Read the two different viewpoints about meat-eating. Are the arguments personal, ethical or cultural? Which point of view is closest to your own?

2 Decide which side of the meat-eating debate you are on. Add your own personal, ethical or cultural arguments to those already provided.

3 Debate the issue in your group. Encourage others to speak and listen to all sides of the debate. Appreciate and acknowledge other viewpoints and different cultural worldviews.

A

Here are *my* reasons, some personal, all logical, why I refuse to stop eating animals.

Firstly, meat is good for you. It contains vitamin B12, which prevents anaemia, as well as plenty of iron. Iron is really important because it helps your body produce two essential proteins, haemoglobin and myoglobin. These proteins deliver oxygen to your cells and keeps them healthy.

Secondly, people are supposed to eat meat. We have the canine teeth and small intestines of an omnivore, and, like all omnivores, we eat meat.

Thirdly, we can eat meat but still care for animals. I buy free-range eggs and chicken, and grass-fed beef, for example.

Fourthly, meat is a part of the traditions of many cultures. We eat meat on special occasions and our national dishes often contain a particular type of meat.

Finally, meat is tasty. I love it!

B

Let's all stop eating animals right now. The arguments against meat-eating are numerous.

Firstly, it costs a lot less to grow vegetables than produce meat. If more people were vegetarian, we could feed the world more effectively.

Secondly, research shows that a vegetarian diet is healthier. Eating meat in large quantities can cause cancer and heart disease, but vegetables are full of food stuffs that are good for us. If you only eat vegetables, you'll keep your weight down too.

Thirdly, the production of meat is a disaster for the environment. Beef, in particular, is a cause for concern. There are a billion cows on the planet, producing phenomenal amounts of methane, which destroys the ozone layer. Cows use up enormous amounts of farmland too, which causes deforestation.

Finally, eating vegetables is fun, as well as healthy. There are great vegetarian recipes and fantastic restaurants.

6 Mediation Ecology news

A Work in pairs. Read the article from an academic news website. What is the main argument?

ECOLOGY NEWS | The news website for environmental scientists

Scientific Evidence for the Decline of Insects

Recently-published research strongly suggests that insect populations are declining at a higher rate than previously believed. There are a number of reasons for this, all of which are of equal importance. In a study by the University of Western Bohemia, researchers investigated how modern agriculture has caused an annual reduction in insects of around 2% every year. In a comparable American study, the research focussed on how deforestation was having an impact. A Korean study pointed to the way that light pollution was causing a decline. It seems that there is no single cause for the decline in insects. Research shows that there are a number of factors.

Humanity's environmental footprint is clearly causing a reduction in the world's insect populations. At the current rate, every ten years, there will be 20% fewer insects. Using pesticide chemicals in farming is to blame, as well as the way that we are cutting down forests, using up land for housing, and producing light pollution that affects the way insects behave. Experts from around the world said that insect populations were suffering severely as a result of human behaviour, including intensive agriculture, urbanization, the use of chemicals, deforestation and light pollution.

In their published papers, scientists recommended ways in which the issue could be tackled. This includes banning pesticides and creating insect-friendly habitats by planting native plants and trees. They noted that some insect populations have been able to do well due to conservation efforts. In areas of high human activity, where insect numbers are falling most rapidly, there is a variety of factors causing the problem, and there is no simple solution. It is important to educate the public, so that people become aware of the problem, and it is important to introduce pesticide bans, limit light pollution, and stop citizens and companies introducing products like detergents to the eco-system.

It will take a long time and a lot of effort to reverse the decline in insect species. However, researchers offer encouragement. 'You have to be optimistic,' said one researcher. 'Insects are essential. Without insects, there isn't enough food in the world.'

B You are going to simplify the article for one of the audiences below. Decide which audience you will write for.

A An opinion column in a national newspaper. Your readers are ordinary adults who take an interest in environmental concerns.

B A website for teenagers. Your readers are young and idealistic, interested in the environment and ready to fight for a cause.

C An article on a sensationalist news website. Your readers aren't particularly interested in ecology, but they enjoy being shocked and entertained.

C Simplify the article for your chosen audience. Follow the instructions (1–3).

1 Select the key points made in the article and make a list. Exclude non-relevant or repetitive information.

2 Paraphrase the key points to make them easier to understand and more relevant to your audience.

3 Choose a title for your article, or invent your own:

Crisis in the insect world
Time to act
Look what we have done

UNIT

7 Mediation Housemates

A **Work in groups of four. Read the situation and instructions.**

You are housemates and you get on well. However, there's an empty room in your house and you can't afford the rent unless you find another person to live with.

Read the descriptions of four potential new housemates. Choose one of the people to describe. Summarize his or her good and bad points for your group. Try to persuade the rest of the group that your chosen person would make the best new housemate.

Jack
Jack is currently unemployed but has had lots of different jobs in the past. He has worked as an electrician and a painter and decorator. He doesn't like cooking and eats fast food most of the time. In the evening, he prefers to stay in because he doesn't have a lot of money. He loves classical music and staying up late, and he has a friendly pet cat. He is very chatty and loves talking about politics.

Rosa
Rosa works as a fitness instructor at a local gym. She gets up at five o'clock every morning for work and likes playing loud pop music to wake herself up. Rosa stays fit and healthy and hopes her housemates will go jogging with her. She is a vegan but doesn't mind other people eating meat in the house. She is a party animal and very out-going. At the weekend, she loves having fun.

Malik
Malik earns a lot of money working for his father's business. He loves playing the guitar and is happy to give free lessons in the evenings. He hates cleaning and says he'll pay extra rent if he doesn't have to do any jobs in the house. His girlfriend lives in another town and plans to visit and stay in the house most weekends. He tends to eat out most evenings and doesn't really want to make new friends.

Clara
Clara works night shifts as a nurse at the hospital. She needs the house to be quiet during the day because that's when she sleeps. Clara is shy and finds it hard to make new friends. She loves cooking and cleaning and is very tidy. In fact, she likes the house to be kept clean and tidy all the time.

B **As a group, order the four people from most to least desirable as housemates. Justify your opinions and give reasons, but consider the opinions of the other people in your group too. By the end of the discussion, you must come to an agreement about who to invite to move into your house.**

PAIR A

A Work in pairs. You have a younger relative who needs to use a cassette player for a school project. They have never used one before and don't understand the instructions. They have asked you for help. Read the operating instructions. Then break down the instructions into a series of smaller steps so that your relative can understand them.

B Work with a new partner. They are your younger relative. Explain how to operate the machine.

How to use a cassette player

Start by checking your cassette player has a power supply. If the player requires batteries, properly install the appropriate batteries into the player according to the diagram printed on the inside of the battery compartment. If the player has a power cable, make sure it is safely plugged into the wall. Connecting speakers or headphones is easy as there are symbols on the machine that show you where they go. If there is a power switch on the player, ensure that it is in the 'On' position. You will need to find and press the appropriate button (labelled 'Eject') to open the cassette door in order to allow you to place a cassette inside. Gently close the tape door, ensuring that it is completely shut. Adjust the volume to a low level and find the 'Play' button, which is usually adjacent to the 'Eject' button. Adjust the volume accordingly. There are options, all on labelled buttons, that allow you to stop or pause, or even perform more advanced functions such as 'fast forward' or 'rewind' the cassette.

PAIR B

A Work in pairs. You have a younger relative who has bought a record player. They have never used one before and don't understand the instructions. They have asked you for help. Read the operating instructions. Then break down the instructions into a series of smaller steps so that your relative can understand them.

B Work with a new partner. They are your younger relative. Explain how to operate the machine.

How to play a record

To play a record, begin by placing the record on the turntable. Since records come with an A and a B side, make sure you place the record on the correct side, based on the song you want to play. If you are using a vertical record player, make sure the record is locked in place and cannot fall off. There is a small lever that you will have to operate in order to lift the arm and move it upwards. Now you can move the arm to the outer edge of the record. Look for the record player's 'on' switch. Once pressed, the record should begin to spin. Make sure you have the record set to the correct speed. If you're using a standard record, it should be 33 1/3 RPM. With the record spinning and the arm in position, you can now use the cue lever to lower the arm. This will bring the needle into contact with the record. Once it makes contact you should begin to hear music. Skipping tracks is easy to do with a record. If you want to skip a track on a record, you'll follow the same process discussed above, except you place the arm above the beginning of the track you want to hear, and not above the beginning of the record.

UNIT

9 Mediation Let's talk it through together

A Work in groups of three. Decide who is A, who is B and who is C. Then read your role card carefully. Who do you think is the most responsible for the failing business?

ROLE CARD A

You opened a bookshop with your friend and partner, B. Unfortunately, it is losing money and may have to close if you don't change your business practice. You have strong views about who is the most responsible and what to do:

- Your partner works fewer hours in the shop than you do – as a result, the shop has to close at six and on weekends. Longer opening hours may be a way forward.
- Your partner orders a lot of academic books. There should be more popular titles and more children's books. There are schools nearby, but children rarely come in.
- People often don't stay in the shop for long. You need a better atmosphere – perhaps a coffee stand in the shop or a reading space with seats.
- Your partner markets the business, but rarely listens to your ideas. You need to spend more money on advertising locally – perhaps by sponsoring local events or having events in the bookshop.

ROLE CARD B

You opened a bookshop with your friend and partner, A. Unfortunately, it is losing money and may have to close if you don't change your business practice. You have strong views about who is the most responsible and what to do:

- You order new stock, market the business and do the accounting. Your partner just works in the shop. You need more help from your partner.
- The shop is near the university. It might be a good idea to sell more academic books and to specialize in books for this market.
- Many people come in, look at books, then leave. They probably go home and buy online. You need reduced prices to get people to buy.
- You need to reduce costs. Too much is spent on the appearance of the shop and that means you can't keep prices low.

ROLE CARD C

Your friends, A and B, opened a bookshop together. Unfortunately, it is losing money and may have to close. They have asked you to help. Read through A and B's views in the role cards above.

B Have an honest and open meeting and discuss ways forward. A and B should try to persuade the others that their ideas are the best but also listen and respond appropriately to the other members of the group. It is the role of C to propose alternative approaches and help A and B come to an agreement.

Mediation Where to go and what to see

A Read about Dubai. Then prepare a presentation on behalf of the Dubai Tourist Office saying why visitors should choose Dubai as a holiday destination.

Group A: prepare a presentation aimed at families with older children.
Group B: prepare a presentation aimed at older couples looking to book a special holiday.

WHY COME TO DUBAI?

1 World records

The world's **largest** shopping centre

6 floors and **1,200** stores

The world's **tallest** skyscraper

828 m, Observation deck on **125th** floor

The world's **largest** performing fountain

90 metres high and **6,600** lights

2 Luxury accommodation

5-star hotels

Spa packages

White sand beaches

3 Fun and adventure

Sky dive

Explore the desert

Watersports at Kite Beach

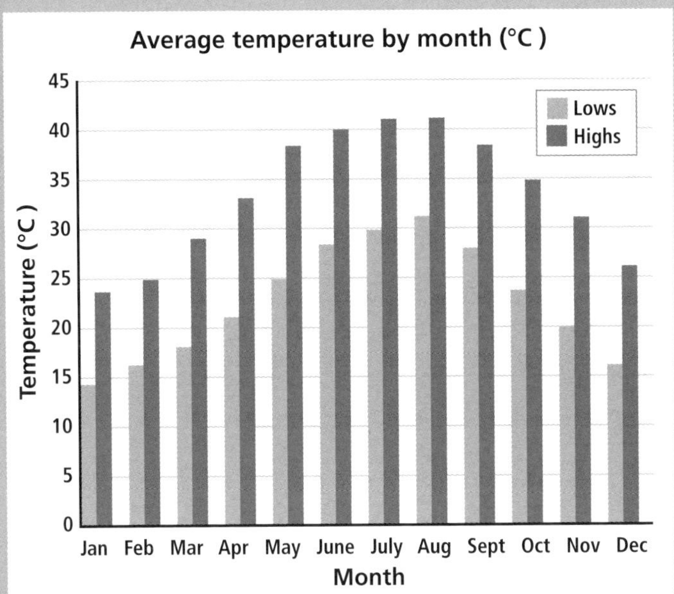

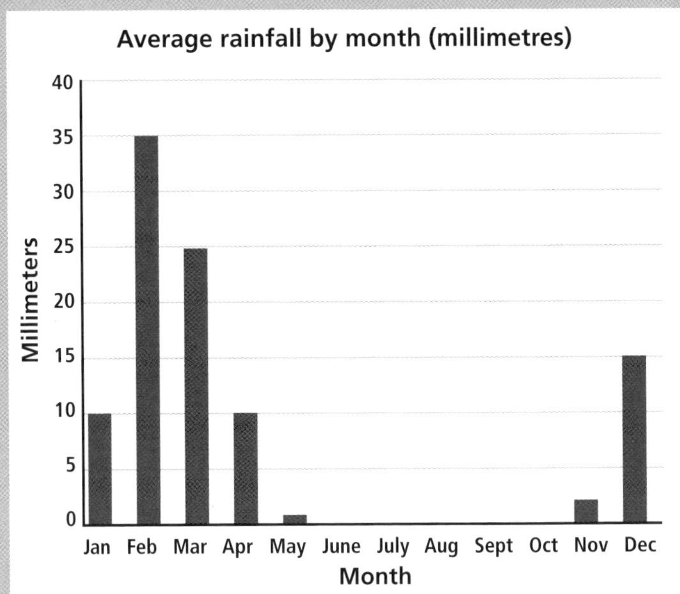

Tips for classroom teaching and management

This section provides general guidance and tips for: understanding learners' needs and expectations; planning lessons; managing classroom interaction; checking understanding; providing feedback and correction. Additional guidance and tips for teaching specific skills covered in the series can be found as part of the *Voices* online resources.

1 UNDERSTANDING LEARNER NEEDS AND EXPECTATIONS

At the beginning of your course, it is important to get to know why your students are learning English, how they want to learn, and what they hope to achieve. Students embarking on a language learning course at Upper Intermediate level are already experienced language learners. However, they are likely to have very different language learning experiences, very different strengths and weaknesses, and potentially very different aims and expectations. It is important to empower higher-level students so that they can express their concerns and preferences and also have a say in what they learn and how they are taught. Here are some suggestions:

1 At the beginning of the course, carry out a written or spoken Needs Analysis and discussion. Create a simple form including questions such as:

A Why are you learning English?

☐ for work ☐ to study ☐ to travel ☐ for fun

☐ other: ______________________

B Which are most important to you? Put the skills in order from 1 to 7.

☐ reading ☐ writing ☐ speaking ☐ listening

☐ pronunciation ☐ grammar ☐ vocabulary

C Which of the skills are you good at? Which are you not good at?

I'm good at ______________________.

I'm not good at ______________________.

D Which of the following are important ways to learn? Choose the three most important.

☐ studying grammar

☐ learning lots of new words

☐ speaking in pairs or groups

☐ reading English texts (articles, blogs, etc.)

☐ watching and listening to real people talking (on TV, radio, video, etc.)

☐ writing real texts (emails, messages, letters, etc.)

Ask students to complete the form individually or ask students to interview a partner and complete the analysis for them. Then ask students to compare their ideas in pairs, then in groups of four, and finally as a class. This encourages students to think carefully about what they need and want, and also makes them aware of how others in their class feel. Collect and keep the Needs Analyses and use them to inform both your class preparation and the way you teach in class.

2 Ask students to write to you about their needs. For homework, they write you a letter or email headed *Dear Teacher …* Write some sentence starters for students to use in the email: *In class, I like … / I don't like … I want to study … I'm good at … I'm not good at … I prefer … to … In the future, I want to …*

3 Ask students to begin and keep a learning journal. They could write each entry and hand them in, or you could ask students to send the journal as emails each week. Begin with the *Dear Teacher* letter as described above. In future diary entries, ask students to write about what they liked in lessons, what they learned, what they had problems with, what they want to do differently. This will give you an ongoing commentary on needs and wants to help you shape lessons. The *Learning to learn: Your journal* sections in the Workbook provide further guidance and ideas for students who are interested in keeping a learning journal.

2 PLANNING LESSONS

Here are some suggestions for adapting the material in *Voices Upper Intermediate* to suit your classroom. More guidance on planning online lessons can be found as part of the *Voices* online resources.

1 Look at the lesson goals. Then, depending on the length of your lesson, divide up the material on the page. So, for example, when planning to teach Lesson C, you may choose to do Listening in one lesson and Vocabulary and Pronunciation in the next. Think about using extra activities in the Teacher's Book to provide extension activities for both lessons.

2 Use the basic notion of 'input/output' to plan lessons. That means a balance between what students study (input) and what they say or write in lessons (output). There should be more output than input in each lesson.

3 Plan your lesson based on your students' learning outcomes. Look at a lesson from the Student's Book and complete this outcome: *At the end of the lesson, my students will be able to …* Base your plan around achieving this outcome. It will mean that you will put emphasis on what students are able to do, rather than on what you have taught.

4 Plan lessons based on your students' needs, priorities and first language. If they have indicated that fluency and speaking practice is of higher importance to them, you may wish to place more attention on Lesson C and D of each unit, and supplement that material with the Communication worksheets in the Teacher's Book. If they have indicated that grammar accuracy is important to them, Lesson B and the additional practice materials provided in the back of the Student's Book, the Workbook and the Grammar worksheets in the Teacher's Book, may be what you place more attention on.

Tips for classroom teaching and management

3 MANAGING CLASSROOM INTERACTION

3.1 Varying classroom interaction

For spoken practice to be useful and meaningful, students should change partners regularly. This builds class relationships and dynamics, and extends spoken practice. Here are some suggestions:

1. In a classroom in which it is hard to move students, put students in groups of four, with students in one row turning to face students in the row behind. Students can practise a conversation with the person next to them, the person opposite, then the person across.
2. In a classroom where students can more easily move their chairs, adjust the physical space. If students are in groups of four, have them move their chairs to the corners of the classroom so groups are away from each other.
3. If you have space, ask students to stand up and walk round and strike up conversations with students they don't know well, or at all. One way of doing this is to play music. When the music plays, students walk. When the music stops, they stop walking and begin talking to the person nearest to them.

3.2 Organizing pairwork

Here are some tips for varying pairwork:

1. Encourage students to speak to different people in the class, and get to know them, by mixing pairs during the initial warmer or lead in parts of the lesson. Use instructions like *Find a partner you didn't speak to in the last lesson* to empower students to seek out new speaking partners. This builds relationships and improves class dynamics.
2. Students often want to sit with a partner they are comfortable with when talking about grammar rules, doing vocabulary exercises, or checking answers to a reading text, for example. However, aim to change pairs when the task is creative or productive. So, students should have a new partner when they do a speaking or writing task.
3. When preparing to do a speaking or writing activity, ask students to prepare with one partner. Then do the activity with another partner. If you have an odd number in class, you could make a pair with one of your students or have a group of three and do one role twice.
4. Encourage students to sit in a different seat at the beginning of each lesson. This may be impractical in some situations, (and, as stated above, adult students sometimes have a strong preference to sit with a partner they know), but if you have an adult evening class or a weekly class, it can be boring if students always sit in the same place. Having to move can be disorientating at first, but students soon recognize that it changes the dynamic of each lesson – a different view, and different partners.

3.3 Managing free group discussions

To develop learners' confidence and fluency, it is useful to balance more structured pair and groupwork activities with freer group discussion. The aim with these activities is to ask students to share opinions or experiences, with the focus on getting meaning across more than on being accurate. Here are some ideas for making them work well:

1. Think about the size of your group. Three students can be good for sharing stories or experiences because everybody gets to talk. Larger groups of five or six can be good for debating or problem solving because there are more opinions to be shared.
2. Set a short time limit for students to read questions or prepare ideas and language before students begin talking.
3. Make one student the group leader. It is this student's job to ask questions, make sure everybody contributes and to draw conclusions or summarize what people said at the end.
4. Give students autonomy to make the activity work for them. For example, students might prefer to talk about fewer questions than are in the text, or focus on the individual experience of a group member.
5. Monitor students' common errors, but don't correct every mistake students make; note a few down, write them on the board at the end of the task, and use them as an error correction activity. (See section 5 for more ideas on error correction.)

3.4 Managing other speaking activities

The more focussed preparation time you give your students, the more accurate and creative their performance will be. So, make sure you leave plenty of time in your lesson for students to prepare ideas, roles and phrases to use. Here are some suggestions:

1. Depending on the speaking activity, give students time to prepare their roles, either by noting ideas or opinions and/or preparing phrases. Set a generous five-minute time limit and ask students to prepare with a partner. Get involved yourself by suggesting things to say or commenting on their ideas.
2. Let students practise what they want to say individually or with a partner before being asked to perform for the teacher or the class.
3. Model the speaking task so students can see what is expected. Either act it out yourself with a student or ask a confident pair of students to model it.

Tips for classroom teaching and management

4 CHECKING UNDERSTANDING

4.1 Giving instructions at higher levels

At this level, students are comfortable with being instructed in English. However, it is still easy to misunderstand instructions, so have a clear and repeated way of managing tasks. Here are some suggestions:

1. Use ICQs (instruction check questions). Ask students to read the instruction of a task in the Student's Book. Then use questions to check understanding. Say, for example, *Are you going to work in pairs? How many words will you write in each space?*
2. Break down instructions. If the instruction is complex – for a speaking roleplay, for example – instruct each stage of the activity separately. Give an instruction, ask students to carry it out, then instruct the next part.
3. Ask students to instruct each other. For example, have pairs read an instruction, then explain the task to each other, or have one student stand up and instruct the class.

4.2 Using concept check questions (CCQs) at higher levels

At higher levels, concept check questions (CCQs) are an important way of checking new words or phrases especially when translation is not an option. If you simply define a word, you don't know if students have understood. Asking questions makes students active and obliges them to show they understand. Here are some example CCQs for the phrase 'hit it off' (introduced in lesson 4C).

hit it off = form an immediate, positive connection with someone

yes/no or *either/or* CCQs:

Do you form a positive friendship with the person? (yes)

Do you form the friendship immediately or over a long time? (immediately)

5 PROVIDING FEEDBACK AND CORRECTION

5.1 Providing feedback on answers

Here are some suggestions:

Whether writing answers to a reading or listening task, or whether doing a grammar or vocabulary exercise, do not assume students have the answers until they can see, check and copy answers. Here are some suggestions:

1. Allow students to check answers with a partner – this provides confirmation, confidence and a degree of peer-teaching.
2. Always write up (or otherwise display) answers on the board. They should be written up clearly (e.g. numbered) so that students can confirm by comparing with what answers they have and can copy the answers if necessary.
3. Monitor closely as students do a task so that you know which answers to focus on – the ones that cause difficulty.
4. Consider involving students in the feedback stage. For example, you could ask individuals to come to the board and write up their answers.

5.2 Using peer teaching

Peer teaching is useful in the language classroom because it develops co-operation and collaboration between students, independent of the teacher and because it recognizes a range of knowledge and abilities which can be made use of. Here are some suggestions:

1. In a vocabulary lesson, ask students to think which English words are the same or similar in their first language or other languages they know. Students can then compare across different languages in the class.
2. Ask students to tick words they know in an exercise, or ask students to say if they understand a grammar point or not. Then pair students with good knowledge with students who are less clear. The more confident students then have the task of helping their classmates with the exercise.
3. In feedback, ask students to make the case for their answer to a specific question. The rest of the class agree or challenge.

5.3 Giving error feedback after fluency

When students are using language from the lesson in a personalized fluency activity, the main aim is to communicate, so you don't want to interrupt the flow by stopping students if they make errors. In this situation:

1. Listen in to what students are saying with a notepad handy so that you can quickly note any errors you hear.
2. Only interrupt if there is a breakdown in communication.
3. At the end, once you have asked questions to find out what students discovered in the activity, incorporate an error feedback stage. This can be very useful, especially if you focus on errors students make in language they have recently been studying, or if you focus on recurring, ingrained errors students continue to make.

Here are suggested procedures for the error feedback stage:

1. Write four or five incorrect short sentences that you heard on the board. Put students in pairs and ask them to correct the sentences.
2. Write short sentences on the board – some correct, some incorrect. Students have to say which are incorrect and why.
3. Write incorrect sentences on the board. Students correct in class or at home. Ask students to explain the error and say why the speaker has made it.

Tips for classroom teaching and management

5.4 Using peer correction and support

As students become increasingly confident and proficient in English on your course, encourage them to take responsibility for helping each other to use new language accurately and creatively. Here are some suggestions:

1 When students do any accuracy work in class, such as a written accuracy practice or a controlled speaking activity, include some reflection in pairs on the activity. With writing, students can compare answers and correct each other. With speaking, they could comment on how well language was used (in L1 if necessary) and suggest corrections.

2 Whenever students prepare language for a roleplay or information exchange activity, ask students to compare what they have prepared with a partner before performing. Use the stage to correct and to suggest other or better things to say.

3 After students have used language in a speaking activity, ask students to work in pairs to correct errors that you noticed while they were speaking.

5.5 Marking written work

Many of the writing tasks in *Voices* are personalized and designed to get students to write something free and fluent about themselves. Since the aim is fluency, it is counter-productive to mark such work strictly, correcting all errors. At the same time, it is a good idea to provide some meaningful feedback on students' work. Here are some ideas:

1 Get students to read each other's work, providing a personal or positive comment and underlining any sections where there is error or confusion. Students can then look at the underlines and rethink their writing. Each Lesson E has a REVIEW activity which prompts students to exchange their writing and give each other feedback.

2 If you collect in work, underline or asterisk any key errors, and write at the bottom what sort of key errors you found. Again, students can choose to respond to this when they get their work back.

3 Provide whole class feedback on an area of error common to students. This, for example, could be the use of articles, punctuation in a text, or tense problems. Students can then look at their text and see if they can find and correct any errors they have made.

Answer key

UNIT 1

Reading

1 3

2 1 a, b 2 a, c 3 b, c, d 4 c, d 5 d

3 1 e 2 f 3 b 4 d 5 a 6 c

4 1 W 2 S 3 W 4 W 5 S 6 W

Grammar

1
1 What makes you smile?
2 This emoticon means 'Hello', doesn't it?
3 Why were you surprised by my news?
4 We'd like to know if you were happy with our suggestion.
5 Don't you love the smell of fresh coffee?

2
1 Can you tell me what this emoji means?
2 I'd like to know if every language uses the same system.
3 Do you know whether you can download these new emojis?
4 Could you show me how you put the symbol in your message?
5 Do you think this symbol looks Japanese or Korean?
6 I wonder if all the emoticons appeared OK in my email.

3 1 What 2 use 3 Who 4 sends 5 Which 6 comes

4 1 is it? 2 aren't they? 3 can we? 4 didn't you? 5 don't you? 6 has he?

5 1 Can't you 2 Didn't you 3 Shouldn't we 4 Wouldn't you 5 Isn't it 6 Weren't they

6 1 isn't 2 does 3 don't 4 Has 5 do 6 Who

Pronunciation

Using stress for emphasis (1)

1 1 angry 2 me 3 your 4 brother 5 sure 6 that

2 a 4 b 1 c 5

Learning to learn: pronunciation

A: Do you know what the difference is between emoticons and emojis?

B: Yes, emoticons are symbols used to represent faces and emojis are actual pictures.

A: Oh, OK!

B: You know you have to be careful with emojis, don't you? What you see when you send it isn't necessarily what the other person sees.

A: Isn't it?

B: No!

Vocabulary

1 1 astonished 2 petrified 3 furious 4 relieved 5 thrilled

2 1 furious 2 astonished 3 relieved 4 petrified 5 thrilled

3 1 motivated 2 impatient 3 thrilling 4 optimistic 5 petrified 6 astonishing 7 concerned 8 relieved

Learning to learn: vocabulary

verb	noun	adjective	antonym
anger	anger	angry	
annoy	annoyance	annoying / annoyed	
astonish	astonishment	astonishing / astonished	
bear		bearable	unbearable
disappoint	disappointment	disappointing / disappointed	
exhaust	exhaustion	exhausting / exhausted	
irritate	irritation	irritating / irritated	
	joy	joyful	
motivate	motivation	motivating / motivated	demotivating/ ed
	optimism	optimistic	pessimistic
please	pleasure	pleasant	unpleasant
sense	sense	sensitive	insensitive
worry	worry	worrying / worried	

Focus on

2 1 really 2 completely 3 slightly 4 relatively 5 a bit 6 quite 7 totally 8 tremendously

Pronunciation

Short and long vowels

1 1 /ɪ/ 2 /aɪ/ 3 /eɪ/ 4 /iː/ 5 /iː/ 6 /ɪ/

Listening

1 a shopping mall, a next-door neighbour, a wedding in the country, coach drivers, a traffic warden, a parking fine

2 1 a, b 2 a 3 c

Writing

1 1 ages 2 drop you a line 3 been up to 4 had no idea 5 catch up 6 be in touch with

2 Write an email to David.

3 Model answer

Hi David

How are things? I'm sorry I haven't been in touch for ages! Especially because I heard you had an accident with your motorbike – I had no idea! Roberto has just sent me an email about it. It sounds terrible. I hope you're OK now.

Guess what? I finished college last month. I'm so happy. I haven't got my final results yet, but I feel quite confident and optimistic about them. We did a final year project and I got a good mark for that. Now I have to decide what to do next. I need a little holiday first, though. I can't go far because I haven't got much money at the moment.

Anyway, I was thinking that it would be great if Roberto and I came to visit you one day. Does that sound OK? Can you get out of the house? We could go for a burger or something. If not, don't worry, we can just see you at home. It will be good to catch up.

Just send me a message and we can arrange something,

See you soon

Alex

Learning to learn: your journal

Students' own answers

UNIT 2

Reading

2 All the words are in the article.

3 1 d 2 a 3 c 4 b

4 1 T 2 F 3 NG 4 T 5 T 6 T 7 NG

5 3 Paragraphs 3, 4 and 5

Learning to learn: reading

Exercise 2 is scanning

Exercise 3 is skimming

Grammar

1 1 I don't find 2 we're trying 3 are they doing 4 she does 5 he's listening to 6 I'm not studying 7 Do you have 8 they learn

2 1 I've been 2 I've been looking 3 have you enrolled 4 I haven't lived 5 I've been working 6 I've been focusing 7 I've finished 8 I've had

3 1 I've been learning Spanish since I was a child.

2 I'm studying from home this year.

3 I've been doing this degree for two years.

4 I've finished five assignments on this course.

5 My class is taking part in this year's open day / the open day this year.

6 We've updated our student website.

7 I've been revising for my exam for five days.

4 1 I've watched 2 I prefer 3 I've turned on 4 I'm not learning 5 I've been experimenting 6 I've doubled 7 speak 8 I'm looking 9 I've been trying 10 haven't got

Learning to learn: grammar

Students' own answers

Pronunciation

Understanding weak forms of auxiliary verbs

1 1 full 2 weak 3 full 4 full 5 weak 6 full

Answer key

Listening

1	live in	first language(s)	other languages	languages used at home
Jordi:	Sweden	Spanish, Catalan	English, Swedish	first languages, English
Chen:	Sweden	Mandarin Chinese	English, Swedish	first language, English

2 1 According to 2 Funnily enough 3 However 4 Which brings me to 5 Essentially

Vocabulary

1 1 bring it up 2 come up 3 make up 4 pick it up 5 point out 6 getting her message across 7 read up on 8 come up with

2 1 come up with 2 read up on 3 make 4 up 5 came up 6 get 7 across 8 point out

Pronunciation

Saying the /r/ sound

1 1 surprised 2 grandparents 3 birds 4 brother 5 try 6 effort

Focus on

1 1 INSEP 2 SEP 3 INSEP 4 INSEP

2 1 picked it up 2 point them out 3 made it up 4 brought it up

3 1 get your point across

2 pointed them out

3 come up with a strategy

4 made it up

Writing

1 **Dear** Mr Fraser

I'm writing about course SY 460.1. **Regarding** the assessment, **I was wondering** if there is a final exam.

Could you tell me where we send our work?

I **look forward to hearing from** you.

Best wishes

Selima Martin

2 She wants information on:

pdfs – does she have to use them?

assessment – how does it work?

group work – how does it work?

dates for assignments – where are they?

3 Model answer

Dear Mr Fraser

I'm a student on course SY 460.1. I am writing to ask about some aspects of the course that I am not clear on. First, could you tell me if we have to use pdf format to send our work? Also I'd like more information about how the assessment system works. I was also wondering if you could explain how the group work is organized. Will we work individually or in groups? Finally, although I have looked at various sections of Campus, I can't find the dates for sending the course assignments. I'd appreciate it if you could send me them or give me a link to the information.

I apologize for sending so many questions.

I look forward to hearing from you.

Kind regards,

Selima Martin

Learning to learn: making the most of English language resources (1)

Students' own answers

1&2 REVIEW 1

Vocabulary

1 1 relieved 2 concerned 3 furious 4 optimistic 5 impatient 6 thrilled

2 1 reading up on

2 come up

3 get my ideas across

4 come up with

5 pointed out

6 making up

Grammar

1 1 haven't 2 Who 3 Did 4 Didn't / Did 5 if 6 Do

2 1 is getting 2 speak 3 are 4 haven't studied 5 don't need 6 translate 7 has increased / has been increasing 8 has changed / is changing

Reading

1 Positive emotions:
smiles excitement enthusiasm calm peaceful feelings more excited feel good

2 1 Y 2 N 3 N 4 Y 5 NG 6 N

Listening

1 1 similar to 2 is active 3 organized 4 known 5 can be part of

2 1 attractive 2 school 3 being asleep 4 video 5 new words 6 remember

Pronunciation

1 1 L 2 S 3 L 4 L

2 2 and 4

UNIT 3

Reading

1 1 c 2 g 3 h 4 f

2 Suggested ideas:
hike along the main motorway, enter a race, go away for a spontaneous weekend, do something in the five-to-nine, e.g. take a train, sleep on top of a hill, wake up jump in a lake then get back on the train and be home by nine o'clock, find a river to go swimming in, sleep in your garden for a night, forage for edible plants in your neighbourhood, pick a random point on a map of your area and go and visit it, do something in the dark.

Learning to learn: reading

Students' own answers

Grammar

1 1 finished 2 spent 3 had been looking 4 found out 5 ended up 6 made 7 had been 8 had been working 9 took 10 travelled 11 was hoping 12 had been

2 1 b 2 a 3 b 4 b 5 c 6 c

3 1 fell 2 hadn't locked 3 had visited 4 disappeared 5 had just begun 6 left

4 1 was working/worked 2 had been 3 set off 4 were going 5 had been driving 6 managed to 7 had stopped 8 brought 9 noticed 10 were smiling and waving/smiled and waved 11 were 12 had shared

5 1 b C 2 c A 3 a D 4 d B

Pronunciation

Pronouncing groups of two or more consonants

1 absolutely 2 angrily 3 completely 4 excitedly 5 incredibly 6 strangely

Listening

1 1 First person to cross the Atlantic Ocean without a sail, the two longest ocean kayak voyages

2 The Atlantic Ocean, three times

3 He went from west to east on the 3rd voyage

2 1 His kayak was damaged in a storm (2nd voyage)

2 The *Baltic Light* crew fixed his kayak (3rd voyage)

3 2, 3, 4, 7, 8

Learning to learn: listening

1 The men had almost completely closed the windows, there was hardly any light in the room, the three men were blocking the front door.

2 No, because they were doing these things to show how the papyrus glowed in the dark.

Vocabulary

1 1 go on 2 set off 3 turn back 4 head for 5 stop over 6 make it 7 steer 8 end up 9 reach

2 1 went on 2 set off 3 stop over 4 make it 5 turn back 6 headed for 7 ended up

Focus on

1 1 f 2 d 3 h 4 c 5 g 6 a 7 b 8 e

Answer key

2 1 went on an exchange trip
2 go on a bike ride
3 am going on a journey
4 are going on … city break
5 go on a bus tour
6 Have … been on a package holiday
7 go on a field trip
8 been on holiday

Writing

1 1 h 2 a 3 d 4 b 5 e 6 c 7 f 8 g

2 1 fascinating 2 headed back 3 truly 4 incredible 5 popped into 6 stunning

3 Model answer

If you only have one day in our town, you really must visit the beautiful old town centre. It has so much to offer, and you can spend the morning there and still have time for a relaxing walk along the river in the afternoon.

Start your day with a delicious breakfast in one of the cafés around our beautiful 13th century cathedral. They all have comfortable outdoor tables and chairs so you can enjoy fantastic views of the old town wall as your drink your coffee. From the cathedral square, you can climb the steps onto the wall and look down into the winding narrow streets, crammed with tiny shops and galleries. There are gorgeous old buildings, such as the market and the bath house, that are well worth visiting. You should pop into the tourist information office near the town gates to pick up all the information you need to plan the rest of your morning.

Before you leave us, don't forget to explore the river bank path, with stunning views into the distant mountains. It really will be one of the highlights of your day!

Learning to learn: your journal

Students' own answers

UNIT 4

Reading

1 2, 3, 5, 6

Relevant sections in article:

2 Things like problem solving, critical thinking and collaboration are all based on creativity. And in fact, creativity was seen as one of the key skills of leadership in a survey of business people.

3 They use their imagination to turn a cardboard box into a castle, a mop into a motorbike or a blanket into the base camp at Everest.

5 Some of them are simple tricks that you probably already know, such as walking around for a few minutes when you are mentally stuck

6 … take a pen and brainstorm your ideas onto a blank sheet of paper

2 Students' own answers

3 pick up a pencil, slowing down, getting out of my comfort zone

pick up a pencil is similar to suggestion in article

4 Model answer

There are many ways you can increase your creativity. For example, you can try techniques such as walking around for a while. Brainstorming is a good way of getting lots of ideas. Using a pencil and paper instead of a computer is also a good idea. Another method is to do regular activities like meditation and relaxation. The main point of many useful techniques is to try something new and give your brain new sensations to process.

5 Can include any of these:
walking around, brainstorming, drawing circles, getting bored, meditating, relaxation activities, swapping computer for pencil /pen and paper, slowing down, getting out of comfort zone

Grammar

1 1 to be 2 to speak 3 me of breaking 4 me to play 5 me for causing 6 telling 7 for being

2 1 persuaded me to contact
2 recommending writing
3 agreed to try
4 invited me to come
5 asked her to suggest
6 offered to meet
7 didn't admit (to) feeling
8 promised to meet

3 1 for not calling 2 Rosa to come 3 to go
4 to make 5 Nikki to put

Changes: for a while, that Friday, supper for them, her in her diary.

4 1 not leaving 2 to sort out 3 for causing
4 to help 5 hiring 6 to pay

Learning to learn: grammar

Students' own answers

Pronunciation

Using stress for emphasis (2)

1 1 accident B
2 bad weather A
3 hotel B
4 ten days B

2 1 The ferry had an accident.
2 The bad weather caused long delays.
3 The travel agency recommended a hotel.
4 We spent ten days in Miyajima.

Listening

1 a 4, b 3, c 1, e 2

2 1 minus 20 degrees
2 hot drink
3 old school teachers
4 ten
5 Ecuador
6 a famous actor
7 every month
8 nearly forty years

3 Students' own answers

Learning to learn: listening

1 number and noun
2 adjective and noun
3 adjective and noun
4 number
5 noun
6 adjective and noun
7 noun
8 number and noun

Pronunciation

Pronouncing long and short 'i'

1 degrees - long
drink - short
given- short
listen - short
seemed - long
seventeen - long
this - short
village - short
winter - short

Vocabulary

1 1 keep in touch
2 get along well
3 reconnecting
4 hit it off
5 lose touch
6 keep in close contact
7 catch up

2 1 reconnected / caught up
2 kept in touch
3 hit it off
4 stick together
5 Losing touch

Answer key

Focus on

1 and 2

1 C / I

2 they don't get along / I

3 Keeping in touch with people / T

4 C / I

5 catching up with old friends / I

6 C / I

7 C / I

8 C / I

3 1 I get along well with my neighbour.

2 I lost touch with my college friends.

3 I promised I would keep in touch with my old teacher.

4 At their first meeting, the new members of the team hit it off with the old members.

5 The party will be a chance for the cousins to reconnect with each other.

Writing

1 1 loudly 2 slowly 3 in delight 4 rapidly 5 with hope 6 without a doubt

2 1 shouting their names – the boy

2 coming towards me – a car

3 not understanding anything – the girl

4 holding his camera – the man

5 shaking – we

6 standing at the window – we

3 1 'Would you like me to / can I / could I take you to a different hotel?' offered the driver.

2 'I don't know your name,' claimed / said the girl.

3 'Remember to keep the photos,' said my friend, smiling / with a smile.

4 'Do you need help?' asked the boy, looking at me.

5 'I'm so sorry for not recognizing you,' I said, taking his hand.

6 'Let's meet tomorrow,' we said, shaking hands.

4 Model answer

The person I would most like to say thank you to is my old English teacher, Mr Moss. He was my favourite teacher in High School and I always remember him, standing at the front of the class, waving his hands around dramatically when he was explaining things to us.

I really had a bad time at school, failing exams continuously, and feeling miserable about it. Generally, the other teachers didn't expect me to do well in their subjects. Mr Moss was different. 'Tom!' he'd shout at me. 'Listen to this. Tell me what you think'. Nobody usually asked my opinion about anything. Often, I didn't really know what I thought about the book or poem we were studying. But Mr Moss always listened, holding his hand to his chin, looking at me as if I was speaking intelligently. 'Good point, good point!' he would say.

That was the beginning of my self-confidence in school and in the world. Everything changed, so thank you, Mr Moss.

Learning to learn: what kind of a language learner are you?

Students' own answers

3&4 REVIEW 2

Vocabulary

1 1 set off 2 head for 3 end up 4 go on 5 stop over 6 make it

2 1 in touch 2 up 3 touch 4 it off 5 along well 6 together

Grammar

1 1 met 2 were volunteering 3 had been 4 hadn't 5 saw 6 'd been looking 7 spent 8 was getting

2 1 Lynne persuaded Jenna to join the/her gym.

2 Fran promised to send the report before Friday.

3 Bill accused Jack of deleting the messages.

4 Leila denied causing the problem.

5 Dani apologized for being/arriving late.

6 Ravi recommended taking the early train.

Reading

1 1 close, intense
2 support, confidence
3 family
4 to talk to, to depend on, to enjoy
Mindmap: Students' own answers

2 1 B 2 C 3 A

Listening

1 1 railway stations 2 second 3 three weeks 4 technical 5 social media

2 1 F 2 F 3 F 4 T

Pronunciation

2 1 reach 2 seat 3 still 4 hit

UNIT 5

Reading

2 1 c 2 b 3 a 4 b 5 c 6 b

3 1 Andrew: Tea and activity
2 Graciela: to stop eating before your stomach felt full and strong social life
3 Arthur: genes and the place you live in and also how hard you work

4 1 cause - I think I owe my career to being an Englishman in Hollywood.
2 correlation
3 cause - Some things change: I now have a quad bike to help me get around.

5 Students' own answers

Grammar

1 1 f 2 d 3 b 4 c 5 a 6 e

2 1 download / will count
2 will feel / take
3 use / help
4 won't be able to / is
5 place / measures
6 doesn't tell / set up

3 1 had told
2 had
3 Would / use, had
4 would have enjoyed

4 1 If we'd done sport at school, I would have been more interested in it.
2 If we'd been fit, we would've gone on the sponsored hike.
3 If my brother had used the gym, he would've renewed his membership.
4 If the Tour de France hadn't gone through my friend's village, she wouldn't have bought a bike.
5 If I hadn't told my friends I was unhappy, I wouldn't have felt better afterwards.
6 If there hadn't been a sale at the sports shop, I wouldn't have bought lots of new sports clothes.

5 1 b 2 d 3 d 4 a 5 c 6 b

Pronunciation

Understanding elision in connected speech

1 1 I'd've 2 She'd've 3 wouldn't've 4 wouldn't've

Vocabulary

1 1 a 2 f 3 c 4 l 5 e 6 h 7 b 8 d 9 i 10 g 11 j 12 k

2 1 take a nap
2 have called in sick
3 symptoms
4 stay in shape
5 Anxiety and depression
6 get over

3 1 stay in shape
2 at risk
3 come down with
4 cope with
5 burn-out

Answer key

Listening

1 Suggested answers

Outdoor places: beaches, gardens, parks, woods

Outdoor jobs: construction worker, gardener, police officer, sports instructor, traffic warden, travel guide

Good things about being outdoors: fresh air, health, physical activity

3 1 N 2 N 3 F 4 T

4 Students' own answers

Learning to learn: listening

1 Few

Although I'm not keen on the idea of being outside in all kinds of weather, getting cold and wet, to be honest.

Yes, well I think that's a bit of an extreme view, actually. Clearly that's not always the case.

'Few' changes the original meaning by specifying quantity. The original text is general, and gives no information about quantity.

2 usually

And I think being at the coast can help with things like depression, can't it?

'usually' changes the original meaning by specifying frequency. In the original text, the speaker says only that he thinks it's possible, but no information about how much/often is given.

3 always

In forestry or gardening, for example, you can find jobs that don't need paper qualifications.

'always' changes the original meaning by contradicting it.

4 All

Like any job, it has to be right for you, otherwise you're going to be stressed and unhappy.

'all' confirms the original meaning because 'like any job' is the same as saying 'all jobs'.

Focus on

1 1 they'd given

2 had

3 worked don't

4 could doesn't

5 had trained

6 had taken do

2 1 had done 2 weren't 3 were 4 didn't pay
5 didn't expect 6 wasn't 7 didn't hurt
8 had listened 9 hadn't been

3 1 hadn't worried 2 had got along 3 had been
4 had followed 5 had taken 6 had spent

Pronunciation

1 1 lock 2 hid 3 set 4 live 5 blog 6 back

Writing

Possible answers

1 1 Recently, there has been greater awareness of the benefits of cycling for our health.

2 Is it the case that children really eat too much fast food these days?

3 It is commonly believed that children eat too much fast food.

4 There is no doubt that cycling is good for your health.

2 Possible answer

1 f 2 c 3 b 4 d 5 a 6 e

5 Model answer

Recently, there has been passionate discussion of the use of bikes and cars in our cities. It has been suggested that towns could make their streets easier to cycle in and more difficult to drive and park in.

Firstly, it's clear that cycling is good for our physical health and also our mental health. In addition, bikes don't pollute the environment. This is especially important in our towns and cities, where air pollution affects residents' health. Respiratory illnesses are more common in urban areas than in rural areas. If it was easier to get around towns on bikes, more people would do so and this would benefit everyone.

On the other hand, there are problems with discouraging people from using cars. Many people live long way from their place of work and have to use a car to get there. Unfortunately, public transport is not always available or quick. Furthermore, encouraging people to cycle may put them at risks of illness, due to the fact that air pollution affects cyclists more than other people.

In conclusion, there is much to discuss and town residents need to be involved in decisions about this issue.

Learning to learn: your journal

Students' own answers

UNIT 6

Reading

2 1 exaggeration 2 true 3 sensationalist
4 gossip 5 opinions 6 factual

3 1 The Roman Empire and 1874, New York stories
2 Britain in the 1700s story
3 1927, European newspapers story
4 1890s news giants and 1903 stories

4 1 S – The Roman empire story
2 S – the Britain in the 1700s story
3 U – the statement, while true, is not specifically supported with evidence in the text

5 Looking online

6 1 dramatic
2 no
3 no
4 online or in scientific or environmental publications

7 2 is the logical conclusion

Grammar

1 1 was reported 2 has been removed
3 are being investigated 4 were / told
5 will be launched 6 have / been banned

2 1 The latest superhero film is expected to break all records.
2 School exam results are understood to be better than ever this year.
3 The suspect is / was believed to have used false identities.
4 The environmental proposals are thought to include ambitious targets.
5 The triathlon is considered to be one of the most challenging sports.
6 Self-drive vehicles are / have been known to have problems in certain situations.

3 1 It is hoped that entry to the concert will be free.
2 It is understood that the awards ceremony might be cancelled.
3 It has been revealed that people spend more time than ever on social media.
4 It is thought that some companies will work a four-day week.
5 It was considered that the customers were lucky to receive a refund.
6 It is recommended that we eat a lot of green vegetables.

4 1 are known to have 2 it has been reported
3 is considered to be 4 have been studied
5 have been found to have 6 It is hoped

Learning to learn: grammar

1 2 and 3

2 a I wonder what this sign means. (direct/indirect question)
b Can I book a place on a coach tour for you? (direct/indirect speech)
c If the TV hadn't been expensive, we would have bought it. (conditional pattern)

Listening

1 2

2 1 how long a story stays in the news
2 second-by-second.
3 specialist
4 television
5 news organizations

3 1 b I 2 a O 3 f I 4 d O

4 1 when all-day 2 had an opportunity 3 as information 4 stories about 5 get a

Vocabulary

1 1 f 2 b 3 d 4 a 5 c 6 e

2 1 tabloids 2 in-depth 3 skim over 4 make
5 top 6 reported

Answer key

Pronunciation

Pronouncing long vowels

1 1 article 2 really 3 rumours 4 sources 5 worldwide

2 1 / ɜː/ worldwide
2 / iː/ really
3 / uː/ rumours
4 / ɑː/ article
5 / ɔː/ sources

Focus on

1 1 c h 2 a f 3 b e 4 d g

2 1 a 2 b 3 c 4 c 5 a 6 c

Writing

1 1 astonishing 2 revealed 3 an unbelievable 4 record-breaking 5 breath-taking 6 chased 7 victory

2 1 The tennis competition will potentially be the most exciting of the year.
2 The study may show what we should do next.
3 Virtually all the experts say that there is only one solution to the crisis.
4 The election results are likely to be announced before midnight.
5 Results suggest that the general public doesn't know anything about the issue.
6 The problems seem to have been caused by the huge rainfall in recent weeks.

3 Model answer

Television star Susie Dent has revealed that she was shocked to find her new book was full of mistakes. Dent is famous for her appearances on TV quiz shows. She is a language expert and she sits in 'dictionary corner'. Millions of viewers watch as she decides if words are OK or not. Dent began her TV career an incredible 25 years ago. She's been on our screens over 2,500 times. In addition to her fantastic TV career, she's a successful writer. She has written several books about English and weird words. Her latest book is called *Word Perfect*, but Dent was astonished to see that it was not perfect at all. She opened the copy that was sent to her from her publisher. To her horror, the first thing she saw was a mistake. Then she found more mistakes. The publisher has promised to correct the errors and print the book again.

Learning to learn: making the most of English language resources (2)

Students' own answers

5&6 REVIEW 3

Vocabulary

1 1 cope with 2 stay in shape 3 burn out 4 at risk 5 come down with 6 get over

2 1 headlines, press
2 skim over, story
3 articles, information

Grammar

1 1 have 2 unless 3 had 4 would 5 If 6 won't

2 1 has been published 2 is understood to be 3 are said to be 4 were analysed 5 are provided 6 is recommended

Reading

1

	claim	evidence
1	feel great	People say/report this
2	leads to ... extra energy	Reaction from temperature shock
3	benefits anxiety and depression	-
4	positive social aspects	People mention/report this

2 1 d 2 e 3 b

Listening

1 All the words except *laugh* are heard

2 1 c 2 b 3 c

Pronunciation

1 1 food 2 leave 3 white 4 lock

2

news	used
dark	far
report	cause
girl	surface
piece	keep

UNIT 7

Reading

1 1 three/multi-generation, skipped-generation, boomerang households

2 Asia, Africa, Latin America, UK; Central America, the Caribbean, Africa; Chile

3 Abdal three-generation household; Doris three-generation household; Tere boomerang household

2 honoured = adjective

the norm = noun

undergo = verb

constraints = noun

orphans = noun

compel = verb

phenomenon = noun

takes me back to = verb

3 honoured d proud and happy

the norm h the usual way

undergo f go though

constraints c limits or controlling factors

orphans a children whose parents have died

compel e force

phenomenon b circumstance

takes me back to g reminds me of

4 Doris

1 She was lonely

2 Moving in to her son's home

3 Positive: she is no longer lonely, she sees her grandchildren more

Tere

1 Her wages were not enough to pay for her own place

2 She returned to her parents' home

3 Possibly negative - she describes how they need to give each other space

5 Students' own answers

Learning to learn: reading

senior - adjective, countable noun, first, B2

Grammar

1 1 to keep 2 slow down 3 to leave 4 from using 5 get 6 from having

2 1 enables / to get

2 helps / save

3 required to change

4 lets / travel

5 prevents / from carrying

6 advised / to pay

7 stops / from getting

3 1 saves me from feeling

2 forces me to be

3 encourages me to build

4 allowed to have

5 don't let us bring

6 stops Josef from coming round

4 Students' own answers

Learning to learn: grammar

Students' own answers

Pronunciation

Stressing multi-syllable verbs

1 1 ad**vise** 2 en**a**ble 3 en**cour**age 4 per**mit** 5 pre**vents** 6 re**quire**

Listening

1 1 religious, millions 2 early one morning, positive 3 discovered, physical health 4 villagers

2 1 anxiety 2 calm 3 form relationships 4 physical 5 energy 6 change

3 1 b 2 d 3 f 4 c 5 a 6 e

4 Student's own answers

Vocabulary

1 1 e 2 d 3 h 4 b 5 f 6 g 7 c 8 a

2 1 top 2 view 3 weather 4 concert 5 tourist 6 sight 7 tourist 8 weather

Answer key

3 1 1 warm and cosy 2 light and airy
3 absolutely stunning

2 1 elegantly decorated 2 narrow
3 cold and damp 4 densely crowded

Pronunciation

Pronouncing /b/, /v/ and /w/

1 1 best 2 wet 3 boat 4 van

Writing

1 1 ↓Ever been to Costa Rica? It's beautiful! Have you

2 We've just got back, but↓would go again tomorrow! We

3 ↓Motorbike broke down again yesterday. My

4 ↓Decided to go home last night after yet another rainy day. I / We / They

5 MacInnes Coffee Shop - ↓ the best value breakfast I've ever had. does / serves / is

6 ↓Ready to join me tomorrow? Are you

7 ↓Any ideas what the problem is? Have you / Have you got / Do you have

8 ↓Looking at next week's weather, ↓ had a great idea –↓camping! I've been, I / I've, let's go

2 1 a bit of a, I'm back

2 ton of, give it a shot

3 got into, way

4 clearing out, loads of, stuff

3 Going paddle boarding for the first time, information about what paddle boarding on the sea is like and what she should know and do

4 Model answer

Hey! Love the photo! Where is it? Never been paddle boarding myself but it looks cool. Seen a few people out on the sea near me in the evenings. How much does a board cost, more or less? Do you have to be super-fit to do it? I gave windsurfing a shot once on holiday, but I didn't have the strength in my arms! I fell off loads too! So, wondering if I need to have really great balance for paddle boarding.

Learning to learn: your journal

Students' own answers

UNIT 8

Reading

1 3

2 1 treatment 2 wristbands
3 contact lenses, hearing aids
4 AI 5 video-based appointments

3 1 c 2 b 3 b

4

unusual	remarkable
problem	issue
focus on	concentrate on
put on	take off (**antonyms**)
information	data
collect	gather
inside	outside (**antonyms**)
simple	complex (**antonyms**)

5 1 and 2

1: 'I'm sure you're thinking there's nothing remarkable in this story.'

2: all the use of what devices 'will' do.

Learning to learn: reading

connect (v)

connection (n) connected (adj) unconnected (adj)	= link, linked
connect to the internet broadband connection	≠ be separate

advance (v)

advance (n) advanced (adj)	= make progress = go forwards = development, progress
make advances in huge advances	≠ go backwards

Grammar

1 1 might 2 must 3 may 4 may 5 can't
6 couldn't

2 1 might / could / may have been

2 shouldn't / must have fallen

3 can't / couldn't have sent
4 should have read
5 can't / couldn't have been
6 must have used

3 1 He can't have told the truth about what happened.
2 The parcel must have arrived in the morning.
3 I shouldn't have parked outside the entrance to the building.
4 The group might have travelled by bus.

4 1 can't have stopped
2 must have dropped
3 can't have broken
4 could / may / might have been
5 shouldn't have kept
6 must have squashed

Pronunciation

Understanding the weak form of *have*

1 1 F 2 W 3 F 4 W

Vocabulary

1 1 pocket-sized 2 innovative 3 outdated 4 user-friendly 5 handy 6 sophisticated

2 1 gadget 2 perform 3 waterproof 4 recharge 5 user-friendly 6 handy

Focus on

1 1 invention memorize
2 silence activate
3 complications simplify
4 strengthen achievement
5 technological affordable
6 universal happiness

2 1 affordable 2 memorize 3 universal 4 silence 5 simplify 6 complication 7 activate 8 strengthen

Listening

1 a 2 b 5 c 3 d 1 e 4

2 a 1 c 2 e 5 g 4 h 3

3 1 kind of 2 to work 3 at a time 4 for only

Pronunciation

Pronouncing long and short 'o'

1 1 L 2 L 3 S 4 S 5 S 6 L

Learning to learn: listening

1 remote sensing
2 huge cities, roads, a whole landscape showing how the people had once lived
3 sometimes he forgets to stop working even to eat
4 remote sensing LIDAR the gadgets he uses regularly

Writing

1 1 long-lasting
2 black and white
3 second-hand
4 on-screen
5 cheap and cheerful
6 one-year

2 1 e 2 b 3 a 4 f 5 c 6 d

3 Model answer

I was given this key finder as a gift and to be honest I didn't really see the point of it at first. It looks nice – very well designed – and it seems quite high-end. I guess it's for people who lose their keys a lot, and that's not me! Anyway, I installed the app on my phone. That's how it works – you attach your keys to the gadget and connect it via Bluetooth. It's pretty user-friendly. If you lose your keys, you click on the on-screen icon and it both lights up and makes a noise. It's supposed to work up to a distance of 100 metres. OK, so what was my experience? It worked fine when I was testing it out, around the house and so on. So I thought that it would be really handy if I ever really did lose my keys. Then, of course, one day I did. I was panicking so much it wasn't until after I found them that I remembered about the finder app!

Learning to learn: using the English you learn

Students' own answers

Answer key

7&8 REVIEW 4

Vocabulary

1 1 crowded 2 damp 3 narrow 4 breathtaking 5 spacious

2 1 outdated 2 sophisticated 3 user-friendly 4 perform 5 waterproof

Grammar

1 1 making us start 2 let you get 3 they allow you to go in 4 stopping us working 5 will force me to go

2 1 can't have lost 2 must have left 3 might/could have stolen 4 shouldn't have been 5 should have looked for 6 might have remembered

Reading

1 1 c 2 b 3 a

2 exploitation noun reside verb medicinal adjective clear verb indigenous adjective

3 a clear b reside c indigenous d exploitation e medicinal

Listening

1 1 c 2 c 3 a

2 1 time 2 annoying 3 use email 4 social media

Pronunciation

1 The second syllable in all of them is stressed

2 1 autumn L 2 always L 3 honest S 4 forest S 5 resources L 6 monument S

UNIT 9

Reading

1 1 Harvard, Guggenheim, Nobel, Bill Gates, Yu Pengnian, Mona Sinha

2 Reese Fernandez-Ruiz

3 Frane Selak

2 1 T 2 NG 3 F 4 F 5 T 6 NG

3 1 a 2 b 3 a

4 1 generous 2 Surely / not a difficult decision 3 just quietly working

Learning to learn: reading

Page 12: 1 T 2 F 3 NG 4 T 5 T 6 T 7NG

Page 20: 1 Y 2 N 3 N 4 Y 5 NG 6 N

Grammar

1 1 In five years' time my family and I will be living by the sea.

2 In ten years' time I will be writing my first book.

3 This time next year I won't be studying any more.

4 Next year I won't be working in my current job.

5 Within two years I'll be running my own social media channel.

6 Next summer my friends and I will be doing a round-the-world trip.

2 1 will have replied

2 Will we have organized, I'll have finalized

3 will have started

4 won't have confirmed, will have heard

3 1 be working 2 have found 3 be cycling 4 have finished 5 have hit 6 be making

4 1 won't be going 2 will have landed 3 will be taking 4 might have invented 5 should have found 6 will be flying

Pronunciation

Pausing

2 A TV kids' channel | recently asked a group of six-year olds | about what life will be like when they are 16. || More than half | (optimistically, perhaps!) | are sure kids won't be going to school every day because | 'everything will be on the internet. || The majority believe that humans will have landed on Mars | and people will be taking 'space holidays' there. || About a fifth of the kids hope that scientists | might have invented | a way for pets to talk to us || and a quarter think it's likely | that doctors should have found cures for all illnesses ||. Finally, | a small | but enthusiastic | number think there's a good chance | we'll be flying with personal jet packs |to get around our neighbourhoods.

Listening

1 1 Joseph 2 Magda 3 Paulo

2 1 b 2 c 3 c

3 1 actually 2 Despite the fact that
3 That being said 4 or at least

4 a then again = that being said (3)
b really though = actually (1)
c even though = despite the fact that (2)

5 Students' own answers

Vocabulary

1 1 tackle 2 achieve 3 it through 4 issue
5 understand 6 made

2 1 through 2 mess 3 problem 4 issue
5 objective 6 understand

Focus on

1 1 a mess 2 for survival 3 all of your objectives
4 a decision 5 with the problem 6 very little

2 1 objectives 2 difficulties 3 tackle 4 overcome
5 crisis 6 make

Pronunciation

Saying /ʃ/, /ʒ/, /tʃ/ and /dʒ/

1 1 /tʃ/ 2 /ʃ/ 3 /dʒ/ 4 /ʒ/

Writing

1 1 valuable 2 part-time 3 proficient
4 knowledge 5 completed 6 graduated
7 regards 8 concerned

2 1 b 2 a 3 d 4 c

3 Model answer

Dear Sir or Madam

I am writing to apply for the position of a tour guide as advertised on your website.

I have attached my CV. As outlined there, I have two years' experience working as a tour guide in Europe and South America. Before this, I spent three years travelling and working around the world, visiting many iconic tourist sites in a total of seventeen countries. I gained valuable experience in problem solving during this time, especially in dealing with the requirements of different countries and cultures.

With regard to my relevant experience, I have worked with all ages and nationalities of tourists and thanks to this, I have developed strong interpersonal skills. In Europe, my experience is mainly in looking after multinational groups on cultural tours of the main cities, while in South America, I worked with younger clients visiting popular cultural sites. I am an enthusiastic and dynamic organizer and enjoy helping clients to have the best holiday experience.

I am physically fit. Moreover, I go swimming, climbing and cycling regularly.

My college diploma is in Business Studies, with additional courses in French and Italian.

I would be very interested in joining your organization as a tour guide. I have had some experience of your tours and have been impressed with your organization's professionalism.

I look forward to hearing from you.

Yours sincerely

Learning to learn: your journal

Students' own answers

UNIT 10

Reading

1 Students' own answers

2 1 coffee, yerba mate 2 coffee, tea 3 coffee, yerba mate

3 1 It helps them to understand a place, its history and its people.
2 Expressions about coffee represent feelings.
3 The taste was probably better than coffee they had drunk before.
4 Being invited to share mate.
5 They worked in remote places or away from family.
6 The tea harvest / tea picking.

4 4 = personification 5 = simile 6 = metaphor

5 1 d 2 c 3 a 4 f 5 e 6 b

6 Students' own answers

Answer key

Grammar

1 1 going, to spend 2 hearing, listening 3 going out, staring 4 to play, stopping

2 1 to meet 2 seeing 3 taking 4 going 5 to leave 6 to have

3 1 getting up 2 not to say 3 not knowing 4 feeling 5 not eating 6 not to go

4 1 welcoming 2 to find 3 to take 4 coming 5 to break 6 watching 7 forming 8 planning

Learning to learn: grammar

Students' own answers

Pronunciation

Aspirating /p/, /k/ and /t/

1 1 ✓ 2 ✗ 3 ✗ 4 ✓ 5 ✓ 6 ✗

Listening

1 3 and 4 are true

2 1 Spain and Portugal 2 street festivals 3 children's festivals 4 Caribbean community 5 children's parade 6 1964 7 two million

3 1 they came 2 who were 3 from the Caribbean, from the Caribbean 4 successful

4 Students' own answers

Learning to learn: listening

1 What about

2 You also mentioned

3 right

4 Coming back to

5 Absolutely! But tell me

show a reaction = Absolutely

refer back to something already talked about = You also mentioned, Coming back to

ask for information = What about, right, But tell me

Vocabulary

1 1 f 2 h 3 d 4 c 5 i 6 b 7 g 8 a 9 e

2 1 like an outsider 2 share / values 3 fit in 4 culturally diverse 5 identify with 6 was raised in

Pronunciation

Saying *th*

1 the other, three

2 thin, than

3 think, father

Focus on

1 1 concerts 2 the countries 3 the majority 4 audiences 5 the places 6 The Irish

2 1 – 2 – 3 – 4 The 5 – 6 The 7 – 8 – 9 the 10 the

Writing

1 1 roughly a third 2 just under half 3 most 4 one in four 5 the vast majority 6 a small number

2 1 identified 2 said 3 agreed 4 chose

3 Model answer

Live shows at the Melbourne International Arts Festival: online ticket purchases

The aim of this report is to summarize the attendance at live shows at the Melbourne Festival, taking into account both local and international visitors. The figures were collected from online ticket purchases. When tickets were sold on the day, there was no information about whether the visitors were local or international.

The most popular events overall were the circus events, with the majority of local visitors choosing these shows and and almost half of the international visitors attending them. The least attended shows were concerts and other music events among international visitors and multimedia performances for both kinds of visitors.

Audiences for dance shows, which includes ballet and modern dance, were the same for both kinds of visitor. About a fifth of the festival's tickets were sold for these events. Roughly a third of international visitors bought tickets for theatre performances. This was much more than the local audience at about ten per cent.

However, it must be noted that many festival-goers chose to buy tickets in person, rather than online. This means that we should be careful about interpreting the results of the survey.

Learning to learn: looking back and looking ahead

Students' own answers

9&10 REVIEW 5

Vocabulary

1 1 struggling 2 overcame 3 make 4 achieve 5 tackle 6 made

2 1 raised in 2 fit in 3 feel like an outsider 4 influenced by 5 share / values 6 identify with

Grammar

1 1 should have finished 2 will have found 3 will be doing 4 won't be working 5 will have changed 6 might be going

2 1 going 2 to win 3 to meet 4 staying 5 having

Reading

1 1 volcanic 2 1959 3 surfing 4 Asia, North America 5 'auana hula

2 d like jewels on a deep blue pillow

a a tropical paradise

b is a melting pot

e is constantly calling for attention

c is a path

Listening

1 1 architect, buildings

2 poet, Ethiopia, the UK

3 Pakistan, Nobel Prize

2 Speaker 1 - b

Speaker 2 - c

Speaker 3 - e

Pronunciation

1

achieve	matches
vision	Polynesians
issue	traditional
manage	project

2 1 ✓ 2 ✗ 3 ✗ 4 ✓, ✗

Credits Student's Book

Illustration: All illustrations are owned by © Cengage.

Cover: © Jim Richardson; **3** David McNew/Getty Images News/Getty Images; **4** (tl1) Yoan Valat/European Pressphoto Agency/Newscom, (tl2) © Gabriele Galimberti, (cl) © Peter Amend, (bl1) Stringer/AFP/Getty Images, (bl2) VCG/Getty Images; **6** (tl1) NASA, (tl2) Olga Kolos/Alamy Stock Photo, (cl) David Ramos/Getty Images News/Getty Images, (bl1) David McNew/Getty Images News/Getty Images, (bl2) pixelfusion3d/E+/Getty Images; **8** (tl) © Edin Whitehead, (tr) © Fernando Caamano, KipperTie, (cl1) Courtesy of Afroz Ahmad Shah, (cr1) © Arianna Soldati, (cl2) © Alec Jacobson, (cr2) © Carolina Chong Montenegro, (bl) Courtesy of Alyea Pierce, (br) Courtesy of Ellie de Castro; **8-9** (spread) Robert Harding Picture Library/National Geographic Image Collection; **9** (tl) Courtesy of Federico Fanti, (tr) Courtesy of Maria Fadiman, (cl1) Courtesy of Francisco Estrada-Belli, (cr1) © Nora Shawki, (cl2) © Eleanor Burfitt, (cr2) © Paola Rodriguez-Troncoso, (bl) © Caio Felipe Santos da Silva, (br) Courtesy of Robbie Shone, (bc) © Tsiory Andrianavalona; **10-11** (spread) Yoan Valat/European Pressphoto Agency/Newscom; **11** (br1) © Tsiory Andrianavalona, (br2) Courtesy of Francisco Estrada-Belli; **13** Benjamin John/Alamy Stock Photo; **15** Source: Google LLC; **16** Andrew Caballero-Reynolds/AFP/Getty Images; **18** Dinodia Photos/Alamy Stock Photo; **20** (tl) DCPhoto/Alamy Stock Photo, (bl) Masterfile; **22-23** (spread) © Gabriele Galimberti; **23** (br1) Courtesy of Maria Fadiman, (br2) © Arianna Soldati; **25** (tl) Christian Ziegler/National Geographic Image Collection, (tc1) George Grall/National Geographic Image Collection, (tc2) zhaojiankang/iStock/Getty Images, (tr) Jon Hilmarsson/Moment/Getty Images, (b) Boscorelli/Alamy Stock Photo, (bl) Atsuo Fujimaru/Minden Pictures; **26** Courtesy of Arianna Soldati; **27** Sam Edwards/OJO images/Getty Images; **28** robertharding/Alamy Stock Photo; **30** Tom Werner/DigitalVision/Getty Images; **32** Anastasia Lembrik/Shutterstock.com; **34-35** (spread) © Peter Amend; **35** (br1) © Fernando Caamano, KipperTie, (br2) Courtesy of Ellie de Castro; **37** © Susan Seubert; **38** Courtesy of Andrej Gajić; **40** (t) AB Forces News Collection/Alamy Stock Photo, (bl1) Andrey_Kuzmin/Shutterstock.com, (bl2) LongQuattro/Shutterstock.com; **43** Elizaveta Galitckaia/Alamy Stock Photo; **44** MarBom/iStock/Getty Images; **46-47** (spread) Stringer/AFP/Getty Images; **47** (br1) Courtesy of Federico Fanti, (br2) © Carolina Chong Montenegro; **49** 501room/iStock Editorial/Getty Images; **50** Michael Hanson/Stock/National Geographic Image Collection; **52** Courtesy of Frederico Fanti; **54** Lucy Lambriex/DigitalVision/Getty Images; **55** (tl) Bojanovic/Shutterstock.com, (tc) jo1/Shutterstock.com, (tr) chwl/Shutterstock.com; **56** skynesher/E+/Getty Images; **58-59** (spread) VCG/Getty Images; **59** (br1) Courtesy of Maria Fadiman, (br2) © Alec Jacobson; **61** (tr) photomaster/Shutterstock.com, (bl) © Mark Henderson; **64** (tl) Lynn Johnson/National Geographic Image Collection, (tr) Jonathan Torgovnik/Getty Images News/Getty Images, (cl) Kieran Dodds/Panos Pictures/Redux, (cr) andresr/E+/Getty Images; **66** Tom Werner/DigitalVision/Getty Images; **68** © Gijsbert van der Wal; **70-71** (spread) NASA; **71** (br1) Courtesy of Afroz Ahmad Shah, (br2) © Eleanor Burfitt; **73** (tl) © Jason Michael McCann/Twitter: @Jeggit, (tr1) Source: First Media, (tr2) Still from Dali Lives © Salvador Dalí Museum, Inc., St. Petersburg, FL, 2020; **74** Herbert Neubauer/AFP/Getty Images; **76** (bc1) (bc2) tanuha2001/Shutterstock.com; **78** Ivy Close Images/Alamy Stock Photo; **80** IRA Block/National Geographic Image Collection; **82-83** (spread) Olga Kolos/Alamy Stock Photo; **83** (br1) © Edin Whitehead, (br2) Courtesy of Robbie Shone; **85** (tl) phichak/Shutterstock.com, (tr) © Paola S. Branco, (b) Peter R. Houlihan/National Geographic Image Collection; **86** SSphotography/Moment Unreleased/Getty Images; **87** (bl) ISA Harsin/SIPA/Newscom, (bc1) AU Photos/Alamy Stock Photo, (bc2) Horacio Garcia Martin/Shutterstock.com, (br) © CJ Worx; **88** Robbie Shone/National Geographic Image Collection; **90** mediaphotos/E+/Getty Images; **92** (bc1) Colorlife/Shutterstock.com, (bc2) safroni safroni/Shutterstock.com, (bc3) Colorlife/Shutterstock.com, (bc4) Eliyev1/Shutterstock.com; **93** (tl1) Andrey_Popov/Shutterstock.com, (tl2) © Bournemouth News and Picture Service, (cl1) (cl2) Andrey_Popov/Shutterstock.com, (bl) dpa picture alliance/Alamy Stock Photo; **94-95** (spread) David Ramos/Getty Images News/Getty Images; **95** (br1) © Nora Shawki, (br2) Courtesy of Francisco Estrada-Belli; **97** (tr) AF archive/Alamy Stock Photo, (b) Atlaspix/Alamy Stock Photo; **98** (bgd) Vadim Sadovski/Shutterstock.com, (c1) Werner Forman/Universal Images Group/Getty Images, (c2) Everett Collection Historical/Alamy Stock Photo, (bc1) ART Collection/Alamy Stock Photo, (bc2) Dinodia Photos/Alamy Stock Photo; **99** (cr) Science & Society Picture Library/Getty Images, (br) © National Museum of the American Indian, Smithsonian Institution (21/0796); **100** © Pacunam/Estrada-Belli; **103** (t) Lukas Rs/Shutterstock.com, (b) Westend61/Getty Images; **104** (tl1) Avijit Sadhu/iStock/Getty Images, (tl2) Dmitry9131/Shutterstock.com, (cl1) Celine Nguyen/EyeEm/Getty Images, (cl2) N8Allen/Shutterstock.com; **106-107** (spread) David McNew/Getty Images News/Getty Images; **107** (br1) Courtesy of Robbie Shone, (br2) © Paola Rodriguez-Troncoso; **109** (tc) Laurent Koffel/Gammo-Rapho/Getty Images, (tr) Francois Nel/Getty Images Sport/Getty Images, (bl) Hulton Deutsch/Corbis Historical/Getty Images, (bc) Tristan Fewings/Getty Images Entertainment/Getty Images; **111** Matthieu Paley/National Geographic Image Collection; **112** makeitdouble/Shutterstock.com; **116** Design Pics Inc/National Geographic Image Collection; **118-119** (spread) pixelfusion3d/E+/Getty Images; **119** (br1) Courtesy of Alyea Pierce, (br2) © Caio Felipe Santos da Silva; **121** © Kike Calvo; **123** © Alyea Pierce; **124** (t) © Helder Shin, (cl) Lisa Kolbasa/Shutterstock.com, (c1) ShustrikS/Shutterstock.com, (bl) Lisa Kolbasa/Shutterstock.com, (bc) Sugiyarto/Shutterstock.com; **126** PeopleImages/E+/Getty Images; **128** Robert Harding Picture Library/National Geographic Image Collection; **130** (tl) Yoan Valat/European Pressphoto Agency/Newscom, (tr) © Gabriele Galimberti; **131** (tl) © Peter Amend, (tr) Stringer/AFP/Getty Images; **132** (tl) VCG/Getty Images, (tr) NASA; **133** (tl) Olga Kolos/Alamy Stock Photo, (tr) David Ramos/Getty Images News/Getty Images; **134** (tl) David McNew/Getty Images News/Getty Images, (tr) pixelfusion3d/E+/Getty Images.

Music: 120 © Kike Calvo.

Text: 37 Source: Heather Greenwood Davis, "Five Ways to Be a Tourist in Your Own Hometown," National Geographic, May 26, 2016. Copyright © 2016 National Geographic; **40/41** Source: Smith, Roff, and Stephen Alvarez, "Beyond the Blue Horizon: Peopling the Pacific," National Geographic Magazine, Vol. 213(3)., March, 2008, p.106. Copyright © 2008 National Geographic; **49** Source: Florence Williams, "This Is Your Brain on Nature," National Geographic, January 2016. Copyright © 2016 National Geographic; Mallory Benedict, "Getting in Touch With Nature, Staying in Step With the World," National Geographic, January 01, 2016. Copyright © 2016 National Geographic; **61** Source: HenPower, Equal arts; **62** Source: Finkel, Michael, and Magnus Wennman. "Want to Fall Asleep? Read This Story," National Geographic Magazine, August, 2018, p. 40. Copyright © 2018 National Geographic; **121** Source: Blog, NGS Newsroom.

Credits Teacher's Book

Illustration: All illustrations are owned by © Cengage.

3 David McNew/Getty Images News/Getty Images; **4** (tl1) YOAN VALAT/European Pressphoto Agency/Newscom, (tl2) © Gabriele Galimberti, (cl) © Peter Amend, (bl1) STRINGER/AFP/Getty Images, (bl2) VCG/Visual China Group/Getty Images; **6** (tl1) NASA, (tl2) Olga Kolos/Alamy Stock Photo, (cl) David Ramos/Getty Images News/Getty Images, (bl1) David McNew/Getty Images News/ Getty Images, (bl2) pixelfusion3d/E+/Getty Images; **8** © Jim Richardson; **18** (tl) Courtesy of Dan Barber, (cl) Courtesy of Heather Marsden (bl) Courtesy of Chia Suan Chong; **19** (tl) Courtesy of Marek Kiczkowiak, (cl1) Courtesy of Stephen Byers, (cl2) Courtesy of Christien Lee, (bl2) Courtesy of Gary Pathare; **220** (tr) Colleen Gara/Moment Open/Getty Images, (cr) wildestanimal/Moment/Getty Images; **224** (tl) ewg3D/iStock/Getty Images, (tc) Ben Stock/Shutterstock.com, (tr) INNA FINKOVA/Alamy Stock Photo, (cl) Image Source/Getty Images, (c) Alicia G. Monedero/Shutterstock.com, (cr) Image Supply/Shutterstock.com; **227** (tc) mariakraynova/Shutterstock.com, (tr) adventtr/iStock/Getty Images, (bc) Vera Aksionava/Alamy Stock Photo, (br) Mahod84/Shutterstock.com; **234** Tom Werner/DigitalVision/Getty Images; **235** Alina Rosanova/Getty Images; **236** Mike Harrington/Stone/Getty Images; **237** (cl) Westend61/Getty Images, (cr) Pheelings Media/iStock/Getty Images; **239** © Dorene Hookey; **248** Justin Lambert/DigitalVision/Getty Images; **249** Solskin/DigitalVision/Getty Images; **250** Westend61/Getty Images; **252** Pollyana Ventura/E+/Getty Images; **254** (tr) Luis Alvarez/DigitalVision/Getty Images, (br) Folio Image/Alamy Stock Photo; **257** Portra/DigitalVision/Getty Images; **260** Gorodenkoff/Shutterstock.com; **276** (tr) Pintai Suchachaisri/Moment/Getty Images, (br) GoranQ/E+/Getty Images; **285** iPics/Shutterstock.com; **290** (cr) ideabug/iStock/Getty Images, (br) NATALIA61/Shutterstock.com.

Text: p284 Source: Gaia Vince. (2016, August 12). The amazing benefits of being bilingual. Retrieved from https://www.bbc.com/future/article/20160811-the-amazing-benefits-of-being-bilingual; **p287** Source: Christina Sterbenz. (2013 October 01). 7 Reasons Why I Refuse To Stop Eating Meat. Retrieved from https://www.businessinsider.com/reasons-to-eat-meat-2013-9?r=US&IR=T; **p292** Source: Dubai Facts. (n.d.). Retrieved from https://www.pinterest.co.uk/uaedxb_/dubai-facts/

Pronunciation chart

VOWELS

iː eat	ɪ it	ʊ put	uː blue
e leg	ə the	ɜː her	ɔː for
æ hat	ʌ but	ɑː car	ɒ from

DIPHTHONGS

ɪə hear	eɪ take	
ʊə tourist	ɔɪ toy	əʊ old
eə where	aɪ why	aʊ how

CONSONANTS

p pay (unvoiced)	b buy	t talk (unvoiced)	d day	tʃ cheap (unvoiced)	dʒ jam	k cap (unvoiced)	g get
f for (unvoiced)	v vet	θ think (unvoiced)	ð that	s sell (unvoiced)	z zero	ʃ she (unvoiced)	ʒ vision
m my	n near	ŋ long	h hot (unvoiced)	l like	r right	w way	j yellow

voiced (grey) / **unvoiced** (white)

The International Phonetic Alphabet (IPA) chart above provides a reference for the pronunciation symbols used in *Voices*. Note that the phonetic transcription of words in *Voices*, and in most British English dictionaries, is based on Received Pronunciation (RP) – the accent traditionally regarded as the standard for British English. However, most people who speak (and teach) English, either as their first or second language, do not speak with an RP accent. When teaching pronunciation in class, consider using the symbols as a guide, but allow students the flexibility to speak with their own accent, providing their pronunciation is intelligible.

Research suggests that the quality of **consonant sounds** is much more important for intelligibility than vowel sounds. Note that not all consonant sounds cause problems of intelligibility. One example is the pair /ð/ and /θ/, as in *bro**th**er* and ***th**ree*. These are very often said (both by first and second language English users) as /d/ and /t/ or /v/ and /f/ with little or no impact on intelligibility. Another sound whose pronunciation can and does vary a lot is /r/, again with no great effect on intelligibility.

There is a lot of variation in **vowel sounds** in Englishes around the world. However, these differences rarely lead to miscommunication. For example, the diphthong /aʊ/ in *h**ous**e* is often said as /uː/ in a Scottish accent, while *way* in Australian English typically rhymes with *eye*. Research on intelligibility in international contexts indicates that it is not so much the quality of the vowel or a diphthong that matters, but its length, such as the difference between the sounds /ɪ/ and /iː/. One exception to this is /ɜː/, as in *t**ur**n*, where it is important to maintain both its quality and length.